CLAIRE SHAEFFER'S
FABRIC SEWING GUIDE

Other books in the Creative Machine Arts Series, available from Chilton:

The Complete Book of Machine Embroidery, by Robbie and Tony Fanning
Creative Nurseries Illustrated, by Debra Terry and Juli Plooster
Creative Serging Illustrated, by Pati Palmer, Gail Brown and Sue Green
The Expectant Mother's Wardrobe Planner, by Rebecca Dumlao
The Fabric Lover's Scrapbook, by Margaret Dittman
Friendship Quilts by Hand and Machine, by Carolyn Vosburg Hall
Know Your Bernina, second ed., by Jackie Dodson
Know Your Elna, by Jackie Dodson and Carol Ahles
Know Your New Home, by Jackie Dodson with Vicki Lyn Hastings and Judi Cull
Know Your Pfaff, by Jackie Dodson with Audrey Griese
Know Your Sewing Machine, by Jackie Dodson
Know Your Viking, by Jackie Dodson with Jan Saunders
Pizzazz for Pennies, by Barb Forman
Sewing and Collecting Vintage Fashions, by Eileen MacIntosh

CLAIRE SHAEFFER'S FABRIC SEWING GUIDE

Chilton Book Company

Radnor, Pennsylvania

Copyright © 1989 by Claire B. Shaeffer
All Rights Reserved
Published in Radnor, Pennsylvania 19089,
by Chilton Book Company

Designed by Culver Graphic Design
Manufactured in the United States of America

Library of Congress Cataloging in Publication Data
Shaeffer, Claire B.
    [Fabric sewing guide]
    Claire Shaeffer's fabric sewing guide.
        p.   cm.—(Creative machine arts)
    Bibliography: p. 517
    Includes index.
    ISBN 0-8019-7802-5
    1. Textile fabrics.   2. Sewing.   I. Title.   II. Title: Fabric
sewing guide.   III. Series: Creative machine arts series.
TT557.S53 1989
646'.11—dc19   88-7845
                                                        CIP

1 2 3 4 5 6 7 8 9 0   8 7 6 5 4 3 2 1 0 9

To everyone who loves beautiful fabrics

Contents

Foreword *by Nancy Zieman*   ix

Letter from the Series Editor   x

Preface   xi

Acknowledgments   xii

Introduction   1

Chapter 1   Basic Guide for Sewing All
             Fabrics   3
    Planning a Garment   3
    Design Ideas and Pattern Selection   8

PART ONE: FIBER CONTENT

Chapter 2   Natural Fiber Fabrics   17
    Cotton   17
    Linen   21
    Ramie   26
    Silk   26
    Wool   38
    Specialty Hair Fibers   59

Chapter 3   Man-Made Fiber Fabrics   62
    Rayon   62
    Acetate and Triacetate   63
    Nylon   65
    Polyester   67
    Acrylic   74
    Spandex   76
    Olefin   78

Chapter 4   Leathers   80
    Leather and Suede   80
    Pigskin   92
    Shearling   92

Chapter 5   Synthetic Suedes   96
    Ultrasuede   97
    Lightweight Synthetic Suedes   105

Chapter 6   Vinyls   107

Chapter 7   Fur   112

Chapter 8   Feathers   120

PART TWO: FABRIC STRUCTURE

Chapter 9   Woven Fabrics   125
    Plain-Weave Fabrics   125
    Twill-Weave Fabrics   127
    Loosely Woven Fabrics   133
    Wash-and-Wear Fabrics   139
    Outerwear Fabrics   142

Chapter 10   Knits   147
    The Knit Family   147
    Jersey/Single Knits   153
    Double Knits   157
    Interlocks   162
    Raschel Knits   163
    Sweatshirt Knits   166
    Mesh   168
    Tricot   170
    Milanese Knits   175

Sweater Knits   175
Ribbing   178
Stretch Terry and Velour   181
Action Knits   184
Power Net   188

Chapter 11   Stretch-Woven Fabrics   190
Stretch Wovens   190
Elasticized Fabrics   192

PART THREE: SURFACE
CHARACTERISTICS

Chapter 12   Transparent Fabrics   197
The Transparent Family   197
Crisp Transparent Fabrics   205
Soft Transparent Fabrics   208

Chapter 13   Special-Occasion
Fabrics   212
Satin and Sateen   212
Ribbed Fabrics   217
Taffeta   220
Decorative Surface Fabrics   223
Prepleated Fabrics   227
Metallics   231
Sequinned and Beaded Fabrics   235
Lace   238
Net   250
White Fabrics   253

Chapter 14   Napped and Pile
Fabrics   255
Napped Fabrics   255
Pile Fabrics   257
Corduroy   261
Velveteen   264
Velvet   267
Panné Velvet   271
Woven Terry and Velour   273
Tufted Piles   275
Fake Furs   276

Chapter 15   Felt and Felted Fabrics   285
Felt   285
Felted Fabrics   287

Chapter 16   Reversible Fabrics   292
Two-Faced Fabrics   292
Double-Cloth Fabrics   297
Double-Faced Quilted Fabrics   311

Chapter 17   Quilted Fabrics   319
Single-Faced Quilted Fabrics   319
Custom Quilting   322

Chapter 18   Fabrics with Designs: Plaids,
Stripes, and Prints   325
Plaids   325
Checks   337
Stripes   338
Border Designs   341
Diagonal Patterns   343
Prints   346

PART FOUR: LININGS AND
INTERFACINGS

Chapter 19   Interfacings and
Battings   353
Interfacings   353
Batting and Insulating Fabrics   369

Chapter 20   Linings and
Underlinings   372

PART FIVE: SEWING TECHNIQUES

Chapter 21   Seams and Seam
Finishes   379
Seams   379
Seam Finishes   410

Chapter 22   Hems and Hem
Finishes   415
Hems   415
Hem Finishes   435

Chapter 23   Edge Finishes   436
Bands   436
Bindings   437
Elastic   444
Facings   446
Ribbings   448

Chapter 24   Closures   449
Button Loops   449
Buttonholes   450
Fly Plackets   460
Snaps   461
Ties and Straps   462
Claire's Super-Easy Zipper   462

Chapter 25   Hand Stitches   464

CONTENTS

PART SIX: FABRIC AND FIBER
DICTIONARY 471

APPENDIX
    Recommended Equipment and
        Supplies 499
    Sewing Machine Needles 500
    Threads 502
    The Sewing Clinic 504
    Tips for Topstitching 511

Glossary 512
Bibliography 517
Index 521
Fabric Worksheet 532

Foreword

by Nancy Zieman, hostess of Public Television's "Sewing With Nancy"

My first sewing project began in 4-H when I was ten years old. I made a simple, gathered skirt from a piece of gold, 100 percent cotton material. Isn't it funny that, after all these years, I still remember the fabric?

But for those of us who love to sew, the fabric is the essential ingredient. We say we choose a fabric because of its color, texture, drapeability—but mostly we choose it because we fall in love with it and *have* to have it.

As I got older and my sewing skills developed, I experimented with different fabric types, often in a trial-and-error fashion. I've made may share of bombs, where the characteristics of the fabric did not match the pattern I chose or I had not known about long-term care of the garment.

Knowing what to expect from a fabric makes working with it much easier. What type of care will it need? How will it drape? What are its particular characteristics? These are a few of the questions that need to be answered in order for us to successfully complete any sewing project. Fortunately, Claire Shaeffer has written a book which will assist us with decisions in buying and working with a wide variety of fabrics.

For me, sewing has been a major part of my life. It is my hobby, my business, my creative release. Browsing through a fabric store and enjoying the colors and textures is a very satisfying experience for me, as it must be for you, too. With Claire's help, this process will now be intensified. I now know more about my favorite fabrics, as well as about those that I've seen but have never tried. I hope that through reading this book and experimenting with a wide variety of fabrics, we can both enjoy sewing even more.

Dear Friend,

Like many of you, I am a self-taught home sewer. Luckily, my mother and aunt are home economists and both love to sew; consequently, I grew up with a good knowledge of technique.

But recently I've felt the need for a better foundation in sewing. I'm too ignorant about many of the fabrics I see or use. What, exactly, is jersey? How do I take care of rayon challis? How is polyester crepe de chine like its silk counterpart? I decided to look around for a college course in the fundamentals of fabrics.

Then Claire Shaeffer's manuscript arrived for editing. It didn't take long before I said "Eureka! This is what I've needed." Not only is the book a thorough treatment of fabrics—their history, characteristics, care, best ways to sew, etc.—but it contains many levels of information. For example, Claire has traveled all over the world to study fabrics and sewing techniques. She has researched in museums, designers' ateliers, and fine clothing stores; she has even apprenticed in designers' sewing workshops. Scattered throughout the book are **Hints,** sharing interesting ways designers finish edges, close seams, combine fabrics.

Claire's book has inspired me in two ways. First, I plan to make a notebook to accompany the book. I will collect fabric samples and paste them into my own personal fabric guide, with notes referring to the appropriate pages in the book. I also plan to make samples of all the seams, hems, finishes, and closures in Part Five: Sewing Techniques. (Don't miss Claire's Super-Easy Zipper—it's clever!) All of this may take years, but I can't think of a more pleasant self-challenge.

Second, Claire's book has inspired me to investigate more kinds of fabric. And don't laugh, but the book has also given me permission to collect fabric without guilt. I now have two hobbies: sewing, and collecting fabrics. Just because I buy a gorgeous hunk of mohair does not mean I have to do anything with it: I'm a collector.

I hope this book inspires you, too.

Robbie Fanning

Series Editor,
Creative Machine Arts, and co-author,
Complete Book of Machine Embroidery

Preface

I am a fabricaholic. I love fabrics, especially beautiful, unusual fabrics. Collecting them, handling them, moving them from one stack to another, showing them to my students and sewing friends, and planning garments—which may or may not be sewn this season—is almost as satisfying as actually sewing my fabrics into beautiful garments.

I know I am a fabricaholic. Since I've accepted my addiction and acknowledged that I like collecting fabrics almost as much as I like sewing them, I'm very well adjusted.

After all, since everyone collects something—recipes, coins, stamps, dolls, wine, guns, woodworking equipment, records, china figurines, records, videos—or has a hobby to enjoy in his or her leisure hours, it's all right for me to collect fabrics.

Unlike most collections, the only constant in mine is change. I am an avid sewer; and unlike many fabricaholics, I have the confidence to cut or sew any fabric in my collection. I've also weeded out any fabrics which no longer meet my standards, are the wrong color, or make me feel guilty.

For me, sewing fulfills both the desire to make something creative and to show it off; and part of my joy is taking a risk to achieve the unexpected and conquer the unknown. I love to experiment, try new techniques, fine-tune old methods, and combine fabrics and designs innovatively.

Most of my results are successful; and some have been stunning creations beyond my wildest expectations. When I have an occasional failure, I remind myself that professionals have them, too; and it really isn't any worse than burning the brownies.

The *Fabric Sewing Guide* began several years ago when I first taught "Sewing Special Fabrics" at the College of the Desert in Palm Desert, California. There was no text; there wasn't even a book that came close to being a text.

As I researched my subject, I realized that in addition to the wealth of material on special fabrics scattered in a variety of different sources, a great deal of information about traditional fabrics was no longer available, and that some of the information provided by the home-sewing industry wasn't correct. So the book mushroomed into this volume, which includes techniques for sewing all fabrics, including leather, suede, fur, and feathers.

The material for the book is based on my experiences as an educator and professional home sewer; interviews with designers, experts, and educators in the home-sewing and fashion industries; research in consumer and trade publications; research in the costume collections at the Victoria and Albert Museum, the Metropolitan Museum of Art, Fashion Institute of Technology, the Phoenix Art Museum, and the Indianapolis Museum of Art; countless snoop-shopping expeditions to examine ready-to-wear in all price ranges; and examining and reexamining the garments in my own small collection.

Acknowledgments

Thank you:

Elaine Bastajian, Betty Bennet, Sandra Betzina, Betty Bornemeier, Gail Brown, Joanne Burnett, Mike Dobrich, Virginia Dobrich, Lora Gill, Arlene Haislip, Rosemary Jameson, Debbie Jensen, Kaethe Kliot, Margaret Komives, Elizabeth Lawson, Mary Lou Luther, Katherine MacMillan, Shirley McKeown, John Montieth, Gale Nehrig, Gail Rachor, Elizabeth Rhodes, Gail Shinn, Susan Schleif, Anne Marie Soto, Ingrid Walderhaug, and Jane Whiteley, for sharing their expertise.

Charles Kleibacker for patiently answering my questions; Michael Novarese for letting me work in his factory; all the staff at Britex Fabrics, G Street Fabrics, and Jerry Brown Fabrics for showing me their treasures; and all the manufacturers of fibers and fabrics who provided me with information and samples.

To the curatorial staff at the Fashion Institute of Technology, the Indianapolis Museum of Art, the Metropolitan Museum of Art, the Phoenix Art Museum, and the Victoria and Albert Museum for their continuing support of my research.

To the many individuals, designers, and retailers who provided or helped me to locate photographs for this book.

To my students for trying new techniques and helping me to refine old ones.

To Pamela Poole for transforming my rough sketches into beautiful diagrams; Robbie Fanning for guiding, supporting and encouraging me at all the right times; and Chilton Trade Book Publishing for its continuing support.

To James, the best editorial assistant I'll ever have. And to Charlie, for being there.

Introduction

The *Fabric Sewing Guide* focuses on the fabrics and materials used to make garments. Designed to give you the confidence to sew fabrics you haven't used before, this single-volume reference includes complete and practical information for sewing all of today's fabrics. Organized for easy reference, the book is divided into six main parts.

Part One, Fiber Content, outlines the characteristics of natural and man-made fibers; Parts Two and Three include specific information and complete details for sewing individual fabrics. Part Four covers linings and interfacings, while Part Five describes basic sewing techniques you need to know. Part Six is a comprehensive textile dictionary listing important textile terms and frequently used fabrics.

Unlike most books, which focus only on sewing techniques, the *Fabric Sewing Guide* focuses on fabrics and their characteristics, as well as how to sew them successfully. It helps you select fabrics and be a more knowledgeable consumer. It addresses fabric-related situations that can't be included on pattern guide sheets, and warns you about problems or mistakes before they occur. It helps you select the most appropriate techniques for individual garments and fabrics, depending on the garment quality and use, as well as your time commitments and sewing experience. (For example, if I'm sewing an everyday cotton blouse, I choose quick-and-easy machine techniques which will launder well; when sewing a cotton tapestry party dress that will be dry-cleaned, I use more hand sewing and design details.)

In addition to broadening your understanding of fabrics and sewing techniques so you can apply your knowledge intelligently, the book includes many fashion photographs to stimulate your imagination for future designs.

HOW TO USE THIS BOOK

The *Fabric Sewing Guide* is organized for easy reference. First, identify your fabric according to the (1) fiber content, (2) fabric structure, and (3) fabric characteristics (texture, weight, transparency, and surface design); then look up each section that applies. For example, if the fabric is a striped, transparent, lightweight silk chiffon, you'd review the following sections: Silk, Woven Fabrics, Lightweight Silks, Stripes, Transparent Fabrics, and Soft Transparent Fabrics.

Each fabric section begins with a list of its characteristics so you will know what to expect. Then the Sewing Checklist summarizes the basic equipment, supplies, and techniques for handling the fabric. The core of the section details specific information on selecting quality fabrics, design ideas, layouts, cutting, marking, sewing details, pressing techniques, and garment care.

If you've never made a particular seam or need a refresher course, look for step-by-step instruction in Part Five, Sewing Techniques. For those who want to expand their knowledge of technique even more, consult my earlier book, *The Complete Book of Sewing Short Cuts,* which includes the largest collection of alternative techniques ever assembled.

If you encounter an unfamiliar textile or fabric term, look it up in the Fabric and Fiber Dictionary. To expand your knowledge, begin a swatch library using the Dictionary as your guide.

At the end of the book, I've included a Fabric Worksheet for you to photocopy. On the worksheet you can record details about the fabric's purchase, its characteristics, notes you've made from this book, and information about the finished garment. I keep two notebooks: Claire's Collection, for my fabrics, and Claire's Creations, for the garments I've made. You may want to do the same.

The *Fabric Sewing Guide* was written for you; to reap the most from it, read it cover to cover and make notes in it. Describe the fabrics you sew, the techniques you like or don't like, and your ideas for future designs or trims. This book is only a springboard, designed to stimulate your creativity and help you sew with confidence. Dare to experiment with new ideas and new fabrics—and share them with me for future editions.

CHAPTER 1
Basic Guide for Sewing All Fabrics

Planning a Garment

The first phase of sewing is one of the most important: planning the garment. Deciding which comes first—the fabric or the design—can be compared to the chicken and the egg. Designs can begin with either the fabric or the pattern; but most develop when the fabric and design are considered together.

For each garment, you'll make a variety of decisions which are affected by (1) the type of garment, its planned use, quality, and current fashion trends; (2) the fabric's characteristics and quality; (3) the garment design and pattern; (4) the compatibility of the fabric and design; and (5) your sewing ability, time available, life-style, and personal preferences.

1. Begin with the garment and its end use. Describe it in detail: identify the type of garment—blouse, skirt, suit, leotard, nightgown, or evening gown; the style of the garment—avant-garde or classic; the garment structure and silhouette—soft, draped, structured, bouffant; the desired quality—luxury or moderate; the relationship of the garment to other garments in your wardrobe; and its relationship to current fashion trends.

Consider (a) where it will be worn—at home, the grocery store, PTA, symphony, or to meet the President; (b) when it will be worn—morning, afternoon, evening, everyday, special occasion, winter or summer, all year; (c) how often it will be worn—once, occasionally, frequently, several years.

2. Once you've described the garment, consider the fabrication. Review the fabrics in your collection, visit fabric retailers, examine the latest mail-order swatches, and survey current trends.

Hint: *Since I believe that good-quality, natural fiber fabrics never go out of fashion, I always have a large collection of them. I particularly like unusual fabrics and frequently purchase materials when I travel. To be on the safe side, I usually buy a little more than I think I'll need—just in case I want to be extra creative.*

I don't have any more storage space than most of you so I have an inventory system. When I purchase a fabric, I list it on a Fabric Worksheet (see Appendix) and file it in my fabric notebook. When I make the garment, I refile the worksheet in my design notebook. (If your storage space is really limited, you'll have to sew more so you can add new pieces!)

My philosophy about collecting fabrics doesn't work for fad fabrics and cheap materials; and I admit that even good-quality fabrics are more fashionable some years than others.

Most fabrics for adult designs, especially luxury and novelty fabrics, are purchased because the fabric design, pattern, or color appeals to you, not because the fabric is durable. When purchasing fabrics for children, durability is usually more important.

To eliminate unsuitable fabrics, evaluate the fabric's quality, type, structure, design, weight, hand (i.e., how it feels), care requirements, comfort factor, and durability, then compare it to the garment you've described. Hold the fabric, crush it, and drape it to determine if it's crisp or soft, thick or thin, heavy or lightweight, loosely or firmly woven, flat or textured, silky or rough, transparent or opaque, sleazy or luxurious.

Evaluate the fabric's suitability for the garment, occasion, and your life-style; how the fabric will fit (or not fit) into your wardrobe; how it will look on you; and whether you have the skills, time, and patience to sew it.

Last, but not least, consider the cost of the fabric and the upkeep for the garment. Determine whether the total cost is appropriate for this type of garment and whether it will strain your budget.

Hint: *Don't be tempted to economize on interfacings, linings, and buttons to save money. Cheap findings frequently spoil an otherwise beautiful design. If necessary, select a less expensive fabric; but finish it with findings appropriate to the quality.*

3. Choose a pattern with a silhouette and design details that will look attractive on you and be appropriate for your age, size, and figure type.

Study the line drawings in the pattern catalog, try on similar garments in your wardrobe, and take a snoop shopping trip to try on some ready-to-wear.

Hint: *Sandra Betzina, author of* Power Sewing, *covers the model's face in the pattern book with a photograph of her own so she can visualize better how the design will look on her.*

4. Before marrying the fabric to a pattern, examine the fabric's character: its fiber content, hand, weight, texture, drape, transparency, and weave. Evaluate its compatibility with the garment design. Review the fabric recommendations on the pattern, analyze successful fabric/design combi-

nations, and survey current fashion trends.

If the fabric isn't perfect for the selected design, can its character be changed with interfacing or an underlining so the fabric and design will work well together?

5. Consider your sewing skills, the difficulty of the design, characteristics of the fabric, the amount of time available, and your patience.

Hint: *When sewing complicated designs, I often select easy-to-sew fabrics; when sewing simple styles, I choose more challenging fabrics. When time is really at a premium, I try to combine easy-to-sew fabrics with easy-to-make designs.*

Every time you sew, you are a designer. And, unfortunately, you will have an occasional failure; it happens to the very best designers so don't be discouraged.

Hints: *Each season, the best fashion designers expand their collections by creating several designs using different fabrications of the same silhouette (pattern). It's as simple as cutting three jackets from the same pattern.*

Designers also expand their collections by making several similar garments using the same fabric. Even when all the designs are gorgeous, the designer usually likes one best.

FABRICS FOR FIGURE FLATTERY

Choose fabrics that will flatter your figure. Select colors you like and think are becoming. Generally, cool hues such as blue, green, and violet are more slimming than warm hues such as red, orange, and yellow. Colors that blend into the background are more flattering to large figures than those that outline the silhouette.

Medium values are usually more slimming than very dark or light values; but, in the Sunbelt states, light and bright colors may be better.

All shiny fabrics (e.g., satin weaves, metallics, and beaded materials) reflect light and make you look heavier; but fabrics such as dull-faced satins, peau de soie, and dull metallics add less weight than acetate satin and shiny sequins.

Although textured materials such as piles, thick woolens and tweeds, mohair, fake furs, and furs add bulk, they can be worn by larger figure types if they are selected carefully. Velour knits are more slimming than woven velours; and short-haired furs have less bulk than long-haired furs. Cotton velvet and velveteen, which absorb light, are more flattering to large figures than rayon velvet, which has light highlights.

Most soft fabrics flatter heavier figures; but, when they are fitted too closely, the fabric clings, emphasizing the size and shape.

Since stiff fabrics stand away from the body, they can be used to hide figure irregularities; but they make the figure appear larger when used for exaggerated silhouettes.

FABRIC QUALITY

To reduce disappointments, learn to recognize fabric quality. Examine the material carefully. Check for flaws in the weave, printing, or finishing.

WOVEN FABRICS

Examine the fabric grain; the warp and filling threads should be straight and at right angles to each other. Many of today's fabrics have permanent finishes which do not allow them to be straightened.

Look for slubs, printing errors, permanent wrinkles, and snags. Good dyes penetrate the fabric well so the color is good on the back as well as the face.

Generally, plain fabrics are judged by the number of threads per square inch. Hold the fabric up to the light and examine the weave. The weave should be uniform; patches of light and dark indicate poor construction, poor-quality yarns, or heavy sizing. The threads should be fine, and closely spaced when the fabric is not a novelty weave.

Test for fraying and seam slippage. Scrape your thumbnail across the warp threads to see if they separate. If they do, the fabric will fray and the threads will pull apart at stress points.

Test for resiliency and the ability to recover from wrinkling. Squeeze the fabric in your hand; it should spring back with very few creases.

Fabrics with the plaids, checks, and stripes woven in are better quality than similar printed fabrics.

KNIT FABRICS

Examine the ribs on knit fabrics; they should be parallel to the edges and at right angles to the course, or horizontal rows on the wrong side of the fabric. If they are badly skewed, the garment won't hang properly if the fabric pattern looks right; and, if it hangs properly, the fabric pattern won't look right.

Check the shape retention. Stretch the fabric to see if it returns to its original shape.

FIBER CONTENT

The fabric's fiber content determines its comfort and care qualities. To determine the fiber content, ask for a small swatch so you can test it. If it's not convenient to take it home for testing, ask the salesperson to burn it for you; or take it outside and test it yourself.

For best results, burn the warp and filling threads separately if you think the fabric is made from more than one fiber.

Hold the swatch securely in a pair of tweezers and work over a sink.

FABRIC SERVICEABILITY

The service of a fabric depends on the kind and strength of the fiber; the tensile strength, twist, and number of plies in the yarn; and the number of yarns per inch, compactness of the fabric construction, and the weave. Natural fiber fabrics with long-staple fibers (e.g., cotton percales and worsted wools) are stronger, smoother, and more serviceable than those with short-staple fibers (e.g., muslin and woolens); they may be more or less serviceable than fabrics made of synthetic filaments.

The twist of the yarns determines the behavior, durability, and appearance. Fabrics made from fine, high-twist yarns (e.g., men's worsted suitings) are stronger, smoother, more durable, more elastic, more absorbent, more resistant to soil, and more crease-resistant than those made from low-twist yarns (e.g., women's soft woolens).

Fabrics made of multi-ply yarns or several strands twisted together are more durable than single-ply

5

Burn Test for Fiber Identification

FABRIC	BURNS	ODOR	RESIDUE
Natural Vegetable Fibers			
Cotton	Rapidly, yellow flame; continues burning; afterglow	Paper	Brown-tinged end; light-colored, feathery ash
Linen	Slower than cotton; afterglow	Rope	Ash maintains shape of swatch
Ramie	Slowly	Rope	Ash maintains shape of swatch
Cellulosic Fibers			
Rayon	Rapidly; afterglow	Paper or rags	Very little; light, fluffy ash
Acetate and triacetate	Fuses and melts; burns quickly; not self-extinguishing	Hot vinegar	Irregular shape; hard, brittle charcoal
Natural Protein Fibers			
Silk	Slowly; sputters; usually self-extinguishing	Hair	Crushable black bead
Wool	Slowly; self-extinguishing	Hair	Small, brittle, black bead
Synthetic Fibers			
Nylon	Shrinks from flame; melts and fuses; self-extinguishing	Celery	Hard gray or tan bead
Polyester	Shrinks from flame; Melts and fuses; Black smoke; self-extinguishing	Sweet smell	Hard black or brown bead
Acrylic	Burns rapidly; hot flame, sputters and smokes; not self-extinguishing	Hot vinegar	Crisp, black mass
Modacrylic	Burns slowly; melts; self-extinguishing	Acrid	Irregular hard, black bead
Olefin	Shrinks from flame; melts and fuses; black smoke; not self-extinguishing	Acrid	Hard, tan bead
Spandex	Burns and melts	Acrid	Soft, sticky gum

yarns. For example, ribbed fabrics woven with several yarns twisted together are more durable than those woven with a single heavy yarn.

Hint: *This is also true of threads. Three-ply thread is more durable than two-ply thread.*

Fabrics with multi-ply yarns are more durable than those with double yarns. Frequently used for ribbed fabrics and novelty wools, double yarns are two or more single-ply yarns that are treated as one yarn during the weaving process. Since the threads are not twisted together, the resultant fabrics tend to be softer and more lustrous; however, they are less resistant to abrasion and snag more readily.

Fabrics woven from long-staple natural fibers (e.g., cottons and worsteds) slip less at the seams than fabrics woven from filament yarns (e.g., silks, nylons, and polyesters).

Fabrics that have slubbed, looped, and novelty yarns for decorative effects (e.g., bouclés and shantungs) are not as serviceable as flannels and silk linens.

Closely woven fabrics that have a high thread count or more threads per inch are more durable, shrink less, and hold their shape better; they also have less slippage at the seams. The closeness of the weave or thread count is determined by adding the number of warp threads per inch to the number of filling threads. Fabrics range from burlap with 20 threads per inch to typewriter ribbons with 350 threads per inch. High-quality percales have 220 threads per inch, while inexpensive muslins have only 128 threads per inch.

Compared to plain-weave fabrics, basket-weave fabrics drape better; but they are not as durable because of the loose weave, low-twist, and low tensile strength of the yarns. Twill-weave fabrics are stronger, firmer, and heavier than plain-weave fabrics; they also drape better. To see for yourself, examine two neckties, one plain-weave and one twill-weave.

Satin-weave fabrics (e.g., Charmeuse) are less durable but more lustrous than plain-weave (e.g., broadcloth) or twill-weave fabrics (e.g., gabardine).

Fabrics woven with fine, tightly twisted yarns into a close weave (e.g., organdy) are more durable than loosely woven fabrics with low-twist yarns and long floats (e.g., damasks).

Fabrics with long floats and open weaves (e.g., embroidered fabrics, lace, quilted materials, and satin) snag easily.

Woven fabrics such as seersuckers are more durable than embossed materials like plissé. Embossed designs are more durable on heat-sensitive fibers such as polyester and nylon than on natural fibers or rayon.

Flocked fabrics are less durable than similar woven designs.

COMFORT AND CARE REQUIREMENTS

Read the information on the end of the bolt. Check the fiber content and care requirements. Generally, natural fibers are more comfortable to wear and synthetic fibers are easier and cheaper to clean.

Blends combine the best, and sometimes the worst, of the fibers used. For example, when polyester is blended with cotton, the new fabric is more comfortable to wear and more resistant to wrinkles, but it pills and stains easily.

TIMESAVERS

If your time to sew is limited, choose fabrics that don't require special handling. For skirts, slacks, and outerwear, select fabrics that don't require underlinings or linings. Firmly woven, opaque, medium-weight materials are good choices. Firmly woven or knit fabrics are easier to sew than slippery, soft, or loosely woven materials. Broadcloths are easier to sew than soft, slippery crepes.

Avoid fabrics that require matching (e.g., plaids), a test garment (e.g., Ultrasuede), single-layer cutting (e.g., velvet), or special seam and hem finishes (e.g., transparent fabrics).

PRICE

Purchase the best quality you can afford. Fine-quality fabrics are not necessarily the most expensive; and, once you've learned to recognize the characteristics of different grades, you'll frequently find that medium-priced fabrics are the best buys.

When your budget is limited, select a good-quality fabric from a less expensive group instead of a poor-quality fabric from a more expensive group. Choose a good-quality polyester blouse fabric over a cheap silk one, velveteen over velvet, or a linen-look or cotton over linen.

Another way to preserve your budget is to combine two different kinds of fabrics—lace with a plain fabric, velvet with a satin, or a novelty wool with a wool jersey.

To figure the real cost of the garment, add the cost of cleaning to the initial cost of the raw materials; then divide by the expected number of wearings.

Garment Care

Garment care depends on the fiber content; the yarn construction; the fabric construction; finishes and dyes applied to the fibers, yarns, or fabric; and the garment construction.

For best results, follow the advice in Rx for Stains (see Appendix) to treat stains and spots when they are fresh. Clean all garments before they are heavily soiled.

Design Ideas and Pattern Selection

Before selecting a pattern, survey the latest in ready-to-wear for design ideas. Don't just look; try on garments, especially if they are new silhouettes or styles you haven't worn in the past.

Analyze the designs you like, to determine what pleases you—is it the fabric, the design, or a detail you can adapt? When shopping, I carry a small note pad to record ideas I want to try.

When selecting a pattern, analyze the design to determine whether it will flatter your body. Look at the line drawings; don't rely on the photograph or fashion illustrations.

Also consider the weight, bulk, texture, opaqueness, drapeability, crispness, surface design, and care requirements of the fabric you plan to use.

Use the fabric suggestions on the pattern envelope as a guide. In addition to specific fabrics, the pattern also indicates whether the style is suitable for crisp or soft fabrics.

If the fabric you've selected isn't listed, compare its characteristics to those which are. If they are similar, continue on. To ensure success when they are not similar, select a different pattern or another fabric; but, if you like to be creative, combine the two anyway. Innovative combinations that aren't recommended can lead to fantastic garments (unfortunately, they can also lead to disaster), but I prefer the "Nothing ventured, nothing gained" route over the safe and dull.

Analyze the design features to determine whether you have the time and ability to sew them well in the fabric you've selected. Features such as set-in sleeves are always more time-consuming than dropped shoulder designs; and, while they are relatively easy to sew in a soft woolen, they are much more difficult to set smoothly in a denim twill.

When sewing a fabric for the first time, select an easy design so you can concentrate on mastering the fabric. I frequently use a pattern I've used before since I've already corrected the fit and practiced my sewing skills.

Hint: *Keep your patterns up-to-date. If they're more than two years old, think twice before using them. Fashion silhouettes change rapidly; frequently imperceptible on the pattern drawing, these changes make the difference between fashionable and passé.*

Preparing and Adjusting the Pattern

Press the pattern with a warm, dry iron, and adjust it before cutting the garment.

There are several ways to check the pattern fit. The easiest is to compare your measurements to those on the pattern envelope; if yours are larger, divide by the number of cut edges (usually four) and add where needed—bust, waist, or hip. Further refinements can be made with pin-fitting.

To pin-fit, trim away the paper margins; match and pin the seamlines together; then try on the pattern. An added advantage of this method is you can check a neckline that might be a little too décolleté.

When sewing intricate designs, fabrics that ravel badly, fabrics marred by pins and needles, or fabrics easily damaged by excessive handling, make a test garment. The test garment provides an opportunity to practice your sewing skills and to experiment with design changes, as well as to perfect the fit.

Hint: *Test garments are usually made in inexpensive muslin or pattern cloth similar in weight to the fashion fabric; if you prefer not to waste the test garment, make a wearable garment in an easy-to-sew fabric.*

DUPLICATE PATTERN PIECES

Most commercial patterns include a tissue pattern for the right side of the garment with instructions to lay out the pattern on two layers of fabric. When cutting expensive fabrics, bulky materials, or fabrics which require matching, you'll save time and fabric by making a complete pattern, i.e., cutting duplicate pattern pieces.

If you made a test garment, carefully rip the fitted test garment and press it flat with a dry iron. Mark the left and right sides of the test garment carefully, and use the garment sections for patterns instead of paper.

If you didn't make a test garment, trace the pattern sections which need to be duplicated onto pattern cloth or paper.

Hint: *If you have a doctor in the family, borrow a roll of examining paper, which is also available from medical supply houses (check the Yellow Pages). Otherwise, use wax paper and a permanent marker to copy the pattern.*

DESIGN CHANGES

Change the pattern design by cutting on the bias, adding seamlines or eliminating them, to utilize the fabric more effectively or to reduce bulk.

Bias-cut sections are particularly attractive on plaids and stripes. Use this easy method to cut a

garment section on the bias when the pattern indicates a lengthwise grain. Fold an envelope diagonally so the end matches one long side. Align the side of the envelope with the grainline on the pattern. Draw the new grainline.

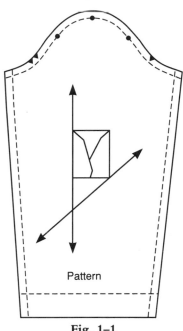

Pattern

Fig. 1–1

ADDING SEAMLINES

Another easy design change is to add a seamline; and, for materials such as leather and suede, which come in pieces, it may be a necessity.

1. Draw the new seamline on the pattern; indicate matchpoints.

Hint: *Make a full pattern when needed.*

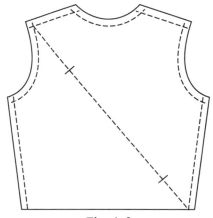

Fig. 1–2

2. Cut the pattern apart; add a seam allowance to both edges. (Most tape measures are 5/8″ wide, if you want to use one as a guide.)

Hint: *Be sure the grainline is marked on both pieces before cutting.*

ELIMINATING SEAMLINES

This change is frequently used at garment edges to reduce bulk.

1. Match and pin the pattern pieces together on the seamline.

2. Cut the garment section in one piece.

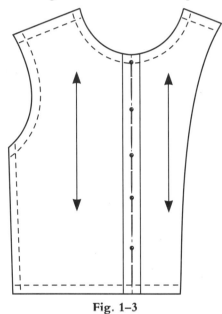

Fig. 1–3

Preparing the Fabric

Most fabrics need to be preshrunk or relaxed before cutting. Using the fiber content, yarn structure, fabric weave and color, manufacturer's recommendations, and garment construction as a guide, decide whether the garment will be laundered or dry-cleaned.

If it will be laundered, wash and dry the uncut fabric the way you plan to wash the garment. To set dark and bright colors, add 1/4 cup vinegar to each gallon of water.

If the garment will be dry-cleaned, steam press it well. This is easy if you have a commercial gravity flow iron; but most household irons don't make

enough steam and the steam isn't dry enough to be certain of the results. In this case, ask the dry cleaner to steam and press the fabric; this is less expensive than dry cleaning.

To preshrink wools, use the London shrunk method (see Chapter 2) or take them to a dry cleaner.

STRAIGHTENING FABRICS

Most fabrics cannot be straightened because they have a heat-set finish; but a few woven from cotton and wool have no special finishes and can be straightened. (See Cotton and Wool.)

To straighten the ends of fabrics with heat-set finishes, spread the fabric on a rectangular table. Align the selvages or the lengthwise fold with one side of the table. Using the table end or cutting board as a guide, mark the fabric end; trim on the marked line.

Hint: *If the end has a large slant and you trim it off, you may be caught short on fabric. Use chalk or a temporary marking pen to mark the straight end.*

Sew Successful
- To save time, stitch it right the first time.
- Sew with a positive attitude.
- Test, test, test; when in doubt, practice before stitching the garment.
- Stitch directionally.
- Stitch with the fabric bulk to the left of the needle.
- Stitch in the direction of the nap, as if you were petting an animal.
- Begin stitching at the point of difficulty (e.g., when stitching reverse corners, begin at the corner; when stitching notched collars, begin at the notch).
- Stitch with the longer layer on the bottom.
- Sew flat; set the pockets before sewing the side seams.
- Sew inside loops, circles, sleeves, pant legs, and collars carefully to avoid inadvertently stitching through unwanted layers.
- When topstitching, stitch right side up unless directed otherwise.
- When straight stitching, use a foot that holds the fabric firmly (not, for example, an all-purpose or embroidery foot).
- Understitch faced edges.

10

STITCHING TIPS

Make a test seam to check the needle size, the thread size and color, and the stitch quality.

Begin with a new needle in the smallest size recommended; there's no need to make a big hole when a little one will work. If skipped stitches or frayed thread are a problem, use the next size larger needle.

Hint: *If several types of needles are suggested, try the Universal-H point, Yellow Band, or Red Band first, depending on your brand of machine. They are most readily available and least expensive.*

LAYOUT AND CUTTING

To avoid stretching and distorting the fabric, spread it on the table so it doesn't hang off the end. Use a nap layout except when you're positive there is no nap or shade difference.

Place all the pattern pieces on the fabric before pinning; and, when cutting a single layer, use *duplicate* pieces.

To avoid damaging the fabric, don't pin the grainline; instead use weights at the ends of the grainline. Place pins within the seam allowances parallel to the grainline.

Hint: *Use small ashtrays, canned goods, dinner knives, and drapery weights if you don't have fabric weights.*

For fine fabrics, use weights only—no pins—or substitute size 10 needles for pins.

Hint: *To avoid damaging your cutting equipment, don't let the pins extend beyond the pattern cutting line.*

Recheck your layout before cutting. Use sharp scissors or a rotary cutter and mat when cutting. Many fabrics are easily damaged by dull cutting equipment.

Hint: *Close your rotary cutter every time you set it down. Your fingers will thank you.*

Identifying the Warp

When you have a fabric scrap with no selvage, use these guides to identify the warp, which runs parallel to the selvage.
- In plain weaves, there are more yarns in the warp.
- In twill weaves, the filling yarns run in the direction of the diagonal.
- In satin weaves, the warp yarns make the floats.
- The direction of the fabric with the least stretch is the warp.
- Inferior or thicker yarns and yarns with slubs, a lower twist, or fewer plies are usually in the filling.
- Plaid fabrics usually have vertical rectangles.

MARKING

The marking method depends on the fiber content, fabric type and quality, time available, and your preference.

CLIPS

Suitable for firmly woven and knit fabrics, clips are the quickest marking method. Don't bother to cut out the notches. Instead, on the raw edge of the garment section, make small 1/8″ clips at the notch center.

CHALK

Suitable for most fabrics, chalk is available in several colors and forms: clay chalk, wax chalk, chalk wheel, or chalk marking pencils.

Hint: *The chalk wheel makes a much thinner line than chalk wedges or pencils and is easy to use.*

Test before using colors; I prefer white or disappearing. Wax chalk is only suitable for wool fabric.

PINS

Pins are suitable for fabrics that are not easily marred, but shouldn't be used on delicate woven fabrics, piles, and some napped fabrics. Use pins to mark placement symbols, dart points, and matchpoints. Remove the pins as soon as possible to avoid a permanent mark. Small safety pins work well for slippery fabrics—they won't fall out.

SOAP SLIVER

Suitable for most fabrics, a sliver of soap can be used instead of clay chalk. To avoid staining the fabric, choose a soap such as Ivory with no oils or cold cream.

TAILOR TACKS

Suitable for all fine fabrics, tailor tacks are accurate, but time-consuming. Use a soft thread such as embroidery floss or unglazed basting thread.

Hint: *Use only white or soft pastels which won't crock or rub off on your fabric.*

To mark matchpoints with tailor tacks, use a double thread without a knot. At the matchpoint, take two stitches through the pattern and fabric layers, leaving a large loop between the first and second stitch. Clip the loop and remove the pattern; carefully separate the fabric layers and clip the threads between them.

Pattern

Fig. 1–4

To mark stitching lines, use a loopy basting stitch to sew through the pattern and fabric layers. Clip the loops and remove the pattern. Carefully separate the fabric layers and clip the threads between them.

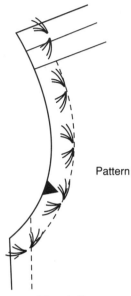

Pattern

Fig. 1–5

TAPE

Suitable for everyday fabrics that have no nap or pile, tape is a quick and easy marking aid for topstitching, buttonholes, and pockets.

Drafting tape is less likely to leave a residue than masking tape, but it's always wise to test.

TEMPORARY MARKING PENS

Temporary marking pens include air-erasable and water-erasable pens. Marks made with air-erasable, sometimes called "48-hour" or "fade-away," pens disappear within twentyfour hours. Marks made with water-erasable pens disappear when touched with water.

Test these pens carefully. Some marks are set permanently when pressed.

THREAD TRACING

Suitable for fine fabrics, use thread tracing to mark details on the body of the garment. If the garment will be pressed before the tracing is removed, use soft basting cotton or silk.

To thread trace, use an uneven or dressmaker's basting stitch.

TRACING WHEEL AND TRACING CARBON

A very accurate marking method that's widely used for fine garments, the tracing wheel and tracing carbon can be used on most fabrics. Test to be sure the tracing wheel won't damage the fabric.

Mark the wrong side only. Use only white tracing carbon on fashion fabrics; use colors on muslins and test garments.

Hint: *Since I don't want to wash my garments before wearing them, I don't use dressmaker carbons which must be washed out.*

Cut the garment sections from a double/lay (two layers), with right sides together, or from a single/lay (one layer), right side up.

Lay the carbon on a resilient surface, carbon side up. For a single layer, place the garment section with the pattern pinned to it on top of the carbon. Using a tracing wheel, trace the marks to be transferred.

When marking a double layer, mark as above, then remove the paper pattern and turn the fabric sections over. Trace the first set of carbon markings.

WAX

Use wax chalks only on wool fabrics. Wax chalks leave grease spots on other materials. They can be purchased at tailoring supply shops.

SEAMS

Seams and seam finishes should be flat and inconspicuous from the right side of the garment, except when they're designed to be decorative.

When selecting the seam or seam finish, consider the fabric type, weight, and transparency; the garment design, type, use, care, and quality; the location and purpose of the seam; and your time commitments and preference.

For lightweight fabrics, I prefer self-finished seams, even when the fabric is not transparent. (See Seams.) For medium- to heavyweight fabrics, plain seams are the flattest.

For heavy wear and a sturdy construction, select a seam with one or more rows of topstitching. For unlined garments, choose a seam or seam finish which looks neat on the inside of the garment. (Lined garments rarely require seam finishes.)

The most professional looking seam on most garments is a serged finish. It's not always my first choice; however, it is used on garments which cost as much as $4000.

The best seam finish for luxury garments is hand overcasting; overcast with mercerized cotton thread.

Hint: *Galanos is the only designer using a Hong Kong finish regularly. (See Chapter 21.) His finish is very narrow and made of a light-weight silk such as chiffon.*

Stretch fabrics require stretch seams.

HEMS

Hems and hem finishes should be flat and inconspicuous from the right side of the garment, except when they're designed to be decorative.

When selecting the hem or hem finish, consider the fabric type, weight, transparency, and drape; the garment design, type, use, care, and quality; and your time commitments and preference.

For better garments made of medium- and heavyweight fabrics, use plain, flat hems. If you have a serger, serge the raw edges before turning them up.

Hint: *Use woolly nylon in the loopers to prevent a thread imprint on the right side of the garment. To avoid melting the thread, use a medium or wool setting when you iron.*

For luxury garments, overcast the edge by hand, using mercerized cotton; hem with silk thread.

When sewing lightweight fabrics, use narrow hems on full garments, flared skirts, shaped edges, narrow trims, and ruffles. Use wide hems on straight and rectangular skirts to add weight and body.

Interface or pad hems to prevent sharp foldlines.

Use machine-stitched hems on garments which will be machine washed and dried, work clothes, children's garments, casual and everyday wear, and uniforms.

Use stretch hems on stretch fabrics. (See Chapter 22.)

Substitute bands, ribbings, and bindings for hems when the fabric is difficult to hem attractively.

BASTING TECHNIQUES

Since I hate to rip, I do a lot of basting; and I use everything from the new water-soluble basting tapes to old-fashioned basting by hand with thread.

Experiment with a variety of basting aids such as washable glues, water-soluble basting tapes, fusible webs, pins, drafting tape, machine basting, and hand basting until you decide which you like best.

PRESSING

Pressing is an essential phase of sewing. Good pressing can enhance a poorly stitched garment; while improper pressing can destroy a well-made design.

Well-pressed garments have flat, carefully shaped edges and straight, unpuckered seamlines. They do not have imprints of construction details on the right side, unwanted creases or wrinkles, or shine and iron marks.

Test press on fabric scraps to determine the heat setting, moisture, and pressure. To press professionally, experiment with various heat settings, damp and dry press cloths, steamers, and clappers.

Press as you go to set seams and darts permanently before crossing them with other seams or hems. Press the seams flat; then press them open.

Use a tailor's ham, sleeve board, seam roll, and point presser to support the garment sections so you can shape and mold them easily.

Hint: *To make a seam roll, cover a tightly rolled magazine with a tube of prewashed muslin or wool; to make a tailor's ham, substitute a small, firm pillow.*

Remove bastings and pins before pressing. Press as much as possible from the wrong side; always underpress collars, cuffs, plackets, and lapels with the wrong side up.

Use a press cloth when pressing the right side of the fabric. To avoid seam imprints, use a seam roll or brown paper strips between the seam or hem allowances and the garment. And remember it's much easier to press again than to remove a shine, crease, or scorch.

PART ONE

Fiber Content

CHAPTER 2
Natural Fiber Fabrics

The natural fiber fabrics are made from materials that grow in nature. Grouped into two categories, cellulosic and protein, they include cotton, linen, ramie, silk, wool, and hair fibers.

Cotton

Sometimes called "the fiber of a thousand faces," cotton is known for its comfort, appearance, versatility, and performance. Available in a wide variety of fabric weights, colors, surfaces, patterns, weaves, and prices, cotton is used to make many fabrics. It is frequently blended with rayon to make less expensive fabrics and with synthetics to make easy-care, wrinkle-resistant fabrics.

Cotton's use in fabrics may have begun in Egypt as early as 12,000 B.C. By 3000 B.C., it was well established in India and Peru. Some fragments found from this later period are actually finer than the finest cottons we have today.

Unlike Europeans, who thought cotton was the fleece from a half-animal, half-plant beast, we know that cotton grows on cotton plants in warm climates with adequate rain. The cotton fibers, which are taken from the boll or seed pod, are sometimes as long as 2 1/2" and sometimes as short as 3/8". The long-staple cottons are the most expensive, hardest to produce, and least abundant.

Creamy white or yellow blooms appear approximately three months after planting. Shortly thereafter (12 to 72 hours) the blooms turn pink, lavender, or red, and fall off the plant, leaving the boll on the stem to go to seed. When the boll

Fig. 2–1 *Designed by Geoffrey Beene, this smashing coat is made of cotton and punctuated with silver metallic dots. (Photographer, Jack Deutsch; photo courtesy of Geoffrey Beene, Spring 1987 Collection.)*

matures 50 to 80 days later, it bursts open, exposing the cotton, which is ready to be picked.

Once the cotton is picked, it is separated from the seeds by ginning. Long fibers are spun into thread; linters, too short for spinning, are made into rayon; and the seeds are used for fertilizer and cottonseed oil.

Today, cotton is blended with many fibers to make fabrics such as poplin, gingham, terry, corduroy, eyelet, Oxford cloth, broadcloth, challis, and batiste, which were all-cotton for thousands of years.

The quality of cotton depends on the fineness of the fiber, its color and brightness, and the amount of foreign matter.

Compared to flax, cotton is weaker; compared to rayon, it is stronger. Mercerized cottons are stronger and more lustrous than unmercerized.

Cotton burns with a yellow flame; when the flame is removed, it continues to burn and has an afterglow. Like other cellulosic fibers, cotton fabrics smell like burning paper and have a fluffy, gray ash.

SEWING CHECKLIST

Machine Needles: Universal-H point or Red or Yellow Band needles; sizes 60/8 to 120/20, depending on the fabric weight.

Thread: Long-staple polyester, cotton-wrapped polyester. Topstitching—regular threads, topstitching, silk (size A).

Hand Sewing Needles: Sizes 5 to 10.

Marking Techniques: All types, except wax.

Seams and Hems: Depends on the fabric transparency, weight, care requirements, and garment use. (See Chapters 21 and 22.)

Interfacings, Linings, and Underlinings: Depends on the fabric weight, garment type and structure, and care requirements.

Fabric Characteristics

- Cotton is comfortable, durable, and very flammable.
- It has a high moisture absorbency, conducts heat well, and resists abrasion, pilling, and moths.
- Cotton drapes well and has good covering power. It is relatively dense, which makes it feel heavier than comparable fabrics.
- It also conducts electricity and does not build up static electricity.
- Cotton is stronger when wet than when dry.
- Cotton has little elasticity and resiliency; it wrinkles easily.
- Cotton fabrics frequently shrink.
- Cottons weaken and deteriorate when exposed to extended periods of sunlight.
- Cotton soils easily.
- Cotton can be laundered or dry-cleaned, depending on the dyes, finishes, fabric structure, and garment design.

PLANNING A GARMENT

SELECTING THE FABRIC

Select cotton fabrics appropriate for the garment type and use. Look for fabrics closely woven with even yarns. For strength and durability, choose sturdy, well-constructed fabrics. For dressy garments, choose lustrous fabrics woven with fine combed-cotton yarns.

Fabrics imported from Switzerland are usually smoother, finer, and more expensive than American-made fabrics.

High-quality cotton fabrics are made from long-staple cotton fibers such as American Peeler, American Pima, Egyptian, and Peruvian cottons. These cotton varieties have the longest fibers and make the finest, most lustrous fabrics.

To determine the fiber length, pull a thread from the fabric and untwist it. If the fibers are longer than 1/2", the fabric will wear well.

Generally, fine fabrics are more closely woven than inexpensive ones. Scrape the fabric with your thumbnail; if the yarns separate easily, the fabric may not wear well.

When durability is desired, rub the fabric vigorously with a smooth surface cloth or self-fabric.

If the fabric roughens, it will not retain its "like new" appearance.

Rub with a contrasting color fabric to check crocking and shedding lint.

Generally better cotton fabrics are softer since they have little sizing while inexpensive cottons are heavily sized to make them appear firmer and heavier. They will lose these qualities when laundered and will not wear well or maintain their appearance. Hold the fabric up to the light and look for sizing or starch between the threads. Or rub the material briskly between your hands. If it feels softer after rubbing or if your hands feel powdery, the fabric is heavily sized.

Mercerized cottons retain their luster even when laundered frequently. Fabrics with cords or ribs in either the warp or filling are weaker than those with cords or ribs in both directions.

Determining the Face Side
- Most cottons are folded right side out on the bolt.
- Generally, the selvage is smoother on the face side.
- The face side has fewer imperfections, knots, and slubs than the back.
- Printed fabrics are brighter on the face.
- Texture, ribs, cords, novelty yarns, flocked designs, and pile are more pronounced on the face.
- Woven dotted Swiss is smooth on the face with the cut ends on the back; flocked dotted Swiss is flocked on the face and smooth on the back.
- Jacquard and dobby weaves may have a more distinct pattern on the face.
- Brocades may have walelike stuffer yarns in the filling on the back which make the fabric three dimensional.
- Generally, the knit rather than purl side is the face of jerseys and single knits. When in doubt, stretch the cut edge; it will curl to the right side.
- Twills on cotton fabrics usually run from right to left.
- The face is the side you prefer.

PREPARING THE FABRIC

Preshrink all cotton and cotton-blend fabrics before cutting. Cotton fibers do not shrink; but cotton fabrics do. During the weaving process, the yarns are held under tension. When the fabric is removed from the loom and washed the first time, the fabric relaxes.

When both sides look the same, mark the face with drafting tape, pins, or chalk to avoid shading differences in the completed garment.

STRAIGHTENING COTTONS

Off-grain fabrics can be straightened if they are all cotton and don't have a special finish. Straighten the ends first by pulling a crosswise thread at each end. Trim on the pulled lines. Hold the opposite corners firmly and pull vigorously to straighten.

Hint: *To avoid being caught short of fabric when the fabric is off-grain several inches, trim only one end.*

Fold the fabric lengthwise with right sides together; baste the straightened ends together. Then baste the selvages together.

Machine wash and damp dry the fabric; iron until dry. Iron with, not across, the lengthwise grain. Iron carefully so the grains will remain straight and at right angles to each other.

Hint: *Use a plant mister or household spray bottle when sprinkling.*

SEWING COTTON

The variety of cotton fabrics ranges from lightweight, loosely woven sheers to heavy, napped velvets; many cotton fabrics do not require special sewing techniques. Only a few sewing suggestions which relate to most cotton fabrics are included in this section. When sewing other popular cottons, see the indicated sections.

Batiste: Transparent Fabrics
Bedford Cord: Ribbed Fabrics
Broadcloth: Plain-Weave Fabrics
Calico: Plain-Weave Fabrics
Cambric: Plain-Weave Fabrics
Canvas: Denim
Challis: Plain-Weave Fabrics
Chambray: Plain-Weave Fabrics

Chino: Denim
Chintz: Plain-Weave Fabrics
Cluny Lace: Lace; Transparent Fabrics
Corduroy: Corduroy; Pile
Covert: Worsted Suitings
Crepe: Soft, Transparent Fabrics
Damask: Reversible Fabrics
Denim: Denim
Dimity: Transparent Fabrics; Plaids
Dotted Swiss: Crisp, Transparent Fabrics
Double-Faced Cottons: Two-Faced Fabrics
Double Knit: Double Knit; Knits
Drill: Denim
Duck: Denim
Durable Press Cottons: Wash-and-Wear Fabrics
Embroidered Cottons: Transparent Fabrics; Border Prints; Decorative Surfaces
Eyelet: Transparent Fabrics; Border Prints
Flannel: Napped Fabrics
Fleece: Napped Fabrics
Gabardine: Denim; Twill-Weave Fabrics
Gauze: Soft, Transparent Fabrics
Ghipure Lace: Lace
Gingham: Checks
Homespun: Loosely Woven Fabrics
Hopsacking: Loosely Woven Fabrics
Jersey: Jersey; Knits
Lawn: Transparent Fabrics
Madras: Plaids; Plain-Weave Fabrics; Stripes
Monk's Cloth: Loosely Woven Fabrics
Muslin: Plain-Weave Fabrics
Net: Net
Organdy: Crisp, Transparent Fabrics
Oxford Cloth: Plain-Weave Fabrics; Transparent Fabrics
Percale: Plain-Weave Fabrics; Transparent Fabrics
Piqué: Ribbed Fabrics
Plissé: Decorative Surfaces
Polished Cotton: Plain-Weave Fabrics

Pongee: Ribbed Fabrics
Poplin: Denim; Ribbed Fabrics
Ratiné: Loosely Woven Fabrics
Rib Knits: Rib Knits; Knits
Raschel Knits: Raschel Knits; Knits
Sailcloth: Denim
Sateen: Satin
Seersucker: Decorative Surfaces
Sheets: Plain-Weave Fabrics
Suede Cloth: Napped Fabrics
Terry: Terry and Velour; Stretch Terry and Stretch Velour; Pile
Ticking: Denim
Velour: Terry and Velour; Stretch Terry and Stretch Velour; Pile
Velvet: Velvet; Pile
Velveteen: Velveteen; Pile
Voile: Transparent Fabrics
Whipcord: Ribbed Fabrics

STITCHING TIPS

Use the fabric weight as a guide when choosing the appropriate needle size and stitch length. Here's an approximate chart; make a sample seam on your own machine.

Stitch woven fabrics with moderate tension on the needle and bobbin; stitch knits with a loose tension.

PRESSING

When pressing cotton blends, lightweights and sheer fabrics, reduce the temperature from the cotton or high setting; then test press on a fabric scrap.

Hint: *Line cotton draperies with cotton/ polyester blend or acetate to reduce yellowing and prevent deterioration.*

FABRIC WEIGHT	NEEDLE SIZE	STITCH SETTING
Lightweights	60/8–70/10	1.5–1.75 mm or 15–18 spi
Mediums	70/10–80/12	2 mm or 12 spi
Heavy	90/14–100/16	2.5 mm or 10 spi
Very Heavy	100/16–120/20	3–4 mm or 6–8 spi

GARMENT CARE

Cotton garments are usually laundered in detergents or soaps, but they can be dry-cleaned when the fabric weave, construction details, or trim make laundering undesirable.

Cotton fabrics frequently shrink. Loosely woven fabrics shrink more than closely woven ones; and all cottons shrink more when they're washed in hot water and are machine dried.

Garments should be cleaned frequently. The short fibers pick up soil easily; and once the dirt is embedded, it's difficult to remove. Most fabrics, except madras and handwovens from Guatemala and Thailand, are colorfast; however, it's better to separate garments according to color as well as soil. Wash whites in hot water, medium colors in warm, and dark colors in cold.

To set colors and reduce fading, add a cup of vinegar to the wash water. To remove excess soil and to whiten whites, use a chlorine bleach; or boil them in water.

Iron damp cottons with a dry, hot iron. Lower the iron temperature for cotton blends. To prevent a shine, iron dark colors from the wrong side or use a press cloth.

Cottons treated with a durable press permanent finish may be damaged when washed in hot water and bleach. To improve the fabric's appearance, press with a warm steam iron.

Cotton is easily damaged by jewelry and pins, which cut the fibers and cause holes.

Cotton stored in warm, damp places will mildew, mold, and rot; be careful to avoid putting garments away damp. Cotton is resistant to moths and carpet beetles, but not to silverfish.

When properly stored, cotton is not affected by age. Acid-free tissue paper is recommended for long-term storage.

GUATEMALAN AND THAI COTTONS

Handwoven cottons from Guatemala, other Central and South American countries, and Thailand are firmly woven. Generally, these handwovens are easy to sew, but they have several characteristics that must be considered.

Sewing Guatemalan and Thai Cottons
- Most handwoven cotton widths range from 17" to 36".
- They require additional yardage. Make a new layout; do not rely on a fabric conversion chart.
- Many handwoven cottons have bold patterns which cannot be matched because they have no regular repeat. (See Plaids.)
- Handwoven cottons shrink as much as 10 percent.
- Some fabrics have small flaws.
- Dye lots and fabric designs may be one of a kind. Be sure to purchase adequate fabric.
- Many are dyed with vegetable dyes which bleed. Set the dye by soaking for half an hour in a mixture of 1/4 cup vinegar to one gallon of water. Rinse well and hang to dry.
- Some are loosely woven. (See Loosely Woven Fabrics.)

Linen

Linen may well be the oldest natural cellulosic fiber, having been used by Swiss lake dwellers as early as 8000 B.C. Egyptian linen fragments have been dated to 4500 B.C.

Made from the stem of the flax plant, linen fibers, which are from 2" to 36" long, are spun into yarn, then woven into fabric.

Available in a variety of weights from handkerchief linen to heavy suitings, linen has a natural luster, high moisture absorbency (12 percent), and no static electricity.

Cool and comfortable to wear in warm climates, linen fabrics are quick drying, lint-free and resistant to moths and the alkalies in detergents, Borax, ammonia, and washing soda. They have good shape retention; and, even though strong when dry, they are even stronger when wet. They shed surface dirt, resist stains, and are not damaged by sunlight, but they yellow with age.

Linen fabrics wrinkle easily, even when treated with a crease-resistant finish. They shrink, have poor elasticity, and are damaged by silverfish and mildew.

Linen dyes well, but it does not dye as easily as

cotton. Darker colors crock badly and fabrics wear and fade at foldlines and edges. Compared to cotton, linen is usually more expensive, more absorbent, and faster drying.

Although flax is a washable fiber, linen garments may not be washable because of the fabric weave or garment structure. When laundered, linen loses some of its crispness.

Fig. 2–2 *Crisp and cool, Don Sayres's all-linen shirt jacket slips over a matching sundress. (Photograph courtesy of Don Sayres.)*

SEWING CHECKLIST

Machine Needles: Universal-H point or Red Band needles; sizes 60/8 to 90/14, depending on the fabric weight.

Machine Setting: 2–3 mm (8–12 stitches per inch).

Thread: Long-staple polyester, cotton-wrapped polyester. Topstitching—regular, topstitching, silk (size A or D).

Hand Sewing Needles: Sizes 5 to 10.

Layout: Double/lay, right sides together.

Marking Techniques: All types, except wax.

Seams: Depends on fabric weight, care requirements, and lining. Lightweight linens—plain, French, false French, standing-fell, flat-fell, topstitched, welt, double/ply. Medium to heavy—plain, flat-fell, topstitched, welt, double-welt, lapped, double/ply.

Hems: Depends on fabric weight, care requirements, and lining. Lightweights—double, shirttail, book, machine-rolled. Medium to heavy—plain, blindstitch, catchstitch, blind catchstitch, machine blindstitch, topstitched, twin needle.

Seam and Hem Finishes: Unfinished, pinked, pinked-and-stitched, serged, zigzag, multi-stitch zigzag, bound, Hong Kong, hand-overcast, turned-and-stitched.

In the United States, a fabric cannot be labeled "linen," "pure linen," or "pure flax" unless it is 100 percent linen. When the fabric is a blend, the percentage of each fiber, according to weight, must be stated. Fabrics labeled "rayon linen" are rayon; those labeled "silk linen," silk. Fabrics labeled "linen-like" frequently contain no linen.

Fabric Characteristics
- Linen fabrics fray badly.
- Linen shrinks.
- Linen does not ease well.
- Linen slicks when pressed on the right side without a press cloth.
- Seam slippage is frequently a problem.
- Some linen fabrics are sheer while others are bulky.
- Linen fabrics lose their crispness when laundered.
- Loosely woven linen fabrics cannot withstand laundering, even though the fiber is washable.
- Linen wrinkles badly.

- Linens have good moisture absorbency and are comfortable to wear.
- Linen dries quickly.
- Linen resists moths and alkalies but is damaged by mold and silverfish.
- Linen yellows with age.
- Linen is strong when wet or dry.
- Linen has poor elasticity.
- Linen wears at creases and foldlines.
- Once pressed, unwanted creases are difficult to remove.

PLANNING A GARMENT

SELECTING LINEN

Available in a variety of weights and suitable for a wide range of fashion silhouettes, from soft, feminine lingerie to sharply tailored suits and coats, linen is a crisp fabric. Most linen dress fabrics are textured, plain-weave materials with fine slubs.

Good quality linens feel cool, firm, wiry, smooth, and supple while heavily sized, inexpensive fabrics frequently feel harsh. To distinguish better fabric, examine the finish and fineness of the yarns as well as the number of threads per inch. Look for fabrics that have straight, even, and smooth yarns and firm, close construction. The finer the yarns and the more threads per square inch, the better the fabric. Some Ancient Egyptian mummy cloths had more than 500 threads per inch. (Fine cotton percale sheets have 220 threads per inch.)

To test for sizing, rub the fabric vigorously between your hands or scratch the surface with your fingernail; look for a fine powder. Hold loosely woven fabrics up to the light and look for sizing; or moisten the fabric with your tongue to check for a starchy taste. Soak the linen in water. If it feels sleazy, it is heavily sized. If it's heavily sized, it will lose its body when it's preshrunk or cleaned.

Since linen is more expensive than cotton, it is important to know the difference between the two. High-quality linens are smoother with less fuzz on the surface than cotton. Linen fibers are longer and more difficult to tear; the torn fiber ends are straighter and smoother, while the fuzzy cotton fibers tend to curl. Incidentally, cotton makes a characteristic shrill sound when torn. Frequently, linen feels cooler to the touch.

To test for linen, unravel several threads; hold securely and pull until they break. Repeat with cotton threads of a similar size. Linen is stronger and harder to break; once broken, the linen ends are pointed; the cotton ends look like brushes.

Another way to test for linen is to drop water on the fabric. If it is linen, it will spread quickly and unevenly along the warp and filling; and it will dry quickly. When you substitute glycerine for water, the linen fabric looks transparent.

Hint: *To improve your knowledge of linen qualities, visit the linen departments in big stores and examine tablecloths in various price ranges. You'll be surprised how much you can learn with very little effort. While shopping, don't overlook the possibilities of designing with tablecloths.*

DESIGN IDEAS AND PATTERN SELECTION

Select patterns with tucks, gathers, pleats, and gores for lightweight linens. For medium-weight fabrics, casual designs and unstructured jackets are good choices. Tailored dresses and separates, coat dresses, jackets, and skirts are perfect for firmer, heavier linens.

Details such as lined yokes, topstitching, and edgestitching enhance tailored designs; they also help to control fraying.

PREPARING THE FABRIC

Steam press linens for garments which will be dry-cleaned. If you don't have a good steam iron, dip the fabric in cold water; do not squeeze. Hang over the shower rod to drip dry.

Wash, dry, and press fabrics for garments which will be laundered.

SEWING LINEN

STITCHING TIPS

Make a test seam. Set the stitch length for 2–2.5mm (10–12 stitches per inch).

Generally linen is not difficult to sew and special

techniques are rarely required. When sewing fabrics with thick slubs, use a straight-stitch presser foot or a jeans foot to hold the fabric firmly. If necessary, use a larger size jeans needle to penetrate the slubs easily.

For smooth, crisp corners on collars and lapels, redraw sharp points so the wiry fabric will turn easily.

Hint: *Use a temporary pen to draw a curve; don't try to take several stitches across the point; it's too difficult to stitch two alike.*

SEAMS AND HEMS

Consider the garment structure and care requirements when selecting seams and hems. For washable garments, choose sturdy seams such as welt, topstitched, felled, double/ply, and topstitched machine hems which will not fray.

Eliminate seam and hem finishes in lined garments which will be drycleaned.

INTERFACINGS, UNDERLININGS, AND LININGS

When selecting interfacings, consider the fabric weight, garment care, garment quality, and amount of crispness desired.

Traditional interfacings such as woven, nonwoven, knit and weft insertion fusibles, sew-in types, self-fabric, muslin, silk organza, polyester organdy, tulle, marquisette, hair canvas, and collar linen are good choices. When hand tailoring, self-fabric works well as an interfacing.

To reduce wrinkling, underline the entire garment with silk organza, polyester organdy or chiffon. For increased crispness, underline with a fusible knit or lightweight fusible weft insertion interfacing. Suitable lining fabrics include rayon, acetate, silk, and cotton.

Hint: *For a special-occasion suit, consider this idea from an Yves Saint Laurent couture suit in my collection. Line the jacket with lightweight silk shantung.*

SLEEVES

Reduce the ease in the sleeve cap as needed to set the sleeves smoothly.

TUCKS AND DARTS

For perfect tucks, pull a thread on the tuck foldline; press the foldline; then stitch. On transparent fabrics, use bobbin-stitched or double-stitched tucks and darts. (See Transparent Fabrics.)

BUTTONHOLES

All types of buttonholes—hand-worked, machine-stitched, and bound—are suitable for linen garments. Reinforce buttonholes with fusible interfacing to avoid fraying.

When making bound buttonholes, use the method of your choice.

PRESSING

Test press. Linens require a hot iron to remove wrinkles; but they are easily slicked.

Use a steam iron or damp press cloth and press from the wrong side.

To set pleats, use a 50/50 solution of white vinegar and water, then press. Test for color-fastness. Once pressed, unwanted creases are difficult to remove.

GARMENT CARE

Depending on the dye, finish, fabric weave, and garment construction, linen garments can be laundered or dry-cleaned. However, many linens lose some crispness and wrinkle more after laundering.

The decision to launder or dry-clean should be made before the fabric is cut. If the finished garment will be laundered, wash the fabric by hand or machine (delicate cycle) to preshrink it. If it will be dry-cleaned, steam press.

Generally, suits, dresses, pants, and other garments made from heavier weight linens require dry-cleaning. Although skirts made of similar fabrics are sometimes laundered, suit skirts should be cleaned by the same method as the corresponding jackets.

Lightweight linens, such as handkerchief linen, wash well. Linens are very strong despite their sheerness; and, while simple designs can be machine laundered and dried, they will lose some of their crispness.

Delicate designs and loosely woven fabrics should be washed gently by hand in a mild detergent like Easy Wash.

White linens can be whitened by drying in the sun and/or soaking in Biz.

Dark shades often fade and the fabric will have an unattractive slick when ironed on the right side.

For best results, use a hot iron while the fabric is still damp. To avoid scorching, reduce the temperature for sheers and linen blends. Use regular or spray starch to restore the crispness and to reduce wrinkling.

Most linen blends can be machine washed and dried. Check the instructions on the bolt end. Remove blends from the dryer while slightly damp, shake well, then hang to dry. Press as needed to remove any remaining wrinkles.

HANDKERCHIEF LINEN

Handkerchief linen is a sheer, lightweight fabric which is frequently used for blouses, skirts, lingerie, handkerchiefs, and children's garments. It ruffles and gathers well.

For sewing suggestions, see Linen and Crisp, Transparent Fabrics.

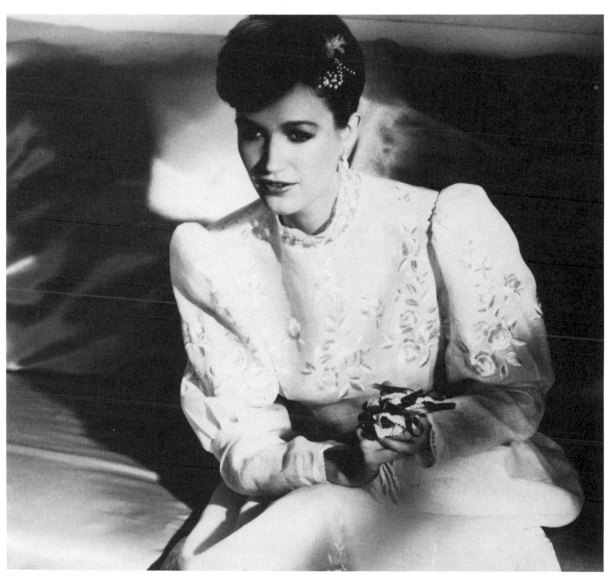

Fig. 2–3 *Designed for a special occasion, this handkerchief linen is intricately embroidered. The delicate beauty of the border is enhanced by the placement on the bodice and sleeves. (Photograph courtesy of Hamilton Adams Imports, Ltd.)*

25

Fabric Characteristics
- Handkerchief linen is a crisp, transparent fabric.
- Handkerchief linen shrinks.
- It frays badly; but better fabrics, which are closely woven with fine yarns, ravel less than inexpensive fabrics.
- Handkerchief linen softens when laundered.
- Linen does not ease well.
- These fabrics are easily damaged in pressing.
- Seam slippage is a problem when the fabric is not tightly woven.

Ramie

Sometimes called "China grass," ramie is a soft, hairy fiber which is less expensive than linen; but, like linen, it is very lustrous, naturally strong, comfortable, and wrinkles easily. It doesn't shrink and it resists mildew.

Ramie is frequently blended with natural and synthetic fibers. It is more absorbent and easier to dye than linen; and it is more resistant to light than either cotton or linen.

Depending on the dyes, fabric weave, finishes, and garment construction, ramie can be laundered or dry-cleaned.

When sewing ramie, avoid designs with creases or pleats; ramie does not wear well at foldlines. (See Linen.)

Silk

The queen of fibers, silk is the only natural filament fiber. According to legend, silk was discovered when a Chinese princess accidentally dropped a cocoon into a cup of hot tea one day. When she removed it, she discovered she could unwind a strong continuous fiber from the outside of the cocoon.

The legend may or may not be true; however, it is recorded that by 2640 B.C. the Chinese Empress Si-Ling-Chi had learned not only how to feed and raise silkworms, but also how to reel and unwind the silk filaments.

The source of silk was so well guarded that the foreigners who purchased the fabrics believed that the fabrics were made from fleeces or flowers grown on trees. It was not until 300 A.D. that the secrets of silk culture trickled into Korea and Japan.

SERICULTURE

Sericulture is the cultivation of silkworms to produce silk. The silkworm goes through four stages of development: the egg, larva, chrysalis, and adult moth.

One moth lays from 400 to 600 eggs on specially prepared sterile papers. The eggs, which are about the size of a pinhead, are stored in a cool, dry place until the breeder is ready to begin their incubation.

The eggs are moved to a warm area to incubate. After about thirty days, they hatch into tiny worms, called "ants." Only 1/8″ long, the young silkworms are fed numerous times a day for 30 to 40 days. During this time, they consume about seventy times their own weight and grow so rapidly that they must shed their skins four times.

When fully grown, the silkworms, now about 3 1/2″ long, begin to rear their heads, looking for a place to attach themselves so they can weave their cocoons. Then they are transferred to a surface of twigs and straw.

The silkworm attaches itself to the straw; then by moving its head in a figure-eight pattern, it surrounds itself with a peanut-sized cocoon made of silk filament.

The silk filament is composed of two strands of silk (fibroin) and sericin, a gummy substance which cements the strands together. When two silkworms spin a cocoon together, they produce a double strand of silk called doupion silk.

Several days later, most cocoons are heated to kill the silkworm inside. This prevents them from maturing and breaking the cocoon into thousands of short fibers.

Fig. 2–4 *Designed by Erik Mortensen for Pierre Balmain, this silk faille evening gown features a bubble or harem skirt. The skirt is backed with a crisp underlining so it will hold the desired shape. (Photo by Francis Kompalitch; courtesy of Pierre Balmain Haute Couture Spring/Summer Collection, 1987.)*

A few selected cocoons are allowed to mature in order to produce new eggs.

After the unbroken cocoons are sorted according to color, texture, size, and shape, they are placed in hot (140°) water to soften the seracin that holds the cocoon together. Once the seracin is softened, the filaments are unwound by a reeling process.

Since the filaments are too fine to be used alone, filaments from two to twenty cocoons are reeled together to make strands of raw silk which are uniform in size and strength. Each cocoon yields only 300 to 1,600 yards of filament, so the reeler is constantly attaching filaments from new cocoons to keep the raw silk even and to make a longer skein. The skeins are combined to make a book; then the books are combined to make a bale—the basic unit for shipping.

Since the raw silk is too fine to be woven, two or more strands are twisted together to make fine filament yarns for weaving. Short fibers from the

outside and inside of the cocoon, fibers from broken cocoons, reeling waste, and gum waste are spun to make spun silk.

Silks which will be yarn-dyed are washed in an olive-oil soap bath to remove the seracin. Degummed silks are white and soft and may weigh up to 25 percent less than before degumming. Better quality silks have less seracin than cheaper quality silks. Some silk fabrics, such as wild silk, have had none of the seracin removed.

Metallic salts are used to weight silks to offset the lost seracin. Although the Federal Trade Commission has ruled that silk fabrics labeled "silk," "all silk," and "pure dyed silk" may be weighted up to 10 percent (15 percent for black), few weighted silks are sold in the United States.

Some silks are woven before degumming; after the fabrics are degummed, they are bleached, dyed, printed, and finished.

WILD SILK

Wild species or tussah silkworms live on oak leaves instead of mulberry leaves. This coarser food produces an irregular, coarse filament, tan in color. Tussah fabrics such as shantung, raw silk, and pongee are durable with a coarse, irregular, ribbed surface. The fabric washes well, but it shrinks badly and should be preshrunk before cutting.

Characteristics of Silk
- Silk is the most luxurious fiber.
- Silk is comfortable to wear, cool in summer and warm in winter.
- Silk is warm but lightweight.
- Silk is resilient and elastic; it holds its shape and resists wrinkling.
- Silk can be used in a variety of fabric constructions from very sheer to very heavy.
- Silk can be supple and drapeable, as well as stiff and bouffant.
- Some silks have a high luster; others have a nap.
- Silk has little static buildup.
- Silk absorbs moisture well and dries quickly.
- Cultivated silks dye and print well.
- Silk does not pill or soil easily.
- It is resistant to mildew, but susceptible to moths and insects.

27

- Silk can be bleached with hydrogen peroxide or sodium perborate-type bleaches but not with chlorine bleaches.
- It is weakened by sunlight, yellows when exposed to light, excess heat, and with age.
- Silk is damaged by perspiration and body oils.
- Silk fiber doesn't shrink, but many silk fabrics do.
- Most silks require dry-cleaning; but some can be laundered, depending on the fabric structure, finish, dye, and the garment structure.
- Silk is easily damaged by strong soaps and detergents, hot irons, acids, and alkalies.
- Silk is easily damaged by improper pressing.
- Silk is the strongest natural fiber; but it is weaker when wet.
- Some silks are very slippery.
- Many silks slip badly at seamlines.

SEWING CHECKLIST

Machine Needles: Universal-H point or Red Band needles; sizes 60/8 to 90/14, depending on the fabric weight.

Thread: Mercerized cotton; topstitching—regular, silk (size A or D); basting—basting cotton and silk (size A); finishing—mercerized cotton and silk.

Hand Sewing Needles: Sizes 5 to 10.

Marking Techniques: All types, except wax.

Seams and Hems: Depends on the fabric weight, transparency, garment use and quality, and care requirements.

Interfacings, Linings, and Underlinings: Depends on the fabric weight, garment type and structure, and care requirements.

PLANNING A GARMENT

SELECTING THE FABRIC

Silk fabrics are selected both for their beauty and durability, but the most important consideration is quality. If you can't afford a good silk, purchase a quality synthetic.

Japan, India, China, Thailand, and Korea produce most of the world's silk, but the best silk fabrics are made in Italy and France.

Learn to recognize and evaluate silk by its hand. Visit a fabric store with a large selection of silks. Examine them and compare the hand and prices until you can identify the characteristic hand of silk—a dry, soft, buttery feel.

Learn to recognize different qualities of the various kinds of silks but don't try to compare them to each other. For example, compare broadcloth to China silk, but don't try to compare broadcloth to chiffon or a silk suiting.

Test the drape and hand of the fabric to determine if it will be suitable for the design you are planning. Crush the fabric in your hand. If it crushes and wrinkles, it is a poor-quality fabric.

Examine solid-color fabrics carefully for imperfections in the weave. Surface variations which are considered attractive in shantung, tussah silk, wild silk, and silk noil are considered imperfections in satin, charmeuse, crepe, chiffon, georgette, and decorative surface fabrics.

Generally fabrics with a higher number of threads per inch have more body, are stronger and more durable; however, they do not drape as well and may wrinkle more.

Fabrics with fewer threads per inch or yarns with little or no twist pick and pull more. And if the garment is fitted tightly or has strain at the seamlines, these fabrics slip more at the seams.

To test for seam slippage, scrape your thumbnail across the fabric; if the warp threads separate, consider another fabric. Twist the fabric; then check the threads for slippage. Sheer fabrics tend to slip more than broadcloth, crepe de chine, and medium-weight fabrics. Also check to be sure the fabric has no flaws and is not printed on-grain. It should be resistant to water spotting.

TEST FOR SILK

If the fabric is not labeled silk, ask for a small swatch so you can test it. Unlike synthetic fabrics which shrink away from the flame, pure silk appears to melt and boil, forming tiny bubbles along the burned edge. Rayon burns quickly with a flame and doesn't leave a round ash. Silk suitings have a distinctive odor.

BLENDS

Frequently blended with other fibers, silk blends are less expensive than pure silk, as well as easier to sew and launder.

When combined with wool, silk is easier to tailor. When combined with cotton, it is less expensive and easier to launder. When combined with man-made fibers, fabrics maintain the look of silk with the advantages of easy care, wrinkle-resistance, and moderate prices.

Determining the Face Side
- Generally silks are rolled on the bolt with the wrong side out.
- The selvage is usually smoother on the face side.
- The face side has fewer imperfections, knots, and slubs than the back.
- Printed fabrics are brighter and solids more lustrous on the face.
- Texture, ribs, cords, twill-weaves, novelty yarns, and pile are more pronounced on the face.
- On silk jersey, the knit side is the traditional face.
- The face is the side you prefer.

PATTERN SELECTION

Consider the hang, drape, weight, hand, surface design, and weave of the fabric as well as the garment use when planning the garment.

Avoid close-fitting designs unless the garment will be underlined to withstand the stress.

PREPARING THE FABRIC AND PATTERN

The decision to launder or dry-clean the garment should be made before the fabric is cut. If the finished garment will be laundered, wash the fabric by hand or machine to preshrink it. If it will be dry-cleaned, press with a good steam iron or ask the dry cleaner to steam press it.

Hint: *A good steaming in the bathroom will also shrink the fabric. Fill the bathtub with hot water; hang the fabric on a rustproof hanger; and leave it to steam for an hour.*

Preshrink the interfacings, linings, and other components appropriately for the garment care.

Since most silks are easily damaged by pins, machine stitching, and ripping, adjust the pattern before cutting. And, if necessary, make a test garment.

SEWING SILK

Since the variety of silk fabrics ranges from soft, fragile sheers to stiff, heavy coatings, only those sewing suggestions which relate to most silk fabrics are included in this section. For additional suggestions, see the sections indicated.

Bengaline: Coatings; Ribbed Fabrics
Brocade: Decorative Surfaces
Charmeuse: Lightweight Silks; Satin
Chiffon: Soft, Transparent Fabrics
China Silk: Lightweight Silks; Transparent Fabrics
Crepe de Chine: Lightweight Silks; Transparent Fabrics
Douppioni: Ribbed Fabrics
Faille: Ribbed Fabrics
Fuji Silk: Lightweight Silks; Transparent Fabrics
Gazar: Crisp, Transparent Fabrics
Georgette: Soft, Transparent Fabrics
Gros de Londres: Ribbed Fabrics; Stripes
Grosgrain: Ribbed Fabrics
Habutai: Lightweight Silks; Transparent Fabrics
Honan: Lightweight Silks; Transparent Fabrics
Jacquard Silk: Lightweight Silks
Jersey: Jersey; Knits

Marquisette: Crisp, Transparent Fabrics
Matelassé: Decorative Surfaces
Moiré: Ribbed Fabrics; Taffeta
Mousseline de Soie: Crisp, Transparent Fabrics
Organza: Crisp, Transparent Fabrics
Ottoman: Ribbed Fabrics; Stripes
Peau d'Ange: Satin Fabrics
Peau de Soie: Satin Fabrics
Pongee: Lightweight Silks; Ribbed Fabrics
Rep: Ribbed Fabrics; Stripes
Satin: Satin Fabrics
Satin-Faced Crepe: Satin Fabrics; Two-Faced Fabrics
Shantung: Ribbed Fabrics; Lightweight Silks
Silk Noil: Lightweight Silks; Ribbed Fabrics; Loosely Woven Fabrics
Suiting: Loosely Woven Fabrics
Surah: Lightweight Silks
Taffeta: Taffeta
Tussah: Ribbed Fabrics
Velvet: Pile Fabrics; Velvet
Voile: Transparent Fabrics

LAYOUT, CUTTING, AND MARKING

Use a nap layout except when you are absolutely sure the fabric has no nap or shading. When both sides look the same, mark the face with drafting tape, pins, or chalk.

Hint: *I used to mark the wrong side of the fabric; but, since I sometimes forgot to remove the tape before completing the garment, I now mark the face side (after testing to be sure the marking method won't leave a scar).*

Spread bulky and thick fabrics in a single layer, right side up. Use weights to anchor the pattern or place fine pins or needles within the seam allowances.

Silks can be marked by any method except wax chalk.

STITCHING TIPS

Make a test seam. For lightweight silks, use small (60/8 to 70/10) needles and a shorter stitch length; for medium-weight fabrics, use medium (70/10 to 80/12) needles; for heavy fabrics, use a large needle and longer stitch.

Keep the tension loose and balanced.

Use mercerized cotton thread whenever possible (sizes 60 for lightweight fabrics and 50 for medium- to heavyweight materials). Since cotton thread is weaker than the silk fabric, the thread will break at stress points before the fabric tears.

BASTING

Use fine pleating pins; and if they leave holes, use size 10 needles.

For most basting, use a soft cotton basting thread. To avoid thread imprints when you press the outside of the garment, baste with silk thread (size A).

SEAMS, DARTS, AND HEMS

Consider the fabric weight, transparency, garment design and quality when choosing seams and seam finishes.

To reduce bulk when sewing medium- and heavyweight silks, grade seams and darts appropriately.

INTERFACINGS

When sewing a luxury garment, use a quality interfacing. In addition to traditional interfacings, self-fabric, silk organza, marquisette, tulle, cotton organdy, and muslin are good choices.

Select an interfacing—sew-in or fusible—that's lighter than the fabric.

Hint: *Examine the interfacing carefully to avoid confusing weight with crispness.*

Experiment with several fusibles before applying them to the actual garment; be sure the interfacing has the same care requirements as the silk. Preshrink as needed before cutting.

LININGS AND UNDERLININGS

Generally, silk and rayon linings are best. Fabrics such as crepe de chine, Charmeuse, good-quality China silk, silk broadcloths, jacquards, and Bemberg are good choices for linings. Try to avoid synthetic fabrics.

Line jackets and coats to hide the garment construction. Underline and/or line pants, skirts, and tightly fitted garments to reduce the stress and seam slippage.

Fabrics such as organza, China silk, silk broadcloth, lightweight self-fabrics are good choices for underlinings. Use a crisp underlining or fusible interfacing to change the character of the fabric.

PRESSING

Test press on a fabric scrap before pressing the garment. Use a cooler setting when pressing lightweight silks.

To avoid spitting and sputtering, be sure the iron has heated properly before using. Since many silks waterspot, test press on a scrap first.

When pressing from the right side of the garment, use a dry press cloth. Use a sleeve board when pressing small detail areas or sleeves.

GARMENT CARE

To minimize staining and expensive or time-consuming cleanings, make dress shields for your silk garments. Allow perfumes and deodorants, which contain alcohol, to dry before you dress.

Let silk garments air overnight before hanging them in the closet. To freshen wrinkled garments, hang them in the bathroom while you bathe. Also, silks shed their wrinkles better when hung on padded hangers in a spacious closet. Store seldom-worn garments on padded hangers in cloth garment bags.

Clean soiled and stained garments as soon as possible. To avoid setting stains on garments that must be dry-cleaned, don't try to remove them yourself. Show the dry cleaner all stains even if they seem to have disappeared, and explain what caused them.

When removing stains on washable garments, don't rub the fabric; blot instead to avoid breaking the fibers and removing the color. To remove grease stains, dust generously with talcum powder. Brush away the powder after an hour; repeat as needed. (Protect your silks from kitchen stains by removing them or wearing an apron.)

LAUNDER OR DRY-CLEAN?

The need for dry cleaning today's silks is somewhat baffling since silks have been worn for thousands of years and dry cleaning wasn't invented until the nineteenth century. But the mystery is easily solved when you know a little about these garments and the people who wore them.

Most silk garments were worn by individuals who did little or no work. Since they were worn over other clothing and had little or no contact with body oils, deodorants, and perfumes, many never required cleaning. Garments which were laundered were frequently ripped apart so the sections could be washed individually. (Ripping wasn't as difficult or time-consuming before the invention of the sewing machine.)

Depending on the dyes, finishes, fabric weave, and garment construction, silk garments can be laundered. But if you decide to launder a fabric labeled "dry-clean only," you do so at your own risk.

Firmly woven, plain-weave fabrics in pastel colors generally wash well, but other fabrics don't: dark and bright colored fabrics fade, lose their luster, and slick when ironed. Crepes shrink badly, suitings lose their body, and satins pick and pull.

WASHABILITY TEST

Consider the garment's use and structure before testing the fabric. If it can be pressed easily, proceed with the test.

1. Cut an 8″ square of fabric.
2. Wash and dry it the way you plan to launder the garment.
3. Examine the square carefully for changes in color, size, sheen, and texture. If you like what you see, preshrink the fabric.

WASHING SILK

Remember that silk is a protein fiber just like your hair. For most silk fabrics, hand-laundering is best. Dissolve a mild detergent like Easy Wash or castile shampoo in warm water. Handle the garment carefully since silk is weaker when wet. Do not rub, bleach, or leave the garment to soak. Rinse thoroughly, and add 1/4 cup of white vinegar to the final rinse. Roll the garment in a towel to remove excess moisture; do not wring. Smooth and straighten the seams; iron the garment or fabric dry.

Hint: *Use a colander to rinse the garment. Place the garment in the colander and rinse with water from the faucet until the water runs clear. Then gently press the excess water out of the garment.*

Some simple designs and close-weave fabrics can be machine washed on the delicate cycle and tumble dried with several terry towels. Remove the silk garments while damp. Smooth and straighten the seams. If they need ironing, iron immediately. If not, hang the garment on a rustproof hanger to dry.

Hint: *I machine wash and dry all my silk lingerie. Clean-finished edges, such as lace and bias fac-ings and bias bindings, dry smoother than tra-ditional loose facings; and ribbon straps dry wrinkle-free, though fabric tubings do need pressing.*

LIGHTWEIGHT SILKS

Crepe de chine, flat crepe, charmeuse, foulard, lightweight satins, silk broadcloth, China silk, jacquard, pongee, Fuji silk, and habutai are the most important lightweight silks.

Luxurious and sometimes expensive, lightweight silks are comfortable to wear year-round. If you follow the guidelines, they aren't difficult to sew.

SEWING CHECKLIST

Machine Needles: Universal-H point, Yellow or Red Band needles; sizes 60/8 or 70/10.

Machine Setting: Stitch length, 1.75–2mm (12–15 stitches per inch); tension, loosely balanced.

Thread: Stitching—mercerized cotton; topstitching—regular, silk (size A or D).

Hand Sewing: basting—basting cotton, silk (size A); finishing—mercerized cotton, silk (size A).

Hand Sewing Needles: Sizes 9 or 10.

Sewing Machine Equipment: Straight-stitch, roller, or jeans foot.

Equipment and Supplies: Very fine pleating pins, small safety pins, weights, well-sharpened shears or rotary cutter and mat, stabilizer, lightweight zippers.

Marking Techniques: Clips, chalk, soap sliver, temporary marking pens, pins, tracing wheel and tracing carbon, thread tracing, tailor tacks.

Seams: French, false French, standing-fell, flat-fell, double/ply, welt, top-stitched, tissue-stitched.

Hems: Shirttail, book, machine-rolled, hemmer-rolled, shell, lettuce edging, topstitched, merrow, mock merrow, plain.

Seam and Hem Finishes: Single/ply—turned-and-stitched, folded, hand overcast, zigzag, multi-stitch zigzag, serged; double-ply pinked-and-stitched.

Edge Finishes: Self-fabric facings, bias bindings, bands, casings, ribbing.

Interfacings: Self-fabric, silk organza, marquisette, cotton organdy, batiste, pima cotton, knit fusibles, lightweight woven and nonwoven fusible, and sew-in interfacings.

Linings: Generally not used, except for outerwear and opaqueness.

Underlinings: Generally not used, except to reduce strain, to change the fabric character or color, or for modesty.

Garment Care: Depending on the dyes and weave of the fabric and garment structure, silk garments can be laundered by hand or machine, or dry-cleaned.

Generally, crisp silk fabrics such as broadcloth and China silk and medium-crisp materials such as jacquards and foulards are easier to sew than soft fabrics such as crepe de chine, Charmeuse, and satin.

Fabric Characteristics

- Lightweight silks are comfortable to wear.
- Firmly woven fabrics do not fray badly.
- Most lightweight silks are easily marred by machine needles, pins, and ripping.
- Puckered seams and skipped stitches are sometimes a problem.
- Seam slippage is a problem at stress points.
- Lightweight silks are easily damaged by improper pressing.
- Soft silks are more difficult to sew than crisp silks.
- Some silks are very slippery.

PLANNING A GARMENT

DESIGN IDEAS AND PATTERN SELECTION

Depending on the fabric hand—soft or crisp—lightweight silks are suitable for soft blouses, tailored shirts, skirts, dresses, lingerie, pants, jackets, and lightweight coats.

Generally, soft designs with gathers, pleats, ruffles, flounces, or drapes are good choices; but more structured styles also work well if the silk is backed with a fusible or sew-in underlining.

Choose from a variety of collars—ties, convertible, two-piece shirt types, ruffles, or flounces—and sleeves—cap, shirt, bishop, puff, leg of mutton, butterfly, raglan, kimono, or dropped shoulder.

Avoid tightly fitted garments unless you plan to use an underlining with strength.

Hint: *A favorite trick of designer David Hayes is to use the same fabric for a crisp, structured jacket worn over a soft dress. For the jacket, he uses a fusible interfacing to change the character of the soft silk.*

SELECTING THE FABRIC

Poor-quality silks, which are frequently cheap, are not worthy of your time and talents; a good fabric is a much better investment.

Learn to recognize different qualities of the various kinds of silks but don't try to compare them to each other. For example, compare China silk to broadcloth, but don't try to compare broadcloth to charmeuse.

Here are some guidelines for evaluating lightweight silks. Generally, the more threads per inch the better the quality; and the finer the threads, the better the quality. Fabrics with open spaces between the threads tend to fray badly and will not wear well.

To test for seam slippage, scrape your thumbnail across the fabric; the warp threads should move little or not at all. Twist the fabric; then check the threads for slippage. Sheer fabrics tend to slip more than broadcloths, crepe de chine, and other medium-weight fabrics.

Look for surface variations, thick and thin yarns and slubs. Although these are natural in silks and add to the character of many silk fabrics, they should not be noticeable in Charmeuse, jacquards, satins, and crepe de chine.

Learn to recognize and evaluate silk by its hand. Visit a fabric store with a large selection of silks. Examine them and compare the hand and prices until you can identify the characteristic hand of silk—a dry, soft, buttery feel.

Test the fabric: hang or drape to see if it will be suitable for the design you are planning. Crush the fabric in your hand; then release it. Better silks will recover well with a minimum of wrinkles. Avoid fabrics that are printed off-grain.

When evaluating silk charmeuse, consider the fabric use and garment design. A fabric with a higher number of threads per inch has more body and is stronger and more durable. However, it will have less drapeability and wrinkle more than lower count fabrics. With fewer interlacings, there will also be more seam slippage, picks, and pulls. The low-count charmeuse might be better for a blouse with a cowl neckline while the high-count fabric is a must for a luxury lining.

When evaluating silk crepes, pull a thread from the filling. The thread should have a crimp or twist. Low-twist yarns have more luster and shrink less during washing while high-twist yarns are more resistant to abrasion and wear better.

PATTERN PREPARATION

Adjust the pattern before cutting since these fabrics are easily damaged by pins, machine stitching, ripping, and excess handling.

SEWING LIGHTWEIGHT SILKS

LAYOUT, CUTTING, AND MARKING

These silks are very slippery and shift off-grain easily. Take care when cutting, since these fabrics will not hang properly if they are cut off-grain.

Cover the cutting table with a flannel-backed vinyl cloth, flannel side up, or use the flannel side of your table pads.

Hint: *I use these nonslip surfaces only with the most slippery fabrics since it is easier to straighten fabrics on a smooth surface. The mat for my rotary cutter has 1" grids on it, but a cardboard cutting board works equally well for straightening.*

Use weights or very fine pins placed in the seam allowances to secure the pattern. For extremely fragile fabrics, substitute fine needles for pins.

Hint: *A new spray, No More Pins™, temporarily glues the pattern to the fabric. Lightly spray the wrong side of the pattern, let it dry; then smooth it in place on the fabric.*

STITCHING TIPS

Cover the sewing machine table with a clean sheet or pillowcase to prevent the silk from slipping and sliding around.

Make a test seam, using a small (60/8 or 70/10), new needle, loosely balanced tension, and a 2mm stitch length (12 stitches per inch). Correct the pressure and shorten the stitch if needed.

For machine stitching, use a fine, mercerized cotton thread which is weaker than the silk fabric

so the seam will rip before the fabric tears at stress points.

Hint: *The stronger threads—cotton-wrapped polyester, polyester, and silk threads—also cause more seam slippage. This isn't a problem if the garment isn't tightly fitted and you always act like a lady. Unfortunately, I frequently wear my silk blouses to shop; and carrying bulky parcels causes stress at the back of the arms. And, since I tend to forget that ladies take small steps, I have to put slits or pleats in all my skirts and slips.*

If necessary, use a stabilizer to reduce skipped stitches and puckered seams.

Hint: *To prevent a hungry machine from eating your fabric, begin stitching on the stabilizer; lay the fabric on top; then stitch the seam.*
Use water-soluble stabilizers. Tear or trim away the excess; steam press to remove the rest.

SEAMS

Plain seams are best for soft, fluid garments. For straight and slightly curved seams on blouses, I frequently use the standing-fell seam because it is not only quick and easy to stitch, but all of the raw edges are enclosed.

For curved seams like the armholes, use a zigzag, multi-stitch zigzag, or serged finish on everyday garments. Use a double/ply bound or hand overcast finish for special garments.

When stitching bias seams, hand baste; then stretch lightly as you machine stitch. Press them back into shape. When sewing a luxury garment, hand baste the seam with basting cotton.

SEAM AND HEM FINISHES

When sewing luxury garments, overcast edges by hand with mercerized cotton. If the fabric ravels badly, serge the edges before seaming the garment; but since the cut edges are normally used as guidelines when stitching, take care to avoid cutting into them when serging.

To prevent thread imprints when serging, use woolly nylon thread in the loopers.

Before using zigzag or multi-stitch zigzag fin-

Fig. 2–5 *Softly draped, this lightweight silk jacquard is from Carven—Haute Couture Collection, Autumn/Winter 1987/1988. (Photo by Baudoin Picart; courtesy of Carven.)*

ishes, test to be sure the stitches aren't too heavy for the fabric, which could cause the seams to sag.

Hint: *To prevent rolling, use an overcasting foot or stabilizer such as tear-away or water-soluble. After stitching, tear away or trim close to the stitched line. For unlined coats and jackets, use a folded edge or turned-and-stitched finish on the hem.*

HEMS

Select a hem appropriate for the garment design and quality. For shirts and tuck-in blouses, use machine-rolled, shirttail, or topstitched hems. On overblouses, use 1 1/4"-wide plain hems.

For ruffles, full skirts, scarves, collars, and sleeves, use the narrow hem of your choice. Since these fabrics are rather springy, hand-rolled hems are more difficult than machine-rolled and mock-merrow hems.

Use a 2"- to 2 1/2"-wide hem on straight-line skirts. Generally, a very flat edge finish is best.

Hints: *Designer Charles Kleibacker uses a hand-overcast finish on his luxurious bias-cut designs. Overcast the edge with mercerized cotton and hem it with silk.*

For a quicker, easier finish, G Street Fabrics teacher Gail Shinn recommends a pinked-and-stitched finish; then she hems the garment to the stitched line on the hem allowance.

EDGE FINISHES

In addition to hems, bands, and self-fabric facings, which are used most frequently, self-fabric bias bindings and ribbings are particularly attractive.

Closures and Trims
- Use lightweight zippers and buttons so the fabric won't sag.
- Select good-quality buttons; cheap plastic ones will spoil the beauty of the garment.
- Use maching embroidery thread for machine buttonholes; try silk (size A) or machine embroidery thread for hand-worked buttonholes.
- For perfect machine-stitched buttonholes, use a water-soluble stabilizer between the fabric and feed dogs.

- Generally, the patch and window methods are best for bound buttonholes.
- Uncorded button loops may be too small and flimsy. Cord them to make loops firmer and larger.
- If you can't make attractive buttonholes or find buttons in a suitable color, hide them under a fly placket. (See Chapter 24.)
- Avoid stiff and/or heavy trims.

INTERFACINGS

All types of interfacings are appropriate for lightweight silks, as long as they are lighter in weight than the fabric. I particularly like self-fabric, silk organza, fusible knit, and lightweight weft insertion interfacings.

When using a fusible, make a sample. If the fusible dots show through on the right side of the fabric, the fusible is too heavy. Use a lighter interfacing, and, if necessary, use two layers to get the desired crispness.

Hint: *Experiment with different brands—one fusible knit fuses softer than another, even if they are both classified the same (e.g., "soft").*

LININGS AND UNDERLININGS

Select lining and underlining fabrics with the same care properties as the silk. Preshrink them before cutting.

Generally garments made in lightweight fabrics are not lined, except when they are used for outerwear—jackets and lightweight coats.

Hint: *I prefer rayon and silk linings which breathe better and are more comfortable than synthetics.*

When a synthetic lining and underlinings can't be avoided, select a polyester blouse fabric for the lining. Better-quality blouse fabrics breathe better than most traditional polyester lining materials, but they usually cost more.

Underlinings are used to reduce strain, maintain the garment's silhouette, change the fabric's character, or increase opaqueness.

Underline closely fitted dresses, pants, and skirts to reduce seam slippage at stress points and to stay draped designs.

Underline jackets, coats, and other structured garments to give them enough body to maintain their shape. Consider the fashion fabric and underlining before deciding if interfacings will also be needed.

Underline light-colored silks with self-fabric, silk broadcloth, crepe de chine, or China silk to make them less revealing. Flat linings work particularly well. (See Chapter 20.)

Hint: *Don't overlook flesh-colored fabrics for underlinings.*

Underline lightweight silks with fusible knits and weft insertion or traditional sew-in interfacings to change the fabric character.

Selecting an appropriate underlining fabric is sometimes a challenge. Cottons are too heavy, synthetics are too hot, and many silks are not sturdy enough. Look at silk organza, other firmly woven lightweight silks, cotton organdy, marquisette, tulle, net, lightweight rayons, blended fabrics, and lightweight sew-in and fusible interfacings.

Hint: *To eliminate unattractive pocket shadows on light-colored fabrics, use flesh-colored pocket sacks.*

PRESSING

Use a clean steam iron. To avoid spitting and spewing, be sure the iron has warmed to the proper setting.

Test press on fabric scraps. These lightweight fabrics frequently require a lower temperature than heavier silks. If the iron isn't warm enough to steam, turn it up and use a press cloth.

To avoid shines, always use a press cloth when pressing the right side of the fabric.

Hint: *My favorite press cloths are old gauze diapers, tablecloth fragments, and old linen handkerchiefs—ladies' or men's.*

Garment Care

Use dress shields to protect the garment from perspiration and deodorant stains.

To remove grease spots, dust them with talcum powder. To avoid damaging the fabric, blot wet spots without rubbing.

Do not try to spot-clean silk garments; you may set the stain permanently. Take soiled or stained garments to the dry cleaner immediately; but, if you know the dry cleaner changes the cleaning fluid on Tuesday, don't take the garment on Monday morning.

WASHING SILK

Depending on the dyes, yarn twist, fabric weave, and garment structure, silk garments can be laundered by hand or machine or can be dry-cleaned. Make your choice before cutting the fabric, preferably before purchasing; preshrink accordingly before cutting.

Generally, garments made of crepe de chine and charmeuse should be dry-cleaned to maintain their freshness, but simple garments and shirts made of light-colored, firmly woven fabrics are usually washable if all the other garment components are also washable.

To test for washability, cut an 8″ square of fabric; wash and dry it exactly as you plan to treat the garment. Examine the square carefully for changes in color, size, and texture. If you like what you see, consider the garment structure and whether it will need to be and can be ironed satisfactorily.

Hint: *I am very conservative about washing silk. I believe that you will keep your silks cleaner if you know you have to dry-clean them. In addition, most silks will not look as good if they must be ironed. Of course, there are exceptions; a few silks—particularly lingerie—can be machine washed and dried. And, if silk is snatched from the dryer before it is completely dry and then dried on a hanger, it can be worn without any pressing.*

Several years ago I purchased a lovely remnant; and, since it was relatively inexpensive, I threw it into the washer and dryer. It shrank and creped. I liked the effect so well, I bought some more at regular price and washed it too. And, even though I'm still enjoying the lovely blouse with a tie collar, I was lucky—most silks cannot be machine dried. (Now would you like to hear about some of my laundry-room disasters?)

To handwash silk garments, use warm water and a mild soap or shampoo. Don't rub, scrub, or wring the garment. Rinse well; then roll it in a light-colored towel to remove excess water. Unfold; shake it well; then hang the garment on a rustproof hanger. Straighten the seams and smooth out wrinkles. When the garment is almost dry, use a steam iron to press from the wrong side.

To set colors which run and fade, add salt or vinegar to the soapy water every time you wash the garment.

Hint: *I use an ample amount—1/4 cup to a gallon of water.*

Wool

The most versatile fiber, wool is a natural animal fiber made of protein.

More comfortable to wear in all climates than any other material, wool is available in a wide range of weights, textures, weaves, and qualities. It can be fleecy, smooth, plain, textured, light, heavy, soft, crisp, sheer, opaque, thick, thin, delicate, strong, spongy, firm, napped, or clear surfaced.

According to legend, wool garments were worn by the Babylonians as early as 4000 B.C.; and by 3000 B.C., Britons were wearing crude woolen garments, which may have been felted instead of woven. In 2000 B.C., the tablets of Ur described women and girls weaving wool.

LABELING

According to the Wool Product's Labeling Act of 1939, the legal definition of wool is "the fiber from the fleece of sheep or lamb or hair of the angora or cashmere goat (and may include the so-called specialty fibers from the hair of the camel, alpaca, llama, and vicuna)."

Technically, there is a difference between wool from sheep and wool from other hair fibers. Wool fibers have more crimp and overlapping scales on the surface, which make them more elastic, more absorbent, and less lustrous than hair fibers. Hair fibers do not have the felting characteristic of wool.

The Labeling Act also defines the kinds of wool and requires that they be listed on the product. "Virgin" or "new" wool applies only to wool fibers taken directly from the fleece of the sheep. "Reprocessed" wool covers wool fibers recovered from woven or felted wool products which have never been worn or used in any way by the consumer. Reprocessed wool is made of cutting scraps from the ready-to-wear industry. "Reused" wool,

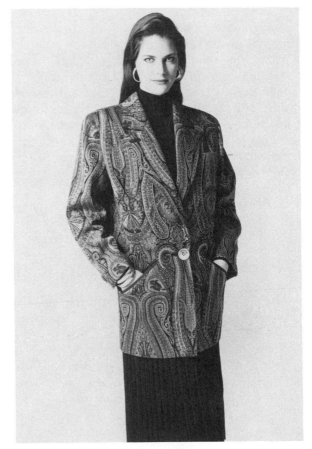

Fig. 2–6 *Trimmed with large buttonholes and pockets outlined in blue grosgrain, Laura Biagiotti's multicolor wool is beautifully cut to showcase the paisley design. The handkerchief pocket is so well matched that it's almost impossible to find the seamlines. (Photograph courtesy of Laura Biagiotti, P.A.P. Fall/Winter 1987/1988 Collection.)*

which covers wool fibers reclaimed from wool products worn or used by the consumer, is used for interlining and cheap garments. It is rarely sold in the home sewing market.

THE ANATOMY OF WOOL FIBERS

Wool fibers, which are composed of the protein keratin, have three parts—the epidermis, cortex, and medulla.

The epidermis or outside layer has two parts: the epicuticle, which is a thin waxlike membrane, and a scale layer.

The epicuticle, the only nonprotein part of the fiber, contributes to the water repellency of wool; but since it has many tiny pores, it also allows wool to absorb water vapors and to release them again into the air. The epicuticle is easily damaged by alkalies, wear, and abrasion; all make it less water-repellent.

The scale layer encircles the fiber shaft and the scales overlap like the scales on a fish. The free ends of the scales point toward the end of the fiber; and when a single fiber is pulled through the fingers, they lie flat against the shaft.

The scales act like tiny springs, allowing the fiber to stretch from one-third to one-half its original length. They also interlock to make it water-repellent and resistant to abrasion, and to cause felting. They are irritating to sensitive skins.

Wool fibers have 300 to 3,000 scales per inch. Fibers with numerous small scales are smoother and finer.

The cortex, the second and major part of the wool fiber, is composed of long, flat, spindle-shaped cells, which are in turn composed of the fibrous components. These cells give wool its natural crimp and contribute to its elasticity and ability to resist wrinkling.

Fine wool fibers have more crimp (thirty per inch) than lower quality wool (five per inch).

The third part of the wool fiber is the medulla or center canal, which is filled with small cylindrical cells. The size of the medulla varies with the fineness of the fiber. It is almost invisible in fine wools, allowing them to be dyed or spun better. The thicker cell-filled medulla in coarse wool fibers causes them to be stiffer and more lustrous.

FROM ANIMAL TO FABRIC

Several hundred breeds of sheep produce wool fibers. Most are bred for wool production and sheared or clipped each spring to remove the fleece.

After the fleece is sorted by length, fineness, color, and quality, the wool is scoured in a warm, soapy, alkaline solution to remove dirt, sticks, burrs, perspiration, and natural oils. Then it is processed on a carding machine, where the fibers are separated to form a fine web.

Short wool fibers are rolled into a loose rope, which is spun into woolen yarns. After carding, long wool fibers are combed to remove short fibers, to straighten the remaining fibers, and to lay them parallel before they are spun into worsted yarns.

Wool can be dyed at any stage: fiber, yarn, or fabric.

THE WOOL FAMILY

WOOLENS AND WORSTEDS

There are two types of wool fabrics: woolens and worsteds. Woolens are woven from woolen yarns; worsteds, from worsted yarns.

Woolens are usually soft, with a rough or fuzzy texture. The yarns are made of short fibers, loosely spun with a low- to medium-twist and are used to make bulkier, heavier, and warmer fabrics such as bulky tweeds, coatings, washable wools, and some flannels.

Compared to worsteds, woolens are easier to sew, less expensive, and better suited to casual designs; they pill, mat, and soil more easily; but stains are easy to remove.

Worsteds are smooth, strong, and more lustrous than woolens. The yarns have a medium- to high-twist and the weave is quite prominent. Worsteds are used to make lighter weight clear-surfaced, hard-textured fabrics such as gabardine, serge, twilled, ribbed, and suiting fabrics.

Worsteds wear longer, crease, and press well. Tightly woven, they rarely sag or bag. They have a smooth, hard surface which wears well but shines easily.

Fabric Characteristics
- Wool is comfortable to wear; it is warm in winter and cool in summer.
- Wool absorbs moisture better than any other natural fiber. It can absorb moisture up to 30 percent of its weight without feeling wet.
- Wool is water-repellent, flame-resistant, elastic, resilient.

- The natural crimp of the fibers allows fabrics to resist wrinkling and to return to their original shape. Wool recovers more quickly when steamed.
- Wool can be stretched as much as 35 percent when dry and 50 percent when wet.
- Wool resists creasing and wrinkling better when dry than when wet.
- Wool felts when exposed to heat, moisture, abrasion, and pressure.
- Wool is lightweight in relation to its bulk.
- It will hold a deep nap without matting.
- Wool tailors well; it is easy to shape, crease, shrink, and stretch with steam.
- It resists static electricity except when the air is very dry.
- Wool can be blended with less expensive wools, other natural fibers, and man-made fibers to reduce the cost or to extend the use.
- Wool resists fading and crocking.
- Wool can be laundered or dry-cleaned, depending on the dyes, finishes, fabric structure, and garment design. Check the end of the bolt and make notes.
- Wool is easily damaged with improper pressing and hot irons.
- Wool is damaged by moths, carpet beetles, alkalies, chlorine bleach.
- Wool is discolored by sunlight; and it will deteriorate with prolonged exposure.

PLANNING A GARMENT

SELECTING THE FABRIC

When selecting wool fabrics, beauty is sometimes more important than durability.

Consider your size when choosing wool fabrics. Bulky, rough surfaces, large prints and plaids, high-contrast colors, evenly spaced stripes, and unusually stiff or clinging fabrics will add pounds to any figure.

Select a fabric appropriate for the garment use. Choose sturdy tweeds for shopping excursions and casual wear; coatings for outdoor wear; fine wools and sheers for dressy garments.

Carefully examine the fabric to be sure it is clean and not shopworn with faded lines at the fold, spots, dust streaks, or pulled threads. Hold the fabric up to the light to check for imperfections and moth holes.

Scrape the fabric with your thumbnail; if the yarns separate easily, the fabric will ravel and may not wear well. Closely woven fabrics are more durable and less flammable.

Squeeze the fabric in your hand, then release it; good-quality fabrics will spring back unwrinkled. When comparing two fabrics, pull a thread from each, and untwist it. The fiber with more crimp will wrinkle less.

Hint: *The fibers are very small and you may need a magnifying glass. I have a small, flat plastic one that fits in my billfold.*

When durability is important for everyday garments, pants, and coats, crush the fabric in your hands and rub it together to see if the surface pills or roughens.

Fabrics with cords or ribs in either the warp or the filling are weaker than those with cords or ribs in both directions.

Worsteds are frequently more expensive than woolens; however, a good-quality woolen is more desirable than a cheap worsted.

Worsteds are better for crisp, tailored fashions, while woolens are more suitable for casual and draped designs.

Hint: *To examine the fabric drape, hold up the corner of one end. Woolens generally drape softly into several bias folds, while worsteds tend to hang stiffly in a cone shape.*

Woolens are well suited for gathers and unpressed pleats, whereas worsteds are better for sharply pressed pleats.

Woolens do not spot, stain, or shine as readily as worsteds.

Soft, textured woolens are easier to sew than tightly woven and clear-finished worsteds, but they don't maintain their shape as well.

Determining the Face Side
- Most wools are folded right sides together on the bolt.
- Generally, the selvage is smoother on the face side.
- The face side has fewer imperfections, knots, and slubs than the back.

- Printed fabrics are brighter on the face.
- Texture, ribs, cords, novelty yarns, nap, and pile are more pronounced on the face.
- Generally, the knit side is the right side of jersey.
- The face is the side you prefer.

FABRIC PREPARATION

Wool fabrics labeled "needle-ready" or "London shrunk" are ready to sew and do not need to be preshrunk.

Do not shrink wool crepes.

Preshrink all interfacing fabrics, linings, and notions.

TESTING FOR SHRINKAGE

To determine if your fabric is needle-ready, cover a corner of the fabric with a dry press cloth and steam thoroughly for ten seconds. Allow the fabric to dry and examine the area. If an imprint of the iron shows, the fabric has shrunk and must be treated before sewing. Examine the nap and finish to determine if there are any other undesirable changes in the fabric's finish or appearance.

SHRINKING WOOL

The easiest way to shrink wool yardage is to ask your dry cleaner to do it. This is also the best method when the test area shows any changes in the surface finish. The fabric doesn't have to be cleaned, just steamed thoroughly. If you are short on space, this is less frustrating.

LONDON SHRUNK METHOD

If you prefer to do it yourself, follow these directions for the London Shrunk Method. You will need a lot of room.

1. Straighten the ends of the fabric and baste them right sides together.

2. Wet a sheet thoroughly and spin it dry in the washer so the moisture will be distributed evenly.

3. Spread the sheet on the floor or a vinyl-covered table.

4. Lay the fabric flat on one side of the sheet. Smooth out any wrinkles and straighten the fabric as needed so the lengthwise and crosswise threads are at right angles.

5. Cover the fabric with the other side of the sheet. Beginning at one end, roll the fabric and sheet together.

Hint: *To avoid wrinkling, make a towel "log" using several towels, and roll the fabric/sheet around it.*

6. Allow the roll to remain several hours or overnight so the fabric will be dampened thoroughly.

7. Unroll the fabric, remove the sheet, and spread the fabric on the floor or over a table or shower rod. Smooth out any wrinkles; and leave the fabric to dry.

8. Steam press, using a dry press cloth.

SEWING WOOL

Since the variety of wool fabrics ranges from lightweight sheers to heavy, napped coatings, only those sewing suggestions which apply to most wool fabrics are included in this section. Additional suggestions for sewing these popular wool fabrics will be found in the sections indicated.

Bedford Cord: Ribbed Fabrics; Worsted Suitings
Blanket Cloth: Coatings
Boiled Wool: Felted Fabrics
Bouclé: Lightweight Wools; Loosely Woven Fabrics; Textured Woolens
Broadcloth: Coatings; Napped; Worsted Suitings
Camel's Hair: Coatings; Hair Fibers
Cashmere: Coatings; Hair Fibers
Challis: Lightweight Wools
Checks, Plaids, and Houndstooth: Checks; Plaids; Worsted Suitings
Cool Wool: Washable Wools; Lightweight Wools
Crepe: Lightweight Wools; Worsted Suitings
Double-Faced Wools: Coatings; Two-Faced Fabrics
Flannel: Napped, Worsted Suitings
Fleece: Coatings
Gabardine: Worsted Suitings
Harris Tweed: Plaids; Stripes; Textured Woolens
Herringbone Tweeds: Stripes; Textured Woolens
H$_2$O: Washable Wools

Melton: Coatings
Mohair: Hair Fibers; Loosely Woven Fabrics; Textured Woolens
Ottomans: Coatings; Ribbed Fabrics; Stripes; Worsted Suitings
Serge: Worsted Suitings
Superwash®: Washable Wools
Tartans: Plaids; Worsted Suitings
Tattersall: Plaids; Worsted Suitings
Tweeds: Textured Woolens
Wadmal: Coatings; Felted Fabrics
Wool Double Knits: Double Knits; Knits
Wool Felt: Felt; Knits
Wool Jersey: Jersey; Knits
Wool Velour: Coatings; Napped Fabrics
Viyella®: Lightweight Wools
Voile: Lightweight Wools
Zibeline: Coatings; Ribbed Fabrics

LAYOUT AND CUTTING

When both sides look the same, mark the face side with drafting tape, pins, or chalk.

Lightweight wool tends to stretch and shift. Use plenty of pins or weights to anchor the pattern securely.

Use a nap layout; the overlapping scales on the wool fibers may affect the shading of the fabric.

Spread bulky and thick fabrics in a single layer, right side up.

STITCHING TIPS

Make a test seam. For lightweight wools, use a small needle (60/8 to 70/10) and a shorter stitch length; for medium-weight fabrics, use a medium needle (70/10 to 90/14) and medium stitch length; for heavy fabrics, use a large needle (80/12 to 90/14) and longer stitch length.

To reduce bulk when sewing medium- and heavyweight wools, grade seams and darts appropriately.

DARTS

Since most wool fabrics are easy to shrink and mold, darts at the elbow and back shoulder are frequently replaced with ease in this manner:

1. Prepare the paper pattern before cutting out. Pin the dart closed; then pin the seamlines together. Mark points *A* and *B* on the seamlines of both

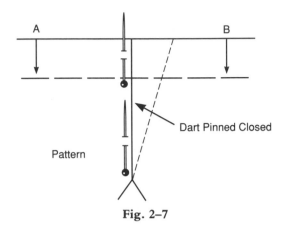

Fig. 2–7

pattern pieces about 1 1/2″ on either side of the dart.

Unpin the pattern and press with a dry iron. Redraw the seamline so it curves slightly.

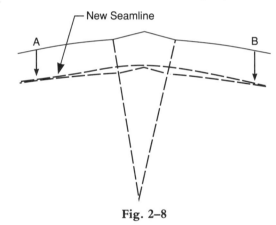

Fig. 2–8

2. Lay out the pattern. Using short clips, mark points *A* and *B* on both garment sections. Mark the point of the dart with a tailor tack or temporary marking pen.

3. Place a row of ease basting on the seamline between points *A* and *B*. Place another row midway between the seamline and raw edge.

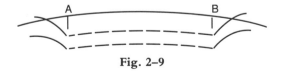

Fig. 2–9

Hint: *To ease baste, lengthen the stitch slightly for medium-weight wools and more for heavy wools; then loosen the upper tension and stitch with the right side up. I use glazed thread or buttonhole twist in the bobbin so it will pull easily without breaking.*

4. Pull up the bobbin thread until the distance between A and B measures 3″. Place pins at A and B; secure the threads by winding the ends around the pins in a figure eight.

Hint: *When you insert the pins, pin a small bite of fabric so the eased section won't grow when you shrink it.*

5. Place the fabric on the ham, wrong side up. Press just the seam allowance between points A and B while you hold the garment section firmly just beyond the dart point. Raise the iron 1/4″ and steam generously; press without steam from the dart point to the eased line. Repeat until all excess fabric has been shrunk away at the seamline. Let it dry thoroughly before moving it.

6. Join the underarm seams, matching points A and B.

Pressing Wool

Test your pressing techniques on a fabric scrap before beginning the garment. The amount of moisture, heat, and pressure varies with the fabric and remember that, since wool is weaker when wet, it should be handled carefully when pressing or steaming.

Use a sturdy, well-padded pressing board which has at least one—the top—layer of wool. My board is padded with an old mattress pad, which is covered with several layers of old wool blankets.

Pressing wool garments takes time; in fact, it is not unusual to spend more time pressing than machine stitching.

Although a good steam iron is a useful time-saver, a dry iron and a damp press cloth will work just as well.

To dampen the press cloth, wet it thoroughly and wring it dry. Then fold it into quarters or eighths; and press until it's damp, not wet.

Most pressing is done with a medium-low temperature (350° F) and steam.

Hint: *If you find pressing with a cloth unwieldy, set the cloth aside and try this method. Hold the steam iron or steamer just above, but not touching, the fabric. Allow the steam to penetrate thoroughly. Remove the iron and cover the steamed area with a clapper. Allow the piece to dry before pressing the next section.*

If you prefer a Teflon iron shoe, take care to avoid slicks and shines.

Dark-colored fabrics—navy, brown, and black—shine easily. To avoid shine, press as much as possible from the wrong side. Use a damp press cloth. Press; do not slide the iron; and do not press the fabric completely dry. Let the section dry before moving it.

To remove a shine, cover the area with several layers of a damp press cloth. Hold the iron against the press cloth and press until damp and steaming. Using the fabric scrap, brush the garment lightly to restore the surface. Repeat if needed.

The face side of wool is rarely, if ever, pressed without a press cloth. When pressing the right side, use a wool press cloth.

Press with the grain; generally, this means pressing from the hem up. Avoid sliding the iron across the grain or the bias. Since wool is very elastic, it can be stretched out of shape with improper pressing.

PRESSING SEAMS

To avoid seam impressions on the outside of the garment, use a seam roll or strips of brown paper between the garment and seam allowances.

For super sharp seamlines, cover the seam allowances with a damp 1″-wide muslin strip; then press.

PRESSING DARTS

When pressing darts, press flat; then press, wrong side up, over a ham or pressing pad. Press carefully to avoid shrinking out the fullness at the end of the dart. Most darts should be slashed open before pressing; wide darts should be trimmed to 1/2″.

PRESSING EDGES AND HEMS

For flat, well-defined edges on flaps, collars, jacket edges, and pleats, cover the edge with a damp press cloth; and press, wrong side up. Remove the iron quickly and cover the edge with a clapper. For springy, resilient fabrics like worsteds and coatings, spank the edge several times with a clapper to beat the steam out of it.

Press skirts and let them hang twenty-four hours or more before marking hemlines. Place strips of brown paper between the hem edge and the garment before pressing the hemline, so you won't imprint the edge on the right side.

To shrink away excess fullness in the hem, press from the hemline up; press with the grain, not across it.

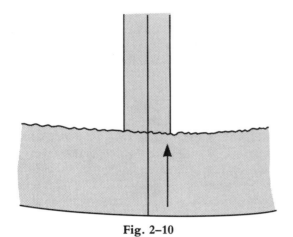

Fig. 2–10

STRETCHING AND SHRINKING

If you've never worked with wool before, experiment with stretching and shrinking. You will use this technique for waistbands, knee treatments, sleeve caps, collars, and lapels.

The weave of the fabric and yarn structure will determine how much the fabric can be manipulated. Generally, woolens are more pliable than worsteds.

Cut a piece 10″ wide and 8″ deep. Steam one long edge so that it is slightly damp; then, with the iron at one end of the fabric, pull on the other. Pull, stretch, and press until the side has a convex curve.

The other side will have ripples and won't lie flat. Steam it well; then press and shrink away the fullness.

When stretching and shrinking the garment fabric, use a press cloth to prevent shines. Use ease basting to shrink evenly without pleating and to avoid shrinking too much.

ALTERATIONS

Before letting out or lowering the hem on wool garments, examine the garment carefully. Most crease lines can be removed; however, soil and wear lines cannot.

PRESSING TECHNIQUES FOR SPECIAL FABRICS

Wool Stretch Fabrics: Lower the iron temperature to synthetic and press with little or no steam. Avoid stretching the fabric when pressing.

Lightweight and Sheer Wools: Lower the iron temperature to prevent scorching.

Wools with a Brushed Nap: Cover the pressing board with a bristle press cloth or large fabric scrap. Press with the nap, using little or no moisture.

Mohair and Mohair Blends: Lower the iron temperature. To avoid matting the mohair, use a dry press cloth next to the mohair with a damp cloth over it. Do not use a steam iron.

Wool Crepe: Avoid excess moisture.

Wiry Worsteds and Heavy Woolens: Use a damp press cloth and increase the pressure. Remove the iron and cover the pressed area with a clapper. Spank vigorously if it still isn't flat.

GARMENT CARE

Since most wools don't soil and spot readily, they are easy to keep clean.

After each wearing, hang the garment immediately, and brush it with a firm, soft brush. To prevent matting, avoid brushing when damp. Allow the garment to rest twenty-four hours between wearings, so it can shed its wrinkles. (Baggy seats and knees will recover with a good steaming and light pressing.)

To freshen garments, air them near an open window or in the shade outside. To prevent soiling, wear a neckline scarf or blouse, and use underarm dress shields.

Occasionally, sponge garments with a damp sponge to remove lint and surface dirt. Rinse the sponge frequently in cool water.

Hang damp garments away from heaters and sunlight, so they can dry naturally. When dry, brush well with the nap. Never put garments away wet.

Hang wool garments on appropriately sized, padded hangers, so they will maintain their shape. Be sure coat and suit hangers extend at least to the shoulder seams.

To prevent wrinkling, fasten the top button, zip zippers, and store garments in a well-ventilated, uncrowded closet.

Store delicate knits flat so they won't stretch out of shape. To avoid creases, fold them with tissue if they are not worn frequently.

Treat spots immediately. Use a clean cloth to absorb any excess liquid; then clean with a mild solution of soap and cool water or cleaning fluid. (Test cleaning solutions on a fabric scrap first.) To prevent pilling and felting, avoid rubbing vigorously. To prevent shrinking or bleeding, use a hair dryer on the cool setting to dry the cleaned area.

Repair rips and tears as soon as possible. And to avoid damage by moths and carpet beetles, clean garments before storing. When using moth balls, do not let them touch the fabric.

Wool fabrics should be dry-cleaned unless specifically labeled otherwise. For washable wools, follow the care directions on the bolt end; handle them carefully when wet to avoid shrinking, matting or stretching them out of shape.

LIGHTWEIGHT WOOLS

Naked wool, challis, batiste, voile, gauze, crepe, albatross, tropical worsteds, and Cool Wool (a brand name) are typical lightweight wools.

Fabric Characteristics
- Although many lightweight wools are firmly woven and easy to sew, most will fray badly if overhandled.
- Some are transparent and should be handled accordingly.
- Puckered seams and skipped stitches are sometimes a problem.
- Lightweight wools are easily marred by too-large needles and ripping.
- Seam slippage may be a problem at stress points.
- All are easy to shape with heat and moisture.
- Lightweight wools are easily damaged with improper pressing techniques.

SEWING CHECKLIST

Machine Needles: Universal-H point or Red Band needles; sizes 60/8 to 80/12.

Machine Setting: Stitch length 1.75–2mm (12–15 stitches per inch).

Thread: Long-staple polyester, cotton-wrapped polyester, mercerized cotton. Basting—cotton, silk (size A); topstitching—regular, silk (size A).

Hand Sewing Needles: Sizes 8 to 10.

Sewing Machine Equipment: Straight-stitch or jeans foot.

Notions: Lightweight zippers, buttons, snaps.

Layout: Double/lay, right sides together.

Marking Techniques: All types.

Seams: Plain, flat-fell, lapped, standing-fell, French, fake French, topstitched, welt, double-welt, double/ply, tissue-stitched.

Hems: Plain, blindstitch, catchstitch, machine blindstitch, double needle, topstitched, shirttail, book, machine-rolled, hand-rolled, fused, interfaced.

Seam and Hem Finishes: Single/ply or double/ply. Pinked, pinked-and-stitched, zigzag, multi-stitch zigzag, serged, hand overcast, Hong Kong, double-stitched fold.

Edge Finishes: Self-fabric facings, bias facings, bindings, bands.

Interfacings: Lightweight interfacing fabrics, silk organza, China silk, organdy.

Linings and Underlinings: Sometimes, to provide support and opaqueness.

PLANNING A GARMENT

DESIGN IDEAS AND PATTERN SELECTION

Frequently used for blouses and dresses, lightweight wools such as challis, naked wool, voile, batiste, and crepe are soft and very drapeable with good body. They are well-suited for gathers, unpressed pleats, cowl necklines, and draped or soft folds.

Tropical worsteds take sharp creases and press well. They are suitable for crisp styles and frequently used for trousers and lightweight jackets.

Fig. 2–11 *By Christian Dior, Tailleur Bar from the Spring/Summer Collection 1947, the "New Look" that revolutionized fashion. Almost ten yards of lightweight wool were used in the skirt. (Photo courtesy of Christian Dior.)*

SEWING LIGHTWEIGHT WOOLS

Preshrink all fabrics, except crepe, if it isn't marked needle-ready. For additional sewing suggestions, see Wool.

STITCHING TIPS

Make a test seam, using a small needle (60/8 or 70/10). Set the machine for a loosely balanced tension, and a stitch length of 1.75–2mm. (12–15 stitches per inch).

Tissue-stitch seams if necessary to reduce skipped stitches and puckered seams.

Avoid overhandling; these fabrics fray badly when mistreated.

SEAMS

Plain seams are best for soft, fluid garments, while self-finished or double/ply seams work well for transparent fabrics and fabrics that fray.

HEMS

Consider the look you want when selecting the hem. Narrow hems have less weight than traditional 2″ plain hems and allow skirts to float and billow more.

Use a narrow hem on scarves.

PRESSING

When pressing lightweight wools, lower the iron temperature to prevent scorching.

When pressing crepes, press with as little moisture as possible.

GARMENT CARE

Most lightweight wools require dry cleaning; however, a few can be handwashed if you pretreated the fabric.

TEXTURED WOOLENS

Widely used for men's and women's informal sportswear, textured woolens and wool tweeds are frequently recommended for beginning tailoring projects because most are easy to sew.

Available in various weaves and textures, all weights, and a variety of qualities, textured woolens are usually woven in a combination of two or more colors or two or more shades of the same color. These fabrics frequently have a rough sur-

Fig. 2–12 *This handsome tailored wool tweed jacket from Krizia contrasts strikingly with the soft wool lace skirt. (Photo by Giovanni Gaste, courtesy of Krizia, Fall/Winter Collection 1987/1988.)*

face, which helps to hide stitching irregularities.

Some fabrics such as Harris, Shetland, Donegal, and Bannockburn tweeds are named after the district in which they are made, while others such as herringbone and salt and pepper are known for their physical characteristics.

One of the most popular textured woolens is the handwoven Harris tweed. Woven on looms in Scottish cottages, the loom and fabric width—27" to 29"—is limited to the door-frame width.

Fabric Characteristics
- Many textured woolens are firmly woven and easy to sew.
- A few are loosely woven and more difficult to handle.
- Many textured fabrics have a nap.
- Some textured fabrics are bulky.
- Woolens are easy to shape with heat and moisture.

- Woolens can be damaged with improper pressing techniques.
- Although most textured wools are woolens, a few are worsteds; and some are wools blended with cotton or synthetics.
- Woolens with slubs and low-twist yarns tend to pill more.

SEWING CHECKLIST

Machine Needles: Universal-H point or Red Band needles; sizes 70/10 to 90/14, depending on the fabric weight.
Machine Setting: Stitch length 2–3mm (8–12 stitches per inch); tension and pressure, adjust as needed.
Thread: Long-staple polyester, cotton-wrapped polyester, mercerized cotton. Basting—Silk (size A), cotton; topstitching—regular thread, topstitching silk (size D).
Hand Sewing Needles: Sizes 5 to 7.
Layout: Nap. Double/lay, right sides together. Heavy tweeds: Single/lay, right side up.
Marking Techniques: All types.
Seams: Plain, welt, double-welt, topstitched.
Hems: Plain, blindstitch, catchstitch, machine blindstitch, double-stitch, fused, interfaced.
Seam and Hem Finishes: Single/ply or double/ply. Unfinished, pinked, pinked-and-stitched, serged, hand-overcast.
Edge Finishes: Self-fabric facings, bias facings, bindings, bands.
Interfacing: Generally used; fusible or sew-in hair canvas, weft insertion fusibles, and appropriate weight sew-ins.
Linings: Generally used for outerwear.
Closures: All types.
Pockets: All types.

PLANNING A GARMENT

PURCHASING THE FABRIC

If the fabric is extremely fibrous, it may irritate your skin.

Wool tweeds should have good color, tensile strength, and elasticity.

Handwoven fabrics may vary in color and have slight irregularities in the weave. To be sure a fabric is handwoven, check the fabric width. Handwoven tweeds such as homespuns and Harris tweeds are 27″ to 29″ wide. Other handwovens will be 45″ or less. (Harris tweeds frequently have a numbered label which identifies the weaver.)

To prepare the fabric, preshrink as needed before cutting.

PATTERN SELECTION

Generally used for coats, jackets, and suits, textured woolens and wool tweeds are well suited for sportswear and informal tailoring.

SEWING TEXTURED WOOLENS

For additional suggestions, see Wool, Coatings, Napped Fabrics, Plaids, and Stripes.

PRESSING

When pressing mohair and mohair blends, lower the iron temperature. To avoid matting the mohair, use a dry press cloth on top of the mohair with a damp cloth over it.

Loosely woven woolens tend to shrink more than tightly woven fabrics.

When pressing wiry woolens and heavy tweeds, use a damp press cloth and increase the pressure. Remove the iron and cover the pressed area with a clapper. Beat it vigorously until it is flat.

WORSTED SUITINGS

Gabardine, covert, pinstripe suitings, serge, cassimere, cheviot, wool poplin, sharkskin, tricotine, tropical worsteds, whipcord, worsted flannel, fancy worsteds, and elastique are some of the most popular worsteds.

Widely used for suitings, worsteds are firmly woven from well-twisted yarns. Most have a clear finish (without a nap) and a prominent weave. Some, such as menswear pinstripes, feature yarn-dyed threads.

Fabric Characteristics
- Worsted suitings are firmly woven with a smooth, hard surface.
- Most are medium-weight, but they range from lightweight tropical worsteds to heavy whipcords.
- They crease and pleat well.
- They are frequently difficult to ease.
- Some fray badly.
- Many worsted suitings are very springy and difficult to press.
- They are easily shined when pressed improperly.
- Most worsted suitings spot badly.

Fig. 2–13 *Designed by Louis Feraud, this crisply tailored, worsted suit is trimmed with embroidery and appliqués on the pocket. (Photo courtesy of Louis Feraud, Paris Autumn/Winter 1987/1988 Collection.)*

PLANNING A GARMENT

PURCHASING THE FABRIC

Worsted suitings with a high thread count and a compact weave will wear better than those with a looser weave. Good quality fabrics have two-ply or three-ply yarns in the warp.

Better suitings, which are woven from finer wools, have a pleasing hand.

If you are an inexperienced seamster, check the fray quality of the fabric before purchasing.

To prepare the fabric, preshrink as needed.

DESIGN IDEAS AND PATTERN SELECTION

Frequently used for tailored designs, coats, jackets, pleated skirts, trousers, tailored dresses, and riding habits, worsted suitings are firmly woven, crisp fabrics. They are well suited to topstitching details, pocket details, and pressed pleats.

On twill weaves avoid bias skirts and details.

SEWING WORSTED SUITINGS

For additional sewing suggestions, see Wool.

STITCHING TIPS

Make a test seam, using a small needle (60/8 or 70/10). Set the machine for 2–2.5mm (10–12 stitches per inch).

Plain seams and hems are best for traditional garments. If the fabric frays badly, finish the seam edges before assembling the garment. To avoid changing the seam width, take care not to trim off any of the seam allowance when serging.

To avoid a thread imprint on the right side of the garment when finishing seams on tropical worsteds, thread woolly nylon thread on the serger loopers.

DARTS AND SLEEVES

For a flatter finish, slash and press darts open.

Shrink and shape the sleeve cap before setting it into the garment. If the fullness can't be eased smoothly, reduce the ease.

PRESSING

Pressing as you sew is more important than ever when sewing difficult, springy fabrics. Press enclosed seams, such as those at collar and garment edges, on a wooden point presser before turning them right side out.

Fig. 2–14 *From Saint Laurent Rive Gauche, Autumn/Winter 1987/1988, this simply shaped jacket is stunning in wool velour. The skirt is suede. (Photo courtesy of Yves Saint Laurent.)*

Hint: *I made a special 18" by 24" press cloth for wools. The two layers of white wool flannel and washed muslin are sewn together on one end.*

· For a sharp press, use a damp press cloth and increase the pressure. Remove the iron and press cloths; cover the pressed area with a clapper. Use the clapper to spank it vigorously until it's flat.

To avoid shine and iron imprints, cover the pressing surface with a wool press cloth and use a damp press cloth. (To reduce shine, sand damaged fabric lightly and cautiously with 000 sandpaper.)

When in doubt, press lightly; then press again if needed.

COATINGS

Coating fabrics are thick, bulky materials which protect the wearer from the damp and cold. Melton, fleece, ottoman, camel's hair and cashmere coatings, heavy tweeds, loden cloth, and jumbo corduroy are most familiar, but alpaca, astrakhan, baize, bolivia, cavalry twill, chinchilla cloth, wool double cloth, gabardine coating, homespun coating, kersey, polo cloth, and ratiné are also worn in many cold-weather climates.

Fabric Characteristics
- Most coating fabrics have a prominent nap.
- Coating fabrics are very bulky.
- Most coating fabrics fray very little so seams and hems are usually left unfinished; however, a few coatings are loosely woven and fray badly.
- Coatings are difficult to press well.
- Coating fabrics wear at the edges and some pill.

PLANNING A GARMENT

DESIGN IDEAS AND PATTERN SUGGESTIONS

Coating fabrics are relatively stiff and retain the silhouette of the garment. They are used to make large, loose-fitting coats and jackets, capes, ponchos, and ruanas.

SEWING CHECKLIST

Machine Needles: Universal-H point or Red Band needles; sizes 80/12 or 100/16.

Machine Setting: Stitch length 3mm (8 stitches per inch); loosely balanced tension; light pressure.

Thread: Long-staple polyester, cotton-wrapped polyester, size 50; mercerized cotton, size 40. Basting—cotton, silk (size A); topstitching—topstitching, silk (size A or D), or two strands of regular thread.

Hand Sewing Needles: Sizes 3 to 7.

Sewing Machine Equipment: Zipper foot, shim.

Equipment and Supplies: Rotary cutter and mat, weights, very long pins, clapper, hardwood board, tailor board, Velvaboard® or needle board, washable glue, water-soluble basting thread, Wonder Under™, Transfuse II™, or Fine Fuse™.

Layout: Nap; single/lay, right side up.

Marking Techniques: Clips, tailor tacks, thread tracing, chalk, soap sliver, temporary marking pens, pins, wax.

Seams: Plain, topstitched, welt, abutted.

Seam and Hem Finishes: Single/ply. Plain/untreated, pinked, pinked-and-stitched, zigzag, serged, bound, Hong-Kong, seam tape.

Hems: Plain, fused, topstitched for casual designs, blindstitch, blind catchstitch, catchstitch, double-stitched, interfaced.

Interfacing: Generally used; fusible or sew-in, hair canvas, weft insertion, woven.

Lining: Usually.

Underlining: Rarely.

Closures: Buttonholes—bound, machine-stitched, or hand-worked; button loops, decorative zippers, toggles.

Pockets: All types.

Simple styles with crisp tailored lines, with or without topstitching, are particularly attractive. Collarless designs, standing, shawl, and padded collars, fur, and velvet collars work well. Notched collars are more difficult to sew.

For a high-fashion look, consider these ideas from three well-known designers: fat pipings from Geoffrey Beene (Fig. 2–16); piped edges and seams with coordinating button loops from Dior (Fig. 2–17); and ribbed knit bands at the hem, wrists, and neckline from Laura Biagiotti (Fig. 2–18).

Avoid self-fabric tie belts, tabs, epaulets, and fussy details, as well as patterns with seams at the garment front edge.

PATTERN PREPARATION

Cut duplicate pattern pieces. Redraw sharp corners on collars and lapels so they will be rounded and turn smoothly (Fig. 2–15).

Make a new pattern for the lining back so the lining will extend to the neckline.

If the pattern has a tie belt, tabs, or epaulets, recut the pattern pieces so these sections can be faced with a lightweight lining fabric.

Remember to preshrink the fabric, lining, interfacing, and notions before you begin sewing.

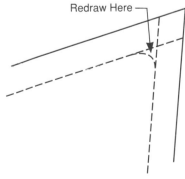

Fig. 2–15

51

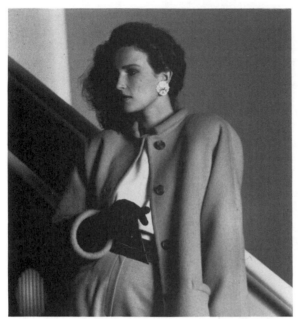

Fig. 2–16 *Career dressing at its best, this go-everywhere coat features softly padded collar and cuffs. (Designer, Geoffrey Beene; photo courtesy of Vogue Patterns.)*

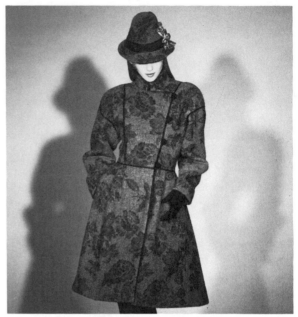

Fig. 2–17 *From Christian Dior Boutique, Autumn/Winter 1987/1988, this Austrian wool coat is outlined with braided piping. (Photo courtesy of Christian Dior.)*

SEWING COATINGS

LAYOUT

Spread the fabric in a single layer, right side up. A doubled layer is not only difficult to cut, but since the fabric is bulky, you may cut some sections too large and others too small.

Lay out the pattern so the nap runs down. Use weights or No More Pins™ to hold the pattern in place. Cut, using a large pair of very sharp shears or a rotary cutter and mat.

Small clips are best for marking the notches. Tailor tacks, thread tracing, chalk, soap sliver, and temporary marking pens also work well. A tracing wheel and tracing carbon are difficult to use on these thick fabrics. If the fabric is wool, use wax chalk.

STITCHING TIPS

Make a test seam using a medium to large needle (80/12 to 100/16). Set the stitch length for 3mm (8 stitches per inch), a loosely balanced tension, and lighter pressure. Hold the fabric taut and stitch with the nap. Adjust as needed by lengthening the stitch, loosening the tension, and lightening the pressure.

To position the fabric, lift the presser foot manually as high as possible. Cover the fabric with a smooth plastic card; then slide it under the presser foot. Remove the card before stitching.

To reduce bulk, trim and grade all seams as needed.

FACINGS

Replace self-fabric facings for collars, tabs, and pockets with lining-weight facings, synthetic suede, or leather.

Replace bulky facings at garment edges with double-fold braid or synthetic suede or leather bindings. Or line the garment edge to edge, simulating a reversible garment.

To secure the edges of the front facings, use strips of Wonder-Under or Transfuse II instead of hand stitching. Cut 1/4″-wide strips; fuse them to the unnotched edge of the facing; remove the paper backing before the lining is attached. During the final press, after the lining is sewn, the Wonder-Under will fuse to the wrong side of the coating.

A houndstooth check jacket tops glen plaid trousers; from Bill Blass, Fall, 1988. Trimmed with bias bands of self-fabric shaped to fit the curved edges, the jacket has in-seam buttonholes and welt pockets. (Photo courtesy Jesse Gerstein, photographer, and Bill Blass, Ltd.)

This elegant suit design lends itself to many fabrications. Here Blass tailors a boldly checked wool. On another design, he featured a white double-cloth jacket and se- *quinned lace pants. (Photo courtesy Bill Blass, Ltd.; Fall, 1988.)*

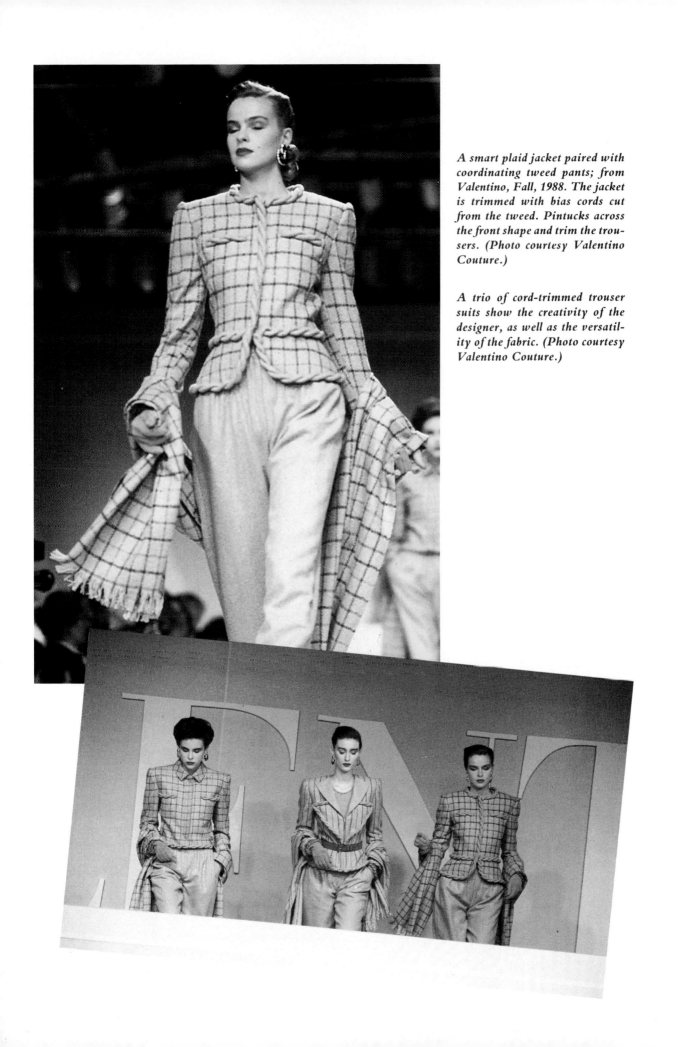

A smart plaid jacket paired with coordinating tweed pants; from Valentino, Fall, 1988. The jacket is trimmed with bias cords cut from the tweed. Pintucks across the front shape and trim the trousers. (Photo courtesy Valentino Couture.)

A trio of cord-trimmed trouser suits show the creativity of the designer, as well as the versatility of the fabric. (Photo courtesy Valentino Couture.)

Louis Feraud's go-anywhere dress is an easy-fitting wool flannel. The sleeves and scarf are trimmed with narrow strips of colored bias. (Photo courtesy Louis Feraud.)

Left: A classic with a difference from Louis Feraud. The plaid design on this traditional jacket is created with strips of grosgrain ribbon. The same ribbon is used to trim the solid-color lapels. (Photo courtesy Louis Feraud.)

Opposite page: One of the most copied looks of our time, this classic Chanel suit from the mid-sixties is made of a handwoven wool and silk fabric, trimmed with braid crocheted from matching yarns. (Gift of Mrs. Joanne Cummings; photo courtesy the Arizona Costume Institute of the Phoenix Art Museum.)

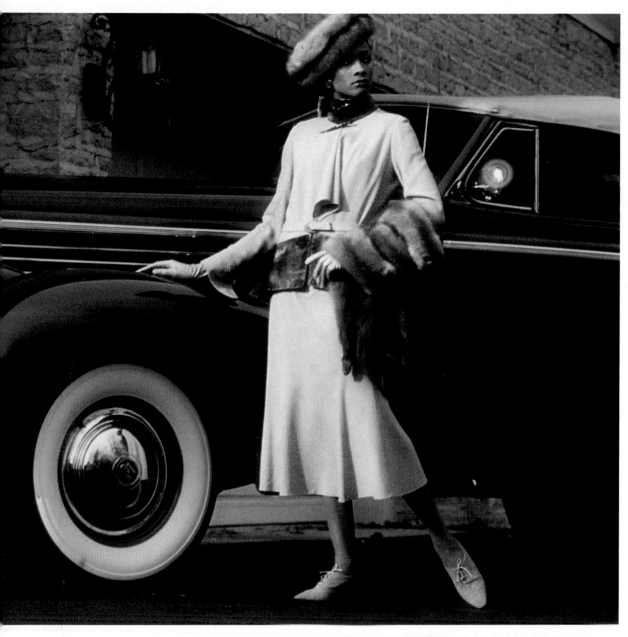

Opposite page, top: *In this avant-garde design from the sixties, Pierre Cardin combines crisp brown and white wools with a simple architectural shape. (Gift of Mrs. Howard Lipman; photo courtesy the Arizona Costume Institute of the Phoenix Art Museum.)*

Opposite page, below: *This innovative dinosaur coat from Zandra Rhodes' 1971 Collection features felt panels which have been cut and seamed to resemble the scaly backbone of a dinosaur. The decorative corsage is made of quilted Matisse-style prints and appliquéd to the coat. (Photographer, Robyn Beeche; photograph from The Art of Zandra Rhodes, © Jonathan Cape, courtesy Zandra Rhodes.)*

Above: *Trimmed with flat fur on the stand-up collar and at the jacket hemline, this wool crepe suit is a timeless fashion from the thirties. (From the Kleibacker Group in the Historic Costume and Textile Collection, Ohio State University; photo courtesy Charles Kleibacker.)*

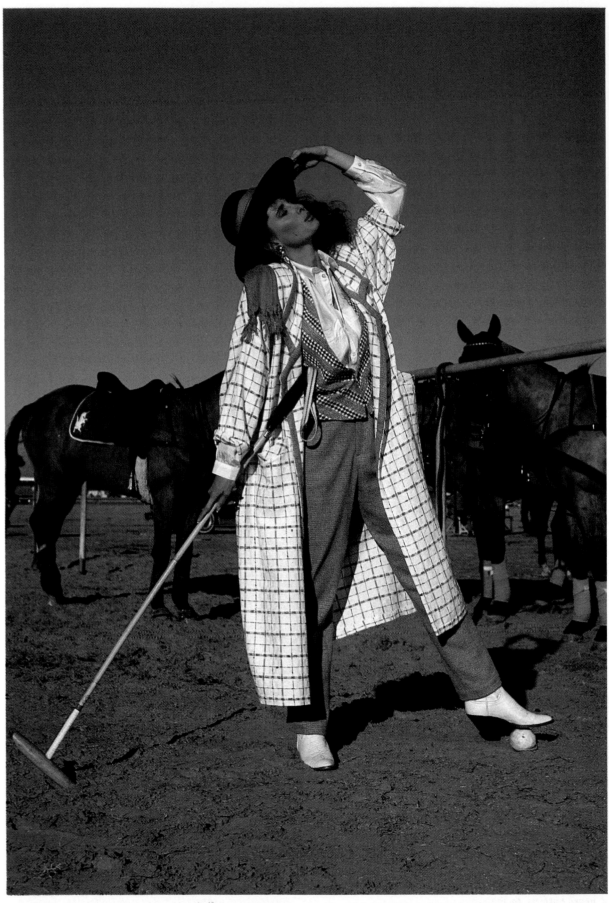

Made of a two-faced fabric, this attractive duster features single-layer lapels and collar. Decorative bands of solid-color fabric trim and finish edges and seams. (Cheryl Coleman, photographer, Palm Springs, California.)

Fig. 2–18 *Laura Biagiotti used wide ribbings and mother of pearl buttons to trim this soft wool jacket. (Photo courtesy of Laura Biagiotti, P.A.P. Fall/Winter 1987/1988 Collection.)*

53

DOUBLE CLOTH

On double cloth, separate the layers on the facing sections to reduce bulk. Before cutting the undercollar, separate the layers; cut the undercollar from only one layer; steam and press well; then cut. For coats with cut-on facings, baste along the foldline through both layers; then separate carefully to the basted line. Cut away the facing on the inner layer.

INTERFACINGS

Some coatings hold their shape so well that interfacings can be eliminated. Interface individual buttonholes if you are not interfacing the entire area. And always use a stay tape at the garment edge to prevent it from stretching.

CLOSURES

Buttons and buttonholes—bound, machine-stitched, or hand-worked—are used most frequently; however, buttons and loops, zippers, and toggles are other considerations.

Bound Buttonholes. Use the strip, modified strip, or window method to make bound buttonholes. In addition to self-fabric, buttonhole welts can be made from contrasting materials such as leather, synthetic suede, grosgrain, and satin. (Contrasting buttonholes are even more attractive when the same material is used to bind the garment edges, replace a self-fabric collar, make welt or slot pockets, or trim patch pockets.) Interface button/buttonhole areas.

Machine-Stitched and Hand-Worked Buttonholes. Generally keyhole buttonholes are preferred on coats and jackets. The large hole allows the button to set better and the front to remain smooth.

For machine-stitched buttonholes, lengthen and widen the stitch. Experiment with regular thread and buttonhole twist on fabric scraps first. For hand-worked buttonholes, use silk thread (size D or F).

Button Loops. If your design has piped seams or bound edges, button loops made from the piping or binding material are very attractive. For instance, when the garment has a braided piping, use a similar braided cord to make the button loops.

If the trim is leather or synthetic suede, consider these quick and easy loops. Cut a 1/2"-wide strip

the desired length. Fold the strip in half lengthwise, wrong sides together; and stitch close to the foldline. Trim the strip so it is 1/8" wide and sew to the garment as usual.

Buttons. Using buttonhole twist, sew buttons on with a stem equal to the garment thickness. Reinforcement buttons underneath are optional. Position the reinforcement button on the facing side. Sew it in place when sewing the regular button.

TOPSTITCHING

Topstitching is especially attractive on plain coatings; and it actually helps control the fabric bulk.

Experiment on fabric scraps. Lengthen the stitch to 4 mm or 6 stitches per inch and use a heavier thread such as silk or polyester buttonhole twist. Or use two strands of regular thread threaded through a single needle.

When using buttonhole twist, experiment with it in the needle, bobbin, or both. Select the look you like best.

Topstitch both sides of the seamline to hold the seam allowances flat; topstitch garment edges 3/8" to 1/2" from the edge.

Hint: *Trim seam allowances so they will be enclosed by the topstitch. Use a zipper foot set to the left of the needle so the foot will remain level when stitching at the edge of the trimmed seam allowances.*

When topstitching over bulky seams, use a shim or folded piece of fabric to balance the foot. As the foot approaches the bulk, place the shim under the heel of the foot; as it leaves the bulk, place it under the toes.

If you have difficulty stitching straight, use water-soluble basting thread or drafting or stitching tape.

Hint: *To remove the tape, pull down in the direction of the nap.*

If you don't like machine stitching at the edges, consider topstitching by hand—perhaps a decorative saddle stitch or a pick stitch.

Hint: *The pick stitch can be made from either the outside of the garment or the inside. When made in the usual manner on the outside, there* *will be a tiny indentation at each stitch. When made from the inside, pick up just the back of the outer layer so the stitches are almost invisible.*

COLLARS

To reduce bulk, replace self-fabric undercollars with a lighter weight melton or Ultrasuede. Trim away the seam allowances on the undercollar; and using a felling stitch, sew the undercollar in place by hand.

POCKETS

Inseam pockets, flaps, welts, and patch pockets are frequently used on coating fabrics. Although inseam pockets are the easiest, plain colored coats frequently need more decorative pockets to enhance the design.

Use lining-weight material to line patch pockets and to make pocket sacks for slot and inseam pockets. Use it to face welts and flaps.

MACHINE-STITCHED FLAPS
AND WELTS

Flaps and welts are easier to set into seamlines than to apply to the garment surface.

Face pocket flaps and welts with lightweight lining fabrics, using either the machine-stitched method, which is used in ready-made coats, or the hand method, which is used for designer garments.

1. Cut the flap facing from lining-weight fabric; trim the outside edges 1/8″.

2. Cut the flap interfacing from hair canvas or a suitable fusible. Trim away all seam allowances. Fuse or catchstitch the interfacing to the wrong side of the flap.

3. Right sides together, match and pin the raw edges together as shown in Figure 2–19. Lining side up, stitch with a 3/8″ seam.

Hint: *Machine baste first with water-soluble thread in the bobbin. Turn the flap right side out to compare the size to the pattern. If it isn't right, do it again. Be sure to replace the basting bobbin before stitching permanently.*

4. Stitch permanently; then steam press the flap on the stitched line. The steam will dissolve the

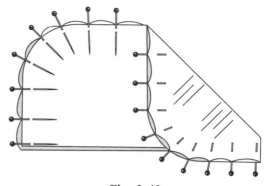

Fig. 2–19

basting thread, as well as marry the stitches. Press the seam open. Trim as needed.

5. Turn the flap right sides out. The seamline should roll to the wrong side. Steam and finger press the edge. Then, place the flap on a smooth, hardwood board; and, from the wrong side, press with lots of steam and pressure. To flatten the edges, pound vigorously with a clapper.

Fig. 2–20

6. Leave the flap to dry. Then join to the garment in the usual manner.

7. Use this method for welts.

HAND-STITCHED FLAPS

This is the method designers use to face flaps, welts, pockets, belts, and even waistbands. At first glance it seems time-consuming, but it really isn't; and the results are fantastic.

1. Cut the flap facing from lining-weight fabric.

2. Cut the flap interfacing from hair canvas or a suitable fusible. Trim away all seam allowances. Fuse or catchstitch the interfacing to the wrong side of the flap.

3. Fold all seam allowances to the wrong side and baste 1/4″ from the edge. If necessary, miter the corners and trim away the bulk. Using a small catchstitch, sew the raw edges to the interfacing.

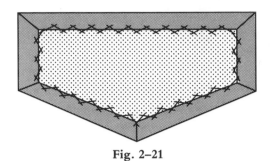

Fig. 2–21

4. Wrong side up, press the edges of the flap with lots of steam and pressure. Use a clapper as needed. This is the only time the flap will be pressed and shaped.

5. Wrong sides together, center the lining over the flap. Place two or three pins in the center. Fold and pin the raw edges of the lining under so you can see a small amount of the flap fabric at each edge. Baste; then slipstitch the lining in place.

6. Right sides up, pin and baste the flap to the garment.

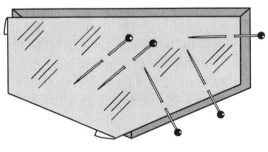

Fig. 2–22

7. Wrong side up, use a running stitch to secure the top edge of the flap to the garment. Try to make the stitches straight and close together so they look like machine stitching.

Hold the flap up; and, using a blindstitch, sew the flap lining to the garment about 1/4″ from the top.

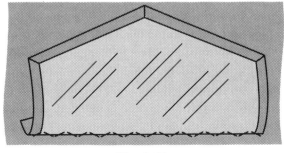

Fig. 2–23

PATCH POCKETS

Patch pockets are very difficult to topstitch in place on bulky coating fabrics so I apply them by hand.

Here are two methods for setting patch pockets by hand.

1. Make and line the pocket. Topstitch if desired.

2. Thread trace the pocket location on the face side of the garment.

3. Baste the pocket in place.

Hint: *Glue baste; then baste by hand with water-soluble basting thread, keeping the stitches an even distance from the pocket edge so you can use them as a guide when securing the pocket from the wrong side of the garment.*

4. Turn the garment section over; and, using either a short running stitch or close diagonal stitch, sew close to the edges of the pocket. Press.

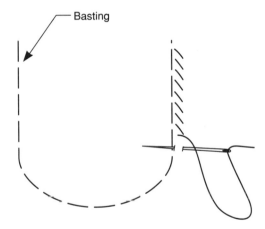

Wrong Side Garment
Fig. 2–24

MAGIC LINED PATCH POCKETS

This patch-pocket method, which Gail Shinn taught me, is slightly more complicated the first time you use it, but it will withstand much more use and abuse than the hand-stitched pocket.

1. Cut a piece of interfacing the size and shape of the finished pocket. Sew or fuse it to the wrong side of the pocket.

2. Right sides together, join the pocket and lining.

3. Press the pocket/lining seam toward the lin-

ing. Then press the seam and hem allowances of the pocket to the wrong side.

Hint: *For a smoother pocket, use a cardboard template when pressing and ease baste the fullness on curved corners. Miter regular corners.*

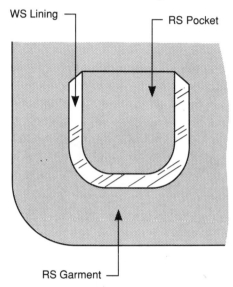

WS Lining — ⌐ RS Pocket

RS Garment —

Fig. 2–25

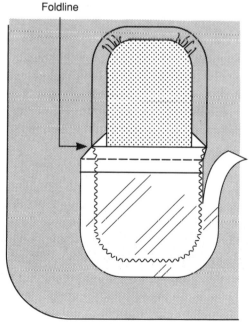

Foldline

Fig. 2–26

4. Right sides up, position the pocket on the garment.

5. Carefully unfold the pocket so that it's upside down; pin the lining to the garment.

6. Stitch (W,2;L,2) around the lining 1″ from the edge beginning and ending at the hemline 3/4″ from the edge.

7. Trim the lining close to the stitched line.

8. Fold the pocket into place; and topstitch or hand sew it from the wrong side.

Hint: *Nancy Zieman uses a machine blind-hem stitch and invisible thread to secure the pocket. Stitch so the straight stitches are on the garment and the zigzag stitches catch the pocket.*

NOTES FROM A NORELL COAT

My Norell coat is made from a wool double cloth. And even though it has a traditional construction with a facing and lining, the fabric has been used unusually.

The front facing, which is cut in one piece with the garment front, has had the inside layer of fabric removed. However, the inside layers are still intact at the hem and sleeve edges.

The only interfacings are the small rectangles under each of the buttonholes. (The collar is described in Double-Cloth Fabrics.)

PRESSING

Cover the pressing board with self-fabric, a Velvaboard®, or needle board. Press from the wrong side to avoid damaging the nap; use steam carefully to avoid shrinking the fabric.

Cover with a damp press cloth; press. Then pound with the clapper. Do not move until dry.

WASHABLE WOOLS

Some wool fabrics are designed to be machine washed and dried under normal conditions without shrinking or fading.

Most washable wools such as H_2O, Featherwool, Silvia, Lana Silk, Crepela, Diana, and Manhattan are blends of wool and one or more synthetics, while a few such as Bellana are 100 percent wools. The all-wool washables have either been treated with chemicals or had the scales removed from the fibers before the fibers are spun into yarns. Both processes allow the wool to be washed without shrinking; however, both affect the malleability of the fiber.

Many washable wools maintain the appearance of traditional wool fabrics such as flannels, broadcloth, double knits, classic plaids, houndstooth checks, tweeds, and twills, while others have added texture and decorative effects. All are easier to maintain, stronger, and more durable than traditional wool fabrics.

The synthetic fibers used in washable wools have many similar qualities, as well as specific individual characteristics which contribute to the finished material.

Nylon is used to increase durability, strength, dimensional stability, and press retention. Often used as a core yarn, it is an aid during the weaving process.

Well-known for adding wash-and-wear properties, polyester is used to add strength and press retention, as well as resistance to wrinkles and abrasion.

Acrylics are used to create new surface textures and to add dimensional stability and bulk without weight.

Rayon is used for decorative effects and as an aid in processing.

Fabric Characteristics
- Washable wools are relatively easy to sew.
- Washable wools look like all-wool fabrics, but most behave like synthetics.
- Skipped stitches may be a problem.
- Washable wools do not ease or tailor well.
- They can be pressed into sharp, permanent pleats and creases.

PLANNING A GARMENT

DESIGN IDEAS AND PATTERN SELECTION

Washable wools are crisp, easy-care fabrics, well suited for children's garments, men's trousers, casual sportswear, collarless coats, and designs for large figures.

Styles with topstitching, pressed pleats, and raglan or cut-on sleeves are particularly attractive.

Avoid blazers and tailored jackets since washable wools cannot be shaped and eased like the all-wool fabrics they resemble.

SEWING WASHABLE WOOLS

Preshrink the fabric and all other components. For additional sewing suggestions, see the applicable sections: Wool, Rayon, Acrylics, Nylon, Polyester, Loosely Woven Fabrics, Napped Fabrics, Textured Woolens, Worsted Suitings, Double Knits, Plaids, and Stripes.

SEWING CHECKLIST

Machine Needles: Universal-H point or Red Band needles; sizes 80/12 or 90/14.

Machine Setting: Stitch length, 2–2.5mm (10–12 stitches per inch).

Thread: Long-staple polyester, cotton-wrapped polyester, size 50. Topstitching—regular, topstitching.

Hand Sewing Needles: Sizes 7 to 9.

Equipment and Supplies: Clapper.

Marking Techniques: All types.

Seams: Plain, topstitched, welt, double-welt, slot, tucked.

Hems: Plain, fused, topstitched, blind-stitch, machine blindstitch, blind catchstitch, interfaced.

Seam and Hem Finishes: Single/ply or double/ply; zigzag, multistitch zigzag, serged.

Interfacings: Usually fusible or sew-in.

Lining: Depends on garment type and design.

Closures: All types.

Pockets: All types.

Garment Care: Wash or dry-clean, depending on construction, garment design, and other components.

GARMENT CARE

Turn the garment inside out. Set the washer for a gentle cycle and wash in warm water with a mild detergent. Tumble dry for 15 to 20 minutes. Remove the garment before it's completely dry to avoid overdrying.

Hint: *Add several terry towels to the dryer to reduce abrasion.*

Machine-washable wools may also be hand-washed in a cold-water soap such as Wooltone. Press—don't wring—out the moisture. Remember wool is weaker when wet and should be supported when it is taken out of the soapy wash water.

Hint: *Place the garment in a large colander for rinsing. Set the colander under the faucet and rinse until the water runs out clear.*

Specialty Hair Fibers

Unlike wool, which is the fleece from sheep, most hair fibers, such as mohair, cashmere, camel's hair, alpaca, llama, guanaco, huarizo, misti, qiviut, and vicuña, are from the goat and camel families. A few hair fibers are from fur-bearing animals: dogs, musk oxen, rodents, and weasels.

And although the annual production of all of these combined is very small, these fibers are important. Most are blended with wool and other fibers for special effects, beauty, softness, drapeability, color, luster, and economy.

Hair fibers vary in quality from the coarse outer hair, which is used in rugs, interfacings, rope, and upholstery, to the fine, soft undercoat, which is used in the most luxurious fabrics.

HAIR FIBERS FROM THE GOAT FAMILY

MOHAIR

Mohair, the best-known and most commonly used hair fiber, is from angora goats, which are raised in the United States, Turkey, and South Africa.

Recognized by its fluffy, lustrous appearance, it feels soft and silky. It resists abrasion and does not shrink, felt, or soil as readily as wool.

Generally used for suitings and novelty fabrics with looped or bouclé yarns, it is frequently more expensive than wool.

Mohair has a nap and should not be steamed.

CASHMERE

Obtained from domesticated Kashmir goats in the Himalayas, Tibet, Iran, Afghanistan, India, and China, cashmere is more like wool than any other fiber.

Obtained by combing the goat during the spring,

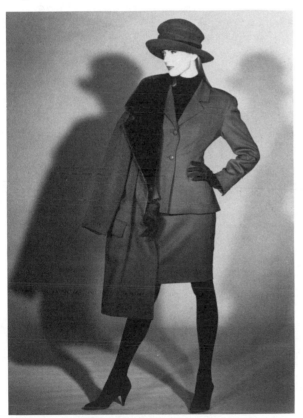

Fig. 2–27 *Trimmed with a beaver collar, this luxurious cashmere coat is from the Christian Dior Boutique, Fall/Winter 1987/1988 Collection. (Photo courtesy of Christian Dior.)*

the yield is very small—only 3 to 5 ounces per animal.

Used in its natural, undyed state—grey, tan, or white—cashmere is extremely fine and soft. The fabrics are warm and comfortable. They drape beautifully, usually have a nap, and are very expensive.

Cashmere is used for making coats, jackets, dresses, and dressing gowns.

HAIR FIBERS FROM THE CAMEL FAMILY

CAMEL'S HAIR

Camel's hair, a hair fiber similar to wool, is taken from the Bactrian (two-humped) camel. Although these camels are found in all parts of Asia, the best quality hair and finest fabrics come from Mongolia.

Known for its warmth without weight and its natural tan color, camel's hair is extremely soft and lustrous.

Each spring, when the camels shed, a trailer follows the camel caravans to collect the large clumps of hair. The clumps—a mixture of soft down and coarse bristly hair—from one camel weigh between 5 and 8 pounds.

Only the soft, downy hair near the camel's skin is used for fine fabrics. The coarse outer hair is used for rugs, blankets, and tent cloths.

Even though camel's hair is more expensive than wool, it is not as durable and wears readily. However, a good-quality fabric is 1 1/2 times as warm as a similar-weight wool.

Camel-hair fabrics have a nap and are frequently blended with wool to make them more durable and less expensive.

ALPACA

A member of the camel family, the alpaca is humpless and only 3 to 3 1/2 feet tall. This domesticated animal is raised for its soft, fine hair in the mountains of Peru and surrounding countries. Strong and lustrous, the long hair—8" to 12"—is sheared every two years.

Used for suitings and dress-weight fabrics, the fleece varies in color from white to reddish brown

to black. It is sometimes blended with silk or cotton and usually has a nap.

LLAMA

Another member of the camel family, the llama is closely related to the alpaca. The fleece is coarser and weaker than alpaca; the colors are usually brown or black.

It is frequently blended with other fibers to make coatings, suitings, and dress fabrics.

GUANACO

Closely related to the alpaca, the guanaco is slightly larger. It is generally supposed that both the llama and alpaca are descendants of the guanaco. The soft, fine fleece is usually reddish brown.

HUARIZO AND MISTI

The huarizo and misti are crosses between an alpaca and a llama. The huarizo has a llama father and an alpaca mother; the misti has the reverse.

VICUÑA

Only two feet tall, the vicuña is the smallest member of the camel family and is known to have the finest fleece.

Since these animals have not been domesticated, they must be killed for their fleece. To prevent their extinction, the Peruvian government has limited the number killed each year.

Vicuña fleece is the lightest, softest and warmest of all the animal fibers. Only the finest hair is used to make fabrics and the yield from one animal is only 4 ounces. Vicuna fabrics cost as much as fur.

HAIR FIBERS FROM FUR-BEARING ANIMALS

Fur fibers from beaver, fox, mink, rabbit, chinchilla, dogs, musk oxen, and rodents are also used in textiles.

Some of these hair fibers—dog, angora, givint—are taken from live animals by shearing and combing while others—chinchilla and fox—are usually taken from the pelts.

More than 50 percent of the fur fibers come from angora rabbits, hares, and plain rabbits. Many are used for felting or to give fabrics a soft hand.

Angora rabbits have long, silky, white fibers. They are clipped every three to four months to obtain 12 to 14 ounces of fiber. The finest angora comes from France, Italy, and Japan. Under the Fur Products Labeling Act of 1951, these fibers must be labeled angora rabbit. Angora is used primarily for knitting and felts.

Hare or jackrabbit and rabbit or coney are used extensively for felts and hatmaking. The soft fibers of the undercoat are used for a soft hand, while the guard or outer hairs are used to create fabrics with a hairy or shiny appearance.

Horsehair is sometimes used in interfacing fabrics. but it is best known for its use in horsehair braid, even though this stiff braid is now made of synthetic materials.

Qiviut (qiviet) is the underwool of the domesticated musk oxen. It is very lightweight, fine, and soft.

Fibers from the weasel family—mink, ermine, marten, and sable—are used for luxury fabrics.

Characteristics of Hair Fiber Fabrics
- Most hair fiber fabrics have a nap.
- Many have a thick pile or fleece.
- Hair fiber fabrics abrade more easily than wool.
- Hair fibers are easily damaged in pressing.
- Hair fibers may be affected adversely by steam.

SEWING HAIR FIBERS

For additional suggestions, see Wool, Coatings, Lightweight Woolens, Textured Woolens, Loosely Woven Fabrics.

CHAPTER 3
Man-Made Fiber Fabrics

Synthetic fabrics are made from fibers manufactured by man. The cellulosic fibers, which include rayon, acetate, and triacetate, are made from wood and other cellulosic products. The synthetics, which include nylon, polyester, acrylic, modacrylic, spandex, metallic, vinyon, and olefin, are manufactured from petroleum, natural gas, coal, alcohol, and limestone.

Rayon

Rayon, the oldest man-made fiber, was introduced in 1889 and called "artificial silk."

A regenerated cellulose fiber, rayon is made when a solution of cellulose—wood pulp and/or cotton linters—is passed through spinnerettes to form filaments.

Well-known for its softness, drapeability, and absorbency, rayon is comfortable to wear, easy to dye, versatile, and economical. It is resistant to moths, static electricity, and pilling.

Much weaker when wet, is should not be used for swimwear, rainwear, or athletic garments. It wrinkles badly and is easily abraded. It may shrink when washed and is susceptible to mildew.

Frequently used to make linenlike fabrics, silk and cotton look-alikes, lining materials, and challis, rayon is used in all kinds of apparel: blouses, coats, dresses, lingerie, sportswear, skirts, suits, and ties. It is the primary fiber used in nonwoven fabrics such as interfacing and disposable hospital gowns.

Most rayons are made by the viscose process. These fabrics are called "rayon" in the United States

Fig. 3–1 *Highlighted with white corded piping, the rayon culottes and jacket are crisply styled and comfortable to wear. (Photo courtesy of Britex Fabrics, San Francisco.)*

62

and "viscose" in the United Kingdom.

High tenacity rayons such as Avron, Avisco XL, Avisco XL II, Comiso, and Zankara are modified viscose rayons. Compared to regular viscose rayon, they are stronger and more resistant to abrasion and wrinkling.

HWM or high-wet-modulus rayons, such as Avril, Avril II, Avril III, Avril Prima Fibers 24, 70 and 400, Moynel, Vincel, Polynosic, Prima, Nupron, Xena, Litrelle, and Zantrel, are modified viscose, which are firmer and react more like cotton when wet. Compared to regular viscose rayon, they have greater dimensional stability during washing, absorb less moisture, and maintain their initial appearance for a long period. They are 50 percent stronger than regular rayon when dry and 100 percent stronger when wet. They are frequently blended with linen, wool, and synthetics.

Cupramonium rayon is made by using copper ammonia to dissolve the cellulose. Compared to viscose rayon, the filaments are much finer and stronger. Although it is used to make chiffon, satin, net, ninon, and other sheer fabrics, it is best known as a high-quality silklike lining or dress fabric. Bemberg is made by the cupramonium process.

Nitrocellulose rayon, the original rayon, is no longer produced.

Fabric Characteristics
- Rayon is absorbent, comfortable, soft, durable, and economical.
- Rayon ravels badly.
- Rayon is 50 percent weaker when wet.
- Rayons fade and deteriorate when exposed to natural and artificial light for long periods.
- Rayons are susceptible to mildew and chemicals, but are resistant to moths.
- It does not accumulate static.
- Most rayons are highly flammable.

- Some rayons wrinkle easily.
- Many rayons shrink.
- Rayon is easily damaged with hot irons.
- Rayon loses its body when machine dried.

PLANNING A GARMENT

SELECTING THE FABRIC

Look for firmly woven fabrics to reduce seam slippage. Avoid materials with long surface floats which will catch and snag, as well as fabrics that aren't colorfast.

SEWING RAYON

A very versatile fiber, rayon can be made to look like cotton, linen, wool, or silk.

When sewing rayon, see Cotton, Lightweight Wool, Loosely Woven Fabrics, Transparent Fabrics, or Velvet.

GARMENT CARE

Garment washability depends on the rayon type, fabric weave, and garment design. Check the label before purchasing. Some rayon fabrics are labeled "wash before cutting."

Using a mild detergent, handwash in lukewarm water; rinse thoroughly. Press the excess water out, but do not wring or twist. Shake well and hang to dry on a plastic hanger. Using a medium temperature, press as needed from the wrong side while the article is still damp. Always use a press cloth when pressing from the right side.

Do not soak colored fabrics.

Acetate and Triacetate

Acetate, a regenerated cellulose fiber, was introduced in 1924. It was the first fabric to melt, not scorch, under the iron.

It is made by combining cellulose and acetate, which form flakes. The flakes are dried, then dissolved in acetone, so they can be extruded through spinnerettes.

Acetate has a high luster and looks and feels luxurious. It drapes beautifully; and acetate taffeta retains its crispness.

Comfortable to wear, it is cool in summer and warm in winter; it resists staining, shrinking, pilling, moths, and mildew. It is also resistant to sunlight and excellent for lining fabrics. However, it

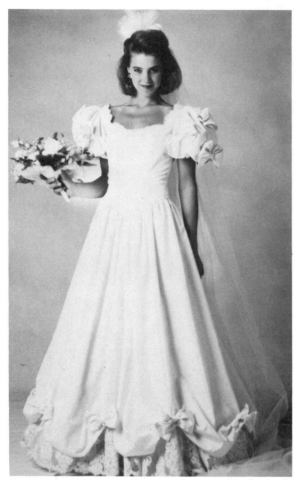

Fig. 3–2 *A frequent choice for wedding and party dresses, acetate is attractive, but inexpensive. (Photo courtesy of McCall Pattern Co.)*

is weaker when wet and does not resist abrasion.

Acetate requires a special type of dye, which can be used to create interesting dyed effects in fabric blends, according to the distribution of fibers.

Used to make a wide range of fabrics, such as antique satin, brocade, crepe, double knits, faille, jersey, lace, satin, and taffeta, from sheer to heavyweights, acetate is used in all types of garments: bridal gowns, evening wear, sportswear, loungewear, foundation garments, lingerie, dresses, blouses, skirts, and linings.

Compared to rayon, acetate dries faster; and, although it is weaker when wet, it is not as weak as rayon.

Triacetate, which is well-known by the trade name Arnel, is washable and resistant to shrinking, wrinkling, and fading. Fabrics can be heat-set for permanent pleat or crease retention.

It is used to make fabrics such as faille, flannel, jersey, sharkskin, taffeta, textured knits, and tricot. It can be brushed, sueded, and napped, and is frequently used to make fabrics such as panné, velour, suede, terry, and velvet.

Triacetate is frequently blended with cotton and rayon for its heat-setting ability and easy care; with wool for its shrink-proof, warmth, and drip-dry properties; and with linen to reduce cost.

Fabric Characteristics
- Acetate and triacetate dissolve in acetone and acetic acid.
- Acetate and triacetate have a luxurious hand and drape well.
- Many acetate fabrics are easily marred by pin holes and ripping.
- Triacetate is resilient and resists wrinkling.
- Acetate is heat-sensitive and melts under a hot iron; triacetate is not heat-sensitive.
- Acetate is resistant to pilling, mildew, and moths, but not to abrasion.
- Acetate can be laundered or dry-cleaned, depending on the dyes, finishes, fabric structure, and garment design.
- Acetate and triacetate are weaker when wet.
- Triacetate can be heat set for permanent pleats and creases.

SEWING ACETATE

Acetate and triacetate are used in a variety of fabrics. Review the sewing suggestions for the fabric types: Taffeta, Satin. Velvet.

GARMENT CARE

ACETATE

Most acetate garments require dry-cleaning; however, a few can be hand-laundered.

Using a mild detergent, handwash in lukewarm water; rinse thoroughly. Press the excess water out, but do not wring or twist. Shake well and hang to dry on a plastic hanger. Using a medium temperature, press as needed from the wrong side while the article is still damp. Always use a press cloth when pressing from the right side.

Do not soak colored garments.

TRIACETATES

Most triacetates can be machine washed and dried; however, the dryer must run cold before it's turned off.

Pleated garments should be handwashed, following the directions for acetates.

If ironing is needed, a high temperature setting can be used. For best results, press from the underside.

Nylon

Nylon, the miracle fiber and first true synthetic, was introduced by DuPont in 1938.

Only a few garments—lingerie, stockings, foundation garments, and men's socks—were manufactured before the beginning of World War II, when it was used extensively to meet military demands for parachutes, tow ropes, tents, tarpaulins, and tires.

Nylon is a polyamide made from hard, white chips, which are melted and extruded through a spinnerette to form solidified monofilaments. The monofilaments are stretched and twisted into yarn.

Well-known for strength and durability, nylon fibers are frequently blended with natural and other man-made fibers to make fabrics in all weights. Nylon and nylon blend fabrics can be woven, knitted, or nonwoven and are used for all types of clothing, from Cordura® to luxury lingerie.

One of the most widely used fabrics, nylon is durable, elastic, easy-care, and naturally water-repellent. It resists wrinkles and travels well.

Nylon is easy to dye, colorfast, and quick drying. Fabrics are not weakened by most chemicals, body oils, perspiration, moths, silverfish, or mildew. They retain heat-set pleats and creases well.

Nylon filament yarn is stronger than a steel wire of the same weight, allowing sheer, filmy fabrics to be practical, as well as glamorous.

Nylon is more resistant to wear and stronger than any other fiber, making it particularly practical for children's clothing, industrial garments, and outerwear. Nylon does not deteriorate with age. It's lighter in weight and absorbs moisture better than polyester.

THE NYLON FAMILY

Some of the newer nylons have been engineered with special qualities for better performance.

Fig. 3–3 *On the right, Cardin's nylon jogging suit is trimmed with an asymmetrical flap. (Photo courtesy of Pierre Cardin Activewear.)*

Type 420: This nylon is frequently blended with rayon or cotton to reinforce and prolong the garment's life.

Antron®: Offers a unique luster, dry hand, and high opacity.

Antron III®: Antron III® has less static.

Cordura®: Lightweight, yet resistant to abrasion.

Qiana®: This elegant cloth can be made in a wide range of fabric types, from chiffon to velvet. Unfortunately, since it was unusually heat-sensitive, it is no longer available.

Helanca: A nylon/polyester blend with two-way stretch.

Fabric Characteristics
- Skipped stitches and puckered seams are frequently a problem.
- Nylon fabrics dull needles and scissors quickly.
- Many woven nylon fabrics fray badly.
- Nylon fabrics do not ease well.
- Nylon fabrics are easily damaged by a hot iron.
- Nylon fabrics pill.
- They collect static electricity so soil and lint cling to the surface; fabrics also cling to the machine needle as you sew.

SEWING CHECKLIST

Machine Needles: Type and size depend on fabric.
Thread: 100 percent nylon fabrics—long-staple polyester; nylon blends—long-staple polyester or cotton-wrapped polyester.
Equipment and Supplies: Straight-stitch or jeans foot, sharp pins, sharp shears or rotary cutter and mat, zippers with synthetic tapes.
Marking Techniques: All types except wax.
Seams: All types, depending on fabric weight and weave and garment construction.
Hems: All types.
Seam and Hem Finishes: All types.
Closures: All types.

PLANNING A GARMENT

DESIGN IDEAS AND PATTERN SELECTION

Nylon fabrics are suitable for a variety of garments: lingerie, foundation, ski clothing, blouses, dresses, casual sportswear, windbreakers, children's clothes, rainwear, outer garments, swimwear, and exercise fashions.

Most nylon woven fabrics are crisp. Generally, styles with a minimum of seams and easing and bias-cut designs are good choices.

Raglan and kimono sleeves are easier to sew than set-in sleeves. Straight seams on the lengthwise grain pucker more than slightly bias seams. Avoid intricate seams and topstitched details.

Nylon fabrics are well suited to the pleated designs made famous by Mary McFadden.

Since nylon is sensitive to sunlight, it is unsuitable for outdoor furnishings, unlined draperies, and drapery linings.

PURCHASING THE FABRIC

Better-quality, woven fabrics which have a dense weave, high-twist yarns and high-thread count fray and pill less than cheaper fabrics.

Smoothly finished nylons, nylon blends, and fabrics with resin finishes reduce the tendency for pilling. Cotton blends pill less than acetate blends.

To distinguish between nylon and polyester, burn a 2″ by 10″ swatch. Nylon will have a celerylike odor and white smoke; polyester will have a heavy black smoke with soot particles and an aromatic odor. Both will melt and form a tan bead.

SEWING NYLON

LAYOUT

Press out the foldline before spreading the fabric. If it can't be removed, refold the fabric and arrange the pattern to avoid the fold.

Spread fabrics right sides together.

STITCHING TIPS

Make a test seam 2–2.5 mm (10 to 12 stitches per inch). Use the appropriate thread matched to size and type needle (see suggestions below). To prevent puckering, loosen the tension on both the needle and bobbin threads and hold the fabric firmly while stitching.

Although Universal-H point needles are suitable for most nylon fabrics, you may prefer Red Band needles for woven fabrics and Yellow Band needles or ballpoint SUK-point needles for knits.

Use small needles (60/8 or 70/10) for sheers and lightweight fabrics, medium needles (80/12) for medium-weight fabrics, and large needles (90/14 or 100/16) for heavyweight fabrics.

Select a thread appropriately sized for the fabric. Use size 50 thread for medium and heavyweight fabrics and 100/3 for sheers and lightweight fabrics.

Begin with a new needle in the smallest recommended size. If skipped stitches are a problem, try the next size larger.

Since nylon fabrics dull needles badly, they should be changed frequently. A new needle per garment is not too often; and some garments will require several new needles.

To reduce seam puckering, use a straight-stitch or jeans foot to hold the fabric firmly when straight stitching. Or use a single hole plate and/or left-needle position. If the feed dogs mar the fabric, reduce the presser-foot pressure.

Hint: *Puckered seams cannot be pressed out.*

Set the machine on low gear or run it slowly when filling the bobbin.

PRESSING

To heat-set pleats and creases, set the iron at a higher temperature; cover the garment with a damp press cloth; then press.

GARMENT CARE

Wash nylon garments frequently. Most garments can be machine washed in warm water with a mild detergent. Machine dry at a low temperature and remove the garment immediately to avoid unwanted wrinkles.

Hint: *Separate garments according to color and soil. Nylon will pick up both during the washing process. To restore whiteness, wash in hot water with a heavy-duty detergent and chlorine bleach.*

To reduce static electricity, use a fabric softener in the final rinse and do not overdry.

Pretreat badly soiled areas with liquid detergent. Use dry cleaning fluid or talcum powder to remove grease stains.

For touch-up ironing, use a moderately warm iron.

Polyester

The most popular synthetic fiber, polyester had a spectacular introduction in 1951 when DuPont exhibited a still-presentable man's suit which had been worn for sixty-seven days without pressing, dunked into a swimming pool twice, and machine washed.

Polyester is a synthetic, filament fiber. Produced from petroleum by-products, it is made by heating hard polyester chips until they melt; then the liquid polyester is extruded through spinnerettes, forming filaments. Initially all the filaments were round, resembling monofilament threads. Today filaments are irregularly shaped so that fabrics breathe and wick, making them more comfortable to wear.

Polyester is frequently blended with natural and other man-made fibers to make fabrics in all weights. Polyester and polyester blend fabrics can be woven, knitted, or nonwoven; they are used for all types of clothing, from heavy outerwear to luxury lingerie.

Dacron, Encron, Fortrel, Kodel, Terylene, Trevira, and Vycron are trade names of popular polyesters.

Recognized for their durability and easy-care properties, polyester fabrics have good shape retention and do not shrink, bag, or stretch. They are equally strong when wet or dry, resist wrinkles, and travel well.

They are easy to dye, colorfast, quick drying and nonallergenic, resistant to most chemicals, moths, and mildew. They retain heat-set pleats and crease well.

Polyester fabrics are crisp and resilient when wet or dry. In fact, they are crisper than the natural fiber fabrics they simulate. The crispness of polyester chiffon is greater than silk chiffon, but slightly less than silk organza. Generally they are also lighter in weight and do not hang the same.

Many polyesters pill badly, do not absorb moisture or wick, attract lint, absorb body odors, and

Fig. 3–4 *Smart and comfortable, this polyester outfit looks good from morning to night. (Photo courtesy of Neil's Apparel; Palm Desert, California.)*

lose their color when abraded. Some do not "breathe," making them hot in summer and clammy in winter.

Some of the newer modified polyester fibers simulate the aesthetics of silk, resist pilling, have a dry, "tactile" hand, and absorb moisture or wick. A new DuPont fiber, Type 720W or Light Spirit Blend, is 50% more breatheable than cotton. Designed to keep the wearer cool and dry, it wicks well and dries easily.

Fabric Characteristics
- Polyester fabrics are easier to sew after laundering.
- Polyester fabrics dull needles and scissors quickly.
- Skipped stitches and puckered seams are frequently a problem when sewing polyester fabrics.
- Polyester fabrics are difficult to ease.
- Polyesters are difficult to press and are easily damaged by a hot iron.

- Polyesters are crisp and resilient.
- Polyesters resist wrinkling.
- Polyesters have good elasticity and recovery.
- They are easy to launder and require little or no ironing.
- Polyesters resist moths, mildew, most chemicals, sunlight, and weathering.
- Polyesters have poor absorbency and may be uncomfortable to wear.
- They pill easily and attract lint.
- Polyester fabrics wear at garment edges and folds.
- Polyester is very elastic but not as elastic as nylon.
- Polyester retains static electricity, pills, and oil-based stains.
- Polyester attracts dust and smoke, requiring more frequent laundering.
- Polyester may be permanently stained by fabric softener sheets.

SEWING CHECKLIST

Machine Needles: Universal-H point, Yellow Band, Red Band, ballpoint (SUK), stretch (HS) needles; sizes 60/8 to 90/14.

Thread: 100 percent polyester fabrics—long-staple polyester; polyester blends—long-staple polyester or cotton-wrapped polyester. Topstitching—regular, topstitching.

Sewing Machine Equipment: Straight-stitch or jeans foot.

Equipment and Supplies: Small pins, sharp shears or rotary cutter and mat, zippers with synthetic tapes.

Marking Techniques: All types, except wax.

Seams: All types, depending on fabric weight and weave and garment construction.

Hems: All types.

Seam and Hem Finishes: All types.

Closures: All types

PLANNING A GARMENT

PURCHASING THE FABRIC

Polyester fabrics are available in a wide range of qualities and prices. Generally, they are less expensive than their natural fabric equivalents.

Choose closely woven fabrics woven with high-twist yarns for better wear and less pilling.

Avoid fabrics that are off-grain; they cannot be straightened. Check to be sure printed patterns, plaids, and checks are aligned with the fabric grains.

Polyester fabrics attract lint, which will show badly on dark-colored fabrics.

When possible, select polyester blouse fabrics for linings; they breathe and absorb moisture better, making them more comfortable to wear. Unravel a yarn; if it is spun from short lengths, it will breathe better than if it is a single filament.

Hint: *To test the moisture absorbency or wicking quality, sprinkle a drop of water on the fabric. The more quickly the water is absorbed, the more comfortable the fabric will be to wear.*

If the fabric will be permanently pleated, you'll need at least three times the recommended fabric requirements.

To distinguish between nylon and polyester, burn a 2″ by 10″ swatch. Nylon will have a celerylike odor and white smoke; polyester will have a heavy black smoke with soot particles and an aromatic odor. Both will melt and form a tan bead.

If you plan to wash the garment, be sure all the components have the same washability.

DESIGN IDEAS AND PATTERN SELECTION

Polyester fabrics are suitable for a variety of garments: slacks, tops, dresses, casual sportswear, menswear, children's clothes, raincoats, outer garments, and lingerie. They are also well suited for draperies.

Most polyesters are crisp fabrics. Generally bias-cut designs and styles with a minimum of seams, easing, and topstitching are good choices for woven fabrics. Gathers, soft folds, and ruffles are particularly attractive.

Raglan and kimono sleeves are easier to sew than set-in sleeves. Straight seams on the lengthwise grain pucker more than slightly bias seams. Avoid intricate seams and topstitched details.

To duplicate Mary McFadden designs, select a simple style and have a professional pleat the fabric permanently.

PREPARING THE FABRIC

Preshrink the fabric to remove excess finishes and relax it. Many polyester fabrics will be softer and easier to sew after preshrinking. Also preshrink notions, linings, interfacings, and underlinings.

PREPARING THE PATTERN

For smooth set-in sleeves, reduce the ease in the sleeve cap or change the grain on the sleeve so that it will be cut on the bias. (See Chapter 1.)

Hint: *If you plan to use bias-cut sleeves, you will probably need extra fabric.*

SEWING POLYESTER FABRICS

LAYOUT

Press out the foldline before spreading the fabric. If it can't be removed, refold the fabric and arrange the pattern to avoid the fold.

Spread fabrics right sides together.

Some fabrics—solid colors, all-over prints, and prints with small irregular patterns—can be used satisfactorily even when they are off-grain since the finish, not the grain, determines the shape. Use the lengthwise grain as a guide and ignore the crossgrain.

STITCHING TIPS

Make a test seam 2–2.5 mm (10–12 stitches per inch). Use the appropriate thread and needle. To prevent puckering, loosen the tension on both the needle and bobbin threads and hold the fabric taut while stitching.

Although Universal-H point needles are suitable for most polyester fabrics, you may prefer Red Band needles for woven fabrics and Yellow Band or ballpoint SUK-point needles for knits.

Use small needles (60/8 or 70/10) for sheers and lightweight fabrics, medium needles (80/12) for medium-weight fabrics, and large needles (90/14 or 100/16) for heavyweight fabrics.

Select a thread appropriately sized for the fabric. Use size 50 thread for medium and heavyweight fabrics and 100/3 for sheers and lightweight fabrics.

Begin with a new needle in the smallest recommended size. If skipped stitches are a problem, try the next size larger; or use a needle lubricant.

Since polyester fabrics dull needles badly, they should be changed frequently. A new needle per garment is not too often; and some garments will require several new needles.

To reduce seam puckering, use a straight-stitch or jeans foot to hold the fabric firmly when straight stitching.

Hint: *Puckered seams cannot be pressed out.*

If the feed dogs mark the fabric, reduce the presser-foot pressure; or tissue-stitch seams.

Set the machine on low gear or stitch slowly when filling the bobbin.

Hint: *If you wind the bobbin on a fast speed, the polyester thread will stretch; it won't have an opportunity to relax until it is stitched into a seam. When it then relaxes, the seam will pucker.*

FACINGS AND INTERFACINGS

Understitch to keep facings from rolling to the outside.

Consider self-fabric interfacings for polyester garments. When using sew-in interfacings, position the interfacing on the wrong side of the garment; for fusibles, position them on the wrong side of the facing.

PERMANENT-PLEATED GARMENTS

Permanent-pleated garments can be dry-cleaned or handwashed in warm water and detergent. Always rinse thoroughly and drip dry.

Hint: *To remove some water before drying, carefully roll the garment so the pleats are parallel. Squeeze the roll gently, working from top to bottom to "push" the water toward the garment hem. Avoid wringing and twisting.*

Press the pleats on the wrong side or with a press cloth. Allow the fabric to cool before moving the garment.

PRESSING

To press seamlines crisply, press with a steam iron; then cover with the clapper until cool.

To heat-set pleats and creases, set the iron at a higher temperature; cover the garment with a damp press cloth and press.

GARMENT CARE

Wash polyester fabrics frequently. To avoid permanent staining, remove oil-based stains as soon as possible.

To avoid permanent perspiration odors, dust with talcum powder and use dress shields. To remove odors, add a cup of baking soda or borax to the wash cycle. Or use a special detergent such as Fab or Surf which will destroy the bacteria which cause the odors.

Most garments can be machine washed in warm water with a mild detergent. Machine dry at a low temperature and remove immediately to avoid unwanted wrinkles. Do not overdry.

To reduce static electricity, use a fabric softener in the final rinse. (Fabric softener sheets may leave permanent spots.)

To clean badly soiled garments, pretreat spots and wash in hot water with a heavy-duty detergent. Whites can be bleached with a chlorine bleach; colors with a nonchlorine bleach.

To remove pills, use a dual-blade razor to shave them away.

For touch-up pressing, use a moderately warm iron.

LIGHTWEIGHT POLYESTERS

Sometimes called silkies or silk look-alikes, lightweight polyesters are more attractive and more comfortable than ever. Equally important, they are generally less expensive, easier to maintain, and easier to sew than the silks they imitate.

Fig. 3–5 *Soft and beautiful, her black charmeuse evening pants and printed blouse are practical, easy-care polyesters. (Photo courtesy of Pierre Cardin Activewear.)*

Compared to silks, polyesters are not as slippery or as easily marred by machine needles, feed dogs, pins, ripping, and fitting. But they are more difficult to ease; seams, stitched on the lengthwise grain, tend to pucker more; and stitching mistakes cannot be pressed out.

Fabric Characteristics
- Lightweight polyesters are wrinkle-resistant.
- Firmly woven polyesters do not fray badly.
- Seam slippage is sometimes a problem at stress points.
- Some polyesters are very slippery.
- Puckered seams and skipped stitches are a problem.
- Lightweight polyesters are easily damaged by high-temperature irons.
- Polyester is difficult to ease.
- Polyesters retain static electricity.
- Some polyester fabrics do not breathe well,

SEWING CHECKLIST

Machine Needles: Universal-H point, Yellow or Red Band needles; sizes 60/8 or 70/10.

Machine Setting: Stitch length, 1.75–2 mm (12–15 stitches per inch); tension, loosely balanced.

Thread: Extra-fine cotton-wrapped polyester, long-staple polyester (100/3).

Hand Sewing Needles: Sizes 9 or 10.

Sewing Machine Equipment: Straight-stitch, roller, or jeans foot.

Equipment and Supplies: Very fine pins, weights, well-sharpened shears or rotary cutter and mat, stabilizer, lightweight zippers.

Marking Techniques: All types, except wax.

Seams: French, false French, standing-fell, flat-fell, double/ply, welt, top-stitched, tissue-stitched.

Hems: Shirttail, book, machine-rolled, hemmer-rolled, shell, lettuce edging, topstitched, merrow, mock merrow, plain.

Seam and Hem Finishes: Single/ply—turned-and-stitched, folded, zigzag, multi-stitch zigzag, serged. Double/ply—pinked-and-stitched, zigzag, multi-stitch zigzag, serged.

Edge Finishes: Self-fabric facings, bias facings, bindings, bands, casings, ribbings.

Interfacings: Self-fabric, knit fusibles, lightweight woven and nonwoven fusibles, sew-in weft insertion.

Linings: Generally not used, except for outerwear or opaqueness.

Underlinings: Generally not used.

making them hot in summer and clammy in winter.

PLANNING A GARMENT

DESIGN IDEAS AND PATTERN SELECTION

Depending on the fabric hand—soft or crisp—lightweight polyesters are suitable for soft blouses, tailored shirts, skirts, dresses, lingerie, sleepwear, pants, jackets, and lightweight coats.

Generally, soft designs with gathers, pleats, ruffles, flounces, or drapes are good choices; but more structured styles also work well if the fabric is backed with a fusible or sew-in underlining.

Choose from a variety of collars—ties, convertible, two-piece shirt types, ruffles, or flounces—and sleeves—cap, shirt, bishop, puff, leg of mutton, butterfly, raglan, kimono, or dropped shoulder. Traditional set-in sleeves are difficult to ease smoothly.

Avoid tightly fitted garments unless they will be underlined.

SELECTING THE FABRIC

Test the fabric hang or drape to see if it will be suitable for the design.

Compared to silks, polyesters are crisper and lighter weight; most do not drape as well.

Avoid fabrics that are printed off-grain.

Fabrics that are loosely woven ravel, pill, and pick more than firmly woven fabrics; they are also more prone to seam slippage.

Satin polyesters not only pick and pull more than plain weave fabrics, they also pill more.

To test the fabric's absorbency or wicking, drop a small amount of water on a swatch. If it spreads to the surrounding area, it will be more comfortable to wear than if it remains in a bubble on the surface.

SEWING LIGHTWEIGHT POLYESTERS

LAYOUT, CUTTING, AND MARKING

When cutting slippery polyesters, cover the cutting table with a flannel-backed vinyl cloth, flannel side up, or use the flannel side of your table pads. Or sandwich slippery fabrics between wax paper; pin your pattern on top, and cut.

STITCHING TIPS

Make a test seam, using a small (60/8 or 70/10), new needle, loosely balanced tension, and a 2 mm (12 stitches per inch) stitch length. Correct the pressure and shorten the stitch if needed.

Hint: *Since polyesters retain static electricity, the fabric is easily drawn into the needle hole at the beginning of the seam and it clings to the needle, causing skipped stitches.*

Begin stitching on a piece of stabilizer; then lay the fabric on top; and stitch the seam.

If necessary, tissue-stitch all seams to reduce skipped stitches and puckered seams.

Wind the bobbin slowly when using polyester thread. When wound at high speed, the thread stretches and it does not relax until it's been stitched into a garment. This is the primary reason for puckered seams; and, unlike puckered seams on silks, puckered seams on polyester fabrics cannot be removed by pressing.

SEAMS

For straight and slightly curved seams on blouses, I prefer self-finished seams such as standing-fell, French, and false French seams.

Hint: *The standing-fell is my favorite because it's quick and easy to stitch.*

Other suitable seams for everyday garments include double/ply seams finished with a zigzag, multi-stitch zigzag, or serged finish on everyday garments.

Seams, such as flat-fell, welt, double-welt, and topstitched, are difficult to topstitch without puckering.

HEMS AND EDGE FINISHES

Select a hem appropriate for the garment design and quality. Use machine-rolled, shirttail, or topstitched on tuck-in blouses. Use 1 1/4"-wide plain hems on overblouses.

For ruffles, full skirts, scarves, collars, and sleeves, use the narrow hem of your choice. Machine-rolled and mock-merrow hems are attractive and easy.

Hint: *Polyester is too springy to make an attractive hand-rolled hem, even if it is a luxury garment.*

Use a 2″- to 2 1/2″-wide hem on straight-line skirts. Generally, a very flat edge finish—pinked, serged, or zigzagged—is best.

For unlined coats and jackets, clean-finish the edge with a fold, turned-and-stitched, zigzag, multistitch zigzag, or serging.

Topstitched hems are easy and frequently enhance the garment. Fold the edge under 5/8″; edgestitch close to the fold. Fold the raw edge in to meet the stitched line and topstitch again 1/4″ from the fold.

Attractive edge finishes include hems, bands, self-fabric facings, and bindings of the same or complimentary fabrics.

CLOSURES

Use lightweight zippers and buttons so they won't cause the fabric to sag.

Select good-quality buttons; cheap plastic ones will spoil the beauty of a good polyester.

Hand-picked zippers are rarely used on polyester fabrics. A very elegant evening or cocktail dress would be an exception.

Use a fly placket instead of buttons and buttonholes if you can't make attractive buttonholes or find buttons in a suitable color. (See Chapter 24.)

SLEEVES

To set sleeves easily, trim away 1/8″ from the sleeve cap and armscye allowances. Join them with a 1/2″ seam. (Stitching a narrow seam is always easier than stitching a wide one.)

If the sleeve cap has more than 1 1/4″ ease, reduce the ease.

Hint: *To reduce the sleeve cap ease, make a horizontal fold across the sleeve cap; a 1/8″ fold reduces the ease 3/8″ to 1/2″. Redraw the cutting lines without reducing the sleeve width.*

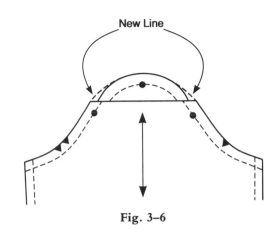

Fig. 3–6

Sleeves are easier to set and more comfortable when cut on the bias. (See Chapter 1.)

INTERFACINGS

All types of interfacings are appropriate; however, they should be lighter than the polyester.

Hint: *I particularly like the self-fabric, fusible knits, and lightweight weft insertion fusibles.*

When using a fusible, make a sample. If the fusible dots show through on the right side of the fabric, the fusible is too heavy. Use a lighter interfacing; and, if necessary, use two layers to get the desired crispness.

Hint: *The easiest way to interface straight edges is to add enough fabric to the garment edge for a facing and interfacing. For a front opening, add 2 1/4″ to the foldline on the pattern front. When assembling the garment, press first on the foldline; then fold the raw edge to the pressed line. Although the buttons and buttonholes will secure it, topstitch if it will enhance the design.*

Use the same technique to interface cuffs. Cut the cuff three times the finished width plus one seam allowance; and apply it using your favorite method.

LININGS AND UNDERLININGS

Generally garments made in lightweight fabrics are not lined, except when they are used for outerwear—jackets and lightweight coats.

Use self-fabric or a good-quality polyester blouse fabric for the lining. Blouse fabrics breathe better than most polyester lining materials, but they cost more.

Use underlinings to reduce strain, maintain the garment's silhouette, change the fabric's character, or increase opaqueness.

Underline closely fitted dresses, pants, and skirts to reduce seam slippage at stress points or to act as a stay for draped designs.

Underline jackets, coats, and other structured garments to give them enough body to maintain their shape.

Underline light-colored fabrics with self-fabric, flesh, or another solid light color to make them less revealing. Flat linings work particularly well. (See Chapter 20.)

Underline lightweight polyesters with fusible knit and weft interfacings or traditional sew-ins to change the fabric character.

Select lining and underlining fabrics with the same care properties as the polyester. Preshrink to remove unwanted finishes before cutting.

Selecting an appropriate underlining fabric is sometimes a challenge. Interfacings, such as nylon ninon, tulle, net, lightweight polyesters, and lightweight sew-in and fusible interfacings are good choices.

PRESSING

Use a clean steam iron. To avoid spitting and spewing, be sure the iron has warmed to the proper setting.

Test press on fabric scraps. Lightweight fabrics frequently require a lower temperature than heavier polyesters. If the iron isn't warm enough to steam, turn it up and use a press cloth.

To avoid shines, always use a press cloth when pressing the right side of the fabric.

GARMENT CARE

Polyesters absorb and retain body odors. Use dress shields to protect garments. Wash garments frequently using Fab or Surf.

Oil-based stains are difficult to remove. Dust grease spots with talcum powder to remove them. Repeat as needed.

To avoid setting stains, pretreat spots before washing. Blot wet spots without rubbing to avoid damaging the fabric.

To reduce static electricity, add fabric softener to the final rinse and avoid overdrying. To remove static cling, spray the garment with a 50/50 solution of fabric softener and water. (Test it first to be sure the solution doesn't stain the fabric!)

Acrylic

Introduced in 1950 as a soft, warm, machine-washable substitute for wool, acrylics are now duplicating the look and feel of cotton.

Acrylic is a synthetic fiber produced from acrylonitrile—a colorless liquid made from elements found in coal, air, water, oil, and limestone. Fibers can be modified to create a variety of yarns from smooth, cottonlike yarns to bulky, fur types.

Known for their warmth without weight, acrylic fabrics can be woven or knitted. They are also resilient, quick drying, and resistant to wrinkling, sunlight, weather, oil, chemicals, moths, mildew, and shrinking. They can be heat-set into permanent pleats and creases.

Many acrylics pill, shrink badly, retain static electricity, and absorb little moisture.

Compared to nylon or polyester, acrylics are warmer, less elastic, not as durable or strong, and pill more. Compared to polyester, acrylics do not retain oil-based stains as tenaciously.

Bulky acrylic yarns pill more than smooth yarns, polyesters, and nylons. Compared to natural fibers, pills cling to the stronger synthetic fibers more tenaciously.

Acrylic fibers—Acrilan, Creslan, Orlon, and Zefran—have a variety of different characteristics and care requirements. Some can be laundered; some require dry-cleaning.

Acrylics are not as strong as polyester and nylon; Zefran is stronger than most acrylics.

Fabric Characteristics
- Acrylic fabrics quickly dull needles and scissors.
- Skipped stitches and puckered seams are frequently a problem when sewing acrylics.

- Acrylic fabrics are easily damaged by hot irons, steam, water extraction (spinning), and hot dryers.
- Acrylics have low moisture absorbency, but they wick well.
- Some acrylics shrink badly.
- Acrylics retain pills and static electricity.
- Acrylics are resistant to abrasion, moths, mildew, sun, and weather.
- Acrylics can be heat-set to maintain pleats and creases.
- Most acrylics are washable.
- Acrylics absorb and hold perspiration odors.

Fig. 3–7 *Developed as a wool substitute, acrylic fabrics are warm and easy to sew. (Photo courtesy of Stretch and Sew, Inc.)*

SEWING CHECKLIST

Machine Needles: Universal-H point, Yellow Band, Red Band, and ballpoint (SUK) needles; sizes 70/10 to 90/14. Type and size depends on fabric.

Thread: 100 percent acrylic fabrics—long-staple polyester; acrylic blends—long-staple polyester or cotton-wrapped polyester.

Sewing Machine Equipment: Straight-stitch or jeans foot.

Equipment and Supplies: Fine pins, sharp shears or rotary cutter and mat, zippers with synthetic tapes.

Marking Techniques: All types, except wax.

Seams: All types, depending on fabric weight and weave and garment construction.

Hems: All types.

Seam and Hem Finishes: All types.

Closures: All types.

Most acrylic fabrics are soft. Generally styles with a minimum of seams and topstitching are good choices.

Since acrylics are not damaged by sunlight, they are good choices for curtains, draperies, and outdoor furnishings.

SELECTING THE FABRIC

Bulky yarns and open-weave fabrics pill more than smooth fabrics; loosely woven and loosely knitted fabrics shrink more than closely structured materials. Check the manufacturer's care instructions on the bolt.

Preshrink the fabric to remove excess finishes and to relax it. Also preshrink notions, linings, and interfacings.

SEWING ACRYLIC FABRICS

When sewing acrylics, see Polyester, Raschel Knits, Jersey, Sweatshirt Fabrics, and Loosely Woven Fabrics.

GARMENT CARE

The care requirements for acrylics differ considerably. Check the manufacturer's suggestions

PLANNING A GARMENT

Acrylics are suitable for a variety of garments: dresses, infant's wear, children's garments, skirts, skiwear, sportswear, and nightwear.

when selecting the fabric.

Since acrylics attract dust, smoke, and dog hair, they should be washed frequently. To avoid perspiration odors, use a deodorant, dust with talcum, and use dress shields. To remove odors, use detergents that destroy odor-causing bacteria.

Wash delicate garments by hand in warm water. When machine washing, use warm water with a mild detergent. Machine dry at a low temperature and remove immediately to avoid unwanted wrinkles.

Hint: *To reduce static electricity, use a fabric softener in the final rinse; do not overdry.*

To remove pills, use a dual-blade razor and shave them away.

For touch-up pressing, use a moderately warm iron.

MODACRYLICS

A modified acrylic fiber used to make fleecy, furlike fabric, modacrylics are warm, soft, and flame-resistant.

Modacrylics are frequently used for children's sleepwear, draperies, and fake furs.

Fabric Characteristics
- Modacrylics are strong, durable, and non-allergenic.
- They are resistant to moths, mildew, sunlight, and weather.
- They absorb little moisture and dry quickly.
- They are easily damaged by heat, hot irons, cigarette ashes, and light bulbs, but they are fire-resistant.

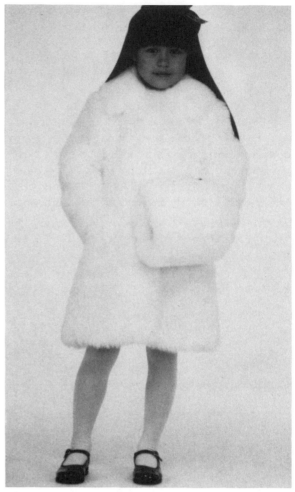

Fig. 3–8 *Designed for the younger set, this fake fur is made of modacrylic fibers which will not burn. (Photo courtesy of McCall Pattern Co.)*

- They can be laundered or dry-cleaned, depending on the dyes, finishes, fabric structure, and garment design.
- Most of the modacrylic fabrics available to home sewers are fake furs. (See Chapter 14.)

Spandex

Used extensively for foundation garments, swimwear, and active sportswear since its introduction in 1958, spandex has revolutionized the fashion industry. Today, small amounts of spandex are being added to many traditional fabrics to improve fit and comfort, as well as to eliminate puckering and bagging.

This lightweight, soft fiber is stronger, more elastic, more durable, and more supple than rubber. It can be stretched more than 500 percent without breaking; it can be stretched repeatedly and still snap back to its original length.

It is resistant to body oils, perspiration, detergents, sun, sand, and salt water.

Spandex is used in small amounts to provide desired stretch, recovery, and holding power. Generally, fabrics for foundation garments, ski-wear, swimsuits, and skating costumes include 15 to 50 percent spandex; other fabrics may include only 3 to 20 percent spandex.

Spandex adds stretch to any fabric, knitted or woven, and improves the look, feel, fit, and comfort. Fabrics can have stretch in the width, length, or in both directions.

Although spandex is frequently called by one of its tradenames, Lycra, there are several other tradenames: Blue C, Cleerspan, Curel, Glospan, Interspan, Numa, Spandelle, Unel, and Vyrene.

Compared to rubber, spandex is more resistant to abrasion, flexing, sunlight, weather, heat, body oil, and perspiration. It can be made into finer threads.

Fabric Characteristics

- Skipped stitches are frequently a problem with spandex.
- Stretch fabrics are very difficult to sew successfully with a straight stitch.
- Seams and edge finishes must stretch with the fabric.
- Seams and hems stitched across the stretch tend to pucker.
- Spandex is strong, durable, lightweight, and very elastic.
- Spandex is easily damaged by heat.
- Spandex is easily damaged by defective or dull needles.
- Spandex is resistant to abrasion, perspiration, body oils, and sunlight.
- Spandex is not damaged by chlorine in swimming pools.

Fig. 3–9 *Designed for active women, these form-fitting bathing suits are made of spandex and nylon. (Photo courtesy of Pierre Cardin Beachwear.)*

PLANNING THE GARMENT

Spandex-blend fabrics are suitable for a variety of garments: lingerie, foundation, skiwear, skating costumes, bicycle pants, exercise apparel, swimwear, golf jackets, pants, skirts, dresses, infant's garments.

Styles with a minimum of seams and topstitching are good choices.

PURCHASING THE FABRIC

Compare the fabric's stretch with the stretch gauge on the pattern envelope. Swimwear fabrics should stretch at least 12 1/2 percent.

Light-colored and white fabrics are more transparent when wet. Most will need a lining to make them opaque.

PREPARING THE FABRIC

Although many spandex fabrics don't need to be preshrunk, they will be easier to stitch.

Allow the fabric to relax at least twenty-four hours before cutting if it isn't prewashed so the garment won't shrink after cutting.

SEWING SPANDEX

See Stretch Wovens, Action Knits, and Tricot.

GARMENT CARE

Garments with spandex can be washed or dry-cleaned, depending on the other fibers and garment construction.

Pretreat stains with a detergent paste. Machine wash in warm water; then tumble dry on low.

Wash white garments separately and avoid chlorine bleach, which discolors and harms spandex.

Handwash fragile garments. Rinse thoroughly; line dry.

Olefin (Polypropylene)

Polypropylene is the most important olefin fiber. Made from petroleum by-products, polypropylene is used for disposable diapers, dishcloths, fishing nets, upholstery fabrics, and insulating materials such as Thinsulate® and bunting fabrics.

Fabric Characteristics
- Polypropylene is very resistant to abrasion, rot, mildew, moths, acids, and alkalies.
- Polypropylene is a light insulating material.
- It does not absorb moisture but allows moisture to escape.
- Polypropylene is strong when wet.

- Polypropylene resists wrinkling.
- Olefin fibers have a low melting point and are easily damaged by warm irons.
- They shrink in hot water and perchlorethylene (dry cleaning fluid).
- They do not dye well.

SEWING POLYPROPYLENE

For sewing suggestions, see Batting and Insulating Materials.

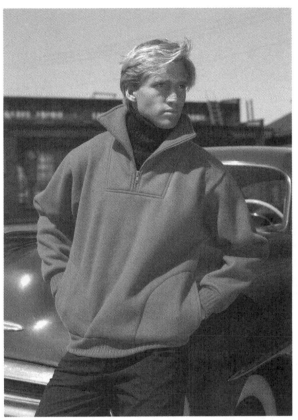

Fig. 3–10 *Easy-to-sew olefin adds warmth without weight. (Photo courtesy of Kwik Sew Pattern Co., Inc.)*

PRESSING

To avoid melting the fabric, use a press cloth and a cool iron; and do not allow the iron to touch the fabric.

GARMENT CARE

Machine wash garments in cool water and air dry. Polypropylene shrinks in hot water.

If the garment must be dry-cleaned, advise the dry cleaner that it contains olefin, which shrinks in perchlorethylene.

CHAPTER 4
Leathers

One of the oldest materials used for clothing, leather is the skin from an animal or reptile—not technically a fabric. After the animal hair is removed, the skin is treated to make it supple and to prevent decomposition. This process, which is called tanning, was named for tannin—a strong, astringent substance frequently used in the process. When the outside or grain side of the skin is tanned and finished, it is called leather. When the inner or flesh side is finished, it is called suede. When the hides are finished with the wool left on, it is called sherpa.

Leather and Suede

Leathers and suedes can be dyed, glazed, buffed, polished, foiled, embossed, patented, beaded, sparkled, printed, perforated, painted stenciled, silk-screened, woven, fringed, or embroidered to create a variety of looks.

Since suede is a kind of leather and is generally sewn like other leathers, this section mentions suede only when particular characteristics or techniques apply exclusively to suedes.

For additional ideas and techniques which can be applied to leathers and suedes, see Chapter 5.

Leathers can be tanned with oil, tannin, alum, or chromium.

Tannin is a strong, astringent substance taken from the leaves and barks of oak trees and other plants. Leathers tanned with the vegetable tannin process are porous, yet resistant to moisture, firm, durable, attractive, and sometimes washable. These leathers are a tan color when they come out of the tanning solution. This characteristic color is easy to see at the cut edges, even after the skins have been dyed other colors.

Leathers tanned with alum are white, soft, and pliable. Unfortunately, they are easily damaged by moisture, which causes them to stiffen, shrink, and waterspot.

Leathers tanned with the metal chromium are less expensive. An examination of a cut edge will reveal a pale, bluish gray color. Chrome-tanned leathers do not resist moisture, but most are washable.

Leathers tanned with formaldehyde are white, soft and supple. They are sometimes washable.

A few leathers—chamois, doeskin, and buckskin—are tanned with oil.

THE LEATHER VOCABULARY

Antelope is a soft, fine, grained leather similar to deerskin. It weighs 2 to 3 ounces per square foot; skins average 5 to 9 square feet.

Buckskin is the flesh or sueded side of deerskin.

Fig. 4–1 *From Mario Valentino, a simple, form-fitting leather dress. (Photo courtesy of Mario Valentino.)*

It is soft, lightweight, and weighs 2 to 4 ounces per square foot; skins average 7 to 9 square feet.

Cabretta is a popular, lightweight goat skin with a fine grain and rich finish. It weighs 2 to 4 ounces per square foot; skins average 6 to 8 square feet.

Calfskin Suede is the underneath layer of calfskin. It weighs 1 to 1 1/2 ounces per square foot; skins average 5 to 7 square feet.

Chamois is the underneath layer of sheepskin, sometimes called **suede chamois.** Best known as a car rag, it's soft, supple, and sueded on both sides. It is inexpensive and can be used for garments. It can be washed with mild soap in lukewarm water. It weighs 2 to 3 ounces per square foot; skins average 7 to 9 square feet.

Cowhide is a smooth grained leather in all weights. Skins average 20 to 24 square feet. Lightweight skins weigh 1 to 1 1/2 ounces per square foot; medium-weights, 4 to 7 ounces; heavy-weights, 8 to 10 ounces.

Cowhide Splits are soft, sueded splits. They weigh 2 to 2 1/2 ounces per square foot; average sizes are 8 to 10 square feet.

Deerskin is the skin side of deer leather. It weighs 2 1/2 to 3 ounces per square foot; average sizes are 8 to 15 square feet.

Deerskin Splits are sueded on both sides. These splits are soft, lightweight, and washable. They are similar to chamois, but stronger. Average size is 6 square feet.

Doeskin is soft, lightweight leather from female deer. It weighs 1 to 2 ounces per square foot; skins average 3 to 5 square feet.

Elk is a soft, supple leather with a coarse grain, similar to deer but more bulky. Skins average 12 to 17 square feet.

Full Grain is the natural grain or texture on the side of the skin from which the hair is removed.

Garment Suede is lightweight, easy-to-sew lambskin suede. It weighs 2 to 3 ounces per square foot; skins average 5 to 7 square feet.

Goatskin is a strong, durable, soft skin. Skins average 8 square feet. It is frequently used for lacings.

Hairsheep is skin from hair-growing, not wool-growing sheep.

Hides are skins of larger animals like cows; skins are over 25 square feet.

Kip is a term for skins of medium-size animals; skins are 15 to 25 square feet.

Lambskin is soft, lightweight leather with a silky feel. It is frequently embossed or tooled. It weighs 1 to 2 ounces per square foot; skins average 8 square feet.

Lambskin Suede is a lightweight, easy-to-sew suede. Sometimes called garment suede, it weighs 1 to 1 1/2 ounces per square foot; skins average 8 square feet.

Leather is the outside of an animal or reptile skin after the hair has been removed.

Morocco is a fine, long-wearing goatskin. It has a rich, red hue.

Naked Leather is an unglazed finish tanned to look natural, with no sheen.

Napa is a soft, thin leather used for fine garments. It may be skin or suede. Skins average 7 square feet.

Ostrich is a leather made from the ostrich. The skin has a characteristic rosette, spiral markings, which are made when the ostrich plumes are pulled from the skin. It is rarely available to home sewers.

81

Peccary Leather is a sheepskin made to look like pigskin.

Patent Leather is made by applying a solution to leather, which becomes hard and shiny.

Pelt is another term for hide or skin.

Pigskin is leather with a grainy texture and a distinctive cluster of three marks where the bristles were located. It can be buffed to a matte finish, polished for a shiny effect, or napped and sueded. It weighs 1 to 3 ounces per square foot; skins average 10 to 12 square feet.

Plonge is leather taken from Japanese cows that were fed a beer diet. It is moderately priced, has few imperfections, drapes, and feels like expensive luxury leathers. It weighs 1 1/2 ounces per square foot; skins average 20 to 30 square feet.

Python Skin is snakeskin with a beautiful scale pattern. Skins average 2 to 4 meters long and 21 cm (8 1/2") wide.

Reptile Skins are small skins from snakes and reptiles.

Shearling is sheep- or lambskin, tanned with the wool intact; a double-faced skin. Skins average 8 to 10 square feet.

Sheepskin is suede from sheep which grow hair, not wool. Sometimes called cabretta, it weighs 2 to 3 ounces per square foot; skins average 8 square feet.

Sheepskin Suede is suede similar to lambskin.

Shirting Suede is a soft, chrome-tanned suede similar to deerskin. Skins average 7 square feet.

Skin is a term for small animal skins; they are less than 15 square feet.

Silk Suede is a lightweight suede that feels like silk. It weighs approximately 3/4 ounce per square foot; skins average 5 1/2 square feet.

Skiver are thin splits of calf, pig, or sheep.

Splits are thin layers of leather made from one

SEWING CHECKLIST

Machine Needles: Universal-H point, jeans (HJ), wedge-point or leather (HLL or NTW) needles 70/10 to 100/16, depending on the leather weight and thickness.

Machine Setting: Stitch length 2.5–4 mm (6–10 stitches per inch); topstitching—3–4 mm (6–8 stitches per inch).

Thread: Long-staple polyester. Topstitching—regular thread, polyester topstitching thread; hand sewing—waxed polyester thread.

Hand Sewing Needles: Glover's or leather needles, sizes 5 to 9.

Sewing Machine Equipment: Roller, Teflon, or leather foot.

Equipment and Supplies: Rotary cutter and mat, sharp shears, thimble, shim, spring hair clips or paper clips, clapper, rubber mallet or cloth-covered hammer, silver knives or ash trays, single-edged razor blade or mat knife, hole puncher, rubber cement, Sticky Stuff™, drafting tape, silicone spray, double-stick basting tape, washable glue stick, and cardboard tube.

Layout: Single layer, right side up.

Marking Techniques: Clips, soap sliver, chalk, temporary marking pens.

Seams: Plain, lapped, tucked, slot, strap, welt, leather seams, laced, tissue-stitched, taped.

Hems: Glued, topstitched, wrong-side-out, interfaced.

Edge Finishes: Leather facings, fabric or ribbon facings, linings, bindings, bands.

Interfacings: Usually sew-in; occasionally fusibles.

Underlinings: Generally not used, except on closely fitted designs.

Linings: Optional; generally used in outerwear and with leathers that crock.

Closures: Buttons and buttonholes, button loops, snaps, zippers, hook and loop tape, ties, eyelets or hooks and lacings.

Pockets: All types.

thick skin. Usually sueded on both sides, they are sometimes called garment split.

Steerhide is heavy, crinkle-grain leather. It weighs 3 to 4 ounces per square foot; skins average 12 to 15 square feet.

Whipsnake is an attractive, affordable snakeskin. Skins average 4 feet long and 3 1/2″ to 4 1/2″ wide.

Characteristics of Leather
- Leather does not fray.
- Leathers are waterproof, but they may spot.
- Leather is sold by the skin, not by the yard.
- Leather frequently has scratches, thin spots, and holes.
- Leather is easily marred by pins and machine stitching.
- Leather garments cannot be let out.
- Many leathers cannot be stitched with regular machine needles.
- Leather may stick to the presser foot.
- Leather is easily damaged by steam and a hot iron.
- Leather may crease permanently when left folded.
- Glues and adhesives may bleed through, causing light or dark spots.
- Sleeves and pant legs on leather garments "shrink" when worn.
- The colors on some leathers crock (rub off).
- When used as a trim, dark-colored leathers may bleed and stain the fabric.
- Blue, green, and brown leathers tend to fade when exposed to light.
- Gold and silver leathers may lose their color when cleaned.
- Leather will mildew and stain permanently when stored in humid areas.
- Suedes have a nap and may require a nap layout.

PLANNING A GARMENT

SELECTING THE LEATHER

Leathers are thinner, softer, more supple, more interesting, more affordable, and easier to sew and clean than ever.

Hint: *Sandra Betzina recommends the soft, pliable leathers such as plonge and cabretta because they drape well and flatter the figure.*

Leather skins are graded by the amount of usable skin, not by the quality. The higher the grade, the fewer scratches, holes, and other flaws. Generally, the more expensive leathers have less waste.

Examine the skins carefully to see how much usable leather there is. Look for large thin areas and flaws which will have to be cut around.

When more than one skin is required, select skins which are most alike in color, texture, and thickness.

Rub suedes and the wrong side of leathers with a white terry towel to determine if the color crocks.

Pigskin frequently loses its color in dry cleaning; and, when combined with fabric, it may bleed on the fabric.

When purchasing suede, use your fingers to examine the surface to see how the nap runs. If your fingers don't leave smooth tracks in one direction, the suede may not require a nap layout.

Avoid leathers which have been tanned with alum.

If you have a limited budget, explore the care requirements and their costs before selecting your skins.

DESIGN IDEAS AND PATTERN SELECTION

You can use leather to make almost anything you can make in fabric—tee tops, tunics, slip or shirtwaist dresses, jackets, coats, skirts, jumpers, pants, vests, belts, handbags, and pillows.

Leather is especially attractive when combined with wool and suede. And now that many of the leathers can be washed or dry-cleaned by regular methods, this is more practical.

The secret to sewing leather successfully is to select the right pattern for the weight, drape, and suppleness of the leather. Compare the hand of the leather to similar fabrics; then consider patterns which suggest those fabrics for the design.

Select a design appropriate for your sewing skills. If this is your first experience with leather, select a simple, easy-to-sew design.

Hint: *Tee tops and handbags are easy and don't require large leather skins.*

Patterns with a minimum of seams are easier to sew, but the pattern pieces may be more difficult to lay out if the skins are small; and there may be more waste.

Choose designs with little or no easing. Styles with kimono or raglan sleeves or dropped shoulders are easier to assemble than set-in sleeves. Seams are easier to stitch than darts. Patterns with small pieces are easier to lay out.

Classic separates are always good. They will be fashionable for several years and are easy to update with different coordinates. But if you like the avant-garde, select a couple of unusual skins to make a smashing tee top, halter, or bustier.

Avoid closely fitted designs unless they are underlined; most leathers will split under stress.

When making trousers in a lightweight leather, select a pattern with pleats or gathers. Pants that are too tight will bag and tear at seamlines.

Patterns designed for synthetic suede or leather can also be used for real leathers.

If you want a more unusual design, consider some of these designer ideas—Yves Saint Laurent's python jacket with leather piping, Princess Stephanie's leather swimsuit, Oscar de la Renta's trapunto jacket, Anne Klein's short skirt with full-length zipper on the side, Carol Horn's quilted baseball jacket, Donna Karan's soft suede shirt (worn with ribbed knit pants). You might also choose a novel closure—eyelets with lacing from Azzedine—or lavish embroidery and appliqué from Gloria Blackburn.

PURCHASING THE LEATHER

Leather is sold by the skin or hide. Skins are pelts or hides of smaller animals such as calves, sheep, goats, pigs, and snakes. Hides are the skins of larger animals such as cows, steers, horses, buffalo, and deer. Large, thick skins are sometimes cut into thin layers called splits.

Unlike fabrics, leather is measured in square feet and is sold by the square yard. Skins are small pieces ranging in size from 5 to 24 square feet. Hides are larger, measuring 40 to 50 square feet. A few leathers like python are sold by the meter (39.37"). Some skins are almost rectangles, while others have definite animal shapes.

To determine how many square feet you need, multiply your yardage requirement by the number of square feet in a yard of fabric, then add an ad-

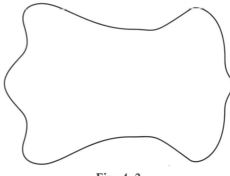

Fig. 4–2

ditional 10 percent to 15 percent to allow for flaws and irregularities on the skins.

For one yard of fabric:

36" wide has 9 square feet
45" wide has 11.25 square feet
54" wide has 13.5 square feet
60" wide has 15 square feet.

Example: For a garment requiring 2 1/2 yards of 45" wide fabric, you'll need 28 1/8 square feet plus 10 to 15 percent (about 3 square feet), to make a total of 31 1/8 square feet. If the skins are 10 to 14 square feet, you will need three skins.

If you are ordering leather by mail, the catalog description frequently includes the weight of one square foot of leather. Leathers which weigh 1 to 1 1/2 ounces are lightweight and supple. Heavier leathers which weigh 2 1/2 to 3 ounces are more suitable for outerwear.

When possible, take the adjusted pattern to the leather store to determine exactly how many skins you'll need. Study the skins and select those which have the same shading and pattern. When purchasing suede, allow for a nap layout if necessary.

Lay the skins flat for storing. If that isn't possible, roll them, right side out, on a cardboard tube until you're ready to sew.

PATTERN PREPARATION

Never overlook the advantages of using a pattern you've already used; you've already ironed out all the fitting wrinkles and practiced your sewing skills.

Or make a test garment to perfect the fit and decide if and where the skins should be pieced. When you've completed all the adjustments on the test garment, rip it apart and press.

Hint: *Use nonwoven pattern fabric or interfacing to simulate the body of light- and medium-weight leathers. Use felt if your leather is stiff or heavy. Construct your test garment with the same seaming techniques you will use on the garment.*

Lengthen jacket sleeves 1/2" to 1" and pant legs 1" to 2". Both will shape to the body and shorten when worn.

For set-in sleeves with more than 1" ease, reduce the sleeve cap when sewing medium to heavy leathers.

Few leather skins are long enough to make slacks. A shallow V-shaped seam just above the knee is the usual solution. Draw the new seamline on the pattern; add one or two matchpoints. Cut the pattern apart and add seam allowances to both sections.

Fig. 4–3

Piece garment sections for more economical layouts. Use the new seamlines to create a slimmer-looking design. Seams at the garment centers or princess lines are always good. Plain or conventional seams can be cut with 3/8" seam allowances, since leather doesn't fray and you won't be letting it out. Lapped seams require no seam allowance on the overlap and a 3/8" to 5/8" seam allowance on the underlap.

Check and correct all seams and seam allowances on your test garment before calculating the leather requirement.

SEWING LEATHER

LAYOUT AND CUTTING

Leather does not have a true grainline. But since it has the least stretch and greatest strength in the length from neck to the tail, the lengthwise grain is considered to be parallel to the backbone.

Lay the skins out flat, right side up. Do not fold the skins or try to cut through double thicknesses.

Examine the skins carefully for imperfections, holes, scratches, and thin spots. Generally, the center or back of the animal is most attractive while the legs and belly may be weak and thin.

Arrange the pattern pieces, placing the tops toward the animal's neck when possible. Most garments will be more attractive when worn the way the animal did, even though leather does not have a nap.

If you aren't using your test garment as a pattern, cut *duplicate* pattern pieces.

First, cut the most noticeable sections—the fronts, collars, and lapels—from the most attractive skins. Try to cut both fronts or backs from the same skin, positioning them so they match nicely.

Lay the largest and most important pieces in the center of the skins where the leather is thickest. Lay small pieces near the edges, shifting off-grain as needed.

For rough suedes and splits which have no nap, consider the color and skin thickness when laying out the pattern.

Examine suedes with a nap carefully to determine the nap direction. Generally, the nap runs from the head to the tail and from the backbone to the legs. A true nap layout may not be required.

For unusual designs, use the suede nap to create differently shaded patterns on the garment.

Use dinner knives or small ashtrays to hold the pattern pieces in place. Pins leave permanent holes and do not penetrate the leather easily. Avoid taping the pieces to the leather; the tape may lift the color.

Cut, using very sharp shears, a mat knife, single-edged razor blade, or rotary cutter and mat.

MARKING

Use a soap sliver or dressmaker's chalk to outline the sections.

Transfer the construction marks to the wrong side of the skins with chalk, soap sliver, smooth tracing wheel, or temporary marking pen. Experiment to be sure they won't show through on the outside of the garment.

Mark notches on plain seams with small clips. Mark lapped seams with chalk, soap sliver, or temporary marking pen.

To avoid confusion later, label the reverse side of pieces that look alike, or clip the pattern and garment sections together until you're ready to sew.

To prevent creasing, use a cardboard tube to save uncut skins and large scraps.

STITCHING TIPS

Experiment with leather scraps and make some test seams.

Always try a Universal needle first—they are the cheapest and most readily available. Then, if you have problems with skipped stitches, change to a small-hole needle plate or alter the needle position. When all else fails, use a leather needle in the appropriate size.

For heavy leathers, stitch seams using polyester topstitching thread; lengthen the stitch to 4 mm (6 stitches per inch), and lighten the pressure as needed.

Hint: *Avoid cotton and cotton-wrapped polyester threads. The tannin causes them to rot.*

To avoid splitting the skins, lengthen the stitch to 2.5 mm (10 stitches per inch) on light- and medium-weight leathers.

Stitch slowly and hold the leather taut to maintain an even stitch length.

If the leather sticks to the bottom of the presser foot, use a roller, Teflon, or leather foot. Or spray the bottom of the foot with a silicone spray.

Hint: *Check to be sure the foot isn't leaving tracks on the leather. If it is, try a different foot.*

Stitch carefully; needle holes cannot be removed from leather.

Hint: *Sometimes needle holes can be hidden on suede by brushing with a toothbrush. Since this doesn't remove the holes, the seam is weaker.*

Backstitching causes the leather to split, unless you can backstitch precisely into the previously stitched holes. Tailor knots are always safe.

When the leather is too thick or tough for machine stitching, use polyester topstitching thread and hand sew with a backstitch. Use a thimble and glover's needle; or make the holes with an awl if necessary.

Hint: *Wax the thread with beeswax; then press the thread so it won't curl and snarl while you're sewing.*

For topstitching, use two strands of regular sewing thread or polyester topstitching thread and a larger needle. Use a roller or leather foot; or dust the leather with talcum powder so the foot will glide smoothly.

For basting, use spring hair clips and paper clips for plain seams and double-stick basting tape for lapped seams. Don't forget to remove the tape after the seam is stitched.

Hint: *Never leave seams basted any longer than necessary.*

Use rubber cement to baste lapped seams and seams which will not be pressed open. Allow the glue to dry before stitching.

When stitching inward or concave curves, clip the curve in several places before stitching.

To avoid stretching, reinforce long seams and seams on the crossgrain with a stay—seam or twill tape or a lightweight selvage.

To reduce creeping when joining leather and a fabric, stitch with the fabric on the top.

SEAMS

When choosing the seam type, consider the leather weight and garment style as well as your personal preference and sewing ability.

When sewing heavy leathers, lapped leather seams have little excess bulk.

Stitch shiny and fragile leathers with a stabilizer between the leather and feed dogs.

Glue or topstitch seams so they will remain flat. Tape all seams which will be stressed during wear. To reduce bulk, bevel or skive the edges of seams with a razor blade or mat knife.

Plain Leather Seams: Cut and stitch plain seams

with 3/8″ seam allowances. Clip or notch as needed so seams will lie flat. Open the seam and press with the handles of the shears or pound with a mallet.

Hint: *If you don't have a mallet, use a clapper or cloth-covered hammer.*

Apply rubber cement to the wrong side of the seam allowances. Wait until the glue is tacky; then press the seam allowances against the garment; and pound again. Test the rubber cement on a scrap first, to be sure it won't show through.

A new product, Sticky Stuff™, can be substituted for rubber cement. When dry, it is softer and more flexible; it is water soluble, but may be dry-cleaned.

For a smoother finish, when stitching corners on collars, cuffs, and garment edges, reshape sharp points so they are rounded.

Hint: *To be sure two points are identical, use a template and temporary marking pen.*

Clip or notch enclosed seams at edges. Apply rubber cement; and, when it becomes tacky, finger press the seam allowances against the garment. Turn the section right side out. Place the clapper just on the edge; then pound the clapper with a mallet or cloth-covered hammer.

Topstitched Seams: Topstitching holds seam allowances flat without gluing; and it adds strength as well. It is particularly attractive on dressy, light-weight leathers when stitched at 2.5 mm (10 stitches per inch) 1/16″ from the both sides of the seamline. Stitch sporty designs with a longer stitch—4mm or 6 stitches per inch—1/4″ from one or both sides of the seamline.

Hint: *Utilize the various needle positions on your machine to help you sew straight and parallel. Then the presser foot remains level on the seamline.*

Lapped Seams: For medium- and heavyweight leathers, lapped seams are the best choice. Trim away the seam allowance of the overlap. Mark the seamline of the underlap with chalk or soap sliver.
Matching the seamlines, lap the seams and baste with rubber cement or a washable glue stick. Top-

stitch 1/8″ from the edge. On sporty designs or outerwear, topstitch again 3/8″ from the edge.

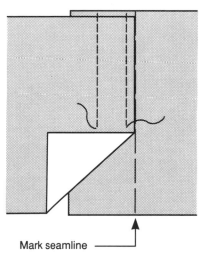

Mark seamline

Fig. 4–4

DARTS

Stitch darts with two or three stitches along the fold at the dart point. Slash and glue the darts open.
If topstitching is used elsewhere on the garment, topstitch the darts also. If the design features lapped seams, lap and stitch the darts. Bevel the edges of the dart as needed to reduce bulk.

HEMS

Hem allowances can vary from 5/8″ to 2″, depending on the garment design and leather weight.
If the garment will be lined, machine stitch 1/4″ from the raw edge of the hem so the lining will be easier to sew to the leather.
Fold the hem in place and pound to set the hemline. Topstitch hems or glue with rubber cement.

Hint: *When topstitching, glue baste with a washable glue stick. When gluing, be sure the glue extends to the foldline.*

On lined garments, glue or stitch the hem allowance close to the foldline so the hem edge remains free, allowing you to machine stitch the lining to it.
To make a flat, smooth hem on curved edges, cut out triangular notches.

Hint: *Don't cut too many notches. You can always cut more or larger triangles later but you can't put them back.*

If the leather is attractive on the wrong side and the edge is straight, make a wrong-side-out hem. Fold the hem allowance to the right side; pound, baste, and topstitch.

Hint: *Be sure the hem allowance is an even depth and the edge is cut smoothly.*

When interfacing the hem, the bias strip can be glue-basted to the wrong side of the leather or machine stitched just inside the hem allowance.

For heavy leathers, replace a traditional hem with a cut-edge facing. Or trim away the hem allowance, and topstitch through a single layer the desired distance from the hemline.

FACINGS

Generally leather facings are used on coats and jackets. To reduce bulk and conserve leather, cut facings on other garments narrower or replace them with fabric or grosgrain ribbon.

Since leather doesn't fray, some facings can be replaced with a narrow hem (the seam allowance). Fold the seam allowance to the wrong side; glue or topstitch to secure. On curved edges, clip or notch the seam allowance so it will lie flat.

SLEEVES

If you haven't already, reduce the amount of ease in the sleeve cap.

Most leathers can be eased by machine. Lengthen the stitch to 4 mm (6 stitches per inch) and stitch, right side up, just inside the seamline and again 1/4" from the edge.

BUTTONS AND BUTTONHOLES

Bound, machine-stitched, slash-stitched, or leather buttonholes, buttons and loops, hook and loop tape, toggles, snaps, zippers, and lacings are suitable fasteners for leather garments.

Using a glover's needle, sew on buttons with heavily waxed thread. Use stay buttons on the facing side if the garment will receive hard wear.

If the leather has an attractive wrong side, use the wrong-side-out hem to finish the front placket.

For machine-stitched buttonholes, mark buttonhole lengths with drafting tape. Stitch; then remove the tape promptly. Always test first to be sure the tape won't mar the leather.

When using traditional machine-stitched buttonholes, lengthen the stitch to avoid damaging the leather.

Bound buttonholes can be made on leather by the strip, modified strip, windowpane, and leather methods.

ZIPPERS

Invisible, slot, lapped, and decorative zippers work well on leather.

For slot and lapped applications, do not baste the opening closed. Glue the seam allowances open before inserting the zipper. Use drafting tape to baste the zipper to the placket.

Exposed zippers are particularly easy since leather doesn't fray. Use a mat knife to cut out the rectangle 3/8" to 1/2" wide and the length of the zipper. Glue or tape the zipper in place and topstitch.

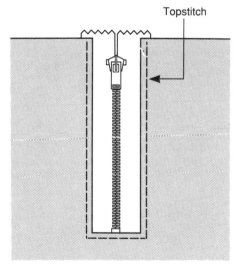

Fig. 4–5

WAISTBANDS

To minimize bulk, use grosgrain ribbon to face the waistband. If the band will be concealed, replace the leather with a grosgrain ribbon band.

POCKETS

All types of pockets—patch, welt, flap, slot, inseam—are suitable for leather.

The novelty inseam pocket for regular or leather lapped seams is particularly attractive. It can be used vertically in a side seam or horizontally in a yoke seam and only requires one pocket sack to form the underlay.

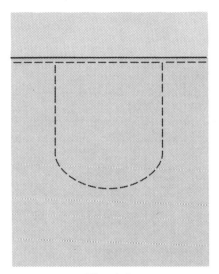

Fig. 4–6

1. Cut one pocket sack from lining fabric.
2. Right sides together, join the pocket sack to the yoke or garment back with a 3/8″ seam. Press.

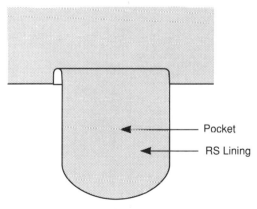

Pocket

RS Lining

Fig. 4–7

3. Stabilize the pocket opening on the front section with a piece of seam tape. With the garment wrong side up, center the stabilizer over the seamline; and glue-baste. (If your garment has lapped leather seams, do not use a stabilizer.)

Right side up, fold the seam allowance under and topstitch the pocket opening so it will match the topstitching of the lapped seam. Pull the threads at each end to the wrong side and knot.

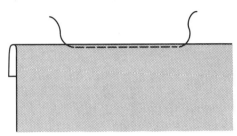

Fig. 4–8

4. Right sides up, baste the garment sections together. Then stitch the seams on either side of the opening, securing the threads with knots at each end.
5. Topstitch through all layers to outline the pocket (but don't close the opening).

INTERFACINGS

Leather stretches and needs interfacing at most edges to maintain its shape.

Hair canvas, woven, and nonwoven sew-in interfacings are easy to use when basted in place with a washable glue stick.

Hint: *Always test the glue first. Try to place the glue only on the seam allowances so it won't show on the right side of the garment. Do not glue the interfacing along the long, unnotched edges.*

Generally, fusible interfacings are best avoided.

LININGS

Line leather outerwear to preserve the garment shape, to reduce clinging, and to prevent the color from crocking onto your skin and other garments.

Linings vary with the style of the garment. They can be made in the traditional style from inconspicuous lining fabrics. Or they can be cut from boldly patterned wool and extended to the garment edge.

Select a good-quality, twill-weave lining in the appropriate weight and fiber for the leather. When the leather is washable, be sure the lining has the same washability.

For a traditional lining, add a full 1″ pleat at the center back if your pattern doesn't have one.

Join the linings of jackets and coats to their facings by hand or machine. Both methods require some advance thought. Creeping is frequently a problem when machine stitching two unlike layers; in hand sewing, the best needle for penetrating the leather will make holes in the lining.

When stitching by machine, use a Universal-H point needle and stitch the lining/facing seam with the lining on top. Pin baste in the seam allowances to avoid creeping; and tissue-stitch if needed.

When stitching the lining hem to the leather, work with the jacket wrong side out. Pin and stitch each side from the front facing to the side seams.

Turn the garment right side out. Reach in between the lining and garment at the hem to grasp the raw edges of the hems. Pull the edges out and stitch, closing the opening as much as possible. Hand sew to finish.

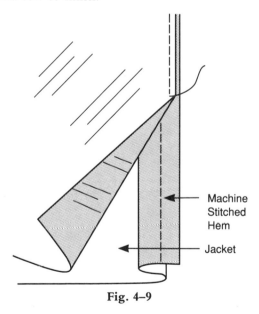

Fig. 4–9

To attach the lining by hand, first machine stitch the facings and hem 1/4″ from the raw edges, then slipstitch the lining to the stitch line.

LINING A LEATHER SKIRT

This easy technique for a skirt lining was used on an Italian suede skirt in my collection.

1. Complete the vertical seams and skirt placket.
2. Baste a stay tape to the wrong side of the skirt at the waistline.

3. Try on the skirt and have the hemline marked.
4. Hem the skirt.

Hint: *If you are using rubber cement, glue along the hemline. Do not glue the raw edge of the hem allowance flat, so you can sew the lining to it by machine.*

5. Complete the vertical seams on the skirt lining.
6. Mark the hemline on the lining and trim on the marked line.
7. Right sides together, stitch the skirt and lining hems together.
8. Wrong sides together, match the waistlines of the skirt and lining; baste.
9. Make two hanger loops for the skirt, to protect it from clip marks: cut a piece of seam binding

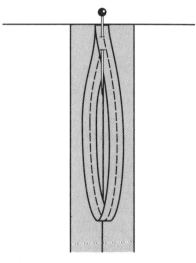

Fig. 4–10

9″ long; fold it in half lengthwise and machine stitch through the center. Fold the loop in half crosswise and pin the ends to the raw edge of the waist at the side seams.

10. Set the waistband.

PRESSING

Pressing leather is quite different from pressing most fabrics. Use a medium temperature dry iron, and always test press on some scraps.

Press from the wrong side, using a press cloth or plain brown paper to protect the leather.

Hint: *Don't use grocery bags with printing; the print may come off on the leather.*

Do not press with steam, which may cause the leather to shrink. To avoid stretching the leather, do not slide the iron.

Most wrinkles will hang out.

SEW DECORATIVE

Use machine embroidery, cutwork, painting, appliqué, patchwork, quilting, piping, beading, fringing, and woven strips to accent the design.

To machine embroider, experiment with these tips from Linda Barker, author of *That Touch of Class: Machine Embroidery on Leather.*

Set the iron on medium; and fuse two layers of wax-coated freezer paper to the wrong side of the leather. Using a small leather needle, a darning foot, and machine-embroidery thread, set the machine for zigzag (W,3 to 4). Lower the foot and embroider.

LEATHER TRIMS

The Italian designers frequently incorporate leather trims on wool garments. But it was an American designer, Bonnie Cashin, who mixed leather and fabrics most innovatively. Capes and kimono coats bound with leather, leather vests lined with wool plaid, and jackets with leather are just a few of the Cashin ideas.

For home sewers, mixing fabrics and leathers was impractical until the introduction of the new leathers, which can be laundered or dry-cleaned by regular methods. Now leather trims on corduroy, velveteen, velvet, canvas, poplin, tweeds, or flannel are not only possible, but easy to sew as well.

Start wih something smashing—a leather collar and cuffs, pipings, bindings, bands, bound buttonhole welts, welt or bound pockets, or just a trim on a patch pocket.

GARMENT CARE

Leather garments will last for years if you care for them properly.

Ask the retailer for care instructions when pur-

Fig. 4–11 *This Bonnie Cashin design for Philip Sills Group was innovative when it first appeared in the mid-sixties. It features a wool jacket with leather trimming and a matching leather skirt. (Photo courtesy of Historic Costume and Textile, The Ohio State University Collection.)*

chasing. If there are none, assume that the leather must be dry-cleaned by a leather method. If the skins are washable, ask for recommendations about the water temperature and brand of soap.

Wear a scarf to protect the leather neckline from soil; and never pin or stick anything to the garment. Make dress shields to protect garments from perspiration.

Hang the garment on a padded hanger and stuff the sleeves with tissue. Protect it with a pillow case or cloth bag. Avoid plastic bags, which cause fading and drying.

Store in a cool, dry place—but not a damp basement or hot attic. Heat causes leather to dry out and stiffen. Moisture causes it to mildew. Many leathers fade when hung in sunlight or artificial light.

Use a clean damp cloth to wipe away surface dirt. To remove dark marks and stains, add a drop of mild detergent to hot water and work the stain in circular motions from the center out. Always test first on an inconspicuous seam allowance for colorfastness.

Do not use cleaning fluids, saddle soap, wire brushes, solvents, steel wool, or other abrasives to remove stains and spots.

Dry a wet leather garment with a soft cloth; then allow it to dry completely away from direct heat. When dry, brush suede garments to restore the nap.

Clean the garment before it becomes excessively soiled. And when you have matching leather pieces, clean them all at the same time, whether they need it or not. Check with the cleaner; and remove or cover any buckles, buttons or ornaments.

To clean leather, use a soft bristle brush, soft gum eraser, dry ball of rubber cement, or dry terry towel to remove surface dirt.

To clean suede, use a stiff plastic bristle brush or Tana Nubuck. If the suede crocks, rub lightly with a dry terry towel to remove some of the excess color.

To remove a grease stain, dust generously with fuller's earth or talcum powder. If all the grease isn't absorbed with the first application, repeat until it is.

Even the best leathers may be less attractive after cleaning. Variation in color, texture, and weight will be more noticeable. They may be stiffer and shrink. Scars, wrinkles, glues, and fusing agents may be more noticeable.

Pigskin

One of the most popular leathers, pigskin is characterized by a cluster of three marks where the bristles were removed. It can be buffed to a matte finish or polished for a shiny effect.

Generally, it is best to sew pigskin like suedes.

Depending on the dye lot, pigskin is often stiff.

Pigskin, particularly blues and greens, loses its color when cleaned; when combined with fabric, it may bleed on the fabric.

To extend the life of pigskin garments, do not hang in sunlight or artificial light.

Shearling

Shearling or sherpa is a reversible sheep- or lambskin which has been tanned with the wool left on. Sheared shortly before slaughter, the wool is short and may not have an obvious nap. The reverse side can be tanned or sueded.

Fake shearling is a two-faced fabric with a man-made lamb's wool one side and vinyl on the other.

Both the real and the fake are called shearling or sherpa. These suggestions can be used for sewing either.

Fabric Characteristics
- Shearling is a reversible material.
- Shearling does not fray.
- Shearling is waterproof, but it may spot.
- Real shearling is sold by the skin; sherpa fabric is sold by the yard.
- Real shearling may have scratches and holes.
- Shearling garments cannot be let out.
- Shearling is easily damaged by steam, hot irons, pins, and machine stitching.
- Some shearlings cannot be stitched with regular machine needles.
- Sleeves will "shrink" when worn.
- Some shearlings stick to the presser foot.

PLANNING A GARMENT

For additional suggestions, see Leather and Suede, Furs, Fake-Fur Fabrics, and Reversible Fabrics.

SELECTING THE SHERPA

Sueded sheepskin with natural wool on the reverse is most readily available. Skins average 8 to 10 square feet. Adjust the pattern and make any design changes before estimating the sherpa needed.

Periodically, fabrics with leatherlike vinyl and fake fur or wool on the reverse are offered to home sewers.

SEWING CHECKLIST

Machine Needles: Universal-H point, jeans (HJ) or leather (HLL or NYW) needles, sizes 70/10 or 90/14.

Machine Setting: Stitch length 2.5–4 mm (6–10 stitches per inch); topstitching 3–4 mm (6–8 stitches per inch); tension and pressure, adjust as needed.

Thread: Long-staple polyester; hand sewing—waxed thread.

Hand Sewing Needles: Glover's, leather, or regular needles, sizes 5 to 7.

Sewing Machine Equipment: Roller, Teflon, or leather foot, shim.

Equipment and Supplies: Sharp shears, thimble, clothespins or large paper clips, clapper, weights, single-edged razor blade or mat knife, hole puncher, rubber cement, silicone spray, washable glue stick, and cardboard tube.

Layout: Single/lay, skin side up.

Marking Techniques: Soap sliver, chalk, temporary marking pens.

Seams: Plain, topstitched, slot, strap, leather seams, laced, taped.

Hems and Edge Finishes: Glued, topstitched, wrong-side-out, unfinished edge, leather facings, fabric or ribbon facings, bindings, bands.

Interfacings, Linings: Rarely used.

Closures: Buttons and buttonholes, button loops, snaps, ties, toggles, lacings.

Pockets: Inseam and patch.

Examine the suede or leather side carefully when it will be skin side out.

DESIGN IDEAS AND PATTERN SELECTION

Generally, sherpa is used skin side out. And, although it can be used for reversible garments, they are not as successful as unlined garments, which look as if they might be reversible.

Vest, coat, and jacket designs are good choices. Let the sherpa do the talking. Choose designs with little or no easing.

Use details such as wrong-side-out hems, fur peeking out at the seamlines, and turned-back cuffs and lapels to emphasize the uniqueness of the material.

SEWING SHERPA

LAYOUT, CUTTING, AND MARKING

The layout and cutting of sherpa is very much like cutting fur.

Use a nap layout. Spread the sherpa with the leather side up. To avoid permanent pin holes, use weights to hold the pattern in place.

Fig. 4–12 *Designed by Mario Valentino, the jacket is made of shearling—a reversible leather which has been tanned with the fur left on. The edges and pockets are trimmed with a dark leather. (Photo courtesy of Mario Valentino.)*

93

Cut carefully. Using the points of very sharp shears, a single-edged razor blade, or mat knife, cut just the skin; then pull the wool apart.

Mark with chalk, soap sliver, or temporary marking pens. Test first to avoid leaving a permanent mark on the leather side.

STITCHING TIPS

Make a test seam, using a new needle. Adjust the tension as needed and use a shim when sewing over uneven layers. Experiment with stitching the shearling so the skin sides are together and the wool sides are together.

Use a roller foot or wrap the toes of the all-purpose foot with transparent tape to avoid snagging the wool.

SEAMS

Most seams can be basted with large paper clips or clothespins. A few, such as leather lapped seams, may have to be pinned; use very fine pins placed in the seam allowance.

Decorative seams, such as nonwoven lapped, slot, wrong-side-out, and laced, are particularly attractive on sherpa fabrics because the fake fur peeks out at the fabric edge, highlighting the novelty of the material.

Use strap, topstitched plain, and welt seams for flat, inconspicuous seaming.

Trim wrong-side-out seams to 1/4″ and let them protrude *à la naturelle;* or topstitch them open.

To make leather-lapped seams, trim away overlap. Lap, matching the edge of the overlap to the seamline on the underlap; edgestitch. Topstitch again 3/8″ away.

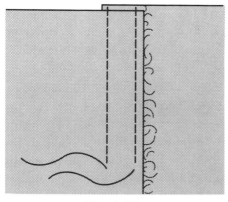

Fig. 4–13

Trim and grade other seams as needed to reduce bulk.

To reduce bulk on topstitched and welt seams, trim away the wool in the seam allowances before topstitching.

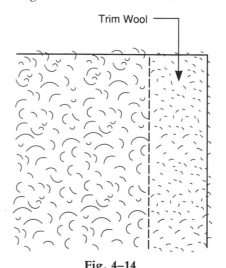

Fig. 4–14

HEMS AND EDGE FINISHES

Finish the edges of cuffs, hems, front openings, and pockets with wrong-side-out hems. Allow a 1″ or wider hem allowance. Fold the hem to the right side of the garment; glue or topstitch close to the raw edge.

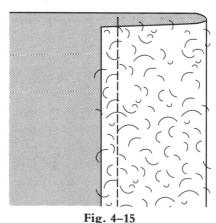

Fig. 4–15

Hint: *Baste, using clothespins and large paper clips.*

To topstitch hemmed edges, trim away the wool in the hem allowance, fold the edge to the wrong side; and topstitch.

To reduce bulk, miter corners when using wrong-side-out and topstitched hems. To prevent curling on an unfinished edge, round the corners.

BUTTONHOLES

Both reinforced bound and stitched-slash buttonholes are attractive on both sides.

STITCHED-SLASH BUTTONHOLES

1. On the skin side, mark the buttonhole location with drafting tape.
2. Cut a rectangular facing 2″ wider and 2″ longer than the buttonhole. Trim away the wool pile on the facing.
3. With the garment wrong side up, center the facing over the buttonhole, wool sides together. Use drafting tape to baste the edges of the facing to the wool.

Hint: *Hand baste on the buttonhole line.*

4. Right side up, stitch (L,2.5–3) around the buttonhole; topstitch again 1/4″ to 1/2″ away.
5. Use a mat knife to slash the buttonhole.
6. Wrong side up, trim the facing strip close to the stitched line.

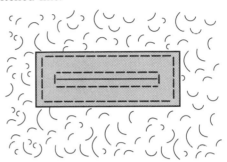

Fig. 4–16

CHAPTER 5
Synthetic Suedes

Sewing synthetic suedes is different, but it isn't difficult. Made famous in 1972 by Halston, Ultrasuede® was the first fine-quality synthetic suede. Frequently used as a generic term for all synthetic suedes, Ultrasuede applies only to specific fabrics trademarked by Springs Mills and marketed by Skinner.

Although there are many other fine-quality synthetic suedes, there are also some inferior fabrics on the market which are difficult to sew, do not wear well, and cannot be cleaned satisfactorily.

When selecting a synthetic suede, first consider the price; good-quality fabrics are not cheap. Then look for a trademark or name of the importer; if you don't recognize either, consider the reputation of the store where you are shopping (i.e., can it be trusted?).

POPULAR SYNTHETIC SUEDES

Several of these fabrics are no longer manufactured; however, since home sewers tend to hoard synthetic suedes, I include them here.

Amara, a Thompson of California product, is no longer available. Compared to Ultrasuede, it feels more like suede.

Belleseime, a Burlington/Klopman product, is no longer manufactured. It is similar in weight but softer than Ultrasuede, with a longer nap. Use conventional seaming and edge finishes.

Caress™, a Skinner product, has the buttery hand of a soft suede. Compared to Facile™, it is much softer. Use conventional seaming and edge finishes.

Facile, a Skinner product, is much softer and easier to sew than Ultrasuede. It has some nap on both sides. Use conventional seaming and edge finishes.

Glore-Valcana is a synthetic suede imported by House of Fabrics and So-Fro Fabrics. Compared to Ultrasuede, it has similar weight and crispness. It has a longer nap on the face.

Lamous®, manufactured by Asahi Chemical Industry Co., Ltd., is marketed by Logantex, Inc. It is softer and lighter than Ultrasuede, and it has a longer nap on the face. Easier to sew and press, garments can be assembled with either the flat method and nonwoven seams and finishes or by conventional techniques.

Lamous-Lite®, another Logantex product, is similar in weight and softness to Facile. Use conventional seaming and edge finishes.

Suede 21™, a Kanebo fabric, is no longer manufactured. Available in two weights, it is softer than Ultrasuede and easier to sew. Use conventional seaming and edge finishes.

Suedemark® II, trade name of Ciao Ltd., has a soft, buttery hand like suede. It is similar in weight to Facile, but is not as crisp. It has less nap on the face and none on the back.

Ultrasuede

Ultrasuede is a unique, nonwoven fabric made of 60 percent polyester and 40 percent nonfibrous polyurethane. It doesn't shrink, crack, peel, pill, or stretch. It is resistant to stains, water, and wind.

These directions are written for Ultrasuede because it's the most difficult to handle. They can be adapted for other synthetic suedes, some real suedes, and leathers.

Fabric Characteristics
- Ultrasuede has no true grain but it does have some give in the width.
- It is a crisp, nonwoven material which does not ease well.
- It has a nap.
- It does not fray.
- It is easily damaged by ashes and hot irons.

- It is not resistant to abrasion, and wears quickly at the elbows.
- It is difficult to penetrate with a regular hand sewing needle.
- Skipped stitches and creeping underlayers are frequently a problem with Ultrasuede.

PLANNING A GARMENT

PURCHASING ULTRASUEDE

Check before you buy. If you want real Ultrasuede, be sure the fabric bolt carries the Skinner Ultrasuede trademark.

SEWING CHECKLIST

Machine Needles: Universal-H point, stretch(HJ) and Yellow Band needles sizes 65/9 to 90/14. Topstitching— Universal or Yellow Band needles; size 90/14, 100/16 or topstitching needle 90/14.

Stitch Length: 2.5–3 mm (8–10 stitches per inch); topstitching—2.5–4 mm (6–10 stitches per inch).

Thread: Long-staple polyester, cotton-wrapped polyester. Topstitching— polyester topstitching or regular thread.

Hand Sewing Needles: Glover's or leather needles.

Sewing Machine Equipment: Even-feed, roller, or Teflon foot.

Equipment and Supplies: Well-sharpened shears, small trimming scissors, rotary cutter and mat, fine pins, thimble, steamer, mat knife, needle lubricant, washable glue stick, Sticky Stuff, water-soluble double-stick tape, fusible web.

Layout: Nap. Single or double layer.

Marking Techniques: Clips, chalk, soap sliver, temporary marking pens, smooth tracing wheel and tracing carbon, drafting tape.

Seams: Plain, topstitched, welt, double-welt, nonwoven lapped, nonwoven flat-fell, nonwoven abutted, wrong-side-out, Zandra Rhodes Seam.

Hems: Topstitched, fused, plain, hand blindstitched, faced, wrong-side-out.

Seam and Hem Finishes: Unfinished.

Edge Finishes: Facings, raw-edge facings, raw edge.

Interfacing: Generally, fusibles are best.

Linings: Generally not used except for outerwear.

Closures: All types.

Pockets: All types, including nonwoven fabric pockets.

Before making a final selection, feel the crispness of the fabric. Since the crispness varies with different dye colors, it will influence the outcome of the final design.

Ultrasuede is expensive fabric. To avoid purchasing extra, fit and adjust the pattern before shopping. Decide whether you'll use regular or nonwoven seams; then make a revised layout to determine the exact fabric requirements.

To plan the most economical layout, use a nap layout, a single layer of fabric, *duplicate* pattern pieces, and the exact fabric width—Ultrasuede is sometimes wider than 45″. For plain seams, reduce seam allowances to 3/8″. For nonwoven lapped seams and finishes, trim away the seam allowance on the overlap; and, for raw-edge facings, reduce seam allowances to 3/8″.

For additional savings, use a tighter layout. Tilt pattern pieces slightly to conserve fabric.

Hint: *I never tilt more than 25 percent; however, Marcia Bryan has had good results tilting pieces up to 45 percent.*

Cut waistbands on either the crossgrain or lengthwise grain. Cut bias sections on the crossgrain. Make a rough sketch of the revised layout.

DESIGN IDEAS AND PATTERN SELECTION

Ultrasuede is a versatile fabric which can be used for a variety of garments from sportswear to outerwear to formals; and since it can be washed or dry-cleaned, it's an excellent fabric for trims.

Garments can be assembled conventionally with plain seams or with techniques for nonwoven fabrics using lapped seams and raw edges. Survey the latest ready-to-wear to determine which method is more fashionable. Generally, lapped seams look sporty, while plain seams look dressy.

Also check the latest ready-to-wear for design ideas. When Ultrasuede was first introduced, it was used for tailored and semi-tailored garments. In more recent years, casual, everyday designs have been more popular.

Some other new looks include an Ultrasuede skirt with a jacket of woven fabric and Ultrasuede trim, an Ultrasuede jacket and a fabric skirt, Ultrasuede tops with machine embroidery and/or

Fig. 5–1 *Synthetic suedes are most attractive in simple designs like this skirt from Style Patterns. (Photo courtesy of Style Patterns Ltd.)*

cutwork designs, and fancy sweatshirts and sweaters with Ultrasuede appliqués.

Designs with simple lines work well and patterns recommended for crisp fabrics such as corduroy, velveteen, faille, and linen are good choices.

Close-fitting, draped, very full, pleated, and gathered designs are rarely successful.

Dropped shoulders, kimono and raglan sleeves are easier to sew than traditional set-in sleeves. Try to avoid darts, which are difficult to stitch smoothly.

Fabric scraps can be used for appliqués, patchwork, belts, and small accessories.

FITTING THE PATTERN

Cut duplicate pattern pieces so the fabric can be cut from a single layer of fabric. And if you haven't used the pattern before, make a test garment in a nonwoven cloth such as felt or a crisp interfacing. Once the design is fitted, mark the seamlines carefully, and rip the test garment apart to use for cutting out. Mark the sections carefully to avoid cutting two right sleeves.

Hint: *Some home sewers prefer to try the design in corduroy or another fabric similar in weight and crispness to Ultrasuede. I prefer making a test garment.*

PATTERN PREPARATION

For plain seams, trim seam allowances to 3/8″.

For nonwoven lapped seams, trim away the seam allowances on the overlap; do not trim the underlap. Generally, lap seams front over back, right over left, and top over bottom. Garment sections that are normally topstitched—waistbands, cuffs, plackets, and pockets—lap the sections which they join.

Trim seam allowances at faced edges to 1/8″.

Trim away the excess tissue and make duplicate pattern pieces if you aren't making a test garment.

FABRIC PREPARATION

Ultrasuede has very little residual shrinkage and really doesn't need to be preshrunk. However, laundering before cutting makes the fabric softer, easier to sew, and reduces skipped stitches.

Before cutting, machine wash the fabric, the lining, and interfacing materials with a load of terry towels. Add fabric softener to the last rinse water. Tumble until almost dry on a medium setting. Remove promptly; hang it so it will dry wrinkle-free.

SEWING ULTRASUEDE

LAYOUT, CUTTING, AND MARKING

Use a nap layout. Cut the garment with the nap going up for a richer, darker look and down for a light shiny look; cut on the crossgrain for the shaded look of real suede.

Spread a single layer of fabric, wrong side up. Mark the wrong side of the fabric with arrows to indicate the nap. Then position the adjusted pattern on the fabric.

If the garment is asymmetrical, check to be sure all pattern pieces are wrong side up.

Before cutting, check once again to be sure all pieces are in position and you are cutting pairs—not two left sleeves.

Use weights to anchor the pattern pieces.

Using very sharp shears or a rotary cutter and mat, cut carefully to avoid zigs and zags. This is particularly important when using lapped seams and raw edge finishes.

When using lapped seams, mark notches with temporary marking pens instead of clips.

STITCHING TIPS

Make a test seam. Lengthen the stitch length to 2–2.5 mm (10 to 12 stitches per inch) and balance the tension. Begin with a new needle in a small size. Do not use leather machine needles.

Hint: *To prevent underlayer creep on plain seams, use an even-feed foot or roller foot. On lapped seams, baste with glue, double-stick tape, fusible web, or Wonder Under.*

Hold the fabric taut when stitching.

If skipped stitches are a problem even though you prewashed the fabric, use a needle lubricant; then try a larger size or a stretch needle.

Hint: *Smaller needles are best. The holes are easier to hide if you have to rip.*

SEAMS

Generally garments are assembled with plain seams, lapped seams, or a combination of the two, but this is only the beginning. The no-fray quality of synthetic suede allows you to create many variations of these two basic seams, as well as a variety of seams which can be used for nonwoven fabrics.

Lapped seams are suitable on sporty designs and work well on vertical seamlines, yokes, and dropped shoulders. However, many seamlines—side seams, sleeve underarms, the armholes for set-in sleeves, shoulder seams, trouser inseams, and trouser front and back seams—look better and are easier to sew with plain seams.

Wrong-side-out seams are particularly attractive when the wrong side is a different shade. Experiment with different seam widths, edgestitch and zigzag stitches.

BASTING

Many basting aids which can't be used on real suede, leather, or vinyl, including glue stick, fusible web, water-soluble double-stick tape, and pins, can be used on synthetic suedes.

Use fine pins for short, easy-to-stitch seams; and glue, fusible web, or Wonder Under for longer, intricate ones.

Hint: *Cut 1/4″-wide strips of Wonder Under. Wrong side up, apply a strip close to the edge of the overlap. Fuse baste the seams together; topstitch.*

Many seamsters like double-stick basting tape—I don't. It dries out, is hard to separate from the paper and can't be removed with steam on synthetic suedes.

DARTS

Darts are difficult to press so they will lie flat and smooth, but they can't always be avoided.

When using plain seams, use plain darts. First, fuse a circle of interfacing at the bust point; then stitch the dart, making several short stitches along the foldline at the point.

When using lapped seams, use lapped darts. Slash horizontal darts on the lower stitching line and vertical darts on the stitching line closest to the garment center.

RIPPING

Try to avoid ripping. If you use fine pins and needles, a few holes won't show, except when you hold the fabric up to the light. However, the holes do not close as they do on regular fabric; so, if you have to rip several times, the needle may chew the fabric badly.

When topstitching with a larger needle, take care to stitch it right the first time. Large needle holes will permanently mar the fabric.

To hide needle holes, steam the area and brush the nap lightly with a soft toothbrush or another piece of Ultrasuede®.

HEMS AND EDGE FINISHES

Garment hems and edges can be topstitched, fused, glued, hemmed by hand, faced, or left raw.

Topstitched Hems. Fold the hem in place and glue baste. Use regular thread to topstitch one or more rows.

Hint: *Fuse the hem before topstitching to give it more body.*

Hand Hemming. Machine stitch 1/4″ from the raw edge of the hem. Using a glover's or leather needle and a thimble, hem the garment with a loose blindstitch.

Hint: *Don't try to sew through the hem allowance; instead, pick up one of the machine stitches.*

Unfinished Hems. Hems left unfinished with a raw edge are frequently topstitched. These hems look better on crisper fabrics; on soft fabrics and certain colors, the material doesn't have enough body to hang neatly.

On some of the Norma Walters' jackets, raw edges are zigzagged (W,4–L,4) through a single layer.

Hint: *The fabric must be very firm for this to be successful. The fabric will stay crisper if it is dry cleaned.*

Faced Edges. Facings are used most often to finish shaped edges. If a facing pattern isn't provided and the facing won't be seen, trace the edge to be faced and cut the facing 5/8″ to 1″ wide. If the facing will be seen, cut as wide as necessary for an attractive finish.

Cut the garment and facing very carefully so the edges will match exactly.

Hint: *This is almost impossible, so I add a 1/8"
seam allowance. Match the raw edges; stitch a
fat 1/8" from the edge; and use your trimming
scissors to trim away the seam allowance.*

Hint: *Gingher's 5" trimmers are super sharp and just
the right size.*

SLEEVES

If the pattern has set-in sleeves with more than
1" ease in the sleeve caps, you may have to decrease
the ease.

Jacket sleeves look better with sleeve heads.

Hint: *On lined jackets, make sleeve heads from
polyester fleece; on unlined ones, make them
from strips of Ultrasuede.*

Sleeve Vents. Face shirt-sleeve vents with a raw
edge finish. Cut the vent facing 2" wide and 1"
longer than the slash. Wrong sides together, fuse
the facing in place; then, using a mat knife or trimming scissors, cut the vent. Edgestitch around the
vent and topstitch again 1/4" away (Fig. 5-2).

WS Sleeve

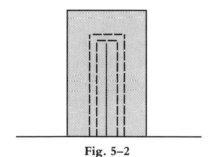

Fig. 5–2

Cuffs. This is the method I like for shirt cuffs;
it can also be used when the sleeves are made of
woven fabrics.

1. Cut the Ultrasuede cuffs with 3/8" seam allowances on all edges. Cut the cuff facing with the
same 3/8" allowance if the sleeve is Ultrasuede; if
the sleeve is another fabric, allow 5/8" for the seam
allowance which joins the sleeve.

2. Right sides up, join the sleeve and cuff facing.
Don't forget the seam allowances on the ends of
the cuff facing must extend 3/8" beyond the sleeve;
press.

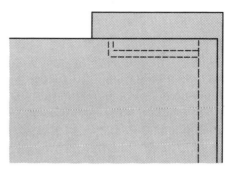

Fig. 5–3

3. With the cuff and cuff facing wrong sides
together, stitch a fat 3/8" from the raw edges to
join the cuff and facing; then topstitch the cuff to
the sleeve. Stitch all edges again 1/4" away.

4. Trim away the 3/8" seam allowances (Fig.
5-4).

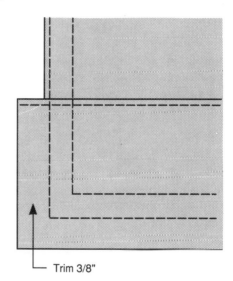

└─ Trim 3/8"

Fig. 5–4

CLOSURES

A variety of fasteners can be used on Ultrasuede:
bound buttonholes, button loops, ties, stitched-
slit, machine-stitched buttonholes, and invisible,
fly, lapped, slot, and exposed zippers.

Use small scraps to cover button forms for
woven, knit, and leather garments. To cover buttons easily, wet the Ultrasuede first.

Do not use Ultrasuede buttons on Ultrasuede
garments; they are a tell-tale sign of "homemade."

Bound Buttonholes. In addition to the techniques
for making bound buttonholes on nonwoven fab-

rics, the strip, modified strip and window methods also work very well.

Button Loops. Cut a 1"-wide strip of Ultrasuede the desired length. Fold in half lengthwise, wrong sides together; edgestitch close to the foldline. Trim close to the stitched line, and you're finished.

Stitched-Slash Buttonholes. Jane Whiteley makes a buttonhole sandwich when sewing synthetic suedes, to reinforce the buttonhole without the interfacing showing. Using silk thread, mark the buttonhole location on both the front of the fabric and the facing. To prevent the interfacing from showing at the slashed edge, cut out a narrow rectangle around the marked line. Since it has already been fused, use sharp scissors and steam to remove it.

Make the sandwich: with the wrong side up, rub glue stick over the location line; cover with a narrow (3/16"-wide) strip of fusible web, then a strip of polyester seam binding with the color matched to the garment fabric. Glue another strip of fusible web to the seam binding. Fuse all of the above to the wrong side of the facing.

Stitch around the buttonhole 1/16" from each side of the marked line. Slash the center carefully with a mat knife.

Zippers. To avoid an unpressed look when using slot and lapped zippers, apply a narrow strip of fusible web to the foldline before setting the zipper.

Lapped Zipper. When using a lapped zipper with plain seams, stitch the seam below it first. Then fuse the seam allowance of the overlap flat before setting the zipper. Be sure the fusible web touches the seamline so the finished placket will be flat.

Use this method for inserting a lapped zipper when the seam below it is lapped.

1. Cut the garment with a 5/8"-wide seam allowance on the underlap and no seam allowance on the overlap.

2. Mark the end of the zipper placket on both the overlap and underlap.

3. In the placket area, trim away 1/2" of the seam allowance on the underlap.

4. Since there is no seam allowance on the overlap, cut a 1"-wide Ultrasuede placket facing the length of the placket.

Hint: *Yes, you could leave the seam allowance on; fold it under at the placket; and trim it away below the placket. But the folded edge won't be as attractive with lapped seams.*

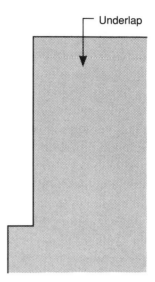

Fig. 5–5

5. Wrong sides together, match the raw edges of the placket facing and overlap; fuse or glue baste. Topstitch 1/16" from the edge, leaving long threads.

6. Right sides up, glue or baste the zipper to the underlap. Edgestitch, leaving long threads.

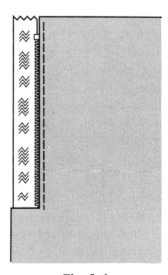

Fig. 5–6

7. Glue, baste, or fuse the lapped seam below the zipper together; edgestitch in place.

8. Close the zipper. Then, using hair-set tape or drafting tape, tape the placket closed. Turn the garment over, wrong side up; and glue or stitch the zipper to the seam allowance.

Hint: *When removing the tape, pull down with the nap.*

9. Right sides up, topstitch the zipper in place; continue stitching to the hem.

10. Pull the loose threads to the wrong side and secure with a tailor's knot.

Slot Zipper. For a smooth zipper placket in a plain seam, fuse the seam allowances flat before setting the zipper. Use the following method with lapped seams:

1. Trim away all seam allowances on both garment sections. Cut a 1 1/2″-wide strip of Ultrasuede® the length of the seam.

2. Wrong sides together, place one garment section on the strip so the strip extends 3/4″; fuse or glue baste. Edgestitch.

Fig. 5–7

3. Right sides up, place the other garment section on the strip so the edges of the skirt butt together, covering the strip; fuse or glue baste. Edgestitch the skirt to the strip.

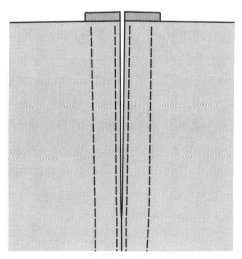

Fig. 5–8

4. Mark the end of the zipper placket and slash the strip to the marked point.

5. Glue baste the zipper in place and topstitch 1/4″ from the seamline; continue stitching to the hem of the garment.

Hint: *Fuse a 1/4″-wide strip of Wonder Under® to each side of the zipper tape; then fuse baste it to the seam allowances.*

NOTCHED COLLAR AND LAPELS

When making a jacket with a faced raw edge, the notched collar and lapels need extra attention so the lapels and the collar will roll nicely.

1. Cut the jacket fronts, the lapels, the collar, and undercollar with 3/8″ seam allowances.

2. On the jacket, measure the distance between the break point—the beginning of the lapel roll line and the top of the lapel; then measure from the roll line to the hem.

The lapel facing should be 1/4″ longer than the jacket above the roll line and 1/8″ shorter below the roll line.

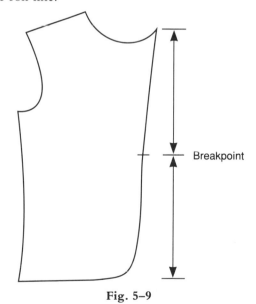

Fig. 5–9

3. Using a fusible interfacing, cut the interfacings for the collar and lapels.

Hint: *The collar can be interfaced in several different ways: only the upper collar, only the undercollar, or both the upper collar and undercollar. Consider the interfacing weight and the finished look before deciding.*

4. If the garment will have a raw edge finish, trim away the seam allowances on the interfacing; then trim away another 1/4″.

Hint: *An easy way to mark the trimming line is to machine stitch 3/4″ from the edge; then trim away the stitched line.*

If traditional seams are used at the edges, the interfacing can be sewn into the seamline without trimming.

5. Mark the lapel roll line on the interfacings; and cut on the marked lines so the lapel will roll properly. Fuse the interfacings to the garment.

Center a piece of twill tape over the roll line, pinning it at each end. Shorten the tape 1/4″ and hand sew it in place.

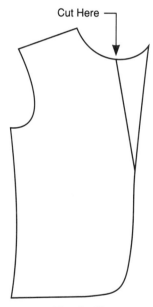

Fig. 5–10

6. Right sides together, join the upper collar and facings; then join the undercollar to the garment. Press the seam allowance open.

Hint: *Gail Shinn uses a press cloth dampened with a vinegar/water solution (2 tablespoons vinegar to 1 cup water) to get a good press.*

7. Wrong sides together, match and pin the collar/facing seamline to the undercollar/garment seamline.

Hint: *Use very fine needles in the well of the seam.*

Fold the facing and garment sections out of the way; using a zipper foot, machine baste the seam allowances together.

8. Place the jacket on a dress form or padded hanger. Match the lapel notches at the beginning of the roll line and pin the layers together. Smooth the collar and facings in place. Above the pin, the underlayer will probably show. Below the pin, pull the facing taut. Using hair clips, a washable glue stick, or fine needles, baste the edges together.

Now examine the collar carefully to determine if the collar/jacket seam will show when you stitch the full seam at the edge. Since you have a 3/8″ seam allowance at the edges, you can easily stitch a narrower seam if needed.

9. Stitch the edges together just inside the seamline about 3/8″ from the edge of the bottom layer. Stitch again 1/4″ away; trim close to the stitched line. Knot ends securely and hide the knot between the layers.

PATCH POCKETS

Ultrasuede patch pockets are very easy to sew.
1. Cut the pockets with a 1″ hem and 1/4″ seam allowances.
2. Fold the hem under (or wrong side out); and topstitch or fuse in place.
3. Right sides up and the pocket on top, topstitch around the pocket a fat 1/4″ from the edge. Topstitch again 1/4″ away.
4. Trim the pocket close to the stitched line.

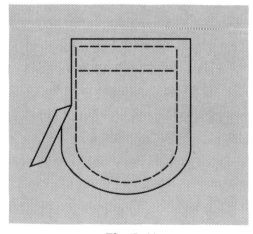

Fig. 5–11

PIPING AND BINDINGS

Ultrasuede pipings and bindings are particularly attractive on other fabrics. Cut strips for either on the crossgrain.

To apply bindings, use the applications for a regular bias-cut fabric binding or those for non-woven materials. (See chapter 23.)

SPECIAL EFFECTS

The special no-fray quality of Ultrasuede makes it ideal for special effects such as weaving, lattice work, cutwork, appliqués, and pinked edges.

I particularly like Ultrasuede for facings on un-lined woven and knit garments. The edges don't have to be finished and it keeps the garment from stretching out of shape. Make the facings narrow and, when possible, straight.

PRESSING

Ultrasuede is very sensitive to heat. To avoid permanently damaging the garment, do not use a regular iron on the face side without a pressing cloth. I prefer a steamer which has a plastic sole-plate and just steams.

Plain seams will not stay pressed open unless they are topstitched, glued, or fused. To fuse them open, insert 1/4"-wide strips of fusible web between the seam allowance and garment; cover with a damp press cloth, and press for ten seconds until the fusible melts.

Hint: *An easy way to cut the fusible into narrow strips is to roll a yard into a cigar-shaped cylinder. Cut the strips across one end.*

To set creases, dip your press cloth in a vinegar/water solution (2 tablespoons vinegar to 1 cup water).

GARMENT CARE

Ultrasuede can be machine washed and dried when the construction allows; however, most garments will retain their crispness better if dry-cleaned.

Do not overdry. Remove the garment from the dryer while it's still damp. Smooth the seamlines. Hang to finish drying.

Be careful when removing spots; it's easy to rub a hole in the Ultrasuede. To remove oil stains, dust with talcum powder. Repeat if needed.

Lightweight Synthetic Suedes

Soft synthetic suedes such as Facile, Suedemark, Lamous-Lite, and Caress, can be gathered, tucked, shirred, smocked, pleated, quilted, and draped into softer designs.

Generally, conventional seams and edge finishes are used for these fabrics, even though they have the same nonwoven, no-fray quality of Ultra-suede.

Fabric Characteristics
- Lightweight synthetic suedes have a nap.
- They are well suited for softly draped designs.

- They are nonwoven fabrics which do not fray.
- They are easily damaged by cigarette ashes and hot irons.
- When torn, they cannot be repaired inconspicuously.
- They are easily damaged by abrasion.
- They can be washed and dried by machine or they can be dry-cleaned by regular dry cleaning methods.
- Facile shrinks badly.

Fig. 5–12 *Lightweight synthetic suedes drape well and hang softly. (Photo courtesy of McCall Pattern Co.)*

SEWING CHECKLIST

Machine Needles: Universal-H point, Red Band or Yellow Band needles; sizes 65/9 or 80/12).

Machine Setting: Stitch length, 2.5 mm (10–12 stitches per inch).

Thread: Long-staple polyester and cotton-wrapped polyester.

Sewing Machine Equipment: Teflon-coated foot, even-feed foot, roller foot.

Notions: Lightweight zippers.

Layout: Nap.

Seams: Plain, topstitched, welt, double-welt.

Hems: Hand blindstitch, topstitched, fused.

Seam and Hem Finishes: Unfinished.

Interfacings: Lightweight fusibles.

Linings: Optional.

Fasteners: Machine-worked or bound buttonholes, button loops, lacings, slot or lapped zippers.

CHAPTER 6
Vinyls

This section focuses on nonwoven fabrics such as vinyl, clear film, vinyl-coated cotton, synthetic leather, resin-coated fabrics, plastic laminates, rubberized coatings. And even though most of them are not true vinyls, the term vinyl is used in this chapter to describe them as a group. Some popular synthetic leathers which should be treated like vinyls include Lamaire™, Soft Skin®, and Ultraleather, and Sofrina.

Films—nonwovens made from fiber solutions—are not true textiles since they contain no fibers or yarns. Used like traditional textiles, films, which are generally called vinyls, are made from chemical polymers such as vinyon and polyester.

During the manufacturing process, the film solution is shaped into sheets instead of being molded into filaments. The resulting products vary in weight, translucence, hand, pattern, color, durability, and quality. Vinyl fabrics are suitable for casual fashions, rainwear, accessories, patio furnishings, and sometimes high fashion.

Fabric Characteristics
- Vinyl does not fray.
- Vinyls have no grain; however, some stretch more in the width than in the length.
- Vinyls are waterproof.
- Unlike leather, vinyl is sold by the yard.
- Vinyls are easily marred by pins and machine stitching.
- Vinyl garments cannot be let out.
- Vinyl tears easily under stress.
- Vinyls stick to the presser foot and do not feed properly.
- Vinyl is easily damaged by a hot iron or direct sunlight.
- Some vinyls crease permanently when left folded.
- Sleeves and pant legs on vinyl garments "shrink" when worn.
- Vinyls are uncomfortable to wear in warm weather.
- Some vinyls crack, yellow, and get sticky with age or dry cleaning.
- Some vinyls stiffen when cold.
- Most vinyls are easy to clean with a damp cloth. Some cannot be dry-cleaned or washed.
- Many vinyls are stained easily by ink or lipstick.

PLANNING A GARMENT

PURCHASING THE FABRIC

Vinyls are available in clear films, knitted backs, and woven backs. They can be grained leather looks, printed animal designs, or vinyl-coated cottons.

Generally translucent films and vinyls with knitted backings are more flexible and easier to sew than transparent films and vinyls with woven backings. Select a soft film for travel organizers and a more durable, stiff film for hats and rain-coats.

When combining the vinyl with another fabric, check to be sure they have compatible care characteristics.

PVC fabrics retain their soft, supple quality for many years. Plastic-coated cottons deteriorate with heat and sun.

To avoid creasing the fabric, roll and store it on a cardboard tube.

DESIGN IDEAS AND PATTERN SELECTION

Frequently used for a variety of outerwear garments and accessories, vinyls are also suitable for trims and accents on tweeds, plaids, knits, furs, fake furs, and synthetic suedes.

Coats, jackets, skirts, pants, tote bags, hats, hand bags, belts, pillows, travel bags, and chair covers are just a few of the many items you can make in vinyl.

Generally, simple designs with a minimum of seams are easiest to sew. When duplicating real leather garments, select patterns with smaller garment sections; or piece large sections so they will look like leather skins.

Garments should have plenty of ease since these fabrics have no give. For best results, shape garments with seams instead of darts and avoid easing, gathers, pleats, and tucks. If necessary, convert easing to darts or to new seamlines.

Raglan sleeves are easier to sew than set-in sleeves.

SEWING CHECKLIST

Machine Needles: Universal-H point, stretch (HS), jeans (HJ) or leather (HLL or NTW) needles, 70/10 to 90/14, depending on fabric weight.

Machine Setting: Stitch length 2.5–3 mm (8–10 stitches per inch); topstitching 3–4 mm (6–8 stitches per inch).

Thread: Long-staple polyester, cotton-wrapped polyester, monofilament nylon.

Topstitching: Regular thread, polyester topstitching thread.

Hand Sewing Needles: Sharps or crewels; sizes 7 to 9.

Sewing Machine Equipment: Roller, Teflon, or leather foot.

Equipment and Supplies: Rotary cutter and mat, spring hair clips or paper clips, clapper or rubber mallet, silver knives or ashtrays, single-edged razor blade or mat knife, smooth tracing wheel, wallpaper roller, drafting tape, double-stick basting tape, water-soluble felt-tip pens, washable glue stick, permanent glue, reinforcement buttons, silicone spray, talcum powder or cornstarch, cardboard tube, eyelets.

Layout: Single layer, right side up; double layer, wrong sides together.

Marking Techniques: Clips, soap sliver, chalk, water-soluble felt-tip pen, smooth tracing wheel and tracing carbon.

Seams: Plain, topstitched, welt, double-welt, tucked, lapped, nonwoven flat-fell, double-stitched, decorative bound, tissue-stitched, taped.

Hems: Glued, topstitched, blind-stitched.

Edge Finishes: Fabric or ribbon facings, bindings, ribbings, bands.

Interfacings: Generally not used.

Linings: Optional.

Closures: Buttons and buttonholes, button loops, snaps, zippers, eyelets or hooks and lacings, hook and loop tape.

Pockets: All types.

Garment Care: Varies with the fabric—washable, regular dry cleaning methods, wipe clean.

Avoid kimono sleeves even though they are easy to sew; the fabric is uncomfortable to wear.

Clear vinyl vests and raincoats are fun garments on which children can display their decal collections.

PREPARING THE PATTERN

Make all pattern adjustments before cutting. For intricate designs, use nonwoven interfacing fabric to make a test garment.

When using set-in sleeves, reduce the ease in the sleeve cap. Reshape sharp corners so they will be attractive on the finished garment.

SEWING VINYL

For additional sewing information, see Leather and Suede.

LAYOUT AND CUTTING

Spread the fabric in a single layer, right side up. When cutting double, spread the fabric wrong sides together.

Vinyls have no grain; however, when bonded to fabrics, use the grain of the fabric as a guide. Vinyls with knit backings have more stretch in the crossgrain.

When cutting films, the grainline can be disregarded. When cutting vinyls which have some stretch across the width, the pattern pieces can be tilted off-grain if it doesn't affect the placement of the fabric motifs.

Use weights or tapes to hold the pattern in place. If pins must be used, place them in the seam allowances.

Cut with sharp shears or a rotary cutter.

STITCHING TIPS

Make a test seam, using a Universal-H point needle (size 80/12) and a stitch length of 2–3 mm (8–10 stitches per inch).

If skipped stitches are a problem, use a larger size needle. If they persist, experiment with leather needles.

Decrease the pressure or tissue-stitch seams if the feed dogs leave tracks.

If the vinyl sticks to the bottom of the presser foot, change to a roller, Teflon, or leather foot, dust the vinyl with talcum or cornstarch, or stitch with tissue paper between the foot and fabric.

Hint: *Coat the bottom of your regular presser foot with silicone spray or needle lubricant for easier stitching. Let it dry before stitching.*

Although other basting techniques—spring hair clips and tape—are preferred, pin basting can be used if the pins are placed within the seam allowances.

When stitching clear films, use transparent, monofilament or invisible nylon thread.

Generally, it's best not to backstitch; however, if you can backstitch so the needle penetrates the previously stitched holes and doesn't make new ones, backstitching is appropriate.

Avoid ripping and restitching.

When topstitching, lengthen the stitch to 3–4 mm (6–8 stitches per inch).

MARKING

Most matchpoints can be marked with small clips.

Mark the wrong side of vinyl-coated fabrics with a soap sliver or chalk. Mark clear films and the right side of vinyl-coated fabrics with a water-soluble felt-tip pen.

Hint: *Test before marking with pens to be sure the mark won't be permanent.*

Although smooth tracing wheels can be used, they are best avoided; and serrated tracing wheels will leave permanent tracks.

Mark intricate topstitching patterns with drafting tape or water-soluble felt-tip pens.

SEAMS AND DARTS

Topstitch seams and darts so they will lie flat. When stitching darts, stitch the point with three or four short stitches on the fold. Tie the threads.

Trim seams and darts on films to 1/8"; or, if the seams are topstitched, trim close to the stitched line.

HEMS

To secure hems, topstitch or use a permanent fabric glue.

A few leather-look vinyls can be blindstitched by hand. Machine stitch 1/4″ from the raw edge. Hem the garment, catching the stitched line. Make the stitches carefully, so they won't show on the outside of the garment.

Since vinyls don't ravel, hems can be eliminated and edges left raw; but this rarely gives a professional finish.

EDGE FINISHES

Bindings of contrast vinyls, bias fabric, purchased bias tape, and ribbons are suitable edge finishes.

Bands and ribbings are attractive on some designs.

Some facings—neckline and arms—can be cut narrower to reduce bulk.

When using fitted facings, topstitch garment edges so they will remain flat.

Replace fitted facings with narrow hems on straight and almost straight edges.

CLOSURES

A variety of buttonholes are suitable for vinyls—machine-stitched, stitched-slash, leather, traditional bound, and nonwoven bound.

Use nonwoven interfacings to interface buttonhole areas except on clear films. Mark buttonhole locations with drafting tape.

Lengthen the stitch for machine-stitched buttonholes. Use drafting tape to baste zippers in place.

COLLARS

Self-finished collars are more attractive and more comfortable to wear than those finished with neckline facings.

On Peter Pan style collars, pink the seam allowances for less bulk.

VENTS

For greater comfort, vent vinyl garments with several eyelets or grommets at the top of the underarm seam.

Fig. 6–1 *This leather lookalike is the perfect choice for a rainy day. (Photo courtesy of Burda Pattern Co.)*

POCKETS

Use drafting tape to hold patch pockets in place for stitching.

WAISTBANDS

Interfacings can be eliminated in most vinyl waistbands when the band is cut on the lengthwise grain.

For improved comfort, use ribbon for waistbands; or face vinyl bands with ribbon.

110

TRIMS

When trimming traditional fabrics, consider using vinyl beltings and decorative vinyls in narrow widths, as well as using vinyl yardage.

To trim curved edges, cut the vinyl the desired shape; it cannot be pressed to shape.

LININGS

Coats and jackets are more comfortable when lined.

Select a wrinkle-resistant fabric; if the garment requires dry-cleaning or cannot be cleaned, choose a dark-colored fabric. If the vinyl is washable, select a washable, permanent-press fabric.

When machine stitching the lining to the vinyl facings, stitch with the lining fabric on top.

PRESSING

Generally, pressing with an iron is best avoided. However, if you must, set the iron on cool and use a press cloth.

Wrong side up, press seams open with the scissor handles or a wallpaper roller; then, right side up, press the seamline.

Topstitch seams so they will stay open.

GARMENT CARE

Check the fabric care characteristics when purchasing the fabric. Some vinyls cannot be laundered or dry-cleaned. Clear, unsupported vinyls can be wiped with a damp cloth and won't need cleaning.

Avoid hot surfaces—radiators, heaters, irons, light bulbs, and cigarettes—which will melt the fabric. Do not leave garments in hot trunks or garages.

When storing vinyl garments, remember that vinyl is a scavenger and will absorb color from newspapers, magazines, and other fabrics.

Ballpoint ink is very difficult to remove from vinyls without damaging the fabric.

CHAPTER 7
Fur

Real fur is an animal skin with the hair still attached; it is not a fabric. All furs have two or more parts: the skin, soft underfur, stiffer overfur, and the guard hair. Tanned and processed to make it soft and supple, fur can be sheared, bleached, dyed, tipped, stenciled, let out, or curled to make it more interesting and more fashionable.

The Fur Family

Astrakhan is a curly fur from the karakul sheep.

Beaver is a warm, soft, and hard-wearing fur. It may be sheared or natural. Redness is undesirable. It is used for jackets, coats, and trims.

Broadtail is soft, fine fur made from unborn, stillborn, or very young lambs of karakul sheep. Used primarily for evening wear, jackets and coats, it is very expensive. In the Soviet Union sheep are killed for their lambs; in America, very young lambs are used.

Calf is a coarse, flat fur with a sheen. It is frequently dyed to imitate other animals.

Chinchilla is a warm, bluish gray fur from the chinchilla, a small rodent. It doesn't wear well and is used for trims and evening wear.

Ermine is a thick, lustrous fur from the weasel family. Often used for evening wear, it doesn't wear well. The winter coat is white, while the summer coat is golden brown. Yellowing whites are undesirable.

Fox is long-haired fur from one of several different foxes. The durability and price vary. Look for thick underfur and silky guard hairs and check for rips and tears. It is used for jackets, coats, and trims.

Leopard is buff-colored fur with black markings. Since it was placed on the endangered species list, it is illegal to sell leopard skins, even if they are secondhand.

Lynx is long-haired fur from the wildcat. Used for coats, jackets, and trims; it is expensive and does not wear well.

Marten is a warm, soft, thick fur. It is frequently available in resale stores, complete with head, eyes and a mouth that clips. It is used for coats, jackets and trims.

Mink is a warm, popular fur with a dark center back stripe, called the grotzen. It should have lustrous guard hairs and dense underfur. Redness is undesirable. It is used for coats, jackets, trims, linings, boas, hats, muffs, stoles, capes.

Mouton is soft, velvety fur made from sheared sheepskin. It is dyed a variety of colors and used for jackets and trims.

Muskrat, also known as the "poor woman's mink," is dyed to look like many other furs.

Fig. 7–1 *From Christian Dior Haute Couture Fall/Winter 1987/1988 Collection, this sensational black chiffon is trimmed with mink bands. (Photo courtesy of Christian Dior.)*

Nutria is South American beaver. It is inexpensive and used for linings and reversible garments.

Ocelot is a fur similar to leopard. Like leopard, it is illegal to sell it.

Opossum is an interesting fur frequently used for sport garments.

Otter is a short, thick, very durable, lustrous brown fur. Used for jackets, coats, and trims, it wears well.

Persian Lamb is soft, curly fur from young karakul lambs. Same as astrakhan.

Rabbit is a popular, inexpensive fur for children's wear. It sheds and is not very durable.

Raccoon is long-haired, warm fur used primarily for trims, linings, jackets, and coats.

Sable is a dense, dark fur from the weasel family. It is very expensive and used for coats, jackets, and trims.

Seal is a warm, sheared fur and always dyed.

Currently, it is very unpopular because of unfavorable publicity about the hunting of the Newfoundland harp seal, although this seal was never used by the American fur industry. Seal is used for jackets and coats.

Shearling is a warm, reversible fur. The leather side is sometimes painted, beaded, or embroidered. Either side can be worn next to the skin. It is used for casual coats and jackets. (See Chapter 4.)

Squirrel is a soft, silky fur used for coats, jackets, linings and children's wear.

TERMS USED IN THE FUR INDUSTRY

Assembled Fur: Large piece of fur made of many small pieces.

Brush: Tail of fox, coyote, or wolf.

Canvas: Test garment made from the pattern to check the fit.

Damaging: Repairing a damaged area by cutting and stitching.

MMBA: Trademark of the Mutation Mink Breeders Association to identify their pelts.

Glazing: Process for adding luster to new or used furs.

GLMA: The Great Lakes Mink Association. Sells only dark-colored pelts.

Grotzen: Dark stripe in center back of a pelt.

Guard Hairs: Long, lustrous surface hair, mixed in with the overfur.

Letting Out: Process of cutting and sewing small sections together to make the pelt longer or wider.

Nailing: Process of shaping fur sections by dampening the skin side and nailing the fur to a wooden surface.

Overfur: Stiff outer covering which protects the underfur.

Plate: Large rectangular piece of fur made by sewing small pieces together.

Reinforcing: Use of tapes and cloth to add strength to fur garments.

Skin on Skin: Method of sewing skins together so the head of one pelt joins the tail of the next pelt.

Shearing: Method of reducing the length of the fur.

Sheen: Lustrous surface.

Sweep: Lower edge of the garment.

Taping: Method for reinforcing edges and staying large areas.

Underfur: Short, thick layer of fur next to the skin.

Special Considerations
- Fur is easy to sew.
- Most mistakes made in cutting can be corrected easily.

SEWING CHECKLIST

Machine Needles: Leather point (HLL or NTW), Red Band, or jeans (HJ) needles, 80/12 to 100/16.

Thread: Long-staple polyester, waxed polyester thread, glazed thread.

Hand Sewing Needles: Glover's and crewel needles.

Equipment and Supplies: Single-edged razor blade, mat knife, or Olfa touch knife, tweezers, staple gun, hammer, tacks, and long T glass-headed pins, thimble, wire dog brush or comb, wallpaper roller, bobby pins or spring hair clips, sponge, push pins, needle lubricant, twill tape, nylon surgical fabric tape, covered hooks and eyes, wadding or polyester fleece, lamb's wool, Seam Seal.

Layout: Nap, single layer, wrong sides up.

Marking Techniques: Chalk, pins, ballpoint, and temporary marking pens.

Seams: Fur, plain/fur, taped.

Hems: Taped.

Edge Finishes: Bands of fabric, leather, or synthetic suedes, ribbings, bindings.

Interfacing: Usually.

Underlining: Muslin, broadcloth, cotton flannel, or silk, depending on condition and fragility of fur.

Lining: Usually.

- Fur has a nap.
- Cut fur sheds badly.
- Fur is a skin which may be difficult to penetrate with regular needles.
- Fur can be damaged by ripped seams.
- Fur is bulky.
- Fur pelts and old garments are uneven in shape.
- All furs oxidize when exposed to light; it is more noticeable on white and light-colored furs which tend to yellow.

PLANNING A GARMENT

PURCHASING THE FUR

There are four sources of fur: fur tails, new pelts, fur plates, and used or secondhand fur garments.

Secondhand garments are the least expensive; however, they can only be used to make garments which are smaller than the original. For a larger garment, you can combine the fur with leather, suede, synthetic suede, or other fur.

Used furs are most readily available to home sewers and can be found in a variety of places—resale shops, garage sales, flea markets, old friends' closets, auctions, and vintage clothing stores.

Generally, new pelts are the most expensive and most difficult to prepare. Rabbit pelts are the exception. They are inexpensive and easy to use.

Fur tails are relatively inexpensive but their use is limited.

Fur plates are available from some furriers; they can be handled like fake-fur fabric. (See Chapter 14.) Although they vary in price, they are usually more expensive than used garments. Since they do not require as much preparation as fur from a used garment, they are easier to use. Generally composed of scraps, paws, bellies, and gills, furriers use plates for less expensive designs.

When purchasing a used fur, your primary concern is how much of the fur can be reused and how much must be discarded. Generally, you will have less waste and find that flat, solid colors such as Persian lamb and some seals are easier to sew than mink and fox.

Examine the overall appearance of the fur carefully. If the fur is badly worn with broken guard hairs and shedding or looks reddish or yellowish, there is little you can do with it except make a fur blanket for a little girl's doll.

If the overall appearance looks good, pull the fur. If it pulls away from the skin, it has dried out. Next, fold it. It should be soft and flexible. If it isn't or if it makes a crackling sound, its use is very limited. Assuming the fur looks good and the price is right, it might work well for something fun and outlandish that you'll only wear a few times. Consider a fur sweatshirt, tee top, muff, or use it for appliqués.

If you are considering the fur for better garments, examine the leather side. If it has dried out or if it tears when you pull on it, its use is limited.

Look for holes and splits on the leather side. Some can be repaired, while others are an indication that the fur is close to falling apart.

If the leather side of the fur passes, look at the fur itself again. Check for worn spots, discolorations, and holes. Some sections can be patched; others will have to be discarded.

Look at the amount of usable fur one more time. Is there enough to make the design you are planning? Is there enough if you use another fabric with the fur? Is there enough fur to make anything?

Remember, when purchasing a used fur for sewing, your criteria isn't exactly the same as when you purchase a secondhand fur to wear "as is" next winter. For example, a badly worn Persian lamb coat priced at $25 might be a good investment if there is enough usable fur for a vest, collar, handbag, hat, or appliqués; but it would be a bad investment if you were going to wear it.

DESIGN IDEAS AND PATTERN SELECTION

Fur can be made into a variety of garments, casual or elegant: cardigans, ski jackets, blousons, ponchos, vests, capes, linings, skirts, and even sweatshirts.

It can have set-in sleeves, raglan sleeves, knitted or synthetic suede sleeves. It can be alternated with bands of leather or suede or trimmed with knitted bands.

Fur will add pounds to any figure and only the very thin should consider double-breasted designs.

Consider your sewing skills when selecting a pattern. It is almost impossible to make a mistake when sewing fur. Simple designs with minimum seaming are quicker and easier to make, but a complex design with subtle seaming might be more fun.

Try to avoid details such as patch pockets and buttonholes, which will show wear before other areas of the garment.

If you're not ready to tackle a complete garment, start with a fur lining or trim—bands, cuffs, collar. Fur pillows and fashion accessories are also easy and quick.

PATTERN PREPARATION

Eliminate nonfitting seams wherever possible. Seams at the side, center back, front/facing, and raglan sleeve center are just a few seams which can be eliminated.

To perfect the fit, make a test garment using a heavy nonwoven interfacing. Consider replacing facings with an edge-to-edge lining.

Make and mark all alterations on the test garment, then carefully rip it apart to use when cutting out. Transfer all matchpoints to the seamline; and trim seam allowances and dart underlays to 1/8".

If you didn't make a test garment, cut *duplicate* pattern pieces.

If you are using an edge-to-edge lining, pin the facing/lining seamline together to make a new lining pattern.

Trim seam allowances to 1/8" if you're using fur seams (see Seams, Chapter 21).

Trim hem allowances to 1/2" or 1".

Indicate the hair direction on the pattern pieces. It usually runs down, but it can be horizontal or diagonal if it enhances the design.

On collars, add a seam at the center back. The hair can run away from the center back, toward it, or down to the floor.

PREPARING THE FUR

Remove the lining, interfacing, and padding. It may not be usable, but don't discard it yet—it may provide some hints for the new construction. To avoid damaging the fur, clip the threads; do not tear the lining out.

To clean the fur, wipe the fur with a sponge dipped in a 50/50 vinegar and water solution. Hang the fur outside to dry and air. Test first to be sure the fur is colorfast. When the fur is dry, brush carefully with an old wig brush or a dog comb or

115

brush. Touch up any discolored fur with a permanent felt-tip marker.

Compare the old and new designs and begin planning the layout.

Remove the sleeves and rip the shoulder seams. Rip the garment just enough so it will lie flat.

Sew the pocket openings together.

Examine the fur again; and, with the layout in mind, replace or repair worn areas as needed.

Hint: *Some sewers prefer to wait to patch and repair until the new garment is cut. This saves patching sections you won't need.*

Patches are easy to hide if they match the larger piece in coloring, pattern, density, texture, nap, and guard hairs.

Examine the seaming on the garment. On long-hair furs, seams are less conspicuous than on short-hair furs. On straight-hair furs, straight vertical seams are less conspicuous than straight horizontal seams. Therefore, most vertical seams are straight, while horizontal seams zigzag. Using the garment seams as a guide, the least noticeable patches are diamond or irregularly shaped (Fig. 7.2); avoid rounded and rectangular patches.

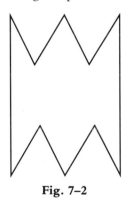

Fig. 7–2

On the fur side, use pins to mark the worn area. Turn the fur over; and using a mat knife, cut out the worn section.

Trace the worn section to make a paper pattern for the new patch. Label the patch pattern to indicate the skin side and the direction of the fur. Using the paper pattern, cut a new patch from a fur scrap.

Use hair-set tape to baste the patch into position. Using a glover's needle, waxed thread, and a whipping stitch, sew the patch in place. Flatten the seams with the scissor handles. Or iron the leather side

carefully with a cool iron. If the iron is too hot to touch with your finger, it will cause the leather to shrivel.

When there are several small areas to be patched, replace the whole section with one large patch.

After patching, place the dry fur on a piece of plywood, fur side down. Stretch the fur; cover the edges with cardboard strips; then, using small upholstery tacks or a staple gun, secure the edges. Sponge the leather side of the patched area with warm water; cover with a thin piece of cardboard to hold the fur flat. Use push pins to secure the cardboard; leave the fur to dry overnight or use a hair dryer to speed the process.

Sewing Fur

LAYOUT AND MARKING

Lay out the fur in a single layer, right side up; and study the fur. Look for markings which need to be matched, differences in the fur density, patterning, and guard hairs. (The guard hair lengths are shorter near the neck and longer near the tail.)

If you're making a jacket from a coat, match the center backs and work around to the front. Lay the new sleeves on the original sleeves.

Turn the fur over, wrong side up; and use a soap sliver to mark the direction and patterning on the skin side.

Use weights or tape to anchor the pattern pieces. Trace around the pattern pieces and mark all matchpoints with chalk, a ballpoint pen, or temporary marking pen.

If the fur is too complicated to match from the skin side, lay out the pattern on the fur side. If the original fur has a vertical pattern, add seams at the underarm, if needed to keep the design on the fur parallel to the front edges. The finished edges should be on a dark stripe. Mark the corner of every pattern piece with a glass-headed pin. Remove the pattern; turn the fur over; reposition the pattern; aligning the pins and corners; trace around the pattern.

CUTTING

Double check the layout to be sure you have a pair of everything.

Using a single-edged razor blade, mat knife, or Olfa touch knife, carefully cut just the skin of the fur.

BASTING

It is a little late to worry about the fit; but it's better now than later. To try on the garment before stitching, "baste" the seams together with 1"-wide drafting tape.

Wrong sides up, butt the edges together; then cover them with the tape. Try the garment on very carefully. After fitting, remove the tape before stitching.

STITCHING TIPS

Make several test seams. Begin with a new, small leather needle or a Red Band size 80/12 or 90/14. Set the stitch for W,4–L,2, a normal to light pressure, and a looser tension. Stitch, with the fur edges centered under the foot, so that the needle swings off the fur. Hold the fur taut when stitching. Stitch with the pile.

Hint: *After stitching, spread the fur wrong side up. Using the scissor handles, press the seam so it lies flat.*

If skipped stitches are a problem, use a larger or different kind of needle.

To avoid damaging the fur, do not backstitch, and stitch it right the first time. If you have to rip and stitch again, the leather may tear.

SEAMS

Furriers have a special machine which makes a tiny seam similar to the rolled or merrow edging on a serger. You can stitch your garment by hand, with a zigzag machine, or with a serger.

To avoid stretching the fur leather out of shape, tape all edges and seamlines with fabric surgical tape or twill tape. Place the tape on the skin side of one edge before stitching the seam.

Hint: *Fabric surgical tape is a good substitute for the furrier's cold tape. Available at drugstores, it has a silky fabric top. When using twill tape, "baste" it in place with a glue stick.*

Baste fur seams with bobby pins, spring hair clips, clothespins, or long, glass-headed pins.

Hint: *To remove pins easily, set them with the heads toward raw edge. Try to avoid stitching over them.*

When basting and stitching, push the pile away from the raw edge toward the body of the garment with the blades of your shears or the back of tweezers.

Hand Sewn Seams. Using a glover's needle, sew the edges together with a small overcasting stitch.

Hint: *If the thread is not waxed or glazed, wax it with beeswax; then press the thread so the wax penetrates it.*

Open the seam flat, skin side up, and press the seam with the handles of your shears or a wallpaper roller. Brush the seam on the right side with a wire dog brush.

Machine Stitched Seam. Set the machine to zigzag (W,4–L,2). Position the seam so the raw edges are in the center of the presser foot. Stitch, allowing the needle to swing off the edge. Press and brush.

Hint: *To control the fur when stitching, use a damp sponge to brush it away from the cut edges.*

EDGE FINISHES

To reduce wear and to create a soft roll line at the edges, interface the edges with polyester fleece or cotton wadding.

Sew 1/2"- to 1"-wide twill tape to all unfaced edges. Place the tape on the fur side, matching the edge of the tape to the edge of the fur. By hand or machine, overcast or zigzag the tape to the fur.

Loosely sew a 1"- to 1-1/2"-wide strip of wadding or polyester fleece to the leather side of the fur at each unfaced edge. Fold the twill tape to the wrong side of the garment, then catchstitch it to the padding, underlining, or skin to prevent sharp creases and "grinning"—the ability to see the leather on the fur side.

If the edge is a fold with a cut-on facing, center the padding strip over the foldline; tack the strip in place before turning the facing to the wrong side.

UNDERLININGS AND INTERFACINGS

Most garments made from used skins wear better if they are underlined. Choose a firmly woven material like broadcloth or muslin to back the fur sections.

Using a glover's needle and a large diagonal stitch, tack the underlining to the back of each section.

Once underlined, many furs do not need to be interfaced. But, if they do, use hair canvas or another sew-in interfacing in a weight appropriate for the fur.

Underlinings also eliminate the need to reinforce the backs of coats and jackets with twill tape.

LININGS

Purchase the best quality lining you can afford. An inexpensive lining in a fur garment is a telltale sign of a homemade garment.

Hint: *Most furriers will sell you a length of lining fabric.*

Sew the lining to the twill tape at the garment edges. To keep linings and facings from rolling to the right side, understitch by hand.

For extra warmth, underline the fur with cotton flannel.

CLOSURES

The simplest closure is to wrap the garment and belt it with a pretty leather belt. Leather or cord button loops, faced and inseam buttonholes, and covered hooks and eyes are also attractive.

Zippers work well when used with short-haired furs; they tend to catch long-haired furs.

If you must use a zipper on long-haired furs, sew the zipper to a band of leather or synthetic suede instead of directly to the fur.

POCKETS

Generally inseam and welt pockets are best, while patch and slot pockets should be avoided; however, flat furs like Persian lamb look particularly attractive with leather-trimmed slot pockets.

For warm, comfortable inseam pockets, use cotton velveteen for the pocket sacks.

To reduce wear at the pocket opening, sew a 1"-to 1-1/2"-wide strip of wadding or polyester fleece to the leather side of the fur.

To avoid tearing when pockets are used, reinforce the corners with twill tape.

COLLARS

Many suit and jacket designs will be enhanced by a fur collar.

1. Allow 1/4" seam allowances on all edges.

2. Tape the edges of the collar. Place the twill tape on the right side of the fur, matching the raw edges; use a small overcast stitch to secure it.

3. For a soft collar, underline the collar with a piece of muslin and a piece of cotton wadding, polyester fleece, lamb's wool, Armo wool or cotton flannel.

Sew the muslin and padding together loosely; then, with the padding next to the collar, use a loose diagonal stitch to sew the muslin/padding layer to the wrong side of the collar.

4. Fold the twill tape to the wrong side; baste it to the muslin.

5. Finish the collar by felling or slipstitching a fabric undercollar in place.

6. Tack the fur collar onto the neckline by hand; or, if you plan to use the same collar on several garments, sew a strip of snaps on the collar facing. Sew corresponding strips to each garment on which you will wear the collar.

FUR LININGS

For coats and jackets with fur linings, choose a loose-fitting design with a raglan sleeve. Since a fur lining is bulky, purchase a pattern one size larger than normal.

Many ready-made coats have an edge-to-edge lining so the fur peeks out at the opening, but a traditional lining with a facing works equally well.

Make the coat according to the directions. Cut the lining sleeves from a regular or quilted lining fabric. Cut the lining front and back from the fur. Eliminate the pleat at the center back and extend the fronts to the edge for an edge-to-edge lining. Assemble the lining and hand sew it to the garment.

TRIMS

Flat fur appliqués add a look of luxury to any plain garment. Givenchy used paisley shapes of Persian lamb to embellish suede jackets and vests one season. These appliqués would be equally attractive on grey wool flannel.

Cut the fur the desired shape and glue baste to the garment. Straight stitch around the appliqué; then cover the raw edge with a pretty cord or braid. Zigzag with matching or contrasting thread over the cord to secure it. This is called couching.

Hint: *Make a small hole with an awl so the ends of the braid can be hidden on the underside.*

GARMENT CARE

Extend the life of your fur with proper care.

Hang the fur on a well-padded hanger and store in a bag of cedar shavings. Don't store it in a plastic bag. To prevent drying, store the fur in a cool closet or fur vault. Don't expose it to direct sunlight or fluorescent lights for long periods.

Allow a wet garment to dry thoroughly away from direct heat. Then shake firmly. If the garment gets completely saturated, take it to a furrier immediately.

Have your fur cleaned periodically by a professional fur cleaner or furrier.

Furs are susceptible to moths, but mothproofing agents will damage the fur if they are in direct contact with them. Put them in a small muslin bag and hang it over the hanger.

Don't pin things to the fur or wear heavy jewelry or chunky bracelets which will cause the fur to wear. Avoid shoulder strap bags, which break and wear the fur.

Avoid spraying the fur with perfume or hair spray. When sitting or driving, unfasten the garment to reduce strain at the seamlines.

CHAPTER 8
Feathers

Lightweight feathers from the marabou and ostrich are sold by the string or boa. Frequently used by designers for linings and full garments, the strips are then hand sewn to a base garment made of a regular fabric and a lining is attached to cover the stitches.

Fabric Characteristics

- Feather strips are very narrow and must be sewn to a backing fabric for linings and full-garment construction.
- Marabou and ostrich feathers are easy to sew.

PLANNING A GARMENT

PURCHASING THE MARABOU AND BASE FABRIC

The feathers are woven onto a cordlike base and sold in two-yard strips which are only 4″ to 5″ wide.

Examine the strings carefully to be sure the feathers are not dried out and breaking or unravelling at the cord base.

Consider the placement design and the density of the coverage when estimating the number of strips needed.

Hint: *Pin the vertical seamlines of the paper pattern together; then draw the design on it with an air-erasable pen. Generally, the feathers are most attractive if spaced 2″ to 3″ apart. Measure the drawn lines. To estimate the number of strips needed, divide that measurement by 72″ (two yards—the length of each strip); and add one extra strip.*

BASE AND LINING FABRICS

Select a fabric for the base which is firmly woven with enough body to support the feather strips. Lightweight fabric, such as taffeta, satin-back crepe, China silk, crepe de chine, organza, chiffon, or wool jersey are best if you want to look and feel as if you're wearing a cloud. The same fabric can be used for the lining.

DESIGN IDEAS AND PATTERNS

For a complete marabou garment, select a simple style to showcase the marabou. Stoles, cocoon wraps, and collarless cardigan jackets and coats are good choices.

Marabou linings for jackets and coats are not only elegant, but surprisingly warm. If that's too flamboyant for you or your budget, use feather strips to trim the neckline and/or hemlines or outline the garment with feathers. The latter suggestion is particularly appropriate for the larger ostrich feathers.

Fig. 8–1 *Red and black strips of marabou form a zebra design on this stunning jacket. (Photo courtesy of Christian Dior Boutique, Fall/Winter 1988/1989.)*

PATTERN PREPARATION

Select a pattern with an edge-to-edge lining or make your own lining pattern by adding 5/8″ seam allowances to edges of all garment sections—front, neckline, lower edge, and sleeve wrists.

Adjust the pattern before cutting.

SEWING A JACKET

1. Using the corrected pattern pieces, cut all major pieces—the fronts, back, and sleeves—from both the base fabric and the lining.

2. Assemble and press the jacket; repeat for the lining; but do not join the two together.

3. On the jacket, fold the seam allowance at all edges to the inside and hand baste.

4. Pin the feather cord, not the feathers, to the jacket, spacing the strips 2″ to 4″ apart.

5. Using a small overcasting stitch, hand sew the feather cord to the garment. Secure the cord ends firmly so they won't stick into the fabric or scratch you.

Hint: *For best results when applying vertical strips, work around the garment from center front to center back so both fronts will match.*

If you haven't decided how the feathers will be arranged on the jacket, put the jacket on a hanger or dress form and experiment with the feather strips to see whether they will look better placed horizontally or vertically.

The strips can outline the lines of the jacket or create a pattern of their own. For example, raglan sleeves can be covered to accentuate the raglan design or they can be covered so they look like set-in sleeves.

6. Attach the lining to the garment. Wrong sides together, pin and hand sew the shoulder seams of the lining and garment together. This can be done in either of two ways: by tacking the seam allowances together between the two layers or by hand sewing loosely in the wells of the seamlines.

Repeat for the side seams.

7. Carefully pin the layers together, working from the center to the edges. Turn under the seam allowances at the edges so they match the garment; pin. Slipstitch the garment and lining together.

GARMENT CARE

If feathers droop or become flattened, steam generously to rejuvenate them.

Dry-clean when soiled.

Do not store feathers in plastic bags.

SEWING CHECKLIST

Machine Needles: Universal-H or Red Band needles; sizes 60/8 or 70/10.

Machine Setting: Stitch length, 2–2.5 mm (12–15 stitches per inch), tension, loosely balanced.

Thread: Extra-fine cotton-wrapped polyester or long-staple polyester (100/3).

Hand Sewing Needles: Sizes 8 to 10.

Seams: Plain.

Lining: Lightweight.

Interfacing and Underlining: Optional.

PART TWO

Fabric Structure

CHAPTER 9
Woven Fabrics

Plain-Weave Fabrics

The plain weave is the simplest and most popular weave. This section focuses on the easy-to-sew fabrics such as chambray, broadcloth, percale, muslin, cotton crepe, calico, and challis, as well as bed sheets.

Compared to plain-weave fabrics, basket-weave fabrics drape better; but they are not as durable because of the loose weave and low-twist and tensile strength of the yarns.

Compared to twill weaves, plain-weave fabrics are lighter weight and print better; they are not as strong or firm and do not drape as well. They ravel less, wrinkle more, and are less absorbent than twill and satin-weaves.

When sewing plain-weave fabrics, review other appropriate sections such as Plaids; Stripes; Pile Fabrics; Ribbed Fabrics; Taffeta; Transparent Fabrics; Soft, Lightweight Silks; Soft, Lightweight Polyesters; Lightweight Wools; and Handkerchief Linen.

Fabric Characteristics
- Most plain-weave fabrics are easy to sew.
- Many plain-weave fabrics shrink and wrinkle badly.
- Seam slippage and fraying are a problem in poor-quality fabrics.
- Most plain-weave fabrics are difficult to ease.

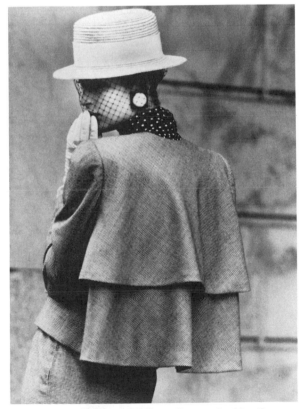

Fig. 9–1 *Bill Blass boldly tailors a double, flyaway jacket in a plain-weave, bird's-eye wool. (Photo courtesy of Bill Blass Ltd., Spring, 1987.)*

- Plain-weave fabrics have poor elasticity and tear easily.
- Many plain-weave fabric garments can be washed successfully while twill or satin fabrics with the same fiber content cannot.
- Sheets are frequently off-grain.

SEWING CHECKLIST

Machine Needles: Universal-H point or Red Band needles; sizes 60/8 to 80/12, depending on the fabric weight.

Machine Setting: Stitch length, 2–2.5 mm (10–12 stitches per inch); tension, balanced.

Thread: Long-staple polyester, cotton-wrapped polyester, mercerized cotton.

Hand Sewing Needles: Sizes 7 to 10.

Equipment and Supplies: Scissors or rotary cutter and mat, pins, weights.

Layout: Double layer, right sides together.

Marking Techniques: All types, except wax.

Seams: Depends on fabric weight; plain, French, false French, standing-fell, flat-fell, topstitched, welt, double/ply.

Hems: Depends on fabric weight; plain, double, shirttail, book, machine-rolled, slipstitch, blindstitch, machine blindstitch, topstitched, twin needle, tucked.

Seam and Hem Finishes: Single/ply or double-ply. Pinked, pinked-and-stitched, serged, zigzag, multi-stitch zigzag, turned-and-stitched, fold.

Edge Finishes: All types.

Interfacings: Fusible or sew-in; self-fabric, organdy, batiste.

Linings and Underlinings: Rarely.

Closures: All types.

Pockets: All types.

PLANNING A GARMENT

SELECTING THE FABRIC

Examine the fabric carefully. Check to see if it has flaws in the weave, printing, or finishing.

Examine the fabric grain; the warp and filling threads should be straight and at right angles to each other. Many plain-weave fabrics have permanent finishes which do not allow them to be straightened.

Look for slubs, printing errors, permanent wrinkles, and snags. Good dyes penetrate the fabric well, so the color is good on the back as well as the face. Check for colorfastness.

Generally, plain-weave fabrics are judged by the number of threads per square inch. Hold the fabric up to the light and examine the weave. The weave should be uniform; patches of light and dark indicate poor construction, poor-quality yarns, or heavy sizing. The threads should be fine, and closely spaced, if the fabric is not a novelty weave.

Closely woven fabrics which have a high thread count, more threads per inch, or an even balance—the same number of warp and filling threads per inch—are more durable, shrink less, hold their shape better, and have less seam slippage.

To test for fraying and seam slippage, scrape your thumbnail across the warp threads to see if they separate. If they do, the fabric will fray and the threads will pull apart at stress points.

To test for resiliency and the ability to recover from wrinkling, squeeze the fabric in your hand; it should spring back with few creases.

Generally, printed plaids, checks, and stripes are less expensive than similar woven fabrics. Check to be sure they are printed on-grain.

Fabrics with long-staple fibers are stronger, smoother, and more serviceable than fabrics with short-staple fibers.

Fabrics woven with fine, high-twist yarns are stronger, smoother, more durable, more elastic, and more crease-resistant.

Fabrics made of multi-ply yarns or several strands twisted together are more durable than single-ply yarns.

Generally, natural fibers are more comfortable to wear and synthetic fibers are easier and cheaper to clean.

When purchasing chintz, test to see if the finish

is permanent. Apply a drop of iodine to a small swatch; it will turn brown if permanent or blue if it isn't. Or dip a swatch in a solution of detergent and water. If temporary, the finish will vanish, and it cannot be restored.

When you've selected an attractive sheet instead of fabric yardage, examine it carefully; the edges and printing may be off-grain. This is rarely a problem when sewing for the home; but it can be when you're making a garment.

If you plan to launder the garment, wash and dry the fabric before cutting out.

PATTERN SELECTION

Suitable for children's garments, casual shirts, blouses, and skirts, plain-weave fabrics are a good choice for beginners. They are easy to gather, pleat, tuck, and topstitch.

Shirt sleeves and dropped shoulders are easier to set smoothly than set-in sleeves. (If the design has set-in sleeves, reduce the ease in the sleeve cap.)

SEWING PLAIN-WEAVE FABRICS

LAYOUT, CUTTING, AND MARKING

Spread the fabric, right sides together. Using weights or pins placed in the seam allowances, cut with sharp shears or a rotary cutter and mat. Mark, using your favorite method.

When cutting prints, the right side is usually brighter; however, a few (e.g., Hawaiian shirt de-signs) are printed so the right side is lighter. If the fabric has writing, it should read left to right.

STITCHING TIPS

Make a test seam. Set the stitch length for 2–2.5 mm (10–12 stitches per inch), depending on the fabric weight.

A few plain-weave fabrics are marred by pins and needles. To test, rip the seam several inches and press with steam; examine the sample. If the fabric retains the needle holes, use pins sparingly and try to avoid ripping.

SEAMS AND HEMS

Finish seams and hems to avoid raveling when the garment is laundered. Double/ply and self-finished seams are good choices for most fabrics.

TOPSTITCHING

Since topstitching irregularities show less on fabrics with small prints than on solids, novices can topstitch without worrying.

INTERFACINGS

Interfaced facings and fusible interfacings are good choices for washable garments.

PRESSING

When pressing cotton, use a hot iron and plenty of steam; for lightweight fabrics, reduce the temperature to avoid scorching.

Twill-Weave Fabrics

Twill is the most durable weave. Produced by a series of floats, the diagonal lines are typical of all twill weaves.

The twill type is determined by the way the filling yarns interlace with the warp. Even or balanced twills have the same number of warps and fillings on the face and the back. Warp-face twills have more warp yarns on the face; while filling-face twills have more filling yarns.

The diagonals or wales vary from very steep to reclining with the 45-degree twill on the true bias.

Generally, twill weaves on wool fabrics run from the upper left to the lower right; twills on cottons run from upper right to the lower left. Fancy twills such as the herringbone and zigzag, which run in both directions, are used on wools, silk suitings, and cottons.

Twill weaves are rarely printed or transparent. Compared to plain-weave fabrics with the same number of threads per inch, twill weaves are softer

127

Fig. 9–2 *From Saint Laurent Rive Gauche, Autumn/Winter 1987/1988, this smart suit is tailored in a herringbone fabric with a broken twill weave. (Photo courtesy of Yves Saint Laurent.)*

and more expensive; they drape better and do not soil as easily; however, once soiled, they are more difficult to clean. Since the twill weave has floats which allow more threads to be woven per inch, it then becomes heavier, stronger, firmer, and more wrinkle-resistant.

Popular twill-weave fabrics covered in this section include gabardine, khaki, chino, covert cloth, serge, drill, and ticking, none of which have prominent ribs.

When sewing other twill-weave fabrics, see the appropriate section: Diagonal Designs, Pile Fabrics, Denim, and Textured Woolens.

Fabric Characteristics
- Most twill-weave fabrics fray badly.
- Balanced twills and some herringbones may not require a nap layout; other twills do.

- Many twill-weave fabrics shrink.
- Some firmly woven twill-weave fabrics are difficult to ease.
- Twill weaves wear and abrade at the edges and foldlines.
- Skipped stitches are sometimes a problem.
- Closely woven twills are naturally water-repellent.
- Some twill weaves are bulky. (See Denim.)
- Some twill weaves have an obvious diagonal pattern. (See Diagonal Designs.)

SEWING CHECKLIST

Machine Needles: Universal-H point or Red Band needles; sizes 70/10 to 90/14, depending on the fabric weight.

Machine Setting: Stitch length, 2–3 mm (8–12 stitches per inch); tension, balanced.

Thread: Long-staple polyester, cotton-wrapped polyester, mercerized cotton.

Hand Sewing Needles: Sizes 5 to 10.

Equipment and Supplies: Scissors or rotary cutter and mat, pins, weights.

Layout: Double layer, right sides together. Some require nap.

Marking Techniques: All types, except wax.

Seams: Plain, topstitched, welt, double-welt, double/ply.

Hems: Depends on fabric weight; plain, double-stitched, blindstitch, machine blindstitch, topstitched.

Seam and Hem Finishes: Single/ply or double/ply. Pinked, pinked-and-stitched, serged, zigzag, multi-stitch zigzag, turned-and-stitched, fold.

Edge Finishes: All types.

Interfacings: Fusible and sew-in.

Linings: Generally for outerwear.

Underlinings: Rarely.

Closures: All types.

Pockets: All types.

PLANNING A GARMENT

Many twill-weave fabrics are tightly woven and firm; but a few are loosely woven. All tend to fray.

Test for resiliency and the ability to recover from wrinkling. Squeeze the fabric in your hand; it should spring back with few creases.

Fabrics woven with fine, high-twist yarns are stronger, smoother, more durable, more elastic, and more crease-resistant.

Fabrics made of multi-ply yarns or several strands twisted together are more durable than fabrics made of single-ply yarns.

Closely woven fabrics, which have a high thread count or more threads per inch, are more durable, shrink less, and hold their shape better.

Generally, natural fibers are more comfortable to wear; and synthetic fibers are easier and cheaper to clean.

Using the fiber content as a guide, preshrink the fabric.

PATTERN SELECTION

Depending on the fabric weight and crispness, twill-weave fabrics are suitable for slacks, skirts, jackets, men's suits, work clothes, uniforms, riding habits, raincoats, and shirts.

For medium to heavyweight fabrics, choose more structured designs with a minimum of pattern pieces. Avoid intricate details. Shirt sleeves and dropped shoulders are easier to set smoothly than set-in sleeves.

SEWING TWILL-WEAVE FABRICS

LAYOUT, CUTTING, AND MARKING

Spread the fabric, right sides together. Lay out the pattern pieces using a nap layout if required. Using weights or pins, cut with sharp shears or a rotary cutter and mat. Mark, using your favorite method.

STITCHING TIPS

Make a test seam. Set the stitch length for 2–3 mm (8–12 stitches per inch), depending on the fabric weight.

SEAMS

Plain seams are best for most designs. Use topstitched, welt, or double-welt seams for work clothes and uniforms, where seams will be stressed.

To prevent fraying on plain seams, serge, zigzag, multi-stitch zigzag, or pink the edges. Use a single/ply finish on heavier fabrics; and a double/ply finish on lightweights.

HEMS

Although topstitched hems are the most durable, plain hems look best on better garments. If the garment is unlined, finish the hem with a fold, turned-and-stitched, bound, or serged finish.

PRESSING

Consider the fiber content when pressing. Avoid pressing the right side without a press cloth; dark-colored twills slick easily.

GARMENT CARE

Depending on the fiber content, dyes, and garment construction, twill-weave fabrics can be laundered or dry-cleaned.

DENIM

Denim is a closely woven, twill-weave fabric available in a variety of weights. Woven with indigo yarns in the warp and white yarns in the filling, it can be identified by the blue and diagonal ridges on the unbleached back.

Originally 100 percent cotton, today denim comes in cotton/polyester blends or cotton/spandex blends with 15 to 20 percent stretch. Although denim is usually plain, it can be printed, striped, brushed, napped, stonewashed, or prewashed in a variety of colors.

Fig. 9–3 *Developing a taste for fashion starts young. Cardin's French-inspired denim for toddlers has embroidered hearts on the knee patches. (Photo courtesy of Pierre Cardin Children's Wear.)*

These suggestions can also be used for other heavy, densely woven materials such as canvas and duck.

Fabric Characteristics
- Denim is a crisp, densely woven fabric.
- It has a twill weave and may require a nap layout.
- Skipped stitches are sometimes a problem.
- Denim can be bulky and multiple layers are difficult to stitch.
- Indigo dyes fade when washed and crock onto lighter colors and your skin.
- Denims will whiten where abraded.
- Denim shrinks when washed.

SEWING CHECKLIST

Machine Needles: Universal-H point, jeans (HJ), or Red Band needles; sizes 80/12 to 100/16, depending on the fabric weight.

Machine Setting: Stitch length, 2–3 mm (8–12 stitches per inch); tension and pressure variable.

Thread: Long-staple polyester, cotton-wrapped polyester; topstitching—regular, topstitching, metallic thread.

Hand Sewing Needles: Sizes 5 to 9.

Equipment: Zipper, even-feed, roller, blind-hem feet; shim.

Layout: Nap, double layer, right sides together.

Marking Techniques: All types, except wax.

Seams: Plain, topstitched, welt, flat-fell, double-stitched, fringed, decorative bound, strap, slot, lapped, tucked. Stretch denim: stretch seams.

Hems: Double, plain, blindstitch, blind catchstitch, machine blindstitch, twin needle, topstitched.

Seam and Hem Finishes: Single/ply or double/ply; pinked, pinked-and-stitched, multi-stitch zigzag, serged, bound, tricot bound, seam tape.

Facings and Edge Finishes: Self-fabric or contrasting fabric facings, bands, ribbings, bindings.

Interfacing: Sew-in or fusible.

Linings: Optional.

Closures: All types.

Pockets: All types.

PLANNING A GARMENT

SELECTING THE FABRIC

Denim is available in many weights from light to heavy. Select a fabric weight suitable for the garment design.

Lightweight and prewashed denims have more drape and are easier to sew than the less flexible medium- and heavyweights.

To reduce shrinkage, be sure the fabric is Sanforized®. (Check the bolt end.)

To test for crocking, rub the denim with a piece of white fabric. If the color comes off, it crocks.

Hint: *Kari Newell uses RIT's "Fast Fade" in her washing machine to get different looks from one piece of denim.*

DESIGN IDEAS AND PATTERN SELECTION

Originally used for jeans and overalls, denim is now a popular fashion fabric used in sophisticated designs.

Depending on the fabric weight and hand, denim is well-suited for crisp, casual designs, as well as soft skirts and dresses.

Heavyweights, 14 to 16 ounces per square yard, are good for jeans, overalls, work clothes, and coats. Medium-weights, 10 to 12 ounce, work well for pants, jackets, skirts, and hand bags. Lightweights, 6 to 8 ounce, are perfect for dresses, prairie skirts, and shirts. Cotton spandex is an excellent choice for pants and jumpsuits.

And if you like high fashion, consider these ideas: a classic Chanel suit in blue denim trimmed with white denim, Laura Biagotti's denim jackets with open cutwork yokes, a sequin-trimmed tuxedo jacket, and Chantal Thomass' mink-lined denim coat.

All denim garments, casual and dressy, are well-suited for topstitching.

FABRIC PREPARATION

Wash and tumble dry the fabric several times to remove excess dye, to preshrink, and to soften the fabric.

Hint: *Machine baste the ends together to prevent fraying.*

PATTERN PREPARATION

Cut extended facings to reduce bulk. Pin the facing and garment front together on the seamline and cut as one piece.

SEWING DENIM

LAYOUT, CUTTING, AND MARKING

Spread the fabric, right sides together, with a lengthwise fold. Use a nap layout. To reduce bulk, cut separate facings from lining or contrasting fabric.

STITCHING TIPS

Make a test seam. Set the stitch length for 2–3 mm (8–12 stitches per inch), depending on the fabric weight. Loosen the tension slightly and lighten the pressure as needed; and begin with a new needle. Hold the fabric taut and stitch with the grain.

When crossing seams, use a shim to balance the presser foot in front and then behind.

Hint: *Multiple thicknesses are easier to penetrate if you:*
- *pound the seams with a hammer before stitching, to break down the fibers;*
- *rub the seams with soap to lubricate the needle;*
- *use a needle lubricant on the needle; and*
- *use a jeans needle.*

SEAMS AND DARTS

To simulate the look of casual ready-to-wear, use flat-fell, welt, double-welt, or topstitched seams on straight and slightly curved seams.

Hint: *Use orange, red, white, gold-colored, or gold metallic thread for greater emphasis. If you don't have topstitching thread, use two strands of regular thread.*

Stitch the inseams of jeans with a double/ply seam. Zigzag or serge the edges.

Use a fringed seam for a novelty finish. To prevent fraying on plain seams, serge or pink the edges. When stitching stretch denim, use stretch seams. To reduce bulk, slash darts open and finish the raw edges.

HEMS

The most popular hems are the topstitched and double-fold hems for casual garments, a plain blindstitched hem for dressier designs, and a fringed edge for a novelty finish.

To reduce curling when making a double-fold hem, first fuse a piece of Wonder Under or Transfuse II to the hem allowance. Fold and fuse the hem in place; then topstitch.

For topstitched hems, finish the edge with a serger or zigzag stitch; fuse the Wonder Under to the hem allowance; topstitch and fuse.

Hint: *For easier stitching, pound the vertical seamlines with a hammer before beginning and use a shim to level the presser foot.*

TOPSTITCHING

Review the Tips for Topstitching in the Appendix. Experiment with various threads, needles, stitch lengths, and fabric thicknesses before topstitching on the garment.

To control the fabric easily and to help you to stitch evenly, try different sewing-machine feet—zipper, even-feed, roller, blind-hem, edge stitch.

Use topstitching thread, two strands of regular thread, or decorative threads for topstitching.

Use a larger, preferably a jeans, needle to prevent skipped stitches. Set the stitch length for 3–4 mm (6–8 stitches per inch). Use a zipper foot, edgestitch foot, or a shim to balance the presser foot, when stitching edges or over uneven layers.

CLOSURES

Machine-worked buttonholes, zippers, and decorative snaps are the most popular fasteners on denim.

When making buttonholes, lengthen the stitch for a more attractive finish.

All types of zippers—fly, slot, lapped, flat-fell lapped, exposed, separating, metal and invisible—are suitable.

Flat-Fell Lapped Zipper. This variation of a lapped zipper is particularly attractive on designs with flat-fell seams.

1. For a neater finish, cut the seam allowances 1" wide in the placket area.

2. Mark the seamlines on the right side with chalk.

3. Wrong sides together, stitch on the seamline from the hem to the zipper placket. Pull the threads to the wrong side and knot.

4. Trim the seam allowance on the skirt back to a fat 1/8".

5. Clip the back seam allowance to the end of the seamline at the bottom of the placket. Continue clipping beyond the seam allowance another 1/4" (see Figure 9–4).

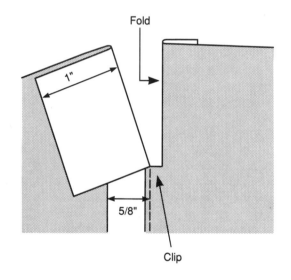

Fig. 9–4

6. Press the seam flat; then, with the garment right side up, press the seam toward the back.

7. Fold the seam allowance of the back placket under; press.

8. In the placket area, fold the seam allowance of the garment front under 3/4"; below the placket, fold under 1/4". Baste. Edgestitch the opening and finish the flat-fell seam.

9. Baste the zipper into the opening; sew it in place by machine. Pull the threads to the wrong side, knot, and trim.

Hint: *On expensive couture designs, all of the topstitching is completed; then the zipper is sewn into the placket by hand. This allows you to have the look of a flat-fell zipper and the ease of hand stitching.*

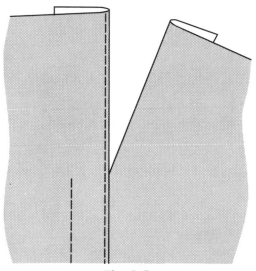

Fig. 9–5

GARMENT CARE

To preserve the denim's appearance, turn garments wrong side out before laundering. To protect other fabrics, wash denims separately.

Add a cup of white vinegar to the wash cycle to reduce fading. And if you don't want any fading, have the garment dry-cleaned.

To minimize wrinkling, remove garments from the dryer while they are still damp. Shake vigorously, smooth, and hang to dry.

Loosely Woven Fabrics

Some of the most beautiful fabrics are loosely woven. Handwovens, bouclés, monk's cloth, hopsacking, and other novelty fabrics are familiar loosely woven fabrics.

Fabric Characteristics
- Loosely woven fabrics are easy to shape and ease.
- Many loosely woven fabrics fray badly.
- Some stretch easily.
- Loosely wovens frequently have a nap.
- Loosely woven fabrics sometimes have slubs which deflect the needle.
- They may have slubs and low-twist yarns, which cause them to pick and pill.
- Many loosely woven fabrics are bulky and/or heavy.
- Many loosely woven fabrics are not needle-ready.
- Most loosely woven fabrics slip badly at the seams.
- Handwoven fabrics frequently have more stretch in the lengthwise grain than machine-woven materials.

Fig. 9–6 *From Carven, this coat is softly styled in a loosely woven mohair. (Photographer, Baudoin Picart; photo courtesy of Carven Haute Couture Collection, Autumn/Winter 1987/1988.)*

PLANNING A GARMENT

PURCHASING THE FABRIC

Many beautiful loosely woven fabrics are hand-woven. If you have a friend who weaves, ask about trading your sewing skills for a fabric length. Although most loosely woven fabrics are selected for their beauty, not their durability, some are more durable than others.

Loosely woven fabrics with metallic threads do not wear well; and those with long floats and slubs pick, pull, and ravel badly.

DESIGN IDEAS AND PATTERN SELECTION

Loosely woven fabrics are suitable for a variety of garments: skirts, coats, slacks, unstructured jackets, tailored jackets, soft suits, dresses, jumpers, ponchos, and ruanas.

To showcase the fabric, choose simple designs with a minimum of seams. Look for patterns which recommend soft fabrics; or, if you plan to change the fabric character, look for designs featuring crisp fabrics.

Design details such as gathers, ease, pleats, darts; dropped shoulders, set-in, kimono, dolman, and raglan sleeves; shawl, standing, and tailored collars are particularly attractive. Avoid closely fitted designs and superfluous details.

If the fabric amount is limited, be creative; combine the loose weave with another fabric with a contrasting texture, such as wool flannel, shantung, poplin, synthetic suede or leather, jersey, or double knit. Or follow the example set by Coco Chanel in her classic suits and line the garment from edge to edge.

SEWING CHECKLIST

Machine Needles: Universal-H point, Red Band, jeans (HJ), or stretch (HS) needles: 60/8 to 90/14, depending on the fabric weight.

Machine Setting: Stitch length, 2–1.75 mm (10–15 stitches per inch); tension and pressure, adjust as needed.

Thread: Long-staple polyester, cotton-wrapped polyester, mercerized cotton. Basting: silk. Topstitching: Regular thread, topstitching thread, or silk (size A or D).

Hand Sewing Needles: Sizes 5 to 7.

Sewing Machine Equipment: Roller or even-feed foot.

Equipment and Supplies: Large, glass-headed pins, twill tape or seam tape.

Layout: Depends on the fabric. A nap layout may be required.

Marking Techniques: Chalk, soap sliver, pens, temporary marking pens, thread tracing, tailor tacks.

Seams: Plain, welt, double-welt, top-stitched, lapped, double-lapped, strap, flat-felled, slot, fringed, bound-and-lapped, bound-and-stitched, piped, decorative serged, wrong-side-out, tissue-stitched.

Hems: Plain, blindstitched, blind catchstitch, figure-eight, catchstitch, machine blindstitched, faced, wrong-side-out, topstitched, book, shirttail, twin needle, fringe, tucked, fused, double-stitched, interfaced.

Seam and Hem Finishes: Single/ply or double/ply. Pinked-and-stitched, zig-zag, multi-stitch zigzag, serged, tricot bound, Hong Kong, seam tape.

Edge Finishes: Self-fabric facings, leather and synthetic suede facings, bias bindings, leather and synthetic suede bindings, bands, ribbings, edge-to-edge linings.

Interfacing: Generally used.

Linings: Generally used for outerwear.

Underlinings: Frequently.

Closures: All types.

Pockets: All types.

One year I made two garments from a gorgeous, loosely woven, handwoven fabric. The first was a loose, unstructured, unlined sweater style, faced with Ultrasuede, and I wore it hundreds of times. It was baggy, warm, and comfortable; I loved it.

The second garment, made from the scraps, was a very structured cardigan-style jacket, underlined with fusible knit interfacing and edged with a silk shantung which matched the skirt. This garment was much dressier and I didn't have as many occasions to wear it; but it looked wonderful, and I felt great in it.

Another choice when you have a limited amount of fabric is to use that fabric as a trim.

PREPARING THE FABRIC

Most garments made of loosely woven fabrics will retain their shape and appearance better if the garment is dry-cleaned.

Generously steam fabrics which must be dry-cleaned or ask your dry cleaner to do it. Steam at least twice to avoid shrinking when the garment is later cleaned.

Think twice before washing a loosely woven fabric; but, if you're determined, remember the fabric may shrink several inches and it may shrink several more inches if tumble-dried.

Preshrink loosely wovens the same way the finished garment will be laundered.

Hint: *To reduce fraying, serge the ends or sew them together to make a loop before the fabric is washed and dried. When machine washing and drying the fabric or garment, make sure the other items have no hooks to snag the loosely woven fabric. Towels are good companions.*

PREPARING THE PATTERN

To eliminate excessive fraying, make a test garment to perfect the garment fit, practice your sewing skills, and experiment with design changes. Use the test garment as a pattern or transfer the changes to the paper pattern before cutting.

If traditional facings or facing/lining combinations are being replaced with edge-to-edge linings, make the lining pattern.

To reduce bulk and to save fabric, eliminate straight, nonfitting seams at the center back and where the front joins the facing.

PLANNING FOR HANDWOVEN STRIPES

Many handwoven fabrics have stripes which do not have a regular repeat and cannot be matched in the traditional manner.

An unmatched stripe design is easier to accept on garments with dropped shoulders than on traditional set-in sleeves; but styles with set-in sleeves can be very attractive when cut on the bias.

If you don't have enough fabric for bias-cut sleeves, match one of the dominant bars on the jacket to the same bar on the sleeve and ignore the bars above and below it.

Hint: *Match midway between the shoulder seam and front notch to broaden the shoulders and narrow the hips.*

When planning straight jackets and skirts, match the bars at the hemline and ignore those above.

Cut small garments in a single width by replacing the seams with darts. Pin the pattern together, matching as many seamlines as possible. The entire seam won't match unless it's straight. Mark and stitch the unmatched portions like darts.

When designing with handwovens, think twice before cutting the garment on the crossgrain. Fold the fabric to see how the hemline will look; the filling yarns may not make a smooth edge.

SEWING LOOSELY WOVEN FABRICS

LAYOUT, CUTTING, AND MARKING

Examine the fabric carefully before cutting. Handwovens sometimes have flaws which must be cut around or placed inconspicuously.

Spread the fabric on a large flat surface. To avoid stretching and distorting the fabric, do not allow it to hang off the end of the table.

Generally, a nap layout is best. If you think the fabric does not have a nap, look again to be sure. The pressing and finishing may cause shading.

If the fabric is bulky or has a pattern to be matched, spread it in a single layer, right side up. If the selvage is flat, use it for straight-edge pattern pieces. To reduce fraying, cut some sections on the bias.

Lay out the pattern carefully. Most loosely woven fabrics have a prominent weave, and off-grain cutting will be very noticeable.

Hint: *To ensure accuracy, cut duplicate pattern pieces; label them "left" and "right." Lay them out, right side up.*

If the fabric stretches or frays badly, spread the fabric right side up on tissue paper; pin. Lay out the pattern pieces; cut both the fabric and tissue. Assemble the garment by stitching through the fabric and tissue; tear away the tissue after stitching.

When cutting soft, spongy fabrics, hold the pattern in place with weights, shallow glass ashtrays, or heavy silverware.

Mark with temporary marking pens, chalk, soap sliver, tailor tacks, or thread tracings. Don't use snips or cut-out notches.

Spray lightly with a fray retardant before proceeding.

PIECING

When working with handwovens, the fabric may not be wide enough to cut a garment section. To piece inconspicuously, make the pieced seams on the lengthwise grain. Piece the seams on skirt side seams near the hem, on trousers at the crotch, and on sleeves at the underarm:

1. Match the grainlines of the two sections.

2. Right sides up, fold under one edge 1/4"; pin so the pins are parallel to and right on the foldline.

3. Rearrange the layers, right sides together; re-pin.

4. Stitch the 1/4" seam. Zigzag or serge the edges together; trim if needed.

STAYS

To prevent stretching and raveling, handle the garment as little as possible after cutting and before seaming.

Staystitch curved edges and shoulder seams to preserve the garment shape.

Stay necklines and shoulder seams so they will hold their shapes. Make a stay from seam tape or lightweight selvage. Measure the paper pattern to determine the length. Pin the stay to the seamline on the wrong side of the garment; machine stitch or hand sew it in place with a short running stitch just inside the seam allowance.

Hint: *For kimono or raglan sleeves, use nylon, tricot, or bias tape as a stay so the seams will have a little give.*

Stay the facing/front seams at the front opening so the hem won't swing toward the side seams. Using the pattern as a guide, measure and mark the seam length on a lightweight selvage. Pin the stay to the seamline and try on the garment. If the hem swings away from the center front, shorten the stay; if the hem laps, lengthen the stay. Stitch the stay into the seamline.

Hint: *If the garment doesn't have a facing/front seam, center a stay tape on the foldline. Use a short running stitch to secure it permanently.*

STITCHING TIPS

Begin with a Universal-H point needle, size 70/10. If skipped stitches are a problem, use a larger needle. If the fabric has hard slubs which deflect the needle, use a Red Band, jeans (HJ) or stretch needle (HS) in an appropriate size.

Make a test seam, using a stitch length of 2 mm (12 stitches per inch) and a loosely balanced tension. When stitching curves and corners, shorten the stitch length to 1.25–1.75 mm (15–20 stitches per inch).

Use a roller foot, even-feed foot or tissue-stitched seams to prevent underlayer creep and to avoid snagging the yarns.

Hint: *When using a straight-stitch or all-purpose zigzag foot, wrap the toes with tape. Some brands of machines have a no-snag foot; ask your dealer.*

SEAMS

Although most decorative seams are attractive on loosely woven fabrics, some—strap, bound-and-lapped, bound-and-stitched, fringed, decorative serged, welt, double-welt, topstitched, and double-lapped—also help control the fraying.

This version of a wrong-side-out seam, designed by weaver Gail Nehrig, emphasizes the fray quality.

1. Cut the seam allowances 1 1/4″ wide.

2. Wrong sides together, stitch on the seamline; press the seams open.

3. Lay a thick yarn pulled from the fabric next to the seamline; zigzag (W,2–4; L,3) over the yarn (Fig. 9-7). Repeat on the other side of the seamline.

4. Fringe the seam edges.

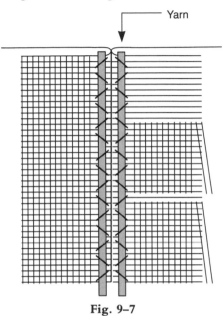

Yarn

Fig. 9–7

Hint: *If a yarn is caught in the seamline, trim it at the seamline.*

To prevent puckering and to avoid vertical seamlines that "hike" at the hemline, stitch side seams with a crooked straight stitch (W,.5; L,2) and sew a weight at the bottom.

Hint: *The leading cause of seamline "hike" is the thread. When using polyester or cotton-wrapped polyester thread, fill the bobbin on slow speed to avoid stretching the thread. Once stitched into a seamline, stretched thread shrinks to its normal length.*

To reduce bulk, clip, notch, and grade seams as needed. To avoid ripping, hand baste seams before machine stitching.

SEAM AND HEM FINISHES

Garments with linings rarely require seam and hem finishes. Finish seams and hems on unlined garments so they will be durable and flat, as well as attractive.

Generally, seams are finished after the garment is assembled; but finishing can be done before stitching the seams. If you finish the edges first, take care to avoid changing or varying the seam-allowance width.

The best seam and hem finish is a serged edge. If you don't have a serger, experiment with these finishes on fabric scraps.

- Coat the edges with a light application of fray retardant, diluted clear nail polish, or a thin solution of white glue before moving the sections from the cutting table. Test these products on a fabric scrap before using them on the garment. Spray retardants such as Fray Stop and No Fray Spray work very well on most fabrics. Test first.
- Stitch with a multi-stitch or regular zigzag stitch; or stitch with a twin needle.
- Fuse 1/4″-wide strips of lightweight interfacing to the edges.
- Bind the seam allowances separately with silk chiffon, organza, or bias tricot. Use a multi-stitch zigzag if possible.
- Trim double/ply seams to 3/8″, bind or use a multi-stitch zigzag or blind-hemming stitch.

HEMS

For an inconspicuous finish, blindstitch the hem, by hand or machine. When hemming garments by hand, hem lightly and loosely so the stitches won't create dimples on the outside of the garment. When hemming by machine, use a small needle and loosen the top tension.

On heavy fabrics, double stitch hems to distribute the weight and to make the stitches invisible. Miter the corners of hems to reduce bulk.

Substitute bindings, bands, ribbings, or fringed hems for traditional hem finishes.

Fringed Hem. For a light, airy look, fringe the hem on dirndl skirts.

1. Determine the depth of the fringe and pull a thread to mark the fringe depth. Stitch (W,2; L,2) just above the pulled thread.

2. To fringe the hem easily, divide it into several small sections instead of trying to pull one long thread. Cut the pulled thread so the cuts are parallel to the lengthwise grain and are spaced 4″ to 6″

apart, depending on the looseness of the weave.

3. Unravel the section to be fringed.

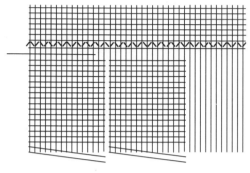

Fig. 9–8

FACINGS

Foldover braids, bias bindings, synthetic suede or leather bindings, ribbon, knitted or crocheted trims, ribbings, bands, and edge-to-edge linings are attractive alternatives to traditional facings. And many loosely woven fabrics have attractive selvages which can be used as edge finishes or trims.

You can substitute suede, synthetic suede, leather, and firmly woven complementary fabrics for self-fabric facings.

Hint: *Use a roller or even-feed foot when joining a loosely woven fabric and a nonwoven.*

CLOSURES

Interface button and buttonhole areas.

Hint: *If you aren't using a fusible interfacing, cut a small rectangle of fusible web for each buttonhole. Insert it between the fabric layers; make the buttonhole; then press to melt the fusible.*

Reinforce all buttonholes with a fray retardant or diluted white glue. Apply it sparingly so it doesn't seep onto the garment; always test first.

When making machine-stitched buttonholes, stitch with a water-soluble stabilizer between the fabric and feed dogs. Cord the buttonholes to prevent stretching.

Button loops of synthetic suede, leather, and contrasting or self-fabric are particularly attractive when the button-loop material is used elsewhere on the garment.

Eyelets, grommets, fur hooks, loops, toggles, and snaps are attractive buttonhole alternatives.

Hint: *Use a circle of synthetic suede, leather, or fusible interfacing under a fastener when it is used in areas which aren't already interfaced.*

INTERFACINGS

Most garments need interfacing to add body and stability to the fabric.

Fusible interfacings change the way the fabric hangs or drapes; and they may change the texture and color. For best results, fuse the interfacing to the facing, to the entire garment section, or to an underlining.

If the fabric has an open weave, experiment with colored interfacings. Fabrics such as batiste, organza, broadcloth, and marquisette are available in a wide range of colors.

LININGS AND UNDERLININGS

Underline loosely woven fabrics to add body, to change the character of the fabric, or to prevent fraying. Line or underline skirts and slacks, so they won't stretch out of shape.

Flat linings control fraying and are particularly attractive on light-colored garments. Many loosely woven fabrics and designs will look better, wear longer, and be easier to sew if the entire garment is underlined.

If the fabric is soft, tack it to the underlining so it won't sag between the seamlines.

The popular Chanel suits in the fifties were frequently made in loosely woven fabrics, then lined in soft silk. To prevent sagging, the garment and lining were machine-quilted together. The quilted vertical rows were usually stitched vertically every 2″ to 4″; however, some were stitched horizontally or in squares to follow the pattern of the fashion fabric. A few were handstitched randomly. Yes, you could sometimes see the stitched rows on the right side of the garment when you looked hard.

Any underlining material will add body and stability. For a soft, light look, consider organza, marquisette, tulle, net, handkerchief linen, cotton batiste, or Armo wool.

For a more structured look, use a lightweight fusible interfacing. Weft insertion and knit fusibles add crispness to most fabrics without overwhelming them.

Cut the fusible and fabric separately; place the fusible on the wrong side of the fabric; and fuse.

Hint: *The loosely woven fabric will be larger than the fusible no matter how carefully you cut. I try to match the cut edges before fusing, but it isn't always possible. I have also fused the underlining to the loosely woven material before cutting; but, since the grain slips and slides, it is difficult to fuse perfectly; also, it takes forever.*

Garments with underlinings may not need interfacings.

PRESSING

Test press to determine the correct amount of heat, moisture, and pressure.

Cover the pressboard with a piece of self-fabric, thick terry towel, or a Velvaboard® to avoid flattening textured fabrics.

To avoid snagging the fabric with the iron point, use a press cloth.

For sharp, well-pressed seams and edges, use lots of steam or a damp press cloth; cover the area with a clapper. Examine the results. If it isn't flat enough, steam again and pound with the clapper. Do not move the section until it is dry.

Wash-and-Wear Fabrics

Wash-and-wear, permanent press, and durable press are just a few of the many names used to identify fabrics which can be worn, washed, tumble-dried, and worn again with little or no ironing.

There are three types of wash-and-wear fabrics: fabrics made of synthetic yarns; blended fabrics which are at least 50 percent synthetic; and natural fiber fabrics which have been treated with special chemical finishes.

The fibers and finishes which make fabrics wash-and-wear also make them less pliable, less durable, springier, and more difficult to alter and sew than traditional natural fiber fabrics. Fabrics frequently have an odor caused by the formaldehyde used to set the finish; they may cause allergic reactions.

When compared to all cotton, polyester/cotton blends have the comfort of cotton and the wash-and-wear properties of polyester. Rayon/cotton blends are more lustrous. Acetate/cotton blends have a smoother, more luxurious hand. Acrylic/cotton blends dry faster; they are softer, wrinkle-resistant, and shrink-resistant.

When compared to 100 percent wool, polyester/wool blends are stronger, and they resist moths, wrinkles, and shrinking; but, even though they look like wool, they handle more like polyester. Acrylic/wool blends are stronger and resistant to wrinkling and shrinking.

Linen/polyester blends retain the sheen of linen without the wrinkles.

Wool, rayon, cotton, and acetate blends with nylon are stronger, resistant to spotting, shrinking, and wrinkling; they are also fast drying. They require minimum ironing and have good heat-set properties for pleat retention.

Fabric Characteristics
- The characteristics of wash-and-wear fabrics are determined by the kind of fibers and the percentage of each.
- Puckered seams and skipped stitches are frequently a problem.
- Some are easily damaged by stitching and ripping.
- Most are easily damaged by hot irons.
- Some are difficult to press.
- Wash-and-wear fabrics are easier to sew after laundering.
- These fabrics quickly dull needles and scissors.
- Wash-and-wear fabrics are difficult to ease.
- They may cause allergic reactions.
- They soil easily and oil-based stains are difficult to remove.

SEWING CHECKLIST

Machine Needles: Universal-H point, Red Band, Yellow Band needles; sizes 60/8 to 100/16.

Thread: Long-staple polyester or cotton-wrapped polyester.

Sewing Machine Equipment: Straight-stitch or jeans foot.

Equipment and Supplies: Small pins, sharp shears or rotary cutter and mat, zippers with synthetic tapes.

Marking Techniques: All types, except wax.

Seams: All types, depending on fabric weight and weave and garment construction; however, plain seams—single/ply or double/ply—are frequently best.

Hems: All types.

Seam and Hem Finishes: All types.

Plackets: All types.

PLANNING A GARMENT

DESIGN IDEAS AND PATTERN SELECTION

Wash-and-wear fabrics are suitable for a variety of garments: slacks, tops, dresses, casual sportswear, menswear, children's clothes, raincoats, outer garments, and lingerie.

Generally, bias-cut designs and styles with a minimum of seams, easing, and topstitching are good choices for woven fabrics. Gathers, soft folds, and ruffles are particularly attractive.

Styles with raglan and kimono sleeves or dropped shoulders are easier to sew than set-in sleeves. Straight seams on the lengthwise grain pucker more than slightly bias seams.

Avoid intricate seams and topstitched details.

PURCHASING THE FABRIC

Wash-and-wear fabrics are available in a wide range of qualities and prices. Generally, they are less expensive than fabrics made of 100 percent natural fibers.

Avoid fabrics which are off-grain; they cannot be straightened. Check to be sure printed patterns, plaids, and checks are aligned with the fabric grains.

To test the moisture absorbency or wicking quality, sprinkle a drop of water on the fabric. The more quickly the water is absorbed, the more comfortable it will be to wear.

PREPARING THE FABRIC

Preshrink the fabric to remove excess finishes and to relax it. Also preshrink notions, linings, interfacings, and underlinings. (If you plan to wear the garment, be sure all the components have the same washability.)

PREPARING THE PATTERN

For smooth set-in sleeves, reduce the ease in the sleeve cap or change the grain on the sleeve so that it will be cut on the bias. (See Chapter 1.)

Hint: *If you plan to use bias-cut sleeves, you will probably need extra fabric.*

SEWING WASH-AND-WEAR FABRICS

LAYOUT

Press out the foldline before spreading the fabric. If it can't be removed, refold the fabric and arrange the pattern to avoid the fold. Spread fabrics right sides together.

Some fabrics—solid colors, all-over prints, and prints with small, irregular patterns—can be used satisfactorily even when they are off-grain since the finish, not the grain, determines the garment shape. Use the lengthwise grain as a guide and ignore the crossgrain.

STITCHING TIPS

Make a test seam with 2–2.5 mm (10–12 stitches per inch). Begin with a new needle. To prevent puckering, loosen the tension on both the needle and bobbin threads; and hold the fabric taut while stitching.

Fig. 9-9 *Trimmed with bias bindings, this polyester/cotton blend jacket feels comfortable, holds its shape, and looks fresh all day. (Photo courtesy of Neil's Apparel, Palm Desert, California.)*

Although Universal-H point needles are suitable for most wash-and-wear fabrics, you may prefer Red Band needles for woven fabrics and Yellow Band needles or ballpoint (SUK) needles for knits.

Use small needles (60/8 or 70/10) for sheers and lightweight fabrics, medium needles (80/12) for medium-weight fabrics, and large needles (90/14 or 100/16) for heavyweight fabrics.

Select a thread appropriately sized for the fabric. Use size 50 thread for medium and heavyweight fabrics and 100/3 for sheers and lightweight fabrics.

Begin with a new needle in the smallest recommended size. If skipped stitches are a problem, try the next size larger.

Since wash-and-wear fabrics dull needles badly, change the needle frequently. A new needle per

garment is not too often; and some garments will require several new needles.

To reduce seam puckering, use a straight-stitch foot or jeans foot to hold the fabric firmly when straight stitching. Use a single-hole needle plate if you have one.

Hint: *Puckered seams cannot be pressed out of wash-and-wear fabrics.*

Set the machine on low gear or stitch slowly when filling the bobbin.

Hint: *If you wind the bobbin on a fast speed, the polyester thread stretches; and it won't have an opportunity to relax until it is stitched into a seam. When it relaxes, the seam will pucker.*

If the feed dogs mark the fabric, reduce the pressure.

FACINGS AND INTERFACINGS

Understitch to keep facings from rolling to the outside.

Consider self-fabric interfacings as well as traditional interfacing fabrics for wash-and-wear garments.

When using a sew-in interfacing, position the interfacing on the wrong side of the garment; for fusibles, position them on the wrong side of the facing.

PRESSING

To heat-set pleats and creases, set the iron at a higher than normal temperature; cover the garment with a damp press cloth; and press.

GARMENT CARE

Wash wash-and-wear fabrics frequently. To avoid permanent staining, remove oil-based stains as soon as possible.

To avoid permanent perspiration odors, use dress shields and wash garments frequently in detergents such as Fab and Surf, which have special ingredients to eliminate odors.

Most garments can be machine washed in warm water with a mild detergent followed by a cold rinse. Machine dry at a low temperature. To avoid unwanted wrinkles do not crowd during washing or drying; when dry, remove immediately.

To reduce static electricity, use a fabric softener in the final rinse.

To clean badly soiled garments, pretreat spots and wash in hot water with a heavy-duty detergent.

Although most whites can be bleached with a chlorine bleach and colors with a nonchlorine bleach, hot water and bleach may damage a permanent-press finish.

To remove pills, use a dual-blade razor to shave them away.

For touch-up pressing, use a moderately warm steam iron.

Outerwear Fabrics

This section focuses on waterproof and water-repellent fabrics, which are used for cold-weather garments, raincoats, parkas, vests, and camping gear.

Most waterproof fabrics such as polyurethane-coated nylon Cordura®, coated nylon pack cloth, coated nylon taffeta, vinyl, coated rubber, plastic, and synthetic leather will keep you dry; but since they don't breathe, they can be very uncomfortable. Another fabric, Gore-Tex™, is waterproof *and* it breathes.

Water-repellent fabrics such as Savina™, nylon taffeta, nylon Taslan®, Mountain Cloth, Tactel®, and Tuftex® have water-repellent weaves, fluorochemical finishes, or silicone treatments, which cause raindrops to roll off. They're more comfortable to wear since they breathe, but they won't keep you dry in a heavy or prolonged rainstorm.

OUTERWEAR FABRICS AND FINISHES

Bion II has a filmlike coating which makes it waterproof, but breathable. Similar to Gore-Tex, it is not weakened by soiling or cleaning.

Cordura is a nylon canvas fabric. Stronger and more resistant to abrasion than cotton canvas and vinyl, it is not affected by rot or mildew and it dries quickly. It is very tough and dense and has little or no rustle. Available in several weights with a polyurethane coating, it is used primarily for soft luggage and packs.

D.W.R. is a durable, water-repellent coating which will wash out in six to eight washings.

Entrant® is a nonstretch fabric with a polyurethane coating. Used primarily for skiwear, it is more waterproof than water-repellent. It is very flexible and tough; and it has a good hand and drape. It can be washed or dry-cleaned.

Zepel® and *Scotchgard®* are fluorochemical finishes which repel water- and oil-based stains. They can be applied by the dry cleaner or by do-it-yourselfers.

Gore-Tex is a filmlike material sandwiched between breathable fabrics. It is engineered with nine billion pores in every square inch. These pores, which are too small for water to enter, allow perspiration to escape. Gore-Tex provides warmth and dryness without bulk or weight. It is used for parkas, fashion rainwear, spacesuits, and athletic wear. Although it is not widely available to home sewers, it is available from The Green Pepper. (See Resources.)

K-Kote, the tradename of Kenyon Industries, is a waterproof polyurethane coating. Called Super K-Kote when applied in a double layer, it is heavier, withstands more water pressure, wears longer than the regular K-Kote waterproof coating, which is applied in a single layer.

Mountain Cloth is a nylon/cotton poplin with a durable water-repellent finish. It is used for windbreakers, skiwear, parkas, and rainwear.

Nylon Antron® Taffeta is woven with Antron nylon fibers. Available in varying thread counts and deniers, it is lightweight, water- and wind-repellent, quick drying, and easy care. Compared to regular nylon taffetas, it has more sparkle, and like most nylon outerwear fabrics, it rustles. It can be machine washed and dried on low heat or dry-cleaned.

Nylon Pack Cloth has finer yarns in the warp than the filling. Lightweight and tough, it is more water-repellent when coated. It is used more frequently for packs and suit bags than garments.

Fig. 9–10 *Perfect for biking, hiking, fishing, or camping, this windbreaker is trimmed with knit cuffs and corded piping. (Photo courtesy of Green Pepper, Inc.)*

Nylon Taffeta is a tightly woven, smooth, plain-weave fabric. Slightly heavier and stronger than ripstop, it is available in many qualities: coated, uncoated, quilted, and unquilted. More densely woven fabrics are more wind- and water-resistant, and downproof; they also fray less. When coated, it is waterproof, does not breathe, and puckers less when stitched. It is used for jackets, windbreakers, rainwear, running suits, vests, and stuff sacks.

Savina DP® is a polyester/nylon blend which is woven 66″ wide, then shrunk to 48″. Wind-repellent and almost waterproof, it has no coating and breathes. Used for running wear, bicycle wear, fashion rainwear, and outerwear, it is softer, more lustrous, and more drapeable than densely woven polyester/nylon blends.

Silicon finishes, which repel water, penetrate the fiber so the pores remain open, allowing the fabric to breathe. Silicon finishes last through five or six launderings and can be renewed by washing in Wash Cycle by Kenyon.

Tactel is texturized nylon with an acetate coating and a matte finish. It is very wind- and water-repellent; and it breathes well. It is lighter weight and rustles less than Taslan. It is used for skiwear, rainwear, windbreakers, and fashion outerwear.

Taslan is a textured nylon with a rough texture and matte finish. It looks like cotton, but it is stronger, quicker drying, and wind- and water-repellent. It is used for skiwear, parkas, outerwear jackets, and pants.

Triblends are blends of nylon, polyester, and cotton. Fast drying, lightweight, and durable, they have a low luster and can be washed or dry-cleaned. They are used for jackets, pants, shirts, jumpsuits.

Ripstop Nylon is a durable plain-weave fabric, which is woven with several threads twisted together at regular intervals to form a grid pattern. The grid resists tearing without adding significantly to the overall weight. Sometimes coated to make it waterproof, it is semicrisp, scroopy, and strong. It is used for stuff sacks, rainwear, and windbreakers.

Fabric Characteristics

- Most outerwear fabrics are very tightly woven.
- Outerwear fabrics are wind-resistant and water-repellent; some are waterproof.
- Stitching outerwear fabrics is sometimes difficult without skipping stitches.
- Puckered seams are frequently a problem during stitching.
- Coated fabrics frequently stick to the bottom of the presser foot.
- Some outerwear fabrics are bulky and multiple layers are difficult to stitch.
- Some fabrics ravel badly; others do not ravel at all.
- Most outerwear fabrics are easily damaged by pins, machine needles, sewing machine lights, and hot irons.
- Most outerwear fabrics resist tearing and snagging.
- Coated fabrics do not breathe as well as uncoated fabrics.

PLANNING A GARMENT

PATTERN SELECTION

Available in a variety of weights, outerwear fabrics are well-suited for raincoats, vests, jackets, pullovers, mittens, gaiters, parkas, racing suits, skiwear, rain pants, bicycle shorts, garment bags, packs and sleeping bags.

One-piece raglan sleeve designs are more water-repellent than set-in sleeves.

When sewing fashion outerwear, check the pattern selection at your favorite retailer. When sewing hard-core athletic designs, choose a pattern from companies such as The Green Pepper, Rain Shed, Donner Designs, Kwik Sew, Daisy Kingdom, Sew Easy, and Rei, who specialize in outerwear patterns.

PURCHASING THE FABRIC

Most retailers do not have large selections of outerwear fabrics; however, these fabrics and the appropriate hardware can be ordered from several mail-order companies. (See Sources.)

When selecting the fabric, consider the wind- and water-repellency of the fabric and its weight, as well as the garment design and use.

Fabrics for down-insulated garments must be downproof—firmly woven so the down won't migrate through the fabric.

Readily available, nylon taffeta is available in a variety of qualities, thread counts, and deniers (fiber size). Densely woven taffetas are usually easier to sew and fray less. They vary in stiffness and drape.

Fabrics with a thread count of 104/88 are only suitable for windsocks and linings where air penetration is desirable.

Taffetas with 112/100 are frequently used as shells over insulating liners. They can be used with Dacron II insulation, but not down, except when calendered or pressed with a hot roller to make them downproof and shiny on one side.

High-count taffetas (160/90) wear well; they are downproof, windproof, and waterproof.

FABRIC PREPARATION

Most outerwear fabrics do not need to be preshrunk. To remove static and to soften washable fabrics, wash with a fabric softener added to the rinse water; tumble dry.

SEWING OUTERWEAR FABRICS

LAYOUT, CUTTING, AND MARKING

Spread the fabric, right sides together, with a lengthwise fold. Most fabrics look the same on both sides. If they don't, select the side which you like better, except when sewing coated fabrics. Then use the uncoated side as the face.

Since the coating stabilizes coated fabrics, you can tilt the patterns off-grain or cut the entire garment on the crossgrain to economize when cutting; however, garments will not perform as well or be as attractive.

Use weights or place pins within the seam allowances. Holes and scratches on the coating will cause the fabric to leak.

STITCHING TIPS

Begin with a new needle in the smallest size that will make a seam without skipping stitches. Large needle holes will make the garment less water-repellent.

Make a test seam. Set the stitch length for 2–3 mm (8–12 stitches per inch), depending on the fabric weight. Loosen the tension slightly and lighten the pressure as needed. Hold the fabric taut and stitch with the grain.

Outerwear designer Arlene Haislip recommends polyester thread. It is stronger and more elastic when wet; and it doesn't rot or mildew like cotton and cotton-wrapped polyester threads.

To avoid jamming the machine when sewing nylon taffeta or ripstop nylon, hold the thread ends firmly at the beginning of seams.

Hint: *The static electricity pulls the threads and fabric into the needle hole.*

To eliminate puckered seams, use stabilizer or tissue-stitched seams.

Nylon fabrics quickly dull sewing-machine needles. To eliminate skipped stitches, pulled threads, and thumping noises, change the needle frequently.

To avoid breaking the fibers when sewing tightly woven Savina DP, use a Universal-H point or Yellow Band needle, size 70/10 to 80/12.

For woven nylon fabrics, use a Red Band needle. Select a small size needle 70/10 to 90/14 which will penetrate the fabric easily. Since nylon dulls needles rapidly, watch for skipped stitches—a signal to replace the needle.

For Cordura, use a Red Band or jeans (HJ) needle, size 90/14.

For Gore-Tex, use a Red Band, size 75/11 or jeans (HJ) needle, size 90/14.

Since coated fabrics tend to stick to the bottom of the foot, use a Teflon foot, talcum powder, cornstarch, or tissue paper on top of the fabric to reduce this problem.

Hint: *Beware—if you've just oiled your machine, a generous application of cornstarch or talcum will make dough in the bobbin case.*

If skipped stitches are a problem when sewing coated fabrics, first wipe the needle with fingernail polish remover; then, if skipped stitches persist, change to a new needle.

SEAMS

Plain seams are best for traditional activewear. Double-stitch seams that will be stressed.

Seams on outerwear are rarely, if ever, pressed open. Double/ply and self-finished seams are frequently used, but many decorative seams are appropriate for casual designs and fashion outerwear.

French, standing-fell, and piped seams repel water better than topstitched, welt, double-welt, and flat-felled seams.

To reduce leaking in a rainstorm, do not pin-baste on the body of the garment. Baste with spring hair clips or pin-baste only within the seam allowance.

When crossing seams, use a shim to balance the presser foot in front and then behind.

Hint: *Multiple thicknesses are easier to penetrate if you pound the seams with a hammer to break down the fibers before stitching. Rub the seams with soap and use a needle lubricant.*

For waterproof fabrics, use a seam sealer so the seams won't leak. Apply seam sealer to the wrong side of the fabric; apply the sealer to both sides of the seam and down the center before crossing it with another seam.

Hint: *The Green Pepper's Arlene Haislip uses two thin coats, which are more flexible than one heavy one.*

Most coated outerwear fabrics do not fray or require a seam finish. To prevent fraying on nylon taffeta and ripstop nylon, sear, zigzag, or serge plain seams. Or use self-finished seams.

Hint: *Use a curling iron or stencil-cutting tool to sear the edges.*

145

CLOSURES

Decorative, separating, and two-way zippers, snaps, grommets, toggles, hook and loop tape, as well as traditional outerwear hardware are good choices. (See Sources.)

Use a nonwoven interfacing to reinforce buttonhole ares.

VENTILATION

Use grommets, eyelets, or nylon mesh at the top of the underarm to improve the wearing comfort of nylon taffeta, ripstop, coated and waterproof fabrics.

Hint: *Some of these fabrics breathe better than others. If a drop of water rests in a well-formed bubble on the surface, you'll definitely need air vents.*

PRESSING

Use a very cool iron to avoid damaging the nylon fabrics. If the fabric has a waterproof coating, don't use an iron at all.

Hint: *To press quickly and easily without an iron, use your scissor handles or finger nail.*

GARMENT CARE

Most outerwear fabrics perform better if washed. When in doubt, check the manufacturer's directions.

Most garments can be machine laundered and tumble dried. Coated fabrics will retain their coating better if they are line dried. A few insulated garments will require dry-cleaning.

Add a cup of white vinegar to the last rinse to be sure all traces of soap are removed.

To avoid damaging other garments being laundered, cover the hook side of hook and loop fasteners with a piece of nylon hose.

To renew the water-repellent finish on fabrics, wash with Kenyon's Wash Cycle or spray the garment with Scotchgard.

Avoid hot irons, light bulbs, campfires, camp heaters, and hot dryers, which will damage the fabric.

CHAPTER 10
Knits

Today, knits are an important part of every wardrobe. All our closets include a variety of knitted garments, from skirts and sweaters to lingerie and swimsuits. Little is known about the origin of knitting. Hand knitting was introduced in Europe about the fifth century, and by the fifteenth century knitted garments were in common use.

The first knitting machine was invented in 1589 by William Lee. Unfortunately, Queen Elizabeth I was afraid it would put many of her subjects out of work and refused to give him a patent. Lee died before the importance of his invention was recognized; but his brother established a successful hosiery business.

Knitted fabrics are made by using needles to interweave yarn to form a series of connected loops. All machine-knit fabrics are divided into two general groups, weft or filling knits, and warp knits. They utilize only four basic stitches: plain, rib, purl, and warp.

The Knit Family

Weft knits are knitted with one continuous yarn, moving back and forth on flat machines or around and around on circular machines. Warp knits utilize many yarns, which move vertically.

Weft knitting machines use only one yarn and three—plain, purl, and rib—of the basic stitches singly or in combination to produce fabrics such as jersey, ribbing, sweater and sweatshirt knits, interlocks, and double knits.

Warp knitting machines use many yarns and one stitch—warp—to produce fabrics such as tricot, milanese, and raschel knits. Generally, the number of yarns equals the number of needles.

Plain stitches are made with one set of needles, which form ribs or knit stitches in one direction on only one side of the fabric.

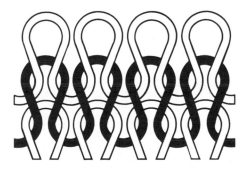

Fig. 10–1

Rib stitches are made with two sets of needles, which form ribs on both sides of the fabric.

Purl stitches are made with one set of needles, which form alternating rows of ribs and ridges on both sides of the fabric.

Fig. 10–2

Fig. 10–3

Warp stitches are made in a systematic zigzag one above the other in a vertical direction.

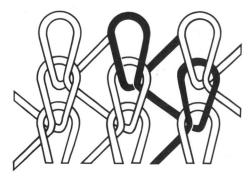

Fig. 10–4

Fig. 10–5   *Soft, simple, feminine knits offer a variety of options. (Photo courtesy of Pierre Cardin Knitwear.)*

Although knits are available in an endless variety of fabrics that vary in texture, stretch, fiber content, weight, and design, most of the knits we sew fall into one of the categories described below. For additional sewing suggestions, see the indicated sections.

Boiled wool is dense wool fabric which has been shrunk and felted. It has limited stretch. (See Felted Fabrics.)

Bunting is a dense fabric made of polyester and polypropylene which has been shrunk and felted. An excellent insulator, it has limited stretch. (See Felted Fabrics and Batting and Insulations.)

Double knits are stable knits with lengthwise ribs on both sides which look the same. Even though they range from very soft to very stiff, all double knits have good body and shape retention. Easy to sew, they have little or no stretch. (See Double Knits.)

Four-way stretch knits have stretch in both the length and width. Compared to two-way stretch

Overleaf: *Velvet evening wrap features a bouquet of large fabric roses. Created by Erik Mortensen for Haute Couture Autumn/Winter 1987–1988 for Balmain. (Photo courtesy House of Balmain.)*

Opposite page: *Mariano Fortuny's Delphos design from the early thirties features his famous pleated silk fabric. Small Venetian beads are used to trim and weight the edges of the tunic. (Gift of Mrs. William Robinson; photo courtesy the Arizona Costume Institute of the Phoenix Art Museum.)*

Above: *A stunning cocktail suit from Givenchy, Pret à Porter, Autumn/Winter 1988–89. Note how the large motifs are positioned and matched so they flow smoothly from one section to another. (Photo courtesy Givenchy.)*
Right: *This elegant cocktail dress from Geoffrey Beene features an elaborately embroidered skirt with a simple black top. (Photo courtesy Geoffrey Beene.)*

From Bill Tice, a breathtaking design fabricated in permanently pleated fabric. (Photo courtesy Bill Tice.)

Opposite page: *Inspired by a visit to Mexico in 1978, the Mexican Fan design was silk screened by hand and then permanently pleated for this Zandra Rhodes' satin jacket. The decorative shoulder seams are finished with satin-stitched lettuce edging. (Photographer, Grant Mudford; photograph from The Art of Zandra Rhodes, © Jonathan Cape, courtesy Zandra Rhodes.)*

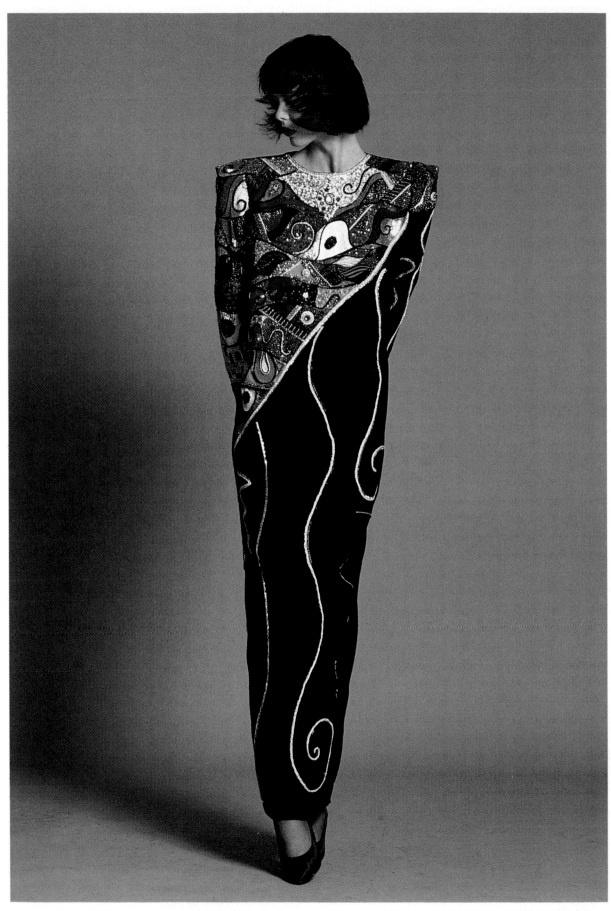

Inspired by the stained-glass windows of Gustav Klimt, this long, black velvet sheath is richly embroidered with gold threads, multicolored paillettes, stones, and fabrics.

From the Louis Feraud Haute Collection, Autumn/ Winter 1985–86. (Photographer, Hervé Nabon; photo courtesy Louis Feraud.)

So simple, so elegant, this satin patchwork coat from Geoffrey Beene reverses to an iridescent. Note the welt pocket on the patchwork side and the patch pocket on *the reverse. All edges are trimmed with gold cord. (Photo courtesy Geoffrey Beene.)*

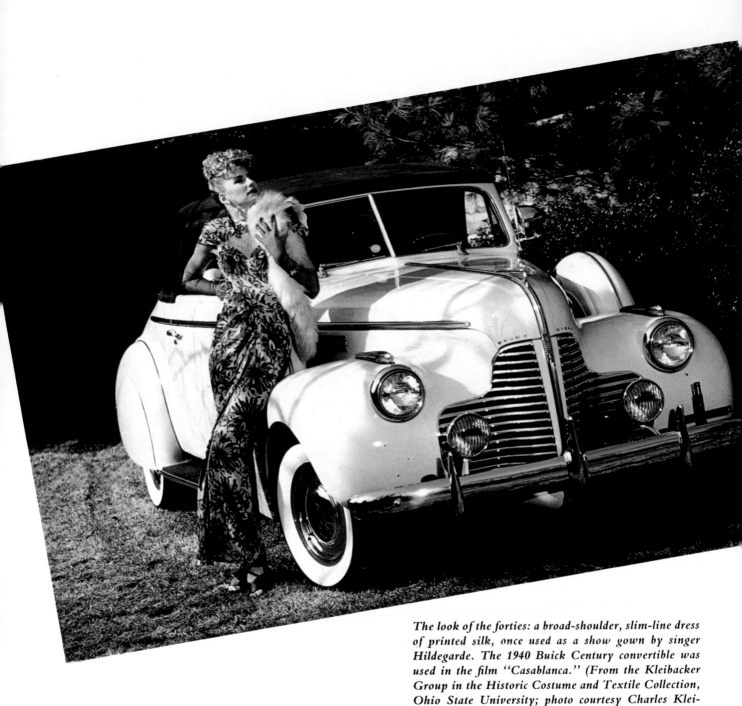

The look of the forties: a broad-shoulder, slim-line dress of printed silk, once used as a show gown by singer Hildegarde. The 1940 Buick Century convertible was used in the film "Casablanca." (From the Kleibacker Group in the Historic Costume and Textile Collection, Ohio State University; photo courtesy Charles Kleibacker.)

knits which are knitted on a tricot machine, four-way stretch knits are knitted on a raschel knitting machine and are usually heavier in weight. They have good stretch and recovery. (See Action Knits.)

Interlock knits are lightweight and drapeable. They have lengthwise ribs on both sides like double knits and little stretch in the width. Compared to jerseys, they are heavier, thicker, and easier to sew. Because of their construction, they curl less and are less likely to be distorted. Interlocks run from only one end when stretched or stressed, while jerseys run from both ends. (See Interlock Knits.)

Jersey is a single knit with lengthwise ribs on the right side and horizontal rows on the reverse. Generally soft and drapeable, jerseys have a moderate amount of stretch. (See Jersey.)

Milanese knits have a fine rib on the face and a diagonal design on the back. (See Milanese and Tricot.)

Power net has superior holding power. Knitted with an elastic fiber, power net has good stretch and recovery. (See Power Net.)

Raschel knits, sometimes called sweater knits, are novelty knits with textured yarns. They are available in a variety of patterns and have little or no stretch. (See Raschel Knits.)

Rib knits have prominent vertical ribs on both sides. Used for closely fitted garments and stretch trims, they have good stretch and recovery. Compared to jerseys, rib knits are thicker, more elastic, and more expensive. (See Rib Knits.)

Single knits are jerseys; they have lengthwise ribs on the right side and horizontal rows on the reverse. They have a moderate amount of stretch. (See Single Knits and Jersey.)

Stable knits have little or no stretch. Boiled wool, double knits, single knits, sweatshirt knits, interlocks, and milanese are popular stable knits.

Stretch knits have moderate to good elasticity. Stretch terry, stretch velour, power net, rib knits, and sweater knits are stretch knits.

Stretch terry has a dense pile with loops on the face and vertical ribs on the back. It has moderate to good stretch. (See Stretch Terry and Stretch Velour.)

Stretch velour has a plush nap on the face and vertical ribs on the back. It has moderate to good stretch. (See Stretch Terry and Stretch Velour.)

Sweater knits look and stretch like hand-knit fabrics. They have moderate stretch. (See Sweater Knits.)

Sweatshirt knits are single knits with a napped surface on the face or back. Used for activewear, the fleece absorbs perspiration. Sweatshirt knits have little or no stretch. (See Sweatshirt Knits.)

Tricot is a lightweight knit with lengthwise ribs on the face. Frequently used for lingerie and loungewear, tricot has moderate stretch. (See Tricot.)

Two-way stretch knits stretch in both length and width. Used for active sportswear, two-way stretch knits have good stretch and recovery. (See Action Knits.)

DIFFERENCES AND SIMILARITIES OF KNITS AND WOVENS

Knits are just as diverse as woven fabrics. To sew them successfully, it's important to recognize the similarities and differences between knits and woven fabrics.

- Generally, knits have more give than woven fabrics, but woven fabrics with stretch yarns may stretch more than stable knits.
- Knits mold and fit the body better than woven fabrics.
- The amount of stretch in a knitted fabric ranges from almost none to 500 percent, depending on the kind of knit, the fiber, yarn, and fabric finish.
- Knits have lengthwise stitches called ribs and crosswise rows called courses instead of a lengthwise grain and a crossgrain.
- Woven fabrics and most knits have more give in the crossgrain than in the lengthwise grain.
- Unlike wovens, some knits have more stretch in the crossgrain than on the bias. And a few knits have more stretch in the length than in the width.
- Garments made from stretch knits don't need as much ease as those made of woven fabrics.
- Pattern selection for both knits and wovens is based on fabric weight, bulk, crispness, drapeability, texture, opaqueness, fabric pattern, and care.
- Generally, knit fabrics are thicker than woven fabrics, but they aren't as wind-resistant.
- Knits do not crease as well as woven fabrics.
- Knits are more resistant to wrinkles.

149

- Knitted and woven fabrics with permanent-press finishes cannot be straightened if they are off-grain.
- On knits, the course or crossgrain cannot be determined by pulling a thread; instead, square the ends of knit fabrics with the edge of a rectangular table.
- Knits shrink more frequently and in larger amounts than woven fabrics.
- Knits have a one-way pattern or nap which is caused by the way the fabric is structured. Shading differences that go undetected in uncut fabric are frequently noticeable in the finished garment.
- Stretch fabrics need stretch seams and hems; when no stretch is desired, seams and edges need to be stabilized with a nonstretch tape.
- Knits do not ravel like woven fabrics; but some run and many curl at cut edges.

SEWING CHECKLIST

Sewing Machine Needles: Universal-H point, Yellow Band, ballpoint (SUK), and stretch (HS) needles; sizes 60/8 to 90/14, depending on the fabric weight.

Thread: Long-staple polyester, cotton-wrapped polyester, woolly nylon, other threads with elasticity.

Equipment and Supplies: Straight stitch, roller or jeans foot; small hole needle plate; lightweight zippers; nonroll elastics.

Layout: Nap

Marking Techniques: All types.

Seams: Depends on the fabric and garment.

Hems: Depends on the fabric and garment.

Edge Finishes: Self-fabric and smooth-fabric facings, lace and bias facings, bindings, bands, false bands, casings, applied elastic, edge-to-edge linings, and ribbings.

- Unlike sewing with woven fabrics, with knits, seam and hem finishes are frequently optional.
- When sewing knits, choose a thread with stretch, such as long-staple polyester, cotton-wrapped polyester, or woolly nylon.
- Generally, knit fabrics are stitched with ball-point needles, which will slide between the yarns instead of penetrating them; while woven fabrics are stitched with sharp-point needles. Needles with sharp or damaged points will make holes and cause runs.
- Generally, knits are stitched with a shorter stitch and looser tension than woven fabrics, so that the seam will elongate with the fabric. Both usually require a balanced tension.
- Knits are less likely to require interfacings, linings, and underlinings than woven fabrics. When selecting interfacings, consider both the purpose—for shaping and supporting—and the relationship of the interfacing to the general characteristics of the fabric.
- For knits and wovens, the fiber content, as well as the fabric structure, determines the garment's durability, pressing temperature, and general care.

PLANNING A GARMENT

SELECTING THE FABRIC

When selecting a knit fabric, consider the end use of the garment and the desired stretch, as well as the fabric's beauty and durability.

Examine knits carefully; the course rows should be perpendicular to the lengthwise ribs. If they are not, select another fabric. Few off-grain knits can be straightened.

If you just love the off-grain fabric or already have it in your collection, look at the fabric again. How would the garment look if the pattern were laid out either on the lengthwise rib or parallel to the lengthwise edge? Although the garment will generally hang better when cut with the grainline parallel to the edge, the lengthwise ribs will then be slanted; and, if the ribs are prominent, the garment will be unattractive. Generally the garment will look best if you lay out the pattern with the grainline parallel to the lengthwise ribs.

Good quality knits have good recovery. Stretch the fabric. if it doesn't return to its original shape, the garment, too, will stretch out of shape and become baggy.

To determine the fabric stretch, fold the fabric crosswise 3″ from the edge. Measure and mark a 4″ length on the foldline; stretch gently.

- Stable knits stretch 1/2″ or less.
- Moderate-stretch knits stretch about 1 1/4″.
- Super-stretch knits stretch 2″ or more.
- Two-way and four-way stretch knits stretch 2″ or more in both directions.

Examine your fabric before purchasing. If it distorts or doesn't stretch far enough, select another pattern or use a different fabric.

PREPARING THE FABRIC

If the knit is washable, wash and dry the fabric as you will the finished garment. Many knits don't actually need to be shrunk, just relaxed; laundering also removes finishes which cause skipped stitches and make the fabric more difficult to sew. Preshrink all trims, interfacings, linings, underlinings, and notions which will be used in the garment.

Steam press knits which will be dry-cleaned. Then lay them flat on a large table or clean floor. Allow them to relax at least twenty-four hours before cutting. If you don't have a good steam iron, ask your dry cleaner to steam the fabric for you.

If you don't know whether your knit is washable, cut a test swatch exactly 4″ square. Wash and dry it as you would the garment. Remeasure after washing and drying and compare it to the unwashed fabric. If it has shrunk or changed substantially, plan to dry-clean the garment.

Square the ends of the fabric. Align the folded edge of the knit with one long side of a rectangular table. Mark the crosswise ends even with the end of the table; trim.

Hint: *If the fabric is off-grain several inches, use the marked line as a guide. If you trim the ends, you may not have enough fabric.*

If the fabric has a prominent crease line, steam press. Reexamine the crease; if it didn't disappear, revise the layout.

PATTERN SELECTION

Select a pattern appropriate to the fabric stretch, weight, texture, and drape. Generally, designs without fussy details work well.

When the stretch factor of the knit is important to the design of the garment, the pattern will indicate how much stretch is required. Often there's a stretch gauge on the pattern envelope.

SEWING KNITS

LAYOUT, CUTTING, AND MARKING

Use a nap layout to ensure uniform color shading in the finished garment. Mark the right side with small pieces of drafting tape if both sides look alike.

If the fabric has a permanent crease line, adjust the layout so the crease line will be located inconspicuously. For easy handling, slit tubular knits along one fold.

To prevent stretching, do not allow the fabric to hang off the edge of the table. If your table is too small, position another at the end to hold the excess fabric—or work on the floor.

Lay out the pattern so the greatest stretch runs around the body. The pattern pieces should be placed so the fabric runs toward points of stress such as the neckline, shoulder seams, and zipper plackets. This is usually from the hem up, but some designs, such as skirts with godets, are an exception.

When cutting bulky knits or fabrics which must be matched, spread the fabric in a single layer, right sides up.

Hint: *Cut duplicate pattern pieces to be sure you don't miss a section or cut two left sleeves.*

Check to see if the knit runs at one raw edge. Stretch both edges to determine the direction of the run. To prevent runs, use weights or new ballpoint pins. Place pins only in the seam allowances.

Hint: *Use a fray retardant on the edge which runs.*

Use a vertical rib as a guide for the straight grain when the selvages or lengthwise edges are irregularly shaped. Thread baste the center foldline, following one continuous rib.

Hint: *If the fabric is off-grain several inches, ignore the lengthwise ribs and fold the fabric in half lengthwise to mark the grainline.*

Cut out the garment with a sturdy pair of well-sharpened, bent-handled shears. Make sure your shears are really sharp, to avoid chewing the fabric.

Most knits can be marked by your favorite method: pins, temporary marking pens, chalk, thread tracing, tailor tacks, tape, tracing carbon, or soap sliver. Use clips only on knits that will not run, and wax only on wool.

STITCHING TIPS

When filling the bobbin, set the machine on low or stitch slowly. When wound at a high speed, polyester and cotton-wrapped polyester threads stretch, causing puckered seams in the finished garment. (Do not use mercerized cotton thread; it doesn't have as much stretch as synthetic threads.)

Begin with a new needle in the smallest size suggested. Use a Universal-H point, ballpoint (SUK), or stretch (HS) needle. The rounded points on these needles separate the yarns instead of piercing them.

Hint: *Check the needle, before inserting, to be sure it has no burrs on it. Place it between your front teeth, bite firmly; then slowly pull it out of your mouth.*

Make a test seam to check the needle, tension, pressure, and stitch length. Hold the fabric taut while stitching. If skipped stitches are a problem, try a larger needle or some needle lubricant.

For a more elastic straight stitch, shorten the stitch length so that more thread will be worked into the seam; loosen the tension on both the bobbin and needle threads; and, if necessary, loosen the pressure.

Hint: *Use a bobbin filled with woolly nylon to make a plain seam more elastic. A crooked straight stitch (W,.5; L,2) also makes an elastic seamline.*

To hold the fabric more firmly, use a straight-stitch foot and small-hole needleplate, or a jeans foot if you have a Bernina. Use a roller foot or all-purpose zigzag foot to zigzag.

When stitching, take an occasional rest. Stop with the needle down; raise the presser foot so the fabric can relax; lower the foot; then continue stitching.

If the feed dogs catch or snag the fabric, tissue-stitch seams. To control edges that roll, first spray with fabric finish; press. Then stitch 1/4" from the edge. Pin baste with the pins at right angles to the edge.

Stitch carefully to avoid ripping, which might damage the fabric. And think twice before stay-stitching. Staystitching is frequently advantageous on necklines, armholes, and waistlines; however, it is occasionally a hindrance and retards the elasticity of the finished garment.

To control facings and linings, understitch, by hand or machine, to hold them flat. To reduce bulk on heavy or bulky knits, clip, notch, and grade seams as needed before crossing them with another seam or hem.

SEAMS

To avoid popped stitches, select a seam with enough stretch for the fabric. (See Stretch Seams.) Plain seams are suitable for stable and moderate-stretch knits. Hold the fabric taut and stretch gently as you stitch.

Narrow double/ply seams are best for light-and some medium-weight knits. Since knits don't fray, they can even be double-stitched and left unfinished. If you have a serger, use a serged finish. For heavier fabrics, use single/ply seams and finish as flatly as possible.

Stabilize shoulder and neckline seams that will undergo stress during normal wear with a stay such as hem tape or a piece of lightweight selvage.

HEMS

Stretch fabrics need stretch hems. Always let the garment hang for at least twenty-four hours before measuring the hem.

Knit garments can be hemmed by hand, machine, or fusing.

Hem everyday garments with fusible web, machine blindstitch, zigzag blindstitch, false band, or twin needle or topstitch; you can even use one or more rows of straight stitching to make the hem a design detail.

Hint: *When topstitching textured knits, a zigzag may look straighter than a straight stitch.*

When blind hemming by machine, use a small needle, so the hem won't show on the right side of the garment.

Hint: *To give the hem more elasticity, use woolly nylon in the bobbin and/or use a twin needle.*

Hem quality garments by hand if you are not using a decorative hem. Use a small crewel needle and a blindstitch, catchstitch, or figure-eight stitch. When hemming by hand, pick up a small stitch on the back side of the fabric and keep the stitches loose.

Hint: *When hemming with a blindstitch, take an occasional backstitch.*

Double-stitch hems on heavy fabrics.

EDGE FINISHES

When choosing an edge finish, consider the fiber content, fabric stretch and opaqueness, and the garment use and care requirements. Most knit garments will be more attractive if alternative finishes are used instead of traditional hems and self-fabric facings.

Bindings and bands in self-fabric, complementary fabrics, synthetic suede, leather, ribbon, and purchased bias tape work well on most knits. Other alternative edge finishes—casings, applied elastic, lace facings, bias facings, false bands, edge-to-edge linings, and ribbings—are also attractive.

When cutting knit bindings, examine the fabric carefully; it may have more stretch on the crossgrain than on the bias.

ZIPPERS

Stabilize the zipper placket just inside the seamline with a piece of seam tape hand stitched to the foldline.

INTERFACINGS, LININGS, AND UNDERLININGS

Knit fabrics are less likely to require interfacings, linings, and underlinings than woven fabrics. The choice of support fabric is determined by both the purpose of the shaping and supporting material and its relationship to the general characteristics of the fashion fabric.

When choosing an interfacing, consider the weight, stretch, and care requirements of the knit as well as the desired finish—crisp or soft.

Hint: *When in doubt, select a lighter weight interfacing. If it's a fusible and not crisp enough, fuse another layer.*

PRESSING

Test press on fabric scraps to determine the correct amount of steam, heat, and pressure. Press carefully—synthetic and wool fabrics are easily damaged by too much heat.

To avoid stretching the knit, do not slide the iron across the fabric. To avoid flattening the surface, cover the ironing board with a thick terry towel, Velvaboard, or fabric; press lightly. When pressing from the right side, use a piece of napped fabric or a terry towel as a press cloth.

To set or remove creases, saturate a brown paper grocery bag with water. Place the bag over the fabric and iron until the paper is dry. Or press with a 50/50 vinegar and water solution.

Hint: *When using vinegar and water, always test first.*

Jersey/Single Knits

Jersey, a weft knit, is the most basic machine-knit fabric. Easily identified by vertical ribs on the face and horizontal purl loops on the back, it is made with one yarn fed to the needles, not unlike hand knitting.

Compared to tricot, jersey is more elastic in the

Fig. 10–6 *Designed by Marc Bohan for Christian Dior Haute Couture Collection, Autumn/Winter 1985/1986, the black jersey drapes softly below the asymmetrical waistline. (Photo courtesy of Christian Dior.)*

width and less stable; it runs easily from both ends and curls at all cut edges.

Available in a variety of weights, fibers, textures, and finishes, jerseys are suitable for casual and dressy designs as well as undergarments.

Fabric Characteristics
- Jersey is soft and supple and will not retain a crisp, structured shape.
- Jersey fabrics have a one-way pattern and require a nap layout.
- Jersey will unravel from both ends but more easily from the last one knitted.
- Jersey runs and is easily damaged by defective needles.
- Ripped seams may leave marks and holes in jersey fabrics.
- Jersey curls to the right side at all cut edges.
- Jersey stretches more crosswise than lengthwise; it may stretch more crosswise than on the bias.
- Topstitched hems may ripple when straight stitched.
- Creases are almost impossible to remove from jersey fabrics.
- Some jersey fabrics shrink badly, while others shrink very little.
- Jersey stretches when worn, causing seams and hems to pop.
- Many jerseys, even expensive fabrics, have small flaws which must be cut around.
- Generally, jersey cannot be straightened if it is off-grain.
- Puckered seams and skipped stitches are frequent problems when sewing jersey fabrics. The machine may also eat the fabric.
- Jerseys have poor dimensional stability—they sag and bag after wearing.

PLANNING A GARMENT

See also Knits for general sewing suggestions.

FABRIC AND PATTERN SELECTION

Closely knit fabrics will stretch and bag less than loosely knit ones. To test the fabric's recovery, stretch it crosswise to see if it will return to its original shape.

Examine the full length before it is cut from the bolt. If the course (cross knit) is off-grain, make another selection.

Most jersey fabrics have less than 20 percent stretch. When selecting a pattern, consider the fabric weight, texture, fiber content, and finish. Designs can be close and skinny, softly draped, or comfortably casual.

Most jerseys are lightweight, supple and elastic. They pleat, drape, and gather well. This makes them a good choice for soft, fluid designs. Lingerie, cotton underwear, evening wear, T-shirts, blouses, dresses, soft jackets and coats are just a few ideas.

When sewing lingerie, see Tricot.

Using the manufacturer's care instructions as a guide, treat the uncut fabric as you plan to treat the garment.

Prepare washable fabrics for sewing by laundering to remove excess finishes. Add fabric softener to the final rinse to eliminate static electricity; machine dry. Preshrink all trims and notions as well.

Fabrics which must be dry-cleaned should be steamed professionally or with a good steam iron at home.

SEWING JERSEY

LAYOUT, CUTTING, AND MARKING

Let the fabric relax overnight before cutting. Find the right side of the fabric by stretching crosswise. The edge will curl to the right side. Before using the selvage or raw edges, examine them carefully to determine if they're straight.

Follow a vertical rib when establishing the true grainline. Try to avoid using the original foldline, which may be permanently creased. If the fabric is tubular, slash along one crease; refold as needed.

Lay out the fabric on a smooth cutting surface, right sides together. To avoid stretching, do not allow the ends to hang off the table unsupported.

Use a nap layout and lay out the pattern pieces so the fabric will run toward stress points. This is usually from the hem up.

Use ballpoint pins placed within the seam allowances or weights to anchor the pattern. Be sure

---

SEWING CHECKLIST

Machine Needles: Universal-H point, stretch(HS), ballpoint (SUK), or Yellow Band needles; sizes 8/60 to 11/75.

Machine Setting: Stitch length 2mm (12 stitches per inch); tension, balanced.

Thread: Long-staple polyester, cotton-wrapped polyester.

Hand Sewing Needles: Sizes 5 to 9.

Sewing Machine Equipment: Straight-stitch foot and small-hole needle plate, roller foot.

Equipment and Supplies: Ballpoint pins, weights, well-sharpened shears, lightweight or invisible zippers.

Layout: Nap. Double lay.

Marking Techniques: Temporary marking pens, soap sliver, chalk, pins, tracing wheel and carbon, tailor tacks, and thread tracing.

Seams: Plain, double/ply, twin needle, tissue-stitched, taped.

Hems: Plain, blindstitch, blind catchstitch, catchstitch, figure-eight, machine blindstitch, zigzag or stretch blindstitch, twin needle, topstitched, lettuce edging, tucked, lace, fused.

Seam and Hem Finishes: Unfinished, pinked, pinked-and-stitched, serged, hand overcast, lace, seam tape.

Edge Finishes: Self-fabric facings, bias facings, bindings, bands, false bands, ribbings.

Interfacings: Used for details, garment openings, buttonholes, waistbands, and pocket areas.

Linings: Generally not used, except on very fitted garments and outerwear.

Closures: Hand-worked, machine-stitched and bound buttonholes, button loops, zippers.

pins are new and undamaged to prevent runs.

When laying out silk jersey, which is more difficult to handle, pin to tissue paper first; lay out the pattern; then cut through the fabric and tissue.

Use very sharp shears when cutting jersey.

STITCHING TIPS

Make a test seam, using a stitch length of 2mm (12 stitch per inch) and a loosely balanced tension. Begin with a new needle; before inserting it, check for burrs.

Use a straight-stitch presser foot and a small-hole needle plate or a roller foot to hold the fabric firmly. Hold the fabric taut while stitching.

If the fabric catches in the feed dogs or puckers, tissue-stitch seams. To reduce curling at raw edges, spray with fabric finish and press. Stitch 1/4″ from the edge.

Hint *Since jerseys do not retain sharp creases, Sandra Betzina edgestitches pleats to help them maintain their shape.*

SEAMS

For everyday garments, narrow double/ply seams are best. If you have a serger, finish seams with serging; otherwise, finish with a zigzag or straight stitch, depending on your equipment.

For a flatter seam, Sandra Betzina uses a crooked straight stitch (W,.5;L,2.5) instead of a stretch stitch.

Since jersey doesn't fray, seam finishes are usually eliminated. For fine garments, plain seams pressed open work well. Finish raw edges with a zigzag, multi-stitch zigzag, or hand overcast, if you'd like. But don't use a turned-and-stitched finish; it's too bulky.

Some seams, such as armholes, necklines, and crotch seams, receive more stress than others when the garment is worn. Sew these with a crooked straight stitch (W,.5;L,1.5); then stitch again 1/8″ away to reinforce the seam.

Stabilize shoulder seams, necklines, and waistlines with nonstretch stay tape.

HEMS

Let garments hang for at least twenty-four hours before marking the hem. Then to avoid runs from the hem up, zigzag (W,.5;L,1) close to the raw edge.

Hint: *Use a stabilizer if necessary to prevent rippling.*

Hem quality garments by hand if you aren't using a decorative finish. Hem lightly and loosely, using a very small crewel needle and a blindstitch, blind catchstitch, catchstitch, or figure-eight stitch.

Hem everyday garments on the machine with a zigzag blindstitch, false band, twin needle, shirttail, or topstitched double-fold hem.

Use lettuce edging to create a soft, feminine look. For more tailored designs, use a tucked hem.

EDGE FINISHES

To prevent facings from rolling to the outside, understitch by hand or machine; then ditch-stitch to secure them at shoulder and underarm seams.

On casual designs, topstitch 1/4″ to 1/2″ from the edge; then trim the facings close to the stitched line. If you have a serger, serge the facings before sewing them to the garments.

Other popular edge finishes include bindings in self-fabric, contrast fabric, bias tape, ribbon, synthetic suede, and leather.

BUTTONHOLES

Reinforce buttonhole areas with a firmly woven interfacing. Position the interfacing so the least amount of stretch is parallel to the buttonhole or use a second piece of interfacing for stability. To prevent rippling, reposition buttonholes so they are parallel to the ribs; or cord the buttonholes.

Machine-stitched buttonholes are appropriate for most garments; lengthen the stitch slightly before sewing. Also consider bound buttonholes on wool jersey, and hand-worked buttonholes or button loops for silk jersey.

ZIPPERS

Slot, lapped, invisible, and exposed zippers are suitable for jersey garments. For fine silk and wool jersey garments, hand stitch the zippers in place. Stabilize the zipper placket with a piece of lightweight selvage.

To avoid a rippling zipper, leave the zipper opening 1/2″ to 1″ longer than the zipper and ease the excess to the zipper tape. Hand baste the zipper in place before stitching it permanently.

INTERFACINGS AND LININGS

Depending on the garment design and interfacing purpose, consider fusible knit, lightweight nonwoven, and woven sew-in interfacings.

Use lightweight, firmly woven sew-in interfacings to stabilize button and buttonhole areas, waist bands, cuffs, collars, and plackets—anywhere stretch is not desired. Use fusible knit interfacing, applied to the facing or entire garment section, when stretch is to be retained.

To preserve the garment shape, line fitted garments with firm, lightweight woven fabrics. To retain the fabric give, use a knit lining, or cut a woven lining on the bias.

DETAILS FROM A PUCCI

In the late fifties, the Italian designer Emilio Pucci introduced his silk jersey skimmers to the world of high fashion. Brightly patterned and comfortable to wear, they were a forerunner of the knit revolution.

Since Pucci developed many of the sewing techniques we take for granted today, you may find this brief review of a dress from the sixties interesting.

- The seams, which were stretched slightly when stitched, are finished with a zigzag (W,2;L,2).
- The back opening has small covered snaps and is interfaced with a lightweight lining fabric cut on the straight grain.

- The empire waistline has a 2″ bias stay of the lining fabric; the shoulder seams are stabilized with a 1/2″-wide lining stay.
- The underarm zipper is set by hand with a short running stitch and silk (size A) thread.
- The hems at the bottom and sleeves are finished with a loose blindstitch.
- The bodice has two darts: one from the empire waist and the other at the underarm. The underarm dart is located on the fabric pattern—a border print—so it's only visible from the wrong side of the garment.

There are some other Pucci firsts we may take for granted today. For instance, he was the first designer to sign his name as a part of the fabric design. This is particularly important because many manufacturers knocked off Pucci-like prints; but only his include the signature. He was also the first designer to outline bold colored prints with a thin black line.

PRESSING AND GARMENT CARE

Always test press on a fabric scrap. Use the fiber content as a guide for selecting the best temperature, but remember that most jerseys require a lower temperature setting than heavier fabrics with the same fiber content. A too-hot temperature can cause melting, slicking, puckering, or scorching. Always use a damp press cloth; be especially careful of overpressing wool and silk jerseys.

Many jersey garments will stretch out of shape when hung and should be stored flat.

Double Knits

An innovation of the Italian knitmakers, fine, expensive double-knit fabrics were first produced for designer garments.

Comfortable to wear, wrinkle-resistant, and economical, double knits were an immediate success when they were introduced to the mass market in the late sixties. In fact, they saturated the market for several years and were manufactured in all qualities and price ranges.

But by the time the popularity of crisp, structured double-knit garments had faded, most of us only remembered the plastic-like quality of the cheaper fabrics. This is unfortunate because good double knits are beautiful, comfortable to wear, and easy to sew.

Available in a variety of weights, yarn types, textures and fibers, double knits are knitted with two or more yarns which interlock in each row. Many look the same on both sides.

Fabric Characteristics
- Double knit fabrics are easy to sew.
- Double knits require a nap layout.

157

- They have little or no crosswise stretch. Most have more stretch on the bias than in the width.
- They don't run or ravel.
- Double knits are stable and firm without being rigid.
- Double knits will retain crisp, structured shapes.
- Most double knits cannot be straightened if they are off-grain.
- Sometimes double knits have a permanent creaseline down the center.
- Skipped stitches are sometimes a problem.
- Double knit is a two-faced fabric that can be used for unlined and reversible garments.
- Double-knit fabrics can be tailored by traditional or shortcut methods.
- Unlike jerseys and sweater knits, they do not stretch when hung in a closet.

PLANNING A GARMENT

See also Knits for general sewing suggestions.

PURCHASING THE FABRIC

All heavy knits are not double knits. When in doubt, examine both sides—double knits look the same on the face and the back. If you still can't decide, pull the raw edge: double knits do not roll; single knits do.

Quality double knits have good stretch and recover their original dimensions when relaxed.

Hint: *To test the recovery, stretch the fabric in both directions. If it doesn't return to its original shape, the garment will stretch out of shape and become baggy if it isn't lined or underlined.*

SEWING CHECKLIST

Machine Needles: Universal-H point, Yellow Band, twin needles; sizes 60/8 to 90/14, depending on the fabric weight.

Machine Setting: Stitch length 2–2.5mm (10–12 stitches per inch); tension, lightly balanced.

Thread: Long-staple polyester or cotton-wrapped polyester, wooly nylon. Topstitching: regular or topstitching.

Hand Sewing Needles: Sizes 5 to 9.

Equipment and Notions: Ballpoint pins, weights, well-sharpened shears, and lightweight, invisible, or decorative zippers.

Layout: Nap.

Marking Techniques: Clips, chalk, soap sliver, pins, temporary marking pens, tailor tacks, thread tracing. Tracing carbon may not mark clearly.

Seams: Plain, double/ply, twin needle, welt, tucked, slot, piped, lapped, double-lapped, bound-and-lapped bound-and-stitched, taped.

Hems: Blindstitch, catchstitch, blind catchstitch, figure-eight, machine blindstitch, twin needle, topstitched, fused, wrong-side-out, double-stitched, interfaced.

Seam and Hem Finishes: Single/ply or double/ply. Unfinished, pinked, pinked-and-stitched, serged, hand overcast, lace, seam tape.

Edge Finishes: Self-fabric facings, lining-fabric facings, bias facings, bias bindings, synthetic suede and leather bindings, bands, and false bands.

Interfacings: Used for details, garment openings, buttonholes, waistbands, and pocket areas.

Linings and Underlinings: Optional, depending on the garment design, quality, and use.

Closures: All types.

Pockets: All types.

Check to be sure the fabric pattern is squared with the lengthwise edges and that there are no unwanted creases. Since it may have a permanent finish which is heat-set, an off-grain fabric cannot be straightened.

DESIGN IDEAS AND PATTERN SELECTION

Since double knits have little or no stretch, the fabric weight, crispness, and texture are more important to the garment design than the stretch factor.

Most double knits have enough body to tailor well and are well-suited for dresses, jackets, coats, pants, and children's wear.

Simple styles with crisp, tailored lines, top-stitching, decorative seams, trims of contrasting fabrics, braids, satin bindings, leather, or synthetic suede are particularly attractive. Darts, seaming details, A-lines, soft pleats, and eased fullness work well.

For medium and heavy double knits, choose a pattern which suggests a crisp fabric; and, if the fabric suggestions don't include double knit, look for suggested wovens such as linen, wool flannel, and corduroy.

For lightweight double knits, choose a pattern which suggests a soft fabric, stable jerseys, or crepe.

It's frequently better to avoid designs with hard, sharp creases and obvious gathers. Also, double knits cannot be used for patterns labeled "knits only."

FABRIC AND PATTERN PREPARATION

Treat the uncut fabric as you plan to treat the garment, using the manufacturer's care instructions as a guide.

Preshrink washable fabrics, all trims, and notions to remove excess finishing solutions which might cause stitching problems. Wash gently with a mild detergent and warm water. Line dry or machine dry on warm.

Fig. 10–7 *Simple, understated elegance, the dress is black and white double knit, designed by Courrèges. (Photographer, Catherine Caron; photo courtesy of Courrèges, Pret-a-Porter Autumn/Winter 1987/1988.)*

159

Steam press wool double knits and fabrics which must be dry-cleaned unless they have less than 1 percent shrinkage or are labeled needle-ready. If you don't have a really good steam iron, send the fabric to the dry cleaner for steaming. It doesn't need to be dry-cleaned.

Steam press the center fold. If it doesn't press out immediately, use a 50/50 vinegar and water solution and a press cloth; press again. If the crease still remains, arrange the pattern pieces so the creaseline will be inconspicuous.

Hint: *Always test for fading and spotting before using the vinegar/water solution on a large section.*

To square the fabric ends, match the folded edge with the long edge of a rectangular table. Mark and cut the crosswise ends even with the table.

Although these knits have some give, and are comfortable to wear, they fit like woven materials. Compare the pattern dimensions and body measurements plus minimum ease before cutting to be sure the garment will be large enough.

SEWING DOUBLE KNITS

LAYOUT, CUTTING, AND MARKING

Let the fabric relax overnight before cutting. Mark the right side with drafting tape.

Use a nap layout. Most double knits are 60″ wide, permitting economical layouts. Use a vertical rib as a guide for the straight grain when the selvages or lengthwise edges are irregularly shaped. Thread baste or chalk the center foldline following one continuous rib.

Fold the fabric on the thread basting with right sides out. If the fabric is unusually bulky, lay it out flat; mark the grainline with thread basting along a lengthwise rib at one edge.

Use ballpoint pins placed within the seam allowances or weights to anchor the pattern. To prevent snags, be sure pins are new and undamaged.

Cut out the garment with a sturdy pair of well-sharpened, bent-handled shears.

Mark using your favorite method—clips, chalk

or soap sliver, new ballpoint pins, temporary marking pens, tailor tacks, or thread tracing. Tracing carbon may not mark clearly.

STITCHING TIPS

Make a test seam, using a stitch length of 2–2.5mm (10–12 stitches per inch), a balanced tension, and regular pressure. Begin with a new needle; adjust the tension and pressure and lengthen the stitch if needed.

When stitching, hold the fabric taut and take an occasional rest stop. Stop with the needle down; raise the presser foot so the fabric can relax; lower the foot; then continue stitching.

Use staystitching only on necklines, armholes, and waistline seams. Reduce bulk by grading and trimming.

Understitch all facings to prevent them from rolling to the outside of the garment. Understitch fine garments with a small hand stitch.

SEAMS AND SEAM FINISHES

Plain seams pressed open are frequently used; since double knits don't ravel, special seam finishes are not necessary. For aesthetics, pink, zigzag, serge, or hand overcast. If the edges of the seam allowances tend to roll, stitch 1/4″ from the edge.

Hint: *When serging seams, use woolly nylon, which is softer than polyester thread. Avoid a turned-and-stitched finish; the fabric is too bulky.*

To make durable crotch and armhole seams, double-stitch on the seamline with a crooked straight stitch (W,.5;L,2). Trim close to the second stitching.

Stabilize shoulder and waistline seams with a nonstretch stay tape. Stabilize necklines and armholes with bias-cut tricot or lightweight lining fabric.

Decorative seams such as the tucked, slot, welt, topstitched, and piped are especially attractive on double-knit designs.

For unlined jackets and coats, consider double/ply, strap, bound-and-lapped, bound-and-stitched, and double-lapped seams.

HEMS

Finish the hem as you did the seams, or leave it unfinished.

Hint: *Lace seam binding works well since it has some stretch; however, lace binding is a tattle-tale sign of homemade; and it may leave an imprint on the right side of the fabric.*

Hem quality garments by hand if you aren't using a decorative treatment. Use a very small crewel needle and a blindstitch, catchstitch, or fig-ure-eight stitch; double-stitch hems on heavy fab-rics. When hemming by hand, pick up a small stitch on the back side of the fabric and keep the stitches loose.

Hint: *When hemming with a blindstitch, take an oc-casional backstitch.*

If the garment is underlined, stitch the hem to the underlining. Interface hems of fine garments with a strip of bias-cut interfacing.

Hem everyday garments with a machine blind-stitch or fusible web. Use a small needle so the hem won't show on the right side of the garment.

For a decorative detail, use regular thread or topstitching thread to topstitch several rows around the hem; or use a twin needle hem, which has a little give.

EDGE FINISHES AND TRIMS

Consider the crossgrain as well as the bias when making self-fabric trims. Although the crossgrain may not have as much stretch as the bias, it fre-quently has enough to be shaped satisfactorily.

When self-fabric facings are too bulky, substi-tute a lightweight lining fabric. To prevent facings from rolling to the outside, understitch by hand or machine.

Hint: *To secure the facings inconspicuously, ditch-stitch, hand tack with a catchstitch, or fuse the facings just to the seam allowances.*

Bindings in self-fabric, satin, faille, grosgrain, ribbon, braid, or synthetic suede look attractive on double knits.

On sleeveless garments, bind both the neckline and armholes or bind the neckline and face the armholes with shaped facings, bias strips, or an all-in-one facing.

Hint: *When using an all-in-one facing, finish the armholes first; then apply the neckline bind-ing.*

If desired, topstitch faced edges 1/4″ to 1/2″ from edge.

INTERFACINGS

Use hair canvas in an appropriate weight to in-terface collars, lapels, and other tailored details on wool suits and coats. Use a washable fusible or sew-in nonwoven interfacing on synthetic double-knit jackets.

Many garments will not need interfacings at faced edges, collars, cuffs, pocket welts, flaps, and waist-bands.

For instance, the twenty-year-old Kimberly knit dress in my vintage costume collection has no in-terfacing in the collar, cuffs, or pocket flaps. The garment is a bit out of fashion, but it has main-tained its original crispness without the help of interfacing. (If you don't remember Kimberly knits, they were the best ready-to-wear had to offer—and very expensive—during the height of the double-knit craze.)

If the fabric does require interfacing, choose a lightweight woven or nonwoven type, muslin, or organdy. When using fusible interfacings, apply them to the facing or to the entire garment section to avoid a demarcation line on the right side of the garment.

Interface pocket areas so the fabric will not tear when the pocket is used.

LININGS AND UNDERLININGS

Generally, outerwear garments are lined. Lin-ings and/or underlinings are optional on other gar-ments, since they may reduce the give and garment comfort.

When lining skirts and trousers, attach the lining at the waist; for dresses, attach only at the neckline and armholes. That way the garment won't lose the stretch and comfort of the fashion fabric.

When lining or underlining garments, consider a lightweight knit or bias-cut woven fabric with the same care properties as the fashion fabric.

Use an underlining to add more body or crispness to a lightweight double knit. Materials such as fusible knit interfacings can be used to change the character of the fabric.

A partial underlining for skirt backs and knees of slacks will help the garment maintain its shape.

CLOSURES

Always interface the buttonhole area with a firmly woven interfacing, positioned so the least amount of stretch is parallel to the buttonhole.

Bound buttonholes are particularly attractive. Loops, machine-stitched or hand-worked buttonholes are also suitable.

Set zippers by your favorite method: slot, lapped, invisible, exposed. On fine wool double knits, hand stitch zippers in place.

PRESSING AND GARMENT CARE

Pressing as you go is particularly important when sewing double knits.

Test press on a fabric scrap to determine the correct amount of heat and moisture.

Use a damp press cloth to prevent shine on wools and heat-sensitive fabrics. Press lightly on the lengthwise grain; do not press across the grain.

To set creases, saturate a brown paper grocery bag with water. Place the bag over the fabric and iron until the paper is dry. Or press with a 50/50 vinegar and water solution.

Always consider the garment construction as well as fiber content when choosing a cleaning method.

Interlocks

A weft knit with fine ribs on the front and back, the interlock is a form of double knit. It looks the same on both sides—smooth. Interlock knits have little elasticity in the width with good elasticity in the length.

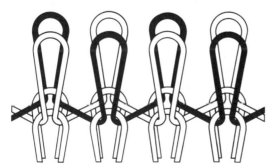

Fig. 10–8

Compared to jersey, interlocks knitted with the same size yarns are more stable and heavier; they have less stretch in the width, do not curl at raw edges, and are more resistant to runs.

Compared to tricot, interlocks have less stretch in the width and more in the length. And, although both run when stressed, interlocks are less runproof.

Fabric Characteristics
- Interlock knits are firm and hold their shape better than jersey.

- They require a nap layout.
- Interlock knits run from the end last knitted and are damaged by defective needles.
- Ripped seams may leave marks and holes in these fabrics.
- Creases are almost impossible to remove.
- Interlock knits shrink little.
- They cannot be straightened if they are off-grain.
- Puckered seams and skipped stitches are frequent problems. The machine also tends to eat the fabric.
- Interlock knits do not curl at raw edges.

PLANNING A GARMENT

For additional information, see Knits and Jersey.

DESIGN IDEAS AND PATTERN SELECTION

Although interlock knits are suitable for dressy designs, lingerie, and evening wear, they are used most frequently for casual garments—T-shirts, dresses, blouses, palazzo pants, and unstructured jackets. Soft, fluid designs, unpressed pleats, gathers, and roll-up sleeves work well.

Interlock knits are rarely mentioned in the fabric suggestions; however, they can be used for designs that feature challis, jersey, lightweight knits, or single knits. Although these knits are easier to sew than jerseys, the same suggestions apply. But be aware that most interlocks are not suitable for "knits only" patterns. Compare the fabric with the stretch gauge on the pattern envelope.

SEWING CHECKLIST

Machine Needles: Universal-H point, stretch(HS), ballpoint(SUK), or Yellow Band, twin needles; sizes 8/60 to 11/75.

Machine Setting: Stitch length 2mm (12 stitches per inch); tension, balanced.

Thread: Long-staple polyester, cotton-wrapped polyester.

Hand Sewing Needles: Sizes 5 to 9.

Sewing Machine Equipment: Straight-stitch foot and small-hole needle plate, roller foot.

Equipment and Supplies: Ballpoint pins, weights, well-sharpened shears, lightweight or invisible zippers.

Layout: Nap. Double lay.

Marking Techniques: All types except wax.

Seams: Plain, double/ply, twin needle, stretch, tissue-stitched, taped.

Hems: Machine blindstitch, zigzag or stretch blindstitch, twin needle, top-stitched, shirttail, lettuce edging, shell, tucked, merrow, mock-merrow, lace, fused.

Edge Finishes: Self-fabric facings, bias and lace facings, bindings, false bands, ribbings, applied elastic, and casings.

Interfacings and Linings: Rarely used.

Raschel Knits

Versatile warp knits, raschel knits run the gamut from four-way stretch fabrics to fine, lightweight machine-made laces and bulky, three-dimensional sweater knits with little or no stretch.

This chapter focuses on the casual, bulky, sweaterlike fabrics which have looped yarns, and the chenille or embroidered-type surfaces with little or no stretch.

Knitted on a warp-knitting machine, which utilizes a variety of stitch formations and yarns to create designs and textures, these fabrics are easy to recognize by the rows of parallel chainstitching on the reverse side.

Fabric Characteristics
- Raschel knits are easy to sew.
- They are firm without being rigid. They do not run.
- Raschel knits have a nap.
- They are frequently lofty and slightly bulky.
- They have little or no stretch and are not suitable for "knits only" patterns.
- They are soft and will not maintain a crisp, structured shape by themselves.
- Raschel knits are frequently made from acrylic fibers, which are washable and warm to wear, but are also subject to pilling.
- Most raschel knits cannot be straightened if they are off-grain.

PLANNING A GARMENT

See Knits for general sewing suggestions.

FABRIC AND PATTERN SELECTION

Raschel knits are well-suited for unlined jackets, coats, straight skirts, slacks, dresses, sweaters, T-shirts, and sweatshirt designs.

Fig. 10–9 *At first glance, these open-weave raschel knits look hand-knit. (Photo courtesy of Pine Crest Knits, Inc.)*

Machine Needles: Universal-H point or Yellow Band, twin needles; sizes 80/12 to 90/14.
Machine Setting: Stitch length 2–2.5mm (10–12 stitches per inch); tension, lightly balanced; pressure, adjust as needed.
Thread: Long-staple polyester or cotton-wrapped polyester or woolly nylon.
Hand Sewing Needles: Sizes 5 to 7.
Sewing Machine Equipment: Roller foot.
Equipment and Supplies: Long glass-headed pins, weights, and invisible, lightweight, or decorative zippers.
Layout: Nap. Single or double layer.
Marking Techniques: Clips, pins, tailor tacks.
Seams: Plain, double-stitched, double/ply, strap, taped.
Hems: Twin needle, topstitched, machine blindstitch.
Seam and Hem Finishes: Single/ply or double/ply. Unfinished, serged, multi-stitch zigzag, zigzag, seam tape, bound, serged.
Edge Finishes: Self-fabric facings, lining-fabric facings, tricot facings, bias facings, ribbings, fold-over braid, synthetic suede and leather bindings.

Let the fabric do the talking. Select a simple design with minimum seaming. Easy fitted shapes, exaggerated sleeves, inseam pockets, elastic waistbands, collarless cardigans, and shawl collars are best.

Consider using decorative ribbings, bindings, bands, and fold-over braids instead of bulky self-fabric facings.

Do not use "knits only" patterns. Also try to avoid pleats, gathers, waistline seams, zippers, buttonholes, slashed pockets, self-fabric facings, topstitching, and fussy details. Ease is better than darts.

When purchasing the fabric, add at least 10 percent to the yardage requirements. Some raschel knits shrink as much as 25 percent. Using the fabric-care recommendations as a guide, preshrink the fabric with the same treatment you plan to give the finished garment.

Raschel knits are usually quite square. Straighten the end if the cutting line is crooked.

These knits fit like woven materials. Compare the pattern dimensions and body measurements plus minimum ease before cutting to be sure the garment will be large enough.

SEWING RASCHEL KNITS

LAYOUT, CUTTING, AND MARKING

Study the fabric to decide whether the garment will be more attractive cut on the crossgrain.

Lay out the fabric with the right sides together or in a single layer with the wrong side up. If there is an obvious crosswise pattern to be matched, use a single/lay, right side up.

Use a nap layout. If you can't decide which way the nap should run from the right side, turn the fabric over. Examine the ends of the vertical chain-stitches; use the end that unravels as the top.

Use weights or long pins to anchor the pattern pieces. To avoid stretching, do not let the fabric hang off the table.

For marking, use snips, long flower or glass-headed pins, or tailor tacks.

STITCHING TIPS

Make a test seam to determine whether the tension needs to be loosened and/or the pressure lightened. To prevent snagging, use a roller foot or wrap the toes of the presser foot with transparent tape.

When stitching, take an occasional rest stop. Stop with the needle down and raise the presser foot so the fabric can relax; then lower the foot and continue stitching.

Staystitch curved edges to prevent stretching. Tape shoulder and waistline seams with a non-stretch stay tape. Stabilize necklines and armholes with bias-cut tricot. Understitch all facings to prevent them from rolling to the outside.

SEAMS AND HEMS

Although raschel knits don't ravel during construction, they will ravel when the garment is worn. Thus double/ply seams are generally best.

Hems can be topstitched, twin needle or machine blindstitched, or zigzag blindstitched. For a quick and easy finish, fold the 5/8″ hem allowance to the wrong side; stitch close to the folded edge and again 1/4″ away. Trim close to the stitched line.

Hint: *If the straight stitch looks crooked, experiment with a narrow zigzag stitch (W,.5–1).*

If the garment has a 2″ hem, stitch again 1 1/2″ and 1 3/4″ from the edge; then trim.

Hint: *To add body to the hem, place a piece of fusible web between the hem and garment layers before stitching; fuse at the final pressing.*

EDGE FINISHES

When using a shaped facing, fuse the interfacing to the facing. Finish the facing edge with a serger, multi-stitch zigzag, or zigzag stitch before sewing the facing to the garment.

To reduce bulk, replace self-fabric facings with lining-weight facings, sheer tricot facings, or bias facings.

For jackets and sweater openings, face the edges with grosgrain ribbon to prevent stretching. For a decorative finish, use ribbings, fold-over braid, synthetic suede bands or bindings, or grosgrain ribbon.

INTERFACINGS, LININGS, AND UNDERLININGS

Most garment designs won't need interfacings; but some will. Select an interfacing with a little give to match the fabric. Use nonwoven, weft insertion, or knitted fusibles or nonwoven sew-ins applied to the facing.

Hint: *To reduce bulk in inseam pockets, cut pocket sacks from a lightweight lining fabric. Reinforce pocket stress points with small pieces of interfacing.*

Omit linings and underlinings on casual garments.

CLOSURES

If buttonholes can't be eliminated, interface the area with nonwoven interfacing. Be sure the interfacing is most stable and stretches least parallel to the buttonhole length.

For machine-stitched buttonholes, lengthen the stitch and cord them to prevent stretching.

Hint: *Gail Brown uses snaps instead of buttons and buttonholes.*

PRESSING AND GARMENT CARE

Test press on a fabric scrap. To avoid matting and flattening the surface yarns, cover the pressing board with a Velvaboard or thick terry towel. Steam press the seamline.

Most raschel knits can be machine washed and dried.

Sweatshirt Knits

Sweatshirt and fleece fabrics are easy to sew and comfortable to wear. Sweatshirt knits have a brushed fleece on one or both sides for warmth; the fleece also absorbs moisture to keep you dry and comfortable. A few sweatshirt knits are finished to be flame-retardant.

Fabric Characteristics
- Sweatshirt fabrics vary in stretch from very little to moderate.
- They are easy to sew.
- Fabrics which contain cotton shrink badly.
- Sweatshirt fabrics are bulky.
- Sweatshirt fabrics require a nap layout.
- Most sweatshirt fabrics cannot be straightened if they are off-grain.

PLANNING A GARMENT

See Knits for general sewing suggestions.

PATTERN AND FABRIC SELECTION

Longtime favorites for active sports, sweatshirt and fleece fabrics became fashion fabrics when Norma Kamali began using them for office dressing—skirts, jackets, and pants—in the late 1970s.

These easy-to-sew knits are good choices for activewear designs, sweaters, skirts, dresses, jogging suits, children's garments, bath robes, coats, and, of course, sweatshirts.

Look for simple designs with darted or seamed shaping. Raglan and kimono sleeves, dropped shoulders, elastic waistbands, collarless designs, shawl collars, topstitched seams, soft pleats, and gathers are just a few of the many design details which work well.

When selecting the fabric, avoid sweatshirt knits that are finished so the ribs and courses are not at right angles.

Fig. 10–10 *For active people, Cardin sweatshirt knits trimmed with exposed zippers and drawstring waists. (Photo courtesy of Pierre Cardin Activewear.)*

FABRIC PREPARATION

These knits shrink both in the length and width; fabrics with some cotton shrink more than all-synthetic fabrics. To avoid being caught short, purchase a little extra fabric.

Preshrink at least twice; additional shrinkage usually occurs after the first wash. To minimize shrinkage, line dry.

SEWING SWEATSHIRT FABRICS

SEAMS, HEMS, AND EDGE FINISHES

Make a test seam using a stitch length of 2.5–3mm (10–12 stitches per inch), a loosely balanced tension, and a new needle.

Stretch slightly as you sew. Use a crooked straight stitch (W,.5;L,2) narrow zigzag, or twin needle seam. An even-feed foot will help reduce creeping.

Hint: *Use woolly nylon thread in the bobbin to put some give in any seam.*

Plain, inconspicuous seams always work well; and, since the fabric does not ravel, they can be left unfinished. Or follow the lead of ready-to-wear manufacturers and accent style lines with decorative seaming: topstitched, welt, flatlocked, piped, decorative serged, and lapped seams are just a few of the many choices.

Use an even-feed foot to reduce drag lines on topstitched and welt seams.

In addition to conventional hem finishes—top-stitched, twin needle, fused, machine and stretch blindstitched, and hand stitched—many decorative hems can be made with stretch-stitch machines.

Experiment with various combinations of stretch stitches and decorative threads. If the threads cannot be used in the needle, put them in the bobbin and stitch wrong side up.

Hint: *Adjust the tension as needed for a more attractive finish.*

Substitute bands or false bands for hems.

For other edge finishes, replace bulky facings with ribbing trims, bindings, or serged or zig-zagged edges.

Hint: *Sweatshirt fabrics are rarely lined; however, one of the cutest designs I've ever seen was a gray 3/4-length coat with a gray and white woven cotton/polyester lining.*

Sweatshirt fabrics are also good background fabrics for machine appliqué or embroidered designs. For best results, stitch with a stabilizer between the fabric and feed dogs.

Hint: *Sewing teacher John Montieth prefers Pellon's Stitch-n-Tear; and, when the fabric is unusually soft, he uses two layers of stabilizer.*

To create novelty designs, use lettuce edging to make ruffled pintucks. Zigzag or satin stitch the edges.

Mesh

Mesh, sometimes called athletic mesh or dishrag, is an open knit with evenly spaced holes.

Fabric Characteristics
- Mesh is easy to sew.
- Mesh is an open-knit, transparent fabric.
- Mesh does not ravel or run.
- Mesh is easily damaged with the point of the iron.

PLANNING A GARMENT

See Knits for general sewing suggestions.

SELECTING THE FABRIC AND PATTERN

Examine the fabric carefully to be sure it is knitted so the mesh rows are at right angles to the

SEWING CHECKLIST

Machine Needles: Universal-H point or Yellow Band, twin needles; sizes 70/10 to 80/12.

Machine Setting: Stitch length 1.5–2.5mm (10–15 stitches per inch); tension, loosely balanced.

Thread: Long-staple polyester, cotton-wrapped polyester.

Sewing Machine Equipment: Jeans or roller foot, small-hole needle plate.

Equipment and Supplies: Long glass-headed pins, weights, rotary cutter and mat, transparent tape, stabilizer.

Layout: Double layer, right sides together.

Marking: Temporary marking pen, tape.

Seams: Narrow, double-stitched, double/ply.

Seam Finishes: Double-stitched, serged, zigzag, multi-stitch zigzag.

Hems and Edge Finishes: Topstitched and twin needle hems, bias and ribbon bindings, fold-over braid, bands, bias facing.

Underlinings: Sometimes.

Fig. 10–11 *For casual elegance, few designs compare with this easy, open-knit mesh pullover trimmed with leather appliqués. (Photo courtesy of Sakowitz Catalog.)*

selvages. If it is more than 1/2″ off, select another fabric.

Select a pattern for an easy pull-on top. Tank tops, long-sleeved pullovers, and tee tops are good choices.

Frequently worn by men and boys *au naturel*, ladies and girls usually wear mesh designs as an overlayer. Or use a little mesh for a yoke or inset to accent crisp summer fabrics.

For a more dramatic treatment, create an interesting design and appliqué it strategically to the garment front. Some ready-mades feature sheepskin appliqués on mesh backgrounds.

Hint: *Use the old standbys—patch pockets—to modesty-proof a mesh pullover.*

SEWING MESH

LAYOUT, CUTTING, AND MARKING

Machine wash and dry the fabric, then spread it in a double/lay, right sides together. Check to be sure the rows of holes will be horizontal, not slanted, on the garment.

Use weights or long glass-head pins to secure the pattern. Cut, using sharp shears or a rotary cutter and mat.

STITCHING TIPS

Make a test seam to determine the stitch length. Shorten the stitch length for mesh with large holes.

Hint: *To eliminate puckered seams, stitch slowly; and, if necessary, tissue-stitch seams.*

169

To avoid snagging the mesh, use a jeans or roller foot; or wrap the toes with transparent tape.

SEAMS AND EDGE FINISHES

Keep the seams narrow since the fabric is transparent; even an easy double-stitched seam works well on these fabrics.

Neckline and armhole edges are particularly attractive finished with smooth fabric or grosgrain ribbon bindings, foldover braids, or ribbings; use a complementary color if you can't match the mesh exactly.

Finish hems with a narrow topstitched or twin needle hem, band, or binding.

Hint: *Press mesh carefully to avoid snagging.*

Tricot

Tricot, everyone's favorite lingerie fabric, is a warp-knit fabric. The loops zigzag vertically up the fabric to form a strong material that's very run-resistant.

Easy to sew and long wearing, tricot conforms smoothly to the body. It is available in a variety of weights, from sheer 15 denier to heavy 60 denier.

One of the most popular weights is 40 denier. A medium-weight fabric, it is opaque and used for slips, nightgowns, panties, and camisoles. The 15-denier sheer is frequently used for overlays and peignoirs, as well as for linings under laces, insertions, edge finishing, and facings.

Some tricots such as Antron III and Lustra have an antistatic finish, which makes them noncling.

Satin tricot is a lustrous, satin-look fabric, while crepe tricots are frosted medium-sheer materials.

When sewing two-way stretch knits, see Action Knits. For pleated sheer tricot, see Prepleated Fabrics and Soft, Transparent Fabrics.

Tricots are also used as backings for laminated fabrics and single-faced quilted fabrics.

Two fusible interfacings—Easy-Knit® and Knit Shape™—are tricot fabrics with a fusible backing.

Fabric Characteristics
- Tricot is easy to sew.
- Skipped stitches are frequently a problem.
- Most tricot fabrics are made of nylon, acetate, or triacetate. All are easily damaged with high heat.
- Tricot fabrics attract oil stains.
- Tricot snags easily.
- Tricot is easily damaged by hook and loop tape.

Fig. 10–12 *Often used for lingerie and sleepwear, nylon tricot is comfortable to wear and easy to launder. (Photo courtesy of McCall Pattern Co.)*

PLANNING A GARMENT

See Knits for general sewing suggestions.

SEWING CHECKLIST

Machine Needles: Universal-H point, stretch (HS), Yellow Band, twin needles; sizes 60/8 to 80/12.

Machine Setting: Stitch length 2mm (12 stitches per inch).

Thread: Long-staple polyester (100/2), extra-fine cotton-wrapped polyester, woolly nylon.

Hand Sewing Needles: Sizes 8 to 10.

Sewing Machine Equipment: Straight-stitch foot and small-hole needle plate or roller foot.

Equipment and Supplies: Super-fine pins, weights, well-sharpened shears and small trimming scissors, loop turner, tapestry needle, small safety pin, washable glue stick, transparent, drafting, or hair-set tape, needle lubricant.

Layout: Nap, double layer, right sides together.

Marking Techniques: Outward notches, temporary marking pens, chalk, soap sliver, pins.

Seams: Double-stitched, stretch seams, twin needle, hairline.

Hems: Lettuce edging, shell, twin needle, lace, machine blindstitch, zigzag or stretch blindstitch, merrow, mock-merrow.

Edge Finishes: Lace facings, bindings, applied elastic, elastic casings.

Linings and Underlinings: Self-fabric or all cotton linings for the panty crotch; sheer tricot lining or underlining for lace.

PATTERN AND FABRIC SELECTION

Although tricot fabrics are used primarily for lingerie, some are suitable for activewear, while others—such as brushed nylon—are used for loungewear and quilts.

Machine wash and dry the fabric to relax it and to remove excess fabric finishes, which may cause skipped stitches. Add fabric softener to the final rinse to eliminate static electicity.

Since most garments are sewn without fitting, adjust the pattern before cutting.

SEWING TRICOT

STITCHING TIPS

Fill the bobbin slowly to avoid stretching the thread.

Make a test seam, using a stitch length of 2mm (12 stitches per inch) and a loosely balanced tension. Always start with a new needle, and be prepared to change needles frequently. Nylon quickly dulls the point, causing skipped stitches.

Use a straight-stitch foot and small-hole needle plate to help hold the fabric firmly. Or use a roller foot and set the needle to the right. If you have a Bernina machine, use a jeans foot.

Static electricity tends to draw the threads into the needle hole, so lower the needle by hand and hold the threads behind the presser foot.

Stitch at a medium speed and hold the fabric taut. The fabric clings to the needle more when stitching fast, causing skipped stitches. A needle lubricant helps prevent this.

Stitch "against" the grain; sew from the waist to the hem. Avoid backstitching; shorten the stitches at the beginning and end of the seam to prevent unraveling. Use transparent tape to baste lace to fabric.

SEAMS, HEMS, AND EDGE FINISHES

Determine the right side of the fabric: stretched crosswise, the edge will roll to the right side. Seams with 1/8" to 1/4" seam allowances are easiest to stitch. For best results, use stretch seams. When sewing sheers, use hairline seams.

171

Hint: *If you have a straight-stitch machine, fill the bobbin with woolly nylon for stretchier seams.*

If the seam ripples after stitching, you stretched too much. Press with a damp press cloth to remove the rippling.

Tricot garments can be hemmed in a variety of ways—lettuce edging, shell, twin needle, applied lace, shirttail, machine blindstitched, merrow or mock-merrow finishes. Consider the garment design as well as your sewing skills and time available when making the choice.

In addition to hems, consider other edge finishes such as lace facings, bindings, and bands. When binding with tricot, cut bindings on the crossgrain or bias. Seams Great and Seams Saver are bias-cut tricot sheers.

ELASTIC

Elastic can be applied to the outside or inside of a garment. Generally elastics 1/4″ and 3/8″ wide are used at leg openings, while 1/2″ and 5/8″ widths are used at the waist.

At waistline edges, elastic can be applied directly to the fabric or inserted into a casing. Around leg openings, the applied method is better.

The casing method isn't as attractive or as professional looking as the applied method, but it's quick, easy, and can be used if you have a straight-stitch machine. It is also a sanity-saver if you have to replace the elastic at a later date.

For casings, use a braided elastic which narrows when stretched. Make the casing, leaving a 1/2″ section unstitched. Insert the elastic, adjust the length, and stitch the ends together.

Hint: *To avoid losing the elastic end, measure and mark the length; but do not cut until after the elastic is inserted and stitched.*

For the applied method, choose a lingerie elastic with one picot edge. Measure the body and cut the elastic at least 4″ shorter. Sew the elastic to the garment.

Hint: *It's easier to join the two while the garment is still flat; but it is neater to sew them into two circles, then join them.*

CROTCH LINING

This is a neat finish for panties with a separate crotch.

1. Right sides together, join the crotch section and the back.

2. Wrong sides up, place the crotch lining on the back and join.

3. Right sides together, join the crotch section and the front.

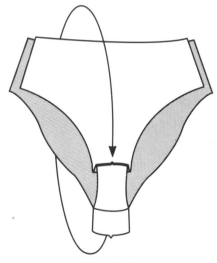

Fig. 10–13

4. Check to be sure the crotch lining will fit smoothly; trim as needed. Wrap the crotch lining around the panties; pin to the front/crotch seam. The right side of the crotch should face the wrong side of the front.

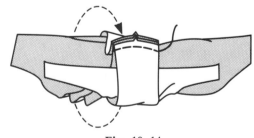

Fig. 10–14

5. Turn the panties over and stitch on the first row of stitching. Turn the garment right side out; press.

STRAPS

Straps for teddies, camisoles, and slips can be plain and functional or very decorative. Use elastic, ribbons, lace, or self-fabric to make garment straps.

1. For each strap, cut a 1 1/2″-wide strip of tricot to the desired length, with the least stretch in the length.

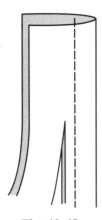

Fig. 10–15

2. Right sides together, stitch 1/4″ from the folded edge. Trim the seam to a skinny 1/4″.

3. Using a small safety pin, loop turner, or tapestry needle and thread, turn the strip right side out.

BRAIDED STRAPS

1. For each strap, make three narrow straps or spaghetti tubes 25 percent to 50 percent longer than the desired finished length.

2. Match and stack one end of each of the straps together; stitch.

3. Anchor the stitched end under the presser foot with the needle down; and braid the strips together tightly.

4. Sew the straps together at the other end; then sew them to the garment.

KNOTTED STRAPS

1. For each strap, make two narrow straps or spaghetti tubes about 25 percent longer than the finished length.

2. Match and stack one end of each strap together; stitch.

3. Knot the straps together, spacing the knots about 2″ apart.

4. Sew the straps to the garment.

TWISTED STRAPS

1. Cut a 1/4″-wide strip of tricot, three times the finished length.

2. Pull 1″ of the tricot end through the hole in the center of the bobbin.

3. Place the bobbin on the spindle so the tricot end is held firmly between the bobbin and the machine.

4. Hold the other end of the tricot firmly. Wind the bobbin so the tricot twists tightly.

5. Using your other hand, pinch the center of the twist; then fold the cord in half. Hold both cut ends firmly and release the center; the cord will twist together.

6. Sew the ends together and smooth the cord with your fingers.

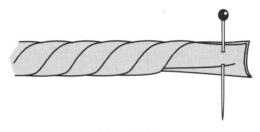

Fig. 10–16

TRICOT BOW

Cut a strip of sheer nylon tricot 1″ wide and 6″ long. Using the sewing machine spool holder as an aid, tightly tie the strip into a bow. Remove the bow and sew it to the garment.

MILLINER'S ROSE

Use purchased or custom-made roses to add a nice finish to lingerie. Roses can be made of sheer tricot or satin ribbon in a variety of sizes to trim camisoles, nightgowns, and peignoirs.

1. Cut a strip on the crossgrain 3″ to 4″ wide and about 15″ long. Fold the strip in half lengthwise, wrong sides together, and trim the strip so it looks like a triangle.

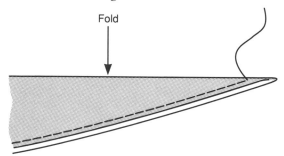

Fig. 10–17

2. Run a gathering thread along the cut edges.
3. Gather and roll the small end to make the center; tack securely.
4. Repeat until most of the strip is gathered, rolled, and tacked. Fold the raw end down to the gathered line and tack. You can also cover the raw edges with a small piece of fabric and add leaves.
5. Change the dimensions of the length and width to make larger or smaller roses.

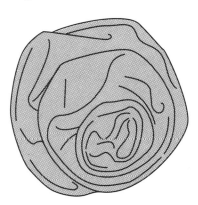

Fig. 10–18

Hint: *I made larger roses in white satin and white faille to decorate the tables for a bridal shower. I put the roses on sturdy wires and arranged them in pots of grape ivy.*
One season Erik Mortensen, the designer at the House of Balmain, used larger velvet roses to trim an elegant evening wrap.

Here's another method you can use to make small leaves and rosebuds. Cut one 2″ to 4″ square, depending on the size of the flower. Fold, wrong

sides together, on the bias. Fold each half so all the points meet at the bottom. Draw a curved line from corner to corner; gather and tack securely. Fold the raw edges under below the gathering.

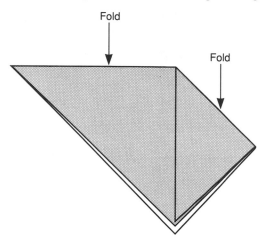

Fig. 10–19

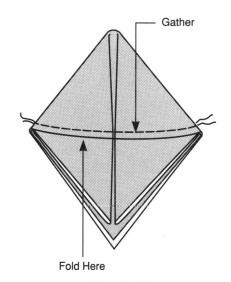

Fig. 10–20

GARMENT CARE

Nylon is a color and dirt scavenger, and will turn gray when washed with dark colors and dirty whites. Wash whites and light-colored nylons separately, since they absorb dark colors so easily.

To prevent yellowing, do not dry in direct sunlight. Use a cool iron if pressing is needed.

Milanese Knits

Milanese, a warp knit, is easily identified by fine ribs on the face and a diagonal design on the back.

Compared to tricot, another warp knit, milanese is more stable, stronger, and smoother; it has more body. Compared to interlock (weft) knits, it has less stretch in the length, but it's run-resistant.

Used for better lingerie, milanese is more expensive and not as readily available as tricot. When sewing milanese knits, see Knits, Tricot.

Sweater Knits

Sweater knits range from fabrics that look and stretch like hand knits to stable raschel knits. This section focuses on knits that stretch and look hand-made. When sewing stable sweater knits, see Raschel Knits.

Fabric Characteristics
- Sweater knits are easy to sew.
- They have a nap.
- Sweater knits run.
- Sweater knits are soft and will not maintain a crisp, structured shape.
- They may be lofty or bulky.
- They vary in stretch.
- They add pounds to most figures.

PLANNING A GARMENT

See under Knits for general suggestions.

DESIGN IDEAS AND PATTERN SELECTION

Available in a variety of fibers, sweater knits are suitable for cardigan sweaters and coats, sweater dresses, tee tops, long-sleeved turtlenecks, sleeveless vests, and full, loose-fitting tops. They combine well with many woven fabrics.

Select a simple design with a minimum number of pattern pieces; check the latest ready-to-wear for design ideas. Easy-fitting shapes, kimono, raglan, dohlman and exaggerated sleeves, inseam pockets, elastic waistbands, and collarless cardigans work well.

Choose slimmer skirts when sewing heavier knits. Try to avoid patch and slashed pockets, zippers,

Fig. 10–21 *From Cardin, these long, lean sweater knits skim the body. On the left, a ribbed knit is used to make the wide cowl collar. (Photo courtesy of Pierre Cardin Knitwear.)*

buttonholes, waistline seams, gathers, darts, and fussy details.

Consider the fabric stretch. If the pattern is designed for knits, compare the fabric to the stretch gauge. Also compare the pattern dimensions and body measurements. The fabric has enough stretch to eliminate ease, but the total stretch should not

be used to cover the body measurements since sweater knits are designed to be worn loose.

For very stretchy fabrics, use a smaller size pattern.

SELECTING THE FABRIC

Sweater knits can be purchased by the yard or as sweater bodies; or they can be knitted by hand or machine. (If you crocheted your yardage, treat the fabric like Raschel Knits.)

Preshrink washable fabrics to relax them and to remove any finishes which will cause skipped stitches. All-cotton fabrics and cotton blends may shrink several inches and should be washed and dried at least twice. Remove acrylics from the dryer immediately to avoid heat-set wrinkles.

Hint: *To reduce pilling and snagging, turn fabrics wrong side out and machine baste the selvages together.*

If the fabric is knit in a tube, cut along one lengthwise rib; many knits are made with a wider rib or something to indicate the best place to cut.

Steam press the creases. If they are permanent, fold the fabric so they will be inconspicuous on the garment.

Steam press fabrics which must be dry-cleaned.

If your fabric is custom-knit, be sure to knit enough. Custom-knit fabrics usually need shrinking and blocking. Straighten the fabric so the ends are at right angles to the edges. Then, wrong side up, pin it to a cardboard cutting board. Hold the iron just above the fabric and steam. Allow the fabric to dry completely before moving it.

SEWING SWEATER KNITS

LAYOUT, CUTTING, AND MARKING

Be sure the knit has time to relax—at least twenty-four hours—before cutting.

Square the ends with the edges of a rectangular table. Use a nap layout; position the fabric in a double/lay with right sides out and the fold on a lengthwise rib.

SEWING CHECKLIST

Machine Needles: Universal-H point or Yellow Band, twin needles; sizes 70/10 to 90/14, depending on the fabric weight.

Machine Setting: Stitch length 2–2.5mm (10–12 stitches per inch), or a crooked straight stitch.

Thread: Long-staple polyester, cotton-wrapped polyester, woolly nylon.

Hand Sewing Needles: Sizes 7 to 9.

Sewing Machine Equipment: Roller or even-feed foot.

Supplies: Sharp shears or rotary cutter and mat, long flower or glass-headed pins.

Layout: Nap.

Marking Techniques: Clips, pins, thread tracing.

Seams: Narrow, double/ply, double-stitched, tissue-stitched, strap, piped, welt, bound.

Hem: Topstitched, twin needle, machine blindstitch, zigzag or stretch blindstitch, hand blindstitch, catchstitch, figure-eight, fused, double-stitched, interfaced.

Seam and Hem Finishes: Double/ply, zigzag, multi-stitch zigzag, serged, tricot bound.

Edge Finishes: Bindings, ribbings, bands, woven-fabric facings, bias facings, decorative facings, elastic casings, grosgrain bands and facings.

Interfacings, Linings, and Underlinings: Depends on the fabric and garment design.

Closures: Zippers (plain and decorative), decorative snaps, snap tape, buttons and buttons and buttonholes; avoid hook and loop tape.

Hint: *If the lengthwise ribs are not obvious, mark them with thread tracing.*

If the fabric is bulky or needs to be matched, use a single/lay with the right side up. When cutting a single layer, use duplicate pattern pieces so the entire pattern can be positioned before cutting.

Lay out the front and back first, matching as needed. Then lay out the sleeves. On some fabrics, the sleeves won't always match. Secure the pattern with weights to avoid losing your pins in the fabric loops.

Hint: *Naomi Baker, author of* Serging Sweaters *(see Bibliography), recommends cutting 1" seam allowances to avoid wavy seams.*

If the fabric has a permanent crease, lay out the pattern so the crease will be inconspicuous on the finished garment.

Cut out the pattern using sharp shears or a rotary cutter and mat. Spray the edges with a fray retardant to prevent runs and shedding.

STITCHING TIPS

Always start with a new ballpoint needle to prevent needle snags and runs. Make a test seam on fabric scraps to determine whether the tension needs to be loosened and/or the pressure lightened.

Staystitch necklines and armholes only if needed to prevent stretching.

When stitching, take an occasional rest stop. Stop with the needle down; raise the presser foot so the fabric can relax. Then lower the foot and continue sewing.

Handle sweater knits carefully to avoid pulling or stretching them out of shape. To prevent snagging, use a roller foot or even-feed foot; or wrap the toes of the presser foot with transparent tape.

For seams with give, stitch using a crooked straight stitch (W,.5;L,2), a twin needle, or woolly nylon in the bobbin. Use tissue-stitched seams or seams stayed with invisible elastic to prevent puckering. If you have serger, consider a serger constriction.

Stabilize shoulder and waistline seams with a nonstretch stay tape.

Hint: *Ingrid Walderhaug uses a fine baby yarn to stabilize these seams. Measure the pattern front with the yarn; then stitch it to the seamlines.*

Stabilize necklines and armholes with bias-cut tricot. Reinforce seams which must stretch with 1/4"-wide invisible (polyurethane) elastic.

SEAMS AND HEMS

Decorative seams—piped, welt, strap, and bound—are particularly attractive on plain sweaterknit fabrics.

Carefully serge or zigzag the edges of knits which ravel and stretch badly before assembling the seams. When serging, stitch carefully to avoid cutting uneven seam allowances; remember the edges will be used as guidelines.

Hint: *When serging, Naomi Baker recommends a wide stitch width and medium to long length, a looser tension, a lighter pressure, and woolly nylon thread in the needle and loopers. The nylon is softer, more durable, and less conspicuous than regular thread.*

Since seam edges tend to roll when pressed open, narrow double/ply seams are best. Straight stitch the seam; then finish the edges with a zigzag, multistitch zigzag, or serger. Trim 1/4" or 3/8".

To prevent wavy seams, be careful not to stretch them as you're sewing. Stabilize shoulder seams with twill tape, selvage strip, or bias tricot. If you're using a serger construction, stitch over the stay when seaming.

Always allow the garment to hang at least twenty-four hours before hemming. Use a flat finish on plain hems. The best choice is serging. If this isn't possible, consider a multi-stitch zigzag or seam tape. Lace tape is a telltale sign of homemade.

Decorative topstitch, machine blindstitch, and twin needle hems work well. On heavy fabrics, double-stitch hems using a blindstitch, blind catchstitch or figure-eight stitch. keep the stitches loose so they won't show on the outside of the garment.

Bindings, ribbings, and bands are attractive substitutes for traditional hems and facings. Consider the weight, fiber, and care requirements when selecting trims.

Bands and ribbings can be applied flat or stretched, depending on the garment design and your preference. Stitch with the ribbing or band on top.

Hint: *To avoid distortion and wavy seams, don't stretch the sweater when applying ribbing or stay with invisible elastic.*

Elastic casings work well for skirts. If the elastic will be applied directly to the fabric, use invisible elastic.

Self-fabric facings are usually too bulky; however, woven-fabric facings and bias facings finish edges neatly.

INTERFACINGS, LININGS, AND UNDERLININGS

Interface openings and buttonhole areas. To prevent stretching at garment front openings, sew a stay tape into the seams or foldlines so they'll hang properly.

Underline lightweight sweater knits with fusible knit interfacing to give them body. To stabilize sweater knits so they look and handle more like double knits and woven fabrics, experiment with underlinings in woven and nonwoven fusibles.

Be sure all interfacings, linings, and underlinings have care requirements which are compatible with the fashion fabric.

PRESSING AND GARMENT CARE

Set the iron temperature appropriately for the fiber. Test press on a fabric scrap. Acrylic sweater knits and ribbing are easily distorted when warm and moist, so be careful.

To avoid stretching, do not slide the iron over the knit. To avoid flattening the surface, steam with the iron held just above the garment; then finger press. Or cover the pressing surface with a Velvaboard or thick terry towel; and, with a damp press cloth, press from the wrong side.

Consider the garment construction as well as the fiber content when determining garment care.

Ribbing

Attractive and easy to sew, stretch ribbing is frequently used instead of hems and bulky facings to finish garment edges at the neck, wrists, waist, and ankles. A longtime favorite for finishing knits, ribbing is now popular for trimming woven fabrics, including silks, and is sometimes used for complete garments.

Made with alternating ribs and wales, rib knits look the same on both sides. More elastic and form fitting than other weft knits, some have more stretch than others. This chapter focuses on those that stretch and recover to their original size and shape.

Fabric Characteristics
- Rib knits vary considerably in stretch, from 25 percent to 100 percent.
- They stretch most crosswise.
- Some rib knits run badly.
- Rib knits have a stripe pattern.
- Ribbings are more difficult to sew attractively with a straight-stitch machine.
- Seams and hems must have built-in stretch to avoid popped stitches.

- Rib knits tend to ripple when topstitched across the ribs.
- Rib knits are easily distorted when pressed across the ribs.
- Dark-colored rib knits frequently fade.

PLANNING A GARMENT

See also Knits for general sewing suggestions.

SELECTING RIB KNITS

Rib knits are sold by the inch in tubular form and in precut strips. Many other rib knits, designed for full garment construction, have enough stretch to be used as substitutes.

Ribbings are available in different weights and many fiber contents—all cotton, polyester/cotton, cotton/Lycra, polyester/nylon, acrylic, acrylic/polyester, silk, and wool. They vary in weight, stretch quality, and care requirements as well as in color.

Hint: *When there is no ribbing to match your fabric, use a complementary color.*

To test ribbing stretch, fold crosswise on the course of the fabric about 3″ below the raw edge. Measure and mark a 4″ section on the fold, then stretch gently as much as possible. It should stretch to 6″ easily if it will be used as a neckline finish.

The ribbing should return to its original shape when released. If it doesn't, it will stretch out when the garment is worn.

Generally, it's better not to preshrink ribbings. Preshrinking makes them difficult to control; and since they shrink only in the lengthwise direction, shrinking will make the rib trim narrower, but not tighter.

To reduce bleeding from dark and bright colors, set the color by dipping it in a vinegar and water solution after the ribbing is cut.

SEWING RIBBING

LAYOUT, CUTTING, AND MARKING

Before cutting, check the fit to be sure the ribbing will be close-fitting but comfortable. Measure and mark the length; then pin it together and try it on.

Waistband ribbing must slide over either your hips or shoulders; neckbands, over the head; wrist and ankle bands, over the hand or foot.

Do not stretch the ribbing when cutting.

Fig. 10–22 *Pierre Cardin's classic knitwear is trimmed with bands of ribbing at the pockets and edges. (Photo courtesy of Pierre Cardin Knitwear.)*

Cut the ribbing smaller than the garment. It will be stretched to fit the garment edge, so it will hug the body.

Use pins, temporary marking pen, chalk, or soap sliver for marking.

SEAMS

Consider the fabric stretch and garment design when choosing the seaming technique. Then use a new needle and experiment with the suggested seams.

Hint: *Double/ply seams work best and are comfortable to wear.*

Use woolly nylon thread to add stretch to any seam. It works especially well when used in the bobbin for twin needle seams or in the serger loopers. When using woolly nylon in the needle, use a needle threader.

Hint: *At edges where ribbing will be applied, trim seam allowances to 1/4".*

If the pattern does not indicate notches, divide and mark both the ribbing and garment into quarters. Match and pin the marked points.

When joining the ribbing to the garment, stitch with the ribbing on top.

HEMS AND EDGE FINISHES

Garments made of rib knit are not easy to hem attractively. Topstitching makes the fabric ripple and the stitches tend to pop when the garment is worn.

Two machine-stitched hems which work well are the twin needle hem and the zigzag blindstitch.

Hint: *For more elasticity, use woolly nylon in the bobbin.*

When hemming by hand, use a blind catchstitch, figure-eight stitch, or regular catchstitch. Keep the stitches loose. And if the fabric is heavy, double stitch the hem.

Use a merrow, mock-merrow finish, or lettuce edging to make a rippled edge.

Use bands, false bands and ribbing trims to replace hems.

Replace bulky facings with bindings, self-fabric ribbing, or contrast-fabric ribbing.

MACHINE-MADE BUTTONHOLES

Always make a test buttonhole. To prevent rippling, position buttonholes parallel to the ribs.

Hint: *Experiment with corded buttonholes if the buttonhole ripples.*

Stabilize the buttonhole area with a light- to medium-weight, nonwoven, sew-in interfacing. Cut the interfacing with the least amount of stretch in the direction of the buttonhole.

Lengthen the stitch so you can see a little fabric between the stitches; use a water-soluble stabilizer between the fabric and feed dogs.

WAISTBANDS

Generally, ribbing trims do not fit snugly enough for waistbands on pants and skirts. For a firmer band, interface the ribbing with nonroll elastic.

1. Select an elastic slightly smaller than the width of the finished ribbed band. Cut the elastic to the desired length plus two seam allowances.

2. Join the ends of the elastic; repeat for the ribbing.

3. Place the elastic on the wrong side of the ribbing and wrap the ribbing around it. Baste the raw edges together and join the ribbing to the garment.

NECKLINE RIBBING—FLAT APPLICATION

Here is the first of two methods for applying neckline trims. These techniques can also be used for ribbed cuffs and hem bands.

1. Cut the ribbing the length indicated on the pattern or measure the neckline and mark the ribbing two-thirds of that measurement.

Hint: *Check to be sure it will fit before you cut. Mark the length with pins, hold the ribbing together, and slip it over your head. If it's too tight, add a little. If it doesn't hug the neck, subtract a little.*

2. Join one shoulder seam.

3. Fold the ribbing in half lengthwise, wrong sides together. Divide and mark the neckline and ribbing into quarters.

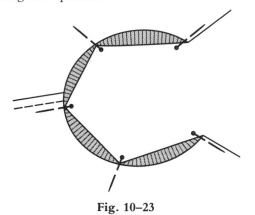

Fig. 10–23

4. Match and pin the marked points.

5. For a round neckline, distribute the stretch evenly. For a boat-shaped neckline, distribute more stretch across the shoulder seams than at the center front and back. For a deep oval, distribute more ease near the center front and center back. With the ribbing on top, stitch in place.

6. Trim the seam 1/4″ to 3/8″ and finish the edges. Finger press toward the body.

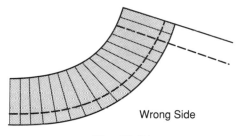

Wrong Side

Fig. 10–24

Hint: *When serging, trim the seam allowances to 3/8″ first. Lengthen and widen the stitch so the seam won't stretch out of shape.*

7. Close the unstitched seam (Fig. 10–24).

Hint: *To ensure that the folded edges of the ribbing and seamlines match perfectly, use a needle to pin baste the seams where they cross the seamline. Begin stitching at the neckline.*

NECKLINE RIBBING—CIRCLE APPLICATION

1. Join the ends of the ribbing, right sides together, to make a circle. Trim away a triangle at each end and finger press the seam open.

2. Fold the ribbing in half lengthwise, wrong sides together; match and baste the raw edges together with a zigzag (W,2;L,3) stitch.

3. Complete the shoulder seams on the garment; press toward the front.

4. Divide and mark the ribbing and garment edge into quarters.

5. For narrow-ribbed bands, begin with the ribbing seam at the left shoulder. For wide ribbing, place it at the center back. Pin, matching the marked points; stitch the ribbing in place.

PRESSING

Press carefully; steam and heat can distort the fabric. Do not slide the iron across the ribs; press only the seam allowances.

Arrange the section as desired; then hold the iron about an inch above the garment and steam. Use your other hand to finger press.

For a professional finish, place shaped edges like necklines over a pressing mitt or tailor's ham; steam into shape.

Stretch Terry and Velour

Available in a variety of fibers and fabric designs, stretch terry and stretch velour are knit fabrics with varying amounts of elasticity. Stretch terry has small loops on the face, while velour has a plush nap on the face. Both have smooth vertical ribs on the reverse.

When sewing woven terry and velour, see Pile Fabrics and Woven Terry and Velour.

Fabric Characteristics
- Stretch terry and stretch velour have a nap.
- They are bulky.

- They always shrink; they may shrink more than 10 percent.
- These fabrics creep badly when stitched right sides together.
- They have variable amounts of stretch; some stretch more in the length than in the width.
- Stretch fabrics need stretch hems and seams.
- Raw edges frequently curl badly.
- The toes of the presser foot may get caught in loops.
- Stretch terry snags easily.

SEWING CHECKLIST

Machine Needles: Universal-H point, or Yellow Band, twin needles, sizes 70/10 to 90/14.

Thread: Long-staple polyester, cotton-wrapped polyester.

Hand Sewing Needles: Sizes 5 to 9.

Sewing Machine Equipment: Even-feed or roller foot.

Equipment and Supplies: Long, glass-headed ballpoint pins, lightweight, decorative, or invisible zippers.

Layout: Nap. Double/lay wrong sides together; single/lay, wrong side up.

Marking Techniques: Clips, temporary marking pens, chalk, soap sliver, pins.

Seams: Plain, stretch, double/ply, strap, piped, welt, taped, tissue-stitched.

Hems: Machine blindstitch, stretch or zigzag blindstitch, topstitched, twin needle, fused, catchstitched, double-stitched.

Edge Finishes: Self-fabric facings, lining-fabric facings, bands, false bands, elastic casings, bindings.

Seam and Hem Finishes: Unfinished, zigzag, multi-stitch zigzag, serged.

Interfacings: Generally not used except for garment openings and buttonhole areas.

Linings and Underlinings: Generally not used.

- Buttonholes will stretch out of shape.
- These fabrics dull needles quickly.

Fig. 10–25 *These vibrant velour robes are trimmed with a leopard print. On the left, the short robe features a hoop hem, an architectural touch from Cardin, while on the right the classic wrap hangs straight. (Photo courtesy of Pierre Cardin Robes.)*

PLANNING A GARMENT

See Knits and Pile Fabrics for general sewing directions.

PATTERN AND FABRIC SELECTION

Soft and comfortable to wear, stretch terry and stretch velour are well-suited for unstructured tee tops, pullovers, skirts, pants, jackets, coats, dresses, and robes.

Select simple designs without fussy details. Consider easy-fitting shapes, inseam pockets, raglan and kimono sleeves, dropped shoulders, elastic waistbands, soft gathers, collarless cardigans, and shawl collars.

And if the fabric has enough stretch consider the designs for "stretch knits."

Check the fabric's stretch and compare it to the stretch gauge on the pattern envelope. To test its recovery, stretch the fabric crosswise. Be certain it will return to its original shape; if it doesn't, the garment will sag and bag.

Machine wash stretch terry and velour to eliminate shrinkage, to relax the fabric, and to remove excess fabric finishes. If the fabric has a high cotton content, launder and dry it several times.

SEWING STRETCH TERRY AND VELOUR

LAYOUT, CUTTING, AND MARKING

Allow the fabric to relax overnight. Use a nap layout; lay out the pattern pieces so the nap will run in the direction you like better. Before laying out the pattern, drape the fabric around your shoulders. Stand back and look at it in a large mirror. The side with the nap going down will look lighter and shinier; the other side, with the nap going up, will be a richer, deeper shade. Most ready-made garments are cut with the nap going down; however, garments can be cut with the nap going up. Decide which you like better.

Lay out the fabric with the wrong sides together or spread it in a single layer wrong side up. Use chalk to mark the direction of the nap on the wrong side of the fabric.

Hint: *When the lengthwise edges are irregular, mark a lengthwise rib.*

To avoid stretching, do not let the fabric hang off the edge of the table. Use weights or long pins to hold the pattern pieces in place. Use well-sharpened shears for cutting.

STITCHING TIPS

Consider the fabric stretch, seam location, and your equipment when deciding the seam construction. Generally, stretch seams are best; however, piped and strap seams are attractive decorative seams.

Make a test seam, using an evenly balanced tension. Hold the fabric taut when stitching and stitch with the pile.

To reduce creeping, use a roller or even-feed foot. If creeping persists, tissue-stitch seams with stabilizer.

To avoid ripping which might damage the fabric, stitch carefully. To reduce curling at raw edges, spray with fabric finish and machine stitch 1/4" from raw edge.

Staystitch curved edges to prevent stretching. Stabilize shoulder seams, V-necklines, and waistline seams with a nonstretch tape to prevent stretching. Trim and grade seams before crossing them with another seam or hem.

SEAMS AND HEMS

Select a seam appropriate for the fabric's stretch. When stitching plain seams, use a crooked stitch (W,.5;1,2).

Let the garment hang for twenty-four hours before measuring the hem. To reduce rolling at the hemline, try one of these techniques.

- Cut the hem allowance at least 1" wide.
- Fuse the hem in place before topstitching.
- Fuse a piece of knit interfacing to the hem allowance before turning it under.

Stretch fabrics need stretch hems so the stitches won't pop when the garment is worn. Topstitch the garment with a straight stretch stitch, decorative stretch stitch, or twin needle. Or use a machine blindstitch or zigzag blindstitch. Use a hand catchstitch hem as a last resort.

EDGE FINISHES

To reduce bulk, replace self-fabric facings with lining-fabric facings, bindings, ribbings, self-fabric bands, or false bands.

When self-fabric facings are used, fuse the interfacing to facing. The interfacing will reduce rolling to the outside and curling at the unnotched edges.

Hint: *Gail Shinn cuts facings from fusible knit interfacing; joins them to the garment as usual; then understitches and fuses them to the wrong side of the garment.*

Most garments do not need interfacing, except in buttonhole areas and at garment openings. To avoid flattening the nap, use nonwoven sew-in interfacings or fuse interfacings to the facings.

CLOSURES

Try to reposition buttonholes so they are on the lengthwise grain. Position the interfacing so there is no stretch in the buttonhole length; or use a second piece of interfacing to stabilize the buttonhole. Lengthen the stitch slightly; and cord the buttonholes to eliminate rippling.

Zippers can be exposed, invisible, lapped, slot, or separating. To prevent stretching and shifting, stay the zipper placket with a narrow (5/8″) strip of fusible interfacing. Fuse the strip to the seam allowance; then set the zipper.

TOPSTITCHING

Experiment with fabric scraps, various stitch patterns, and different sewing machine feet to achieve an attractive topstitching that will stretch when you move without rippling the fabric.

Lengthen the stitch length to 2.5–3mm (8–10 stitches per inch) and topstitch with the nap, even though it may be against the grain.

When topstitching necklines and patch pockets, stitch one half with the nap; then break and fasten your stitches before stitching the other half with the nap.

To reduce creeping when topstitching, pin or baste carefully; and place a piece of stabilizer between the fabric and feed dogs.

PRESSING

Pressing as you sew velours is particularly important since this may be the last time the garment is pressed.

Test press on a fabric scrap to determine the best temperature. Press the face side to create mottling and crushing; then try to remove it. If it is permanently changed, pressing right side up may be disastrous.

To avoid crushing the nap, cover the pressing board with a Velvaboard or thick terry towel. Steam the seamline and press lightly.

When pressing the right side of the fabric, use a napped press cloth. Do not let the iron touch the face side.

Action Knits

Action knits, sometimes called two-way and four-way stretch knits, are used for swimwear, dance, skating, and cycling costumes, leotards, tights, and skiwear.

Readily available in a variety of high fashion prints and colors, most of these fabrics are knit with yarns which have an elastomeric fiber core called spandex or elastane.

Two-way and four-way describe knits which stretch in both the width and length. Generally, four-way stretch knits are raschel knits and two-way stretch fabrics are tricot knits. Four-way stretch fabrics are heavier, cover better, pill less, and do not run.

This section focuses on swimwear; however, you can apply the same techniques to any garment made of action knits.

Fabric Characteristics
- Action knits have a nap.
- They are easily snagged by damaged pins and needles.
- Action knits require stretch seams, hems, and edge finishes.
- Thin fabrics and light colors may be revealing when wet.
- Lining fabrics must have as much stretch as the fashion fabric.
- Action knits are easily damaged by hook and loop tape.

PLANNING A GARMENT

See also Knits for general sewing directions.

FABRIC AND PATTERN SELECTION

Be sure the fabric has adequate stretch for the

184

pattern. And if the garment will be lined, select a two-way stretch lining.

Nylon/spandex blends are quick drying and good choices for swimwear, while polyester/cotton blended with spandex is cool and comfortable for exercising. Nylon has more stretch and resists abrasion better than other synthetics.

Four-way stretch fabrics are heavier than two-way stretch fabrics. The stretch in action knits also varies. Compare the amount of fabric stretch with the amount required for the pattern.

Wash and line dry the fabric to preshrink and to remove any excess finishes which might cause skipped stitches. Mark the right side of the fabric with drafting or hair-set tape.

Most action knits are designed to fit snugly and have no ease or minus ease. One piece swimsuits and leotards will measure about 2″ shorter than the body measurement. And if the fabric is extremely stretchy, it can measure up to 6″ shorter.

Fig. 10–26 *Designed by Emilio Pucci, these action knits are printed with geometric design of medieval inspiration. (Photo courtesy of the photographer, Lorenzo Allisio-Florence, and the designer, Emilio Pucci.)*

Hint: *Swimsuits and leotards fit most figures better if they have a seam at the center back.*

Compare your body measurements—bust, waist, hips, and back of the neck to waist—to the measurement chart on the pattern envelope. Shorten or lengthen the pattern before cutting out.

Also check the depth of the neckline and armholes to be sure they are not too low. Adjust as needed.

Hint: *When in doubt, Gail Brown cuts extra-wide seam allowances, which can be trimmed away after pin fitting.*

SEWING CHECKLIST

Machine Needles: Universal-H point, ballpoint (SUK), stretch(HS), and Yellow Band or twin needles; size 70/10 for most sewing; size 90/14 for sewing heavy materials and elastic.

Machine Setting: Stitch length 2.5mm (10 stitches per inch).

Thread: Long-staple polyester, cotton-wrapped polyester, woolly nylon.

Hand Sewing Needles: Sizes 8 or 9.

Sewing Machine Equipment: Roller foot.

Equipment and Supplies: Fine ballpoint pins, well-sharpened shears, rotary cutter and mat, drafting or hair-set tape, elastics unaffected by chlorine, salt water, or body oils; bra cups (optional).

Layout: Nap.

Marking Techniques: Chalk, soap sliver, temporary marking pens, clips, pins.

Seams: Stretch, twin needle.

Hems: Topstitched, twin needle, lettuce edging.

Edge Finishes: Applied elastic, casings, self-fabric bindings, ribbings, snap tapes, bands and false bands.

Lining: Depends on the garment and fabric transparency.

Closures: Zippers, hooks and eyes, ties.

Once the pattern is altered and the garment fitted, cut a permanent pattern for future garments from pattern cloth or inexpensive nonwoven interfacing.

SEWING ACTION KNITS

LAYOUT, CUTTING, AND MARKING

Use a nap layout. Spread the fabric right sides together; or, if the fabric has a print, spread a single layer right side up so the print can be placed attractively.

Determine which grain has the most stretch. Generally, the greatest stretch goes around the body. However, ski pants, jumpsuits, unitards, tights, and pants for vigorous activities such as dancing, ice skating, and skiing need more stretch in the length.

Some swimsuit patterns have a bias grainline. Since you're sewing an action knit, bias-cuts are unnecessary except when the fabric is a stripe; otherwise, position the pattern pieces so the stretch goes around the body.

Use weights or fine, ballpoint pins placed in the seam allowances. Use well-sharpened shears or a rotary cutter and mat when cutting.

STITCHING TIPS

Make a test seam, using a new ballpoint needle. Stretch the fabric moderately when stitching. If the finished seam ripples, you've stretched too much.

Cut; then baste with a wide zigzag. Many commercial patterns have too much ease and will have to be taken up.

SEAMS AND HEMS

Seams should be strong, stretchy, and narrow. Try several seam methods before making a decision.

All seams should have some stretch so they won't rip. Seams such as the center back and crotch seams, which receive a great deal of stress, should be very strong.

Swimsuit necklines, armholes, and leg openings are usually finished with applied elastic. Ruffles and skirts are finished with narrow hems, lettuce edging, or merrow finishes.

For a lettuce edging, stretch the fabric as much as possible while stitching the edge with a satin stitch (W,2;L,.1), zigzag (W,2;L,2), or narrow serging.

Finish the hems of tights and pants with a twin needle hem or false band.

ELASTIC EDGES

Choose a cotton/spandex or invisible elastic which is resistant to perspiration, body oils, sun, salt water, and chlorine. Avoid rayon elastics.

Generally elastic is applied directly to the fabric; however, it can be inserted into a casing. Use knitted, woven, or invisible elastics for direct applications and braided elastics in casings.

When sewing elastic directly to the garment, cut it 10 percent to 25 percent shorter than the body measurement.

Self-fabric bindings are an alternative to elastic. Cut the binding on the crossgrain to the desired finished length plus 1/2" seam allowances. Stretch the binding as you stitch it in place.

LININGS

Linings are optional; however, they are frequently used for modesty or comfort. Suitable lining fabrics include lightweight two-way stretch fabrics, self-fabric, two-way stretch banlon, lightweight girdle fabrics, and nylon tricot.

Hint: *For slimmer tummies, line the front with lightweight power net or girdle fabric.*

Line tightly fitted garments to protect the body from construction details which might irritate the skin. Make lined garments about 1" longer and 1/2" wider, so they won't be too tight.

Line swimsuits which are light-colored or made of thin fabrics to preserve their opaqueness when wet. For unlined swimsuits and leotards, line the crotch. Also line ice skating costumes to avoid nipple bumps on the cold ice.

ROSEMARY'S QUICK AND EASY LINING

Designer Rosemary Jameson uses this easy method to line swimsuits and skating costumes.

1. Right sides together, cut out the swimsuit front and back from the fashion fabric.

2. Fold the lining fabric right sides together. Lay the two fronts, which are still right sides together, on top of the lining fabric. Align the grains; and pin the four layers together. Cut out the lining.

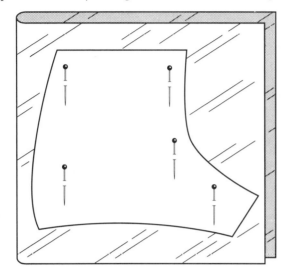

Fig. 10–27

3. Without unpinning the four layers, stitch the center front seam, using a straight stretch stitch. Unpin.

4. Repeat for the back.

5. Right sides together, join the side seams of the swimsuit; then join the side seams of the lining.

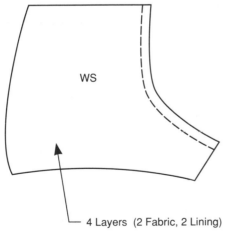

WS

└─ 4 Layers (2 Fabric, 2 Lining)

Fig. 10–28

6. Stitch the crotch and hem the legs and waist.

Here's another lining method that works well when you need to fit as you sew.

1. Complete the seams of both the swimsuit and lining.

2. With both wrong sides out, place the swimsuit on the table with the back up. Place the lining on top of the suit so the wrong side of the lining back is next to the wrong side of the swimsuit. Match and pin all four layers of one of the side seams together; stitch (W,2;L,2).

3. Continuing with the lining and swimsuit wrong sides together, stitch the center front seams together. Repeat for the other side and center back seams. Turn the garment right side out.

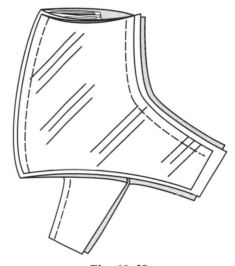

Fig. 10–29

4. Complete the garment.

WAISTBANDS

Cut waistbands on the grain with the most stretch. This is usually crosswise.

Use elastic or self-fabric to interface waistbands.

CLOSURES

The design of many two-way stretch garments allows them to be pulled on without a fastener.

If a fastener is needed or desired, consider zippers, eyelets and lacing, loops and lacing, fabric ties, swimsuit bra hooks, buttons and buttonholes.

GARMENT CARE

Action knits are machine-washable. Do not bleach. Line dry if recommended by the manufacturer.

187

Power Net

Made of spandex, an elastomeric fiber, power net is frequently referred to by its tradenames—Lycra, Blue C, Nuna, Interspan, Unel, Vyrene, Spandelle, Spanzelle, Cleerspan, Curel and Glospan. (These elastomeric fibers are called elastane in Europe.)

Lightweight, figure-controlling, and resistant to abrasion and chlorine, these fabrics are used most often for foundations—bras and girdles—and tummy-flattening underlinings. However, several innovative designers are using them for swimsuits.

Power net can be plain netting, a jacquard knit, or allover lace. It is available in several weights; and, unlike most fabrics, heavier doesn't mean greater control since heavier fabrics don't return to their original shape as well.

Fabric Characteristics
- Some power-net fabrics shrink.
- Skipped stitches are frequently a problem.
- Seams and edge finishes must have built-in stretch.
- Power net is difficult to sew successfully with a straight stitch.

SEWING CHECKLIST

Machine Needles: Ballpoint (SUK), stretch (HS), Yellow Band, twin needles; sizes 75/11 to 90/14.

Machine Setting: Zigzag, stretch stitch.

Thread: Long-staple polyester, woolly nylon.

Hand Sewing Needles: Sizes 7 to 9.

Layout: Nap, double layer, right sides together.

Notions: Stretch lace, lingerie elastics with a velvety underside.

Seams: Stretch, topstitched, strap.

Edge Finishes: Applied elastic, twin needle hem.

Garment Care: Machine or handwash; line dry or machine dry on low setting; avoid chlorine bleach.

SEWING POWER NET

See Knits for general sewing directions.

LAYOUT, CUTTING, AND MARKING

Lay out the fabric with right sides together. When in doubt, the right side is usually smoother than the wrong side.

Lay out the pattern with the most stretch going around the body. To determine the direction with the greater stretch, stretch the fabric and look at the holes. They close in the direction with the most stretch and open in the opposite direction.

SEAMS AND EDGE FINISHES

Make a test seam using a new ballpoint or stretch needle. Check the stretch before stitching the garment.

Unlike seams on other two-way stretch fabrics, seams on garments made of power net are generally topstitched so they will be flat and nonirritating on the inside of the garment.

Stitch seams with a narrow zigzag (W,1;L,1) or straight stretch stitch. Then, open the seam and topstitch across the seamline with a multi-stitch zigzag (W,4;L,.5) or decorative stretch stitch. Or fold the seam to one side and topstitch with a zigzag or multi-stitch zigzag.

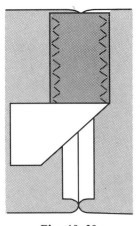

Fig. 10–30

To reinforce seams, make a self-fabric strap. Cut a lengthwise, 5/8″-wide strip. Zigzag (W,3;L,1.25) the edges in place (Fig. 10–30).

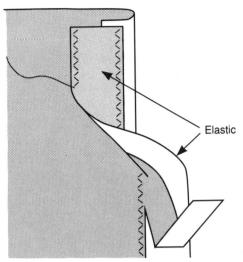

Fig. 10–31

For a neat, comfortable edge finish, use applied elastic. Join the elastic to the garment so the raw edges of the power net are enclosed between the elastic and fabric. The elastic can be on either the inside or the outside of the finished garment.

For a quick and easy finish, lap the elastic over the garment edge 1/4″ and zigzag in place (Fig. 10–31).

CHAPTER 11
Stretch-Woven Fabrics

Stretch Wovens

Stretch-woven fabrics have the ability to extend and recover. Made by blending cotton, wool, or synthetic fibers with a stretch fiber such as spandex or Lycra, or by weaving the fabric from core-spun yarns, stretch wovens combine the appearance of traditional woven fabrics such as denim, satin, batiste, lace, poplin, seersucker, broadcloth, gabardine, corduroy, velveteen, and flannel with the comfort and fit of knits.

Compared to traditional woven fabrics, stretch wovens have better shape retention with 25 percent to 40 percent stretch. They are more comfortable to wear and wrinkle-resistant; they fit better and move with the body.

Compared to knits, they have better shape retention, do not run, are less bulky, and are lighter weight.

Fabric Characteristics
- Stretch wovens are easy to sew.
- They are stable and firm without being rigid.
- Stretch fabrics are easily damaged by dull shears, pins, and needles.
- Skipped stitches are sometimes a problem.
- Stretch-woven fabrics require stretch seams and hems in the direction of the stretch.
- Stretch wovens can have stretch in one or both directions.

- Stretch wovens are easily damaged by hot irons and improper pressing.

PLANNING A GARMENT

Many suggestions for sewing knits and double knits can be used on stretch wovens, even though the fabric structure is different.

PATTERN AND FABRIC SELECTION

Stretch wovens are particularly well-suited for suits, trousers, straight skirts, jackets, casual sportswear, and uniforms.

Simple designs with crisp, tailored lines are usually best. If the pattern doesn't recommend stretch wovens, look for patterns that recommend fabrics such as linen, wool flannel, corduroy, denim, and gabardine.

For lightweight fabrics, choose a pattern which suggests a soft fabric, stable jerseys, or crepe de chine. Avoid patterns labeled "knits only."

Good-quality stretch wovens have good stretch and recover to their original dimensions when relaxed. To test the recovery, stretch the fabric in both directions. If it doesn't return to its original shape, the garment will sag and bag.

190

Check to be sure the fabric pattern is squared with the lengthwise edges, since off-grain fabrics can rarely be straightened.

Allow the fabric to relax overnight; and if it is washable, preshrink and dry according to the manufacturer's recommendation.

Preshrink all washable trims, interfacing, linings, and notions.

Steam press wool fabrics unless they are labeled needle-ready.

SEWING STRETCH WOVENS

LAYOUT, CUTTING, AND MARKING

Mark the right side of the fabric with drafting tape. Use ballpoint pins placed within the seam allowances or weights to anchor the pattern. Be sure pins are new and undamaged.

Cut out the garment with a sturdy pair of well-sharpened, bent-handled shears. Mark, using your favorite method, but use wax only on wool.

STITCHING TIPS

Make a test seam, using a stitch length of 1.75mm (14 stitches per inch), a balanced tension, and regular pressure. Adjust the tension and pressure and lengthen the stitch if needed.

Begin with a new Universal-H point needle, which will slide between the stretch fibers without weakening them.

Stitch slowly and use a needle lubricant to prevent slipped stitches. When stitching, hold the fabric taut and take an occasional rest stop. Stop with the needle down; raise the presser foot so the fabric can relax; lower the foot; and continue stitching.

Understitch all facings to prevent them from rolling to the outside of the garment. Use staystitching only on necklines, armholes, and waistline seams. Reduce bulk by grading and trimming.

SEAMS AND HEMS

Most stretch wovens need stretch seams.

Hint: *If you don't have a zigzag machine, fill the bobbin with woolly nylon thread.*

191

When finishing seams, use woolly nylon on serger loopers or in the bobbin of your regular machine to avoid a thread imprint on the right side of the garment.

To make durable crotch and armhole seams, stitch first with a crooked straight stitch (W,.5; L,2); then stitch again 1/4" away. Trim the seam to 1/4" and finish the edge so it won't ravel.

Stabilize shoulder and waistline seams with a nonstretch stay tape. Stabilize necklines and armholes with bias-cut tricot or lightweight lining fabric.

For unlined jackets and coats, double/ply, topstitched, welt, and flat-felled seams are best.

Hem quality garments by hand if you are not using a decorative hem. Use a very small crewel needle and a blindstitch, catchstitch, or figure-eight stitch. (When hemming with a blindstitch, take an occasional backstitch.) Double-stitch hems on heavy fabrics. When hemming by hand, pick up a small stitch on the back side of the fabric and keep the stitches loose.

Hem everyday garments with a machine blindstitch or fused hem. Use a small needle when hemming by machine so the stitches won't show on the right side of the garment.

For a decorative detail, use regular thread or topstitching thread to topstitch several rows around the hem; or use a twin needle hem which has a little stretch.

Hint: *For more stretch, use woolly nylon in the machine bobbin.*

INTERFACINGS, LININGS, AND UNDERLININGS

Many garments will not need interfacings at faced edges. Most will need it for collars, cuffs, pocket welts and flaps; and all garments need interfacings for waistbands, garment openings, and button/buttonhole areas.

Generally, an interfacing with stretch is better, except for waistbands and buttonholes. Always interface the buttonhole area with a firmly woven interfacing, positioned so the least amount of stretch is parallel to the buttonhole.

Outerwear garments are generally lined. Linings and/or underlinings are optional on other garments since they may retard stretch and reduce the garment comfort.

Select lining fabrics with the same care properties as the fashion fabric. Tricot and other stretch fabrics are good choices. For nonstretch lining fabrics make a deeper pleat or add extra fullness to the lining.

When lining skirts and trousers, attach the lining only at the waist.

PRESSING

Pressing as you go is particularly important when sewing stretch wovens. Test press on a fabric scrap to determine the correct amount of heat and moisture. Use a damp press cloth to prevent shine, discoloration, and stretching.

To set creases, saturate a brown paper grocery bag with water. Place the bag over the fabric and press until the paper is dry. Or press the garment with a 50/50 vinegar and water solution.

Elasticized Fabrics

Available in lightweight cottons, silks, and satins, elasticized fabrics have two-way stretch. The puckered face has an attractive allover puckered pattern; while the back has an intricate pattern of elastic threads.

Easy to sew and comfortable to wear, elasticized fabrics frequently have nonelasticized companion fabrics.

Fabric Characteristics
- Elasticized fabrics have two-way stretch.
- They require stretch seams and hems.
- Depending on the base fabric, they may require a nap layout.
- Elasticized fabrics are very narrow.
- Elasticized fabrics require more yardage and a revised layout.

SEWING CHECKLIST

Machine Needles: Universal-H point or Red Band, twin needles; sizes 60/8 to 80/12, depending on the fabric weight.

Machine Setting: Stitch length 2–2.5mm (10–12 stitches per inch); tension, balanced.

Thread: Long-staple polyester, cotton-wrapped polyester, mercerized cotton.

Hand Sewing Needles: Sizes 7 to 10.

Equipment and Supplies: Rotary cutter, sharp scissors, pins, weights.

Layout: Single layer, right sides up.

Marking: All types, except wax and tracing wheel.

Seams: Plain, double-stitched, double/ply, taped.

Hems: Plain, catchstitch, topstitched.

Seam and Hem Finishes: Serged, zigzag, multi-stitch zigzag, bound.

Edge Finishes: Ribbings, bands, bindings, smooth-fabric facings, edge-to-edge linings.

Interfacings: Rarely, except for buttonholes.

Linings: Depending on the base fabric and type garment.

Closures: Best avoided.

PLANNING A GARMENT

FABRIC AND PATTERN SELECTION

Most elasticized fabrics are less than 30″ wide. Depending on the base fabric, elasticized fabrics are used for casual play clothes, special-occasion designs, and elegant casual wear.

The moderately priced cotton elasticized fabrics are most readily available; however, a few finer fabrics, made of shirred voiles, silks, velvets, and satins, are available in specialty shops.

For best results, select a pattern for a pull-on garment with a minimum number of pieces. For fun dressing, look at the stretch patterns for closely fitted halters, camisoles, tank tops, and pull-on skirts which can be worn with plain fabric coordinates. If your figure can't stand the close-fitting exposure, make a plain fabric sweatshirt with elasticized trims.

For more elegant fabrics, consider body skimmers—not huggers—with a minimum number of pieces. Valentino showed a satin elasticized tee top with a plain satin skirt.

Preshrink fabrics which will be laundered.

SEWING ELASTICIZED FABRICS

LAYOUT, CUTTING, AND MARKING

Spread the fabric in a single layer, right side up. Using weights or pins placed in the seam allowances, cut with sharp shears or a rotary cutter and mat. Most fabrics can be marked with a temporary marking pen and clips.

STITCHING TIPS

Make a test seam. Set the stitch length for 2–2.5 mm (10–12 stitches per inch), depending on the fabric weight. Stretch as you stitch.

Tape seams which need to be stabilized. If you have a serger, finish seams and hems with a serger.

Hint: *Be sure the cutting blade is sharp and begin with a new needle.*

If you don't have a serger, use a zigzag or multi-stitch zigzag for seams. For most fabrics, double/ply seams work well; for heavy fabrics, use single/ply seams.

Use a machine topstitched hem on casual designs. On luxury garments, secure the hem with a catchstitch or bind the edges with a plain fabric.

PRESSING

Steam press from the wrong side. Hold the iron above the garment; steam; then press with your fingers.

PART THREE

Surface Characteristics

CHAPTER 12
Transparent Fabrics

A variety of transparent and semitransparent fabrics are available in all fibers. Fabrics range from very soft to crisp, lightweight to heavy, and dressy to casual.

Transparent fabrics fall into three categories: crisp, soft, semicrisp. The crisp fabrics—organdy, organza, dotted Swiss, marquisette, and handkerchief linen—are the easiest to sew, while the soft ones—chiffon, georgette, and crepe chiffon—are the most difficult. Semicrisp and semisoft fabrics—voile, leno, lawn, dimity, shirtings, batiste, eyelash voiles, eyelets, gauze, rayon challis, and Viyella—may or may not be difficult to sew, depending on the looseness of the weave.

Other transparent fabrics such as athletic mesh, dishrag and crochet-type knits, net, sheer tricot, lace, and open-weave fabrics are woven or knitted with medium to heavy yarns to form open-work patterns. A few fabrics, such as challis, Viyella, and shirtings are transparent in some colors.

This chapter focuses on the basic techniques for semicrisp and semisoft fabrics. For additional information, see Crisp, Transparent Fabrics; Soft, Transparent Fabrics; Lightweight Silks; Lightweight Polyesters; Handkerchief Linen.

The Transparent Family

For additional sewing suggestions, see the indicated sections.

Batiste is a semisoft, lightweight, plain-weave fabric. Available in a variety of fibers and blends, it varies in sheerness. It is used for lingerie, infants' garments, little girls' dresses, blouses, dresses, handkerchiefs, linings, and underlinings. (See Cotton and Plain-Weave Fabrics.)

Challis is a semisoft, plain-weave fabric made of rayon, cotton, or wool. Lightweight and easy to sew, challis may not be transparent in dark hues.

Chiffon is an elegant, sheer fabric. Woven from highly twisted yarns in a plain weave, most chiffons are very soft and slippery, but strong. Compared to georgette, it is smoother and more lus-

trous. It is available in natural and man-made fibers and is used primarily for special occasion, cocktail, and evening dresses; scarves; and linings and underlinings. (See Soft, Transparent Fabrics.)

Crepe chiffon is a very lightweight, sheer crepe. Used for formal wear, it is softer than georgette and particularly difficult to sew. (See Soft, Transparent Fabrics.)

Crochet-type knits are knitted fabrics with an open-work pattern. Depending on the knit design and fiber content, they are suitable for a variety of garments, from casual to dressy. (See Mesh.)

Dimity is woven with multi-ply yarns to create stripes or checks on a transparent, plain-weave fabric. Semicrisp to crisp, dimity is used for blouses,

197

dresses, children's and infants' wear, and curtains. (See Stripes and Plaids.)

Dishrag knits are open-weave raschel knits which look like dishrags. Sometimes called fishnets or

athletic mesh, they are used for casual tops, athletic wear and children's wear. (See Mesh.)

Dotted Swiss is a crisp fabric with woven, flocked, or printed dots at regular intervals. It is used pri-

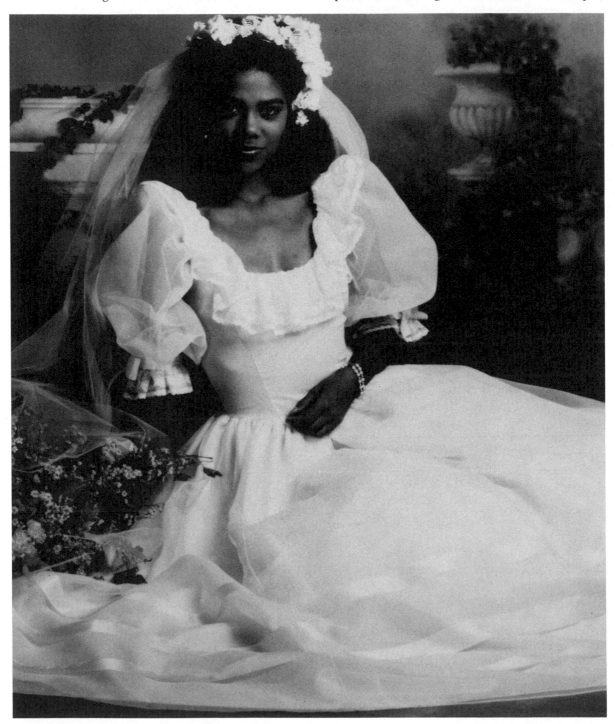

Fig. 12–1 *Frequently a choice for brides, transparent fabrics range from very soft to very crisp. (Photo courtesy of McCall Pattern Co.)*

marily for little girls' dresses, summer blouses, wedding dresses, and nightgowns. (See Stripes.)

Double sheer is a lightweight crisp fabric tightly woven with twisted yarns. Almost opaque, it looks like moiré and is used for evening wear.

Eyelash voile is a reversible fabric with clipped yarns on the fabric surface which look like eyelashes. Semicrisp to crisp, eyelash voile is used for blouses, dresses, children's and infants' wear, and curtains. (See Stripes, Two Faced Fabrics.)

Eyelet is an embroidered open-work design on organdy, organza, chiffon, or batiste. Soft to crisp, depending on the background fabric, eyelet may have an allover pattern or a border design. It is suitable for blouses, dresses, special formal wear, children's and infants' wear, and curtains. (See Borders, Lace.)

Gazar is a heavy organza. Almost opaque, it has a linenlike coarseness.

Gauze is woven with tightly twisted yarns in a plain or leno weave. Available in a variety of fibers, the quality and ease of sewing depends on the number of threads per inch and the weave. It is suitable for casual garments and curtains.

Georgette is loosely woven double sheer with highly twisted yarns in both the warp and filling. Compared to crepe de chine and chiffon, it has less luster and more crepe. Usually made of silk or polyester, it is suitable for evening wear, blouses, dresses, and scarves. (See Soft, Transparent Fabrics.)

Handkerchief linen is a light, crisp, fabric used for blouses, dresses, lingerie, baby dresses, and handkerchiefs. (See Crisp, Transparent Fabrics and Handkerchief Linen.)

Lace is an open-work, decorative fabric. It is available in a variety of fibers and patterns, ranging from very formal to very casual. (See Lace.)

Lawn is a fine, lustrous sheer with a high thread count. Usually semicrisp, it is not as soft as voile and batiste or as crisp as organdy. It is used for infants' and children's wear, blouses, collars, cuffs, and handkerchiefs.

Leno is a loosely woven, but firm, open-weave fabric. Sometimes called gauze, it is used for casual garments and shirtings.

Maline is a fine, open mesh with a diamond shape. (See Net.)

Marquisette is a crisp, sheer, open-weave fabric.

It is suitable for underlinings, interfacings, evening wear, dresses, children's wear, curtains, and trimmings. (See Crisp, Transparent Fabrics.)

Mousseline or silk muslin is a crisp, sheer. Compared to chiffon, it is more closely woven and not as soft. It is used for evening wear and trimmings. (See Crisp, Transparent Fabrics.)

Net is a mesh fabric. Available in a variety of meshes, it is used for evening wear, petticoats, interfacing, costumes, millinery, and trimming. (See Net.)

Ninon is a sheer, crisp voile with a smooth finish. It is used for curtains and evening wear. (See Crisp, Transparent Fabrics.)

Nun's veiling is a sheer, semicrisp wool. Woven with finely twisted yarns, it has a firm hand. It is used for dresses and mourning veils. (See Lightweight Wools.)

Open-work raschel knits are open knits with little or no stretch. They are used for casual garments. (See Raschel Knits.)

Organdy is a sheer, crisp fabric woven with fine, tightly twisted cotton yarns. It is used for blouses, dresses, evening wear, children's dresses, curtains, interfacings, and facings. (See Crisp, Transparent Fabrics.)

Organza is a sheer, plain-weave fabric. Made in silk, rayon, or polyester yarns, it is not as crisp as organdy. It is used for evening wear, children's dresses, blouses, dresses, interfacings, underlinings, linings, and facings. (See Crisp, Transparent Fabrics.)

Point d'esprit is a fine net with rectangular dots spaced at regular intervals. (See Net.)

Sheer tricot is a transparent tricot knit. It is used for lingerie and edge finishes. (See Tricot.)

Tana lawn is a semisoft cotton manufactured by Liberty of London. (See Plain-Weave Fabrics.)

Tarlatan is an open, plain-weave fabric with a crisp finish. Frequently used for costumes, it is sometimes used for interfacings and to back quilted material. (See Crisp, Transparent Fabrics.)

Tulle is a fine, hexagonal mesh. (See Net.)

Viyella is a soft, twill-weave fabric made of 55 percent wool and 45 percent cotton. (See Lightweight Wool.)

Voile is a sheer, semicrisp fabric made of highly twisted yarns in natural and synthetic fibers. It is used for lingerie, blouses, and children's clothes.

Fabric Characteristics

- Transparent fabrics allow seams, hems, and

SEWING CHECKLIST

Machine Needles: Universal-H point, stretch (HS), Red or Yellow Band needles; sizes 60/8 to 70/10.

Machine Setting: Stitch length 1.25–2mm (12–20 stitches per inch); light tension.

Thread: Extra-fine cotton-wrapped polyester, long-staple polyester (100/3), fine mercerized cotton (60/3).

Hand Sewing Needles: Sizes 8 to 10.

Sewing Machine Equipment: Straight stitch, jeans, or roller foot.

Equipment and Supplies: Very fine new pins, weights, well-sharpened shears or rotary cutter and mat, lightweight zippers, and stabilizer.

Marking Techniques: All types, except wax.

Seams: Narrow—French, false French, hairline, standing fell, machine-rolled, flat-fell, whipped, edgestitched, self-fabric bias binding, double/ply, lace insertions, tissue-stitched.

Hems: Very narrow hems—machine-rolled, rolled-hemmer foot, hand-rolled, shell, lace, shirttail, book, mock-merrow, merrow, wired, horse hair, lace. Wide—double-fold hems, satin stitched.

Edge Finishes: Bindings, bands, bias bindings, bias and tricot facings, lace and net facings, edge-to-edge linings, decorative facings, self-fabric shaped facings on underlined garments.

Interfacings: Optional.

Linings and Underlinings: Optional.

Closures: Machine-stitched and hand-worked buttonholes, button loops, frogs, zippers, snaps, hooks and eyes, and ties.

---

facings to show on the outside of the garment.

- Light colors are more transparent than dark ones.
- Transparent fabrics can be made opaque by adding an underlining, lining, or multiple layers of self-fabric.
- Many transparent fabrics are sheer and fragile.
- Seam slippage is a problem on closely fitted garments.
- Some transparent fabrics ravel badly.
- Some are very slippery and elusive.
- Some transparent fabrics have a sheen and should be treated like napped fabrics.
- Some sag when sewn to firmly woven lining fabrics.
- Skipped stitches and puckered seams are frequent problems.
- Some transparent sheers are easily damaged by the presser foot and feed dogs, by ripping, and by overhandling.
- Many transparent fabrics are permanently marred by large or defective needles.
- Sheer fabrics require a lower iron setting than heavier fabrics with the same fiber content.

PLANNING A GARMENT

FABRIC AND PATTERN SELECTION

Leno-weave fabrics tend to slip and fray less than plain-weave fabrics. When selecting plain-weave fabrics, choose closely woven materials with fine yarns to reduce fraying and seam slippage.

Hint: *To test for seam slippage, scrape your thumbnail across the fabric to determine whether the warp threads separate.*

Avoid heavily sized materials, which lose their crispness when the garment is cleaned. To test for sizing, scrape your nail across the fabric to see if it releases the sizing. Hold the fabric up to the light and look for starch between the yarns.

If the garment has wide double-fold hems or multiple layers, you'll need additional fabric.

Generally, a pattern with a minimum number of seams is best, since all construction details can be seen from the right side of the garment. Avoid intricately shaped seams, fitted garments, slim silhouettes, and fussy details.

When choosing the pattern, consider the hand of the fabric, its softness and crispness, as well as the type of garment. Generally, gathers, pleats, tucks, and ease are more attractive than darts.

Details such as a tucked bodice or patch pockets over the breasts make garments less revealing while maintaining the transparent quality of the fabric.

Synthetic fabrics can be permanently pleated, then used for a variety of designs. (See Pleated Fabrics.)

For a rich, luxurious look, use multiple layers of a sheer fabric. This also makes the garment more opaque. For large figure types, underline the garment body and use sheer sleeves.

FABRIC AND PATTERN PREPARATION

The fabric care for transparent fabrics ranges from dry-clean only to machine wash and dry. Check the manufacturer's recommendation for fabric care and then consider the garment structure.

Generally, silk sheers require dry cleaning. Cotton organdy and synthetic fabrics are washable, depending on the garment structure.

Fit and adjust the pattern before cutting. If necessary, make a test garment, using a similar weight fabric.

When using deep-fold hems, add the hem allowance—twice the finished width—to the garment hemline. When using doubled sleeves, skirts, or bodice sections, make a new pattern for that section. (See Doubled Sleeves, later in this chapter.)

To avoid a facing/front seamline, eliminate the seam by cutting the bodice with an extended facing. Pin the pattern for the facing to the bodice front, matching the seamlines.

Redraw shaped facings on shirt fronts so the facing shadow will be a straight line. Measure the distance between the center front and the finished edge. Make the finished facing twice this width.

Hint: *To eliminate the need to finish facing edges, cut the front sections so the edge is on the selvage.*

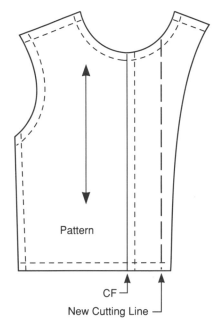

Pattern

CF ⌐
New Cutting Line ⌐

Fig. 12–2

Or make the new facing twice as wide to make a facing and an interfacing. On the finished garment the raw edge of the interfacing will meet the fold at the garment edge.

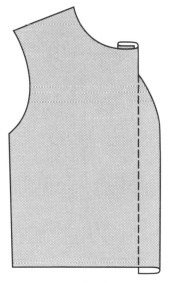

Fig. 12–3

201

An edge-to-edge lining made of self-fabric is another solution to the facing problem. Cut the garment/lining with a fold at the hemline or front edge. Or cut two separate sections and join them at the outside edges.

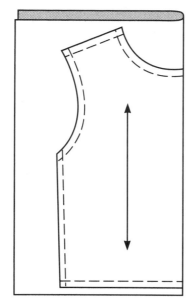

Fig. 12–4

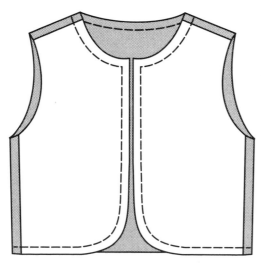

Fig. 12–5

SEWING TRANSPARENT FABRICS

LAYOUT, CUTTING, AND MARKING

To control elusive sheers, cover the cutting surface with a flannel-backed tablecloth or table pads, flannel side up.

Cut, using well-sharpened shears or a rotary cutter and mat. If the fabric frays badly, apply a fray retardant sparingly to all edges immediately after cutting.

Experiment with marking techniques to determine which is best for your fabric. Avoid dark-colored tracing carbon.

STITCHING TIPS

Generally, natural fiber fabrics are easier to sew than synthetics.

Change to a straight stitch or roller foot and a small-hole needle plate to avoid dragging the fabric into the needle hole. If you must use a zigzag foot, decenter the needle.

Hint: *My Bernina has a jeans foot which holds lightweight fabrics securely.*

Make a test seam, using a new needle, a short stitch length—1.25–2mm (12–20 stitches per inch)—and a loosely balanced tension.

To prevent the fabric from being drawn into the needle hole when beginning, stitch onto a small piece of stabilizer; then place the fabric on top of the stabilizer; stitch the seam. Hold thread ends securely as you begin stitching to avoid a thread bubble.

To prevent puckered seams, tissue-stitch seams and hold the fabric taut when stitching. Remove the tissue carefully to avoid distorting the stitches.

Secure threads at the beginning and end with a knot or several short stitches. Try to avoid backstitching.

Hint: *Silk sheers are generally more forgiving and easier to stitch than synthetics.*

SEAMS

When choosing seams and seam finishes, consider the fabric quality, weight, and tendency to fray, the garment style and use, care requirements, and your time and sewing ability.

Hint: *Generally, seams on transparent fabrics should be very inconspicuous and quite narrow—less than 1/4".*

Make several sample seams; then hold them up against your body so you can view them as they will be worn. Examine the way the sample seams hang as well as the way they look.

Plain seams, which are stitched only once, are softer than self-finished seams, which are stitched twice. French, standing-fell, and flat-fell seams are softer when hand stitched.

The best choices for better garments and lightweight woven fabrics are French, false French, standing-fell, flat-fell, machine-rolled, hairline, whipped, double/ply bound, and double/ply overcast.

Avoid using French and flat-fell on curved seams such as armholes, necklines, and princess lines; instead use false French, standing-fell, double ply/overcast, or double/ply bound seams.

Use double-stitched seams on fabrics which don't ravel. For casual garments and less expensive fabrics which ravel, use double/ply seams finished with a zigzag, multi-stitch zigzag, or serging.

Hint: *After all of that wonderful advice, I must confess I recently saw double/ply serged seams on a garment which cost $5325.*

Trim seams inside collars and cuffs evenly to 1/8" or 1/4", depending on how badly the fabric frays. When using the selvage edge as a seam finish, clip at intervals so seams will hang properly.

Substitute lace insertions for seams on lingerie, children's wear, and delicate blouses and dresses.

DARTS

When darts cannot be avoided, use double-stitched, bobbin-stitched, or hairline darts to make them less conspicuous.

To double-stitch a dart, stitch to the dart point; raise the presser foot; turn the dart around; and restitch the dart line.

To bobbin-stitch a dart, thread the machine and draw up the bobbin thread as usual. Knot the bobbin and spool thread; carefully pull the knot through the needle. Pull up more of the bobbin thread and wind the thread onto the spool until the knot reaches the spool. Stitch the dart, beginning at the point. Rethread before stitching the next dart.

HEMS

Allow garments to hang at least twenty-four hours before measuring hems; and, if the fabric is a soft sheer, let it hang at least twice that long.

If the garment has a straight skirt, use a very narrow hem, a wide double hem, a wide satin-stitched hem, or a double skirt with a fold at the hemline. If the skirt is flared or circular, use only narrow hems or a complete lining.

Hem children's garments with deep double-fold hems. These hems can be as deep as one-third the total skirt length.

Use horsehair braid so the hem will stand away from the body. Lace hems are particularly attractive on wedding dresses and lingerie. (See Lace.)

EDGE FINISHES

Replace traditional shaped facings with bindings, bands, edge-to-edge linings, or lace, bias, or tulle facings.

For lingerie and infants' garments, consider lace facings on the right side of the garment; for casual designs, consider bias facings on the right side of the garment.

Apply bindings by hand or machine, depending on the garment quality and time factor.

Hint: *To eliminate ripping, I hand baste bindings in place before stitching.*

INTERFACINGS, UNDERLININGS, AND LININGS

Traditional interfacing fabrics are rarely used. Self-fabrics and flesh-colored organzas, tulles, and marquisettes work well. Generally, fusibles are best avoided; if you are considering using one, always test first before applying a fusible.

When possible, eliminate interfacings; reshape them so they will be a part of the overall design; or replace them with an underlining or flat lining.

Cut pocket sacks for inseam pockets from flesh-colored fabric, so they will be inconspicuous.

The success of a transparent garment depends as much on its lining, underlining, or custom-designed undergarment as the construction techniques used on the garment itself. Select underlinings and linings which have compatible fiber and care qualities.

Linings may or may not be used with underlinings. Underlining and lining fabrics can reduce transparency, provide support, and eliminate the need for special seams and hems. They range from sheer tulles and chiffons to opaque satins and printed linens. When selecting these fabrics, consider the color, texture, and surface pattern as well as the opaqueness desired.

Cotton fabrics cling to the figure and do not work well; and shiny acetates and satins may overwhelm the outer material.

The three most obvious ways to make a garment less transparent are an edge-to-edge lining, a complete underlining, and a separate or built-in slip for a particular garment.

Let's examine each individually and consider some of the variations.

EDGE-TO-EDGE LINING

The edge-to-edge lining duplicates the garment section which it lines, finishes all edges, and eliminates the need to finish seams. It also provides opaqueness for all but the lightest colored fabrics. And when a sheer lining fabric or self-fabric is used, it maintains the illusion of sheerness that attracted you initially.

Some suitable fabrics for edge-to-edge linings include self-fabric, tulle, chiffon, organza, marquisette, satin-backed crepe, satin, or taffeta. For the lining, select the same color in a lighter or darker shade, a flesh color, or a complementary color.

The doubled skirt or sleeve, which has a fold at the hemline, is a variation of the edge-to-edge lining. Use these directions for the sleeve pattern for any garment section or group of sections which have a straight hemline.

1. Make a new pattern. Fold a piece of pattern paper in half; then align the hemline of the sleeve pattern with the fold on the paper. Trace the sleeve pattern; mark the notches and grainline. Cut out the pattern.

Hint: *Use wax paper and a tracing wheel to trace the pattern.*

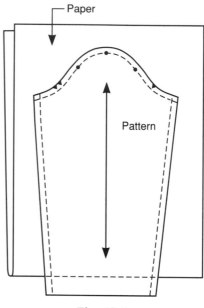

Paper

Pattern

Fig. 12–6

2. Open out the pattern and use it to cut a pair of sleeves.

3. To assemble the sleeve, begin right sides together. Fold the sleeves lengthwise; stitch the underarm seam. Press and trim to 1/4".

4. Wrong sides together, match and baste the edges of the cap together. Ease baste between the notches.

5. Set the sleeves and bind the edges.

6. When making a doubled skirt, join all vertical seams first; press; then fold at the hemline, wrong sides together.

UNDERLINED GARMENT SECTIONS

Generally, an underlining duplicates the section which it backs. Complete underlinings hide the structure of the garment, eliminating the need for special seams and edge finishes. They also provide support.

Underlinings range from light organzas to heavy satins. These fabrics are sometimes used to create a new fabric in color and texture. The usual combinations—a printed sheer over a solid backing, solid sheer over a print, or two solids—are frequently used for bridesmaids' dresses.

When underlinings are used for draped and shirred designs, the underlining is usually more fitted than the sheer and serves as a base garment or large stay.

Underlinings may back only a portion of the garment—an underlined bodice and skirt with sheer sleeves—or they may underline a portion of a section. These partial underlinings are frequently used for modesty on the bodice.

To retain the sheerness of chiffons and crepes and to stabilize them for easy handling, underline with flesh-colored tulle or net.

Hint: *Net is stiffer than tulle and may be so scratchy that the seam edges will have to be bound.*

Designers Galanos and Stavropolous are known for their multilayer sheers. Usually separate skirts are sewn together at the waistline and separate bodices are joined at the neckline. These designs are a variation of underlining. Multilayered designs can be all one color, different shades of the color, or different colors.

In addition to finishing the raw edges on vertical seams, flat linings have the added advantage of allowing minor alterations. (See Chapter 20.)

CUSTOMIZED UNDERGARMENTS

A custom-made undergarment can be a separate or built-in slip. Generally, built-in underpinnings are better for soft fabrics and for designs which need support. Choose a flesh, complementary, or matching color fabric to create the desired effect.

To make the undergarment almost invisible under the garment, use a flesh-colored fabric and design the undergarment so its edges fall immediately beneath the seamlines of the garment.

Hint: *Shoulder pads are less noticeable when covered with a flesh-colored fabric.*

CLOSURES

Bound buttonholes should be avoided, except when the fabric is somewhat opaque or the garment is underlined.

When making machine-stitched buttonholes, place a piece of water-soluble stabilizer under the fabric before stitching. When possible, use a machine-embroidery hoop to hold the garment section taut.

If button loops made from self-filled bias tubing are too small, cord the tubing to make the loops larger and firmer.

Fabric-covered snaps and thread-covered hooks and eyes work well in some plackets.

Hint: *Use two layers of fabrics when covering button forms so the metal or plastic doesn't show through.*

Try to avoid zippers on light-colored sheers. Insert zippers by hand on after-five and evening wear. If the garment is underlined, sew the zipper only to the underlining.

PRESSING AND GARMENT CARE

Test press on fabric scraps. Use a cooler iron to avoid scorching the fabric.

When pressing eyelet, cover the pressing surface with a towel; press the fabric, wrong side up.

Washable garments made of transparent fabrics require shorter wash cycles.

Crisp Transparent Fabrics

The crisp transparent fabrics—cotton organdy, silk organza, gazar, polyester organdy, and dotted Swiss—are the easiest to sew.

For additional information, see Transparent Fabrics.

Fabric Characteristics
- All construction details—seams, hems, and facings—show on the outside of the garment.
- Some crisp sheers fray badly.
- Many are easily damaged by the sewing machine feed dogs.
- Puckered seams are sometimes a problem.
- Natural fiber fabrics are frequently easier to handle than synthetics.

SEWING CHECKLIST

Machine Needles: Universal-H point or Red Band needles; sizes 60/8 or 70/10.

Machine Setting: Stitch length 2–2.5mm (12–15 stitches per inch).

Thread: Long-staple polyester (100/3), extra-fine cotton-wrapped polyester, mercerized cotton.

Sewing Machine Equipment: Straight-stitch, jeans, or roller foot.

Equipment and Supplies: Very fine pins, well-sharpened shears, lightweight zippers and buttons.

Marking Techniques: All types, except wax.

Seams: Very narrow—French, false French, standing-fell, machine-rolled, flat-fell, hairline, French whipped, double/ply, tissue-stitched.

Hems: Narrow—machine-rolled hem, rolled-hemmer foot, hand-rolled hem, shirttail, book, mock-merrow, merrow, lace, horsehair. Wide—double-fold hem, wide satin-stitched, horsehair braid.

Edge Finishes: Bindings, bands, net and bias facings, decorative facings, self-fabric facings, edge-to-edge linings.

Interfacings: Optional.

Linings and Underlinings: Depends on garment design.

Closures: Machine-made and hand-worked buttonholes, button loops, covered snaps, hooks and eyes.

Pockets: Patch; avoid slashed and in-seam.

PLANNING A GARMENT

FABRIC AND PATTERN SELECTION

Choose closely woven fabrics with fine yarns to reduce fraying and seam slippage. Avoid heavily sized material. Frequently loosely woven and inferior in quality, it loses its crispness when the garment is cleaned.

Generally, patterns with a minimum of seams are best. Crisp sheers stand away from the body and are most attractive when the fabric is used generously. Avoid closely fitted designs.

Hint: *If the garment has wide double-fold hems or self-fabric linings, you'll need additional fabric.*

Preshrink the fabric before cutting. Machine wash and dry synthetic fabrics; steam press silk organza and gazar.

Soak cotton organdy in a basin of hot water. When the water cools, drain the basin and press out as much water as possible; do not wring or twist the fabric. Roll the fabric in a thick towel to remove more moisture. Hang the fabric, smoothing out as many wrinkles as possible. When almost dry, press as needed. Use spray starch to restore crispness.

Hint: *Before sewing expensive fabrics, make a test garment and alter the pattern, to avoid ripping which may damage the fabric.*

SEWING CRISP TRANSPARENT FABRICS

LAYOUT, CUTTING, AND MARKING

Most crisp sheers do not have a nap and will not be permanently marred by pin holes, if you use new, fine pins.

Pin the pattern in place with very fine pins. I use weights on the grainlines and position all pins within the seam allowances parallel to the grainline.

Cut, using very sharp shears. To mark, use pins, chalk, soap sliver, temporary marking pens, tailor tacks, or thread tracing.

STITCHING TIPS

Generally, natural fiber fabrics are easier to sew than synthetics.

Make a test seam, using a new needle, a short stitch length—1.25–1.75mm (15–20 stitches per inch)—and a loosely balanced tension. Hold the threads firmly behind the presser foot to begin stitching. Hold the fabric taut while stitching.

Change to a straight-stitch foot, jeans foot, or roller foot with a small-hole needle plate to hold the fabric firmly. If you must use a zigzag foot, decenter the needle.

Secure threads at the beginning and end with a knot, spot tack, or shorter stitch. Do not backstitch.

SEAMS, DARTS, AND HEMS

Seams on transparent garments should be very inconspicuous and quite narrow—less than 1/4". Suitable seams include French, false French, standing-fell, machine-rolled, flat-fell, hairline, French whipped, and narrow double/ply.

Darts should be as inconspicuous as seams. Use one of the above seaming techniques to accomplish this.

Hint: *To avoid a knot at the end of a dart, bobbin-stitch or double-stitch the dart.*

Generally, it's better to hem garments and linings separately. Hems can be very wide, very narrow, or eliminated completely.

FACINGS AND EDGE FINISHES

Replace traditional shaped facings with straight facings, decorative facings, narrow bias facings, bias bindings, tulle or self-fabric edge-to-edge linings. Avoid fusibles.

Sheers are particularly attractive with decorative facings; since crisp fabrics have plenty of body, they're easy to appliqué.

These directions for an organdy collar can be used to trim a variety of garments, placemats, and tablecloths.

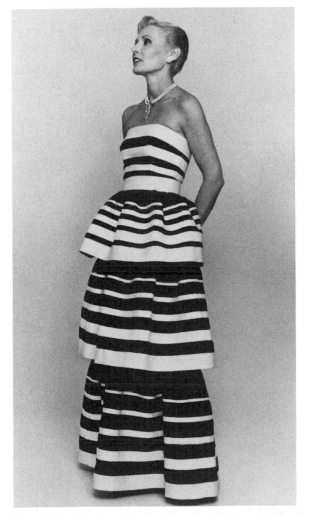

Fig. 12–7 *Designed by Los Angeles designer Michael Novarese, the tiers on the silk organza design are trimmed with five widths of grosgrain. (Photo courtesy of Michael Novarese.)*

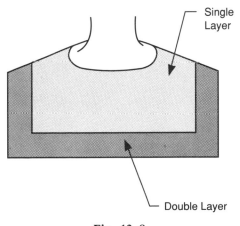

Single Layer

Double Layer

Fig. 12–8

207

1. Make the pattern for the facing. Trace the collar pattern and draw the finished facing shape on the traced pattern. Add a 1/4″ seam allowance at the unnotched edge—the outer edges already have seam allowances.

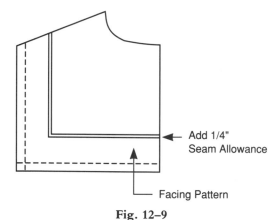

Add 1/4″ Seam Allowance

Facing Pattern

Fig. 12–9

2. Cut out the collar and facing.

Hint: *Cut the facing from self-fabric, another crisp sheer, or an opaque fabric.*

3. Wrong sides up with the facing on top, join the outer edges with a hairline seam. Trim the seam as closely and evenly as possible.
4. Turn the collar right side out. Press.
5. Using a short stitch (1.75mm or 15 stitches per inch), stitch the facing to the collar 1/4″ from the unnotched edge. Trim close to the stitched line.

Hint: *Use either 5″ trimmers or appliqué scissors to trim closely.*

6. Using matching or coordinating machine-embroidery thread, satin stitch (W,2; L,almost 0)

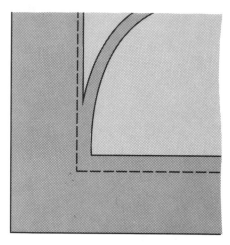

Fig. 12–10

over the stitched line. This is particularly attractive when the stitch is narrow; but it must be wide enough to cover the stitched line and the raw edge.
7. Sew the collar to the garment.

CLOSURES

Button loops, hand-worked or machine-stitched buttonholes are good choices. Avoid bound buttonholes, unless the section is underlined.

Hint: *Machine-stitched buttonholes are particularly attractive when stitched with machine-embroidery thread.*

Zippers are frequently used on underlined and casual designs. Select a lightweight coil. Apply zippers by hand on cocktail and evening wear. Apply by machine on washable organdy and dotted Swiss.

Soft Transparent Fabrics

Soft, transparent fabrics like chiffon, georgette, and crepe chiffon are the most difficult transparents to sew. They are probably among the most difficult fabrics you'll ever encounter.

For additional suggestions, see Transparent Fabrics.

Fabric Characteristics
• All construction details—seams, hems, and

facings—show on the outside of the garment.
• Soft fabrics are very elusive. They are easily distorted and fray badly.
• Soft, transparent fabrics are very fragile and are easily damaged by machine needles, the presser foot, feed dogs, ripping, overhandling, and overfitting.

- They sag with age and weight.
- They are easily damaged by hot irons and steam.

PLANNING A GARMENT

PATTERN AND FABRIC SELECTION

Soft, transparent fabrics drape beautifully, so designs featuring shirring, soft tucks, and gathers are particularly attractive. Strapless designs with sheer yokes are always popular.

If this is your first soft, sheer design, choose a relatively simple design with a minimum number

Fig. 12–11 *Yards and yards of silk satin-striped chiffon and a true bias cut combine to form a masterpiece. The Kleibacker signature— tiny bias strings—holds the silhouette close to the body in front. (Photo courtesy of Charles Kleibacker.)*

of seams. For a more luxurious-looking garment, use several layers of the fabric instead of a lining fabric to make the garment opaque.

Hint: *Large figure types can wear soft sheers better than they can wear crisp ones.*

SEWING CHECKLIST

Machine Needles: Universal-H point or Red Band needles; sizes 60/8 to 70/10.
Machine Setting: Stitch length 1.25–2mm (12–20 stitches per inch); tension, lightly balanced.
Thread: Extra-fine cotton-wrapped polyester, long-staple polyester (100/3). On silks—fine mercerized cotton.
Hand Sewing Needles: Sizes 8 to 10.
Sewing Machine Equipment: Straight-stitch, jeans, or roller foot.
Equipment and Supplies: Very fine new pins, weights, well-sharpened shears or rotary cutter and mat, lightweight buttons and zippers, and stabilizer.
Marking Techniques: All types, except wax.
Seams: Very narrow—French, false French, standing-fell, machine-rolled, flat-fell, whipped, double/ply, tissue-stitched, taped.
Hems: Narrow—machine-rolled, rolled-hemmer foot, hand-rolled, shell, merrow, mock-merrow—or wide double hems.
Edge Finishes: Bindings, bands, net and bias facings, edge-to-edge linings.
Interfacings: Generally not used.
Linings and Underlinings: Both opaque and sheer linings and underlinings are used.
Closures: Button loops, zippers, snaps, hooks and eyes.

Press silk chiffons and georgettes quickly and lightly with a dry iron.

Fit and adjust the pattern before cutting; make duplicate pattern pieces. If necessary, make a test garment in a similar weight fabric.

Eliminate facings at edges to be bound.

SEWING SOFT TRANSPARENT FABRICS

LAYOUT, CUTTING, AND MARKING

Cover the cutting surface with a flannel-backed tablecloth or table pads, flannel side up. Then cover it with large sheets of tissue or wax paper taped together.

Hint: *Some wax papers can be fused together with a warm dry iron—put aluminum foil over sole plate if you're worried about wax on your iron.*

Spread the fabric in a single layer, right side up, on the tissue. Straighten it carefully; and, if necessary, clip the selvages so the edges will lie flat.

Lay out the pattern pieces. Use weights, or pins only in the seam allowances, to hold the pattern in place.

Hint: *Whenever possible, use the selvage as a seam finish and reduce seam allowances to 1/4" before cutting out. Use a very narrow selvage to stabilize seams.*

Cut, using well-sharpened shears. Pick up the pattern pieces; then, with the fabric still pinned to the paper, prepare the sections—right sides together—for stitching.

STITCHING TIPS

Generally, natural fiber sheers are more elusive and softer than synthetic fabrics.

Make a test seam, using a new needle, a short stitch length—1.25–1.75mm (15–20 stitches per inch)—and a loosely balanced tension. To avoid a thread bubble, hold thread ends securely as you begin stitching.

Change to a straight-stitch, jeans, or roller foot and a small-hole needle plate to avoid dragging the fabric into the needle hole. Or use a zigzag foot and decenter the needle.

Hint: *To prevent the fabric from being drawn into the needle hole, first stitch onto a small piece of stabilizer. Then place the fabric over the stabilizer and stitch the seam.*

To prevent puckered and stretched seams, stitch the seams with the fabric sandwiched between two tissue paper layers. Tear the paper away carefully to avoid distorting the stitches. To avoid distorting necklines and armholes, staystitch through the tissue paper.

Secure the threads at the beginning and end with a knot, spot tack, or shorter stitch. Do not backstitch.

Hint: *For best results, don't skimp on hand basting.*

SEAMS, HEMS, AND EDGE FINISHES

Simple seams—whipped, French, false French, double-stitched—are generally best. Concentrate on making them narrow and sturdy.

Hint: *Hand-stitched seams are softer and hang better.*

Before marking hems, allow the garment to hang as long as possible, preferably several days, but at least twenty-four hours.

Very narrow hems are usually best, but double 2" hems sometimes work well on narrow skirts. Generally, double hems and wide hems are too heavy for soft, transparent fabrics.

Narrow bias bindings are the best finish, but they must be handled carefully. To prevent unwanted fraying, do not trim away the seam allowance until the binding has been basted and stitched to the edge.

Hint: *Most soft sheers are sewn to a slip if they aren't underlined.*

CLOSURES

Buttons and button loops, lightweight zippers, covered snaps, and hooks and eyes work well. Use a zipper for security and hide it with a series of buttons and button loops. Make the button loops from teeny-weeny, self-filled bias tubing.

Do not use a zipper unless it can be sewn to the lining or underlining—it will make the garment sag. Instead, substitute a continuous-bound placket and covered snaps or hooks and eyes if the fabric is too soft for a zipper.

CONTINUOUS BOUND PLACKET

1. Cut the placket strip 2 1/2″ wide and at least twice the length of the opening.

Hint: *The placket is easier to sew if the strip is cut on the lengthwise grain.*

2. Stitch the skirt seam below the placket. Fasten the threads securely at the placket end; and clip the seam allowances to the end of the stitched line.

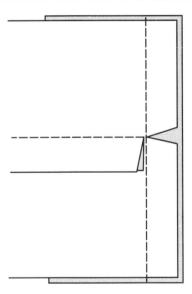

Fig. 12–12

3. Right sides together, pin and baste the strip to the skirt opening, matching the raw edges; stitch.

4. Wrap the strip around the raw edges; press lightly, fold under the raw edge of the strip and slipstitch in place.

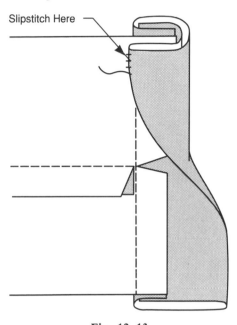

Slipstitch Here

Fig. 12–13

PRESSING

Test press on fabric scraps, using a cool iron. Work quickly with little pressure; try to avoid moisture which may cause the fabric to shrink.

CHAPTER 13
Special-Occasion Fabrics

Satin and Sateen

Satin fabrics have a smooth, lustrous surface. Woven in a satin weave from low-twist yarns, satin features long floats on the fabric face. The floats are in the warp or lengthwise grain, except on sateen. (Many satin-weave fabrics are not called satin.)

Satins range from soft, drapeable fabrics to heavy, stiff ones. Some have a high sheen, while others have a dull luster. Originally made of silk, today many are made of rayon, acetate, nylon, polyester, and long-staple cottons.

THE SATIN FAMILY

For additional sewing suggestions, see the indicated sections.

Antique satin has a dull back and lustrous face. Woven with slubbed yarns in the filling, either side can be used as the face. It is frequently used for evening wear and draperies. (See Ribbed Fabrics and Two-Faced Fabrics.)

Baronet satin, the most lustrous satin, has a rayon warp and cotton filling.

Canton satin is a soft, heavy fabric with a cross-rib, crepe back. (See Ribbed Fabrics.)

Charmeuse is a soft, light- to medium-weight fabric with a dull back. It is frequently used for blouses, lingerie, and nightgowns, as well as evening gowns and dresses. (See Lightweight Silks.)

Ciré is a waxed-finish satin with a smooth, lustrous finish similar to patent leather. The wax finish makes it stiffer than other similar-weight satins.

Cotton satin is woven with long-staple, combed cottons in the warp.

Crepe-backed satin, sometimes called satin-back crepe, is a reversible fabric with a satin face and crepe back. It is frequently used for linings, blouses, and dresses. (See Two-Faced Fabrics.)

Cut velvet is woven on a jacquard loom to create a distinct pile pattern on a satin background.

Double-faced satins look the same on the face and back. (See Two-Faced Fabrics.)

Duchesse satin is a very heavy, stiff satin. It is usually made of silk or acetate.

Messaline is a lightweight, loosely woven satin. It is usually made of silk or acetate. (See Lightweight Silks and Transparent Fabrics.)

Panné satin has a very lustrous, stiff face.

Peau d'ange is a medium- to heavyweight satin with a dull finish. It is usually silk and heavier than peau de soie.

Peau de soie is medium-weight satin with a dull finish. It looks the same on both sides. Originally silk, today it is frequently made of synthetic fibers.

Sateen is a dull-luster, cotton fabric with filling, instead of warp floats.

Fig. 13–1 *From the Kleibacker Group in the Historic Costume and Textile Collection, at The Ohio State University, a superb wedding dress of crepe-backed satin. The deep neck-yoke and edging on the sleeves are an incredible maneuver of hand work—small bias pieces of the satin lined by hand and joined by hand-worked "bars" to show the skin. (Photo courtesy of Charles Kleibacker.)*

Satin-stripe sheers are sheer fabrics with satin-weave stripes. (See Transparent Fabrics and Stripes.)

Satin-faced silk is reversible with a very lustrous face and a dull, cross-rib back. (See Two-Faced Fabrics, Silks, Lightweight Silks.)

Skinner Satin is the tradename for a heavy, durable lining satin.

Slipper satin is a stiff medium- to heavyweight satin.

Fabric Characteristics
- Satins snag easily.
- Satin fabrics are easily marred by pins, needles, rough hands, rough sewing surfaces, and ripping.
- Some satins ravel badly.
- Some satins are very slippery.
- Puckered seams are frequently a problem.
- Satins are easily damaged with improper pressing.
- Satins are susceptible to seam slippage.
- Some satins are easily damaged by folding.
- Satins are difficult to ease.
- Some satins waterspot; many will show perspiration stains.

PLANNING A GARMENT

FABRIC AND PATTERN SELECTION

Most satin fabrics are selected for their beauty, not their durability. Yarns with low-twist, filament yarns have more luster than those with high-twist, staple yarns.

The best, and most expensive, satins are silk or silk-faced. Satins with longer floats are more lustrous, but less resistant to abrasion and snagging.

Satins with a tighter weave fray less, are more durable, and more resistant to seam slippage; those with a looser weave have longer floats, more luster, and drape better.

Hint: *Scrape your thumbnail across the fabric. If the warp yarns separate, the seams will slip and the fabric will ravel.*

Satins are easily bruised by folding. Ask for an empty cardboard tube when you make your pur-

213

chase. If you don't plan to use the fabric immediately, wrap the rolled satin in white tissue paper, an old white sheet, or a pillowcase.

SEWING CHECKLIST

Machine Needles: Universal-H point and Red Band needles; sizes 60/8 to 80/12, depending on the fabric weight.

Machine Setting: Stitch length, 2–2.5mm (10–15 stitches per inch).

Thread: Long-stable polyester, cotton-wrapped polyester, mercerized cotton; size depends on fabric weight. Serging—woolly nylon; hand sewing—silk A, basting cotton.

Hand Sewing Needles: Sizes 8 to 10.

Sewing Machine Feet: Straight-stitch, roller or jeans foot.

Equipment and Supplies: Sharp shears, extra-fine pins, lightweight zippers, covered snaps.

Layout: Nap, double layer, right sides together. Silk satins—nap; single layer.

Marking: All types except wax.

Seams: Plain, double/ply, self-finished, tissue-stitched, appliqué.

Hems: Plain, blindstitch, blind catchstitch, catchstitch, horsehair braid, faced, lace, narrow hems, interfaced, double-stitched.

Seam and Hem Finishes: Luxury garments—hand overcast, Hong Kong. Others—pinked, pinked-and-stitched, zigzag, multi-stitch zigzag, serged.

Edge Finishes: Self-fabric and lining-fabric facings, bias bindings, bias facings, lace.

Interfacings: Sew-in interfacings.

Linings: Generally.

Underlinings: Frequently.

Closures: Buttons and buttonholes, button loops, thread loops, snaps, hand-stitched zippers, invisible zippers.

Traditionally, satin is used for special-occasion garments such as bridal gowns, prom dresses, evening gowns and coats, cocktail dresses and jackets. Many of today's satins are used for daytime blouses and dresses, lingerie, negligees, sleepwear, and linings.

The pattern selection will depend on the particular fabric, since satins range from soft to stiff, from transparent to opaque and from lightweight to heavy. Generally, tightly fitted designs are best avoided or underlined to prevent seam slippage at stress points.

For crisp, heavy fabrics, choose sculptured shapes with simple lines, unusual seaming, and A-line skirts. Avoid eased seams and traditional set-in sleeves when possible.

For soft fabrics, draped styles, gathers, soft pleats and flares, ruffles, and cowl necks are good choices.

The slipperiness of satins makes them well-suited for linings in coats and jackets and a joy to wear next to your skin.

Make a test garment to perfect the fit, practice your sewing techniques, and avoid overhandling the satin fabrics.

Reduce the ease in the sleeve cap as needed or cut the sleeve on the bias. (See Chapter 1.)

SEWING SATIN

LAYOUT, CUTTING, AND MARKING

To avoid snagging these delicate fabrics, cover your cutting table and work areas with a clean white sheet.

Use a nap layout; satin fabrics sometimes reflect the light differently when cut without nap. Spread the fabric right sides together. If the fabric will be bruised by folding, spread it right side up.

Instead of pins, use weights or fine needles. When using needles, place them only in the seam allowances. Use weights at the top and bottom of the grainline.

Mark lightly and as little as possible. Test the marking technique on a scrap before using it on your fabric. Some materials are easily damaged with a tracing wheel, while others are not.

STITCHING TIPS

Hint: *Before you begin sewing, smooth rough hands by rubbing them with a teaspoon of sugar and a teaspoon of cooking oil; rinse. Repeat if needed.*

With a new needle, make a test seam. Set the stitch length for 2–2.5 mm (10–15 stitches per inch); loosen the tension slightly and lighten the pressure. Hold the fabric taut when stitching, to avoid puckered seams. Use a straight-stitch roller, even-feed or jeans foot to hold the fabric firmly so it won't go into the needle hole or creep.

Seams on the lengthwise grain are more difficult to stitch without puckering than those on the bias.

Hint: *Redraw the cutting lines. At the garment hem, mark a point 1/2″ from the cutting line. Connect this point and the cutting line at the hipline or top of the garment.*

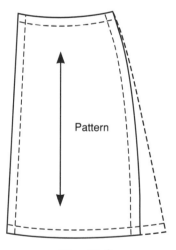

Fig. 13–2

SEAMS AND SEAM FINISHES

Hand baste the seams on luxury garments to avoid having to rip a machine-stitched line. Baste with silk thread to avoid pressing imprints; or remove the basting before pressing. Use fine needles instead of pins when pin basting.

Self-finished and double/ply seams are suitable for lightweight satins. (If the fabric is lightweight or transparent, see Lightweight Silks and Transparent Fabrics.) Eliminate seam finishes on lined garments.

Finish seams on heavy and crisp fabrics as flatly as possible. Generally single/ply finishes—pinked, pinked-and-stitched, zigzag, multi-stitch zigzag, and serged—are good choices. Hand overcasting with silk or cotton thread is best on luxury garments; other finishes may show on the outside of the garment, especially if it isn't underlined.

Hint: *To avoid thread imprints when serging, use woolly nylon in the loopers.*

To hide needle holes when you have to rip, scratch the fabric lightly with your thumbnail or a fine needle.

Generally, topstitching is best avoided.

HEMS

When hemming luxury garments, make the hem 2″ or wider. Interface the hem for a softer and crisper finish. If the skirt is flared, make small pleats as needed to control the extra fullness in the hem allowance.

On prom dresses and bridal gowns, use very narrow or horsehair hems. Hem heavier satins inconspicuously with a blindstitched or catchstitched hem; or interface the hem with cotton flannel or lambswool and quilt with three to seven rows of machine stitching spaced 1/4″ to 1/2″ apart.

FINE POINTS

To avoid unwanted perspiration stains, use dress shields. Make lingerie straps to keep bra and slip straps out of sight.

To avoid drooping skirts, insert a ruffle at the waistline:

1. From a crisp, lightweight fabric, nylon net, or tulle, cut the ruffle 4″ to 8″ wide and two to three times the seamline measurement. If the fabric is woven, cut the ruffle on the bias.

2. Gather the ruffle approximately 2″ from one edge.

3. Distribute the gathers evenly and pin the ruffle to the seamline, so the longer edge is next to the wrong side of the skirt.

Hint: *To distribute the gathers evenly, divide and mark both the skirt and ruffle into quarters. Match and pin the marked points.*

LININGS AND UNDERLININGS

Most special-occasion garments are lined, underlined or both. Linings eliminate the need for seam and hem finishes.

Satin linings are more supple than taffeta ones. Fabrics with more threads per inch split less and have less seam slippage.

Underlinings not only support heavy skirts and lightweight fabrics, they also cushion seams and hide hemming stitches, so they don't show on the right side of the garment.

Hint: *Interface garment edges and hems for a softer, more luxurious finish. Also interface button and buttonhole areas.*

CLOSURES

Jeweled and decorative buttons are particularly attractive on special-occasion garments. Buttonholes can be bound, hand-worked, or machine-stitched.

To avoid damaging the garment with rough buttons, sew the button to the buttonhole and fasten the garment with cloth-covered snaps.

If the fabric ravels badly, make bound buttonholes, using the patch or modified-patch method.

Thread or fabric loops and ball buttons are also attractive on special-occasion and everyday designs. Fabric loops can be used on all weight fabrics, but thread loops should be reserved for soft, lightweight satins.

Consider current fashions carefully before using fabric-covered buttons. Generally, full ball buttons are more fashionable than flat and semiball ones.

Hint: *Full ball buttons are particularly attractive on wedding gowns, at short neckline plackets, and at wrist openings.*

For best results, have a professional cover the buttons for you.

When you prefer the security of a zipper and a look of buttons on the back of a wedding dress or ball gown, use a mock button loop closure. Sew a lapped zipper into the placket; then sew the buttons to the lap.

Use only lightweight coil zippers. Hand stitch zippers on special-occasion garments. Machine stitch zippers on daytime and washable garments.

PRESSING

Satins are easily damaged with improper pressing. Take care to avoid seam and hem imprints, glazing on the right side, and unwanted pressed lines.

Test press on a fabric scrap to determine the heat setting, moisture, and pressure. Generally, a warm, dry iron and light pressing is best.

Press from the wrong side as much as possible. To avoid glazing, always use a press cloth when pressing the right side. Press with the satin floats.

Use a seam roll and brown paper strips to avoid seam and hem impressions on the outside of the garment.

GARMENT CARE

Most satin garments require dry-cleaning, but satin lingerie, nightgowns, blouses, and some dresses can be machine washed and dried. To protect them and reduce snagging, place each garment in a separate cloth bag for washing.

Hint: *For each bag, you'll need one muslin rectangle 22" by 44" and one 22" zipper. Right sides together, join one end of the muslin to the zipper tape with a 1/4" seam; right sides up, topstitch 1/4" from the seamline. Repeat for the other side of the zipper. Unzip the zipper and make French seams on each side of the bag.*

To avoid abrasion and snags, store satin garments on well-padded hangers in garment bags.

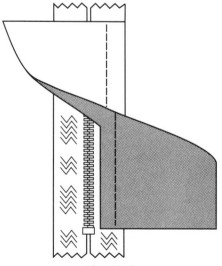

Fig. 13–3

Ribbed Fabrics

Ribbed fabrics are created by grouping several yarns together or by using heavy or thick yarns in one direction, with fine yarns in the other. Cross-rib fabrics have horizontal ribs, while lengthwise-rib fabrics have vertical ribs.

A variety of ribbed fabrics are available in all fibers. Fabrics range from soft to stiff, lightweight to medium heavy, sheer to opaque, and everyday to special occasion, while the ribs vary from very fine to very prominent.

THE RIBBED-WEAVE FAMILY

For additional sewing suggestions, see the indicated sections.

Antique satin is a reversible satin-weave fabric. The back, which is frequently used as the face, is dull with a slubbed cross-rib. (See Satin and Two-Faced Fabrics.)

Bengaline is woven with groups of filling yarns to form the rib. Compared to poplin, the ribs are finer.

Broadcloth has the finest ribs of all ribbed fabrics. The ribs on cotton and rayon broadcloths are formed by grouping filling yarns, while the ribs on silk are heavier than the warp yarns. The best cotton broadcloths are closely woven from long-staple cottons to produce a soft, lustrous fabric. (See Plain-Weave Fabrics.)

Canton crepe is a silk crepe with a slight cross-rib. (See Silk and Lightweight Silks.)

Dimity is a lightweight, sheer fabric woven with multi-ply yarns to create fine cords. It can be striped or checked. (See Transparent Fabrics, Stripes, and Plaids.)

Douppioni, a cross-rib silk, is woven with an uneven, irregular slubbed yarn from two cocoons nested together. (See Silk.)

Faille, sometimes called *faille taffeta,* has a more pronounced cross-rib, which is frequently woven with staple yarns. Compared to grosgrain, faille is softer, with larger, flatter ribs. (See Taffeta.)

Grosgrain is a hard-finished, closely woven, cross-rib fabric. It is frequently used for trims and stiffening.

Gros de Londres is a closely woven cross-rib fabric

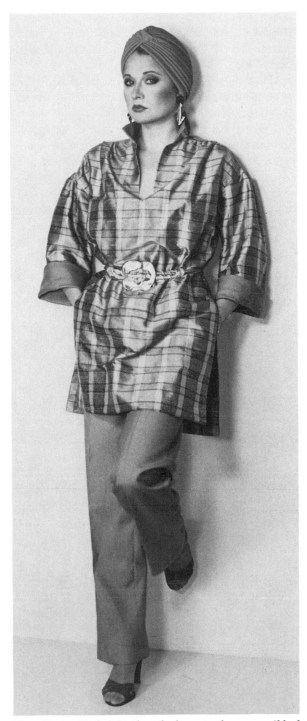

Fig. 13–4 *Understated and elegant, the cross-ribbed silk shirt, which tops the silk shantung pants, is made of Thai silk. (Photo courtesy of Britex Fabrics, San Francisco.)*

217

which is easily distinguished by its alternate thick and thin ribs. Ribs are formed by groups of filling yarns. (See Stripes.)

Marocain, a heavy crepe fabric, has slightly wavy cross ribs, produced by thick, twisted crepe yarns. Compared to Canton crepe, it is much heavier. (See Silk.)

Moiré faille or *moiré taffeta* is easily identified by its rippled, watermark pattern, which may or may not be permanent. (See Taffeta.)

Ottoman, a heavy, cross-ribbed fabric, has round, prominent ribs. The ribs, which are formed by groups of filling yarns, are larger than most ribbed fabrics. (See Stripes and Coatings.)

Pinwale piqué has vertical raised cords or wales of various widths and thicknesses, according to the yarns used. Better quality cotton piqués are tightly woven from combed cotton yarns. (See Stripes, Plain-Weave Fabrics.)

Pongee is a light- to medium-weight cross-rib fabric woven with filaments from wild silkworms or synthetics in the filling. (See Lightweight Silks and Lightweight Polyesters.)

Poplin is a lightweight, firm, cross-rib fabric. The ribs, which are almost as fine as those on broadcloth, are formed by grouping filling yarns.

Repp is a medium to heavyweight fabric with prominent rounded cross ribs. (See Stripes and Coatings.)

Shantung, a cross-rib fabric, is woven with slubbed filling yarns. It may be dull or lustrous, soft or firm, lightweight or heavy.

Taffeta, a firm, close-weave fabric, has a fine cross rib formed by a heavier yarn in the filling. (See Taffeta.)

Tussah is a cross-rib fabric made with irregular filaments from uncultivated silkworms or synthetic look-alikes in the filling. (See Silk.)

Upholstery fabrics with ribbed designs are heavy fabrics. (See Coatings.)

Wild silk is a heavier, cross-rib fabric with irregular filaments in the filling. (See Silk.)

SEWING CHECKLIST

Machine Needles: Universal-H point and Red Band needles; sizes 70/10 to 90/14, depending on the fabric weight.

Machine Setting: Stitch length, 2–3mm (8–15 stitches per inch); tension, loose; pressure, adjust as needed.

Thread: Long-stable polyester, cotton-wrapped polyester, mercerized cotton; size depends on fabric weight. Basting—silk A, basting cotton.

Hand Sewing Needles: Sizes 5 to 10.

Sewing Machine Equipment: Straight-stitch, jeans, even-feed or roller foot.

Equipment and Supplies: Sharp shears, extra-fine pins, weights, covered snaps.

Layout: Nap. Heavy fabrics—single/lay; light- to medium-weight fabrics—double/lay, right sides together.

Marking Techniques: All types except wax.

Seams: Plain, double/ply seams, self-finished, piped, tucked, and slot.

Hems: Plain, blindstitched, blind catchstitch, catchstitch, faced, interfaced, double-stitched.

Seam and Hem Finishes: Luxury garments—hand overcast; others—pinked-and-stitched, zigzag, multi-step zigzag, serged.

Edge Finishes: Self-fabric and lining-fabric facings, bias bindings, bias facings.

Interfacings: Generally used.

Linings and Underlinings: Generally used for outerwear and luxury garments, depending on fiber content, fabric, and garment design.

Closures: Dressy garments—buttons and buttonholes, button loops, thread loops, covered snaps, hand-stitched zippers, invisible zippers. Washable garments—all types.

Fabric Characteristics

- Ribbed fabrics are much weaker than un-ribbed fabrics.
- Many ribbed fabrics require a nap layout.
- Cross-ribbed fabrics with ribs 1/4"-wide or wider must be matched like stripes.
- Cross-ribbed fabrics with alternating thin and thick ribs must be matched like stripes.
- Some ribbed fabrics are easily marred by pins, needles, and ripping.
- Fabrics with pronounced ribs fray more readily than those with fine ribs.
- Ribbed fabrics are susceptible to seam slippage, particularly at seams which are parallel to the ribs.
- Puckered seams are sometimes a problem on lighter weight fabrics.
- Some ribbed fabrics creep badly when stitched.
- Closely woven ribbed fabrics are difficult to ease.
- Some ribbed fabrics are easily damaged in pressing.
- Some moiré patterns are not permanent.
- Some ribbed fabrics waterspot; many will show perspiration stains.
- Generally, cross-rib fabrics add pounds; some lengthwise rib fabrics are slimming.

PLANNING A GARMENT

See Satin and Sateen for general sewing directions for special occasion fabrics.

FABRIC AND PATTERN SELECTION

Most ribbed fabrics are selected for their beauty, not their durability. Fabrics with large, pronounced ribs are less durable than those with smaller ones; however, they can be underlined to improve durability.

Upholstery fabrics are frequently stiffer, bulkier, heavier, and less durable than garment-weight fabrics. When dry-cleaned, colors may run and finishes disappear. Dark-colored fabrics tend to become shiny with wear.

This section focuses on dressy fabrics with prominent ribs, such as antique satin, bengaline, Canton crepe, douppioni, faille, grosgrain, gros de Londres, marocain, moiré, ottoman, pongee,

repp, shantung, taffeta, tussah, wild silk.

When using these fabrics for special-occasion and dressy garments, consider the hand. Generally, lightweight ribbed fabrics are softer and drape better than heavier materials with large ribs.

For light- and medium-weight fabrics, full, gathered or pleated skirts, gathered sleeves, ruffles, and even soft, draped designs are good choices.

When sewing fabrics with large, prominent ribs, showcase the fabric on a simple style with a minimum of seams. For stiff, heavier ribs, choose sculptured shapes with simple lines, straight or A-line skirts, and little or no easing.

Generally, tight fitted designs are best avoided or underlined, to prevent seam slippage at stress points.

To create more interest or to improve the design, change the grain on one or two garment sections. To avoid seam slippage, select sections which will not be stressed. Yves Saint Laurent repositioned the ribs on the lapels of an ottoman jacket so the ribs and edge of the lapel were aligned. Christian Lacroix cut a gathered faille skirt on the crossgrain.

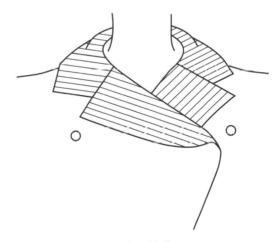

Fig. 13–5

Generally, changing the grain on the entire garment so the "stripes" will run vertically will cause the garment to pull apart at the seams.

Make a test garment to perfect the fit, practice your sewing techniques, and avoid overhandling the fabric.

Reduce the ease in the sleeve cap as needed.

219

SEWING RIBBED FABRICS

LAYOUT, CUTTING, AND MARKING

Use a nap layout. Use weights or fine pins to anchor the pattern. Place pins only in the seam allowances. Use weights at the top and bottom of the grainline.

Mark lightly and as little as possible. Test the marking method on a fabric scrap before using it on the fabric.

STITCHING TIPS

Make a test seam. Set the stitch length for 2–2.5mm (10–15 stitches per inch); loosen the tension slightly; lighten the pressure if needed; and begin with a new needle. Hold the fabric taut when stitching. Use a straight-stitch, jeans, even-feed, or roller foot to hold the fabric firmly so it won't creep.

SEAMS AND HEMS

Hand baste the seams on luxury garments; then stitch. Baste with silk thread to avoid pressing imprints; or remove the bastings before pressing.

Use fine needles instead of pins when pin basting.

Eliminate seam finishes on lined garments; finish seams on heavy and crisp fabrics as flatly as possible. Generally, hand finishes—single/ply pinked, pinked-and-stitched, zigzag, multi-step zigzag, and serged—are good choices.

Hint: *Grading, trimming, and clipping are particularly important when sewing heavy fabrics.*

Double/ply seams are suitable for lightweight failles and moirés.

Flat, hand-stitched hems are usually best for all fabric weights. Interface the hem for a padded look and double-stitch heavy fabrics.

LININGS, UNDERLININGS, AND INTERFACINGS

Most special-occasion garments are lined, underlined or both. Linings eliminate the need for seam and hem finishes; underlinings reduce seam slippage and help give a garment the desired shape.

For soft padded edges and hems, see Interfacings (Chapter 19). For closures, review that section in Satin and Sateen fabrics.

PRESSING AND GARMENT CARE

Ribbed fabrics, particularly dark colors, are easily glazed in improper pressing. Test press on a fabric scrap to determine the heat setting, moisture, and pressure. Generally, a warm, dry iron and light pressing is best.

Hint: *When pressing moiré, it's especially important to test on a fabric scrap before pressing the garment; steam may damage the moiré pattern.*

Press from the wrong side as much as possible. Always use a press cloth when pressing the right side. Use a seam roll and brown paper strips to avoid seam and hem impressions on the outside of the garment.

Most ribbed fabrics require dry-cleaning; store garments on well-padded hangers.

Taffeta

Taffetas are crisp, fine-rib fabrics with a distinctive rustle or scroop. Tightly woven with high-twist filament yarns in a plain weave, taffetas have approximately the same number of yarns in both the warp and filling.

A variety of taffetas are available, ranging from soft to stiff, lightweight to medium-heavy, in solids, prints, plaids, and iridescents. Originally made of silk, today many are rayon, acetate, nylon, polyester, or combinations.

THE TAFFETA FAMILY

For additional sewing suggestions, review the indicated sections.

Antique taffeta is a stiff fabric with slubs in the filling. (See Ribbed Fabrics.)

Faille taffeta, sometimes called *faille,* has a more pronounced cross rib; it is frequently woven with staple yarns. (See Ribbed Fabrics.)

Iridescent or *changeable taffeta* is woven with one color of yarn in the warp and a different color in the filling. (See Napped Fabrics.)

Moiré taffeta or *moiré faille* is easily identified by its rippled, watermark pattern, which may or may not be permanent. (See Ribbed Fabrics.)

Paper taffeta is a very lightweight taffeta with the finest cross ribs. (See Crisp, Transparent Fabrics.)

Pigmented taffeta is a dull-surfaced taffeta, which is woven with delustered or pigmented yarns.

Tissue taffeta is a lightweight transparent taffeta.

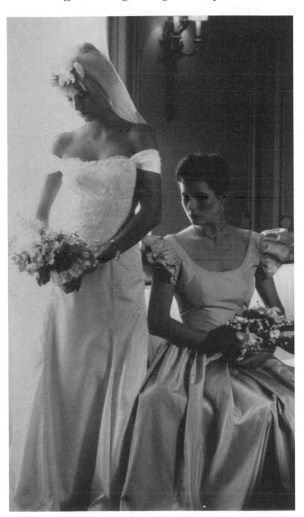

Fig. 13–6 *A popular fabric for formal wear and bridal gowns, taffeta has a fine rib-weave and a characteristic rustle. (Photo courtesy of McCall Pattern Co.)*

Compared to paper taffeta, it is softer. (See Crisp, Transparent Fabrics.)

Fabric Characteristics

- Taffeta is easily marred by pins, needles, and ripping.
- Some taffetas ravel badly.
- Taffetas are susceptible to seam slippage.
- Puckered seams are frequently a problem.
- Taffetas crease easily and can be permanently damaged by folding.
- Taffetas are very difficult to ease.
- Taffetas are easily damaged in pressing.
- Some moiré patterns are not permanent.
- Some taffetas waterspot; many will show perspiration stains.

PLANNING A GARMENT

See Satin and Sateen for general sewing suggestions.

FABRIC AND PATTERN SELECTION

Most taffeta fabrics are selected for their beauty, not their durability. The best—and most expensive—are tightly woven silks. Taffetas with more threads per inch hold their shape better, fray less, and have less seam slippage.

When in doubt, scrape your thumbnail across the fabric. If the warp yarns separate, the taffeta is loosely woven, seams will slip, and the fabric will ravel.

Many taffetas, particularly silks, are easily bruised by folding. Ask for a long cardboard tube when you make your purchase, to avoid permanent fold marks.

If you don't plan to use the fabric immediately, wrap the rolled taffeta in white tissue paper, an old white sheet, or a pillowcase.

Frequently used for special-occasion garments, such as bridal gowns, prom dresses, evening gowns and coats, cocktail dresses and jackets, taffetas are well-suited for crisp designs.

The pattern selection will depend on the particular fabric since taffetas range from soft to very stiff, transparent to opaque, lightweight to medium-heavy.

For lightweight and medium fabrics, consider full, gathered or pleated skirts, gathered sleeves,

221

ruffles, and draped designs. For stiff, heavier taffetas, choose sculptured shapes with simple lines, unusual seaming, A-line skirts, and little or no easing.

Generally, tightly fitted designs are best avoided or underlined, to prevent seam slippage at stress points.

Hint: *Taffeta is well-suited for lining coats if you don't mind the rustle.*

Make a test garment to perfect the fit, to practice your sewing techniques, and to avoid overhandling the taffeta.

Reduce the ease in the sleeve cap as needed or cut the sleeve on the bias. (See Chapter 1.)

SEWING TAFFETA

LAYOUT, CUTTING, AND MARKING

Use a nap layout for iridescent and moiré taffetas.

Hint: *I prefer a nap layout for all taffetas, but that is sometimes too expensive.*

If the fabric is easily marred by folding, spread it right side up. Spread other fabrics right sides together.

Instead of pins, use weights or fine needles to anchor the pattern. When using needles, place them only in the seam allowances. Use weights at the top and bottom of the grainline.

Hint: *Extend both ends of the grainline so it can be pinned in the seam allowances.*

Mark lightly and as little as possible. Test the marking method on a fabric scrap before using it on the taffeta. Some materials are easily damaged with a tracing wheel, while others are not.

Before you begin sewing, smooth rough hands by rubbing them with a teaspoon of sugar and a teaspoon of cooking oil; rinse. Repeat if needed.

STITCHING TIPS

Using a new needle, make a test seam. Set the stitch length for 1.75–2.5mm (10–18 stitches per inch); loosen the tension slightly; and lighten the pressure. Hold the fabric taut when stitching. Use a straight-stitch or jeans foot to hold the fabric firmly so it won't go into the needle hole.

Hand baste the seams on luxury garments, then stitch. Baste with soft, cotton basting thread, or silk thread to avoid imprints. Remove the bastings before pressing.

Use fine needles instead of pins when pin basting.

To hide needle holes when you have to rip, scratch the fabric lightly with your thumbnail or a fine needle.

SEAMS AND HEMS

Enclosed and double/ply seams are suitable for lightweight taffetas. (If the fabric is lightweight or sheer, see Transparent Fabrics and Lightweight Silks.)

Eliminate seam finishes on lined garments; finish seams on heavy and crisp fabrics as flatly as possible. Generally, hand overcasting with mercerized cotton is best on luxury garments; other finishes may show on the outside of the garment, especially if they aren't underlined.

When sewing a luxury garment, make the hem at least 2″ wide. Interface the hem for a softer finish. If the skirt has a flare, make small pleats as needed to control the extra fullness in the hem allowance.

On prom dresses and wedding gowns, use very narrow horsehair, lace, or wide hems.

LININGS, UNDERLININGS, AND INTERFACINGS

Most special-occasion garments are lined, underlined or both. Linings eliminate the need for seam and hem finishes.

Underlinings not only support heavy skirts and lightweight fabrics, they also cushion seams and hide hemming stitches.

Interface garment edges and hems for a softer, more luxurious finish.

To avoid drooping skirts, insert a ruffle at the waistline.

For closures, review that section in Satin and Sateen fabrics.

PRESSING AND GARMENT CARE

Taffetas are easily glazed in improper pressing. Seam and hem allowances may show through. And once a line is pressed, it can rarely be removed.

Test press on a fabric scrap to determine the heat setting, moisture, and pressure. Generally, a warm, dry iron and light pressing are best. (When pressing moiré, it's especially important to test on a fabric scrap before pressing the garment; steam may damage the moiré pattern.)

Press from the wrong side as much as possible. Always use a press cloth when pressing the right side. Use a seam roll and brown paper strips to avoid seam and hem impressions on the outside of the garment.

Most taffeta garments require dry-cleaning, even when made of washable fabrics.

To avoid unwanted perspiration stains, use dress shields. Store taffeta garments on well-padded hangers to avoid foldlines at the shoulders.

Decorative Surface Fabrics

Fabrics with decorative surfaces are made in several different ways. Fabrics such as brocade, brocatelle, matelassé, and tapestry are woven with one or more extra sets of yarns to create a permanent puckering on the surface; while seersucker is woven with slack tensions to form puckered stripes or checks.

Fabrics such as cloque, embossed fabrics, and plissé have special finishes applied to the surface to form durable patterns.

A variety of fabrics are available in all fibers. Fabrics range from soft to stiff, lightweight to heavy, sheer to opaque, and dressy to casual.

For additional sewing suggestions, see the indicated sections.

Brocade is an elegant, floral-patterned fabric woven on a jacquard loom with an extra set of yarns. When compared to damask, which is flat and reversible, brocade has a low relief pattern on the face and long floats on the back. It frequently has

223

Fig. 13–7 *This elegant dinner dress from Oscar de la Renta features textured silk cloque trimmed with velvet sleeves. (Photo courtesy of Jesse Gerstein, photographer, and Oscar de la Renta, designer, Fall 1987.)*

long satin floats and/or metallic threads. Woven in several weights, it is suitable for dresses, suits, coats, draperies, and upholstery. (See Satin, Metallics, and Large Prints.)

Brocatelle is a tightly woven, high relief fabric similar to brocade. It is usually heavier than brocade and used for draperies and upholstery. (See Satin, Metallics, and Large Prints.)

Cloque is a lightweight crepe which has been specially finished to create a blistered or puckered surface. It is usually silk. (See Lightweight Silks.)

Embossed fabrics are heat-set to create raised decorative designs. Generally used on synthetic fabrics, the durability of the puckering depends on the thermoplastic qualities of the fabric.

Imperial brocade is a brocade woven with metallic yarns. (See Metallics, and Large Prints.)

Matelassé is woven on a jacquard loom with two extra sets of crepe yarns. When the fabric is finished, the underlayer of crepe yarns is shrunk to create a quilted or padded effect. Compared to brocade, it is usually lighter and rarely has distinguishing floral or figure patterns.

Plissé is printed with caustic soda to create a blistered surface. Usually woven in cotton or man-made fibers, the plissé pattern can be in stripes, checks, or an overall design. The puckered finish is durable, but may not be permanent. (See Stripes and Plaids.)

Seersucker has permanent crinkle stripes or checks which are woven into the fabric by using slack tensions. Generally used for children's and casual wear, it ranges from sheers to heavyweights and may be printed. (See Stripes and Plaids.)

Tapestry is woven with one or more extra sets of yarns to create a pictorial or floral pattern. Compared to brocade, tapestry is stiffer and heavier with a rougher surface. (See Coatings and Large Prints.)

Upholstery fabrics include heavyweight brocades, brocatelles, and tapestry. (See Coatings and Large Prints.)

Fabric Characteristics
- Fabrics with woven decorative surfaces are permanent; others are only durable.
- Fabrics with large floral or decorative designs should be matched horizontally.
- Brocade, brocatelle, cloque, matelassé, and tapestry require a nap layout.
- Some fabrics are easily marred by pins, needles, and ripping.
- Some fabrics fray badly.
- Some fabrics creep badly when stitched.
- Woven decorative surfaces are frequently thick and bulky.
- Most fabrics are difficult to ease.
- Decorative surfaces are easily damaged in pressing.
- Generally, cross-rib fabrics add pounds; some lengthwise rib fabrics are slimming.
- Decorative surfaces with long floats pick and snag easily.

PLANNING A GARMENT

See Satin and Sateen for general sewing suggestions.

SELECTING THE FABRIC

Formal fabrics, such as brocade, brocatelle, and matelassé, are selected for their beauty, not their

224

durability. Loosely woven fabrics and fabrics with long floats are the least durable.

The surface design on these fabrics is permanent; and, even though it may flatten when worn, steam will restore it. Dark-colored fabrics tend to become shiny with wear.

Tapestry fabrics are more durable when the warp and filling yarns are the same size.

Upholstery fabrics are frequently stiffer, bulkier, heavier, and more tightly woven than garment-weight fabrics. When dry-cleaned, colors may run and finishes disappear. Many upholstery fabrics that are beautiful to look at may be scratchy to wear.

Decorative surfaces such as those on embossed fabrics and plissés are durable, but not permanent. The blistered surface frequently becomes less pronounced after sitting and laundering.

To prepare special-occasion fabrics for sewing, press them lightly with steam. If the fabric is easy-care, machine wash and dry it.

DESIGN IDEAS AND PATTERN SELECTION

When sewing fabrics which also have fine ribs, see Ribbed Fabrics.

Used for special-occasion and formal garments, brocade, brocatelle, matelassé and tapestry fabrics are frequently combined with satins and taffetas.

Select a pattern with simple lines. Avoid intricate seams and small details. Remember most of the fabrics are difficult to ease and are somewhat bulky.

Tapestry waxes and wanes as a casual, daytime fabric. When fashionable, consider jackets, coats

---

SEWING CHECKLIST

Machine Needles: Universal-H point and Red Band needles; sizes 70/10 to 90/14, depending on the fabric weight.

Machine Setting: Stitch length 1.75–3mm (8–15 stitches per inch); depending on the fabric weight; tension, loose; pressure, light.

Thread: Long-stable polyester, cotton-wrapped polyester, mercerized cotton; size depends on fabric weight. Hand sewing—silk A, cotton, long-staple polyester.

Hand Sewing Needles: Sizes 5 to 10.

Sewing Machine Equipment: Straight-stitch, jeans, even-feed, or roller foot.

Equipment and Supplies: Sharp shears, extra-fine pins, weights, covered snaps.

Layout: Heavy fabrics—nap, single/lay; Light- to medium-weight fabrics—nap, double/lay, right sides together.

Marking Techniques: All types, except wax.

Seams: Plain, double/ply seams, piped, tissue-stitched.

Hems: Plain, blindstitch, blind catchstitch, catchstitch, horsehair braid, faced, narrow hems, interfaced, double-stitched.

Seam and Hem Finishes: Single/ply or double/ply, depending on fabric weight. Unfinished, hand overcast, Hong Kong, pinked, pinked-and-stitched, zigzag, multi-step zigzag, or serged.

Edge Finishes: Self-fabric facings, lining-fabric facings, bias bindings, bias facings, lace.

Interfacings: Sew-in interfacings.

Linings: Generally used for brocade, brocatelle, matelassé, and tapestry. For other fabrics, it depends on the fiber content, fabric, and garment design.

Underlinings: Depends on the fabric and garment design.

Closures: Formal garments—buttons and buttonholes, button loops, thread loops, snaps, hand-stitched zippers, invisible zippers. Washable garments—all types.

225

and handbags. Designs with simple lines are easiest, but blazers are sometimes very "in."

For softer, lightweight cloque and matelassé, consider draped designs as well as simple sculptured shapes which showcase the fabric.

Hint: *Soft fabrics can be underlined to give them enough body for a crisp silhouette.*

Plissé, embossed fabrics, and seersucker are well-suited for casual blouses, skirts, dresses, slacks, nightgowns, robes, pool cover-ups, and children's garments. Avoid intricate seaming and let the fabric do the talking.

When sewing brocade, brocatelle, or matelassé, make a test garment to perfect the fit, to practice your sewing techniques, and to avoid overhandling the fabric.

When possible, eliminate separate facings by cutting an extended facing to reduce bulk. When this isn't possible, use an edge-to-edge lining or lining-fabric facings.

Reduce the ease in the sleeve cap as needed.

SEWING DECORATIVE SURFACES

LAYOUT, CUTTING, AND MARKING

Use a nap layout. Examine the fabric carefully to determine if it has a pattern to be matched.

Use weights or fine pins to anchor the pattern. Place pins only in the seam allowances. Use weights at the top and bottom of the grainline.

To retard fraying, dab a fray retardant on all raw edges immediately after cutting.

Mark formal fabrics lightly and as little as possible. Generally, tailor tacks and thread tracing are best, but snips, chalk, and pins sometimes work well.

On washable fabrics, use your favorite marking method.

STITCHING TIPS

Use a new needle to make a test seam. Set the stitch length for 1.75–3mm (8–15 stitches per inch); loosen the tension slightly; and lighten the pressure. Hold the fabric taut when stitching. Use a straight-stitch, jeans, even-feed or roller foot to hold the fabric firmly so it won't creep.

SEAMS AND HEMS

Eliminate seam finishes on lined garments.

Finish seams on heavy and crisp fabrics as flatly as possible. Single/ply finishes—hand overcasting, pinked, pinked-and-stitched, zigzag, multi-step zigzag, and serging—are good choices.

Hint: *Grading, trimming, and clipping are particularly important when sewing heavy fabrics.*

Both single/ply and double/ply finishes are suitable for lightweight and washable fabrics. For casual fabrics, flat hems—hand- or machine-stitched—and narrow topstitched hems are appropriate.

For formal fabrics and cloque, flat hand-stitched hems are best. Interface hems for a padded look and double-stitch heavy fabrics.

LININGS, UNDERLININGS, AND INTERFACINGS

To eliminate the need for seam and hem finishes and to hide the garment construction, line special-occasion garments. Linings also eliminate picks and pulls in the long floats on the back of brocade, brocatelle, and matelassé fabrics.

When sewing cloque and matelassé, use underlinings to give the garment the desired shape.

Hint: *Garments made of plissé, embossed fabrics, and seersucker are not usually lined.*

PRESSING AND GARMENT CARE

Fabrics with decorative surfaces are easily flattened during pressing. Cover the pressing board with a thick terry towel, piece of self-fabric, or a Velvaboard.

Hint: *Do not use a needleboard; it may damage the fabric.*

Consider the fiber content and test press on a scrap to determine the heat setting, moisture, and pressure before pressing the garment. Watch for shrinking when steaming.

Press from the wrong side as much as possible. When pressing from the right side, always use a press cloth. This is particularly important when pressing dark colors, which are easily glazed.

Hint: *To avoid flattening the surface design, use a piece of self-fabric; then steam press.*

Use a seam roll and brown paper strips to avoid seam and hem impressions on the outside of the garment.

Dry-clean garments made of brocade, brocatelle, matelassé, tapestry, and cloque. Some upholstery fabrics should not be dry-cleaned. Try to avoid mishaps and spot clean as needed, to delay the trip to the dry cleaner.

Most garments made of plissé, embossed fabrics, and seersucker can be machine washed and dried.

Store special-occasion garments on well-padded hangers.

Prepleated Fabrics

Pleating is an ancient practice. The Egyptians used heated stones to pleat heavily starched materials semipermanently. And for centuries, ruffs and garment details were pressed into fancy pleats or fluting with heated crimping irons.

In 1909 Italian designer Mariano Fortuny developed a process by which silk could be permanently pleated. He used these pleated silk fabrics to create the Delphos—a classic design of dress similar to the Greek chiton.

Numerous versions of the Delphos were produced, with different neckline and sleeve treatments, but they were all long, cylindrical in shape, with holes for the head and arms, with a cord to adjust them to the shoulders. Today Fortuny's dresses are as permanently pleated as they were when he created them more than fifty years ago.

In recent years, Mary McFadden has revived this classic look with accordian pleating (sometimes called Marii or mushroom pleating) in polyester, and occasionally silk, fabrics.

Some permanently pleated materials can be purchased by the yard; others are pleated to order by a pleating company.

The fabric is placed between two pleating papers; pleated; then heat-set to make the pleats permanent. Since almost any fabric can be pleated, the variety in custom-pleated fabrics is almost limitless and matching, unpleated fabrics are readily available.

Most fabrics pleat well. A few materials, such as some rayons, silks, and wools, shrink during the pleating process; but, since they shrink uniformly, this is not a major problem. Wool gabardine is an exception.

According to one pleating company, when wool gabardine shrinks, a small impression is made at the edge of the pleats, which many home sewers find unattractive.

Pleat durability depends on the fiber content. If the fabric has a high percentage of polyester or nylon, the pleat retention is exceptional.

Synthetic fabrics, including chiffon, Charmeuse, organza, taffeta, georgette, tissue lamé, and satin, pleat well. Wool and silk fabrics must be dry-cleaned and pressed to maintain sharp pleats; they are easily damaged by liquid spills.

All-cotton fabrics should not be pleated. They do not hold the pleating well and sometimes yellow.

There are several different kinds of pleats, but there are only two basic types: flat pleats and raised pleats. Box and knife pleats are flat; while accordian, mushroom, crystal, and sunburst pleats are raised.

The flat pleats—box and knife pleats—vary in size and can be used on medium- and lightweight fabrics. Raised pleats are used on light- and medium-weight fabrics.

Fabric Characteristics
- Prepleated fabrics stretch 300 percent to 500 percent in width.
- Most prepleated fabrics do not have a one-way design; however, they should be handled as if they do.
- Pleated garments can be shortened but not lengthened.
- Natural fiber fabrics don't hold their pleats as well as synthetic materials.

227

- Synthetic fabrics dull the needle quickly.
- Prepleated fabrics can be stretched out of shape easily when handled carelessly.
- Prepleated fabrics do not drape well when you sit.

Fig. 13–8 *Designed by Bill Blass, Spring 1987, this fuschia silk taffeta is trimmed with a cascade of knife-pleated ruffles. (Photo courtesy of Bill Blass.)*

SEWING CHECKLIST

Machine Needles: Universal-H point or Red Band needles; sizes 60/8 to 80/12.

Machine Setting: Stitch length 2–2.5mm (10–12 stitches per inch); tension loosely balanced; pressure, light.

Thread: Long-staple polyester, cotton-wrapped polyester, nylon monofilament.

Hand Sewing Needles: Sizes 5 to 10.

Sewing Machine Equipment: Hemming foot.

Supplies: 20-pound fishing line.

Layout: Nap, single layer, right side up.

Marking Techniques: Clips, pins, temporary marking pens, chalk, tailor tacks, and thread tracing.

Seams: Plain, double/ply.

Hems: Plain blindstitch, machine blindstitch, machine-rolled, hemmer-rolled, lettuce edging, Fortuny hem, merrow, mock-merrow.

Seam Finishes: Double/ply, zigzag, multistitch zigzag, serged.

Hem Finishes: Zigzag, multi-stitch zigzag, hand overcast, serged.

Edge Finishes: Plain-fabric facings, bands, bindings, casings.

Interfacings: Generally not used; avoid fusibles.

Linings and Underlinings: Optional.

PLANNING A GARMENT

SELECTING PREPLEATED FABRICS

Consider the fiber content and fabric construction when selecting prepleated fabrics. Synthetic fibers can be heat-set and retain pleats best. Silk and wool retain pleats when dry-cleaned, but linen, cotton, and rayon do not.

Woven fabrics hold pleats better than knits; firmly woven materials better than loosely woven ones; and worsteds better than woolens.

The Mary McFadden mushroom pleating is most readily available; however, you will occasionally find exciting novelty fabrics with small box or knife pleats.

Most prepleated yardage is pleated on the crossgrain. Make a revised layout before shopping.

If you decide to have a fabric custom-pleated, to avoid disappointment and expensive dry cleaning bills, first discuss your fabric and design with the pleater and your local dry cleaner. Tell the pleater everything you know about the fabric—its fiber content, dyes, manufacturer, etc. If you want knife or box pleats tapered between the hips and waist, tell the pleater when the fabric is shipped.

If the garment will be machine or handwashed, preshrink the fabric before pleating.

Custom-pleated fabrics can be pleated on either the lengthwise or crossgrain. Generally, flat pleats are hemmed before pleating and raised pleats are hemmed after pleating.

The required time for pleating varies from several days to a couple of weeks. Some pleating companies specialize in small custom jobs, while others work them in between their industry accounts. This is very important to know if you need several bridesmaids' skirts quickly.

Although pleating is relatively inexpensive, most pleating companies have a minimum charge plus shipping. The total charge is based on the length of the unpleated fabric; which means narrow strips cost just as much as wide ones.

DESIGN IDEAS AND PATTERN SELECTION

To showcase the fabric, select a simple pattern with a minimum number of pieces. Easy tunic tops, pull-on skirts, one-shoulder or halter dresses, and simple sheaths let the fabric speak for itself. Pleated fabrics retain their pleats better if the garment is not tightly fitted.

Box and knife pleats are long-time favorites for classic skirts. For sharper, longer-lasting pleats, pleat fabrics on the fabric grain.

Make ordinary designs exciting with details such as pleated inserts on blouses, pleated sleeves, cascades of pleated ruching, horizontally pleated cummerbunds and band collars, or pleated godets.

SEWING PREPLEATED FABRICS

LAYOUT, CUTTING, AND MARKING

Lay out the pattern pieces so the grainline is parallel to the pleats, unless the garment design requires a different positioning.

Note: In this section, the lengthwise grain refers to a line parallel to the pleats, even though they may not be the lengthwise grain of the fabric.

Use a nap layout, and spread the fabric in a single layer, right side up.

STITCHING TIPS

Make a test seam using a stitch length of 2–2.5mm (10–12 stitches per inch); and a loosely balanced tension. Tissue-stitch as needed with a stabilizer under and/or on top of the fabric.

To stabilize crossgrain and bias seamlines, hand sew a firmly woven stay tape to the seamline. Avoid staystitching, which distorts the seamline.

Hint: *If you have a serger, stay and join the seams simultaneously. Pin the stay tape to the seamline of the top layer; and serge. Be sure the pins are placed so they can be removed as you sew.*

HEMS

Use a traditional 2"- to 2 1/2"-wide hem when sewing classic pleated skirts, wide pleats, and medium- to heavyweight fabrics.

Choose the hem finish carefully to avoid a ridge on the outside of the garment. If the fabric doesn't ravel, leave the edge raw. If it does, use a zigzag, multi-stitch zigzag, hand overcast, pinking, or serging. Make some samples and test press to see which is least likely to show through.

Hint: *Use woolly nylon for serging; it is softer than regular sewing thread and less likely to show through.*

Use very narrow hems on lightweight fabrics, garments with narrow pleats, and ruffles. The machine-rolled, hemmer-rolled, lettuce edge, merrow, mock-merrow, and Fortuny hem are good choices.

For fluted edges, stitch (L,2 or W,2;L,2) a machine-rolled hem using monofilament nylon. For more fluting, enclose 20-pound fishing line between the hem layers.

To duplicate the hems used on Fortuny designs, fold under 1/4″ and blindstitch loosely. For ravelly fabrics, overcast the edge by hand before hemming.

Hint: *Mario Fortuny sewed small Venetian glass beads to the hemline edge of overblouses. In addition to making a pretty border, they served as a weight so the hem would cling to the body.*

EDGE FINISHES

Use a narrow bias binding or bias facing to finish V-shaped, jewel, bateau and surplice necklines, as well as to finish other edges on the bias or crossgrain.

Stay necklines before finishing to preserve the shape.

Use a self-fabric or complementary fabric to bind the edges. When using self-fabric, use a very hot iron. Stretch and pin the fabric flat; then spray with white vinegar. Cover with a damp cloth and press until dry. Repeat until the fabric lies flat.

Net, organza, and sheer nylon tricot work well as facing fabrics.

Replace waistbands with elastic casings.

CLOSURES

Buttons and loops are more attractive than buttons and buttonholes. If the fabric doesn't press flat enough to make a pretty loop, use a complementary fabric or decorative cording.

Set zippers by hand. On raised pleat fabrics, use a slot application. On traditional pleated skirts, cut a wide underlap, and replace the zipper with snaps.

If the pleats are perpendicular to the zipper placket, bind the edges of the placket.

CUSTOM-PLEATED TRIMS

Pleated trims can be hemmed before or after a fabric is custom-pleated.

For a flat finish at the trim edges, hem the strips before pleating. For a fluted edge, pleat; then hem.

Trims with a flat finish cost more, since the cost of pleating is based on the number of linear, not square, yards to be pleated. And you must estimate very accurately the minimum number of yards you'll need.

For economy, some fabrics can be cut in double-width strips and pleated. Hem both sides before pleating. After pleating, cut the wide strip into two narrow ones.

Hint: *Pleated trims are perfect for ruffles. Machine baste the ruffles in place on the seamline before permanently stitching them.*

CUSTOM-PLEATED SKIRTS

Decide on the finished skirt length; add 3″ for the hem and waist seam allowance. Remember the skirt can be shortened, but not lengthened.

To estimate the total skirt width, use a 3 to 1 ratio for lightweight fabrics and a 2 to 1 or 2 1/2 to 1 for heavier weights. Multiply the ratio fullness by your largest measurement, usually the hip, and add 10″. For example, if your hips are 40″ and the ratio is 3, the total skirt width will be 130″.

To determine how many skirt lengths you'll need, divide the total skirt width by the fabric width. Round fractions off to the next whole number. For a 130″ skirt width, you'll need three lengths of fabric 54″ wide and four lengths of 36″-wide fabric. Fabrics 45″ wide will require three or four lengths, depending on the amount of waste for matching the fabric pattern.

Before sending the fabric to the pleater, lay out the skirt in the usual manner on the unpleated material, so the pleats will be on the lengthwise grain. Match and join the sections, leaving the placket seam open so the fabric will lie flat for pleating. Press the seams well and hem the skirt.

Cut the waistband from the skirt scraps. For a 1″-wide band, cut the strip 3 1/4″ wide and your waist measurement length plus 3″.

Hint: *I cut the band on the lengthwise grain, but you may prefer the crossgrain. If the fabric has a pattern, cut the band so it will be most attractive.*

Send the skirt, but not the waistband, to the pleater, along with the measurements for your waist, hip, and length. Many pleaters will taper the pleats from the hip to the waistline, but you must request tapering.

The skirt will return about three weeks later with easy directions for finishing.

SUNBURST PLEATING

Sunburst pleating is a favorite for bridal gowns and bridesmaids' skirts. Sometimes called fan or concertina pleating, the pleats, which radiate from the circle center, are small at the top and wider at the hem.

Sunburst pleating is used on full circle or half-circle skirts; and most pleating machines will pleat fabrics up to 60″ wide. Each pleating company has specific instructions for sunburst pleating. Check with them before purchasing the fabric.

To prepare the skirts for sunburst pleating, cut out the skirt, and let it hang for at least twenty-four hours. Try the skirt on and have the hem measured. Trim as needed, but do not hem.

Send the skirt to the pleaters. Some pleaters also hem sunburst-pleated skirts without charge. Be sure to ask when you're comparing prices.

PRESSING AND GARMENT CARE

Avoid overpressing. Once pressed flat, most prepleated fabrics cannot be repleated attractively.

Use plenty of steam and light pressure. Hold the iron about 1″ above the fabric and give it several shots of steam.

To reduce dry cleaning costs on pleated garments, consider a bulk cleaner. Or ask your cleaner to "dry-clean only" and do your own pressing. When in doubt, avoid disappointment by trying different cleaning processes on your pleated fabric scraps.

To avoid unwanted wrinkles on washable garments, do not crowd too many garments into the machine; and spin lightly.

Metallics

Precious metals have been woven into cloth since Biblical times, with some evidence that silver was used as early as 2000 B.C.

For centuries luxurious textiles were woven with real gold and silver. When the garments were discarded, the fabrics were burned to reclaim the precious metals.

Today's metallic fibers include metal, metal-coated plastic, plastic-coated metal, or a metal-wrapped core yarn. Many, which are made of colored aluminum and plastic, bear little resemblance to their predecessors. Other metallics, such as Lurex and Metlon, are better known by their trade names.

In addition to being lighter in weight, more flexible, and much more affordable, the new metallics don't tarnish and are easier to sew. Combined with other fibers such as polyester, nylon, rayon, silk, wool, and cotton, metallic fabrics vary in weight from tissue lamé to heavy brocades. They can be woven or knitted and are available in a variety of fabric structures.

For additional suggestions when sewing metallic fabrics, see the indicated sections. Popular metallics include lamé, brocade, and matelassé (see Decorative Surfaces), lace (see Lace), sheer metallics (see Transparent Fabrics), stretch lamé (see Stretch Wovens and Knits), and metallic knits (see Knits, Double-Knits, Tricot). Other metallics include Indian saris (see Borders) and Egyptian asutes.

Fabric Characteristics
- Metallic fabrics dull shears and sewing-machine needles.
- Metallic fabrics fray and snag easily.
- Metallics have a sheen, requiring a nap layout.
- Some metallics are very scratchy.
- Silver and brass threads in older metallic fabrics tarnish.
- Metallic fabrics are easily damaged by needle and pin holes.

231

- Sewing-machine needles do not penetrate metallics easily and frequently cause pulls.
- Metallic fabrics are easily damaged by heat and moisture.
- Some metallics cannot be dry-cleaned.

SEWING CHECKLIST

Machine Needles: Universal-H point, stretch (HS point), Red or Yellow Band needles (knits); sizes 60/8 to 90/14, depending on the fabric weight and structure.

Machine Setting: Stitch length 2–3mm (8–12 stitches per inch); tension, loosely balanced; pressure, light.

Thread: Long-staple polyester (100/3), extra-fine cotton-wrapped polyester.

Hand Sewing Needles: Sizes 7 to 10.

Equipment and Supplies: Old, well-sharpened shears, weights, fray retardant, acid-free tissue.

Layout: Nap; double layer, right sides together; single layer, right side up.

Marking Techniques: Snips, thread tracing, temporary marking pens.

Seams: Plain, double/ply, self-finished, taped, tissue-stitched.

Hems: Depends on fabric weight. Plain, blindstitch, topstitch, shirttail, book, machine-rolled, double-stitched.

Seam and Hems Finishes: Zigzag, multi-stitch zigzag, serged, tricot bound, folded.

Edge Finishes: Bindings, bands, ribbings, lining-fabric facings, bias facings, ribbon bindings.

Interfacings: Sew-in types, depending on the garment design and fabric structure.

Closures: Most types of lightweight fasteners.

Linings: Generally used for outerwear, formal designs, and scratchy fabrics.

PLANNING A GARMENT

FABRIC AND PATTERN SELECTION

Most metallic fabrics are selected for their beauty; and since many will be worn so little that they will never require cleaning, shrinking is rarely a problem.

Depending on the other fibers and fabric structure, metallics can be laundered or dry-cleaned. Use the manufacturer's care recommendations to preshrink washable fabrics. Press fabrics which must be dry-cleaned with a warm, dry iron.

Traditionally, metallics were reserved for evening and formal wear. Now they are seen everywhere at almost any time of day.

Select a simple design with a minimum number of seams to showcase the fabric. Intricate details, darts, and complex seaming break up the fabric design unnecessarily.

Avoid close-fitting designs unless you plan to underline the garment; designs which slip over the head are easiest. When sewing soft metallics, consider a draped design if you're an experienced seamstress.

Perfect the fit before cutting the fabric, even if you have to make a test garment.

Hint: *Metallic fabrics are easily marred by stitching and ripping; and, if you handle the fabric excessively, it frays badly.*

SEWING METALLIC FABRICS

LAYOUT, CUTTING, AND MARKING

Use a nap layout, and spread out the fabric, right sides together. If it has a pattern to be matched, spread it in a single layer, right side up.

Check to be sure the foldline is not permanent. If it is, arrange the pattern pieces so it will be inconspicuously located or avoided.

Use weights to secure the pattern pieces; metallics are easily damaged by pins.

Hint: *Use No More Pins spray to hold the pattern in place.*

Cut with an old pair of well-sharpened shears. To reduce raveling, don't cut until you are ready to sew; then cut, and handle the sections as little as possible. Or use a fray retardant on all raw edges immediately after cutting.

Fig. 13–9 *This black and gold brocade evening jacket makes a glamorous evening statement. Notice the unusual cut of the sleeves and front and the perfectly matched front sections. (Photo courtesy of Carolina Herrera, Fall/Winter 1988.)*

Hint: *Fray retardants may discolor the metallics and should be applied carefully. Or apply them to the entire section.*

Mark with thread tracing, chalk, soap sliver, or temporary marking pens.

STITCHING TIPS

Generally, very fine Universal-H point or ball-point needles are best. Since it is very difficult for the needle to penetrate the metallic fibers, the ball-point will slip between the threads without causing a distortion, even when you're sewing woven fabrics.

Begin with a new needle in a small size. Change the needle frequently so it will penetrate the fabric easily; stitching these fabrics dulls needles quickly.

Make a test seam, using a stitch length of 2.5 mm (10 stitches per inch) and a loosely balanced tension. Lengthen or shorten the stitch as needed.

Hint: *Some metallics, such as tissue lamé, are very difficult to penetrate. Debbie Jensen, an owner of Jehlor Fantasy Fabrics, recommends that you position a hair dryer so it will blow on the fabric and presser foot. The warm air softens the fabric, making it easier to stitch.*

Try to avoid ripping. Many fabrics will be permanently marred by needle holes, while others will fray badly when handled excessively.

SEAMS AND HEMS

Generally, plain seams are best on heavier fabrics; while double/ply seams work well on light- and medium-weight metallics.

To avoid skin irritations on unlined garments, bind the seams with tricot binding or line the garment. If irritation isn't a problem, finish double/ply seams with a zigzag, multi-stitch zigzag, or serging.

On medium- and heavyweight metallics, use bias-faced hems to avoid snagging your hose. Or line the garment to the edge. On lightweight fabrics, shirttail, book, and topstitched hems are best.

Finish the edges of plain hems with a zigzag, multi-stitch zigzag, serging, or tricot binding, if needed.

INTERFACINGS, LININGS, AND FACINGS

Avoid fusible interfacings. Generally outerwear and formal designs are lined for aesthetics; however, any garment can be lined to eliminate skin irritation.

Also avoid self-fabric facings which will irritate the skin. Instead, line the garment to the edge or use smooth fabric facings.

Bias facings, ribbon, and ribbings, as well as satin or taffeta bindings and bands are particularly attractive on some designs.

CLOSURES

Before using buttonholes or zippers, make several samples, to be sure the metallic threads will not be distorted.

Insert zippers by hand.

Replace buttonhole closures with loops or a fly placket.

ASUTE

Asutes are handmade stoles produced by blind women in the village of Asute Egypt. The background is white or black cotton net and the design is made by folding 1/8″-wide pieces of metal around the individual holes of the net. Originally made for belly dancers, they were very popular in the '20s. Today, azutes and azute fragments are sometimes used to make evening wraps.

The asute is relatively heavy and will sag if it isn't firmly tacked to a backing. Hand tack parallel rows every 4″ to 5″ to stabilize it.

The size and location of the metal pieces makes machine stitching difficult and sometimes impossible. Examine the seamline to be stitched. If there is little or no metal in it, machine stitch. If there is a lot of metal, use a hand backstitch.

Finish the garment with an edge-to-edge lining, sewn in place by hand.

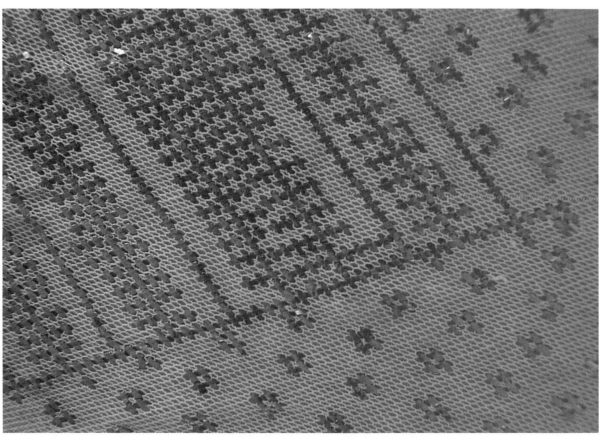

Fig. 13–10 *Earlier in this century, asutes were made by blind women in the Asute Valley, Egypt. Narrow* *strips of silver- or gold-colored metal were folded around the cotton net to make the pattern.*

PRESSING AND GARMENT CARE

Test press on scraps. Metallics are very sensitive to heat and moisture. Steam may tarnish or discolor the fabric; and high heat will melt plastic-coated threads. Even when the fabric isn't completely ruined, it may be permanently dulled.

Hint: *Fabrics with a high metallic content are more sensitive to heat.*

Use a press cloth and press from the wrong side. Some metallic fabrics are easy to press with the handles of your shears.

Hint: *Another suggestion from Debbie Jensen is to use your blow dryer to open and press seams. Before you laugh, try it!*

Check the label when you purchase the fabric. Some metallics cannot be dry-cleaned; others cannot be washed or dry-cleaned.

To clean garments made of metallic foil, hand-wash and drip dry. Press with a warm iron, using a cotton press cloth between the iron and fabric.

To clean bonded lamé, which is fused to a woven cotton backing, wipe with a damp cloth.

To prevent tarnishing, wrap real metal fabrics in acid-free tissue before storing.

Sequinned and Beaded Fabrics

Sequinned and beaded fabrics, which are among the most glamorous fabrics, can be used for complete garments or accent trims.

Beads, small sequins, large paillettes, and sparkling chips are sewn or glued to background fabrics such as taffetas, wool knits, open raschel knits, satins and delicate chiffons to create a variety of beaded designs. Sometimes applied individually and sometimes in strips to create allover patterns or individual motifs, the designs vary in intricacy.

This section focuses on fabrics which have sequins, beads, or glitter applied to the surface. When sewing fabrics such as cracked ice, beaded laces, and beaded border designs, review other appropriate sections.

Fabric Characteristics
- Sequinned fabrics are scratchy and irritate the skin.
- Sequins are frequently applied with a chain stitch which, when inadvertently pulled from one end, will unravel a large section.
- Sequins dull scissors and sewing machine needles.
- Ripping is at best difficult.
- Sequinned fabrics have a nap and should be cut from a single layer.
- Some sequinned fabrics are easily marred by pins and ripped seams.
- Sequinned garments may pick or scratch satin fabrics.
- Some sequinned fabrics have large motifs which should be matched. (See Large Prints.)
- Others have striped or plaid designs which require matching. (See Plaids and Stripes.)
- The weight of the beads and sequins may cause the fabric to sag.
- Sequinned fabrics are sometimes bulky.
- Sequinned fabrics are easily damaged by heat, moisture, and dry cleaning.

PLANNING A GARMENT

FABRIC AND PATTERN SELECTION

Check the fabric width before purchasing. Many sequinned fabrics are 45″ wide; however, the sequin design may be less.

When combining beaded fabrics with other fabrics, be sure the weights are similar, so the garment will hang properly.

Most sequinned fabrics will not shrink. To prepare the fabric, press it from the wrong side with a warm, dry iron.

Hint: *Moisture makes the sequins curl and lose their sheen.*

Select a simple style with a minimum of seams to showcase the fabric. Intricate details, darts, and complex seaming break up the fabric design unnecessarily.

When sewing stiff fabrics, generally designs with flares are better than those with gathers and pleats. Styles with kimono and raglan sleeves or dropped shoulders are easier to sew than set-in sleeves.

Adjust the pattern before cutting the fabric. If necessary, make a trial garment to perfect the fit and your sewing skills. Fit the test garment; then carefully rip it apart and use it as your pattern.

Replace self-fabric facings with edge-to-edge linings or lining-fabric facings, bindings, bands, or ribbings.

Fig. 13–11 *Perfect for holiday dressing, a simple design showcases the sequin-trimmed fabric best. (Photograph courtesy of the Simplicity Pattern Co.)*

SEWING SEQUINNED FABRICS

LAYOUT, CUTTING, AND MARKING

Lay out the fabric in a single layer right side up. Make duplicate pattern pieces if you aren't making a test garment.

Use a nap layout; the sheen and shading on sequins may not be noticeable until the garment is made up. The sequins should feel smooth as you run your hand from the neckline to the waist.

If the sequinned fabric has motifs that must be matched, see Prints and Lace. If it has a striped or plaid design, see Plaids and Stripes. If it has a border design, see Borders.

Use weights or place pins within the seam allowances.

To avoid damaging your best shears, cut with an old pair of well-sharpened ones. Immediately after cutting, bind raw edges with 1″-wide drafting tape to prevent ravelling during construction.

Mark with pins, thread tracing, chalk, soap sliver, or temporary marking pens.

STITCHING TIPS

Begin with a new needle in a small size. Universal-H point needles can be used on most woven and knit fabrics. A few wovens will require a Red Band needle. Change needles frequently; stitching through sequins dulls and damages them. Since the sequins frequently break when stitched through, try to avoid ripping.

When plain seams are used, line the garment to cover scratchy seams. Avoid fusible interfacings; the heat and moisture required to apply them will damage the sequins.

Select a seam appropriate to the quality, use, and life expectancy of the garment. For quick and easy designs, use plain seams. For fine garments or exquisite fabrics, consider the sequin-appliqué seam or a woven-appliqué seam.

SEQUIN-APPLIQUÉ SEAM

In this method the sequins are removed from the seam allowances, making the garment more comfortable to wear and easier to sew.

1. Use a temporary marking pen, chalk, or soap sliver to mark the seamlines on the reverse side of the fabric.

If that isn't possible, mark with thread tracing placed on the garment itself 1/8″ away from the seam. (For 5/8″ seam allowances, place the thread tracing 3/4″ from the edge.)

2. Carefully remove the sequins from the seam allowances plus 1/8″. Knot the sequin threads to avoid further unraveling.

Hint: *Sequins are sewn on with a chain stitch and one end unravels easily. To determine which end unravels, rub your hand over the sequins; if they feel smooth, you are rubbing toward the edge that ravels. If not, try again.*

3. Right sides together, use drafting tape to hold the sequins out of the way and pin or baste the edges together. Stitch the seamline.

Hint: *To avoid breaking sequins, use a zipper foot set to the right of the needle.*

4. Finish sheer fabrics with a hairline seam. Trim the seam to 1/8″ and zigzag (W,2; L,1) the edges together.

Leave seams unfinished if the garment will be lined.

5. On the face side of the garment, restitch the sequins over the seamlines by hand. Trim away the extra sequins.

HEMS AND EDGE FINISHES

To avoid skin irritation and scratching other delicate fabrics, replace self-fabric facings with lining-fabric facings, an edge-to-edge lining, bands, bindings.

Interface hemlines for a softer look. To avoid damaging your nylon stockings and legs on unlined garments, face the hemline, finish it with a band, or bind the edge. For lined garments, extend the lining to the edge and slipstitch the folds together.

HEM BANDS

In addition to finishing the edge, hem bands serve as a buffer between sequins on the garment and the body; and they can be used to lengthen the garment.

Use a regular waistband application or this easy method to sew a band to the skirt hem.

1. Shorten the garment the width of the band then add a 5/8″ seam allowance. For a 2″-wide band, shorten the garment 1-3/8″.

2. Remove the sequins from the seam allowance.

3. Cut the band the desired length plus two seam allowances and twice the desired width plus two

SEWING CHECKLIST

Machine Needles: Universal-H point or Red Band needles; sizes 60/8 to 90/14, depending on the fabric weight and structure.
Machine Setting: Stitch length 2.5mm (10 stitches per inch); tension, loose; pressure, light.
Thread: Long-staple polyester or cotton-wrapped polyester.
Hand Sewing Needles: Sizes 5 to 9.
Sewing Machine Equipment: Zipper foot.
Equipment and Supplies: Old, well-sharpened shears, weights, pins, 1″-wide drafting tape, nylon tricot binding.
Layout: Nap, single layer, right side up or double layer, right sides together.
Marking Techniques: Snips, pins, tailor tacks, thread tracing, temporary marking pens, chalk, soap sliver.
Seams: Plain, hairline, sequin-appliqué, double/ply, tissue-stitched, taped.
Hems: Faced, blindstitched, interfaced.
Seam and Hem Finishes: Single/ply bound, Hong Kong, double/ply bound.
Edge Finishes: Bands, bindings, ribbing lining-fabric facings.
Closures: Lightweight zippers, button loops, hooks and eyes, snaps.
Pockets: Inseam.
Interfacings: Sew-in types; frequently not used, except for garment openings.
Linings: Generally used on outerwear, formal designs, and scratchy fabrics.

seam allowances. For a 2″-wide band, cut the band 5-1/4″ wide.

4. Right sides together, join the ends of the band and press.

5. Wrong sides together, fold the band in half lengthwise; and machine baste the raw edges together.

6. Tape or pin the sequins away from the hem allowance. Place the band on the face side of the garment, matching the raw edges; pin or baste. Turn the garment over with the inside out; and stitch the band to the hem. Press.

7. Hand stitch the sequins so they lap the band about 1/2″.

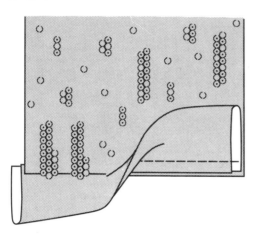

Fig. 13–12

Lace

Lace is a decorative fabric originally handmade by knotting, interlacing, looping, or twisting threads.

The Sumerians used a lacelike trim on their garments as early as 4000 B.C., but it wasn't until the Renaissance that lace became an important feature of fashionable dress. Machine production began in the early nineteenth century with the invention of the Leavers machine.

Laces run the gamut from very fine, sheer materials to heavy, coarse fabrics. Available in a variety of fibers—nylon, polyester, linen, wool, cotton, and rayon, lace is used for all types of garments, from casual clothes to formal bridal gowns.

Compared with other fabrics, lace is fragile; and, although it should be handled with care, it is easier to sew than you might think. Lace is very forgiv-

CLOSURES

When possible, use button loops, hooks and eyes, snaps, or a zipper instead of buttonholes.

To simulate a button/buttonhole closure, sew the buttons on the overlap; and fasten the garment with fabric-covered snaps or replace the button/buttonhole closure with a fly placket.

Insert zippers by hand.

PRESSING AND GARMENT CARE

Test press on fabric scraps. Sometimes finger pressing or pressing with the handle of your shears is enough.

Use a dry, warm iron. Steam and high heat discolor and melt sequins. Press seams open on a seam roll.

Sequinned and beaded fabrics should not be laundered and many cannot be dry-cleaned satisfactorily. (If the garment gets wet, hang it to dry away from heat and sunlight.)

Fold and store sequinned garments in a drawer. When hung, they sag, stretch, and may even tear. And save your scraps! Sequins tend to fall off the garment after several wearings. Remove the sequins as needed from the scraps to cover bald spots.

Hint: *Alcoholic beverages, perfumes, and deodorants discolor sequins.*

ing; if you make a mistake, it can frequently be hidden.

THE LACE FAMILY

Originally named for the centers where they were produced, laces have hundreds of names; but most lace fabrics fall into these groups: allover, guipure, and fine laces such as Alençon, Chantilly, Cluny, and Schiffli.

For additional information, see the indicated sections.

Fig. 13–13 *Designed by Philippe Venet, Autumn/Winter 1987/1988, the black iridescent lace is underlined with a flesh color fabric. (Photo courtesy of Philippe Venet.)*

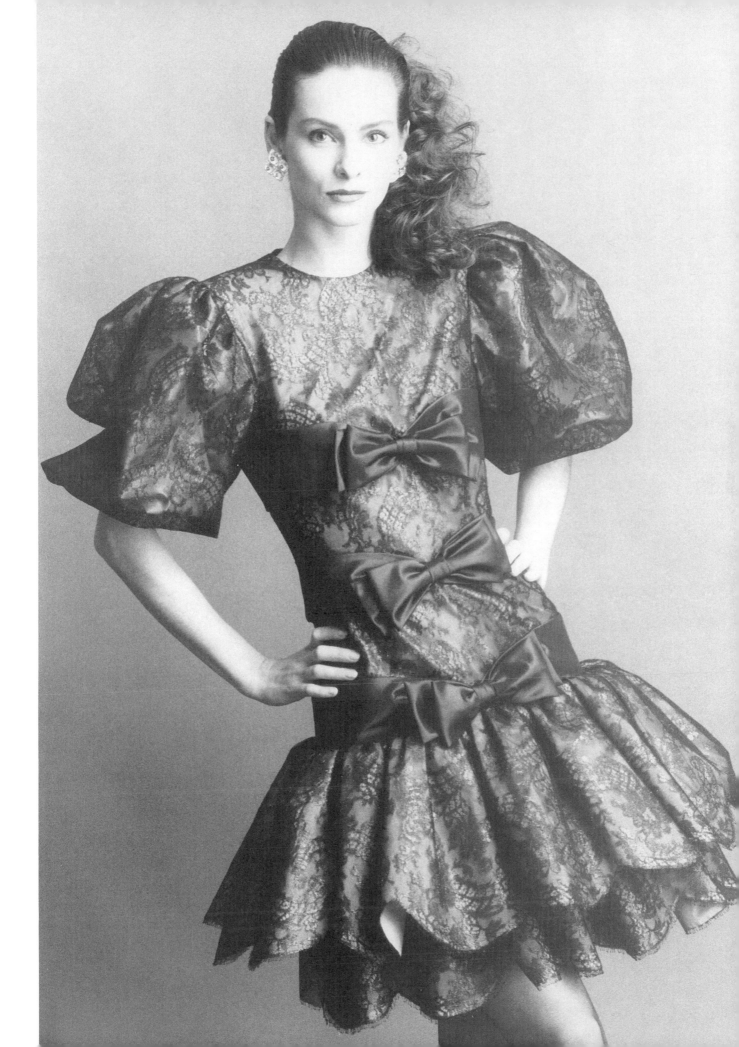

Alençon lace has a floral design on a clear net ground. Originally a needle lace, it has a classical design of flowers and swags which is precisely arranged on the net ground. The individual motifs are outlined with a heavy thread. Available in all forms and widths, it is frequently clipped to make individual appliqués. Alençon lace is used for wedding gowns, lingerie, and formal wear. When compared to Chantilly, the Alençon motifs are more

Fig. 13–14 *Alençon lace has delicate flowers and swags outlined with cord; the gently scalloped edges are chained beading.*

delicate and are always completely outlined with cord; the scallops at the edge are less pronounced; and the edge has chained beading, instead of a picot.

Allover lace has an allover, repetitive pattern similar to a printed material. The edges are straight—sometimes with a selvage and sometimes left unfinished. Available in wide widths, most of today's allover laces are inexpensive; but this wasn't always the case. Allover laces are cut and sewn like other sheer fabrics with a surface design. (See Stripes and Transparent Fabrics.)

Fig. 13–15 *Allover lace has a repetitive pattern.*

Chantilly is a fine, open lace which features a delicate design of branches and flowers held together by flowing ribbons or scrolls. Originally a bobbin lace, the pattern is often outlined with thick, silky threads. Frequently used for bridal gowns, cocktail dresses, and formal wear, it is readily

Fig. 13–16 *Chantilly lace features branches and flowers. Finished with picots, the edges are more deeply scalloped than Alençon lace.*

available in a variety of qualities and prices.

Cluny lace is a coarse lace made with cottonlike yarns. Readily available in narrow and wide widths, Cluny is used for trims, curtains, tablecloths, and casual garments; it is frequently combined with heavier, less formal fabrics. (See Transparent Fabrics and Mesh.)

Fig. 13–17 *Cluny lace is a coarse lace made of cotton-like yarns.*

Filet, a square mesh design, is available in narrow-width trimmings.

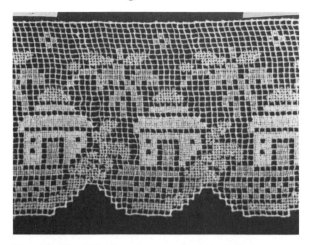

Fig. 13–18 *Filet lace has a square mesh design.*

Guipure, sometimes called *Venise,* point de Venise, chemical, or burned-out lace, is a firm, stiff lace. Unlike most laces, it does not have a net background. It is an embroidered design made, usually with cotton, on Schiffli machines. Originally, the design was worked on foundation materials which would dissolve in a lye bath. Today it is embroidered on water-soluble films. (See Transparent Fabrics.)

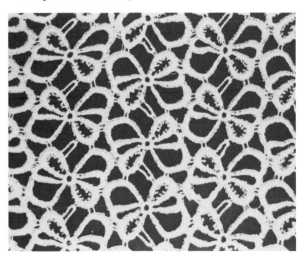

Fig. 13–19 *Guipure lace is actually an embroidered material. It is made on a foundation material which is later dissolved.*

Metallic laces feature metallic threads. (See Metallics.)

Peau d'ange is a kind of Chantilly lace. Unlike many laces, it was never made by hand.

Re-embroidered lace is any lace embroidered with a heavy cord, lace, ribbons, beads, or sequins on the surface. (See Sequinned Fabrics.)

Schiffli or *Breton lace* is a delicate, transparent net with an embroidered design. Readily available in trims, it is more difficult to find in wide widths. (See Nets and Borders.)

Fig. 13–20 *Schiffli lace features chain-stitch embroidery on a net background.*

Fig. 13–21 *Tape lace, sometimes called Battenberg, utilizes a tape to create the design.*

241

Tape lace, sometimes called *Milanese* or *Batten-berg,* utilizes a tape or tape effect to create the design on a sheer background. Available in narrow widths, collars, and cuffs, it is frequently made by talented seamsters.

Val lace, the common name for *Valenciennes,* is a narrow, flat lace with a fine floral design on a diamond or round-shaped net. A dainty lace, it is frequently used for French hand sewing and heir-loom machine stitching on children's designs, lin-gerie, and blouses.

Fig. 13–22 *Val lace has a fine floral design. From top to bottom: a beading insertion, an insertion, an edging.*

The Lace Vocabulary

À jours is the ornamental work introduced into the enclosed spaces of the motifs.

Background or *ground* is the foundation of net or brides which forms a basic part of the fabric.

Bead edge is a decorative edge made of a series of tiny buttonhole loops instead of picots. Some bead edges are almost straight; however, when compared to selvages, they are slightly scalloped and more attractive.

Beading is a lace or embroidery with slits, through which ribbon can be laced. It can be an edging, insertion, or galloon.

Brides, sometimes called bridges or bars, are con-necting threads between the motifs. They are used instead of net.

Cordonnet is the cord which outlines the pattern.

Edgings have one selvage edge and one decora-tive edge with scallops or picots. They can be wide or narrow, flat or gathered.

Footing is the straight or selvage edge of lace.

Galloons are laces with two decorative edges. They can be wide or narrow, flat or ruffled. Many can be separated into two borders; and, if there are motifs or a band between, they can also be used individually.

Insertion is a narrow lace with two selvage edges in various widths from 1/4" to 12". It can be used decoratively to join fabrics and other trims or to eliminate seams.

Motifs, sometimes called medallions or appli-qués, are individual lace designs which can be sewn to the fabric. They can be clipped from wide laces or purchased individually.

Picots are tiny loops along the edges.

The *reseau* is the background of net which fills the open spaces of laces such as Alençon, Chantilly, and Valenciennes. Embroidered laces such as gui-pures do not have reseau.

A *set* is a group of laces with the same design in several widths and different forms—insertions, edgings, beadings, and galloons.

The *toile* is the design of the lace as distinct from the ground.

Wide lace is any lace 36" or wider. Laces with one decorative edge are flounces, with two deco-rative edges, galloons. Laces with two selvage edges are usually allover laces.

Fabric Characteristics

- All laces are transparent. (See Transparent Fabrics.)
- Most laces don't ravel; but Cluny and some allover laces do.
- Laces don't have a grainline, but they have more stretch in the width than in the length.
- Some laces have no selvage.
- Most laces have horizontal and vertical mo-tifs which must be matched like plaids. (See Plaids and Prints.)
- Many laces have a one-way design and will require a nap layout. (See Napped Fabrics.)
- Most laces will require extra fabric.
- Lace scraps can be used for appliqués and other projects.
- Many laces shrink.
- Laces are sized and frequently become softer when washed or dry-cleaned.
- Lace is easily damaged by hot irons and care-less pressing.
- Some laces tear easily.

PLANNING A GARMENT

SELECTING LACE

Consider the garment design and use when selecting lace. If it's for a special occasion, purchase the best you can afford—even if you have to combine it with another fabric. If it's for a casual or fad design, select a good-looking, inexpensive lace.

In addition to traditional wide laces, flounces, and galloons, consider secondhand garments, tablecloths, curtains, and home decor laces as sources for unusual laces. Or make your own lace fabric by joining narrow strips of insertions or edgings.

Hint: *To join edgings, overlap the selvage edge of one edging with the decorative edge of another; topstitch. To join insertions, butt the selvage edges together; and zigzag (W,2;L,1).*

When using lace with another fabric, it should be similar in weight, texture, and color.

Better laces are made of finer threads and smaller stitches. Good quality laces have a variety of textures, net designs, and motifs, which can be clipped to make borders, panels, and individual motifs. In comparison, inexpensive laces have a flat, monotonous look.

Allover laces are less expensive than flounces and galloons. Generally, the quality of allover laces is inferior; however, they can be exceptional.

The fiber content is also an indication of quality. Silk or linen fibers used in fine laces are frequently replaced with acetate in inexpensive laces. Nylon and polyester are used for fine and low-cost lace. Nylon dyes better than polyester.

Generally, laces made on the Leavers machine are finer and more expensive than those made on raschel machines.

Better quality guipure laces utilize fine threads and small stitches to create a variety of depths and textures. Less expensive guipure is flat and monotonous.

Machine-clipped lace, allover lace, and low-cost guipure frequently have short thread ends left on the motifs.

Most laces have a one-way design, as well as motifs which require matching. To accurately determine the amount required, plan your layout before making the purchase. If that isn't possible,

243

purchase 1/2 to one yard extra to allow for matching.

Check the fabric width before making your purchase; some laces are only 36″ wide, while others are 54″.

When making several garments for a wedding party, be sure all the lace is from the same dye lot.

DESIGN IDEAS AND PATTERN SELECTION

Select a pattern which will showcase the lace. Depending on the lace, designs can range from casual tee tops to formal wedding gowns.

For Cluny and allover laces, simple designs are particularly attractive. Consider designs with a minimum of seams, designs for transparent fabrics, and designs with dropped shoulders, bat-wing, or kimono sleeves.

For fine laces such as Alençon and Chantilly, consider more complex designs and princess seaming, which can be assembled invisibly with appliquéd seams.

For the heavier guipure, simple, elegant designs are best. Pattern designs with straight edges—necklines, dirndl and straight skirts, and straight jackets—allow you to utilize any scalloped edges on the lace fabric.

Hint: *When planning the dresses for a bridal party, remember that the garments will probably be seen more from the back than the front.*

Lace is just as attractive when used in unexpected places as it is when used traditionally. Some of the new looks include a V-shaped insert on a tee top worn with a lace skirt, lace yokes on sweaters, lace front on a sweatshirt-style garment, lace sweatshirts in allover lace, oversized shirtdresses in cotton and casual laces, large satin appliqués on lace sweatshirts.

Some of my favorite ideas from designers include a Lanvin-Castillo evening gown with the scalloped edge at the top of the full skirt and a Thea Porter black lace blouse with the dominant motifs on the sleeve cap.

To shrink "dry-clean only" lace, steam press with the wrong side up.

Hint: *Before shrinking metallic and embellished laces, read the manufacturer's directions or test*

press. Sequins and some metallics are easily harmed by steam and heat.

To avoid tangling when shrinking washable lace trimmings, put them into the foot of an old stocking. Pin or tie the top; machine wash and dry.

To shrink washable lace fabrics, put them into a pillow case and machine baste the top closed. Wash and dry, using the care recommendations of the manufacturer.

SEWING LACE

LAYOUT, CUTTING, AND MARKING

Lace is smoother on the wrong side. To identify the right side easily, mark it with strips of drafting or hair-set tape.

Hint: *If it takes more than thirty seconds to determine which is the right side, it doesn't matter.*

Plan the motif placement before cutting and, when possible, before purchasing the fabric. If the design is large and regularly spaced, position the motifs like a large print and match the pattern horizontally like a stripe.

Generally, the garment will be more attractive if the motifs are balanced on each side of the garment centers. Avoid placing large motifs on the bust points.

Hint: *If the garment is transparent, motifs are sometimes placed over the bust for modesty.*

Spread light-colored fabrics in a single layer on a dark table; and use duplicate pattern pieces so the entire garment can be planned before you begin cutting.

Hint: *I use the flannel-backed table pads from my dining room table. When working with dark-colored fabrics, I use a light-colored, flannel-backed table cover.*

Use a modified nap layout, positioning the tops of all pattern sections more or less in the same direction.

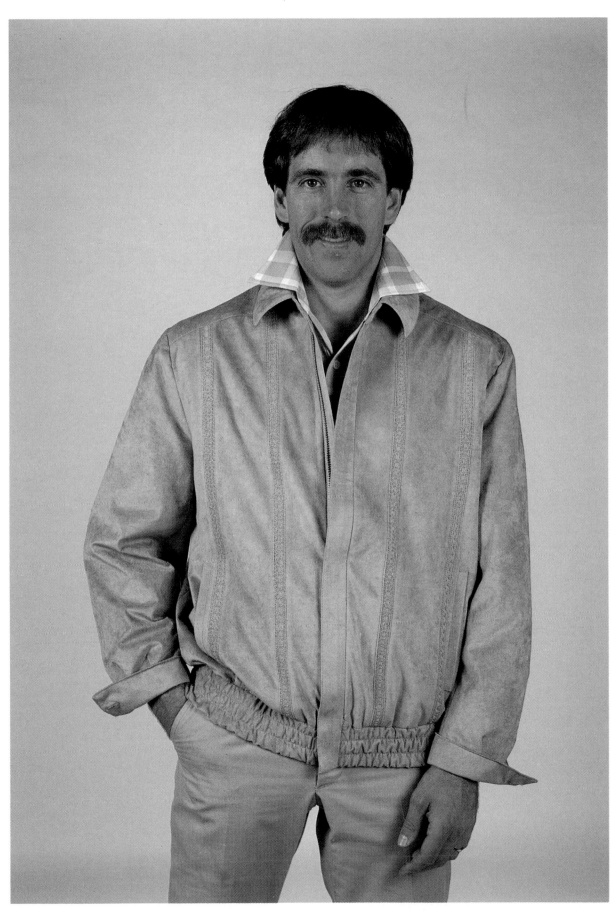

Facile, a buttery soft synthetic suede, makes a handsome and comfortable jacket. (Photo courtesy Neil's Apparel, Palm Desert, California.)

From Bill Tice, this dramatic coat is a quilted masterpiece. (Photo courtesy of Bill Tice.)

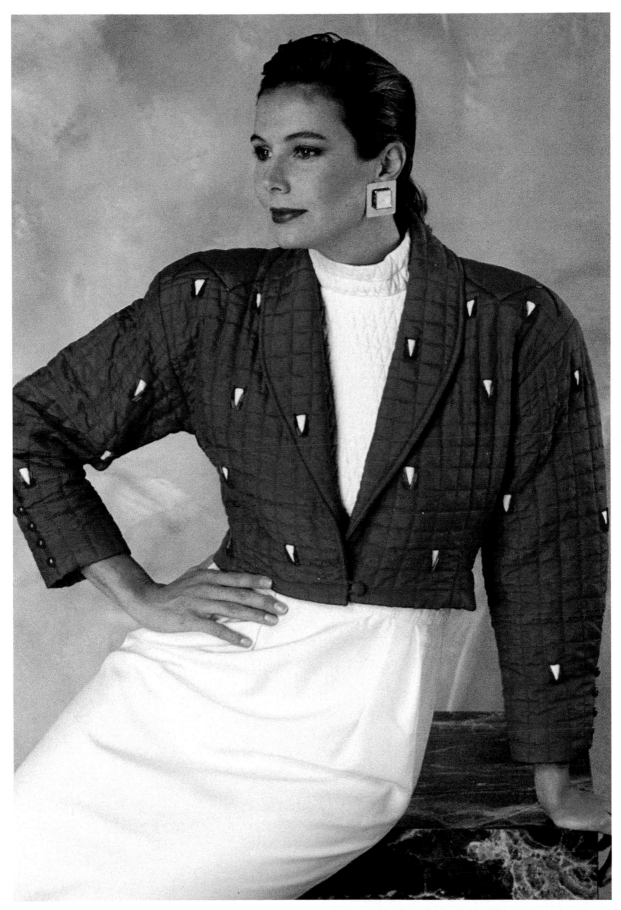

Created by wearable art designer Richard Farnell for the 1987–1988 Shining Star Fashion Show, this all-silk jacket utilizes Poly-fil Cotton Classic Batting. (Photo courtesy Fairfield Processing Corp./Poly-fil.)

Right: *Eight fabric layers are stacked and quilted. Seven layers are slashed, leaving the lining unslashed. When washed, the cotton fabric "blooms." (Photo courtesy Pattie Frazer.)*

Below: *Designer Pattie Frazer used a quilt-then-slash technique to create this interesting cotton coat. The coat reverses to quilted pink lining. (Photo courtesy Pattie Frazer.)*

Above: *Designed by hand weaver Mary Kay Stoehr, this undulating herringbone twill resembles snakeskin. Bias bands are used as a dramatic accent to finish the edges and armscyes. Joe Coca, (photographer; reprinted with permission of Interweave Press.)*

Left: *Albert Nipon's fashionable top features wide bands of color seamed together to create a different look. (Photo courtesy Albert Nipon.)*

Opposite page, lower right: *A classic two-piece dress from Albert Nipon. Trimmed with solid-color bands, the small floral print becomes a sophisticated daytime outfit. (Photo courtesy of Albert Nipon.)*

A classic Chanel suit from 1959. The bias-trimmed flaps and sleeve cuffs, blouse-fabric lining, edge-to-edge lining, and fake blouse cuffs are Chanel signatures which have inspired other designers and creative seamsters for several decades. (Photo by the author.)

An appliquéd seam from a Balenciaga design. I always take my camera along when I travel; even though my photos aren't perfect, they inspire me, refresh my memory, and recapture ideas for future designs. (Photo taken by author at "Memorable Dress: Ohio Women," Ohio State University, 1986.)

Designer Marianne Triese specializes in one-of-a-kind jackets. This chintz design features three-dimensional flowers. (Photo courtesy Marianne Triese.)

This handwoven fabric from Bianculli features 1"-wide bias strips, as well as a variety of yarns. Sleeves are cut on the bias so the watermelon-colored strips match the front. The jacket is banded with bias pulled from the fabric and fused to the edges. (Design by the author.)

Pattie Frazer's macaroni coat is made of hundreds of narrow jersey strips. When cut, the fabric edges curl into "macaroni" tubes. (Photo courtesy Pattie Frazer.)

A red velveteen rose on a zebra print costume worn by Phyllis Diller. (Photo taken by the author at "Memorable Dress: Ohio Women," Ohio State University, 1986.)

Pattern pieces can be shifted off-grain if the motif placement will be attractive on all pieces. Generally, it is best to avoid cutting some sections on the crossgrain and others on the lengthwise grain. If the lace has no selvage or straight edge, use the lengthwise motifs to establish a grainline.

Arrange and rearrange the pattern pieces until the design is located as desired; then anchor the pattern pieces with weights or glass-headed pins.

Arrange the straight edges of pattern pieces along the scalloped edge of the lace. When using the scalloped edge at the hemline, determine the finished length before cutting.

Hint: *Double check the skirt length before cutting.*

If it is impractical or impossible to lay out the pattern pieces with the straight edge(s) on the lace scallops, trim away the scalloped edge; lay out the pattern; then reapply the edging as desired.

If your lace has large open areas, use hair-set tape as needed to fill in the gaps. Using a temporary marking pen, transfer the pattern markings to the hair-set tape. Remove the tape after basting or stitching.

STITCHING TIPS

Make a test seam. Set the machine for 2mm (12 stitches per inch) and a loosely balanced tension. Begin with a new needle. Wrap the toes of the presser foot with transparent tape or use a roller foot to avoid snagging the lace. Use a small-hole needle plate except when zigzagging.

To eliminate puckering, stitch slowly; hold the fabric taut; and/or use a stabilizer.

Hint: *When sewing heavier guipure laces, use a Red Band, jeans, or larger needle to penetrate the dense lace.*

Shorten the stitch length when sewing more open-weave laces.

Use flower or safety pins; or baste seams with hair clips or hand basting if pins won't stay in.

SEAMS

Narrow seams are the best choice for most garments made of allover, Cluny, and inexpensive Chantilly and Alençon laces.

Lace appliqué seams are the best choice for your finest designer creations in fine Chantilly and Alençon laces, as well as in some guipure laces. Time-consuming and almost invisible, these seams are used on elegant designer garments which cost thousands of dollars.

When cutting garments with appliqué seams, cut the underlap with a 1/4″-wide seam allowance. On the overlap, cut around the edge of the motifs, leaving 1/4″ seam allowances.

Hint: *Most seamlines have some flare, taper, or shaping, which will prevent the motifs on the two layers from overlapping exactly.*

If there is a bald spot with no motifs near or on the seam, cut a motif from a scrap and appliqué it over the bald spot.

Finish darts like the seams. If the garment has narrow seams, stitch the dart again 1/8″ from the first stitching line; and trim to a skinny 1/4″.

APPLIQUÉD DARTS

One of the beauties of fine Chantilly and Alençon laces is that they can be darted inconspicuously as needed to make the garment fit perfectly.

1. Thread trace the stitching lines of the dart.

2. Clip around the motifs through the center of the dart.

3. Lap the dart, matching the stitching lines; baste.

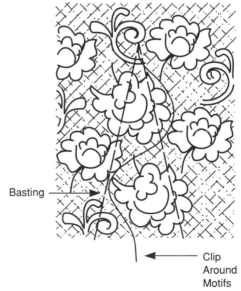

Basting

Clip Around Motifs

Fig. 13–23

Hint: *If it will enhance the design, lap part of the dart in one direction and part in the other.*

4. Appliqué, by hand or machine, around the edges of the motifs. Trim away the excess.

HEMS

Allow the garment to hang for several days before marking the hemline.

Generally, lace, topstitched, horsehair, 1/4″-wide book hems work best. Plain hems are a good choice for underlined garments. Machine-rolled and hand-rolled hems are more difficult to sew on laces because the lace motifs do not fold as smoothly as the net background.

When sewing fabrics with scalloped edges, eliminate hemming by laying out the pattern so the finished edge of the fabric is at the hemline. Place the hemline, not the cutting line, of the pattern pieces on the motifs.

Hint: *The exact placement of the scallops depends on the depth of the lace scallops and the garment edge. The relationship of the garment edge to the scallop can be at the inner edge of the scallop, the outer edge, or somewhere between the two.*

This method may be the easiest way to finish garment edges, but it isn't always possible. A more practical hem is the lace hem. For this method, use purchased lace edgings or the finished scalloped edge, which has been trimmed from the fabric. Mark the hemline; then apply the edging by hand or machine.

EDGE FINISHES AND FABRIC BANDS

Eliminate traditional shaped facings, except when the garment is underlined. Some attractive finishes for the edges include lace trims, satin or taffeta bindings, narrow bias or tulle facings, and edge-to-edge linings.

Satin and taffeta bindings and narrow facings are particularly attractive on allover and guipure laces.

A fabric band made from the slip, lining, or coordinating fabric is one choice when lengthening a lace garment. Here are three different ways to make a fabric band.

- Apply it like a waistband.
- Sew it to a slip so it will show below the lace.
- Sew it to the wrong side of the skirt.

Cut the band width twice the finished width plus 4″. Join the ends of the band so it equals the skirt width. Fold the band in half, wrong sides together; and finish the raw edges by hand, zigzagging, or serging. With the skirt wrong side up, position the raw edge of the band 2″ above the hem. If the hem is scalloped, position it so there are no ugly gaps between scallops. Hand tack the raw edge of the band to the wrong side of the skirt.

INTERFACINGS, UNDERLININGS, AND LININGS

Most lace designs do not need interfacings. If they do, interface lightly with a sheer or flesh-colored marquisette, voile, organza, organdy, net, or tulle; avoid fusibles.

Depending on the lace, garment design and use, and your personal preference, lace garments can be lined and/or underlined; or they can be worn over a slip. Sleeves are frequently left transparent even when the rest of the garment is lined or underlined.

Use matching, contrasting, or flesh-colored fabrics to make the lace opaque. Select a color and fabric which will complement, not overwhelm, the lace.

When selecting underlining and lining fabrics, consider the garment design and use, as well as the design, weight and care properties of the lace. Some suitable fabrics include satin, taffeta, crepe, organdy, organza, tulle, marquisette, and batiste. Generally, it's best to avoid cotton, except for very casual designs; cotton clings to the body.

Guipure laces are underlined more frequently than Chantilly, Alençon, and allover laces.

To preserve the transparency of lightweight laces, underline with sheer fabrics, such as marquisette, tulle, silk chiffon, and organza.

Place the right side of the lining next to the wrong side of the lace; on some designs, construction details can be marked on the wrong side of the underlining.

246

CLOSURES

Always interface buttonhole areas. If the garment is all lace, use thread button loops. If it's trimmed with another fabric, use the trimming fabric to make the button loops.

To strengthen the zipper placket and eliminate stretching, reinforce the opening with a strip of tulle or sheer selvage. Replace zippers with snaps or hooks and eyes if the lace isn't underlined.

Hint: *To hide small hooks, use pliers to bend them so the small sewing holes are on top of each other.*

LACE-BORDER APPLIQUÉS

Lace borders with a scalloped edge at the bottom and an irregular or reverse scallop at the top can be purchased by the yard or cut from wide lace, edgings, and galloons.

Frequently used around the hems of wedding dresses and formal wear, they can be used on other fabrics or on all-lace designs. And, although they are usually appliquéd to the garment, they can be applied like an insertion. They are particularly easy to shape and ease around curves.

This technique is for appliquéing lace borders to garment hems. Generally, the border is positioned so the entire scallop is below the garment edge; however, if the scallop is more than 1″ deep, you may want to raise the border.

1. Complete the garment hem.

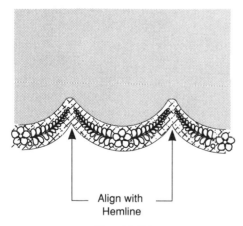

Align with
Hemline

Fig. 13–24

Hint: *To avoid a limp hem on full skirts, use a horsehair or wire hem.*

2. Right sides up, pin the border in place, aligning the top of the scallop with the garment edge. Pin the border close to the hemline where the garment is fullest. Then pin the top of the border to the skirt hem; clip and shape the upper edge as needed so it will lie flat. Baste the border in place and whip stitch any clipped sections together.

3. By hand or machine, stitch the top of the border to the garment, leaving the lower edge free on skirt hems; hand tack occasionally on other edges.

LACE-BORDER INSERTIONS

Use these directions for a more transparent application.

1. Mark the hemline and trim on the marked line.
2. Using the directions for a lace border appliqué, pin and baste the border to the garment.
3. Using a satin stitch (W,1;L,.5) stitch the top of the border in place.

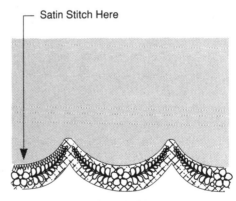

Satin Stitch Here

Fig. 13–25

4. With the garment wrong side up, carefully trim away the fabric under the border.

Hint: *Use small trimming or appliqué scissors.*

LACE APPLIQUÉS AND INSERTIONS

Lace motifs are frequently used individually as appliqués and insertions on other fabrics.

Generally, small motifs are placed on smaller garment sections such as collars, yokes, sleeves, and bodices; large motifs are placed on large sections such as skirts. When large and small motifs are used on the skirt, place the large motifs toward the hem. A frequent exception is a lace-covered bodice with a few scattered motifs on the skirt.

Hint: *To position motifs attractively, put the garment on a dress form or on the body. Pin; then baste before stitching permanently.*

This application method can also be used for galloon insertions.

1. Select a fine lace with attractive motifs. It can be a new good-quality lace, such as Chantilly or Alençon, or a fragment of an antique lace.

2. Clip around the lace motif, leaving a 1/4" seam allowance.

3. If the garment fabric will be trimmed away for a transparent effect, cut a backing from marquisette, tulle, or organza. Baste the backing to the wrong side of the lace.

4. Right sides up, position and baste the motif to the garment.

5. For a machine application, stitch (L,1.5) around the edge of the motif.

Hint: *Use an embroidery foot if the lace is re-embroidered; otherwise, use a roller foot or straight-stitch foot with tape around the toes.*

6. Using appliqué or small trimmers, trim away the excess net around the motif.

7. Using a satin stitch (W,1; L,.5) and an embroidery foot, follow the design of the motif and stitch around the edge.

Hint: *For best results, use a stabilizer between the appliqué and the fabric; or place the section in a machine-embroidery hoop.*

8. For a hand application, whip stitch the edges in place, using silk (size A) or extrafine cotton-wrapped polyester thread.

9. For a transparent look, turn the garment wrong side up, and trim away the fabric under the motif.

Hint: *To avoid cutting into the lace or backing, trim when you feel fresh and unrushed. Pinch the garment fabric; insert your scissors into the center of the motif; clip to the satin stitch; then*

clip around the motif. Duck-billed appliqué scissors may make the job easier.

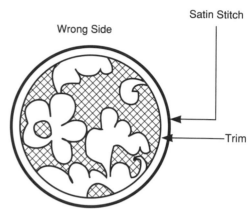

Fig. 13–26

FUSING APPLIQUÉS

1. Clip the motif from the lace.

2. Place the motifs, wrong side up, on a Teflon pressing sheet.

3. Cover with a piece of Wonder Under that's slightly larger than the motif; fuse it in place.

4. Trim around the motif; then fuse it to the fashion fabric or veiling.

Hint: *When fusing motifs to tulle, place a Teflon pressing sheet under the tulle.*

LACE INSERTIONS

Lace insertions are not only decorative, but functional; they can be used to replace traditional seams.

Here are two easy techniques for the insertions. If the garment will be worn frequently or machine washed and dried, finish the fabric edge before applying the lace using the technique for insertion seams. If it will be worn only occasionally, hand-washed, or dry-cleaned, follow the directions above for motif appliqués.

Hint: *To avoid being caught short when applying insertions, stitch the lace in place before cutting the lace. It sometimes "shrinks" when you stitch it.*

When stitching, do not stretch the lace.

248

LACE CUT-OUTS

These clever insertions were used by California designer Michael Novarese on his red silk dresses.

1. Right side up, draw a 5" circle on the garment section with chalk or a temporary marking pen.

2. For each insertion, cut a 10" square of silk organza and a 6" square of lace.

3. Place the organza on the right side of the fabric. Stitch (L, 1.75mm) on the marked line. (You can see the line because organza is transparent.)

4. Cut out the center of the circle and trim the seam to 1/4"; turn the organza to the wrong side. Press.

5. Center and pin the lace under the opening; and edgestitch around the cut-out.

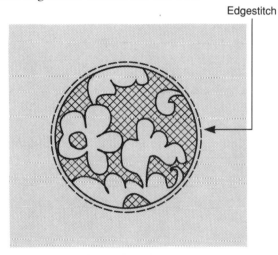

Edgestitch

Fig. 13–27

LACE RUFFLES AND EMBELLISHED LACE

Depending on the desired fullness of the finished ruffle, you'll need two to three times the finished length.

Hem ruffles of allover lace with a merrow or mock-merrow finish, machine-rolled hem, binding, net facing, or horsehair before gathering.

Beads, rhinestones, pearls, and sequins can be sewn on or glued in place with a permanent fabric glue.

Hint: *To glue beads quickly, use tweezers and a permanent fabric glue. Pour a small amount of glue onto a piece of wax paper; then, holding the bead with the tweezers, dip it into the glue; and apply the bead to the lace.*

Use ribbons, narrow laces, lace motifs, fabric appliqués, and horsehair braid to decorate the lace. Sew in place by hand or machine.

THREE-DIMENSIONAL EFFECTS

Lace Flowers: Use lace motifs in matching or different patterns to create three-dimensional effects. Tack lace flowers at the center only.

Hint: *To save time, use a machine tack (L,0;W,2) or permanent fabric glue.*

Appliqués: Another interesting effect can be created by stuffing lace appliqués with fiberfill to make them soft and puffy. Satin stitch the appliqué to the garment; then, from the wrong side, make a slit in the background fabric under the appliqué. Stuff lightly; close the slit with a few hand stitches.

If you prefer, make flat appliqués. Use lace, satin, or taffeta for the appliqués and apply them to casual, as well as to dressy designs.

Buds and Roses: Use purchased fabric flowers or custom-made buds and roses (see Chapter 10, Tricot) to embellish the lace.

Lace Scraps: Save even the tiniest lace scraps to use on lingerie, evening bags, infants' wear, blouses, pillows, and handkerchiefs.

If you have an old lace garment or tablecloth, examine it carefully to see what can be salvaged.

Hint: *To whiten old cotton and linen laces, soak in Biz. Do not use Biz on wool, silk, nylon, or acetate.*

TEA DYEING

Use a strong solution of tea to dye white laces ecru. But, before you dye, remember that the tannin may cause the fabric to deteriorate in twenty years.

1. Cover four to six tea bags with two cups of boiling water; let steep ten minutes.

Hint: *For more even and faster dyeing, cover the lace with hot water, stir, and leave it to soak for five to ten minutes.*

2. Put the lace into the tea and add water if it isn't completely submerged. Let it soak about thirty minutes.

Hint: *When dyeing large pieces, stir occasionally to avoid streaking.*

3. Remove the lace, wring, and look at the color. It will dry lighter.

4. Hang to dry or put in a laundry bag and machine dry.

5. If it isn't dark enough when dry, wet the lace, heat the tea, and dye it again.

PRESSING AND GARMENT CARE

Test press, using a warm, dry iron. A hot iron will melt synthetic laces and scorch silk or cotton laces. Use a press cloth to avoid snagging the lace with the point of the iron.

Use only the iron tip when pressing seams; press narrow seams toward the front of the garment.

To avoid stretching the lace, don't allow it to hang off the ironing board unsupported. Press with an up-and-down motion, not across the fabric.

To avoid flattening the lace when pressing re-embroidered laces and guipure, cover the ironing board with a thick towel; press from the wrong side.

To restore some of the lace's crispness, cover with a piece of wax paper and press.

A few laces can be machine washed and dried; most require dry-cleaning. Consider the garment construction as well as the manufacturer's care recommendations to determine the best cleaning method.

Hang lace garments on padded hangers in an uncrowded closet. Cover with a pillowcase or garment bag. For long-term storage, stuff with tissue paper—preferably acid-free—and store flat in a large, sheet-lined box. Refold the garment annually.

Hint: *When storing a bridal gown, store fabric scraps, extra buttons, and leftover lace with the garment so they will age together.*

Net

One of the oldest fabrics, net relics have been found in most prehistoric ruins. Originally made by knotting, today most nets are made on tricot or raschel knitting machines.

Net is available in a variety of natural and man-made fibers and is well suited for bridal and formal wear.

THE NET FAMILY

English net is a cotton net. Available in several sizes of mesh, it is used for undergarments and yokes on bridal gowns.

Illusion is a very fine tulle used for bridal veils.

Maline is a very fine net with hexagonal holes. Made of silk, rayon, nylon, or cotton, it is used primarily for millinery.

Net is an open-mesh fabric. Sometimes called *bobbinet,* it is made of rayon, silk, polyester, nylon, or cotton and ranges from very sheer to heavy. It is used for evening gowns, bridal veils, petticoats, costumes, millinery, trimmings, interfacings, and underlinings.

Point d'esprit is a fine net with rectangular dots spaced at regular intervals.

Tulle is a fine, hexagonal net. It is used unstarched for wedding veils, petticoats, millinery and interfacing; it's starched for ballet tutus. Nylon tulle is crisper than silk tulle.

Fabric Characteristics
- Net is easy to sew.
- Net is transparent. (See Transparent Fabrics.)
- Net does not fray.
- It does not have a grain; however, it has more give in the width than in the length.
- Net tears easily and cannot be repaired successfully.
- It is easily damaged with the point of the iron.

SEWING CHECKLIST

Machine Needles: Universal-H point, Yellow Band needles; sizes 60/8 to 80/12.

Machine Setting: Stitch length 1.75–2.5mm (10–15 stitches per inch); tension, loosely balanced.

Thread: Fine long-staple polyester (100/3), extra-fine cotton-wrapped polyester, woolly nylon, topstitching.

Sewing Machine Equipment: Straight-stitch, jeans, or roller foot, small-hole needle plate, embroidery foot.

Equipment and Supplies: Flower or safety pins, transparent tape, stabilizer.

Seams: Plain, French, double/ply, bound, hairline, tissue-stitched, serged, double-stitched.

Edge Finishes: Unfinished, bound, horsehair, lace, mock-merrow, merrow, wired, net facings, hemmer-rolled.

SEWING NET

LAYOUT AND CUTTING

Net and tulle do not have a grain; but they do have more stretch in the width than in the length.

Cut most garments conventionally on the lengthwise grain. To economize, tilt pattern pieces as needed. Avoid cutting some pieces on the lengthwise grain and others on the crossgrain.

For undergarments, cut two layers—one on the crossgrain and one on the lengthwise grain.

Since these fabrics tend to be elusive when you're cutting several layers, use flower or safety pins to hold the layers together.

STITCHING TIPS

Make a test seam to determine the stitch length. Shorten the stitch length for nets with large holes.

Fig. 13–28 *Carolina Herrera's tulle and velvet cocktail dress features strips of horsehair to shape the undulating skirt ruffles. (Photo courtesy of Carolina Herrera, Fall/Winter 1987/1988.)*

To avoid snagging the net, use a jeans or roller foot, or wrap the toes with transparent tape. If necessary, tissue-stitch seams so the feed dogs will not tear the fabric.

To prevent puckering and unwanted gathers, stitch slowly; and, if your machine has a slow speed, change speeds.

To gather, set the machine for 2.5mm (10 stitches per inch) and stitch. When there are several layers, gather each individually; then stitch them together.

SEAMS AND HEMS

Since nets don't ravel, seams do not have to be finished; however, they should be narrow since net is transparent. Some nets are scratchy and irritate the skin. Bind them with sheer tricot for comfort.

If both sides of the garment will show, use a tiny 1/8″ French seam. Or press a plain seam to one side; topstitch (W,1;L,2); and trim closely.

Tissue-stitch seams to avoid tearing the fabric on the feed dogs and to prevent puckering.

Many edges can be left unfinished, but finish the edges of petticoats with bindings so they won't snag your nylons.

To give hems more definition and body at the hemline, use a horsehair hem or zigzag over wire.

Finish hems on evening gowns with a decorative satin stitch, a hemmer-rolled hem, or merrow finish.

HEMMING VEILS

Leave the hems on veils raw or finish with a narrow satin binding, ribbon lace hem, beaded edge, mock-merrow or merrow finish. Survey the latest bridal magazines to determine which is most fashionable.

Finish hems on bridal veils before gathering them. When stitching a merrow finish, use woolly nylon thread in the overlock loopers. For a mock-merrow finish, use woolly nylon in the bobbin of your regular machine.

1. Cut the veil with a 1/2″ hem allowance.
2. Position white topstitching thread on the hemline. Using an embroidery foot, zigzag (W,1;L,1) over the thread.
3. Trim away the tulle below the stitched line; press.

Hint: *Fine-tune the stitch so it is just wide enough to cover the twist. To avoid a fluted edge, guide, don't pull the tulle. If the fabric doesn't feed smoothly, tissue-stitch using strips of water-soluble stabilizer between the tulle and feed dogs.*

FACINGS, INTERFACINGS, UNDERLININGS, AND LININGS

Net and tulle are excellent fabrics for facings, interfacings, underlinings, and linings. They add crispness without weight and are particularly well-suited as a base fabric for lace appliqués.

Use net or tulle instead of bias facings on sheer and lace garments. Cut the net on the crossgrain instead of on the bias.

Hint: *When making bubble skirts, stuff the skirts with balls of net so they will hold their shape.*

EMBROIDERING NET

1. Draw the design on water-soluble stabilizer.

Hint: *Use a Deco-Color pen. This is a permanent color pen, but it disappears when the stabilizer dissolves.*

2. Put the tulle in a machine-embroidery hoop; and pin the stabilizer to the wrong side.
3. Right side up, embroider the design, using a decorative thread.

Hint: *When embroidering white on white, use a shiny rayon thread.*

You can also use lace appliqués to add a touch of elegance to bridal veils and formal gowns. Cut the motifs from a lightweight lace and then fuse them to the tulle.

Hint: *Cover the pressing board with brown paper; then, using a rectangle of Wonder Under larger than the motif, fuse. The excess will transfer to the paper; discard the paper.*

PRESSING

Press with a warm, dry iron. To revive limp veils, cover with wax paper and press.

White Fabrics

Always a favorite for brides and summertime freshness, white fabrics are seasonless. They are available in every fiber and a variety of weaves and knits, and can be used for all types of garments.

Frequently used alone or as an accent, whites must be handled with care throughout the construction process to maintain a pristine appearance.

Although whites vary in transparency from very sheer to opaque, all are more transparent than similar fabrics in darker colors. (See Transparent Fabrics.)

Fabric Characteristics

- White fabrics soil easily.
- Whites are easily damaged by improper pressing and dirty irons.
- Many white fabrics are transparent; and construction details—seams, hems, and facings—will show on the outside of the garment.

SEWING WHITES

LAYOUT, MARKING, AND CUTTING

Before beginning, clean everything—the carpet, floor, table tops, sewing machine, sewing equipment, and your hands—thoroughly.

Hint: *Lora Gill has her students wash their hands every hour when working on white.*

Cover the clothes you are wearing with a white or pastel smock.

Cover the cutting table with a clean sheet before spreading the fabric.

Mark as little as possible; experiment with marking techniques on fabric scraps first. Fine pins, chalk or soap sliver, clips, thread tracing, tailor tacks, and white tracing carbon are best.

Hint: *I mark white with white tracing carbon, even though it is sometimes difficult to see. Disappearing marking pens and colored chalks may not come out. Colored threads—even pastels—*

Fig. 13–29 *Trimmed with lace at the hem and midriff, this elegant gown is made of silk organza. (Photo courtesy of Carolina Herrera Couture Bridal Collection, Spring/Summer 1988.)*

sometimes fade onto the white fabric when the cloth is steamed. And colored tracing carbons rarely disappear completely. If you can't see the white, use another marking method.

Use only new, fine stainless steel pins. Old and brass pins may leave a dark residue on the fabric.

Clean your scissors before cutting the fabric to be sure they don't harbor lint or fabric fuzz from previous garments.

STITCHING TIPS

Clean your machine before beginning. Check twice to be sure there is no oily residue around the feed dogs.

If you have a portable machine, cover the table under it with a clean white sheet. If you have a cabinet model, cover the wood with a clean white pillow case.

253

At the end of the sewing day, wrap the garment in a clean white sheet.

SEAMS AND HEMS

Consider the fabric transparency, weave, and weight; garment design and use; and care requirements when selecting seams and hems. Generally, narrow seams look best.

FACINGS AND UNDERLININGS

Cut facings and pocket sacks from flesh-colored fabrics, to avoid telltale shadows.

Most white fabrics have some transparency. Underline or flat line (see Chapter 20) the sections to make them opaque.

PRESSING

Before pressing, clean the iron soleplate with hot iron cleaner or silver polish. Use a cotton swab to clean the steam holes.

Hint: *Use denatured alcohol to remove fusible resins.*

If the soleplate is beyond cleaning, cover it with a detachable nonstick soleplate, available in fabric stores.

If the iron is clogged and doesn't steam properly, clean the water reservoir. Fill it with 1/4 cup white vinegar and 1/4 cup water; allow it to heat for three to five minutes. Unplug and adjust to a steam setting. Place the iron flat on a rack in the sink to allow the solution to drip for half an hour. Rinse several times. Repeat if necessary.

Replace the ironing board cover with a clean, white sheet. When pressing large pieces of fabric or bouffant garments, spread a clean sheet on the floor under the ironing board.

Always test press on fabric scraps to determine the correct temperature, moisture, and pressing techniques. Use a press cloth to protect your fabric when pressing from the right side.

GARMENT CARE

Wash whites separately. Separate heavily soiled fabrics. Whites pick up colors and dirt from other garments.

Pretreat wax and oil-based stains before laundering. Before bleaching or removing stains, experiment with fabric scraps. Always read the manufacturer's directions before beginning. Do not soak for more than thirty minutes without changing the water.

Be sure garments are clean but not starched before putting them away. To prevent silks and wools from yellowing, store in a cool, dry closet away from light.

CHAPTER 14
Napped and Pile Fabrics

Napped Fabrics

In garment construction, the term "nap" is used very loosely to describe pile fabrics, fabrics with one-way designs, and knits, as well as the true napped fabrics described in this section.

Technically, napping is a finishing process applied to one or both sides of woven or knitted fabrics. It raises the fiber ends to the surface, so they can be clipped, brushed flat, or left erect. Originally used for a softer finish on wool, today napping is also applied to cotton and man-made fibers to make them look like wool.

Compared to tightly woven fabrics which have no nap, napped fabrics are warmer and more stain-repellent. However, they mat, pill, and show wear more readily.

Napped fabrics reflect the light differently when held in different positions. They vary in weight and amount of nap from cotton flannel, which has a light, soft fuzz, to wool coating fabrics with very thick naps.

Melton, wool broadcloth, wool flannel, doe-skin, serge, camel's hair, mohair, cotton outing, sweatshirt fleece, suede cloth, brushed denim, and lamb's wool are napped fabrics.

Fabric Characteristics
- Napped fabrics require a nap layout.
- Napped fabrics usually require more fabric.
- On some fabrics, the direction of the nap is difficult to determine.
- Napped fabrics vary in weight, bulk, fiber content, nap length, use, difficulty to sew, and care requirements.
- Some napped fabrics are easily marred by pins, the sewing machine presser foot, and/or pressing.
- Napped fabrics show wear first at fold and creaselines.

PLANNING A GARMENT

PURCHASING THE FABRIC

A napped finish is sometimes used to camouflage a poor quality fabric. Hold the fabric up to the light to examine the fabric weave for closeness and/or defects.

Tightly woven and twill fabrics generally wear better than loosely woven materials. Knitted and loosely woven fabrics also pill and mat more quickly.

Fabrics with longer naps wear, pill, and mat more quickly than those with short naps. Napped fabrics made with hair fibers mat and wear more quickly than those made with wool.

Rub the right sides of the fabric together vigorously; shake it to see if fibers fall off. Then examine the surface for loose pile and pilling.

Fig. 14–1 *Designed by Courrèges, the trapeze-line jacket is made of napped wool and cashmere. (Photo courtesy of Courrèges, Autumn/Winter Collection, 1988/1989.)*

SEWING CHECKLIST

Sewing Machine Needles: Universal-H point, Yellow Band or Red Band needles; sizes 70/10 to 100/16, depending on the fabric weight and construction.

Machine Setting: Stitch length 2–3mm (8–12 stitches per inch); tension and pressure, variable.

Thread: Long-staple polyester, cotton-wrapped polyester, mercerized cotton, silk.

Hand Sewing Needles: Sizes 5 to 9.

Sewing Machine Equipment: Roller or even-feed foot, zipper foot, shim.

Layout: Nap. Double/lay—right sides together; single/lay, right side up.

Marking Techniques: Chalk, soap sliver, clips, tailor tacks, thread tracing, tracing wheel and carbon.

Seams: Depends on the fabric weight and structure, garment type and quality, and care requirements. Plain, welt, double-welt, topstitched, standing-fell, slot, tucked, lapped, taped, double/ply.

Hems: Plain, blindstitched, blind catchstitched, topstitched, double-stitched, interfaced.

Seam and Hem Finishes: Depends on the fabric weight and structure, garment type and quality, and care requirements.

Interfacing: Depends on the fabric and garment design. Usually woven or nonwoven sew-in.

Linings and Underlinings: Optional.

Closures: All types.

Pockets: All types.

Preshrink the fabric before cutting, using a method appropriate to the fiber and fabric structure.

SEWING NAPPED FABRICS

LAYOUT, CUTTING, AND MARKING

To determine the direction of the nap, use your hand to stroke the fabric parallel to the selvage. It will feel smooth when you stroke with the nap and rough when you rub against it.

If you cannot determine the nap by rubbing it with your hand, drape the fabric around your shoulders so the two ends hang down on each side in front. Study the color values in the mirror to determine which is lighter.

Hint: *Most napped fabrics are cut with the nap running down so they will wear better and pill less.*

Spread the fabric right sides together with a lengthwise fold. If the fabric has a pattern to be matched or is heavy, spread the fabric in a single layer, right side up.

Avoid crosswise folds. If the pattern layout indicates a crosswise fold, cut the fabric on the foldline. Then turn the top layer around to reposition it, right sides together, so the nap on both layers runs in the same direction.

Lay out the pattern pieces so the tops of all pattern pieces are toward the same end of the fabric. Cut waistbands, collars, and cuffs on the crossgrain if it will enhance the design.

Cut light- and medium-weight fabrics with the grain; cut bulky, thickly napped fabrics in the direction of the nap.

STITCHING TIPS

Make a test seam. Set the stitch length for 2mm (12 stitches per inch) for lightweight and medium fabrics and 3mm (8 stitches per inch) for heavier materials. Lighten the pressure and loosen the tension if needed.

Stitch thickly napped fabrics with the nap; stitch all others directionally with the grain.

PRESSING

Experiment with heat, moisture, and pressure on fabric scraps before pressing the garment.

To avoid damaging the nap during pressing, cover the pressing surface with a fabric scrap, piece of wool, or thick terry towel.

Press from the wrong side. When pressing the right side use a self-fabric or wool press cloth; and press with the nap.

To avoid flattening wools, cover the pressing board with wool. When pressing mohair, use a cooler iron and a dry cloth next to the mohair to avoid shrinking and matting.

Use a seam roll to prevent seam impressions on the right side of the garment. To remove impressions, begin wrong side up; slip the iron under seam and hem allowances; press.

Pile Fabrics

Frequently called napped fabrics, pile fabrics are knitted or woven with an extra set of yarns to produce a pile on one or both sides of the fabric. The pile can be cut or uncut, allover or patterned, high, low, or varying in depth.

Like napped fabrics, pile fabrics reflect the light differently, depending on the direction of the pile. When it runs up, the fabric looks darker and richer; when it runs down, it looks lighter and shinier.

Pile fabrics range from very delicate, elegant cut velvets to rugged, casual fake-fur fabrics. Other typical pile fabrics include corduroy, fleece, terry, chenille, velour, and velveteen.

For additional information, see the indicated sections.

Chenille is a tufted pile fabric with a woven ground. (See Tufted Pile Fabrics.)

Corduroy is a filling pile fabric. It is usually woven with vertical wales or ribs. (See Corduroy.)

Fleece has a deep, soft pile. Usually made with wool or hair fibers, it can be woven with pile or be heavily napped. (See Coatings.)

Fig. 14–2 *Bill Blass drapes this narrow, cut-velvet beauty into a deep V back. (Photo courtesy of Bill Blass Ltd.)*

Terry is a warp-pile fabric. Unlike other piles, the loops are uncut and the fabric has no nap. (See Terry and Velour.)

Velour is a warp-pile fabric used for casual garments. (See Terry and Velour.)

Velvet is a warp-pile fabric used for elegant designs. (See Velvet.)

Velveteen is a filling-pile fabric with a short, close pile. (See Velveteen.)

Velveteen plush, sometimes called plush, has a filling pile that is longer than 1/8″. (See Coatings and Velveteen.)

Fabric Characteristics

- Pile fabrics vary in weight, bulk, fiber content, pile length, use, difficulty to sew, and care requirements.
- Pile fabrics have a nap.
- Pile fabrics usually require extra fabric.
- On some fabrics, the direction of the pile is difficult to determine.
- Pile fabrics are easily marred by pins, ripped seamlines, alterations, and improper pressing. Some piles are marred by fingermarks.
- Pile fabrics creep badly and sometimes pucker during stitching.
- Pile fabrics ravel and shed.
- Some pile fabrics are bulky.

Planning a Garment

FABRIC AND PATTERN SELECTION

The quality of pile fabrics is determined by the fiber, density, evenness, and luster of the pile, the closeness of the weave in the ground fabric, and the construction—"V" or "W"—of the pile.

Unravel a few threads at the end of the fabric; the greater the number of pile yarns, the better the fabric. W-shaped yarns, which pass under-over-under the interlacing yarns, are more durable than V-shaped yarns, which pass under one yarn.

Hint: *Fabrics with some nylon in the pile are easy to maintain and resist liquid stains and wrinkling.*

Preshrink the fabric before cutting out, using a method appropriate to the fiber and fabric structure.

Simple designs which emphasize the fabric's surface interest are usually best. Try to avoid tightly fitted garments and designs with seams on the lengthwise grain.

Refine the fit before cutting out to avoid marring the fabric with fitting and ripping. If necessary, make a test garment.

Eliminate unnecessary straight seams. Pin the pattern pieces together, matching the seamlines; and cut the two garment sections in one piece.

Sewing Pile Fabrics

LAYOUT, CUTTING, AND MARKING

Pile fabrics look deeper and richer when the pile runs up from the hem. When the pile runs toward the hem, fabrics look lighter, smoother, and shinier.

To determine the direction of the pile, stroke the fabric parallel to the selvage. It will feel smooth when you stroke with the pile and rough when you rub against it. Use white chalk or a soap sliver to mark arrows on the wrong side of the fabric indicating the direction of the pile.

Generally, piles are cut up for beauty (e.g., velvet) and down for wear (e.g., corduroy and velveteen). However, the pile can run in either direction, if you are consistent.

To decide which is better, drape the fabric around your shoulders so the two ends fall down on each side in front. Study the color tones in the mirror.

To avoid shifting when cutting, spread the fabric in a single layer, wrong side up. If there is a pattern to be matched, spread fabric right side up. Use duplicate pattern pieces for easier, more accurate cutting. (You'll also use less fabric.)

To save time, use a lengthwise fold; fold the fabric wrong sides together. Avoid crosswise folds. If the pattern layout indicates a crosswise fold, cut the fabric on the foldline. Turn the top layer around to reposition it, right sides together, so the nap runs in the same direction.

Use a nap layout; lay the pattern pieces so the tops of all pieces are toward the same end of the fabric. Cut waistbands, collars, and cuffs on the crossgrain if it will enhance the design.

Pile fabrics with printed or woven designs such as plaids, large prints, or corduroy wales, should be matched appropriately (see Plaids and Prints.)

Place fine pins or needles in the seam allowances. Remove pins from the fabric as quickly as possible to avoid marring the pile.

Mark as little as possible, using clips, chalk, temporary marking pens, tailor tacks and thread tracing. Avoid tracing wheels and tape on the face side of the fabric.

Mark buttonhole locations and patch pockets with tailor tacks or thread tracing. Use silk thread to thread trace on velvets.

Cut light- and medium-weight fabrics with the grain; cut bulky, thickly napped fabrics in the direction of the pile.

STITCHING TIPS

Make a test seam with two 10″ fabric scraps. Set the stitch length for 2mm (12 stitches perinch) for lightweight and medium fabrics and 3mm (8 stitches per inch) for heavier materials. Loosen the tension slightly and lighten the pressure as needed. Stitch with the nap and hold the fabric taut when stitching. The test seam should be smooth without puckers and even at the ends.

If you have a creeping underlayer, experiment with these remedies. The pile, grain, and seam length will determine which works best on a particular fabric.

- Stitch with the pile, disregarding the grainline. Stitch collars and necklines from the center out.
- Hold the fabric taut when stitching.
- Pin baste with fine needles, placing them at right angles to the seamline in the seam allowance only.
- Use a roller or even-feed foot, but check carefully to be sure it doesn't leave tracks on the right side of the fabric.
- Stitch with strips of tissue paper or a stabilizer between the layers and/or between the fabric and feed dogs.
- Hold the top layer up so the pile on the two layers can't lock together.
- Use a diagonal basting or double baste.

- Stop periodically; raise, then lower the presser foot; begin stitching again.

Hint: *To minimize bulk, grade, trim and notch seams, slash and press darts open.*

For seams, hems, and facings, see Corduroy sewing directions in the following section.

GATHERS

Use buttonhole twist, glazed or waxed thread, or a heavy cord in the bobbin. Use a long stitch (4 mm or 6 stitches per inch). On the right side, stitch two rows—one on the seamline and one midway between the seamline and raw edge. Pull up bobbin threads to gather.

PRESSING AND GARMENT CARE

Experiment with heat, moisture, and pressure on fabric scraps before pressing the garment. Some fabrics require a very light touch, maybe steaming only; others need a firm press; and a few may be damaged by steam.

All-cotton fabrics can withstand higher temperatures than blends.

To avoid damaging the pile during pressing, cover the pressing surface with a Velvaboard, needleboard, thick terry towel, or fabric scrap, right side up.

Press the garment from the wrong side. When pressing the right side, use a self-fabric, velveteen, or wool press cloth; press with the nap. Do not allow the iron to touch the pile.

Use a steamer when pressing from the right side. Steam thoroughly and brush with the nap.

Use a seam roll to avoid seam impressions on the right side of the garment. To remove impressions, slip the iron under the seam or hem allowance and press.

To keep garments clean, vacuum and brush away loose dirt after wearing. Freshen pile with steam by hanging the garment in the bathroom and filling the bathtub with hot water. Keep the door closed; let the garment dry completely before wearing or handling. Brush if needed.

Hint: *You can raise the pile of washable fabrics in the dryer. Tumble fifteen to twenty minutes with several damp towels.*

To protect skirts and pants from hanger marks, sew skirt hanger loops into the waistband. Or place a fabric scrap, right sides together, between the garment and the hanger.

Before laundering, turn the garment inside-out; use a fabric softener to reduce lint. Machine wash and tumble dry; remove while slightly damp. Straighten seams and hang to dry.

Corduroy

Always popular for casual garments, corduroy is a very durable fabric. Corduroy is made in a variety of weights and wale designs.

Manufactured with an extra set of filling yarns to form the pile, corduroy can be woven with a "V" weave or "W" weave. Distinctive ribs are formed when the extra set of pile loops are cut and brushed to form wales.

Corduroy is usually described by the size of the wales. Miniwales have more than 21 wales per inch; pinwales, 16 to 21 wales per inch; midwales, 11 to 15 wales; and jumbo or wide wales, three to 10.

Novelty patterns have ribs in various widths and heights; and no-wale corduroy is ribless. Stretch corduroy has a small amount of spandex to make it a stretch fabric.

In addition to solid colors, corduroy can be printed with plaid, floral, or paisley patterns.

Fabric Characteristics

- Corduroy is relatively easy to sew.
- It is used for casual garments.
- Corduroy has a pile and requires a nap layout.
- Corduroy usually requires extra fabric.
- Corduroy may be marred by pins, ripped seamlines, alterations, and improper pressing.
- Some corduroy fabrics creep badly and sometimes pucker during stitching.
- The corduroy pile sheds.
- Wide and midwale corduroys are bulky.
- Wide wale and novelty corduroys have prominent vertical stripes which may require matching. (See Stripes.)
- Many corduroys are 100 percent cotton and shrink when laundered.
- Corduroy can be laundered or dry-cleaned.
- Corduroy fabrics may not be as attractive after laundering.

Fig. 14–3 *From Saint Laurent Rive Gauche Autumn/Winter 1987/1988, this classic corduroy jacket tops an ottoman skirt. (Photo courtesy of Yves Saint Laurent.)*

261

PLANNING A GARMENT

FABRIC AND PATTERN SELECTION

Corduroy can be used for everything from sturdy children's garments to elegant evening fashions, but it's used most frequently for sportswear, jackets, coats, skirts, slacks, children's wear, pillows, and bedspreads.

It combines well with many different fabrics—wool, fleece, cotton, calico, synthetic suede and leather, and even satin. It can be cut on the crossgrain to create an ottoman effect or on the bias for chevrons.

Corduroys vary in weight and the fabric should be appropriate for the garment. Use these suggestions as a guide.

Use pinwales for dresses, blouses and children's wear; midwales for skirts, jackets and trousers; and jumbo wales for coats and outerwear.

Generally, long-staple, combed, mercerized cotton is used for the pile. The ground on good-quality corduroys is long-staple cotton, polyester/cotton, or 100 percent polyester.

The polyester and polyester-blend fabrics are stronger and shrink less.

Examine the wrong side of the fabric. The pile will shed and pull out more if the weave is loose. Twill-weave fabrics wear better and have a denser pile than plain-weave fabrics.

Unravel the end and examine the pile. W-shaped piles are anchored better and usually wear better.

For greater warmth in coats and jackets, select a corduroy with a high, dense pile. Corduroys with a dense pile resist crushing, stand more erect, and cover the base fabric better than those with low-count piles.

Deep-colored reds, blues, and blacks bleed badly.

Compared to velveteen, the pile of no-wale corduroys is woven into uniform rows while the pile of velveteen is interlaced randomly. The corduroy will have a more distinct break at vertical foldlines. When sewing, the difference between no-wale corduroys and velveteens is minimal.

All-cotton corduroy shrinks; preshrink the fabric before cutting out. For garments which will be laundered, wash and dry the fabric using the method you plan to use on the garment.

For garments which will be dry-cleaned, spread the fabric in a single layer, pile side out, over the shower rod. Fill the tub with hot water, close the door; and leave the fabric to dry; or steam with a steamer.

Adjust the pattern before cutting the fabric. Compare the upper collar and undercollar patterns for tailored garments. The undercollar should be 3/4″ to 7/8″ smaller.

Sewing Corduroy

See Pile Fabrics for additional suggestions.

LAYOUT

Spread light- and medium-weight corduroys with a lengthwise fold, wrong sides together. Spread heavier fabrics in a single layer, wrong side up.

For better wear, lay out children's garments so the nap runs down.

Wide wale and novelty corduroys have vertical stripes to be matched.

STITCHING TIPS

Always make a test seam with two 10″ fabric scraps. Set the stitch length for 2 mm (12 stitches per inch) for pinwale corduroy, 2.5 mm (10 stitches per inch) for midwale, and 3 mm (8 stitches per inch) for wide wale. Loosen the tension slightly and lighten the pressure as needed.

Hold the fabric taut and stitch with the nap. The test seam should be smooth without puckers and even at the end.

SEAMS AND HEMS

Plain, open seams are usually flattest. I prefer serged or multi-stitch zigzag; however, tricot binding prevents shedding pile. Topstitch hems and seams for very casual designs. Topstitch with the nap.

When topstitching, use two strands of regular thread or topstitching thread and a needle one size larger. Set the stitch length to 3mm (8 stitches per inch) or 4mm (6 stitches per inch) for heavier fabrics. Stitch with the pile. Use a zipper foot or a shim when stitching over uneven layers.

Double-stitch hems on heavy fabrics; interface hems for a soft edge.

Hint: *Use a stiff brush or a hand vacuum to remove loose pile at the raw edges.*

FACINGS, INTERFACINGS, AND LININGS

Replace self-fabric facings on heavier corduroys with facings cut from a lighter weight fabric or a complete lining.

Before applying fusibles to the garment sections, experiment with fabric scraps. Apply fusibles to the facing or entire garment section.

Hint: *For a better bond, cut fusibles on the cross-grain.*

Linings eliminate the need for seam finishes and shedding pile; they also keep slacks from riding up. Outerwear garments are more comfortable and easier to slip into when lined.

Twill linings are more durable than plain weave linings.

Hint: *All types of pockets—inseam, welt, bound, trouser, and patch—work well on corduroy. On heavy fabrics, use a twill lining fabric to line patch pockets and make pocket sacks.*

CLOSURES

Most fasteners—except hand-worked buttonholes and hand-stitched zippers—are appropriate for corduroy.

When making bound buttonholes, cut the welts on the bias and cord them. Lengthen the stitch for machine-worked buttonholes.

PRESSING AND GARMENT CARE

Experiment with the heat, moisture, and pressure on fabric scraps. All-cotton corduroys can withstand a higher heat than blends.

To revive the nap after fusing or construction pressing, hang it in a steam-filled bathroom. Or steam the face side with a steamer or steam iron held about 1/2″ away. If necessary, use a stiff brush and brush against the pile.

Use a no-wale corduroy press cloth when pressing the right side. Do not allow the iron to touch the pile.

To fluff the nap between wearings, tumble in the dryer with several damp towels for fifteen to twenty minutes. Remove and hang immediately.

Depending on the garment type and structure, corduroy garments can be laundered or dry-cleaned. Most will retain a new appearance longer when drycleaned.

Turn the garment inside out for washing, and use a fabric softener to reduce lint. Machine wash, and tumble until almost dry. Straighten the seams and hang to dry.

Velveteen

A popular fabric for dressy and casual garments, velveteen is made in a variety of weights and designs. Manufactured with an extra set of filling yarns to form the pile, the pile loops are cut by circular knives revolving at high speed.

In addition to solid colors, velveteen can be printed with plaid, floral, or paisley patterns.

Fabric Characteristics
- Velveteen is relatively easy to sew.
- Velveteen has a pile and requires a nap layout.
- It usually requires extra fabric.
- Velveteen may be marred by pins, ripped seamlines, alterations, and improper pressing.
- Some velveteen fabrics creep badly and sometimes pucker when stitched.
- The velveteen pile sheds at raw edges.
- Some velveteens are bulky.
- Many velveteens are 100 percent cotton and shrink when laundered.
- Velveteen can be laundered or dry-cleaned.
- Velveteen fabrics may not be as attractive after laundering.

PLANNING A GARMENT

FABRIC AND PATTERN SELECTION

Velveteen can be used for everything from dressy children's garments and elegant evening fashions to linings. It is used most frequently for sportswear, jackets, coats, skirts, slacks, bedspreads, and pillows.

Fig. 14–4 *Velveteen is a classic fabric for little girls' special-occasion dresses. (Photo courtesy of Vogue Pattern Co.)*

It combines well with many different fabrics—wool, fleece, cotton, calico, synthetic suede, leather, and satin.

Long-staple, combed, mercerized cotton is used for the pile; on good quality velveteens, it is also used for the ground. Examine the wrong side of the fabric. A twill or closely woven plain weave holds the pile more firmly and sheds less. Twill-weave fabrics generally wear better and have a denser, more luxurious pile than plain-weave fabrics.

Velveteens with a dense pile will resist crushing, stand more erect, and cover the base fabric better than those with low-count piles.

Compared to corduroy, velveteen has a finer, denser pile. When magnified, the pile of no-wale corduroy is woven into uniform rows while the pile of velveteen is interlaced randomly. This causes the no-wale corduroy to have a more distinct break at vertical foldlines; while velveteen, a filling pile, breaks at the horizontal foldlines. When sewing, the difference between no-wale corduroys and velveteens is minimal.

For greater warmth in coats and jackets, select a fabric with a high, dense pile.

Compared to velvet, velveteen has more body and does not drape as well; its pile has less sheen and is never more than 1/8″ high. The back of velveteen has a slight nap.

To distinguish between velvet and velveteen, unravel the fabric on two adjacent sides. The velveteen pile will unravel on the crossgrain between two filling rows. The velvet pile will unravel on the lengthwise grain between two warp rows.

Hang velveteen fabrics when storing; do not leave them folded.

All-cotton velveteens shrink; always preshrink the fabric before cutting. For garments which will be laundered, wash and tumble dry the fabric using the method you plan to use on the garment.

For garments which will be dry-cleaned, spread the fabric in a single layer, pile side out, over the shower rod. Fill the tub with hot water, close the door, and leave the fabric to dry or steam with a steamer.

Adjust the pattern before cutting the fabric. Compare the upper collar and undercollar patterns for tailored garments. The undercollar should be 3/4″ to 7/8″ smaller.

SEWING CHECKLIST

Sewing Machine Needles: Universal-H point, or Red Band needles; sizes 70/10 to 90/14, depending on the fabric weight.

Machine Setting: Stitch length 2–2.5mm (10–12 stitches per inch); tension and pressure, variable.

Thread: Long-staple polyester, cotton-wrapped polyester, topstitching thread.

Hand Sewing Needles: Sizes 7 to 9.

Sewing Machine Equipment: Roller or even-feed foot, zipper foot, shim.

Layout: Nap. Light and medium weight—double/lay, wrong sides together; heavyweight—single/lay, wrong side up; patterns to be matched—single/lay, right side up.

Marking Techniques: Chalk, soap sliver, clips, disappearing marking pens, pins, tailor tacks, thread tracing.

Seams: Plain, welt, topstitched, lapped, piped, tissue-stitched.

Hems: Plain, blindstitch, blind catchstitch, topstitched, double-stitched, interfaced, faced.

Seam and Hem Finishes: Unfinished, pinked, pinked-and-stitched, multi-stitch zigzag, serged, tricot bound, bound, Hong Kong.

Facings: Self-fabric facings, smooth-fabric facings, bands, ribbings, bindings.

Interfacing: Usually sew-in; depends on the fabric and garment design.

Linings: Optional.

Underlinings: Rarely.

Closures: All types.

Pockets: All types.

SEWING VELVETEEN

See Pile Fabrics for additional suggestions.

LAYOUT

Spread light- and medium-weight velveteens with a lengthwise fold, wrong sides together. Spread heavier fabrics in a single layer, wrong side up. Spread fabrics with patterns to be matched in a single layer, right side up.

For better wear, lay out children's garments so the nap runs down.

STITCHING TIPS

Always make a test seam with two 10″ fabric scraps. Set the stitch length for 2mm (12 stitches per inch) for lightweight velveteens and 2.5mm (10 stitches per inch) for heavier fabrics. Loosen the tension slightly and lighten the pressure as needed.

Hold the fabric taut and stitch with the nap. The test seam should be smooth without puckers and even at the end.

If the underlayer creeps, use a roller or even-feed foot.

Hint: *Examine the fabric carefully. If there are feed dog tracks, tissue-stitch seams.*

SEAMS AND HEMS

Use a stiff brush or a hand vacuum to remove loose pile at the raw edges.

Finish seams and hems on unlined outerwear with a serger, or use binding. Double-stitch hems on heavy fabrics; and interface hems for a soft finish.

Topstitch hems and seams for casual designs. Topstitch with the nap, using two strands of regular thread or one strand of topstitching thread. Lengthen the stitch for heavier fabrics and sporty garments. Use a zipper foot or a shim when stitching over uneven layers.

FACINGS, INTERFACINGS, AND LININGS

Replace self-fabric facings on heavier velveteens with facings cut from lighter weight fabrics; or use a complete lining.

Before applying fusibles to the garment sections, make some samples. Generally, fusibles are applied to the facings.

Outerwear garments are frequently lined; but other garments are not. Linings eliminate shedding pile and the need for seam finishes. They also keep slacks from riding up. Generally, twill linings wear better.

Hint: *All types of pockets—inseam, welt, bound, trouser, and patch—work well on velveteen. On heavy fabrics, use a twill lining fabric to line patch pockets and make pocket sacks.*

CLOSURES

Most fasteners are appropriate for velveteen. Hand-worked buttonholes and hand-stitched zippers should be avoided except on fancy evening wear.

Slot, invisible, and fly zippers are usually better than lapped zippers. Use an invisible or hand-stitched zipper on dressy velveteen garments.

When making bound buttonholes, experiment with different methods and fabrics to see which welts look best. When making bound buttonholes with velveteen welts, cut the welts on the bias and cord them.

PRESSING AND GARMENT CARE

Experiment with heat, moisture, and pressure on fabric scraps. All-cotton velveteens can withstand a higher heat than blends.

To revive the nap after fusing or construction pressing, hang the sections in a steam-filled bathroom. Or steam the face side with a steamer or steam iron held about 1/2″ away. Don't touch the pile until it dries.

Use a velveteen press cloth when pressing the right side. Do not allow the iron to touch the pile.

Depending on the garment type and structure, velveteen garments can be laundered or dry-cleaned.

Turn the garment inside out for washing and use a fabric softener to reduce lint. Machine wash and tumble dry.

To fluff the nap between wearings, tumble in the dryer with several damp towels for fifteen to twenty minutes. Remove and hang immediately.

Velvet

Fig. 14–5 *Known for sumptuous ball gowns, this elegant contrast of black velvet is typical of the House of Balmain. Designed by Erik Mortensen for Pierre Balmain Haute Couture, Autumn/Winter 1987/1988. (Photographer Jacques Peg; photo courtesy of Pierre Balmain.)*

Woven with an extra set of warp yarns which form the pile, velvets range in weight from chiffon to heavy upholstery fabrics. Originally made of silk, velvet is now available in cotton, rayon, acetate, polyester, and blends.

Velvet and other warp-pile fabrics are usually woven as double cloth. Two layers of fabric are woven simultaneously, one on top of the other; the pile, which joins the two layers, is cut after the fabrics are woven.

This weaving method causes the pile to stand very erect; in fact, it is sometimes difficult to feel the difference in the nap.

Bagheera velvet is a soft velvet with uncut loops.

Brocaded velvet or *voided velvet* looks like cut velvet; however, it is made by removing areas of the pile to create the pattern.

Chiffon velvet is a very lightweight velvet which drapes well.

Crushed velvet is pressed in different directions to create a pattern with various color shades.

Cut velvet is woven on a jacquard loom to create a distinct pattern in pile on a plain background. Background fabrics range from sheer chiffons to heavy satins.

Faconné velvet generally describes any fancy-weave velvet; more specifically, it describes brocaded velvet.

Lyons velvet is a heavier, crisp velvet that does not drape well. The background is closely woven and the pile is short, thick, and erect. True Lyons velvet is woven in Lyons, France.

Mirror velvet is pressed in different directions to create a pattern with various color shades. Compared to crushed velvet, it is softer and lighter weight.

Nacré velvet is an iridescent fabric with a background of one color and the pile of one or two others.

Panné velvet is pressed in one direction so the pile lies flat. Soft and shiny, it sometimes has a knitted base.

Sculptured velvet is trimmed to various heights to create a sculptured pattern in the pile.

Transparent velvet is woven with fine yarns. It is very lightweight, lustrous, and translucent when held up to the light. It drapes well.

Sewing Machine Needles: Universal-H point, Red Band needles; sizes 60/8 to 80/12, depending on the fabric weight.

Machine Setting: Stitch length 2–3mm (8–12 stitches per inch); tension and pressure, variable.

Thread: Long-staple polyester, cotton-wrapped polyester. For silk velvets, mercerized cotton for machine stitching and silk thread for hand basting over the pile.

Hand Sewing Needles: Sizes 7 to 9.

Sewing Machine Equipment: Roller or even-feed foot, zipper foot, shim.

Equipment and Supplies: Very sharp shears, new, fine pins, mat knife or single-edged razor blade, steamer.

Layout: Nap. Single layer, wrong side up.

Marking Techniques: Chalk, soap sliver, clips, temporary marking pens, tailor tacks, thread tracing.

Seams: Plain, taped, piped, tissue-stitched.

Hems: Plain, blindstitched, catch-stitched, blind catchstitched, double-stitched, interfaced, faced.

Seam and Hem Finishes: Single/ply; unfinished, pinked, pinked-and-stitched, multi-stitch zigzag, serged, tricot bound, hand overcast, Hong Kong, seam tape.

Facings: Self-fabric facings, smooth-fabric facings, bands, ribbings, bindings.

Interfacing: Cotton velvets: fusibles or sew-ins. Other velvets: sew-ins.

Linings: Generally.

Underlinings: Rarely.

Closures: All types.

Pockets: All types.

Fabric Characteristics

- Velvet is more difficult to sew than corduroy.
- Velvet has a pile and requires a nap layout.
- It usually requires extra fabric.
- Velvet is easily marred by pins, ripped seamlines, alterations, heat, moisture, and improper pressing.
- Most velvet fabrics creep badly and sometimes pucker during stitching.
- The velvet pile sheds badly at raw edges.
- Some velvets fray badly.
- Some velvets are bulky.
- Most velvets must be dry-cleaned.
- Cotton velvet is most durable.
- Acetate velvet is easily damaged by moisture and pressure.

PLANNING A GARMENT

SELECTING THE FABRIC

Available in a variety of weights from very light to heavy, velvet is used primarily for elegant, dressy designs.

Most dress velvets are made of filaments of rayon, nylon, polyester, or silk and have a rich sheen. Cotton velvets, frequently used for upholstery, are made of long-staple, combed, mercerized cotton.

Examine the wrong side of the fabric. A close weave will shed and fray less than a loose weave. Fold the fabric wrong sides together. Better quality fabrics with denser piles have less break along the foldline.

Hint: *When you want the fabric to drape well, select a light, transparent velvet which does not have a dense pile.*

If you can't afford a good velvet, select a good-quality velveteen. Generally, velvets and velveteens can be distinguished by fiber content. Velveteen has a nap on the back; the velvet pile is usually shorter, denser, and more erect than velveteen.

Velvet has less body and drapes better than velveteen; but velvets, with the exception of cotton velvets, will not wear as well as velveteen. When folded wrong sides together, velveteen will break on the lengthwise grain and velvet on the cross-grain.

Another way to identify the fabrics is by unraveling them on two adjacent sides. The velveteen pile will unravel on the crossgrain between two filling rows. The velvet pile will unravel on the lengthwise grain between two warp rows.

Always preshrink the fabric appropriately for the fiber content before cutting.

For garments which will be dry-cleaned, spread the fabric in a single layer, pile side out, over the shower rod. Steam with a steamer, and leave the fabric to dry. Acetate velvet should be steamed only from the wrong side. To avoid damaging the pile, do not touch fabric while damp.

Pin one selvage edge to a hanger for storing; do not store the fabric folded.

DESIGN IDEAS AND PATTERN SELECTION

Generally velvet garments—dresses, jackets, coats, capes, skirts, and slacks—look best in simple, classic designs with a minimum of darts, seams, buttonholes, and topstitching.

Soft gathers, pleats, piped seams and piped edges are nice details, while tightly fitted garments, horizontal seams, tucks, pressed pleats, and vertical seams on the lengthwise grain are best avoided.

Velvet combines well with a variety of other fabrics—wool, flannel, tweed, challis, taffeta, satin, faille, tulle, and brocade.

Adjust the pattern before cutting the fabric. And, if necessary, make a test garment to perfect the fit and to practice your sewing skills.

SEWING VELVET

For additional suggestions, see Pile Fabrics.

LAYOUT, CUTTING, AND MARKING

Determining the direction of the nap is sometimes difficult on velvet. Drape the fabric around your shoulders and decide which end you like better. Unlike other pile fabrics, velvet will often wear better and mat less when cut with the pile up.

Spread the velvet in a single layer, wrong side up. Place fine needles instead of pins within the seam allowance. Remove immediately after cutting so they won't leave permanent dents.

Try to limit marking to the wrong side of the fabric. When marking the right side, use silk thread.

STITCHING TIPS

Always make a test seam with two 10″ fabric scraps. Set the stitch length for 2mm (12 stitches per inch) for lightweight velveteens and 2.5mm (10 stitches per inch) for heavier fabrics. Loosen the tension slightly and lighten the pressure as needed.

Hold the fabric taut and stitch with the nap. The test seam should be even and smooth without puckers. Use an even-feed or roller foot to prevent underlayer creep. If it leaves a track along the seamline, tissue-stitch seams.

When joining velvet to a smooth fabric, stitch with the velvet on top. Take care to avoid underlayer creep.

Understitch by hand.

Topstitching is best avoided. When that isn't possible, practice on scraps first. Use a longer stitch length, a looser tension, and hold the fabric taut while stitching.

Hint: *Double baste with water-soluble thread to avoid a drag line.*

SEAMS AND HEMS

To avoid shifting when stitching, double baste. After stitching, use a stiff brush or a hand vacuum to remove loose pile at the raw edges.

Double-stitch hems on heavy velvets with a blindstitch or blind catchstitch.

Interface hems with cotton flannel, lamb's wool, or Armo wool for a soft finish.

To press the hem, steam wrong side up; pat the folded edges with the bristles of a stiff brush.

FACINGS, INTERFACINGS, AND LININGS

On heavy velvets, replace self-fabric facings which won't show with facings cut from a lightweight fabric; or use a complete lining.

Understitch facings and linings by hand. After facings are understitched, baste, using silk thread and a diagonal stitch, to hold them while pressing.

For interfacings, silk organza, hair canvas, muslin, and traditional sew-in types are good choices.

Avoid fusibles on most velvets, but experiment with them when sewing cotton velvet. They can be applied to the facing or to the entire garment section.

Most velvet garments are lined. Linings eliminate shedding pile and the need for seam finishes. Linings also keep pants from riding up.

Select a lining appropriate for the weight and fiber of the velvet.

POCKETS

Although inseam pockets are best for most velvets, other pocket designs—welt, bound, trouser and patch—also work well, especially on cotton velvet. To reduce bulk, use a lining-weight fabric to line patch pockets and to make pocket sacks on other pocket types.

Apply patch pockets by hand. Using silk thread, baste in place. Then, wrong side up, secure the pocket with a short running stitch. If the pocket will receive a great deal of use, secure with a backstitch.

CLOSURES

Most fasteners are appropriate for velvets. Buttons and button loops, buttonholes, zippers, hooks and eyes, and covered snaps are good choices. Consider current fashion trends and make several samples to see which looks best on your fabric.

For bound buttonholes, use the strip or window method; cut self-fabric welts on the bias and cord them.

Satin, faille, wool, and grosgrain are also good choices for the welts; they are particularly attractive when the same fabric is used as an edge binding or piping on the garment.

For easier construction and more durability, make false bound buttonholes and use covered snaps to fasten the garment. Complete the buttonholes on the outside of the garment, but leave the facing side unfinished. Sew the button into the buttonhole. Then sew the snap socket at the button location and the snap ball on the facing side of the buttonhole.

For machine-stitched buttonholes, lengthen the stitch; and, if possible, widen it. To avoid marring the pile, do not use a buttonhole attachment for machine-stitched buttonholes. If you have a straight-stitch machine, use bound or hand-worked buttonholes; or replace the buttonholes with button loops or a zipper.

For hand-worked buttonholes, machine stitch 1/8″ from each side of the buttonhole and across each end. Cut the buttonhole length with a single-edged razor blade or mat knife. Finish the buttonhole with small buttonhole stitches around the opening.

Use lightweight coil zippers if you opt for this kind of closure. Invisible or hand-stitched zippers are best.

DECORATIVE TRIMS AND BINDINGS

Narrow braid is an attractive decorative trim. Pin the braid by placing the pins parallel to the edge of the braid; baste. Using a zipper foot, machine stitch or hand sew the braid in place. To ease flat trims around corners, use a small running stitch to gather the inside edge of the curve. Press, baste, and stitch.

Cording and round braids are also attractive. Baste them in place; then hand stitch permanently. Or couch them with a zigzag (W,4;L,2) stitch—use matching or contrasting thread.

Faille, satin, and ribbons are good choices for binding garment edges. Use bias strips of the faille and satin.

Hint: *For a professional finish, use a steam iron to shape the bias or ribbons before sewing them to the garment. Hand baste; then stitch, using a zipper foot.*

When joining bias strips of velvet, be sure all strips are seamed on the same grain—preferably the lengthwise grain. Otherwise, the piping will be different shades.

You can also use velvet as a trim to accent garments made of other fabrics. Velvet collars and cuffs, yokes, and piping are just a few ideas.

To eliminate bulk, face velvet collars and cuffs with a firmly woven nonpile fabric such as lining fabric, silk or polyester blouse fabric, or lightweight taffeta or satin.

PRESSING AND FUSING

Experiment with the heat, moisture, and pressure on fabric scraps. All-cotton velvets can withstand a higher heat than filament fibers and blends.

Cover the pressing surface with a Velvaboard, needleboard, thick terry towel, or velvet scrap—pile side up. Place the velvet face down on it; then press the wrong side lightly with a steam iron or steamer. Do not touch the pile when it is damp.

Press rayon, and silk pile velvets from the wrong side. Use only the point of the iron on the stitched line. Do not rest the iron on the fabric. Use a velvet press cloth when pressing the right side and press with the nap. Never allow the iron to touch the pile.

Hint: *For easier and safer pressing, sew a large velvet scrap to a heavy-duty press cloth. The heavier cloth protects the garment from too much moisture.*

To remove shine caused by overpressing, steam and brush with the pile of a velvet scrap.

To revive the nap after fusing or construction pressing, hang it in a steam-filled bathroom. Or steam the face side with a steamer or steam iron

held about 1/2″ away. When dry, brush with a soft brush or self-fabric.

GARMENT CARE

Most velvet garments should be dry-cleaned and steamed, but not pressed. To keep garments clean, vacuum and brush away loose dirt after wearing.

Cotton velvets can be washed when the garment construction, dyes, and other fabrics allow. Some fabrics will actually look richer when washed and tumble dried. Remove the garment from the dryer while it's still damp. Straighten seams and hang it to dry.

Hint: *Turn the garment wrong side out so it won't collect lint.*

Freshen the pile with steam by hanging the garment in the bathroom and filling the bathtub with hot water. Close the door; let the garment dry completely before wearing or handling.

To protect skirts and pants from hanger marks, sew skirt hanger loops into the waistband.

Panné Velvet

Panné velvet is a lightweight pile fabric with the pile pressed in one direction. It can have a knitted or woven backing. (See Velvet and Pile Fabrics for additional sewing suggestions.)

Fabric Characteristics
- Most panné velvets are easy to sew.
- Panné velvet is used for casual and dressy garments.
- Panné velvet has a pile and requires a nap layout.
- It usually requires extra fabric.
- Panné velvet is marred by pins, ripped seamlines, alterations, heat, moisture, and improper pressing.
- Most fabrics creep badly and sometimes pucker during stitching.
- Generally, they don't shed or fray badly.
- Some panné velvets are bulky.
- Some panné velvets curl at raw edges.

PLANNING A GARMENT

DESIGN IDEAS AND PATTERN SELECTION

Panné velvet is a soft, supple fabric with good drape. Designs with unpressed pleats, soft folds, insets, or gathers are particularly attractive. Try to avoid darts.

Select a simple style with a minimum of surface details and structured seaming.

Preshrink the fabric before cutting out, according to the manufacturer's care instructions; adjust the pattern before cutting the fabric.

GARMENT CARE

Check the care recommendations when purchasing to determine the appropriate care. Some fabrics—100 percent rayon panné velvets—require dry-cleaning, while others—triacetate/nylon blends—can be machine washed and tumble dried.

To keep garments clean, vacuum and brush away loose dirt after wearing. Freshen pile with steam by hanging the garment in the bathroom and filling the bathtub with hot water. Close the door; let the garment dry completely before wearing or handling.

To protect skirts and pants from hanger marks, sew skirt hanger loops into the waistband.

SEWING CHECKLIST

Sewing Machine Needles: Universal-H point, Yellow Band, or stretch (HS) needles; sizes 60/8 to 80/12, depending on the fabric weight.

Machine Setting: Stitch length, 2–3mm (8–12 stitches per inch); tension and pressure, variable.

Thread: Long-staple polyester, cotton-wrapped polyester.

Hand Sewing Needles: Sizes 7 to 9.

Sewing Machine Equipment: Roller or even-feed foot, zipper foot.

Layout: Nap; double layer, wrong sides together.

Marking Techniques: Chalk, soap sliver, clips, temporary marking pens, tailor tacks, thread tracing.

Seams: Plain, taped, tissue-stitched.

Hems: Plain, blindstitch, blind catchstitch, machine blindstitch, double-stitched, interfaced, faced.

Seam and Hem Finishes: Single/ply or double/ply, unfinished, pinked, pinked-and-stitched, multi-stitch zigzag, serged, tricot bound, hand overcast, Hong Kong, seam tape.

Facings: Self-fabric facings, smooth-fabric facings, bands, ribbings, bindings.

Interfacing: Usually sew-ins, depending on the fabric and garment design.

Linings: Optional, generally used for outerwear.

Underlinings: Rarely.

Closures: All types.

Pockets: All types.

Fig. 14–6 *From the Kleibacker Group in the Historic Costume and Textile Collection at The Ohio State University, this silk panné velvet fits snugly across the derriere, then explodes into two deep tiers of handkerchief points. (Photo courtesy of Charles Kleibacker.)*

Woven Terry and Velour

Several different fabrics are called velour and terry. Some are stretch fabrics with a knitted base, while others are nonstretch fabrics with a woven base. This section focuses on nonstretch velour and terry. (When sewing stretch terry or velour, see Stretch Terry and Velour.)

Terry and velour are warp-pile fabrics. Some terry cloths have uncut loops on one side with a plain back; others have uncut loops on both sides. Terry velours have cut loops on one side which look like velveteen; and some velours have a sculpted pattern.

Fabric Characteristics
- Terry and velour are easy to sew.
- Both are used for casual garments.
- Terry and velour have a pile and may require a nap layout.
- They usually require extra fabric.
- Some sculptured terry cloths and velours are bulky.
- Velour puckers and creeps when stitched; terry does not.
- Velour sheds.
- Terry and velour shrink and should be laundered before cutting.

PLANNING THE GARMENT

FABRIC AND PATTERN SELECTION

Generally, terry cloth is more absorbent than terry velour; terry velour is more attractive, but has more lint.

Cotton fabrics are most absorbent, followed closely by cotton blends. Synthetic materials are least absorbent.

Better quality fabrics have a closely woven background with closely-packed loops.

Terry and velour are well-suited for very casual garments, tee tops, shorts, slacks, pool or beach cover-ups, bathrobes, and towels. Hoods, wrap fronts, elasticized waists, slip-on tops, and patch pockets are good design features.

Select a pattern with a minimum of seams. To reduce bulk and trim your design, use less bulky easy-care fabrics for bias bindings and front bands. Or use ribbing bands for garment openings, necklines, hems, and sleeve cuffs.

Preshrink the fabric before cutting. Wash and dry the fabric using the method you plan to use on the garment.

SEWING VELOUR AND TERRY

See Pile Fabrics for additional suggestions.

LAYOUT, CUTTING, AND MARKING

Use a nap layout. Spread the fabric with a lengthwise fold, wrong sides together. (To identify the warp, pull a loop.)

Fig. 14–7 *Her terry velour wrap is perfect for relaxing at home or wearing at the pool. (Photo courtesy of Pierre Cardin Beachwear.)*

Some terry fabrics do not require a nap layout. Check twice before cutting.

For better wear, lay out children's garments so the nap runs down.

Most marking can be done with clips.

SEWING CHECKLIST

Sewing Machine Needles: Universal-H or Red Band needles: sizes 70/10 to 100/16, depending on the fabric weight.

Machine Setting: Stitch length, 2–3mm (8–12 stitches per inch); tension and pressure, variable.

Thread: Long-staple polyester, cotton-wrapped polyester, topstitching thread.

Hand Sewing Needles: Sizes 5 to 9.

Sewing Machine Equipment: Roller or even-feed foot, zipper foot, shim.

Equipment and Supplies: Transparent tape.

Layout: Nap, double layer, wrong sides together.

Marking Techniques: Clips, temporary marking pens, pins.

Seams: Plain, double/ply, welt, top-stitched, standing-fell, flat-fell, strap.

Hems: Plain, machine blindstitch, top-stitched, faced, and wrong-side-out.

Hem and Seam Finishes: Single/ply or double/ply; double-stitched, zigzag, multi-stitch zigzag, bound, serged, folded, turned-and-stitched.

Facings and Edge Finishes: Smooth-fabric facings, decorative facings, bindings, ribbings, casings, and bands.

Interfacing: Rarely.

Linings: Rarely.

Closures: Buttons and button loops, machine-stitched buttonholes, zippers, toggles, ties.

Pockets: Inseam and patch.

STITCHING TIPS

Always make a test seam with two 10″ fabric scraps. Set the stitch length for 2.5mm (10 stitches per inch) and a loosely balanced tension. Lighten the pressure if needed.

The test seam should be even, smooth, and without puckers.

SEAMS AND HEMS

Many terry and velour garments are worn as outerwear, so the insides of the garments should be finished attractively. For bulky fabrics, strap and decorative bound seams work well.

Flat-fell, standing-fell, and double/ply serged seams are good choices for lightweight terry fabrics.

For a decorative finish, use a wrong-side-out hem or decorative facing on the outside of the garment.

Generally topstitched hems are best. Finish the raw edge of the hem with serging, multi-stitch zigzag, or a binding; then topstitch.

Topstitching is more attractive on terry than velour. If you don't have a roller foot, wrap the toes of the presser foot with transparent tape to avoid catching the loops. (Some brands have no-snag feet.)

Topstitch with the pile. To emphasize the topstitching, use two strands of regular thread or topstitching thread. Lengthen the stitch for heavier fabrics.

Hint: *Use a zipper foot or a shim when stitching uneven layers.*

FACINGS AND POCKETS

On bulky fabrics, replace self-fabric facings with bindings, bands, or ribbings. To keep facings from popping out, ditch-stitch shoulder and side seams.

Patch and inseam pockets are usually best on terry and velour. When making patch pockets, bind and trim the opening with a lightweight, easy-care fabric. Or face it with a decorative band or ribbon on the outside of the pocket.

CLOSURES

Many designs are more attractive without a fastener; however, ties, machine-stitched buttonholes, and zippers work well if the fastener can't be eliminated.

Depending on the garment design, exposed, slot, and separating zippers are good choices.

Interface button and buttonhole areas.

PRESSING AND GARMENT CARE

Experiment with the heat, moisture, and pressure on fabric scraps. All-cotton velour and terry can withstand a higher heat than blends.

Use a fabric scrap when pressing the right side. Do not allow the iron to touch the velour pile.

To revive the nap after fusing or construction pressing, tumble dry with several damp towels.

Since both fabrics are usually 100 percent cotton, cotton/blend, or synthetic blend, they do not require special treatment. Turn the garment inside out; machine wash and tumble dry. Use a fabric softener to reduce lint.

Tufted Piles

Chenilles have a tufted pattern design. Tufted fabrics are made by punching tufts into a previously woven fabric. Once pulled through, the tufts bloom or untwist, to hold them in place.

Although sometimes available as yardage, they are more often available in the form of bedspreads.

Tufted fabrics are much cheaper and quicker to sew than other pile fabrics.

SEWING CHECKLIST

Sewing Machine Needles: Universal-H point or Red Band needles; sizes 80/12 to 90/14.

Machine Setting: Stitch length 2–2.5mm (10–12 stitches per inch); tension, loosely balanced.

Thread: Long-staple polyester or cotton-wrapped polyester.

Hand Sewing Needles: Sizes 7 to 9.

Layout: Nap, single layer, right side up.

Seams: Plain, double-stitched, double/ply.

Seam and Hem Finishes: Single/ply or double/ply, double-stitched, zigzag, multi-stitch zigzag, serged.

Hems: Plain, blindstitch, topstitched.

Edge Finishes: Casings, bands, ribbing, smooth-fabric facings, bias facings.

Interfacing: Rarely.

Linings: Rarely.

Fabric Characteristics

- Chenille bedspreads shrink and should be laundered before cutting.
- These fabrics have a pile and require a nap layout.
- They have an uneven surface with thick and thin sections.
- Some areas are bulky.
- They frequently have a pattern which must be positioned attractively. (See Prints.)

PLANNING A GARMENT

DESIGN IDEAS AND PATTERN SELECTION

These fabrics are ideal for elegant, casual designs—slipover tops, blouson jackets, swimsuit toppers, and loungewear.

Select a pattern with a minimum of seams. Look for ribbed band trims, elastic waistbands and sleeve finishes, wrap designs, and exposed zippers. Avoid patch pockets and topstitched details.

Preshrink the fabric before cutting out. Wash and dry the fabric using the method you plan to use on the garment.

SEWING TUFTED PILE FABRICS

For additional suggestions, see Pile Fabrics and Corduroy.

LAYOUT

Use a nap layout. Spread the fabric in a single layer, right side up. If you're using a bedspread, the hemmed edges may not be on the straight grain and should not be used like selvages. Mark the lengthwise grain and crossgrain with a temporary marking pen or thread tracing.

STITCHING TIPS

Always make a test seam with two 10″ fabric scraps. Set the stitch length for 2–2.5mm (10–12 stitches per inch), with a loosely balanced tension. Lighten the pressure if needed.

The test seam should be even and smooth without puckers.

Hint: *Make inseam pockets from lightweight, smooth fabric. Pocket openings should be stayed to prevent stretching.*

CLOSURES

Machine-stitched buttonholes and zippers work well if the fastener can't be eliminated.

Depending on the garment design, exposed, slot, and separating zippers are good choices. Stay the zipper plackets with a strip of fusible interfacing on the seam allowance before setting the zipper.

PRESSING AND GARMENT CARE

Experiment with heat, moisture, and pressure on fabric scraps. All-cotton fabrics can withstand a higher heat than blends.

Since fabrics are usually 100 percent cotton or a cotton/blend, they do not require any special treatment.

Machine wash and tumble dry. Use a fabric softener to reduce lint. If the pile becomes crushed, tumble dry with several damp towels.

Fake Furs

Fake-fur fabrics are not just fakes, but fashion fabrics in their own right. Many of these fabulous fabrics look like the real thing—mink, sable, seal, beaver, broadtail, Persian lamb, leopard, jaguar, tiger, zebra, python, pony, fox, chinchilla, and otter—while others are frankly fakes, wild and imaginative.

Fake furs are pile fabrics on a woven or knitted backing. Available in a variety of weights, thicknesses, and pile depths, most have a modacrylic, acrylic, or polyester pile with a backing of a different fiber. Some are as lightweight and easy to handle as corduroy, while others are very stiff and bulky.

The first fake furs, introduced in 1929, were made of mohair, alpaca, or wool blended with rayon for luster. Usually gray or tan, they had a woven base and were used for inexpensive winter coats.

By the mid-forties, fake furs were beginning to resemble real pelts. Piles were furrier and denser, but not heavy. Many fabrics had knit backings, which made them more pliable.

Since then, the versatility of synthetic fibers and finishes, combined with human ingenuity, have led to a variety of prints and sculptured fake furs,

as well as to a combination of long "guard hairs" and short underfur.

Today most fake-fur fabrics are made of modacrylic fibers which are flame-resistant.

Fabric Characteristics
- Fake-fur fabrics are easy to sew.
- Most fake-fur fabrics have a nap.
- Mistakes, distortions, and crooked seams can frequently be hidden in the pile.
- Fake furs have a lot of lint and fuzz, which can damage your machine if it isn't brushed off frequently.
- Fake furs are bulky and will add pounds to your figure.
- Modacrylic fabrics are very heat-sensitive and are easily damaged in pressing.
- Some shed and/or mat.
- Fabrics with cotton-knit backings may shrink excessively.
- Less expensive to clean than real fur, fake furs are more porous, nonallergenic, and mothproof.
- Fake furs are not as warm as real furs.
- Fake furs are difficult to topstitch.

Machine Needles: Universal-H point, Red Band, or jeans(HJ) needles, 80/12 to 100/16, depending on the fabric weight.

Machine Setting: Stitch length, 2.5–3mm (8–10 stitches per inch), depending on the fabric weight; tension, loosely balanced; pressure, light to normal.

Thread: Long-staple polyester or cotton-wrapped polyester for light- and medium-weight fabrics; heavy-duty or topstitching thread for heavy fabrics.

Hand Sewing Needles: Sizes 5 to 7.

Sewing Machine Equipment: Roller or even-feed foot, zipper foot, shim.

Equipment and Supplies: Very sharp scissors, glass-headed pins, wire dog brush or comb, wallpaper roller, bobby pins or spring hair clips, sponge, push pins, awl, tapestry needle, Velvaboard or thick terry towel, twill or seam tape, transparent or drafting tape, wadding or polyester fleece.

Layout: Nap, single layer, wrong side up.

Marking Techniques: Pins, temporary marking pens, chalk, pencil, felt-tip pens, clips.

Seams: Fur, plain/fur, taped.

Hems: Plain, faced, double-hemmed, and interfaced.

Facings: Self-fabric, plain fabrics, synthetic suedes, and leathers.

Edge Finishes: Bands (fabric, leather, or synthetic suedes), bindings, ribbings.

Interfacing: Optional; avoid fusibles.

Underlining: Sometimes, depending on fabric and design.

Lining: Usually on outerwear; traditional facing/lining or edge-to-edge. Optional on other garments.

Closures: Large, covered hooks and eyes; covered snaps; decorative buttons with loops made of elastic, smooth fabrics, or synthetic leathers and suedes; frogs; leather tabs; toggles; decorative fasteners; large zippers; faced and bound buttonholes.

PLANNING A GARMENT

PURCHASING FAKE FURS

Although fake furs—like most fabrics—are usually purchased because the pattern, design, or color appeals to you, some knowledge of fabric quality will reduce disappointments.

Better quality fabrics have a dense, resilient pile. Fold the fabric, wrong sides together. If the backing shows through, it will probably show at garment edges.

Feel the pile with your hand; then brush the fabric in all directions with your hand. It should move easily and spring back without a separation. If it mats, sheds, or feels sticky, select another fabric.

Examine the backing, which may be knitted or woven. It should be firm and supple, not too soft or too stiff. If it's soft and stretchy, it can be underlined so it will hang attractively; if it's stiff and heavy, it will be difficult to sew.

Generally, fabrics with a knit base are easier to sew than those with a woven backing; the exception is knits which have been coated with a resin finish.

Fake-fur fabrics look more expensive if, when examined closely, the individual fibers are of several shades instead of a single color.

Select lining and interfacing fabrics with the same care properties. Since most fake furs do not soil easily, dark-colored linings are usually best.

DESIGN IDEAS AND PATTERN SELECTION

A few patterns are especially designed for fake furs, but many others are suitable. Some of the many choices include coats, capes, ponchos, ruanas, blazers, bomber jackets, cardigans, vests, hats, muffs, pillows, and bedspreads.

Generally, the best looking garments are simple, uncluttered designs with interesting silhouettes. Avoid intricate details, pleats, gathers, sharp creases, and double-breasted styles. Details such as darts, tabs, yokes, buttonholes, and welts will disappear into the pile.

Let the garment style guide you in selecting an appropriate facing. Self-fabric, synthetic suedes, leathers, and medium-weight plain fabrics are all appropriate.

Most fake-fur garments will be more attractive and more comfortable if lined. Edge-to-edge linings, as well as traditional facing/lining combinations, are good choices.

FABRIC PREPARATION

Read the manufacturer's care instructions carefully. Some fake furs can be machine washed and dried, some must be line dried, and a few require dry-cleaning.

Preshrink the fabric, either by steam pressing or laundering, before cutting. To avoid matting, treat the material as a fine fabric and handle as little as possible.

When laundering, use a delicate wash cycle, mild detergent, and fabric softener in the rinse water. Roll the fabric in a terry towel to remove excess moisture. Shake vigorously and gently stretch to the original measurements. Hang over a shower rod or on a plastic hanger to dry. Use a dog brush or comb to restore the pile's fluff.

Hint: *Be careful when line drying. The weight of the water can stretch the fabric out of shape.*

PATTERN PREPARATION

Adjust the pattern before cutting. Some pile fabrics are difficult to rip and restitch without marring.

To perfect the fit, preview the design, and perfect your sewing skills, make a test garment in a heavyweight muslin or canvas. When making a coat or jacket, try it on over your regular clothing; and, if it will have shoulder pads, pin them in for the fitting. Make all adjustments on the muslin and mark all stitching lines with a lead pencil. Carefully rip the muslin apart and use it as the pattern.

If you didn't make a test garment, cut separate pattern pieces for the right and left sides of the garment to avoid cutting mistakes. Trim away any excess tissue if you haven't already, and mark the pattern with arrows to indicate the pile direction.

Eliminate decorative flaps, tabs, and epaulets. For easy construction, replace patch and slashed pockets with inseam pockets, unless they are important to the overall garment design.

When using fake fur as a lining, purchase the pattern one size larger to allow for the additional lining thickness. Check the sleeve width before cutting to be sure it won't be too tight.

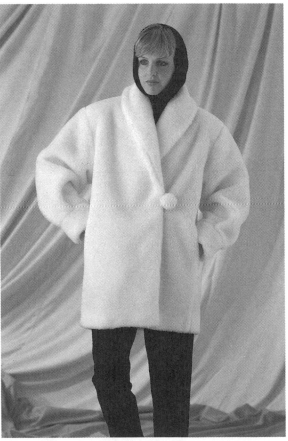

Fig. 14–8 *Made of modacrylic fibers, fake fur fabrics are fun to wear and easy to sew. (Photo courtesy of Kwik Sew Pattern Co., Inc.)*

Hint: *Measure the sleeve width; then measure and mark this amount on the fabric. Wrap the fabric around your arm with the "fur" toward your arm to check the size. If necessary, increase the width of the sleeve and the body of the garment.*

To reduce bulk, eliminate straight garment/facing seamlines and cut facings in onepiece with the garment. Or eliminate facings and use an edge-to-edge lining.

Eliminate back neck facings and recut the back lining pattern so it will extend to the neckline. When possible, eliminate nonfitting seamlines such as those at the center back.

If using the fur seam which has 1/8" seam allowances, trim the seam allowances on the pattern first.

SEWING FAKE-FUR FABRICS

LAYOUT, CUTTING, AND MARKING

Drape the fabric over a chair and stand back to study it. Notice any special design or pile characteristics which will influence the fabric's placement on the figure.

Fabrics with prominent fur marking patterns may require large amounts of additional yardage. The precise amount of fabric needed is sometimes difficult to estimate.

Use a nap layout. Generally long piles run down; some piles can be run horizontally; and sheared fur lookalikes such as beaver and seal can run up.

Spread the fabric in a single layer with the wrong side up. A double thickness is not only more difficult to cut, it's so bulky you may inadvertently increase or decrease the garment size.

Mark the pile direction and any pelt markings with chalk on the wrong side of the fabric, then lay out the entire pattern wrong side up. Using long pins, pin through the backing only; or use tape or weights to hold the pattern pieces in place. To avoid stretching, don't let the fabric hang off the edge of the table.

Hint: *For easier cutting, trace around the pattern pieces with a lead pencil or felt-tip pen and remove the pattern.*

If the fake fur has stripes, see Stripes; if it has a plaidlike pattern, see Plaids.

Fabrics with intricate pelt markings are more difficult to match and cut when they don't have the design printed on the reverse side of the fabric. If you can't transfer the pelt markings to the reverse, spread the fabric, right side up; then place the pattern pieces on the fabric so the design will be positioned attractively on the garment. Using weights to secure the pattern, cut out the garment sections with 1" seam allowances. Remove the pattern; turn the cut sections over; and reposition the pattern on the back of the fabric. Trim away the excess seam allowances by cutting through the backing only.

Before cutting the collar, consider how it will look on the garment front. The pile can run down, toward the center back, or away from the center back.

Double-check to be sure there is a pair of each section before cutting. Cut carefully through the fabric backing with the shears' points. Hold the fabric up off the table, separating the fur as you cut, to avoid cutting through the pile.

Hint: *Fake furs can also be cut with a single-edged razor blade, mat knife, or Olfa Touch Knife; but I find using the tips of the shears easiest.*

Mark the fake fur using the method of your choice: pins, temporary marking pens, pencils, or chalk. And, if you're using conventional plain seams, short clips work well.

Hint: *Use a small hand vacuum to pick up loose pile fibers. Vacuum the cut edges of the garment sections to reduce shedding at the sewing machine.*

STITCHING TIPS

Make several test seams. Set the stitch length for 2.5–3mm (8–10 stitches per inch), a normal to light pressure, and a looser tension. Hold the fabric taut when stitching. Stitch with the pile, even when you must stitch against the grain.

During construction, clean the machine frequently to remove the accumulated lint and pile.

Use long flower or glass-headed pins, clothespins, spring hair clips, bobby pins, or wooden toothpicks to baste seams together.

Hint: *To remove pins easily, set them with the heads toward the raw edge. Try to avoid stitching over them.*

SEAMS

There are two basic seams for fake fur fabrics: the traditional fur seam, which has 1/8″ seam allowances; or the conventional plain seam with 5/8″ seam allowances. Both are frequently used in the same garment.

Use the plain seams when sewing the fake fur to a lining or facing.

When basting, push the pile away from the raw edges toward the body of the garment. I use the blades of my scissors to stroke the pile away from the seamline. A damp sponge also works well on some fabrics.

To match intersecting seams, insert a needle into the seamlines and pin.

Examine the seam after stitching; and, if necessary, pull the pile out of the seam with a dog comb or brush.

Stabilize shoulder, neckline, and long side seams with preshrunk twill seam tape stitched into the seamline. Or, for a more flexible seam which will also protect the lining from abrasion, hand stitch the tape over the seam allowances after the seam is stitched.

Stabilize the front/facing foldline with twill tape so the front edges will hang perpendicular to the

floor. Center the preshrunk tape over the foldline and tack in place with a short running stitch.

Stabilize the openings of inseam pockets with tape, so they will not stretch out of shape.

FUR SEAM

This seam works particularly well for fur toys and seamlines which are not at garment edges.
1. Trim the seam allowances to 1/8″.
2. Brush the pile toward the garment.

Hint: *An easy way to keep the pile out of the seamline is to tape it. Place strips of drafting tape 1/2″ from the raw edges.*

3. Right sides together, zigzag (W,4;L,2) the two edges together. The needle will swing off the fabric when it swings to the right.

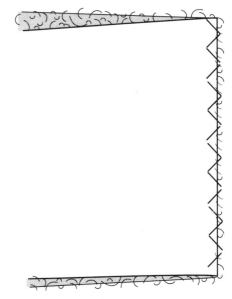

Fig. 14–10

Hint: *Overcast the edges together by hand if the fabric is unusually bulky and seamlines are converging. Or serge the seams with a loosely balanced stitch. An abutted seam also works well. Begin with the sections wrong sides up. Butt the edges to be joined and zigzag (W,3;L,2) them together.*

4. Lay the garment out flat wrong side up; press the seam with the scissor handles or a wallpaper roller, to flatten the seamline.

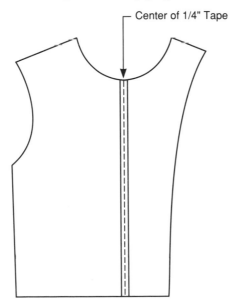

Center of 1/4″ Tape

Fig. 14–9

PLAIN FUR SEAMS

Many seamsters prefer this seam, which can be used if you don't have a zigzag machine. It also works well for garment edges and garment/lining seams.

1. If you don't have a zigzag machine, stitch a plain seam right sides together.

2. Using small trimming or appliqué scissors to reduce the bulk, trim away the fur pile on the seam allowances.

Fig. 14–11

Hint: *If the fabric has a deep pile, trim away the pile in the seam allowances before stitching. Stitch using a zipper foot.*

3. Steam the seams open and finger press. If the seams won't stay pressed open, use a loose catchstitch to sew them to the fabric backing; or use a permanent glue to glue the seam allowances to the backing.

4. Brush the seamlines with a wire dog brush to pull the pile out.

DARTS

To mark darts, insert a pin straight down through each matchpoint. Carefully remove the pattern and mark the pin locations with a marking pen.

Stitch the darts using the fur or plain seam technique. When using a plain seam, slash the dart through the center after stitching and trim away the pile in the seam allowances. Glue or catch stitch the dart open.

COLLARS, LAPELS, AND SLEEVES

Face fake-fur collars and lapels with self-fabric, synthetic suedes, or smooth, plain-weave fabrics.

For a luxurious, big-fur look, use self-fabric facings. Experiment with both the fur and plain seams to see which produces the best finish.

When using synthetic suede or a smooth fabric facing, assemble the collar like real fur with taped edges and a hand-sewn facing (see Chapter 7). Or assemble it in the usual manner by machine stitching the fake fur and facing, right sides together.

Most sleeves can be eased into the armholes without difficulty. Make sleeve heads from polyester fleece so the sleeve caps will hold their shape for the life of the garment.

If the sleeves have excessive ease, make small darts in the caps or reduce the ease.

EDGE FINISHES AND HEMS

For a decorative finish, bind the edges of the collar, lapel, and/or hems. Experiment with different applications and various bindings made of bias strips, ribbon, synthetic suede, or leather. If you plan to bind the edge, shear the pile at the edge to reduce bulk.

Hint: *To avoid shearing away too much, stitch a row of guide stitching the desired distance from the edge.*

Before applying the binding to the edge, steam press to shape it.

Depending on the pile length, use a plain hem or a faced hem on fake-fur garments. Mark the hemline with long, glass-headed pins. Interface the hem for a softer finish.

PLAIN HEM

Use a plain hem 2″ to 2 1/2″ wide for fabrics with short- or medium-length pile.

1. Measure and trim the hem allowance to the desired depth.

2. Finish the edge with seam tape, tricot binding, serging, or a zigzag stitch.

Hint: *If the garment is lined, leave the edge unfinished.*

3. Interface the hem, if desired, with a bias strip or polyester fleece 2″ to 2 1/2″ wide.

4. Using a catchstitch, hem twice—once midway down the hem allowance and again, at the edge.

FACED HEM

To reduce bulk on medium-length and long-pile fabrics, use a faced hem.

1. Measure and trim the hem allowance to 1/2" to 1" wide.

2. Cut a bias facing 2 1/2" to 3" wide; or, if garment is lined, use 1"-wide twill tape.

3. If the garment is flared, press the facing so it curves to fill the edge of the hem.

4. Right sides together, stitch the facing or twill tape to the raw edge of the garment with a 1/4" seam.

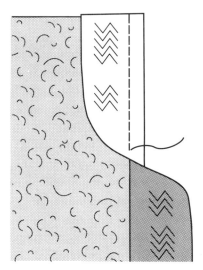

Fig. 14–12

5. Press the facing toward the raw edge.

6. Fold the hem into position; and, using a catchstitch, hem twice.

7. If the garment is lined, sew the lining to the twill tape.

CLOSURES

Although other fasteners and button loops are usually better, buttonholes are possible and sometimes the perfect answer for a particular garment.

When using hooks and eyes on fake-fur fabrics, insert them between the layers of the garment and facing; or cut a small slit in the fake fur and push the hook through. From the reverse side, sew the hook securely to the fake-fur backing.

Always interface button and buttonhole areas. On short pile and flat fake furs, use faced openings, machine-stitched buttonholes, or traditional bound buttonholes. On medium-and long-pile fakes, use faced openings or bound buttonholes. Machine-stitched buttonholes aren't recommended since they will be hidden in the pile of the fur fabric, but they are a viable answer for unusual situations.

To machine stitch buttonholes, mark the buttonhole location on the face side of the fabric with pins. Then, with the pile held away from the marked line, stitch around the buttonhole. Pull out any pile caught above the buttonhole.

When making bound buttonholes, use either the traditional strip method or the windowpane method. (See Chapter 24.) Use smooth fabrics, synthetic suedes, leathers, or ribbons instead of self-fabric for the buttonhole welts. Catchstitch the edges of the welts to the fabric back. If the fabric is too bulky to machine stitch around the buttonholes, use a short hand backstitch.

Suitable for all fake-fur fabrics, the faced buttonhole is an inconspicuous buttonhole alternative.

FACED BUTTONHOLE

1. Mark the buttonhole on the reverse side of the fabric with a pin at each end of the buttonhole.

2. Using the pins as a guide for the buttonhole location, pin or tape the nap away from the buttonhole.

3. From a firmly woven lining or nonwoven interfacing fabric, cut a facing 2" wide and 2" longer than the buttonhole.

4. Right sides together, center and pin the facing over the buttonhole.

5. Turn the garment section over; with the wrong side up, machine stitch around the buttonhole, using a short stitch (1.25mm or 20 stitches per inch). Take two stitches across each end.

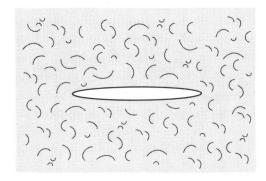

Fig. 14–13

6. Check under the facing to be sure the pile was not caught in the stitching. If it was, use a tapestry needle to pull it out.

7. Slash the buttonhole and turn the facing to the reverse side (Fig. 14–13).

8. Catchstitch the edges of the facing to the fabric back.

9. To finish the garment facing, slash the facing and overcast the edges by hand; then slipstitch the facing to the wrong side of the buttonhole.

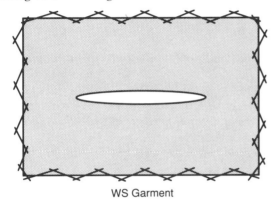

WS Garment

Fig. 14–14

BUTTONS AND BUTTON LOOPS

The buttons on fake furs can be very distinctive or very inconspicuous. For designs with button closures, consider covering button molds with leather, synthetic suede, self-fabric, or smooth fabrics to match trims on the pockets or buttonholes.

When sewing on buttons, make the thread shank as long as the fabric layers are thick.

Using topstitching or waxed thread, sew the button securely through more than one fabric layer. If the garment is for a child or will be handled roughly, sew a backing button to the facing side of the garment.

Make button loops from leather, synthetic suede, round elastic, cord, or plain fabrics. Cut loops 2" longer than the finished button loop. Using an awl, make a hole in the garment foldline. Insert the ends of the loop into the holes. Hand sew the ends of the button loops securely to the back of the fake fur.

ZIPPERS

To make zippers easier to use and sew, finish the edges of the opening with smooth fabric facing,

bands, ribbings, synthetic suede or leather. Then sew the zipper into the placket. For a more attractive finish when the zipper is sewn directly to the fake fur, sew it in place by hand.

Set the zipper into a conventional slot placket with the zipper teeth concealed or exposed; or use an invisible zipper.

To reduce bulk at the zipper placket and to prevent the pile catching in the zipper, shear away the pile on the seam allowances.

BELTS AND BELT CARRIERS

Depending on the garment design and prevailing fashion, belts can be synthetic or real suede, leather, fabric, or fake-fur fabric.

To make belt carriers from synthetic suede, real leather, woven braid, or grosgrain ribbon, cut the carriers 1/2" wide and twice the width of the belt. Fold the carrier in half, wrong sides together; and edgestitch along both sides.

Using pins, mark the locations for the belt carrier ends on the side seams of the garment. Rip the seam at each marked point about 1/4". Insert the belt carrier ends into the openings and adjust the length. Restitch the side seams and secure the ends of the carriers by hand or machine.

POCKETS

Inseam pockets are usually best; however, welt, slot, and patch pockets can be also used. On slot pockets, cut the welts from synthetic suede, leather, ribbon, or a smooth fabric. On welt pockets, the welts can also be cut from self-fabric and lined with a lining fabric or ribbon.

Line patch pockets with lining material. Apply them by hand or by machine.

INTERFACINGS, UNDERLININGS, AND LININGS

Some fake-fur fabrics have enough body to be used without interfacing; however, most garments will maintain their shape and look more like real fur designs when interfacings are used.

Use the crispness and weight of the backing as a guide when considering the need for underlinings. Underline lightweight or soft fake-fur fabrics with muslin or a medium-weight interfacing material.

For warmth without weight, underline with lamb's wool or Armo wool. For a warmer garment, underline with needlepunch, lightweight Thinsulate, or polyester fleece.

Select a lining fabric to complement the fake fur in style, weight, quality, and care requirements. Firmly woven satin, brocade, crepe, sateen, taffeta, poplin, denim, wool flannel, synthetic suede, and lightweight corduroy are good lining choices.

If the fake looks like the real thing, avoid a tattletale lining by choosing a good-quality, classic lining fabric that might be used to line a real fur.

If the fake is a fun fur, the sky is the limit. The lining can be a wild contrasting color or an inconspicuous neutral.

Understitch edge-to-edge linings by hand to prevent them rolling to the outside. Try to avoid machine understitching.

PRESSING

Test press on a scrap of fabric. Fake-fur fabrics are sensitive to heat and moisture. Some fabrics can be pressed with steam while others cannot; experiment with fabric scraps to determine the best pressing technique.

Do not let the iron touch the pile side of the fabric. To avoid flattening the pile, cover the pressing table with self-fabric, a Velvaboard, or thick terry towels.

Always press in the direction of the pile; use a clapper, if needed, to flatten the seams. When pressing lapels, facings, or collars, use self-fabric or a thick towel as a press cloth.

GARMENT CARE

Although many fake-fur fabrics can be machine washed and dried some must be dry-cleaned. Consider the garment construction and other materials used before laundering washable fakes.

To freshen the appearance between cleanings, use a wire comb or brush. Gently stroke the pile with the nap.

Fake-fur fabrics are very sensitive to heat. Cigarette ashes, curling irons, light bulbs, hot radiators, and warm irons may melt and flatten the fibers.

Fake-fur fabrics repel rain but an excessive amount of moisture will mat and flatten them. Shake the garment to remove excess moisture; then hang on a padded hanger away from direct heat until dry.

Store the garment on a padded or shaped hanger. Try to avoid crushing it in a full closet. For long-term storage, a cool, dry, uncrowded closet is best.

CHAPTER 15
Felt and Felted Fabrics

Felt

True felt is made from wool, fur, mohair, cotton, rayon, or synthetic fibers. The fibers are pounded, compressed, shrunk, and felted by the application of moisture, temperature change, pressure, and abrasion.

Since felt has a unique no-fray quality, it is very easy to sew.

Fabric Characteristics
- Felt does not ravel.
- It is easy to sew.
- Felt is difficult to dry-clean.
- It is susceptible to abrasion in wear and dry cleaning.
- Felt may tear under strain.
- Felt cannot be mended easily.
- Felt does not recover well and will bag at knees, elbows, and seat.
- Felt is easily damaged by steam.
- Some felts have a nap.

PLANNING A GARMENT

PATTERN AND FABRIC SELECTION

Felts are fun fabrics, which make wonderful one-of-a-kind garments. Let your imagination run wild

Fig. 15–1 *Make it fun; make it fancy; but make it felt. (Photo courtesy of the Simplicity Pattern Co.)*

and create something outlandish, to utilize the unique no-fray quality of these inexpensive materials.

Choose jacket, coat, cape, poncho, vests, sportswear, skirt, hat, bag, and children's patterns designed for crisp fabrics.

Simple lines and a minimum of pattern pieces are best. Since the fabric will tear when stressed, avoid close-fitting designs and patterns with ease or darts. Designs with gathers and flares are good choices.

Hint: *Don't overlook patterns for synthetic suedes and bathrobe patterns that can be used for jackets and coats.*

One of my favorite designs was a "dinosaur coat" created in the early seventies by English designer Zandra Rhodes. Rhodes used white felt with seams on the outside cut to simulate the scaly backbone of a dinosaur. She also added a large "corsage" of Matisse-inspired silk-screened flowers which had been embroidered and quilted.

Many felts are 72″ wide—the same width as a twin sheet. To determine the yardage requirements, lay out the pattern on a sheet. Then measure the sheet from the top of the first pattern piece to bottom of the last one.

Trim away the seam allowances on all edges which will be bound. Reduce seam allowances to 1/4″ for raw-edge finishes.

Eliminate straight seams by overlapping and pinning the pattern pieces together. Since felt has no grain, changing the grain on one or both of the garment sections will not affect the hang of the garment. When possible, change darts to seamlines.

SEWING FELT

LAYOUT, CUTTING, AND MARKING

Steam press the fabric before laying out. Steam carefully to avoid shrinking the fabric unevenly.

If the felt has a nap, use a nap layout.

Felt has no grain. Tilt pattern pieces slightly if needed for fabric economy.

STITCHING TIPS

Make a test seam, using a stitch length of 2.5–3mm (8–10 stitches per inch). Adjust the pressure if needed.

Staystitch 1/4″ from the neckline, armscye, front, waistline edges.

SEAMS, DARTS, AND EDGE FINISHES

Seams can be quite plain or very fancy, depending on the garment design, seam location, and your mood.

Plain, double/ply, topstitched, and welt seams are good choices for inconspicuous seaming. They look particularly nice in unlined outerwear.

Use the no-fray quality of the fabric to create variations of the strap and nonwoven lapped seams by pinking the edges. Or stitch plain seams on the outside and pink the edges. For something really different, try the Zandra Rhodes seam (see Chapter 21).

If the design has darts, stitch the darts as usual and press. Slash the dart, stopping 1/2″ from the point; press open. Topstitch each side 1/16″ from the dart line. Trim close to stitching on the underside.

If desired, assemble felt garments using the techniques for Ultrasuede.

Attractive edge finishes include bindings made of leather, felt, or synthetic suede; braids; and pinked edges.

Hint: *For more body, fuse a facing to edges which will be pinked.*

CLOSURES

The slashed buttonhole is the easiest fastener, but regular machine-stitched buttonholes, button loops, toggles, frogs, ties, decorative clasps, and zippers—plain or decorative—are also attractive.

When regular machine-stitched buttonholes are used, lengthen the stitch around the buttonhole; and stitch only once.

Use reinforcement buttons on children's garments.

PRESSING AND GARMENT CARE

Use little or no moisture when pressing.

When purchasing true felt, check the care requirements on the bolt end. Most felts have a very limited life and discarding the garment is frequently more feasible than cleaning it.

Felted Fabrics

Unlike true felt, which is made by felting raw fibers, felted fabrics—boiled wool, wadmal, loden, melton, and bunting fleece—are made from fabrics which have been shrunk and fulled to produce a feltlike material. Compared to felt, they are frequently less dense, drape better, and are more resistant to abrasion.

This section focuses on felted wovens such as duffel, frieze, loden, and wadmal, which are finished on both sides, but many of the techniques can be applied to face-finished fabrics such as beaver, broadcloth, kersey, and melton. When sewing this latter group, review the section on Coatings.

Boiled wool, sometimes called Geiger, is made of 100 percent merino wool which has been dyed, knitted, shrunk, and fulled. Readily available by the yard in two weights—medium (16 ounces) and heavy (24 ounces), it has the suppleness and comfort of a knit as well as the stability, shape retention, and warmth of a woven fabric. It is resistant to wind and rain and wears like iron.

Bunting fleece is another knitted fabric which has been shrunk and felted. Made of Dacron polyester or polypropylene (olefin), it is a deep-pile, reversible fabric with good shape retention. Warm, soft, and lightweight, it retains its insulation properties when wet, dries quickly, and breathes. The best known bunting fabrics are Chinella®, Polarfleece®, Polarplus™, and Polarlite®.

Duffel is a dense, twill-weave woolen with a heavy nap. Originally made in Duffel, Belgium, it was used during World War II to make waterproof, hooded coats for sailors.

Felted wovens are shrunk and fulled 20 to 50 percent so the weave is obscured. Frequently stiff and thick, these heavy coatings can be finished on one or both sides.

Frieze is a heavy, twill-weave coating with a rough nap. Made in Ireland for several centuries, it may have originated in the Netherlands.

Loden is a fleecy, waterproof coating woven from coarse, oily wool. Originally made in Loderers, Austria, the most popular color is a shade (loden) of green.

Wadmal is a coarse, twill-weave fabric made in the Scandinavian countries.

All felted fabrics have the unique no-fray quality of felt, making them very easy to sew. And felted fabrics are relatively easy to make at home if you have the time and patience (instructions later in this chapter).

Fabric Characteristics
- Felted fabrics do not fray.
- They are very easy to sew.
- Some felted fabrics are very thick and bulky.
- Most felted fabrics are expensive.
- Felted fabrics have a nap.

Fig. 15–2 *Louis Feraud's super-short felted wool jacket is trimmed with black binding. (Photo courtesy of Louis Feraud—Paris, Haute Couture Autumn/Winter Collection, 1987/1988.)*

SEWING CHECKLIST

Machine Needles: For boiled wool and bunting fleece—Universal-H point or Yellow Band needles. For felted wovens—Universal-H point or Red Band needles; sizes 70/10 to 90/14.

Machine Setting: Stitch length 2.5–3mm (8–10 stitches per inch); tension, loosely balanced.

Hand Sewing Needles: Sizes 6 to 9.

Thread: Long-staple polyester, cotton-wrapped polyester, mercerized cotton.

Equipment and Supplies: Sharp shears, extra long pins, drafting tape.

Layout: Nap. Medium weights—double/lay; heavyweights—single/lay, right side up.

Marking Techniques: Clips, temporary marking pens, pins.

Seams: Plain—topstitched, double/ply, welt. Decorative—abutted, strap, slot, nonwoven lapped, bound-and-lapped, bound-and-wrapped, wrong-side-out, and serged.

Edge Finishes: Braid, bias bindings, synthetic suede or leather bindings.

Interfacings, Underlinings, Linings: Generally not used.

- Boiled wool has residual shrinkage and must be preshrunk.
- Bunting fleece is machine-washable and dries quickly.
- Bunting fabrics do not absorb odors.
- Polarfleece is heavier and tends to pill more than Polarplus.
- Polarlite is lighter than Polarfleece.
- Chinella is softer and drapes better than Polarfleece and Polarplus. It has a nubby texture which does not pill.

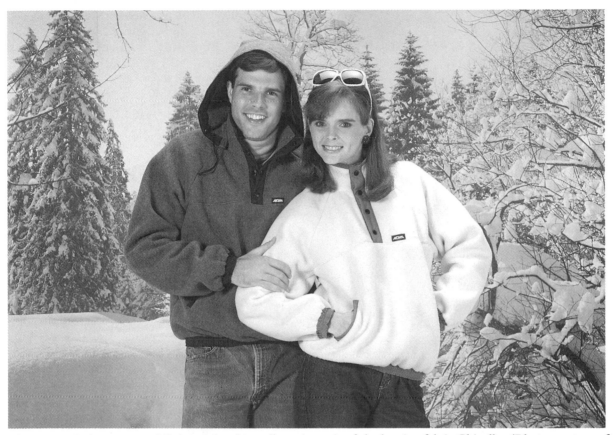

Fig. 15–3 *Soft, warm, and lightweight, this pullover is made of the bunting fabric Chinella. (Photo courtesy of Altra, New Richmond, Indiana.)*

PLANNING A GARMENT

PATTERN AND FABRIC SELECTION

Boiled wool and felted wovens are well-suited for vests, coats, capes, ponchos, skirts, skiwear, and children's garments.

Bunting fabrics are suitable for lightweight wraps, sweatshirts, pullovers, jackets, and robes, as well as paddings for bicycle shorts, linings, and insulating shells worn under windbreakers or windproof outer garments.

The classic, unlined, braid-trimmed jacket, made famous by the Austrian manufacturer Geiger is one of the most popular garments for boiled wool.

Hint: *When making a washable garment of boiled wool, purchase an additional 1/4 yard of fabric.*

Choose a pattern with simple lines and a minimum number of pattern pieces. Eliminate all facings, linings, and interfacings. Trim away the seam allowances on all edges which will be finished with a braid or binding.

If the fabric is more than 1/4″ thick and too bulky for conventional seams, trim away the seam allowances and make abutted, slot or strap seams.

Preshrink the fabric and braid before cutting. You can send it to the dry cleaner or do it yourself with a good steam iron and press cloth.

Most felted fabric garments require dry cleaning. If you plan to handwash the garment, handwash the fabric and braid in Wooltone before cutting out. Roll it in a towel to remove excess moisture; lay it flat to dry.

SEWING FELTED FABRICS

LAYOUT, CUTTING, AND MARKING

Boiled wool, felted wovens, and buntings look the same on both sides; select and mark the "face" side with drafting tape.

Use a nap layout. When cutting heavy, bulky fabrics, spread the fabric, right side up, in a single layer.

STITCHING TIPS

Make a test seam, using a stitch length of 2.5–3mm (8–10 stitches per inch) and a loosely balanced tension, stretching slightly as you stitch. Adjust the pressure if needed.

Staystitch 1/4″ from the neckline, armscye, front, waistline edges.

If the design has darts, stitch the darts as usual. Slash the dart, stopping 1/2″ from the point; press the dart open. Topstitch each side 1/16″ from the dartline; then trim close to the underside.

SEAMS AND SEAM FINISHES

Use plain seams for inconspicuous seaming. Trim to 1/4″ or 3/8″. Since the fabric doesn't fray, you can leave seams unfinished or overcast them by hand or machine, separately or together.

Topstitched and welt seams are especially attractive on light- and medium-weight fabrics. Generally, the fabrics have enough give that curved seams will lie flat without clipping.

For decorative seams, consider abutted, strap, bound-and-lapped, bound-and-stitched, or wrong-side-out. All of these seams work especially well on thick felted fabrics.

And if you have a serger, don't overlook decorative serged seams.

HOW TO MAKE FELTED FABRICS

HAND METHOD

If you want a special, one-of-a-kind design with plain knitted panels and perfectly matched braid,

it isn't difficult to make your own boiled wool. And although the directions are for knitted materials, they can be used on wovens as well.

For best results, use a good quality, 100 percent wool or merino yarn to knit your fabric. Do not use a washable wool. You will practice on a knitted swatch. Read through all the instructions before you begin, so you understand the process.

1. Before beginning the fabric, knit a swatch 100 stitches by 100 rows so you can accurately determine the amount of fabric needed. Working with the swatch has some other advantages as well. You'll develop a better technique and expose dyes that fade and run.

2. Soak the fabric in lukewarm water for 30 minutes to saturate the fibers. This causes them to swell and helps the fabric to shrink more uniformly.

3. Fill the sink with very warm water. Add 1/8 cup of soap for each gallon of water; if you're using merino wool, don't use soap.

Fill a second sink or large dish pan with cold water. Add 12 to 20 ice cubes.

4. Place the fabric in the hot, soapy water; then, using a circular movement, rub the fabric between your hands and work methodically to "scrub" the entire piece. Put the fabric back into the warm water; remove and squeeze dry. Then put it into the cold water and rub some more. Remove and squeeze dry. Repeat the entire process six times.

Hint: *Nancy Keenan, author of* The "Boiled Wool" Jacket and Vest, *uses an old-fashioned washboard to rub the fabric.*

5. Drain the sinks; remove the fabric and roll it in a large towel to remove excess moisture.

6. Look at the fabric. Don't be alarmed if the rectangle has shrunk more at the center than at the ends and sides. Note its measurements.

Fine fibers and merino wools begin to felt very quickly; and it's possible, though unlikely, that your fabric may already be felted enough. Remember, it will shrink a little more during the final rinse and drying process.

You can stop anytime; but you can't reverse the process. Once it is felted, you cannot unfelt it. Check your fabric frequently and decide whether or not you want to continue.

When the fabric is felted enough, squeeze it out; then put it into the washing machine to spin out the remaining water. Remove the fabric; shake briskly; and gently stretch sideways.

7. Machine dry on hot. Check every 10 minutes to avoid shrinking too much. If necessary, take the fabric out before it's dry, and lay it flat to finish drying.

8. The dry fabric should be well matted, dense, and opaque. If you like the way it looks, press with a steam iron. If you don't think it has felted enough, wet the fabric and start over. Measure again and note the measurements.

9. Use the information and measurements you've noted while working with the swatch to determine the total amount of shrinkage, as well as the amount of shrinkage that occurred during the final rinse and drying. Then calculate the amount of fabric you'll need to knit.

10. Knit the fabric and repeat the shrinking process to felt it.

Hint: *If the edges ripple badly, spread the fabric on a flat surface and steam the edges thoroughly. While still damp, cover the edges with long boards to hold them flat; leave the fabric to dry.*

MACHINE METHOD

This method features the three basic elements for felting—temperature change, moisture, and abrasion—in a home washing machine.

The washing-machine method is definitely easier, but the felting is more difficult to control in both amount and evenness.

1. Select a loosely woven wool fabric, preferably with loosely twisted yarns. Wool blankets and older pieces of wool shrink best. Avoid washable fabrics. Be sure you start with enough fabric, since it may shrink as much as 75 percent.

2. Sew the ends together to make a loop.

3. Fill the washer with tepid water and soak the fabric 20 to 30 minutes. Spin and drain the machine.

4. Remove the fabric and begin filling the machine until the water is very warm (about 120°F). Drain the machine and fill immediately with hot water and 1/2 cup soap. Put the fabric back in and agitate two or three minutes. Untangle and check the felting. Repeat if desired. Spin dry and rinse in cold water.

Hint: *For more felting during the wash cycle, add a few other clothes, so the fabric won't slosh around in too much water.*

If your washer can be stopped and opened while the fabric is in the water, you can combine the hand and machine method. Stop the machine during the wash cycle. Rub the fabric between your palms, working systematically to cover the entire piece. Return the fabric to the washer, spin dry, and rinse.

5. Remove the fabric from the washer. Snap the selvage edges to straighten them. Then line dry—in a breeze, if possible. If you want to shrink it some more, machine dry.

6. Examine the dry fabric. If you want more felting, repeat the process.

7. Steam press to remove any wrinkles.

CHAPTER 16
Reversible Fabrics

Sewing with reversible two-faced, and double-cloth fabrics is particularly exciting. Since these materials are equally attractive on both sides and since either or both sides can be used for the outside of the garment, they are especially well-suited for reversible and unlined garments.

All reversible fabrics fall into two broad categories—those which can be separated into two layers and those which cannot.

In this chapter, true double-cloth fabrics which can be separated are called double-cloth fabrics. Fabrics which have two attractive faces but cannot be separated are called two-faced fabrics. These include double knits, jacquards and damasks, duplex prints, boiled wool and other felted fabrics, woven plaids and stripes, plain fabrics that look the same on both sides, satin-back crepe, and double-ply fabrics which are woven so both sets of warps and fillings move back and forth between the layers.

Two-Faced Fabrics

Two-faced fabrics have two attractive faces but cannot be separated into two layers. These include double knits, some jacquards and damasks, satin-back crepe, duplex prints, boiled wool and other felted fabrics, woven plaids and stripes, plain single/ply fabrics that look the same on both sides, and double/ply fabrics which are woven so both sets of warps and fillings move back and forth between the layers.

They are well-suited for reversible and unlined garments or for designs which use both sides of the fabric on the outside of the garment. Most of these fabrics are light to medium in weight and relatively easy to sew.

This chapter focuses on sewing these fabrics into reversible garments or unlined jackets and coats; when using them in the conventional manner or

making lined garments, review the appropriate section for the fabric. For example, use the suggestions in this chapter to make a reversible wrap-around skirt in linen. Use the suggestions for linen and/or plain-weave fabrics for making a traditional linen sheath skirt.

By definition, two-faced fabrics do not have a wrong side; however, for clarity in these directions, the right side is the technical face—the side which is usually worn on the outside—and the underside is the technical back—the side usually worn next to the body.

Fig. 16–1 *From Emanuel Ungaro Parallele, Autumn/Winter 1987/1988 Collection, a traditional jersey is used as a two-faced fabric to create this interesting jacket. (Photographer, Guy Marineau; photo courtesy of Ungaro.)*

Fabric Characteristics
- Two-faced fabrics have two attractive faces.
- Reversible garments are more attractive on one side than the other.
- The inside of reversible garments should be as attractive as the outside; however, the garment doesn't have to be worn inside out.
- The unique construction techniques for reversible garments eliminate the need for traditional facings, interfacings, linings, and underlinings.

PLANNING A GARMENT

FABRIC AND PATTERN SELECTION

Many reversible designs require less fabric than conventional garments because facings, linings, underlinings, and interfacings are eliminated; but special features like turnback cuffs and double hems will require additional yardage.

SEWING CHECKLIST

Machine Needles: Universal-H point, Red Band or Yellow Band needles; sizes 70/10 to 90/14, depending on the fabric weight.

Machine Setting: Stitch length 2–2.5mm (10–15 stitches per inch).

Thread: Long-staple polyester, cotton-wrapped polyester, mercerized cotton. Topstitching—regular thread, silk (sizes A and D), topstitching.

Hand Sewing Needles: Sizes 7 to 10.

Sewing Machine Equipment: Zipper foot, shim.

Layout: Double layer, right sides together. Nap, if needed.

Marking Techniques: Chalk, soap sliver, temporary marking pens, tailor tacks, thread tracing, and pins.

Seams for Reversible Garments: Strap, lapped, decorative French, French-topstitched, flat-fell, double-lapped, bound, wrong-side-out, decorative serged, serged-and-lapped, bound-and-lapped, bound-and-stitched.

Seams for Unlined Garments: All seams for reversible garments, topstitched, welt, double/ply.

Seam Finishes for Unlined Garments: Double/ply—zigzag, bound, tricot bound, multi-stitch zigzag, or serged. Single-ply—bound, tricot bound, serged.

Hem Finishes for Unlined Garments: Bound, tricot bound, zigzag, multi-stitch zigzag, serged, folded edge.

Edge Finishes for Reversible Garments: Clean-finished hems, double hems, wrong-side-out hems, shaped, bias or lace facing, tucked hems, fabric binding, synthetic suede and leather bindings, decorative braids, ribbon binding, ribbon facing, serging.

Closures for Reversible Garments: Machine-stitched or hand-worked buttonholes, bound buttonholes, fabric and ribbon ties, lacings, button links, toggles, frogs.

Pockets: Patch, inseam, topstitched inseam, welt, false welt, flaps.

To avoid purchasing excess fabric, buy the pattern first. Make all desired changes for special seams, edge finishes, sleeve cuffs, collars, and other fashion details. Eliminate all pattern pieces which will not be used. Then, using the adjusted pattern, make a revised layout to determine the amount of fabric you'll need.

When sewing satin-back crepe, damask, and duplex prints, consider the two sides of the fabric as two different fabrics. Look at designs with contrast trims; skirts with gores, godets, or yokes; and jackets with bands. Explore the possibilities of how you can combine two perfectly matched fabrics.

Use two-faced fabrics for vests, jackets, coats, capes, ponchos, skirts, and robes. Simple designs with a minimum of seams, darts, and intricate details are most attractive.

First decide whether the garment will be truly reversible and worn with both sides out. In reality, very few garments are equally attractive on both sides since one side is always a little more interesting as well as more smoothly constructed than the other.

Remember, since facings and linings are eliminated, seams, darts, hems, pockets, and closures should be equally attractive on both sides of reversible garments.

When selecting the pattern, consider the fabric weight. Two-faced fabrics range from lightweight shirtings to medium-weight double/ply materials.

Collarless designs are the easiest; while garments with standing or shawl collars are less difficult than those with notched collars.

Designs with shawl collars and turned-back cuffs do have the advantage of showcasing the uniqueness of the fabric, and thus are particularly attractive.

Cut-on, raglan, kimono, and shirt sleeves are the best choices for reversible designs, but traditional set-in sleeves are suitable for unlined garments. Designs with dropped shoulders work well for either.

Wrap styles—coats, jackets, and skirts—are particularly attractive and always popular. (Generally gathers and pleats are best avoided except in wrap skirts.)

If the fabric isn't bulky, gathers and ease are easier to sew than darts. Generally, patch pockets are easier to sew than inseam, welt, and slot pockets. Replace kick pleats with vents.

For unlined garments, most designs suitable for crisp fabrics are good choices.

PATTERN AND FABRIC PREPARATION

Refine the fit and correct the length before cutting out the pattern. Reshape the unnotched edges of facings so they will resemble a straight band when topstitched in place. Add fold-back cuffs and double hems.

Preshrink fabrics appropriately for the fiber content, fabric weave, and garment construction.

SEWING TWO-FACED FABRICS

The sewing techniques in this section focus on reversible or unlined garments. When sewing two-faced fabrics in conventional designs, review the appropriate section.

LAYOUT

Spread the fabric in a double/lay, with right sides together. Use a soap sliver, chalk, tailor tacks, thread tracing, temporary marking pens, or pins for marking. Avoid clips and tracing carbon.

SEAMS AND DARTS

Make a test seam, using a stitch length of 2mm (12 stitches per inch). Adjust the stitch length as needed for the fabric weight.

For reversible and unlined garments, select a seaming technique which will be attractive on both sides. Frequently, several different seam types are used on the same garment.

Good choices for reversible garments include the strap, flat-fell, decorative French, decorative bound, double-lapped, decorative serged, bound-and-lapped, bound-and-stitched, wrong-side-out.

To determine the most appropriate seaming technique, consider the garment type and design, fabric weight, seam location and shape, and desired effect.

To join a standing collar to the garment, use a strap or decorative bound seam.

For reversible garments, stitch small darts on the right side of the garment as part of the design.

295

For unlined garments, stitch darts as usual on the inside; then topstitch, so they will lie flat.

EDGE FINISHES AND POCKETS

Generally, all edges—hems, pockets, flaps, collars, front edges, cuffs, and belts—are finished the same way.

Bias bindings, decorative ribbons, fold-over braids, decorative fabric facings, ribbon facings, double hems, wrong-side-out hems, and serged edges are attractive finishes. Bindings of synthetic suedes and leathers, as well as real suedes and leathers, are attractive and easy to apply.

If you have a serger, experiment with different threads and edge finishes to create unusual finishes.

When using facings and hems to finish garment edges, they can be turned to the inside for an inconspicuous finish or to the outside for a decorative trim. Neaten the unnotched facing edges with a fold, decorative serging, or interfaced facing.

Most pocket types can be used on unlined garments, but patch, inseam, fake flaps, and fake welts are the neatest. On reversible garments, decorative inseam pockets are most attractive.

YAMAMOTO INSEAM POCKET

This clever pocket was used on an unlined jacket by Japanese designer Yohji Yamamoto.

1. Pin the pocket pattern to the jacket front on the seamline; cut the front and pocket in one piece. Repeat for the back.

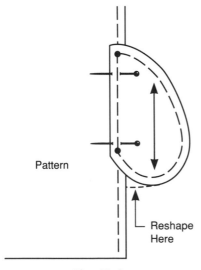

Fig. 16–2

Hint: *Reshape the pocket as needed so it will be more attractive.*

2. Join the front and back with French seams. Clip as needed. Press.

3. If desired, topstitch the pocket to the jacket front.

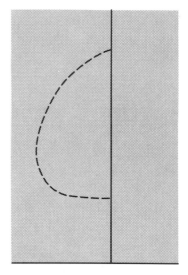

Fig. 16–3

CLOSURES

Most fasteners look better on one side than the other. Fabric and ribbon ties, lacings, button links, and bound buttonholes are the best choices.

Buttons and machine-made buttonholes or decorative fasteners, such as toggles, frogs, and zippers, are appropriate for unlined garments.

When using buttons, a reversible garment can have two sets of buttonholes—one on each front—and can be fastened with button links, two sets of buttons, or buttons sewn to a strip of ribbon. Or, if you can accept a left-over-right lap when the garment is worn inside out, make one set of buttonholes and two sets of buttons.

Hint: *Experiment on fabric scraps until the buttonhole samples look as good on the wrong side as on the right.*

LACINGS AND TIE CLOSURES

Lacings are attractive for casual garments. Lace them through grommets or machine-made eyelets on the garment or bias tubing or corded button loops at the edge.

Hint: *Use a double-stitched hem or faced facing at the opening, so the edge won't sag from the weight of the lacing (see Fig. 21-3).*

A tie closure is also attractive on casual garments. Use ribbon, bias tubing, or fabric to make the ties.

1. To make fabric ties with one finished end, cut a fabric strip four times the finished width. Fold under 1/2″ at one end; press. Then fold the strip in half lengthwise, wrong sides together; press.

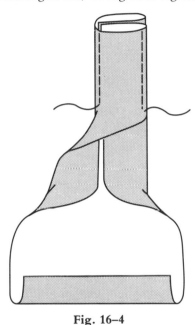

Fig. 16–4

Fold the raw edges in to meet the pressed line; edgestitch both sides of the tie.

2. If the garment has a double-fold hem at the edge, insert the unfinished tie end into the edge before it is topstitched. If it has a binding or braid trim, insert the tie end under the braid or binding before it is stitched in place.

SLEEVES

Sleeves are particularly difficult on reversible garments. Kimono and raglan sleeves and dropped shoulders are the easiest.

When sewing set-in sleeves, reduce the ease in the cap, so the edge will be less curved and easier to set.

For unlined garments, consider a traditional sleeve application with the seam on the inside of the garment. Trim the seam allowances to 1/4″ and bind the edges.

Hint: *To make the garment reversible, select a binding which matches the trim on the garment edges; press the bound seam toward the body of the garment. Edgestitch it flat.*

Double-Cloth Fabrics

Double-cloth fabrics are made by stitching or fusing two separate fabric layers together. Sometimes called double-faced, these fabrics are exciting and different, but not necessarily difficult to sew.

This section focuses on fabrics which are woven separately and fused together, as well as on fabrics which are woven with five sets of yarns. Fabrics woven with five sets of yarns have one set of warp and filling yarns for each of the two fabrics with an additional set of binder or interlacing yarns in either the warp or filling to join the two layers together.

Since the two faces are woven separately, different weaves, colors, and textures can be used to create endless variations. Two contrasting plains, a plaid reversing to a solid, or a nap reversing to a smooth are just a few of the possibilities. These fabrics can be separated into two single/ply layers by clipping the binder yarns.

Fused fabrics are more difficult to separate, but it can be done; and, if the fabrics are fused together off-grain, it may be better to separate them completely.

Most double-cloths are coating weights; however, a few are lighter suit and skirt weights. Lighter weight fabrics can be assembled using the double-faced techniques described in this chapter or by traditional sewing methods.

297

Fabric Characteristics

- Double-cloths are reversible; however, most fabrics have one face which is much more attractive than the other.
- Double-cloths are firmly woven, crisp materials which hold their shape.
- Most double-cloths are medium- to heavy-weight; most are wool, wool blends, or synthetics which look like wool.
- Some double-cloths are difficult to separate.
- Some fabrics will have a demarcation line when the layers are separated.
- Some are bulky and difficult to ease.
- The inside of reversible garments should be as attractive as the outside; however, the garment doesn't have to be worn inside out.

- The unique construction techniques for double-cloths eliminate the need for facings, interfacings, linings, and underlinings.

PLANNING A GARMENT

See Two-Faced Fabrics for additonal suggestions.

PATTERN AND FABRIC SELECTION

Well-suited for reversible and unlined garments, double-cloths can be used for vests, jackets, coats, capes, ponchos, skirts, and robes.

SEWING CHECKLIST

Machine Needles: Universal-H point, Red Band or Yellow Band needles; sizes 80/12 to 100/16, depending on the fabric weight.

Machine Setting: Stitch length, 2.5–3mm (8–12 stitches per inch).

Thread: Long-staple polyester, cotton-wrapped polyester, mercerized cotton. Topstitching—regular thread, silk (sizes A and D), topstitching thread. Basting—silk and basting cotton.

Hand Sewing Needles: Sizes 5 to 8.

Sewing Machine Equipment: Zipper foot, shim.

Equipment and Supplies: Long, glass-headed pins, weights, single-edged razor blade, mat knife, clapper.

Layout: Nap. Medium to heavy fabrics—single/lay, right side up; light-weight fabrics—double/lay, right sides together.

Marking Techniques: Chalk, soap sliver, temporary marking pens, tailor tacks, thread tracing, and pins.

Seams for Reversible Garments: Strap, double-cloth seams (plain, flat-fell, lapped, insertion) decorative serged, bound-and-lapped, bound-and-stitched.

Seams for Unlined Garments: All seams for reversible garments, topstitched, serger flatlock, welt, double/ply.

Seam and Hem Finishes for Unlined Garments: Single/ply or double/ply unfinished, zigzag, multi-stitch zigzag, serged.

Edge Finishes for Reversible Garments: Double-cloth finishes, self-bound, decorative hems, fabric bindings, synthetic suede and leather bindings, decorative braids, ribbons, serging.

Closures: Inseam, machine-stitched, hand-worked, faced, and bound buttonholes, fabric and ribbon ties, lacings, button links, toggles, frogs, zippers.

Pockets: Patch, inseam, topstitched inseam, welt, false welt, flaps.

First decide whether the garment will be truly reversible and worn with both sides out. In reality, very few garments are equally attractive on both sides, since one side is always a little more interesting, as well as more smoothly constructed, than the other.

For a reversible garment, choose a simple design. Designs with shawl collars and turned-back cuffs showcase the uniqueness of the fabric and are particularly attractive. Cut-on, raglan, and kimono sleeves are easier than set-in sleeves; darts are best avoided.

Remember, since facings and linings are eliminated, seams, darts, hems, pockets, and closures should be equally attractive on both sides.

Wrap styles—coats, jackets, and skirts—are particularly attractive and always popular. Collarless designs are the easiest; while garments with standing or shawl collars are less difficult than those with notched collars.

If the fabric isn't too bulky, gathers and ease are easier to sew than darts. Generally, patch pockets are easier to sew than inseam, welt, and slot pockets. Replace kick pleats with vents.

If the garment will not be reversible, most designs suitable for crisp fabrics will be attractive.

Generally, double-cloths are more expensive than traditional fabrics; however, the overall cost of the garment may actually be less.

Most reversible designs require less fabric than conventional garments because facings, linings, underlinings, and interfacings are eliminated. Most hem allowances are reduced to 5/8" and some are eliminated entirely.

Special features like turned-back cuffs will require additional yardage. To avoid purchasing excess fabric, buy the pattern first. Make a test garment to refine the fit. Make all desired changes for special seams, edge finishes, sleeve cuffs, collars, and other fashion details. Eliminate all pattern pieces which will not be used. Then, using the adjusted pattern, make a revised layout to determine the fabric amount.

Press the fabric with a generous amount of steam if it isn't needle-ready.

SEWING DOUBLE-CLOTHS

LAYOUT AND STITCHING TIPS

To insure accuracy, cut medium to heavyweight fabrics from a single layer, right side up. For bulky

Fig. 16–5 *From Philippe Venet Haute Couture Collection, Autumn/Winter 1987/1988, the classic spencer design is made of cashmere double cloth. (Photo courtesy of Philippe Venet.)*

299

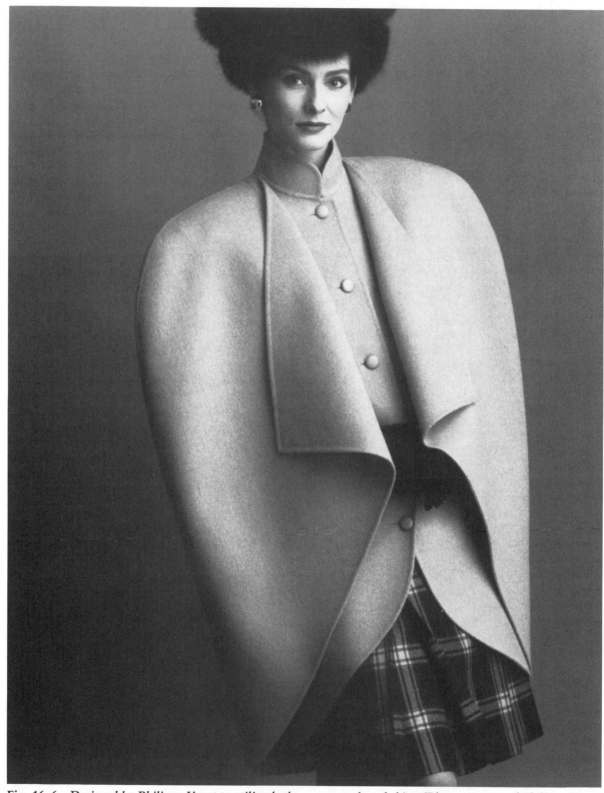

Fig. 16–6   *Designed by Philippe Venet to utilize both sides of the double cloth, this beautiful cashmere cape tops a pleated skirt. (Photo courtesy of Philippe Venet, Autumn/Winter 1987/1988.)*

fabrics, use long (1 3/8″) quilter's pins or weights.

Use a soap sliver, chalk, tailor tacks, thread tracing, temporary marking pens, or pins for marking. Avoid clips and tracing carbon.

Make a test seam, using a stitch length of 2.5mm (10 stitches per inch) and a loosely balanced tension. Lengthen the stitch as needed for heavier fabrics; shorten it for lightweights. Lighten the pressure as needed.

When the fabrics are two different colors, use appropriately colored threads in the needle and bobbin.

SEAMS AND DARTS

For reversible and unlined garments, select a seaming technique which will be attractive on both sides. Frequently, several different seam types are used on the same garment.

Good choices include the strap, lapped, topstitched, and decorative serger seams as well as special seams for double-cloths—plain, flat-fell, lapped, and insertion.

To determine the most appropriate seaming technique, consider the fabric weight, seam location and shape, and desired effect as well as the difficulty of separating the fabrics.

For set-in sleeves, waistbands, and cuffs, the double-cloth insertion seam is best. For standing collars, use one of the special double-cloth seams or a strap seam.

DOUBLE-CLOTH PLAIN SEAM

Suitable for any reversible fabric which can be separated into two layers, the plain seam is sometimes called a slipstitched or clean-finished seam.

1. All seam allowances are 5/8″.

2. Separate the layers at each edge to be seamed. Clip the interlacing binder yarns with small, sharp scissors for 1 1/4″—twice the seam width.

Hint: *Baste—by hand or machine—a guideline 1 1/4″ from all edges to be seamed. Then, when you separate the layers, you won't clip too far.*

If the fabric layers are fused together, pull them apart.

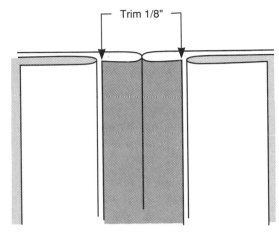

Fig. 16–7

Hint: *If you don't pull them apart an even distance from the edge, there will be an ugly, irregular demarcation line on the finished garment.*

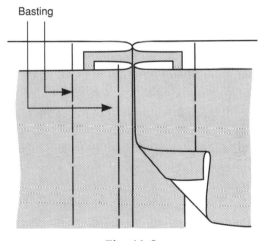

Fig. 16–8

3. Right sides together, machine stitch the outer layers together. Press the seam open and trim to 1/2″ (Fig. 16–7).

4. To finish the seams on the inside of the garment, trim the remaining seam allowances to 3/8″; turn in one raw edge so the fold is on the seamline (Fig. 16–8). Baste 1/4″ from the folded edges. Repeat for the other edge. Press lightly.

5. Slipstitch the seam together. You can also topstitch both sides of the seamline 1/2″ away.

Hint: *I like the topstitching because it hides the demarcation line.*

6. Remove the basted guideline; press.

DOUBLE-CLOTH FLAT-FELL SEAM

Suitable for any reversible fabric which can be separated, the double-cloth flat-fell seam is particularly attractive on lightweight fabrics.

1. All seam allowances are 5/8″.
2. Separate the layers for 1″ at each edge to be seamed.
3. Right sides together, machine stitch the outer layers together with a 5/8″ seam. Press the seam to one side and trim to 1/4″.

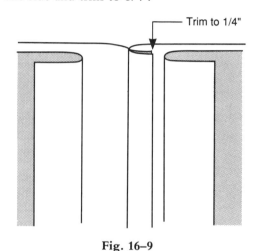

Trim to 1/4″

Fig. 16–9

Hint: *I like to press the side and shoulder seams toward the front, center seams to the left, and all seams in between toward the center. Do it anyway you like, but be consistent.*

4. To finish the seams on the inside of the garment, trim the remaining seam allowances to 1/4″. Lay one seam allowance flat over the first seam, aligning all the cut edges. Then fold the remaining seam allowance under 1/4″. The folded edge will be at the seamline. Baste 1/8″ from the folded edges and press lightly.
5. Slipstitch or fell the folded edge to the seamline.

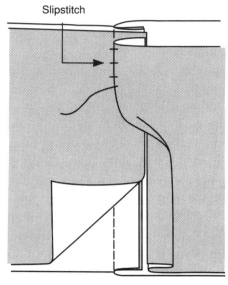

Slipstitch

Fig. 16–10

6. Topstitch so the seam allowances are between the seamline and topstitching.
7. Remove the basting stitches and press.

DOUBLE-CLOTH INSERTION SEAMS

Suitable for any double-cloth which can be separated, the insertion seam is frequently used for collar/neckline seams, armscyes, waistbands, and cuffs. The seam allowance of one garment section is hidden between the layers of the corresponding section.

1. Trim seam allowances to 1/4″.
2. First decide how the seam will look on the finished garment, since all of the seam allowances will be on one side of the seamline.

Hint: *When making this decision, consider these questions. Does one garment section have more fullness than the other? How would the seam be pressed if this were a plain, single-faced fabric?*

For example, since sleeves and skirts have more fullness than the sections which they join, sleeves are inserted into the armholes and cuffs; and skirts are inserted into waistbands.

Flat, notched, and shawl collars are usually inserted into the garment neckline; but since a standing collar is just a band collar, the neckline is inserted into the collar.

302

3. On the section to be inserted, staystitch through both fabric layers. Staystitch a skinny 1/4″ from the edge, just inside the seamline.

4. Baste the corresponding edge of the other section 5/8″ from the raw edge. Separate the layers to the basted line.

Hint: *Be careful when clipping the layers apart, to avoid stretching the neckline. And, if necessary, staystitch the separated layers with a short running stitch.*

5. Right sides together, pin the insertion to the outer layer; stitch on the seamline 1/4″ from the raw edges. To avoid catching the inner layer in the seamline, stitch with the insertion on the bottom. Press.

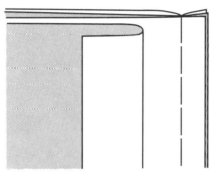

Fig. 16–11

Hint: *Some seamsters like this alternate method better. Slip the raw edge of the insertion into the corresponding seam. Turn in the raw edge of the outside layer on the seamline. Baste 1/8″ from the folded edge and press lightly; edgestitch or slipstitch the edge permanently.*

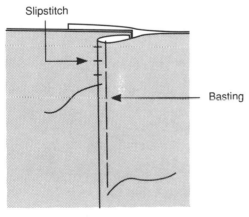

Fig. 16–12

6. To finish the seam on the inside of the garment, turn in the remaining seam allowance. Baste 1/8″ from the folded edge. Press lightly and slipstitch or fell the folded edge to the seamline.

7. Topstitch so the seam is between the seamline and topstitching. Remove the bastings and press.

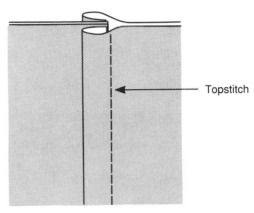

Fig. 16–13

8. Variation: Piping is very attractive on these seams. Use a purchased rayon piping or custom-made silk piping with a 1/4″ seam allowance. Using a zipper foot, stitch it to the seam allowance which will be inserted; then join the sections together.

DOUBLE-CLOTH LAPPED SEAM

Suitable for fabrics which can be separated, the lapped seam is the flattest and is particularly attractive on thick fabrics.

1. Allow 5/8″ seam allowances.

2. Mark the seamline with thread tracing.

3. Separate the layers between the edge and thread tracing.

4. Decide how the seam will lap. This is usually front over back at side and shoulder seams and right over left at the garment centers. On the overlap, trim away the seam allowance of the inner layer; and on the underlap, trim away the seam allowance of the outer layer.

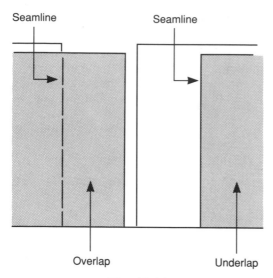

Fig. 16–14

5. Match and baste the seamlines together.

6. Turn under the raw edge of the outer layer so it touches the basted line. Baste; press lightly.

7. Turn the garment reverse-side-out and repeat on the inner layer; press.

8. Topstitch along both folded edges.

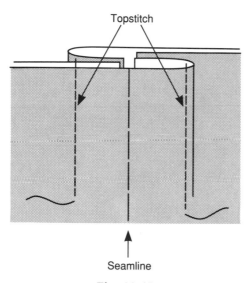

Fig. 16–15

Hint: *Use the zipper foot, positioned so the edge of the foot is at the fold.*

9. Remove the bastings and press.

EDGE FINISHES

Generally, all edges—hems, pockets, flaps, collars, front edges, cuffs, and belts—are finished the same way.

Special double-cloth finishes—double-fold, piped, and self-bound edges—as well as bias bindings, decorative braids and ribbons, and serged edges are attractive finishes. Bindings of real or synthetic suedes and leathers also look good and are easy to apply.

If you have a serger, experiment with different threads and edge finishes to create unusual finishes.

DOUBLE-FOLD FINISH

The double-fold is one of the most popular double-cloth finishes. It is sometimes called a plain, clean-finished or slipstitched edge.

1. Trim seam and hem allowances to 1/4". If the fabric is thick and bulky, trim to 3/8".

2. At each edge, separate the layers for 3/4" (1" on bulky fabrics). This is twice the seam width plus 1/4" at each edge. If the layers are fused together, pull them apart.

Hint: *Baste a guideline 3/4" (1" on bulky fabrics) from the edge by hand or machine. Then, when you separate the layers, you won't clip too far or have an ugly, uneven demarcation line on the finished garment. If the basting is neat and attractive, it can be left in the garment permanently.*

3. To prevent stretching and to ensure that the edge hangs correctly, tape and edge with linen tape or a piece of selvage cut from a lightweight fabric. Position the edge of the tape on the seamline; pin and sew it in place with a small diagonal stitch. Stitch lightly so it will be invisible on the right side of the garment.

Hint: *Try on the garment before sewing the tape in place. If the edges swing away from the center at the hem, shorten the tape; if they overlap, lengthen it.*

4. Turn in the edges and baste. If the edge has a curve, notch or clip it as needed, so the seam allowances will be flat and inconspicuous when

turned in. Edgestitch or slipstitch the folds together. Remove the bastings. Press; spank the edges with a clapper to flatten them. Topstitch the hem depth—1/4″ to 3/8″ from the edges—if you'd like.

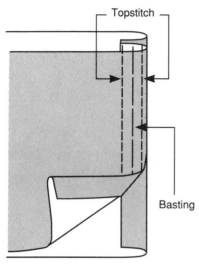

Fig. 16–16

Hint: *Ferragamo, an Italian manufacturer, frequently uses this edge finish without the topstitching. I rather like the topstitching at the edge of the hem because it covers the demarcation line and makes a professional looking garment.*

When topstitching, lengthen the stitch and use a zipper foot. When crossing seams and stitching edges, use a shim to keep the presser foot level.

When the edges are slipstitched, sew loosely and try to make the stitches even, like machine stitches.

DOUBLE-CLOTH PIPED EDGES

Suitable for any reversible fabric which can be separated into two layers, the double-cloth piped edge is particularly attractive on lightweight garments with piped seams.

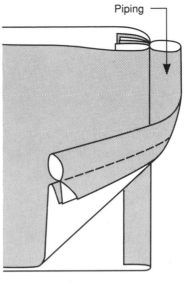

Fig. 16–17

1. Trim seam and hem allowances to 1/4″ and separate the layers 3/4″.
2. Make the piping with a skinny 1/4″ seam allowance.
3. Baste the piping to the seam allowance of the outer layer. Stitch.
4. Turn in the edges on the seamline; baste; and slipstitch the folds together. Remove the bastings and press. If desired, topstitch the hem 1/4″ from the edges.

Hint: *Don't worry if your hand sewing is not perfect; the piping will hide it nicely.*

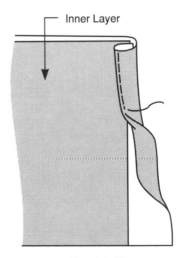

Fig. 16–18

DOUBLE-CLOTH
SELF-BOUND EDGE

Suitable for fabrics which can be separated, this attractive edge finish is plain on one side.

1. Allow 1"-wide seam and hem allowances. If the fabric is thick and bulky, allow 1 1/4".

2. Baste on the seamline and separate the layers to the basted line.

3. For a plain finish on the outside and a binding on the inside, trim away the inner layer to the basted line.

4. Fold the outer layer to the inside; turn in the raw edge and baste. Slipstitch or topstitch in place.

5. Reverse the last two steps for a binding on the outside.

DARTS

Darts are tricky to make on reversible garments. If the garment is reversible, separate the two layers from the seamline to the point of the dart or slash through the center of the dart and separate the layers on either side of the slash.

After the layers are separated, complete the dart using either the technique for a double-cloth plain seam or the double-cloth flat-felled seam. Press the two darts in opposite directions.

If the garment is not reversible, stitch a regular dart; then, wrong side up, topstitch. The topstitching can be placed parallel to the dartline or along the folded edge.

POCKETS

Finish pocket edges like the hems and edges or separate the layers. Line the pockets using a traditional method.

Hint: *After separating the fabric, Ingrid Walderhaug fuses a piece of interfacing to the wrong side of the pocket to stabilize it; then she adds the lining.*

Patch pockets are particularly easy to apply and can be added to most designs, with limitless variations.

To be creative, use patch pockets on the outside of the garment and welt pockets, welts without pockets, or flaps on the reverse.

For unlined garments which are not reversible, inseam pockets, trouser pockets, and fake flap or welt pockets are attractive. Always finish the edges of pockets that show so they're compatible with the rest of the garment.

When applying patch pockets to both sides, sew them by hand. Make the pockets. Stitch the first pocket in place. Then position the other pocket precisely on the reverse side. Using a fell or slipstitch, stitch lightly through only one layer of fabric.

PATCH POCKET WITH WELT

When making a patch pocket on one side and a welt on the reverse, make the welt opening first.

1. Mark the pocket opening; it should be at least 1/2" shorter than the width of the welt.

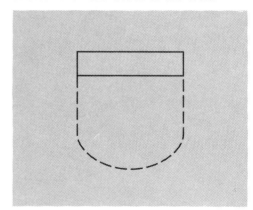

Fig. 16–19

2. Baste 1/2" from both sides of the pocket opening. Using a mat knife or single-edged razor blade, slash the opening. Clip the binder yarns to the basted line and turn the raw edges in. Slipstitch the edges together; the opening will be oval shaped, not rectangular.

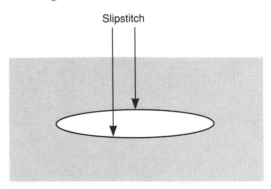

Slipstitch

Fig. 16–20

3. Check to be sure the welt will cover the pocket opening, then finish all the edges. Sew the facing to the welt.

Hint: *I miter all the corners of the welt and sew a lightweight facing in place by hand.*

4. Baste the welt in place just below the opening; sew the welt ends and bottom to the coat with a fell stitch.

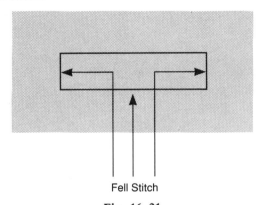

Fell Stitch

Fig. 16–21

Hint: *Using a fell stitch, stitch through only one fabric layer. Try to make the stitches look like machine stitches on the welt side.*

5. Turn the garment over and apply the patch pocket so that it covers the welt opening. Stitch lightly so the stitches won't show on the other side.

CLOSURES

Choosing a fastening for reversible garments is difficult, since very few will be attractive on both sides. Fabric and ribbon ties, lacings, button links, and inseam buttonholes are the best choices.

Buttons and machine-made buttonholes and decorative fasteners such as toggles, frogs, and zippers, are appropriate for unlined garments.

There are several different ways a garment can be fastened with buttons. The garment can have two sets of buttonholes, one on each front, and can be fastened with button links, two sets of buttons, or buttons sewn to a strip of ribbon. Or, if you can accept a left over right lap when the garment is worn inside out, make one set of buttonholes and two sets of buttons.

FACED BUTTONHOLES

1. Baste around the buttonhole 1/2″ from each side and end.

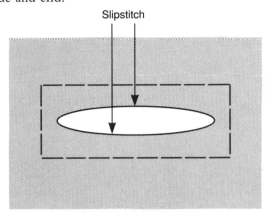

Slipstitch

Fig. 16–22

2. Carefully slash the buttonhole opening with a mat knife or single-edged razor blade.

3. Separate the layers between the slash and basted line.

4. Using a fine needle, fold the raw edges in 1/8″; and slipstitch the edges together.

Hint: *Begin in the center of the buttonhole; and, instead of making teeny-weeny stitches, go around it twice. Use the needle point to shape the ends; then make several overcast stitches to keep the corners square.*

BOUND BUTTONHOLES

Well-made bound buttonholes look fantastic on lightweight double cloth; unfortunately, they are the most difficult kind to make.

1. Make 5″ of corded piping for each buttonhole. Trim the seam allowance to a skinny 1/4″.

2. For each buttonhole cut two piping strips the length of the buttonhole plus 1″.

3. Baste around the buttonhole 1/2″ from each side and end.

4. Carefully slash the buttonhole opening with a single-edged razor blade.

5. Separate the layers between the slash and basted line.

6. Insert one corded strip between the separated layers. Then, using a short, fine needle, turn under one edge 1/8″; baste and slipstitch the edge to the stitched line on the piping.

7. Repeat on the other side; then finish the back-side.

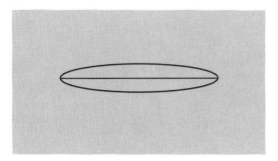

Fig. 16–23

For hand-worked buttonholes, overcast the raw edges of the buttonhole with cotton thread. Then use silk buttonhole twist and a buttonhole stitch to make the buttonhole on the outside of the garment. If the garment will actually be reversible, turn the finished buttonhole over and make buttonhole stitches around the hole again, stitching only through the inside fabric layer.

INSEAM BUTTONHOLES

Inseam buttonholes work best on plain seams which have been pressed open.

1. Mark both ends of the buttonhole precisely.
2. Stitch the seam, leaving the buttonhole open. Backstitch or tie knots at both ends.

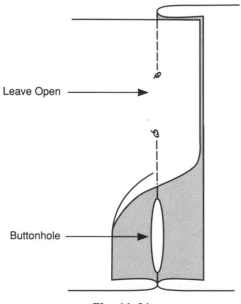

Leave Open ⟶

Buttonhole ⟶

Fig. 16–24

Hint: *I use a lightweight selvage to stay the buttonhole so it won't stretch out of shape. Cut a 1/4"-wide length 1" longer than the buttonhole. Pin it in place so the edge of the selvage is on the seamline. Secure permanently with a running stitch.*

3. Finish the seams on the inside of the garment, and slipstitch the two layers together at the buttonhole.

BUTTON LINKS

Appropriate for dressy designs, this closure can be fastened with purchased cuff links or custom-made button links.

1. You'll need two buttons with shanks for each button link. Join the shanks with a 1/2" swing tack.
2. For each button link, make a machine-stitched buttonhole on each garment section.

Hint: *Experiment on fabric scraps until the buttonhole samples look as good on the wrong side as the right.*

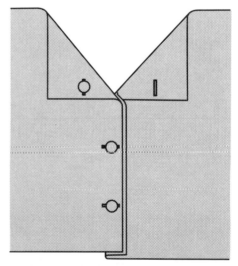

Fig. 16–25

3. Fasten the garment so both buttons are on the outside. The laps will protrude between the buttons.

RIBBON TIES AND LACINGS

A tie closure is particularly attractive on casual garments. Use ribbon, bias tubing, or fabric to make the ties. (See Two-Faced Fabrics.)

If the garment has a double-fold finish at the edge, insert the unfinished tie end into the edge before it's slipstitched. If it has a binding or braid trim, insert the tie end under the braid or binding before it is stitched in place.

Lacings are attractive for casual garments. Lace them through grommets or machine-made eyelets on the garment or bias tubing or corded button loops at the edge.

ZIPPER

This slot zipper is appropriate for lightweight reversible fabrics which can be separated into two layers.

1. Open the zipper and measure the width of the zipper tape from the edge of the tape to the edge of the coil. Cut the seam allowances in the placket opening this width.

2. Separate the layers for twice the seam width plus 1/4".

3. Turn in the edges of the outer layers on the seamline; press lightly.

4. Slip the zipper between the layers; and align the coil of the zipper with the folded edges. Baste.

5. Topstitch the zipper in place 1/4" from the edge. Remove the bastings and press again.

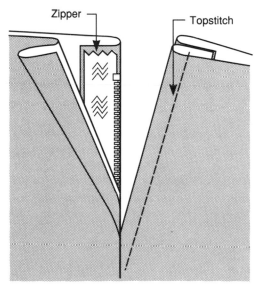

Fig. 16–26

HAND-STITCHED ZIPPER

This zipper is particularly attractive on garments which have double-cloth plain or piped seams and edges; however, since it isn't inserted between the fabric layers, it cannot be used on reversible garments.

1. Cut the seam allowances in the placket opening the same width as the seam below it.

2. Separate the layers accordingly (twice the seam width plus 1/4").

3. Complete the seam below the placket. If the seam will be topstitched, wait until the placket is finished so the stitching can be completed without breaking the threads at the bottom of the zipper.

4. Turn in the edges of the placket on the seamline; baste 1/8" from the edge; press lightly, and slipstitch the folds together. Remove the bastings; press and pound the edges to flatten them as much as possible.

If the seam is to be topstitched, topstitch the desired distance from the seamline and placket opening. When double-cloth flat-fell seams are used, topstitch the placket opening on both sides, even though the seam below is only stitched on one side.

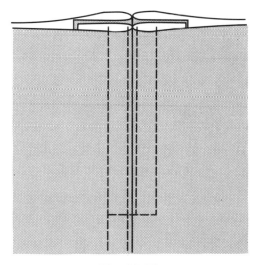

Fig. 16–27

5. Baste the zipper into the placket. Use a small running stitch to sew the zipper to the seam allowances. Remove the bastings and press.

COLLARS

Collars can be set to the neckline by several different methods. This is the insertion method for standing or mandarin collars.

1. Finish the outer edge of the collar unless it has a binding.

2. Trim the seam allowances of the garment and collar necklines to 1/4″.

3. Baste the collar neckline 5/8″ from the raw edge. Then clip the threads between the layers to the basted line.

Hint: *Ingrid Walderhaug stabilizes the neckline with yarn. Measure the length from the pattern. Handstitch yarn to the wrong side of the garment just inside the seamline.*

4. Turn in the raw edges of the collar on the seamline and baste each layer separately 1/8″ from the edge.

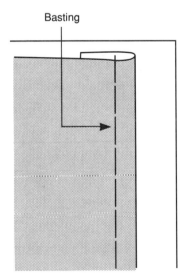

Basting

Fig. 16–28

5. Slip the raw edge of the garment into the collar. Pin, then baste. Slipstitch or machine stitch the neckline seam permanently. Press.

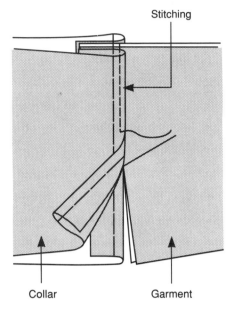

Stitching

Collar   Garment

Fig. 16–29

NORELL COLLAR

This technique taken from a Norell coat is an easy collar finish for unlined double-cloth coats and jackets.

1. Using the pattern, cut one undercollar and one upper collar.

2. Separate the undercollar and discard the inside layer.

3. Right sides together, join the outer edges of the uppercollar and undercollar. Press and turn the collar right side out.

4. Sew the collar to the garment.

HAND-TAILORED COLLARS

For a tailored collar on unlined double-cloth coats, the undercollar use traditional padding stitches on.

1. Cut one undercollar and one upper collar.

2. Separate the fabric layers of the undercollar and discard the inner layer. Then, using hair canvas to interface it, shape the collar with small, diagonal padding stitches. Trim away the hair canvas from

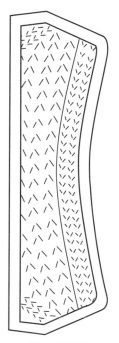

Fig. 16-30

SLEEVES

Sleeves are particularly difficult on reversible garments. Kimono and raglan sleeves and dropped shoulders are the easiest.

When sewing set-in sleeves, reduce the ease in the cap so the edge will be less curved and easier to set.

For unlined garments, consider a traditional sleeve application with the seam on the inside of the garment. Trim the seam allowances to 1/4″ and bind the edges.

Hint: *To make the garment reversible, select a binding which matches the trim on the garment edges; press the bound seam toward the body of the garment. Edgestitch it flat.*

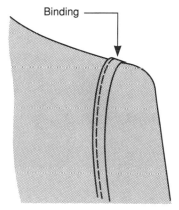

Fig. 16-31

the seam allowances. Steam and shape the collar over a tailor's ham.

3. Separate the fabric layers of the upper collar if the fabric is heavy or stiff.

4. Complete the outer edges of the collar by hand or machine. Turn the collar right side out and press.

5. Sew the collar to the garment.

Double-Faced Quilted Fabrics

Double-faced quilted fabrics have two face fabrics with a layer of filling, usually polyester batting, in between. When sewing single-faced quilteds, see Single Faced—Quilted Fabrics. Also read Chapter 17, because double-faced quilteds have as many similarities to quilted fabrics as to reversible fabrics. Many suggestions apply to both.

Readily available, these fabrics have enough body to create attractive unlined and reversible garments.

In this section, the fabric which will usually be worn on the outside is called the right side or outside; the other fabric is called the inside or wrong side.

Fabric Characteristics
- Double-faced quilteds are usually thick and bulky.
- For reversible garments, seams and edge finishes should be equally attractive on both sides.
- For unlined designs, seams and edge finishes should be neat and inconspicuous on the inside.
- Many double-faced quilted fabrics have a nap or one-way design.
- Some quilted fabrics ravel badly.

311

Fig. 16–32 *From Geoffrey Beene Spring 1987, this quilted cotton shirting jacket reverses to gazar. (Photo courtesy of Geoffrey Beene.)*

PLANNING A GARMENT

Review suggestions for Single-Faced Quilted Fabrics, Two-Faced Fabrics, and Double-Cloth, as well as chapter 17.

FABRIC AND PATTERN SELECTION

Fabric quality is closely related to the closeness of the quilted design, the strength of the stitches, and the quality of the quilted thread, as well as the face fabrics themselves. The fabric should be printed and stitched with the grain.

Hint: *When choosing old quilts, check the joins. Most were sewn with cotton thread, which may have rotted.*

SEWING CHECKLIST

Machine Needles: Universal-H point or Red Band needles; sizes 80/12 to 100/16.

Machine Setting: Stitch length, 2.5–3mm (8–10 stitches per inch); tension, loosely balanced.

Thread: Long-staple polyester, cotton-wrapped polyester. Basting—water-soluble basting thread.

Hand Sewing Needles: Sizes 5 to 9.

Sewing Machine Equipment: Zipper foot, walking or roller foot.

Equipment and Supplies: Weights, long glass-headed pins.

Layout: Nap, single layer, right side up.

Marking Techniques: Clips, pins, chalk, soap sliver, temporary marking pens, thread tracing, tailor tacks.

Seams for Reversible Garments: Flat-felled, strap, false French, bound-and-lapped, bound-and-stitched, double-lapped, decorative serged.

Seams for Unlined Garments: All seams for reversibles, plus topstitched, welt, double/ply.

Edge Finishes: Bindings, bands, fold-over braids, decorative facings.

Interfacing: Generally not used except for collars.

Linings and Underlinings: Not used.

Fasteners: Buttons and buttonholes, button loops, faced-slit buttonholes, toggles, frogs, ties, conventional zippers and decorative zippers.

Pockets: Patch, topstitched inseam pockets.

Depending on the face fabrics, quilted materials are suitable for casual, dressy, and at-home designs. Robes and loungewear, skirts, vests, jackets, and coats are frequent choices.

If the quilted material has an unquilted companion fabric, consider mixing the two together on the same garment.

If it doesn't, don't overlook the possibility of creating companion fabrics by ripping the layers apart and using one of the separated fabrics. Separate a small piece first; steam press; then examine it carefully for permanent needle holes.

Choose a simple design with a minimum number of pieces. Most patterns designed for corduroy are good choices.

Avoid pleats, tucks, and gathers. If that isn't practical, replace tucks and pleats with gathers; then reduce the gathers.

Designs without collars are the easiest, but standing and shawl collars are only slightly more difficult.

Styles with kimono, raglan, or dropped shoulder seams are easier than set-in sleeves.

Turned-back cuffs are attractive on jackets and pants; and they will extend the life of children's garments.

Preshrink the fabric. Wash and dry washable fabrics. Steam press nonwashables.

Hint: *To prevent the quilting from unraveling and the filling from coming out, edgestitch or zigzag the edges together before shrinking.*

Alter the pattern as needed and make a complete pattern. When facings or hems are replaced with bindings, trim away the seam or hem allowances on all edges to be bound.

Eliminate straight seams wherever possible by overlapping and pinning the seamlines of the pattern pieces together.

Lengthen sleeves and pants legs from turned-back cuffs.

SEWING DOUBLE-FACED QUILTED FABRICS

LAYOUT, CUTTING, AND MARKING

Examine the fabric to determine if either the quilted stitches or the fabric pattern needs to be matched or if the fabric has a nap or one-way design.

If the fabric is printed off-grain, determine whether the grain, quilted stitches, or fabric pattern should be the primary concern when positioning the pattern.

Use a nap layout for napped and one-way designs. Spread a single layer of fabric, right side up. Position the pattern pieces so the fabric pattern, grain, and quilted stitching will be most attractive on the finished garment.

Use weights or pin the pattern only to the top layer of the fabric. Cut, using very sharp shears. Try to avoid using clips to indicate match points when using flat-felled or double-lapped seams.

After cutting old quilts, machine stitch 1/4" from all edges so the hand-sewn seams won't unravel.

Hint: *I stitch each edge separately without pivoting at the corners.*

SEAMS

To select the most appropriate seams, consider the kind of garment, the seam location and shape, the fabric, and your personal taste.

For reversible garments, flat-fell, strap, false French, bound, bound-and-lapped, bound-and-stitched, decorative serged, and double-lapped seams are good choices. For unlined garments, welt, topstitched, double/ply, and serged seams are also suitable.

Make samples of several seams to decide which you prefer. And don't hesitate to change the seam allowance or binding widths to customize your garment.

For ease in handling armscye seams, stitch the sleeve to the garment before joining the underarm seams.

FLAT-FELL SEAMS FOR QUILTED FABRICS

This traditional seam is inconspicuous on both sides of the garment. Position the two rows of stitching on the side of your choice.

Hint: *The side with two rows of stitching is more difficult to finish neatly, so I prefer to have it on the inside, though most sewing experts recommend the reverse.*

1. Allow 3/4″ seam allowances.

2. For two rows of stitching on the outside, stitch, wrong sides together, on the seamline.

3. Trim one seam allowances to 1/8″. Trim away the batting and backing from the other seam allowance. Press.

4. Wrap the larger seam allowance around the raw edge of the smaller one; pin. Using water-soluble basting thread, hand baste on the first seamline.

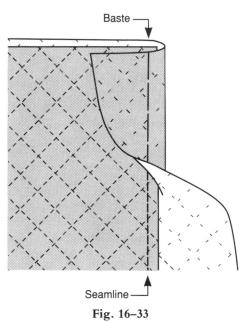

Fig. 16–33

5. With the garment right side up, edgestitch the fold to the garment, enclosing the raw edge.

Hint: *Use a zipper foot when edgestitching. To stitch the sleeve underarm easily, turn the garment wrong side out; and stitch inside the sleeve. Begin stitching at the garment hem, continuing until you reach the sleeve hem.*

6. Steam press to remove the water-soluble thread.

STRAP SEAMS FOR QUILTED FABRICS

Decorative as well as utilitarian, strap seams are always good choices for reversible garments. And, although the strap is usually on the outside of the garment, it can be on the inside.

Bias tape, coordinated or matching unquilted fabrics, vinyls, synthetic suede, ribbon, and decorative braid are attractive materials for the straps.

Choose materials which can be shaped to fit curved seams such as bias tape, or cut materials such as vinyl and synthetic suede to match the seam shape.

1. Stitch the seam, wrong sides together; press it open.

Hint: *If the strap is narrow, press the seam to one side, instead of open.*

2. Trim away the batting and backing from both seam allowances. Trim the face fabric to 1/4″.

3. Cover the seam with the strap and edgestitch in place; press.

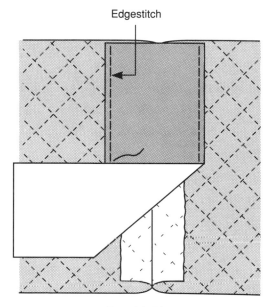

Fig. 16–34

BOUND SEAMS FOR QUILTED FABRICS

Bound with a bias strip, this seam stands away from the garment. The binding can be on either the outside or the inside of the garment.

1. Allow 5/8″ seam allowances.

2. From a solid color, matching or coordinating print, cut a 1 1/4″-wide bias binding.

3. Garment right sides together, stitch on the seamline. Press and trim the seam to 1/4″.

4. Wrong side up, match and pin the raw edges of the binding and the seam; stitch again on the seamline.

5. Trim away one of the garment seam allowances. Wrap the bias around the seam; fold and pin the raw edge under so the folded edge of the bias touches the original seamline. Baste as needed. Edgestitch the fold in place; press.

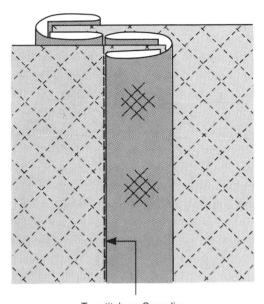

Topstitch on Seamline

Fig. 16–36

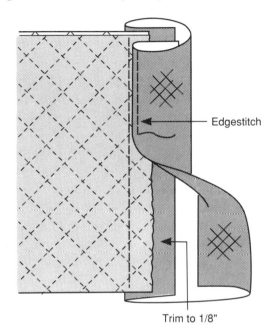

Edgestitch

Trim to 1/8"

Fig. 16–35

Hint: *Hand baste with water-soluble basting thread.*

BOUND-AND-LAPPED SEAMS FOR QUILTED FABRICS

1. Allow 1/4" seam allowances.
2. Using 1 1/4"-wide bias binding, bind the raw edges of each of the two sections to be joined.
3. Right sides up, lap one section over the other, matching the seamlines. Stitch on the seamline.

Hint: *The seamline is at the edge of the binding.*

DOUBLE-FOLD BIAS SEAMS FOR QUILTED FABRICS

This quick and easy method features purchased double-fold extra-wide bias tape. The seam stands away from the garment and can be on either the outside or the inside.

1. Allow 5/8" seam allowances.
2. Right sides together, stitch on the seamline.
3. Trim away the batting and backing from the seam allowances; then trim the seam to 1/2". Press flat.
4. Slip the seam into the bias binding. The narrow side of the binding should touch the seamline. Baste.
5. With the narrow side of the tape up, edgestitch in place.

Hint: *When stitching across a bound seam, fold the shoulder seams and side seams to the back; fold horizontal seams down.*

6. If desired, enclose the binding fold with another binding in a different color.

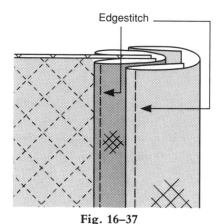

Fig. 16–37

TOPSTITCHING AND EDGE FINISHES

When making welt and topstitched seams on unlined garments, trim away as much of the bulk as possible before topstitching.

When darts can't be avoided on reversible jackets, stitch the darts as usual; press to one side. Topstitch the dart flat.

For edge finishes, consider fold-over braids, ribbon, bias bindings, bands, and decorative facings.

If the edges will be bound, staystitch 1/4" from the raw edge.

DECORATIVE FACINGS

Do not trim away the seam allowances on edges to be faced.

1. Draw the facing shape on the pattern, adding a 3/8" seam allowance at the free edge.

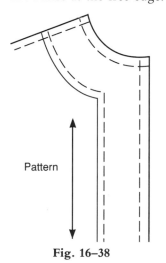

Fig. 16–38

2. Seam and press the facing in the usual manner.

3. Gauge stitch a skinny 3/8" from the free edge of the facing. Fold under the edge and press.

Hint: *Crimp convex curves so they'll fold under easily.*

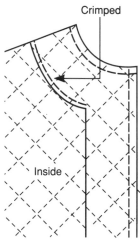

Fig. 16–39

4. Wrong sides up, join the facing and garment. Press and trim the seam allowance; then turn the facing right side out. Press.

5. Fold under the raw edges of the facing; baste and edgestitch the facing to the garment.

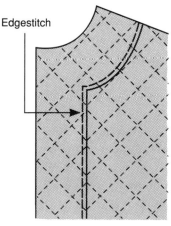

Fig. 16–40

Hint: *If you face the facing, you can concentrate on the topstitching since the edge has already been neatly finished.*

Avoid fusible interfacings unless they are applied to a separate facing.

CLOSURES

Although traditional designs feature button loops or buttonholes, also consider toggles, frogs, ties, and plain or decorative zippers.

Cord machine-stitched buttonholes so they will maintain their shape for the life of the garment.

Hint: *If you don't have topstitching thread in a matching color to use for cord, make your own with four to six strands of regular thread.*

Use the binding fabric or double-fold bias tape to make ties.

POCKETS

Finish patch pockets by lining them to the edge, binding all edges, hemming the opening and binding the remaining edges, or lining the pocket and binding the opening.

For reversible garments, hand sew the patch pockets through only one layer of fabric.

For unlined garments, edgestitch the pocket by machine, if desired.

The topstitched inseam pocket works well on unlined garments, but it's tricky to finish professionally on reversible ones.

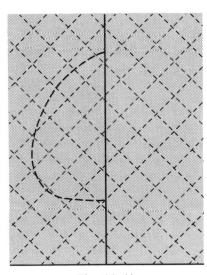

Fig. 16–41

1. Reshape the pattern for the pocket sack as needed so it will look attractive.
2. Pin the pattern to the garment back, overlap-

ping the seamlines, so the pocket and back will be cut in one piece.

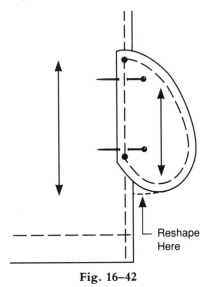

Fig. 16–42

3. Cut the other pocket sack from an unquilted or lining fabric.
4. Right sides together, join the lining sack to the garment front on the seamline. Trim and press.
5. Right sides together, join the garment front and back on the seamline; when stitching the pocket, stitch only a 1/4″ seam.
7. Bind the seams, mitering the corner at the top of the pocket.

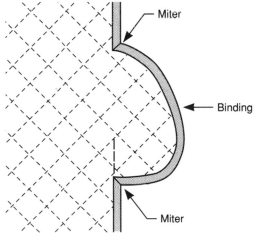

Fig. 16–43

8. Baste the pocket to the inside of the garment.
9. Right side up, topstich next to the basted line. Steam press.

317

Hint: *Use water-soluble thread to baste.*

PRESSING AND GARMENT CARE

Press lightly with the tip of the iron on the seam line.

Consider both the fiber content and garment structure when determining the garment care. Most quilted fabrics can be machine washed and dried; however, a few will require dry-cleaning.

Dry-clean garments made from old quilts if the piecing is fragile.

CHAPTER 17
Quilted Fabrics

This chapter focuses on single-faced quilted fabrics and custom-quilting fabrics. When sewing double-faced quilted fabrics, see Reversible Fabrics.

Single-Faced Quilted Fabrics

Quilted fabrics are composed of three different fabrics—a face fabric, a backing, and a filling—which have usually been machine quilted together.

Versatile and easy to sew, quilted fabrics are available in a variety of materials, such as broadcloth, calico, corduroy, nylon, satin, and velveteen. Most quilted materials are crisp and stand away from the body.

Some are single-faced with a lightweight tricot or gauze backing, while others are double-faced with two different face fabrics. Most have a filling of polyester batting; and a few are offered with coordinating unquilted fabrics.

This section focuses on single-faced quilted fabrics. When sewing double-faced quilteds, see Chapter 16 (Double-Faced Quilted Fabrics).

Some quilteds are much thicker than others, depending on the weight and bulk of the separate layers.

Fabric Characteristics
- Quilted fabrics are bulky.
- Many quilteds have a nap or one-way design.
- The feed dogs on the sewing machine may damage the backing fabric.
- Some backing fabrics do not wear well.

PLANNING A GARMENT

FABRIC AND PATTERN SELECTION

All quilted fabrics will add a few pounds to your figure.

Examine the fabric carefully. If either the printed pattern or quilted pattern is off-grain, consider another fabric. The closeness and quality of the stitches is as important as the fabric design. Better quality fabrics are backed with tricot, not gauze.

Depending on the face fabric, garments can be casual, dressy, or at-home designs. Robes and loungewear, skirts, vests, jackets, and coats are good choices.

If the quilted fabric has an unquilted companion fabric, consider mixing the two on the same garment. A wide quilted hem or a quilted belt on an unquilted garment, quilted sleeves with a plain bodice or vice versa, a quilted garment with a plain lining, or a quilted bodice and a plain skirt are just a few ideas.

Choose a simple design with a minimum of seams. Generally, patterns designed for quilted fabrics or corduroy are good choices.

When possible, avoid pleats, tucks, and gathers; if that isn't practical, replace tucks and pleats with

---

SEWING CHECKLIST

Machine Needles: Universal-H point or Red Band needles, sizes 80/12 to 100/16.

Machine Setting: Stitch length 2.5–3mm (8–10 stitches per inch); tension, loosely balanced.

Thread: Long-staple polyester, cotton-wrapped polyester.

Hand Sewing Needles: Sizes 5 to 9.

Sewing Machine Equipment: Roller or walking foot.

Layout: Nap, usually single/lay, right side up.

Marking Techniques: Clips, pins, chalk, soap sliver, temporary marking pens, thread tracing, tailor tacks.

Equipment and Supplies: Weights, transparent tape.

Seams: Plain, double/ply, welt, strap, tissue-stitched.

Seam and Hem Finishes: Single/ply or double/ply; double-stitched, zigzag, multi-stitch zigzag, serged, seam tape or bound.

Hem: Plain, blindstitch, machine blindstitch, topstitched.

Hem Finishes: Zigzag, multi-stitch zigzag, serged, lace or seam tape, tricot bound.

Edge Finishes: Bindings, edge-to-edge linings, lining-fabric facings, braid.

Interfacing: Generally not used.

Linings: Generally.

Fasteners: Buttons and button loops, bound buttonholes, decorative zippers, frogs, toggles, ties.

Pockets: All types.

---

gathers; then reduce the amount of gathering. Collarless designs and standing and shawl collars are easier than notched collars; styles with kimono, raglan, or dropped shoulder seams are easier than set-in sleeves.

To reduce bulk, eliminate straight seams, such as those which join facings to garment fronts. Overlap and pin the seamlines of the pattern pieces together and cut the garment section.

Alter the pattern as needed; then make duplicate pattern pieces for easy cutting.

Preshrink the fabric. Wash and dry washable fabrics. Steam press nonwashables.

Hint: *To prevent the quilting from unraveling and the filling from coming out, edgestitch or zigzag the edges together before shrinking.*

SEWING SINGLE-FACED QUILTED FABRICS

LAYOUT, CUTTING, AND MARKING

Examine the fabric to determine if either the quilted stitches or fabric pattern need to be matched or if the fabric has a nap or one-way design.

If the fabric is printed off-grain, determine whether the grain, quilted stitches, or fabric pattern should be the primary consideration when positioning the pattern.

Spread the fabric, right side up. Use a nap layout for napped fabrics and one-way designs. Position the pattern pieces so the fabric pattern, grain, and quilted stitching will be most attractive on the finished garment.

Use weights; or pin the pattern only to the top layer of the fabric. Cut, using very sharp shears.

STITCHING TIPS

Make a test seam, using a stitch length of 2.5–3mm (8–10 stitches per inch) and a loosely balanced tension. If necessary, reduce the pressure.

Stitch, using a stabilizer underneath to avoid damaging the fabric with the feed dogs. Hold the fabric taut when stitching. Staystitch curved edges just inside the seamline to reduce raveling.

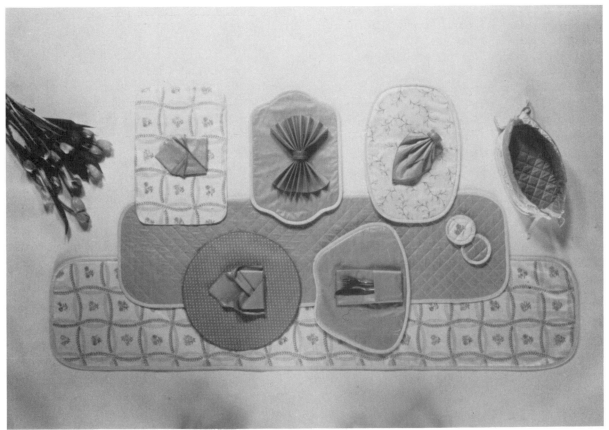

Fig. 17–1 *Quilted fabrics are a popular choice for placemats and table accessories. (Photo courtesy of McCall Pattern Co.)*

SEAMS, DARTS, AND HEMS

When selecting the seam or finish, consider the kind of garment, whether it will be lined or unlined, the fabric, and your personal taste.

Plain seams can be used on any seam—straight or curved. Welt and topstitched seams also work well on straight and slightly curved seams.

On unlined garments, double/ply seams look best. On lined garments, bevel single/ply seams to reduce bulk.

Stitch the darts on unlined garments as usual; slash on the foldline; and trim out the batting. Press open; then topstitch 1/4″ from the dartline; trim close to the topstitching.

Finish the edges of plain hems on unlined garments with zigzag, multi-stitch zigzag, serging, lace, seam tape, or tricot binding. Using a hand or machine blindstitch, catch only the backing fabric.

COLLARS

Most collars are easier to sew and less bulky if you use an unquilted fabric for either the undercollar or the upper collar. If there is no companion fabric, make one by separating the face from the backing.

CLOSURES

Button loops, toggles, ties, frogs, and other decorative fasteners look attractive. Generally, machine-stitched buttonholes are best avoided because the filling peeks out.

Bound buttonholes are usually too dressy but they are very attractive. Replace self-fabric welts with welts of unquilted fabrics or grosgrain ribbon.

INTERFACINGS, LININGS, AND UNDERLININGS

Crisp quilted fabrics rarely need interfacings except in button/buttonhole areas and collars.

If the quilted fabric is soft, interface garment edges. Use a sew-in applied to the garment or a fusible applied to the facing.

Quilted garments are more comfortable and last longer when lined. Edge-to-edge linings are less bulky than conventional facing/lining finishes.

To tame lining fabrics which want to roll to the outside, topstitch garment edges; understitch; cut 1/8" smaller; or use a corded piping on the edges.

To reduce bulk, use lining-weight fabrics for patch pocket linings and inseam pocket sacks.

To make single-faced quilteds double-faced, use unquilted plain colors or companion prints to flat line or underline them.

1. Using the pattern pieces for each section to be backed, cut out the underlining sections.

2. Wrong sides together, baste the underlining and quilted fabric together.

Hint: *Machine stitch 1/4" from the edge to baste and to retard fraying.*

3. For unlined garments which are not reversible, experiment with fusing the layers together; however some fabrics do not fuse well; and some that do fuse well are not attractive.

4. Handle the underlined fabric like a double-faced quilted.

PRESSING AND GARMENT CARE

Set the iron temperature appropriately for the fiber content. Press seamlines lightly with the tip of the iron.

Consider both the fiber content and garment structure to determine the garment care. Many quilteds can be washed; however, a few will require dry-cleaning.

Custom Quilting

One of the joys of sewing is the ability to create unique designs; custom quilting is one of the easiest ways to do it.

If this is new to you, quilt a section or two to trim an unquilted garment; or quilt a jacket or vest to match a quilted dress or skirt.

This chapter is a small tip of a very large iceberg. For a more in-depth look at quilting, you'll enjoy *The Complete Book of Machine Quilting* by Robbie and Tony Fanning.

Fabric Characteristics
- Small areas are easier to quilt than large ones.
- Quilting takes time.
- Quilting stiffens the fabric.
- Quilting fabrics with closely spaced rows are stiffer than those with widely spaced rows.
- Fabrics "shrink" when quilted.
- Quilted fabrics are warmer than unquilted ones.

SEWING CHECKLIST

Machine Needles: Size and type depend on the fashion fabric. Use one to two sizes larger than you would in garment sewing the same fabric.

Thread: Invisible nylon, mercerized cotton, topstitching thread, silk (Sizes A and D), machine embroidery, metallic, long-staple polyester, cotton-wrapped polyester in a matching or contrasting color.

Sewing Machine Equipment: Quilting gauge, walking or roller foot.

Marking Techniques: Soap, chalk, temporary marking pins, thread tracing, drafting tape, pouncing.

PLANNING A GARMENT

SELECTING THE FABRIC

For the fashion fabric, choose a material which is firmly woven, so the padding won't show or migrate through the stitched holes. Fabrics with soft sheens are particularly attractive.

Select a batting appropriate for the design and function; some are very soft and thin, while others are thick and stiff. And if the garment will be washable, check the care requirements of the padding.

Padding materials such as lamb's wool, cotton flannel, cotton batting, Armo wool or Armo Rite, polyester fleece, or polyester batting range from very soft and thin to thick and semicrisp. Experiment with different battings, as well as with several layers of the same batting. And always check the care requirements of the batting to be sure it is compatible with the fashion fabric.

When making single-faced quilting, use the stabilizer of your choice.

When making double-faced fabrics, consider fusible interfacings, gauze, voile, organdy, organza, percale sheets, broadcloth, self-fabric, lining fabrics, and similar companion fabrics for the backing.

Most custom quilting emphasizes the pattern design, outlines the motifs on a print, or highlights the stripes or checks on the fashion fabric, but you can create your own designs. In addition to the old standbys—parallel rows, squares, and diamonds—try any interesting design on a plain fabric. Hand quilting books are full of possibilities.

Designs with small sections such as yokes, lapels, collars, cuffs, pockets, and bands are good choices for beginning quilters.

The more adventurous should consider simple jackets and coats with a minimum number of pattern pieces.

SEWING NOTES

Always quilt the fabric before cutting the garment. Quilting reduces the size of the fabric both in the length and the width. Although the actual amount of shrinkage depends on the thickness and

Fig. 17–2 *From Laura Biagiotti, the silk taffeta dress and parka are custom quilted in a chevron design. (Photo courtesy of Laura Biagiotti, P.A.P. Fall/Winter 1987/1988 Collection.)*

type of batting, it is approximately 1″ for every 8″ of unquilted material.

LAYOUT, MARKING, AND CUTTING

Lay out the pattern pieces so the fabric can be cut into rectangles or blocks for the individual pattern pieces. Be sure the rectangles are larger than the pattern pieces so they won't "shrink" too much.

Cut and quilt blocks; then lay out the pattern pieces on the blocks and cut out the garment pieces.

When the quilting is inspired by the fabric design, you probably don't need to mark the lines to be quilted.

When quilting straight lines, chalk, chalk wheels, temporary marking pens, and drafting tape work well. When quilting a silhouette or shaped design, make a pattern from quilting plastic, art frisket paper, or a manila file folder.

PRICK AND POUNCE MARKING

When quilting intricate designs, use a pricked pattern and a pounce bag. The method described here is a cross between Robbie Fanning's technique and the method used in the European embroidery houses.

1. Draw or trace your design on one of those plastics that come in a bacon package or a manilla file folder. (I like the plastic better because it's translucent.)

2. To prick the pattern, use an unthreaded needle (80/12) and machine stitch (L,3) all the lines of the design.

3. Place the pricked pattern on the right side of the fabric; and rub a pouncing bag over the pattern.

Hint: *Cut an 8" circle of muslin and fill with cornstarch (dark fabrics) or cinnamon (lights.)*

4. Carefully remove the pattern and connect the dots with a temporary marking pen.

STITCHING TIPS

Experiment with different types and sizes of needles, a variety of threads, and several different stitch lengths before quilting the garment. If the garment is washable, be sure the thread is also washable.

When quilting large pieces, use safety pins to hold the layers together. Or baste with silk thread, which doesn't drag the fibers through the fashion fabric as badly as does cotton or polyester.

If you're having stitching problems, consult The Sewing Clinic, in the Appendix.

CHAPTER 18
Fabrics with Designs: Plaids, Stripes, and Prints

Plaids

Plaid fabrics have woven, knitted, or printed bars and spaces running both lengthwise and crosswise.

Ethnic plaids such as Scottish tartans and Indian madras are among the most distinctive. Unlike the madras plaids, which are woven only in cotton, tartans are woven in all types of fabrics from lightweight cottons to silk taffetas and heavy wools.

All plaid fabrics fall into two categories—even or uneven, depending on the arrangement of the color bars which make the plaid design.

Very few plaids are even. Some plaids, which appear even at first glance, are balanced crosswise and lengthwise, but they are rectangular instead of square. Generally, this is because the filling yarns or picks are not as close together as the warp yarns or ends; but it can be because the warp and filling yarns are different sizes.

Even plaids are the easiest to match and the best choice for beginners. Garments made up in even plaid fabrics look exactly the same on both sides of the center. Many seamlines can be matched perfectly, both horizontally and vertically; and chevron effects are easy to achieve.

Unbalanced plaids are more difficult to work with, but the basic concept is the same—balance dominant heavier bars on either side of center, disregarding lighter bars. More important, uneven plaids can be used to create very interesting effects and designs. Generally, the plaid pattern continues in one direction around the body.

Fig. 18–1 *From Adele Simpson's Fall 1987 Collection, this three-piece costume coordinates plaids in three sizes. Notice that the bias-cut skirt echoes the design lines of the belt. (Photo courtesy of Adele Simpson, Inc.)*

Sometimes it's difficult to determine whether a plaid is balanced or not. When working with large or multicolored plaids, I number each bar and space so I can read the pattern easily without getting confused. A plaid that reads 543212345432l2345 is balanced; while another plaid, 123451234512345, is not.

Handwoven plaids are the most challenging. Many are unbalanced lengthwise and crosswise; and most don't have a regular repeat.

PLAID VOCABULARY

Balanced: A symmetrical arrangement of color bars and spaces. When folded through the center of the repeat, the two halves are identical. Plaids can be balanced crosswise, lengthwise, or both.

Even Plaid: A perfect square. The color bars and spaces are balanced: the same size, color, and sequence both horizontally and vertically. When the fabric is folded diagonally through the center of the repeat, the fold is on the true bias and the bars and spaces match. Very few plaids are even; and most even plaids are cotton fabrics.

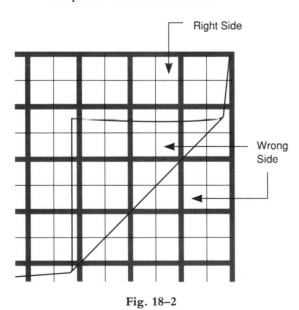

Fig. 18–2

Repeat: One complete plaid pattern. (A few plaids don't have repeats.)

Unbalanced Plaid: An uneven plaid which, when folded into quarters, has four different quarters. Unbalanced plaids have no center of design, but they usually have a repeat.

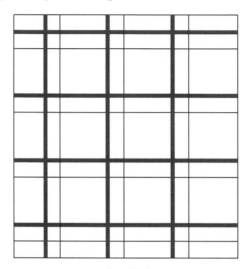

Fig. 18–3

Uneven Plaid: A rectangular repeat which is not a perfect square. It can be balanced crosswise, lengthwise, both, or neither.

Uneven Plaid—Balanced Crosswise: An uneven plaid with a symmetrical arrangement of vertical bars. When folded vertically through the center of the repeat, the two halves are identical.

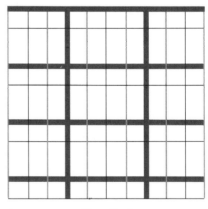

Fig. 18–4

Uneven Plaid—Balanced Lengthwise: An uneven plaid with a symmetrical arrangement of horizontal bars. When folded horizontally through the center of the repeat, the two halves are identical.

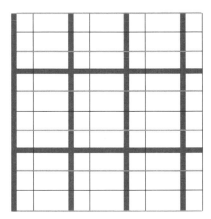

Fig. 18–5

Uneven Plaid—Balanced in Both Directions: An uneven plaid with a symmetrical arrangement of horizontal and vertical bars. When folded into quarters, all four quarters are identical but they do not make a perfect square. Balanced plaids frequently look like even plaids, but they are rectangles instead of squares.

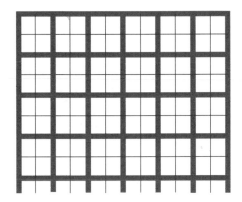

Fig. 18–6

Fabric Characteristics
- Plaids must be matched.
- Some plaids have a nap or one-way pattern.
- Few plaids which are off-grain can be matched satisfactorily.
- Plaids can be knitted, woven, or printed.
- Plaids may require a nap layout.
- Plaids require additional yardage.

SEWING CHECKLIST

Machine Needles: Size and point type depend on the fabric weight and structure.

Machine Setting: Depends on fabric weight and structure.

Thread: For most fabrics—long-staple polyester, cotton-wrapped polyester; for silks—mercerized cotton; for basting—water-soluble, basting cotton, silk.

Sewing Machine Equipment: Even-feed, roller, and zipper feet.

Equipment and Supplies: Dual tracing wheel.

Marking Technique: Tracing wheel and tracing carbon, pins, temporary marking pens, chalk, soap sliver.

Basting Aids: Glue stick, water-soluble thread and doublestick tape, Sticky Stuff, transparent tape, drafting tape, pins, cotton basting thread.

Seams: Plain, lapped, welt, decorative bound, piped tucked, slot.

Edge Finishes: Plain hems, facings, bias facings, bindings, bands.

Closures: All types.

Pockets: All types.

PLANNING A GARMENT

SELECTING PLAIDS

Select a plaid that is appropriately scaled for you and the garment. Generally, petite figures look best in smaller plaids while tall, willowy types can wear big blanket plaids.

Small plaids are more appropriate for blouses while large plaids make beautiful coats.

Avoid plaids which are printed, woven, or knitted off-grain more than 1/4″. Since most off-grain fabrics cannot be straightened, the finished garments will either have unmatched seamlines or twisted seams.

327

Generally, woven plaids are more expensive and less likely to be off-grain than printed or knitted plaids.

Examine the plaid from a distance, as well as up close. Plaids which are interesting when closely inspected may be uninteresting from a distance. Hang the plaid vertically first flat, then with folds, to see how it will look on a garment.

You always need extra fabric for matching plaids. Exactly how much depends on the plaid design, whether it's balanced or not, its size, the garment design, and the amount of waste.

Usually, an extra 1/4 to 1/2 yard will be enough for small plaids and 1/2 to one yard for large ones. To calculate more precisely, count the number of main pattern pieces—skirt front and back, bodice front and back, sleeve, etc.—and add one. Multiply by the length of the repeat—the length of one complete plaid pattern from top to bottom.

For example, if the fabric is 45" wide with a repeat of 6" and you need three lengths for a jacket and two for a skirt (a total of five lengths), multiply six (five lengths plus one extra) by 6" (the length of the repeat) for a total of 36" or one yard extra.

Occasionally, when there is a lot of waste in the fabric width, you'll need another garment length.

Many plaids require a nap layout; estimate the fabric requirement accordingly.

DESIGN IDEAS AND PATTERN SELECTION

The most attractive garments are simple, uncomplicated designs which showcase the fabric. Bias bindings, bands, and piping are particularly attractive on plaid designs.

For easy sewing, choose a pattern with a minimum of pieces and avoid those that are "not suitable for plaids." For best results, select a pattern which lists plaids among the suggested fabrics or illustrates the design in plaid on the pattern envelope.

To determine if a pattern design is suitable for plaids, most pattern companies make a trial garment in a plaid fabric; styles which are particularly attractive have one view illustrated in plaid.

Evaluate the pattern carefully to see how much gathers and darts will interrupt the plaid design. Darts parallel to the fabric grain are more attractive than those on the bias. Bust darts beginning at the

armscye or high on the side seam are most attractive.

Double-pointed darts, used to fit suits at the waistline, look best and are most slimming when centered between two prominent bars.

Designs which keep the crossgrain level at the bust and hips, allowing the plaid to flow uninterrupted around the garment, are attractive.

Underarm seams allow the horizontal lines to continue around the body without interruption. Underarm darts look better when located near the armscye.

Set-in sleeves are easier to plan than raglan sleeves; however, raglan sleeves can be very effective on large bold plaids or perfectly matched on even plaids.

When the plaid is balanced crosswise, kimono and raglan sleeve designs, which have shoulder curves cut exactly the same, will match at the shoulder seams.

Hint: *The design will probably need a seam at the center back and/or center front.*

Avoid kimono, raglan sleeves, and full, gored skirts if the plaid is unbalanced crosswise.

Reverse curves, such as princess lines and round yokes, interrupt the pattern both vertically and horizontally.

Closely fitted styles and rounded edges on collars, cuffs, and pockets look best in small-sized plaids.

The side seams of bias-cut designs and A-line skirts cannot be matched horizontally and vertically unless there is a center front opening or center back seam, since the garment front is usually 1" wider than the back.

The hemlines on straight, slim, and pleated skirts will distort the plaid less than those on flared or circular skirts.

If you are an inexperienced seamster, start with a blouse with a bias yoke, dress with a bias skirt, or a jacket with bias sleeves.

DESIGNS FOR HANDWOVENS

Designs with dropped shoulders and dohlman sleeves work well; or, if you have enough fabric, cut regular set-in sleeves on the bias.

Hint: *If you can match the color bars at the front armhole with the bias on the sleeve, the results will be stunning.*

Many small garments can be cut in a single width if darts are substituted for seams. Align the pattern pieces so the grainlines are parallel. Lap the pattern pieces and match the seamlines where possible without tilting the grainlines; pin. Lay out the pattern and mark the stitching lines.

Cutting the garment on the crossgrain is always a consideration; however, most handwovens will have an uneven and unattractive hemline.

PLACING THE COLOR BARS

The placement of the color bars is extremely important for a professional-looking garment. And for most garments, you will have to make some compromises, since you can rarely match everything.

All plaids have dominant stripes or bars, both vertically and horizontally. For best results, carefully consider where these bars will be positioned on the garment, so the design will produce an attractive optical illusion.

Don't try to match every seamline; the total effect is most important. Study the fabric and pattern design to determine which matchpoints have top priority and which can be compromised.

To identify the dominant bars, drape the fabric over the back of a chair. Stand back and squint to see which stripes stand out most.

VERTICAL BARS

First determine the placement of the vertical dominant bars on the garment front.

Generally, it is best to locate the center front midway between two prominent bars, but sometimes it is more pleasing to locate a prominent vertical bar at the center. And, occasionally, the center is located at the edge of the most prominent bar.

Stand in front of a full-length mirror and drape the fabric over your figure to see which position gives the best illusion of height and slimness.

Generally, when the vertical plaid placement begins at the front and forms chevrons at vertical seamlines, the center back will not be in the center of either the plaid square or most dominant bar. When this is the case, the garment will require a seam at the center back.

If you don't like the way the bars will look at the center back, start over. This time begin at the center back and work toward the front.

Do you like the way the bars meet at the center front? If you don't, try this last and least preferred placement—positioning the center front and back on the same color bar. This leaves the matching of the vertical bars at the sideseams to chance; and they will rarely, if ever, form chevrons at the side seams.

HORIZONTAL BARS

Next, determine the placement of the dominant horizontal bars on the garment.

To create the illusion of broad shoulders and narrow hips, position the most dominant horizontal bar just below the shoulder seams. To keep the bars away from the bust area, place large bars nearer the shoulder seam.

Drape the fabric over your figure and move it up and down to determine the best location for you. Try to avoid dominant horizontals at the bust, waist, hips, and hemline.

The garment hem should be midway between two prominent bars, though this is not always possible when the bars are optimally placed at the shoulder.

SLEEVES AND TROUSERS

To create the illusion of wider shoulders, locate the sleeve center midway between two dominant verticals. Or locate the sleeve center on the center of a dominant bar.

Hint: *An examination of several French couture suits revealed that vertical color bars on the sleeve continued the design of the jacket.*

On trousers, locate the center-front seam midway between two prominent bars. Hopefully the crease or pleat foldlines will fall on prominent bars. If not, shift the fabric slightly for better placement. Match the side seams horizontally and vertically to position the prominent verticals on the back of the trousers.

Once the basic placement for dominant horizontals and verticals is established, the rest of the garment can be matched.

ENSEMBLES AND TWO-PIECE GARMENTS

When making an ensemble with a plaid jacket and corresponding bolder plaid coat, match the vertical bars at center front and the prominent horizontal bars just below the shoulders.

Generally, larger garments have larger plaids, i.e., coats have larger plaids than jackets.

When making a two-piece garment, match the vertical bars at the garment centers of the skirt and blouse or jacket. The horizontal pattern should continue smoothly from head to toe. Match the horizontals at the waistline so the spacing between the last horizontal on the top and the first one on the skirt is approximately the same as the spacing on the uncut fabric.

LAYOUT IDEAS FOR BALANCED AND EVEN PLAIDS

To avoid a homemade look, plaids must match horizontally at the garment centers, all vertical seams, and the front armscye notches.

Plaids which are balanced crosswise and lengthwise are almost as easy to plan and sew as even plaids. Compared to even plaids, balanced plaids will not match when the crossgrain and lengthwise grain are joined; and a line drawn through opposite corners will not be on the true bias.

Uneven plaids which are only balanced crosswise have a one-way design and require a nap layout.

Make a trial garment; correct the fit; and duplicate the pattern pieces to make a complete pattern. Carefully label the pieces "right" and "left" to avoid cutting two right sleeves. Transfer all matchpoints to the seamlines by drawing a line through the center of each notch.

Hint: *Since all matching is done at the seamlines, I trim away the seam allowances on the pattern so I can see the plaid pattern better.*

Use a transparent ruler and colored pencils to trace the dominant plaid bars onto the trial garment. Then, starting with the garment front, lay one pattern piece on the fabric. Draw the lengthwise and crosswise bars at important notches and matchpoints, such as the front armscye notch and the hemline of the side seam.

Hint: *Sarah Bunje uses wax paper for the pattern and traces the plaid lines with a tracing wheel.*

Trace the plaid bars onto the other front. On garments with a front opening, match plaids at the garment center, not the garment edge.

If the front has a double-pointed dart at the waistline, try to center the dart between two vertical bars. You may have to move the dart 1/4" to 1/2".

Underarm darts are more attractive when one stitching line is on a prominent bar.

Lay the adjoining section—the side front, underarm panel, or back—on top of the front and align the corresponding notches. If the two sections have the same slope, the vertical bars on horizontally balanced plaids will be an even distance from each side of the seamline and form chevrons. Trace the horizontal and vertical bars across the hemline.

SLEEVES

Lay the sleeve pattern on top of the front; match the horizontal bars at the front notch. Examine the prominent vertical bars on the sleeve front and their relationship to the horizontals and verticals on the garment. On the sleeve, locate a prominent vertical bar so it will interface homogeneously with the horizontals and verticals on the bodice. The sleeve center does not have to be on a dominant vertical—the overall design is usually more pleasing if it isn't.

Examine the horizontal bars below the armscye. It is to be hoped the bars on the sleeve front will match those on the garment body. If they don't, you may be able to shift the sleeve up or down so they will. The horizontal bars on the sleeve seldom match those on the bodice back. When they do, it's just luck.

Once you're satisfied with the overall placement, trace the horizontal and vertical bars at the front armscye notch onto the sleeve pattern.

Hint: *Margaret Komives allows '1"-wide seam allowances on the sleeve cap so that if the cap doesn't quite match, it can be recut.*

On a two-piece sleeve, match the front seamline if you cannot match both.

Hint: *When working with wool, both can usually be matched. Fold the ease out of the sleeve front pattern. Cut the fabric; then stretch and shape the edge to put the ease back in.*

On dropped shoulder designs, match either the dominant horizontal bars below the armscye with the corresponding bars on the garment body or match the bars at the front armscye notch.

SKIRTS

Match skirt side seams so the horizontal bars match from the hemline to the notches and so the seamlines are centered between the vertical bars on the skirt front and back. To do this, the skirt must have a seam at the center back since the skirt front is wider than the back.

On skirts with straight hemlines, the hemline looks best midway between two prominent bars. A prominent horizontal bar at the hemline appears to shorten and broaden the figure.

Hint: *Determine the best placement for the dominant horizontal lines in the bodice or jacket; then let the hemline take care of itself.*

On flared skirts, the hemline should be in the least conspicuous bar of the plaid.

When making a pleated skirt, space the pleats for the plaid and disregard the marks on the pattern. Position the same color bar, preferably the dominant bar, at the edge of each pleat.

Cut the waistband to continue the design (1) on the skirt or pants, (2) on the most prominent bar, (3) centered between the bars, or (4) on the bias.

Hint: *Wait until the garment is assembled to cut the waistband. It can be cut on the lengthwise grain, crossgrain, or bias; experiment with the fabric scraps before deciding.*

Use a fusible interfacing to stabilize bands so stretchy bias and crossgrain bands are just as easy to sew as those cut on the lengthwise grain.

DETAILS

Cut all major pattern pieces first. Then experiment with scraps to decide how to position the pattern for facings, collars, cuffs, pockets, welts, yokes and flaps.

The facings for tailored collars and lapels are usually cut on the same grain as the garment so the fabric pattern matches at the beginning of the roll line. With this positioning, the horizontal bars on the facing fall below those on the garment front when the lapel is folded into position (Fig. 18–7).

On some Saint Laurent jackets, the plaid pattern is moved up so the lapel bars match the horizontal bars on the jacket when the lapel is folded back (Fig. 18–8).

You may also want to relocate the prominent vertical bars on the lapel if they aren't positioned at the edge. When the lapel isn't straight, cut the facing parallel to the edge of the lapel instead of parallel to the center front.

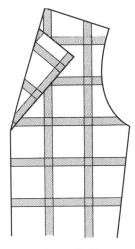

Fig. 18–7

Cut tailored collars on the crossgrain to match the garment back, on the bias for a novelty effect, or on the lengthwise grain to match the bar at the lapel edge.

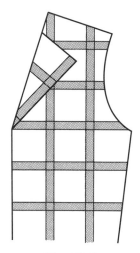

Fig. 18–8

When the garment back is not centered on a dominant vertical or between two, the collar will need a center back seam. When the collar is centered at the back, the progression of horizontal bars on the back can continue on the collar or a prominent bar can be placed at the edge of the collar. The latter placement may look better with the plaids on the lapel.

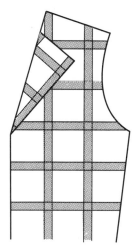

Fig. 18–9

Plaids may not match on shoulder seams, back armholes, trouser inseams, side seams above darts, and skirt side seams above the hipline.

BIAS COLLARS

Bias collars sometimes fit better and offer a variety of pleasing variations. Pay particular attention to the plaid bars at the collar corners. Plan a seam at the center back and be sure both sides are cut on the same grain.

Experiment with your scraps; consider how the collar will look where it joins the lapel. Since the center back seam doesn't have to be on the true bias, you can be very creative when planning a bias collar.

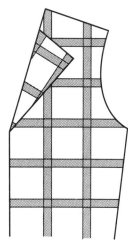

Fig. 18–10

If it will enhance the design, change the outside edge of the collar from a shaped edge to a straight edge.

BANDS AND YOKES

When the garment has a band at the front opening, cut the band on the bias or lengthwise grain.

Cut back yokes with the grainline perpendicular to the center back; only even plaids match adjoining sections—front, back, or sleeves. Locate a prominent vertical bar at the yoke seamline, midway between the seam and shoulder point, or just below the shoulders—this may not be at the top of the yoke.

BIAS-CUT DESIGNS

Some of the most attractive effects are created with bias-cut plaids. Four-gored skirts will chevron at garment centers and side seams.

For a perfect match, select a balanced plaid fabric and be sure that the skirt panels are exactly the same size and shape.

To make a bias pattern, see Chapter 1.

LAYOUT IDEAS FOR PLAIDS— UNBALANCED CROSSWISE

Position plaids in the usual way with the plaid pattern moving around the body to create stunning designs (Fig. 18–11). Or create a mirror image design if the plaid looks the same on both sides or if it has no nap or one-way pattern. For mirror image designs, the pattern must have seams at both garment centers (Fig. 18–12).

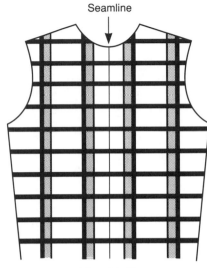

Seamline

Fig. 18–12

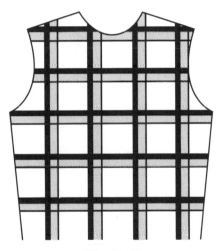

Fig. 18–11

If the fabric looks the same on the top and underside, lay out and cut the garment with two right sides. After cutting, flip one section over to make the left half of the garment.

If the fabric does not have a nap or one-way pattern, lay out the fabric with a crosswise fold. Or cut the sections for the right side of the garment with the tops in one direction; cut the sections for the left side of the garment in the other direction.

If the pattern doesn't have a seam at the center back and front, replace the foldline by adding a 5/8″ seam allowance to both sections.

Mirror image designs are particularly attractive on four-gored bias-cut skirts.

On regular flared skirts, uneven plaids can be matched horizontally at the side seams; but they won't form a perfect chevron unless a mirror-image technique is used.

Use a nap layout for plaids which are unbalanced crosswise and lengthwise. Fabrics such as seersucker plaids, which have no nap and are reversible, can be cut with a mirror image.

SEWING PLAIDS

LAYOUT, CUTTING, AND MARKING

Before laying out the pattern, pin the marked pattern pieces together and try them on; this is your last opportunity to rearrange the plaids.

Spread the fabric in a single layer with the right side up; position the pattern pieces, face up, on it. Be sure the plaids match at the seam lines, not the cutting lines. To mark the matchpoints on the seamline, connect the points of the notches and extend the line to the stitching line.

Hint: *Trim away the seam allowance on the pattern to make matching easier. Mark the cutting line using a dual tracing wheel.*

333

Use a nap layout for plaids which are unbalanced lengthwise.

Hint: *When I have enough fabric, I use a nap lay-out. Even when the plaid appears balanced, fabric finishes may change the shading; and it is rarely evident before the garment is sewn. This is particularly true on handwoven fabrics.*

If the fabric is printed or woven off-grain and can't be straightened, follow the plaid pattern and ignore the grainline.

When possible, lay out the pattern pieces so adjoining seams are next to each other. Be sure to leave enough space between the pattern pieces to add seam allowances.

Lay out all the large pieces—the fronts, backs, and sleeves—first. Then lay out the smaller pieces—pockets, flaps, welts, facings, collars, and cuffs. In fact, you may want to delay cutting some of the smaller pieces until later.

Hint: *To cut difficult fabrics, cut the right front bod-ice first; flip it over; align the plaids, and cut the left bodice. Then cut the bodice backs, sleeves and skirt.*

When working with even plaids, be careful to avoid confusing the crossgrain and lengthwise grain.

To avoid too much of a good thing, don't get carried away cutting small sections on the bias.

Generally, on better garments, details—pockets, flaps, and welts—are cut to match the garment. To do this accurately, lay the pattern piece for the detail on the garment section and trace the plaid pattern. Then lay out pattern for the detail.

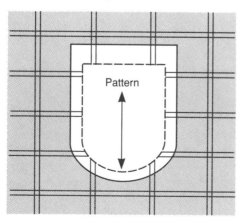

Fig. 18–13

Hint: *When there is a dart under a pocket, match the pocket edge nearer the center front to the gar-ment.*

When the layout is complete, pin the pattern pieces in place and add seam allowances, using chalk, temporary marking pen, soap sliver, or tai-lor tacks.

Hint: *If possible, take a break before cutting. When you return, check one last time to be sure ad-joining pieces match at the beginning and end.*

STITCHING TIPS

Select a machine needle in the correct size and type for the fabric. Select a thread that will blend with the plaid colors. It may or may not exactly match one of the colors in the fabric.

Stitch directionally. Whenever possible, stitch with the same section on top. For example, when stitching the skirt side seams, stitch both with the skirt front on top. To do this and to stitch directionally, stitch one seam in the usual position with the bulk to the left; stitch the other with the bulk to the right.

Use a roller foot, even-feed foot, or basting aids when stitching, so the plaids won't shift.

For short, easy-to-match seams, offset the top layer 1/8″, just so you can see the bottom layer. Insert a few pins; and stitch with an even-feed foot.

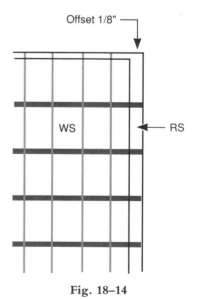

Fig. 18–14

Hint: *Try to avoid stitching over the pins. If you must, turn the hand wheel manually.*

Plain seams are the most common treatment. However, lapped seams are easier to stitch accurately; and they can be topstitched again to look like double-welt seams. For a sporty look, use welt seams. When the plaids do not match exactly, use piped seams.

JOINING SEAMS

1. Press under one seam allowance.

Hint: *I machine stitch each section just inside the seamlines so I'll know exactly where to press and match.*

2. Right sides up, align the plaid bars and baste the two sections together.
   For piped seams, sew the piping to the seamline before pressing.
3. For a plain seam, turn back the pressed section so right sides are together; machine stitch along the pressed line.
   For lapped seams, edgestitch the folded edge.

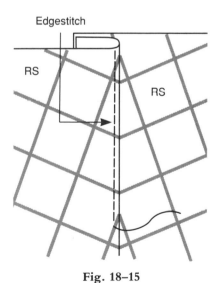

Fig. 18–15

To make double-welt seams, trim one layer and topstitch again 1/4″ from the foldline.

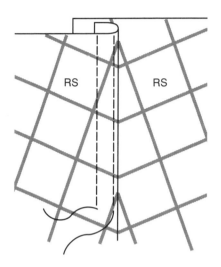

Fig. 18–16

Hint: *Use a zipper foot to stitch lapped seams.*

4. Remove the basting; press the seam open or to one side as desired.

BASTING TECHNIQUES FOR PLAIDS

Now that you've cut the fabric to match, it's easy to baste and sew it to match.
   Consider the complexity of the plaid, the texture of the fabric, and the garment design, as well as your sewing skills, when selecting a basting method.
   For best results, baste with right sides up. Fold and press one seam allowance under.

Hint: *Mark the seamlines with chalk or machine basting.*

Glue stick and water-soluble doublestick tape are easy basting techniques which work well on some fabrics. Position the glue or tape just inside the seamline on the right side of the unpressed section. Align the plaid bars and press the layers together. Let the glue dry before stitching.
   Another easy basting method is to use drafting or transparent tape. With the right sides up, align the bars and tape the sections together. Then, right

sides together, stitch from the wrong side on the seamline.

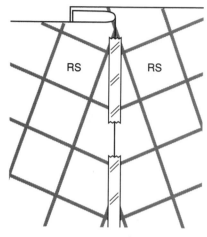

Fig. 18–17

Hint: *Before using tape, test to be sure the tape won't mar the fabric or pull off the nap.*

When pin-basting, try to avoid stitching over the pins. Begin right sides together; insert pins on the seamline at major matchpoints. For best results, stab the pin straight down; check the location of the pin on the underneath; then set the pin.

Machine basting works well on fabrics which are not marred by needle holes. Right sides up, align the bars and pin the sections together. Set the machine for a blind hemming stitch (W,2;L,2.5) and a loose tension; stitch next to the foldline. Only the zigzag stitch will catch the foldline.

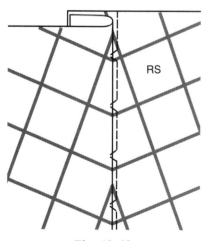

Fig. 18–18

Hint: *Use water-soluble basting thread in the bobbin. Be careful—this thread dissolves in hot moist hands and when wound onto a bobbin at high speed. (That's why you can't use it on top— the heat from the needle will melt it.)*

For difficult seams, hand baste. Right sides up, align and pin the sections together. Then use short slipstitches or fell stitches to baste.

Hint: *The fell stitch tends to hold the fabric a little more securely; however, the stitches slant on the wrong side; and if you aren't using a water-soluble thread, they are more difficult to pull out.*

When using slipstitches, I frequently turn the garment over and put in a second row of basting, from the wrong side; so there are no spaces between the stitches.

CLOSURES

Buttonholes can be machine-stitched, hand-worked, or bound. Cut welts for bound buttonholes on the bias, straight grain, or crossgrain to match the garment design.

Hint: *Use either the strip or windowpane method to make bound buttonholes which match the garment. Double baste them in place so they won't shift when you stitch.*

Cord bias buttonhole welts so they won't stretch out of shape.

TARTANS

Generally used to describe the plaids and checks used by Scottish clans for kilts, coats, and shawls, the word "tartans" technically describes the cross-stripe pattern. Woven in all types of fabrics from lightweight cottons to silk taffetas and heavy wools, tartans usually have a twill weave.

When sewing tartans, see Plaids.

Checks

Checks are closely related to plaids. Like stripes, they are easier to handle because the fabric pattern is simpler.

Checks such as gingham and windowpane checks are usually even; while checks such as houndstooth and tattersall checks are uneven. Fabrics vary in weight from very lightweight dimity checks to heavy windowpane wools.

When sewing checked fabrics, see Plaids.

Fig. 18–19 *Oscar de la Renta's bold checked coat is beautifully cut with minimum seaming. (Photo courtesy of Jesse Gerstein, photographer, and Oscar de la Renta, designer.)*

Stripes

Striped fabrics are closely related to plaids, but they are much easier to handle, since the colored bars run in only one direction.

Stripes can be found in virtually every major fiber and fabric weight. They can be woven, knitted, or printed, equal or varying widths, one, two or many colors, smooth or textured, subtle solid-color cross-ribs, vertical cords, bold contrasting colors, corded or flat, woven or printed. They are available in every size, from the tiniest pinstripe to bold awning stripes.

Fabrics such as dimity, ottoman, seersucker, pinstripes, pillow ticking, oxford stripes, corduroy, Bedford cord, ribbed piqué, and awning stripes are examples of the many striped patterns.

The basic concepts for sewing plaids also apply to stripes and are not repeated in this section. (See Plaids.)

Fig. 18–20 *Gertrude Lawrence wears a classic striped knit from the thirties. (Photo courtesy of Paul Tanqueray, photographer, and the National Portrait Gallery, London.)*

Fabric Characteristics
- Horizontal stripes must be matched.
- Some stripes have a one-way pattern, requiring a nap layout.
- Most off-grain fabrics cannot be matched satisfactorily.
- Stripes frequently require additional fabric.

SEWING CHECKLIST

Machine Needles: Size and point type depend on the fabric weight and structure.

Machine Setting: Depends on fabric weight and structure.

Thread: For most fabrics—long-staple polyester, cotton-wrapped polyester; for silks—mercerized cotton; for basting—water-soluble, silk, cotton.

Sewing Machine Equipment: Even-feed, roller, zipper feet.

Marking Techniques: Tracing wheel and tracing carbon, pins, disappearing marking pens, chalk, soap sliver.

Basting Aids: Glue stick, water-soluble thread and double-stick tape, transparent tape, drafting tape, pins, silk and cotton thread.

Seams: Plain, lapped, welt, double-welt, piped, decorative bound, slot.

Edge Finishes: Traditional hems and facings, bias facings, bindings, bands, and ribbing.

Closures: All types.

Pockets: All types.

KNOW YOUR STRIPES

Balanced Alternating Stripe: Sometimes called a balanced even stripe, this two-color pattern alternates equal-width bars and spaces.

Balanced or Mirror-Image Stripe: A symmetrical

338

arrangement. When folded in the center of the most dominant bar, the two halves are in sequence, color, and/or size.

Fig. 18–21

Even Stripe: A pattern with equal-width color bars and spaces.

Fig. 18–22

Repeat: One complete stripe pattern.

Unbalanced Even Stripe: A three or more color pattern with progressive or consecutive arrangement of equal-width bars and spaces.

Fig. 18–23

Unbalanced Uneven Stripe: A pattern with progressive or random multicolor bars.

Fig. 18–24

Uneven Stripe: A pattern with bars and spaces of unequal widths.

PLANNING A GARMENT

For additional suggestions, see Plaids.

READING STRIPES

The stripe arrangement on intricate patterns and multicolored fabrics is sometimes difficult to decipher. To determine the type of stripe, label each color bar with a number and write down the number as you read the pattern across the repeat.

For example, 1212 is an alternating, two-color stripe. 12321 is a balanced, mirror-image stripe. 12341 is an unbalanced, progressive multicolor stripe. 12324242526784242489l is an unbalanced, random multi-stripe.

A few fabrics, such as handwovens, have random stripes and do not repeat the pattern.

Hint: *To quickly check a striped pattern, fold through the center of the repeat; turn back one corner on the bias. If the stripes match at the fold, the pattern is balanced.*

SELECTING STRIPED FABRICS

Examine the fabric to be sure the stripes are printed or set on-grain. When folded lengthwise, horizontal stripes should match at the selvages and vertical stripes should match at the ends.

339

Generally, vertical stripes, which run up and down parallel to the selvage, slim and flatter most figures. Horizontal stripes, which run crosswise from selvage to selvage, shorten the figure.

However, thin, vertical stripes are more slenderizing than bold, widely spaced stripes; thick vertical stripes tend to add pounds and inches.

When considering striped fabrics, stand three or four feet from a full-length mirror; drape the fabric over your figure and examine your image.

When considering railroading the fabric (cutting the garment on the crossgrain), check to be sure the fabric will drape attractively.

Purchase extra fabric as needed for matching. Consider the stripe width and design, number of pattern pieces, and design layout to determine the additional amount needed.

Hint: *To quickly estimate the amount required for matching horizontal stripes, multiply the width of the stripe repeat by the number of major pattern pieces.*

DESIGN IDEAS AND PATTERN SELECTION

Almost any pattern—except those labeled "not suitable for stripes"—can be made from a striped fabric; and many interesting effects are easily obtained with little effort. Patterns labeled "not suitable for stripes" will not match at the seamlines.

For a first garment, consider a simple design with few pattern pieces and trim it with a bias piping or binding.

For more interest and challenge, choose a design with a separate band or yoke. Change the stripe direction on one or two pieces to create a different look.

For a one-shouldered sun dress or evening gown, create a new look by locating the stripe parallel to the neckline.

Make an easy, but unusual, collarless jacket or simple dress by cutting one half with vertical stripes and the other with horizontal stripes.

Tuck the stripes to make a solid color or rearrange the colors for collars, cuffs, yokes, and other small garment sections. Tucks can be on the outside or inside of the garment.

For simple two-color stripes, use released tucks or pleats to create positive/negative effects.

Add new seamlines and change the grainlines to create miters, assymetrical/bias miters, and bulls-eyes.

Change the skirt grainline so it will be parallel to the yoke/skirt seamline.

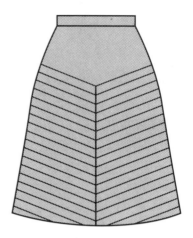

Fig. 18–25

For jackets with lapels, enhance the design with one of these designer ideas: Yves Saint Laurent cut the facing on an ottoman jacket with the stripes (crossgrain) parallel to the lapel edge (Fig. 18–26). Courregés cut the facing on the crossgrain; when folded back, the stripes are parallel to the bodice.

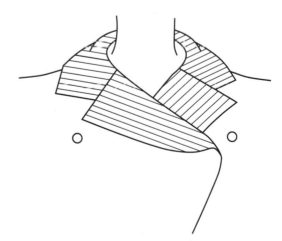

Fig. 18–26

SEWING STRIPES

LAYOUT, CUTTING, AND MARKING

Use a nap layout for uneven stripes, unless you plan a mirror-image design.

When cutting horizontal patterns and uneven stripes, use duplicate pattern pieces and lay out on a single layer of fabric. Reposition the pattern if a bold stripe falls at the bust, waist, hipline, or hem.

For even vertical designs, use a double layer with a lengthwise fold. Carefully pin the layers together so the stripes are aligned. For fabric economy, use a "without nap" layout.

On cuffs, waistbands, and plackets, enter the dominant stripe or position it at one edge to create a banded look.

Match two-piece garments and dresses with waistline seams where the bodice or top meets the skirt or bottom.

UNBALANCED STRIPES AND MIRROR IMAGES

Like plaids, unbalanced stripes can be cut to progress around the garment. They will not match at the shoulders. And a match at the sideseams may have to be sacrificed for a more attractive placement on the front and back.

If the fabric doesn't have a one-way pattern or looks the same on both topside and underside, balance uneven vertical stripes to create a mirror image.

First, add seams at garment centers if there are none. Cut two rights for each garment section.

Reverse one to use for the left side; then assemble the garment.

When the fabric doesn't have a one-way design or nap, fold the fabric crosswise; then cut.

SEAMS

Seams on striped fabrics can be decorative, as well as utilitarian. Welt, double-welt, piped seams, decorative bound seams, tucked and slot seams are good choices.

To piece garment sections invisibly, locate the seamline at the edge of one stripe in an inconspicuous area—near the hemline or under the arm.

POCKETS AND BOUND BUTTONHOLES

Cut pockets and bound buttonholes on the bias for a diagonal effect, on the same grain so the stripes match, or on the opposite grain.

On vertical stripes, locate buttonholes horizontally or vertically.

On horizontal stripes, buttonholes don't have to, and probably won't, fall on the same stripe. On wide horizontal stripes, bound buttonholes can be all one color or can match the stripe.

On bias-cut designs, locate buttonholes on the grainline.

Cut welts for bound buttonholes on the lengthwise grain, crossgrain, or bias. They can match the stripe or be a contrasting color or pattern.

Generally, all machine-stitched buttonholes are stitched with the same color thread; however, they can be stitched with different colors to match the striped bars. Covered buttons can also match or contrast with the stripe.

Border Designs

Most border designs have a printed, embroidered, woven, or knitted design along or instead of one selvage. A few are printed panels with the border on the crossgrain.

Available in all fibers and fabrics, typical border designs include printed fabrics, lace, eyelet, embroidered, sequinned, cut velvet, and other formal fabrics. Many have coordinating fabrics without the border design.

Materials such as sheets, tablecloths, scarves, and towels are also border designs.

Fabric Characteristics
- Most borders run the length of the fabric and garments are cut on the crossgrain.
- Some borders have a one-way design and require a nap layout.

- Some fabrics with border designs must also be matched like stripes. (See Stripes.)
- Some border designs are transparent. (See Transparent Fabrics.)
- Some borders are lace. (See Lace.)
- To optimize the fabric design, you may need additional fabric.
- Few patterns are designed for border designs.

Fig. 18–27 *Emilio Pucci's cotton batiste cover-ups are made from two of his famous scarf designs in typical Pucci colors—yellow, pink, and red. (Photo courtesy of the photographer, Lorenzo Allisio-Florence, and the designer, Emilio Pucci.)*

SEWING CHECKLIST

Machine Needles: Universal-H point or Red Band needles; sizes 60/8 to 80/10.

Machine Setting: Depends on the fabric.

Thread: Long-staple polyester or cotton-wrapped polyester. Silk fabrics—mercerized cotton or extra-fine cotton-wrapped polyester.

Hand Needles: Sizes 5 to 10.

Layout: Nap, single layer, right side up.

Marking Techniques: All types, depending on the fabric.

Seams: Depends on the fabric. Plain, French, false French, standing-fell, double-stitched, appliqué, self-finished, tissue-stitched.

Seam and Hem Finishes: Single/ply or double/ply, depending on the fabric—turned-and-stitched, pinked, pinked-and-stitched, zigzag, multistitch zigzag, serge, and bound.

Hems: Depends on the fabric. None, plain, faced, shirttail, book, machine-rolled.

Closures: All types, depending on the fabric.

PLANNING A GARMENT

DESIGN IDEAS AND PATTERN SELECTION

Select a simple design to showcase the fabric. Pattern designs with at least one straight edge work best.

Avoid A-line, gored, and circular skirts. Safe choices include simple dirndl skirts, dresses, and blouses with the border around the hem; shirtwaist dresses and shirts with the design at the garment opening. Or create a more unusual design by running the border vertically on the side or side front of a dirndl skirt.

Hint: *Don't forget, when the border is used at the hemline, the skirt or garment length is limited to the fabric width, unless you plan to piece the fabric.*

On tee tops, simple dresses, and camisoles, place the border horizontally across the shoulders like a yoke or vertically for an off-center design.

On asymmetrical designs, such as surplice and off-center closures, use the border only on the overlap. On a four-gored skirt, position the border to form chevrons.

Create an unexpected focal point by placing the border at the sleeve cap instead of at the wrist or at the top of a skirt instead of at the hem.

Cut the border into smaller widths for collars, cuffs, front bands, and pockets. Use the border on the facing or front band and collar of a shirt instead of at the hem.

Create a mirror image above and below the waistline on dresses and jackets by joining two border sections together at the waist.

PATTERN ADJUSTMENTS

To determine the fabric requirement, plan the layout before purchasing the fabric. Most designs will require 1/2 to one yard additional fabric.

Adjust the pattern before cutting. Establish the garment length when placing the border at the hemline. If the fabric isn't wide enough to cut the skirt or dress, recut the pattern for piecing.

Cut duplicate pattern pieces for a single/lay.

Cut a separate facing pattern if the fabric isn't wide enough for an extended facing or if the design on the facing will be unattractive.

Trim away the hem allowance on the pattern if the fabric is embroidered or finished at the edge.

SEWING BORDER DESIGNS

LAYOUT

Spread the fabric in a single layer right side up. Using duplicate pattern pieces, lay out the pattern so dominant motifs are positioned attractively. When laying out the pattern, also be sure to align the finished edge, not the cutting line, with the edge of the border.

Don't overlook the rest of the design on the fabric. Occasionally, it's even more attractive than the border.

Hint: *When positioning some pattern pieces on the crossgrain and others on the lengthwise grain, check twice to be sure the fabric pattern works well together.*

Don't be tempted to have too much of a good thing. Generally, using the border in two, or maybe three, areas looks best.

SEAMS AND HEMS

Use appliqué seams to join the borders on embroidered, cut velvet, sequinned and other elegant fabrics.

When seaming border designs with a finished edge, such as on tablecloths and scarves, use self-finished seams—French, false French, flat-fell, or standing-fell seams.

When matching border designs, begin stitching at the border—the point of difficulty.

When the border extends to the selvage, face the edge, so the border won't be cut off in the hem allowance.

When pressing eyelets and embroidered fabrics, cover the pressing board with a thick terry towel. Press the eyelet, wrong side up.

Diagonal Patterns

Diagonal designs have printed lines or woven ridges in a diagonal formation on the right side of the fabric. If the diagonal design is not obvious, handle the fabric like plain-weave materials or ordinary twill weaves.

Woven diagonals have ridges in the same or contrasting color. Formed as a part of a twill weave, the angles of diagonals vary from low to very steep; and a few are on the true bias.

Generally, diagonal weaves run from the upper

left to the lower right on wools and from right to left on cotton. Diagonal prints run in either direction.

Fabric Characteristics
- Diagonal weaves range from very inconspicuous to very distinctive.
- Diagonal designs are usually planned so the lines progress around the body in one direction.
- Matching diagonals is impractical on many garments.
- Diagonals can only be matched at straight seamlines which are on the lengthwise grain. They cannot be matched on curved or bias seams.
- Diagonals do not chevron except in rare instances.
- Reversible diagonal fabrics can be matched to chevron.
- Diagonals may slant in either direction.
- Diagonals do not require a nap layout; however, other characteristics of a diagonal fabric may.
- Generally, bias-cut sections are unattractive unless the diagonal design is a true bias or 45-degree angle.

PLANNING A GARMENT

DESIGN IDEAS AND PATTERN SELECTION

Fabrics with steep diagonal designs make you look taller and slimmer.

Since diagonals are difficult to match at seamlines, pattern companies rarely recommend diagonal design fabrics.

Simple designs with basic rectangular shapes, straight or almost straight seamlines, and set-in sleeves work well.

Try to avoid collars with a fold at center back, turned-back lapels, long bias darts, V-necklines, kimono and dohlman sleeves, gored and A-line skirts.

Avoid bias trims if the diagonals are not on the true bias or cut the bias on the opposite bias so it looks like a crossgrain.

Fig. 18–28 *Daytime sophistication from Oscar de la Renta: a dramatic cape and chemise dress with asymmetrical button closure. The fabric is a twill weave with a pronounced diagonal design. (Photo courtesy of Jesse Gerstein, photographer, and Oscar de la Renta, designer.)*

When in doubt, chart the pattern pieces. Trace the miniature pattern pieces from the pattern guide sheet; make duplicates; and draw diagonal lines on them. Match the seamlines and survey the results. If you like what you see, use the pattern.

Note: In recent years, couturier Emanuel Ungaro always has diagonal-weave fabrics in his collection; he disregards all of the above rules and uses large collars, kimono sleeves, and bias trims which look off-grain.

Straight underarm darts are more attractive than long bias darts. If the design has bias darts, change them to underarm darts with the following method:

1. Draw the location of the new dart; and slash it to the bust point.

2. Close the original dart.

3. Mark the end of the new dart about 1 1/2″ from the bust point; and connect the end of the dart and two openings on the side seam.

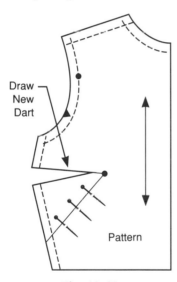

Fig. 18–29

When the fabric width permits, eliminate straight seamlines. Overlap and pin the pattern pieces together on the seamlines; then cut the garment.

SEWING DIAGONAL DESIGNS

LAYOUT

Twill weaves and printed diagonals do not require nap layouts unless they have a nap, sheen,

Fig. 18–30

pile, knit, etc. However, I prefer nap layouts whenever possible.

To match the diagonal design on straight, lengthwise seams, begin with duplicate pattern pieces.

Do not cut collars with a fold at the center back; the collar points won't match and will look unattractive. Add a seam at the center back; cut one collar half on the lengthwise grain and the other half on the crossgrain.

Bias collars won't look good if the stripes are not on the true bias; and if the collar is cut on the diagonals, disregarding the grain, the collar won't roll properly.

When making a tailored jacket or coat, cut the undercollar on the bias as indicated, even though it looks peculiar; it won't be visible when the garment is worn.

MATCHING DIAGONALS

The diagonal pattern can be matched if the seams are on the lengthwise grain. Although this occurs most frequently at garment centers, straight side seams on straight skirts, blouses, and boxy jackets will also match.

1. Make duplicate pattern pieces.

2. Begin with the garment front. If it has a seam at center front, match and pin the pattern seamlines together. If it opens at center front, match and pin the pattern centers together.

3. Pin the pattern backs and fronts together, matching the vertical seamlines. Lay the pattern on the fabric. Trace several prominent diagonals on each pattern piece and identify the colors on the pattern.

4. Unpin the side seams and pin the pattern backs together, matching the center seamline. Lay the pattern on the fabric to be sure it matches properly at the center; large designs may not.

If it doesn't match, you can ignore it; but I prefer to match the center back and have one unmatched sideseam. Remark the pattern with stripes if needed.

5. Unpin the remaining pattern pieces; and lay out the pattern on the fabric, matching the diagonals on the pattern to those on the fabric.

REVERSIBLE FABRICS

Two-faced fabrics can be cut so the diagonals chevron at the garment centers.

1. Add seam allowances to the pattern at the garment centers.

2. Lay the pattern on the fabric and trace several prominent diagonals on the pattern.

3. Spread the fabric in a single layer; lay out the pattern for the right side of the garment; cut. Repeat to cut a second set of right sides.

4. Flip one set of rights to make the left side of the garment.

BIAS TRIMS

Bias trims are particularly attractive on jacket and collar edges. If the diagonals are on the true bias, bias trims can be cut with lengthwise or crosswise stripes.

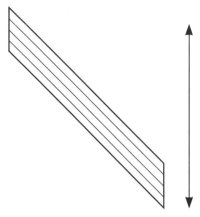

Fig. 18–31

If the diagonals are not on the true bias, cut the trim with crosswise stripes.

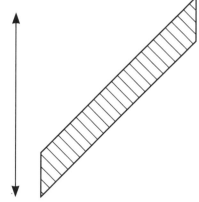

Fig. 18–32

Prints

It is generally believed that the Egyptians used resist printing as early as 2100 B.C., even though very few prehistoric textiles have been unearthed.

Today various printing methods are used to decorate fabrics with florals, stripes, geometrics, polka dots, paisleys, abstracts, op-art, tropical designs, borders, ink blots, graffiti, ethnic patterns, and calicos.

Available on all types of fabrics and weaves, prints enliven every wardrobe.

Fabric Characteristics
- Large prints require careful placement.
- Large-scale prints should be matched like stripes. (See Stripes.)

- Many prints have a one-way design and require a nap layout.
- Prints with one-way designs and large motifs require additional fabric.
- Small-scale prints frequently look like a neutral solid from a distance.

Fig. 18–33 *From Emanuel Ungaro Parallele, Autumn/Winter 1987/1988 Collection, two black and white silk prints are combined to create a smashing bustier with harem skirt. (Photographer, Guy Marineau; photo courtesy of Emanuel Ungaro.)*

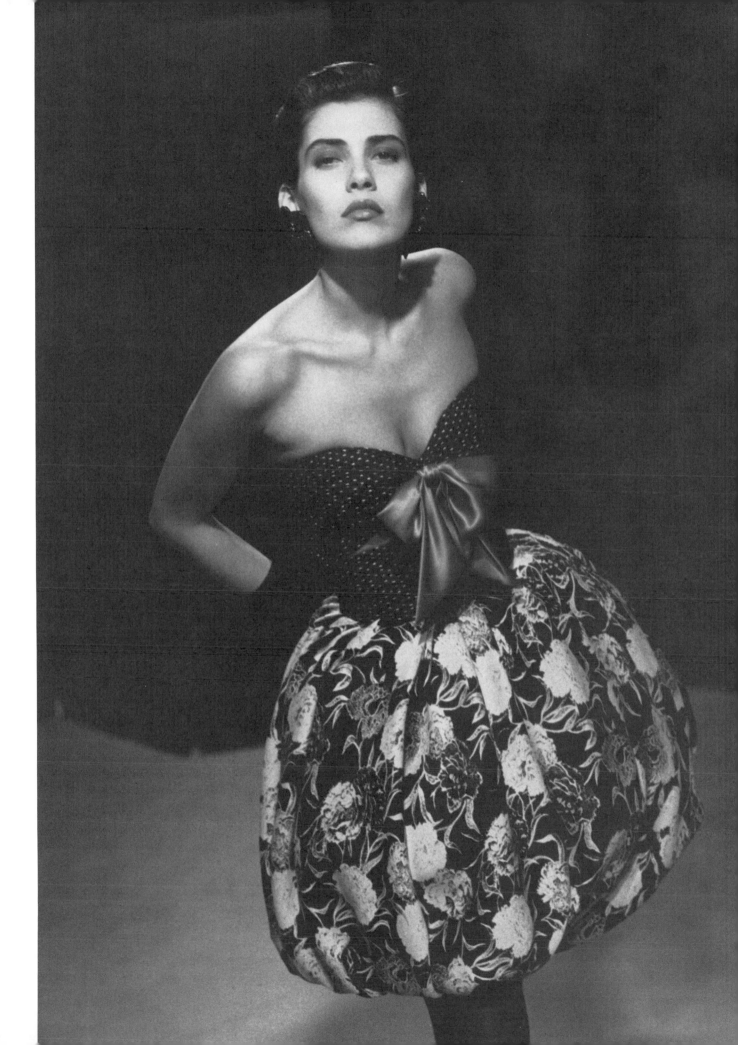

PLANNING A GARMENT

PATTERN AND FABRIC SELECTION

When sewing large prints, select a simple design with a minimum of pieces. Avoid fussy details.

When sewing small prints, the design will depend on the silhouette, since the seamlines will be "lost" on the fabric.

Designs with pipings, applied bands, decorative facings, and contrast ribbings are particularly attractive for most prints.

If you're a sewing novice, small-scale prints will hide a multitude of sins. But try to avoid purchasing prints from a small swatch. Unroll a couple of yards of fabric. Examine the colors up close; then view the fabric from a distance to be sure it doesn't turn gray.

Hang the fabric in folds, as well as flat, to see how the print will look when made into a garment.

Any print can be worn by any figure type, if it fits your personality; but these suggestions will enhance most figures.

Bold, large-scale prints in bright colors are more attractive on tall, slender figures; small-scale prints in medium values are good choices for short, heavy figures; and medium-scale prints in medium values work well for large, heavy figures. Petite figures look good in small- to medium-sized prints in light or pale colors.

MIXING PRINTS

Mixing prints successfully takes practice. Study ready-made garments for the latest trends and design ideas. Look for separates that harmonize to make an attractive ensemble, as well as for garments with multiple prints.

Hint: *Don't overlook men's fashions; they've been mixing prints and patterns for years.*

For best results, begin with something simple. It's easier to mix two prints than to mix five; and prints are easier to mix with separates than within one garment.

Look at fabric collections which include coordinated prints; or visit a retailer who specializes in quilting materials.

Choose prints with the same color values or intensities in different scales. Mixing the same type print, such as two florals or two geometrics, is usually safer than mixing a floral and a geometric.

When using several prints in the same garment, select fabrics with similar care requirements, fiber content, weight, drape, and colorfastness.

This idea, developed by Anne Marie Soto, is particularly helpful when mixing different prints. Cut a large window in the center of a sheet of typing paper; then stack several bolts of printed fabrics with the window in front. Stand back and squint, so only the window is visible.

Hint: *This is particularly helpful when looking at small-scale prints; the individual colors blend together, creating a different color.*

Use these time-tested combinations to stimulate your imagination:
- foulard and paisley
- foulard and plaid
- plaid and paisley
- stripes and dots
- two jacquard patterns in the same color
- one jacquard pattern in different colors
- plaids and stripes in the same colors with similar scales
- two plaids in different scales
- plaids and checks
- a positive and a negative print
- two geometrics with the same colors.

Once you've made your selection, consider solid-colored pipings, bindings, borders, belts, or scarves to pull the outfit together.

Almost as challenging as choosing the prints is deciding which to put where. When you survey ready-made designs, you'll see that even though there are no firm, easy-to-follow rules, these two are frequently used.

1. The scale of the print is directly related to the size of the garment. Generally, coats feature larger plaids than jackets; but on a suit, sometimes the jacket is made of the larger plaid and other times the skirt is.

2. The dominant prints draw the eye. Generally bold prints add inches to the smallest hips, so instead they are used for tops to broaden the shoulders and to narrow the hips.

Plan your layout before purchasing the fabric to

348

avoid purchasing too much or being caught short. Make duplicate pattern pieces if the print has large motifs. Preshrink all fabrics.

SEWING PRINTS

LAYOUT

If both sides look almost the same, mark the right side of the fabric with drafting tape. Use a nap layout if the print has a one-way pattern.

When laying out small-scale prints, spread the fabric in a double/lay, right sides together.

LARGE-SCALE PRINTS

When sewing large-scale patterns, decide which motifs are dominant; then drape the fabric in front of you and stand about six feet from a full-length mirror. Try several placements.

Hint: *Generally, locating the dominant motifs equidistant from the garment centers is most attractive. I try to have one motif located on the left shoulder like a corsage; but, if that positions a motif at a major body curve such as the bust, hips, or elbows, I regroup.*

A few designs look best with the motifs located at the garment centers.

To match and position large motifs easily, spread the fabric right side up; then, using duplicate pattern pieces, lay out the pattern.

Try to match the motifs so the design flows smoothly from one section to another. Remember to match the seamlines, not the cutting lines.

PART FOUR

Linings and Interfacings

Interfacings and Battings

The interfacing, an essential ingredient for most garments, is an additional layer of fabric placed between the outer shell and the facing or hem. The primary reason for using interfacings is to add support, body, and shape, or to eliminate stretch. Secondary reasons include shadow proofing seams and taming facings at garment edges. Use interfacings to prevent sagging at necklines and button closures; to add softness to hemlines; to add body, shape, or wrinkle resistance to entire garments or garment sections; and to stabilize and emphasize details, such as collars, cuffs, midriff inserts, pockets, vents, flaps, welts, and epaulets.

Interfacings

TYPES

Interfacings are described in two ways: by the fabric structure (woven, nonwoven, knit, weft-insertion), and by the method of application (sew-in and fusible).

METHOD OF APPLICATION

Sew-in interfacings are sewn into the garment by hand or machine. Available in most fibers, they can be woven or nonwoven materials.

Fusible interfacings have a resin on one side and are bonded to the fabric when you apply heat, moisture, and pressure. They can be woven, nonwoven, tricot knit, or weft-insertion knits. All fusibles are crisper after fusing. The size of the fusible dots increases with the weight of the interfacing; if the fusible is too heavy for your fashion fabric, the dots will show through.

Fusibles cannot be used on all fabrics. Some materials, such as metallics, leathers, vinyls, furs, crepes, seersuckers, and cloques, are damaged by the heat, moisture, or pressure required for fusing. Fusibles destroy the tactile quality of most fabrics.

FABRIC STRUCTURE

Woven interfacings are woven fabrics with a stability in the lengthwise grain and a slight give in the crossgrain. Available in many fibers, they are suitable for all woven fabrics.

Nonwoven interfacings are feltlike materials which do not ravel. Well-suited for washable garments and knits, nonwovens can be machine washed and dried or dry-cleaned.

Stable nonwoven interfacings have no grain and no give. They are very firm and can be cut in any direction.

Stretch nonwoven interfacings have crosswise stretch. They are suitable for knits, bias-cut fabrics, and stretch wovens.

All-bias nonwoven interfacings have some give in all directions. Some can be cut in any direction; others have more give in the bias. They are suitable for supple, unstructured shapes.

Tricot knit interfacings are fusibles and can be used to interface or underline knit and woven fabrics.

Weft-insertion interfacings are fusible knit interfacings with weft insertions. This structure produces stability in the crossgrain and stretch and recovery in the length. Well suited for tailoring, weft-insertions are more supple than woven fusibles and more stable than knits.

Fig. 19–1

Fusible woven interfacings describe themselves. The limited selection in the interfacing department can be expanded by applying a fusible web to the back of any woven fabric. Use Wonder Under, Transfuse II, or a Teflon release sheet to apply the fusible web.

Hair canvas is the traditional interfacing for tailoring. Woven with wool, goat's hair, and other fibers, it is available as a sew-in or a fusible. The quality improves with the amount of the wool and hair.

Fusible web is a mesh of polyamides which melt. With heat, moisture, and pressure, fusible webs can join two fabric layers permanently for hemming, appliqués, or interfacing. It may be applied to a single layer of fabric with a Teflon release sheet. Some fusible webs such as Wonder Under

and/or Transfuse II are packaged on a paper release sheet.

Release sheets are Teflon-type sheets which allow you to bond a fusible web to a fabric without gumming up the iron.

Stabilizers are nonwoven fabric, paper, or water-soluble materials. Technically they are not interfacings; however, they support the fabric during construction for tissue stitching, appliquéing, and embroidery. They tear away or dissolve easily after stitching.

PLANNING A GARMENT

SELECTING THE INTERFACING

The interfacing is an important part of the garment; this is no time to economize. Purchase the best interfacing you can afford; and by all means, avoid economy-package interfacings such as the four yards for $2.00 you frequently see advertised.

Choosing the perfect interfacing is a challenge; but, with practice, any home sewer can do it well. For each garment you sew, you'll need to make several decisions.

These decisions are affected by (1) the quality, design, and use of the finished garment; (2) the quality, weight, hand, color, care requirements, and special characteristics of the fashion fabric; (3) the reason for interfacing; (4) the characteristics of the interfacing materials; and (5) your sewing ability, time available, and your preferences.

When selecting interfacings, I consider all the above factors; then I experiment with my favorite interfacing materials, which I always have on hand.

Here are some things to consider as you use this procedure for choosing interfacings.

1. **Consider the finished garment.** Will it feature a fine fabric or moderately priced material, designer techniques or serger methods? Will it be soft or structured, avant-garde or classic, casual or dressy, an everyday design or special-occasion garment, for daytime or evening wear? Will special interfacing treatments be required to achieve the finished look? Will it be washed or dry-cleaned?

2. **Consider the fashion fabric**—its quality, structure, weight, hand, transparency, and care requirements. Generally, sew-ins are used for more expensive fabrics and quality garments; however,

fusibles such as Armo Weft, Whisper Weft, Easy-Shaper, Pel-Aire, Suit-Shape, and knit or weft-insertion fusibles are the preferred interfacings for expensive synthetic suedes.

The fabric quality is particularly important when selecting interfacings for tailored garments. Expensive wools, silks, and linens deserve fine-quality, woven sew-in interfacings. Everyday and washable fabrics may actually be more attractive with knit or weft-insertion fusibles.

Examine the structure of the fashion fabric and consider the reason for the interfacing.

To maintain the fabric character, stretch wovens, knits, and bias-cut fabrics need interfacings that give with the fabric or stretch in some area; but, to maintain the garment's shape and prevent unwanted stretching at shoulder seams and buttonholes, they need interfacing materials which stabilize.

Evaluate the fabric's weight, drape, and hand. To avoid overwhelming the fabric, select an interfacing that is slightly lighter in weight and a little crisper. To change the fabric's character, select a very crisp or fusible interfacing. Avoid interfacings which are heavier in weight than the fashion fabric.

Self-fabric, silk organza, organdy, voile, tulle, or marquisette are frequently good choices for featherweight and lightweight fabrics.

When considering woven interfacings, drape one layer of fabric over a layer of interfacing. If the interfacing is almost perfect, but a little too crisp, cut it on the bias to make it more flexible. If it is too soft, create a new interfacing material by sewing or fusing together two layers of the same or different interfacing materials. One layer may be on the straight grain and the other on the crossgrain or bias; or one layer may be a sew-in and the other a fusible.

Hint: *On shirt collars, Milwaukee teacher Margaret Komives applies a fusible interfacing to a sew-in woven to add crispness to the collar points while retaining the suppleness of the sew-in in the rest of the collar.*

Consider the transparency or opaqueness of the fashion fabric. For transparent fabrics, consider the interfacing color and shape and reconsider the need for the interfacing. Select an interfacing that will blend into the total design. My favorite interfac-

Fig. 19–2 *With the help of some very stiff interfacing, Bill Blass boldly entwines a drape of pink and red satin to frame the face in this dramatic evening gown. (Photograph courtesy of Bill Blass Ltd., Fall Collection 1988.)*

355

ings include self-fabric, silk organza, organdy, voile, or marquisette.

Hint: *I frequently reshape the interfacing so it will look more attractive from the outside of the garment (e.g., the front of a transparent blouse is more attractive when the interfacing and facing are straight instead of shaped). Sometimes I eliminate the interfacing completely.*

Be sure the care requirements of the interfacing are compatible with the fashion fabric. Permanent press interfacings can be used in dry-clean-only garments, but all-cotton interfacings and interfacings that require dry-cleaning or ironing aren't suitable for wash-and-wear designs.

3. **Evaluate the use of the interfacing in the finished garment.** You may want to interface sections which were not indicated on the pattern or you may eliminate the interfacing entirely.

Interfacings are used to add durability (e.g., button and buttonhole areas); protect the fashion fabric from stress (e.g., armscye seams); improve the appearance (e.g., garment edges and sleeve heads); preserve the shape (e.g., shoulder seams, sleeve vents, and hems); and create special effects (e.g., bubble or harem skirts and decorative bows or drapes).

Sometimes it's necessary to use several different interfacing materials in the same garment. A tailored jacket may have hair canvas in the lapels, linen in the collar, muslin in the hemline, and lamb's wool in the sleeve heads. The skirt of an evening gown may be interfaced with Armo-Press while detail areas such as large bows may be interfaced with hair canvas.

Or you can cut the same interfacing on different grains. The lengthwise grain has the least amount of stretch. The crossgrain has some give and is frequently more comfortable to wear. The bias has the most stretch and flexibility.

4. **Review the characteristics of the individual interfacing fabrics**—the fabric structure, fiber content, method of application, color, and care requirements. The interfacing fabric structure—woven, nonwoven, knit, weft-insertion, or net—affects its fray quality, washability, hand, drape, stretch, and cost. The decision to use interfacings with particular fabric structures is frequently a matter of preference. I prefer woven interfacings for better

garments because they drape and hang more like fashion fabrics, but they do ravel.

Hint: *When using woven sew-ins, I use a faced facing for a neater edge on my garments, especially washable designs.*

The fiber content affects the care requirements, flexibility, malleability, and cost of the interfacing.

The method of application—sew-in or fusible—affects the fray quality, hand, and drape of the fabric; and it sometimes affects the serviceability of the garment.

Generally, it's difficult to evaluate fusibles without making a test sample. Fusing makes all fabrics crisper and more wrinkle- and fray-resistant; they may bleed through and look "boardy," blister after laundering, or have a demarcation line at the edge of the interfacing.

Hint: *Many consider using fusibles a timesaver, but basting nonfusible interfacings with a glue stick runs a close second; and it isn't nearly as hot—important to me, since I live in the desert. To avoid blobs, use the glue sparingly.*
Seattle teacher Jane Whiteley, who uses even more glue sticks than I, wears jeans when sewing so she can wipe the glue off her fingers onto her jeans to save time. At the end of the day she washes the jeans.

If the fusible dots bleed through when you test, the interfacing is too heavy. If there is a demarcation line, try a lighter interfacing or interface the entire garment section. If the interfaced area is a different color or texture from the rest of the fabric, interface the entire section and, if needed, the entire garment.

5. **Consider your sewing skills, time available, and personal preferences.** It's your garment and you are the designer.

Generally, hand-tailoring techniques and hair canvas interfacings are preferred to quick fusible interfacings for fine-quality tailored garments; but if you don't have the talent, time, or patience to use them, use those which will give you a professional-looking finish.

After considering all the above, make some test samples using your favorite interfacings—the fabrics in your stockpile. Experiment with several interfacings which vary from crisp to soft. And,

356

if necessary, review your interfacing library and test additional interfacing fabrics which you don't usually use.

Hint: *After narrowing my choice to two or three interfacings, I usually choose the crisper, lighter weight material.*

INTERFACING LIBRARY

Begin an interfacing library. Each time you try a new fabric, buy several 1/8 yard cuts to test on it. Make several samples with fabrics in your scrap box or your fabric drawer.

1. Cut a 6″ square of fabric; cut a 2″ by 6″ strip of interfacing with one straight edge and one pinked edge.

2. Place the interfacing on the wrong side of the fabric, align the straight edge with the center of the fabric.

3. Fuse or stitch the interfacing in place.

4. Fold the sample in half at the straight edge of the interfacing; examine it for weight, crispness, and a demarcation line at the pinked and straight edges.

Fold the sample in the middle of the interfacing. If it folds like cardboard, or with wrinkles, it's too heavy.

If the fusible dots are visible, the interfacing is too heavy.

5. Label the sample and file it for future reference.

PREPARING THE INTERFACING

Stockpile your favorite interfacing in three- to five-yard lengths; preshrink them immediately.

All interfacings shrink; and, if the fabric and interfacing shrink different amounts, the fusible will separate, blister, or ripple when cleaned. Once the fusible blisters, pressing with a steam iron will improve the appearance but it won't eliminate the blisters.

To preshrink washable sew-in interfacings, machine wash. Tumble dry interfacings for wash-and-wear designs; line dry interfacings for hand-washable and dry-clean-only garments.

To preshrink washable fusible interfacings, fill a basin with hot water. Place the folded interfacing in the basin. Remove the interfacing when the water

cools. Roll in a towel to remove excess moisture; hang over a shower rod to dry.

To preshrink tailor's linen, use the procedure for fusibles and soak in warm water. To preshrink hair canvas, steam press.

To preshrink nonfusible dry-clean-only interfacings, steam vigorously.

STORING INTERFACINGS

Label all interfacings before putting them away.

Hint: *Jane Whiteley writes the name on the selvage at one end with a laundry pen. Then she uses the interfacing from the other end. When it's time to purchase more she cuts off the name and takes it to the store.*

Use the plastic direction interleafs to make storage bags for the fusibles they accompany. Fold in half lengthwise and sew up the sides.

PREPARING THE PATTERN

If the pattern doesn't include an interfacing pattern, use wax paper to make one. (See the next section for seam allowance directions.)

When using self-fabric interfacing on transparent fabrics, reshape the blouse front facing so it looks attractive.

SEWING INTERFACINGS

CUTTING

Using the interfacing pattern or garment section pattern, cut most interfacings with 5/8″ seam allowances. Trim away the seam allowances for hair canvas and collar linen.

Trim away the seam allowances plus 1/8″ on fusible interfacings for synthetic suedes and other nonwoven materials when the garment is to be finished with cut edges. This will prevent the interfacing from showing at the edges and lapped seams.

When cutting a tailored collar, be sure the interfacing has a center back seam so the points will be on the same grain.

APPLYING INTERFACINGS

Woven interfacings are applied to the garment so they will shadowproof the seams and cause the seamline to roll to the underside.

Hint: *Use a washable glue stick to glue-baste the interfacing to the seam allowance.*

Fusible interfacings are frequently applied to the facing to avoid a demarcation line on the garment; or interface the entire garment section—front, collar, and cuffs.

Hint: *Use the abutted or lapped seaming method to stitch darts in interfacing.*

Apply the interfacing to the upper collar and cuffs. Trim away the seam allowance of the interfacing completely; glue in place; and use the trimmed edge as a guide for stitching the seams. Topstitch the finished section to secure the interfacing.

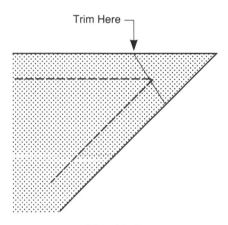

Fig. 19–3

Hint: *To minimize bulk, trim away the corners just inside collar points.*

For a crisper interfacing, fuse two or three layers or fuse two sew-ins together with fusible web. For a softer interfacing, cut woven interfacings on the bias.

Interface buttonholes with the least amount of stretch parallel to the buttonhole. Use leftover pieces of waistband fusibles to stabilize buttonholes. Firmly woven, lightweight fabrics left over from blouses are particularly nice.

Most waistband interfacings are too heavy to use on both the waistband and its facing. Interface only the outside of the waistband.

INTERFACED EDGES

For softer edges, use 1"- to 2"-wide bias strips to interface necklines, armscyes, and hems.

If there is a seamline, stitch the bias into the seamline; clip as needed so it will lie flat. If there is a fold, center the interfacing over the foldline and blindstitch it in place.

FACED FACING

To interface washable garments with a woven interfacing, face the facing. Right sides together, join the interfacing and facing on the unnotched edge with a 1/4" seam. Fold and press the interfacing to the wrong side; trim and clip as needed, so the interfacing is the same size as the facing. Join the faced facing to the garment.

SELF–FABRIC INTERFACINGS

Self-fabric interfacings are particularly attractive for button closures on transparent fabrics.

To reshape the pattern for self-fabric facings, measure the distance between the center front and the garment edge. Multiply by four to add a facing

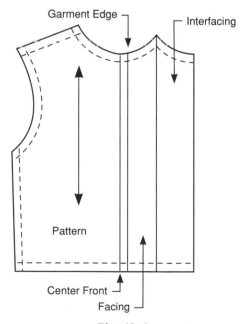

Fig. 19–4

and an interfacing. Add this amount to the garment edge.

When sewing, press the interfacing/facing to the wrong side on the garment edge. Fold the raw edge in to meet the pressed line; press again. Baste across the top and bottom. Topstitch, if desired; however, the buttons and buttonholes will secure it.

FUSING INTERFACINGS

While heat and moisture melt the resin, the pressure pushes it into the fibers.

1. Read the directions which came with the interfacing.

2. Place the fabric, wrong side up, on the pressing board.

3. Place the interfacing, resin side down, on the fabric.

4. Cover with a press cloth, dry or wet, depending on the interfacing instructions.

5. Baste press lightly in several areas if the section is large.

6. Set the iron on "wool." Press hard with steam, unless the directions indicate otherwise, for 10 to 15 seconds. Overlap the fused areas carefully to avoid a bare section. Do not slide the iron.

Hint: *Elizabeth Lawson, my boss at the College of the Desert, is from Tennessee, so she counts Tennessee 1, Tennessee 2, etc.*

7. When fusing tightly woven materials, such as synthetic suede, denim, and gabardine, fuse one side; then turn the section over and fuse the other. Always use a press cloth when fusing from the right side. For synthetic suedes, use a damp, not wet, cloth to avoid creating permanent bubbles.

8. Allow the fabric to cool before moving it.

9. Test to be sure all corners are securely fused.

TO REMOVE INTERFACING

1. Cover the interfacing with a damp cloth.

2. Press with the iron set on "wool."

3. Pull the interfacing away from the fabric before it cools.

4. Discard the interfacing; it can't be reused.

UNDERLINING WITH INTERFACINGS

Most interfacing materials can be used to underline the garment. Use underlinings for body or to completely change the character of soft and loosely woven fabrics.

Hint: *Use knit fusibles to underline sleeves in unlined garments so they'll be easier to slip on.*

INTERFACING CHECKLIST

There are approximately 100 different interfacings. The Interfacing Checklist names interfacings, their manufacturer, and traditional fabrics which can be used as interfacings.

The interfacings are grouped first according to weight, then according to type: Woven Sew-in, Woven Fusible, Nonwoven Sew-in, and Nonwoven Fusible.

Abbreviations for interfacing structure: W–woven; K–knit; WI–weft insertion; N–nonwoven. Abbreviations for application method: S–sew-in; F–fusible.

Interfacings for Featherweight Fabrics

Suitable for tissue-weight fabrics, chiffon, georgette, crepe de chine, silk organza, and marquisette.

INTERFACING STRUCTURE	INTERFACING APPLICATION	INTERFACING NAME	WEIGHT	COLORS	COMMENTS
W	S	Silk Chiffon Georgette Crepe de chine	Featherwt.	All	Soft; use for same and similar featherweight; dry-clean
W	S	Silk organza Marquisette Tulle	Featherwt.	All	Crisp; dry-clean or wash and dry

Interfacings for Very Lightweight Fabrics

Suitable for sheers, handkerchief linen, voile, crepe de chine, Charmeuse batiste, very lightweight polyesters, wools, and silks.

W	S	Batiste Sheath lining	Very ltwt.	All	Use in same fabric and sheers; various weights; 100% cotton or polyester/cotton blends; sheath lining less expensive than batiste; same care requirements, usually wash and dry
W	S	Crepe de chine	Very ltwt.	All, flesh	Soft; use in same fabric; varies in weight; generally dry-clean
W	S	Handkerchief linen	Very ltwt.	All, flesh	Crisp; washable, not durable press
W	S	Nylon ninon	Very ltwt.	All, flesh	Very crisp; machine wash and dry
W	S	Organdy	Very ltwt.	All, flesh	Crisp; heavier than organza; unstitched corners tend to curl; 100% cotton or polyester/cotton; washable; may not be durable press

INTERFACING STRUCTURE	INTERFACING APPLICATION	INTERFACING NAME	WEIGHT	COLORS	COMMENTS
W	S	Polyester chiffon	Very ltwt.	All, flesh	Crisper than silk chiffon; softer than silk organza; machine wash and dry
W	S	Self-fabric	Very ltwt.	All	Same color; same care properties
W	S	Silk organza Marquisette	Very ltwt.	All, flesh	Crisp; dry-clean or wash and iron
W	S	Tulle Illusion veil Net	Very ltwt.	All	Varies from medium crisp to very crisp; care depends on fiber
W	F	Silk-weight interfacing	Very ltwt.	Cream, black, white, beige	Very soft, lightweight; 100% cotton or 100% polyester; machine wash and dry
N	S	Nonwoven #905 (Pellon)	Very ltwt.	White, beige	Soft, very light; crosswise stretch; 100% polyester; machine wash and dry
N	S	Sheer Sew-in (Stacy)	Very ltwt.	White, beige, charcoal, print blender	Very soft; drapeable; little crosswise stretch; 100% polyester; machine wash and dry
N	F	Jiffy Flex (Staple)	Very ltwt.	White	Crisp; machine wash and dry
N	F	Nonwoven #906F (Pellon)	Very ltwt.	White, beige	Very light; medium crisp; crosswise stretch; 100% polyester; machine wash and dry
N	F	Poly-O (Staple)	Very ltwt.	White, beige, charcoal	Crisp; machine wash and dry
N	F	Sheer Blenders #907F (Pellon)	Very ltwt.	Charcoal, red, blue, silver	Soft; crosswise stretch; 100% polyester; machine wash and dry
N	F	Sheer Fuse (Stacy)	Very ltwt.	White, beige, charcoal, print blender	Soft; crosswise stretch; 100% polyester; machine wash and dry
N	F	So-Sheer (Crown)	Very ltwt.	White, beige, charcoal	Soft; crosswise stretch; 100% polyester; machine wash and dry

361

Interfacings for Lightweight Fabrics

Suitable for lightweight cottons, wools, silks, synthetics, linens, shirtings, broadcloths, and handkerchief linens.

INTERFACING STRUCTURE	INTERFACING APPLICATION	INTERFACING NAME	WEIGHT	COLORS	COMMENTS
W	S	Organza Organdy Marquisette Batiste Sheath lining	(See Interfacings for Very Lightweight Fabrics)		
W	S	Polyester organza	Ltwt.	All, flesh	Varies in crispness; 100% polyester; machine wash and dry
W	S	Utica linen	Ltwt.	Tan	Crisp; nice for collars; dry-clean
N	S	Add-Shape Featherlite (Stacy)	Ltwt.	White, charcoal	Medium crisp; flexible; crosswise stretch; 90% polyester/10% rayon; machine wash and dry
N	S	Featherweight Bias (Crown)	Ltwt.	White	Soft; crosswise stretch; 70% polyester/30% rayon; machine wash and dry
N	S	Interlon bias (Stacy)	Ltwt.	White	Medium crisp; bias stretch; 70% polyester/30% rayon; machine wash and dry
K	F	Easy Knit (Stacy)	Ltwt.	White, beige, black, gray	Crisp, crisper than Knit Shape; crosswise stretch; 100% nylon tricot; machine wash and dry
K	F	Knit Shape (Pellon)	Ltwt.	White, black	Crisp, softer than Easy Knit; crosswise stretch; 100% nylon tricot; machine wash and dry
WI	F	Whisper Weft (Crown)	Ltwt.	White, beige	Soft; stable; bias give; 60% polyester/40% rayon

Interfacings for Light- to Medium-Weight Fabrics

Suitable for light- to medium-weight wovens in cottons and blends, knits, piqué seersucker, shantung, denim, poplin, lightweight suitings, raw silk, double knits, wool dress-weights.

INTERFACING STRUCTURE	INTERFACING APPLICATION	INTERFACING NAME	WEIGHT	COLORS	COMMENTS
W	S	Armo Press Firm (Crown)	Ltwt.	White	Very crisp; 50% polyester/50% cotton; durable press; machine wash and dry

362

INTERFACING STRUCTURE	INTERFACING APPLICATION	INTERFACING NAME	WEIGHT	COLORS	COMMENTS
W	S	Armo Press Soft (Crown)	Ltwt.	White, black	Soft; 50% polyester/50% cotton; durable press; machine wash and dry
W	S	Collar linen	Ltwt.	Tan	Medium crisp; used for tailoring collars; dry-clean
W	S	Shape-Flex Woven (Stacy)	Ltwt.	White, black	Soft and lightweight; 100% cotton; machine wash and dry
W	S	Siri	Ltwt.	White, black	Crisp; wash or dry-clean
W	S	Super Siri Light-weight	Ltwt.	White	Soft; wash or dry-clean
N	S	Featherweight #910 (Pellon)	Ltwt.	White, black, gray	Soft; use for subtle shaping; all bias; 100% polyester; machine wash and dry
N	S	Interlon Light-weight (Stacy)	Ltwt.	White, black	Crisp; stable; 100% polyester; machine wash and dry
N	S	Interlon Bias Lightweight (Stacy)	Ltwt.	White	Crisp; bias stretch; 70% polyester/30% rayon; machine wash and dry
N	F	Detail Fusible	Ltwt.	White	Crisp; detail areas; 70% polyester/30% rayon; machine wash and dry
N	F	Fashion Former Lightweight (Crown)	Ltwt.	White	Medium crisp; stable; 70% polyester/30% rayon; durable press; machine wash and dry
N	F	Featherweight to midweight #911FF (Pellon)	Ltwt.	White, charcoal	Very crisp; all-bias; 80% polyester/20% nylon; machine wash and dry
N	F	Jiffy Flex Light-weight (Staple)	Ltwt.	White, black	Machine wash and dry
N	F	Sof-Shape #880F (Pellon)	Ltwt.	White, charcoal	Soft; changes the hand very little; 100% nylon; machine wash and dry

W—Woven   WI—Weft Insertion   S—Sew-in
K—Knit   N—Nonwoven   F—Fusible

INTERFACING STRUCTURE	INTERFACING APPLICATION	INTERFACING NAME	WEIGHT	COLORS	COMMENTS
N	F	Soft-Fuse (Stacy)	Ltwt.	White	Ultra soft; crosswise stretch; not recommended for silks & sheers; machine wash and dry
N	F	Uni-Stretch Lightweight	Ltwt.	White	Soft; crosswise stretch; 75% polyester/15% nylon/10% rayon; machine wash and dry
W	S	Sta-Shape Durable Press (Stacy)	Med.wt.	White, black	Very crisp; 50% polyester/50% rayon; durable press; machine wash and dry
W	S	Formite II (Crown)	Med.wt.	White	Crisp; machine wash and dry; durable press
W	S	Shapewell, 70 (Pellon)	Med.wt.	White	Very crisp; 100% cotton; machine wash and dry
W	S	Veriform (Stacy)	Med.wt.	White, black	Very crisp; 50% polyester/50% rayon; durable press; machine wash and dry
W	S	Super Siri Mediumweight	Med.wt.	White	Soft; wash or dry-clean
W	S	Wigan	Med.wt.	Gray, black	Soft; used for tailoring and interfacings; 100% cotton; wash or dry-clean
W	F	Fusible Formite	Med.wt.	White	Soft; 100% cotton; machine wash and dry
W	F	Fusible P-91 (Crown)	Med.wt.	White	Soft; 100% cotton; machine wash and dry
W	F	Kuffner	Med.wt.	White, black	Crisp; 100% cotton; machine wash and dry
W	F	Shape-Flex All Purpose (Stacy)	Med.wt.	White, black	Medium crisp; 100% cotton; machine wash and dry
W	F	Shape-Flex 50/50 (Stacy)	Med.wt.	White, black	Crisp; 50% polyester/50% cotton; durable press; machine wash and dry
W	F	Shapewell #70F (Pellon)	Med.wt.	White	Crisp; 100% cotton; machine wash and dry
N	S	Add-Shape Mediumlite (Stacy)	Med.wt.	White	Crisp; crosswise stretch; 90% polyester/10% rayon; machine wash and dry

INTERFACING STRUCTURE	INTERFACING APPLICATION	INTERFACING NAME	WEIGHT	COLORS	COMMENTS
N	S	Interlon Durable Press (Stacy)	Med. wt.	White	Crisp; crosswise stretch; 100% polyester; machine wash and dry
N	F	Easy-Shaper Lightweight (Stacy)	Med. wt.	White, charcoal	Medium crisp; crosswise stretch; lighter than suitweight; 90% polyester/10% rayon; durable press; machine wash and dry
N	F	Easy-Shaper Suitweight (Stacy)	Med. wt.	White, charcoal	Firm, crosswise stretch; heavier than Easy-Shaper Lightweight; 90% polyester/10% rayon; durable press; machine wash and dry
N	F	Fashion Former Medium-weight (Crown)	Med. wt.	White	Medium crisp; stable; 70% polyester/30% rayon; machine wash and dry
N	F	Jiffy Flex Suit-weight (Staple)	Med. wt.	White, black	Medium crisp; machine wash and dry
N	F	ShirTailor #950 (Pellon)	Med. wt.	White	Crisp; stable; lighter than Shirt-Fuse; used for collars and cuffs; 100% polyester; durable press; machine wash and dry
N	F	Shirt-Fuse (Stacy)	Med. wt.	White, beige, charcoal	Crisp; stable; heavier than ShirTailor; 100% polyester; machine wash and dry
N	F	SRF (Crown)	Med. wt.	White, charcoal	Soft; crosswise stretch with recovery; 75% polyester/25% nylon; machine wash and dry
N	F	Stretch & Bounce (Staple)	Med. wt.	White, charcoal	Soft; crosswise stretch; 50% polyester/50% rayon; machine wash and dry
N	F	Stretch-Ease #921F (Pellon)	Med. wt.	White	Medium crisp; bias and crosswise stretch; 20% polyester/10% nylon; machine wash and dry

W—Woven   WI—Weft Insertion   S—Sew-in
K—Knit   N—Nonwoven   F—Fusible

Interfacings for Medium- to Heavyweight Fabrics

Suitable for bottom weights, medium to heavy wools, double knits, suitings, and some tailored designs.

INTERFACING STRUCTURE	INTERFACING APPLICATION	INTERFACING NAME	WEIGHT	COLORS	COMMENTS
W	S	Muslin	Various weights	Cream	Medium crisp; may not be durable press; 100% cotton or cotton/polyester; always preshrink; machine wash and dry
W	S	Linen	Various weights	All	Crisp; 100% linen not durable press; wash and dry or dry-clean
N	S	Interlon Regular Weight (Stacy)	Med.wt.	White	Stiff, for detail areas; 100% polyester; machine wash and dry
WI	F	Suit-Shape (Stacy)	Med.wt.	White, gray	Medium crisp; suitable for speed tailoring; 60% polyester/40% rayon; machine washable
N	F	Pel-Aire #881F (Pellon)	Med.wt.	Natural, charcoal	Medium crisp; suitable for soft tailoring; 100% nylon; machine wash
N	F	Shape-Flex Nonwoven (Stacy)	Med.wt.	White	Crisp; 70% polyester/30% rayon; machine wash and dry
N	F	Tailor's Touch (Stacy)	Med.wt.	White, gray	Medium crisp; suitable for speed tailoring on pile fabrics; 50% polyester/50% rayon; machine wash and dry
N	F	TriDimensional Med.- to Heavywt. #931 (Pellon)	Med.wt.–heavy	White	Medium crisp; crosswise stretch; 50% polyester/50% nylon; machine wash and dry
N	F	Uni-Stretch Suitweight (Crown)	Med.wt.	White	Soft; crosswise stretch; 75% polyester/15% nylon/10% rayon; machine wash and dry
WI	F	Armo Weft (Crown)	Med.wt.	White, black, beige, gray	Medium soft; flexible length, stable crosswise; used for soft tailoring knits & wovens; 60% polyester/40% rayon; machine wash and dry

Hair Canvas

The wiry goat hair in hair canvas allows you to create a soft, uncreased roll which will last for the life of the garment. The quality of hair canvases varies, depending on the fiber content. Hair canvas with larger amounts of wool and goat hair are easier to shape, better quality, and more expensive.

INTERFACING STRUCTURE	INTERFACING APPLICATION	INTERFACING NAME	WEIGHT	COLORS	COMMENTS
W	S	Acro (Crown)	Med.wt.	Natural	Crisp; used for med.- to heavywt. wools & wool blends; 51% polyester/ 43% rayon/6% goat hair; machine wash
W	S	Fino II (P-1) (Crown)	Med.wt.	Natural	Crisp, good quality with high wool content; used for med.- to heavywt. wovens; warp: 50% rayon/50% polyester; filling: 35% rayon/15% polyester/15% goat hair; dry-clean
W	S	Hair Canvas 77 (Stacy)	Med.wt.	Natural	Stiff; difficult to tailor; used for med.- to heavy-wt. fabrics; 63% rayon/ 20% goat hair/ 17% nylon; dry-clean
W	S	Hymo	Med.wt.	Natural	Crisp; used in the industry; varies in quality depending on amount wool/goat hair; dry-clean
W	S	P-26 Red Edge (Crown)	Med.wt.	Natural	Very crisp; moderately priced; used for med.- to heavywt. wovens; 62% cotton/30% rayon/ 8% goat hair (goat hair only in filling); dry-clean
W	S	Sewer's Choice (Pellon)	Med.wt.	Natural	Crisp; good quality; used for med.- to heavy-wt. fabrics; 43% cotton/36% rayon/21% goat hair; dry-clean
W	F	Fusible Acro (Crown)	Med.wt.	Natural	Crisp; moderately priced; 51% polyester/ 43% rayon/6% goat hair (goat hair only in filling)

W—Woven   WI—Weft Insertion   S—Sew-in
K—Knit   N—Nonwoven   F—Fusible

Waistband Interfacings

INTERFACING STRUCTURE	INTERFACING APPLICATION	INTERFACING NAME	WEIGHT	COLORS	COMMENTS
W	S	Armoflex (Crown)		White	Widths 1″; 1 1/4″; 1 1/2″; 2″
N	F	Fuse-N-Fold (Pellon)		White	same
N	F	Jiffy Waistband (Staple)		White	same
N	F	Waist-Shaper (Stacy)		White	same

Specialty Interfacings

INTERFACING STRUCTURE	INTERFACING APPLICATION	INTERFACING NAME	WEIGHT	COLORS	COMMENTS
W	S	Armo Rite (Crown)		Cream	Soft; used for underlinings, quilting, hems, sleeve heads; 100% polyester; machine wash and dry
W	S	Armo Wool (Crown)		Cream	Soft; used for underlinings, quilting, hems, sleeve heads; 100% wool; dry-clean
W	S	Canvas Unlimited (Stacy)		White	Use for ties, underlinings; 90% polyester/ 10% rayon; machine wash and dry
W	S	Buckram		White, black	Very stiff; width 42″; dry-clean
W	S	Crinoline		White	Very crisp; width 38″; dry-clean
K	S	Domette		White	Sometimes called lamb's wool, llama wool; very soft; knitted with a fleece; used for sleeve heads, quilting, hems, shoulder pads; various fibers; dry-clean
N	F	Craft-Fuse (Stacy)		White	Very crisp; width 22″; used for belts, handbags, hats; 100% polyester; machine wash and dry
N	F	Style-A-Shade (Stacy)		White	Very crisp; widths 36″ and 45″; used for hats, handbags, belts, shades; 100% polyester; machine wash and dry

W—Woven	WI—Weft Insertion	S—Sew-in
K—Knit	N—Nonwoven	F—Fusible

STABILIZERS

Stitch-n-Tear® (Pellon)
Trace Erase™ (Stacy)
Water-soluble stabilizers Aqua-Solv, Solvy, WSS, Washout, Rensit.

FUSIBLE WEBS AND TRANSFER SHEETS

Sometimes called fusing agents, fusible webs are webs of polyamide, which melt when heat is applied. Generally used between two fabric layers, they can be applied to a single layer with a nonstick transfer sheet.

Five Fuse™ (Solor-Kist Corp.) Fusible web.
Fusible web (Armo)
Jiffy Fuse™ (Staple) Fusible web.
Wonder-Web™ (Pellon) Fusible Web.
Stitch Witchery (Stacy) Fusible web.
No Stick Applique Press Sheet (Solar-Kist Corp.) Transfer sheet.
Trans-Fuse II™ (Stacy) Transfer sheet for fusible web.
Wonder Under™ (Pellon) Fusible web with transfer sheet.

Batting and Insulating Fabrics

Batting and insulating fabrics are used to create a raised quilted design and add warmth.

Some insulating materials such as down, bunting, Thinsulate, Thermalite, needlepunch, and Polarguard are used primarily for cold-weather garments and sleeping bags; while others such as lamb's wool, cotton and silk battings, and polyester fleece are used primarily for decorative quilting.

The efficiency of insulating materials is determined by the amount of dead air trapped within the fabric and the ability of the fabric to wick. Hollow-core fibers entrap the air to build a shield around the body, conserving body heat. At the same time, the fibers allow body moisture to dissipate into the atmosphere, preventing a buildup of heat robbing moisture.

TYPES

Aluminized Mylar needlepunch is made with a thin piece of aluminized Mylar sandwiched between two layers of needlepunch. A good insulator with reflective qualities, aluminized Mylar needlepunch is used for window shades, mittens, and slim-line garments.

Armo Wool is a loosely woven fabric made of 90 percent wool and 10 percent synthetic. Sometimes incorrectly called lamb's wool, it is 54″ wide and available by the yard. It is a good interlining fabric for fashion garments and is sometimes used for decorative quilting.

Bonded batting is a polyester batting. Coated with a light resin on both sides to keep the fibers from migrating, it has a higher loft and fluffier appearance than unbonded batting. An excellent choice for quilts and comforters, it can be quilted every 4″ to 6″ without matting. It washes and wears well; and the addition of the resin coating makes it easy to sew by hand or machine.

Bunting fabrics are made of Dacron polyester or polypropylene (olefin) knits. Warm, soft, and lightweight, these deep-pile insulators have good shape retention. They also retain their insulation properties when wet, and are most effective when used with a tightly woven outer shell. They dry quickly, absorb body moisture, and breathe. The best known bunting fabrics are Chinella, Polarfleece, Polarplus, and Polarlite.

Cotton batting is a thin sheet of cotton held together with a glaze. It's used primarily for sleeve heads, shoulder pads, and quilting. When quilted, the rows must be spaced no more than 2″ apart to prevent matting and bunching when laundered. It is soft and drapes well; it does not beard or pill.

Down, the best natural insulator, is the soft, fluffy feathers from the breast or belly of geese and ducks. It breathes and allows body moisture to evaporate quickly; however, it is expensive, difficult to handle, does not insulate when wet; it also shifts and mats.

Hollofil® and **Hollofil II** are short polyester fibers with a hollow core which has been treated with a silicone finish. Compared to down, it is odorless, nonallergenic, moth- and mildew-resistant, and almost as warm. It retains its insulating properties when wet and resists matting and lumping. Although it is frequently used for prequilted nylon taffeta fabrics, Hollofil can be a loose batting which is handled like down or a lightly bonded, easy-to-handle batting. It is machine washable.

Lamb's wool, sometimes called **Domette** or **Eskimo,** is an open-weave or knit with a long nap on one side. Available by the yard in 54″ widths, it is soft, fluffy, and particularly attractive when quilted. It is also used to interline fashion outerwear.

Milium lining is a rayon lining with a milium backing. Used primarily to line draperies, it does not wear well in garments. It is stiff and the metallic Milium will dull your shears.

Needlepunch is a dense, nonwoven sheet of polyester which has been punched with thousands of hollow-core polyester fibers. Suitable for cold-weather garments and skiwear, it can be machine washed or dry-cleaned.

Polarguard is a long-filament insulation. Generally used for sleeping bags, it is washable, lightweight, and has a high loft. It insulates when wet but does not compact as well as Hollofil II and Quallofil®.

Polyester batting is made of nonallergenic polyester fibers. Available in sheets for standard quilt sizes or by the yard, it is lightweight, resilient, inexpensive, washable, and easy to sew. Since it pulls apart easily, it is frequently wrapped with cheesecloth to keep the fibers from migrating. It is more suitable for decorative quilting than insulating.

Polyester fleece is a needlepunch fabric which has been punched with needles to entangle the fibers. Unlike needlepunched fabrics which have been punched with hollow-core polyester fibers, polyester fleece has no insulating qualities. Compared to polyester batting and lamb's wool, it is denser and flatter. It is an excellent choice for quilts and comforters; however, quilted designs on garments will look flat.

Quallofil the best Du Pont insulating fiber, has four hollow cores in each fiber. It is almost as warm as down and retains its insulating properties when wet. It compacts, but not as much as down.

It is nonallergenic, odorless, quick drying, and machine washable.

Quilted linings have a layer of batting quilted to the satin or taffeta lining fabric. Available in various qualities with different insulating properties, it is used to insulate and line outerwear. It is frequently used just to line the sleeves.

Silk batting is a very light batting. Sold in leaves instead of sheets, it is used for quilting luxury garments and accessories. It must be quilted closely to keep the fibers from shifting. It can be hand-washed or dry-cleaned.

Sunback is a rayon satin lining fabric backed with fleece. Used to line fashion outerwear, it must be dry-cleaned.

Stretch needlepunch has hollow-core polyester fibers punched into a stretchy foam core. It is used to insulate stretch garments and skiwear.

Thermax, a DuPont product made of Thermolite, is made from thin, hollow-core polyester fibers which reduce the rate of heat transfer and block radiation. Compared to Thinsulate, it is not as warm.

Thinsulate, a thermal insulation from 3M Company, is a thin, but effective, insulator made of polyester and olefin (polypropylene). Compared to polyester fiberfill, down, or wool, an equal thickness provides twice the insulation. It retains its insulation properties when wet and is most effective when used with a tightly woven outer shell. It can be machine washed or dry-cleaned without bunching, matting, or thinning. It is easier to handle when it's attached to scrim.

Wool batting is sold in large sheets for quilts and comforters. It is resilient, durable, and comfortable. When used for comforters, it can be tufted successfully; for garments, it must be quilted closely to keep the fibers from shifting. It must be dry-cleaned and is susceptible to moths.

Wool blankets can be recycled for quilting or insulating. Resilient and comfortable, blankets do not mat, shift, or migrate, but they are susceptible to moths. When preshrunk, wool is washable.

SELECTING INSULATING FABRICS

When choosing batting, first consider the design and end use of the garment, the need for insulation, the desired thickness, the desirability of nonallergenic fibers, and the care requirements. Consider also the following characteristics:

- Thermolite and Thinsulate are well-suited for slim-line parkas and vests.
- Polarfleece tends to pill more than Polarplus; and it's heavier.
- Polarplus has a high loft and is bulky.
- Polarlite is lighter than Polarfleece.
- Chinella is softer and drapes better than Polarfleece and Polarplus. It has a nubby texture which does not pill.
- Cotton and silk battings must be quilted more closely than polyester fleece, Thermolite, Thinsulate, lamb's wool, cotton flannel, wool blankets, wool interlinings.
- Most garments insulate better when used with firmly woven windproof fabrics.
- When insulating with down and loose Hollofil, be sure the outer shells are firmly woven so the fibers won't migrate through them.
- Use lamb's wool, silk batting, or cotton batting for more tactile, softer quilted designs. For firm, flat quilting, use polyester fleece. For something in between, consider Armo wool, wool blankets, and cotton flannel.

SEWING BATTING AND INSULATING FABRICS

STITCHING TIPS

When sewing quilted fabrics, lengthen the stitch length.

When sewing polypropylene/Lycra blends, use a small zigzag or stretch stitch.

Piece battings for luxury garments, quilts, and comforters by hand. Butt the edges together and secure with a catchstitch.

GARMENT CARE

Repair rips and tears before cleaning.

To fluff insulated garments, tumble for about fifteen minutes on low heat.

To reduce static electricity, add a fabric softener to the rinse water; do not overdry.

Do not bleach insulated garments.

Hang rain-dampened garments on a plastic hanger until dry.

To machine wash garments with polyester and olefin insulations, wash in warm water on the gentle cycle; tumble dry with low heat. Press as needed with a warm iron; do not steam press.

Thinsulate shrinks 7 percent when dry-cleaned.

Most down-filled garments can be laundered; check the care requirements before proceeding.

To machine wash down-filled garments, dissolve a mild soap in warm water; then add the garment and several bath towels. Wash on a gentle cycle; add fabric softener to the final rinse. Do not use bleach, enzymes, or phosphate detergents which will cause the down to deteriorate.

Hint: *There are special soaps for washing down garments; or you can use Ivory Flakes or a nondetergent shampoo.*

To machine dry, add a pair of tennis shoes or tennis balls and several dry bath towels. Using a low heat setting, tumble until dry. Be sure the garment is completely dry before putting it away.

Hint: *Down has a distinctive odor when it's wet. If it smells wet, it is.*

To avoid compacting the fibers and a subsequent loss of insulating qualities, do not store down garments compressed.

CHAPTER 20
Linings and Underlinings

Linings and underlinings improve the durability, comfort, and quality of a garment. Simply explained, linings cover the seams and construction details to finish the inside of garments while underlinings do not. Assembled separately, linings are sewn to the garment at the neckline, armholes, garment opening, waistline, and sometimes at the hem. In addition to adding comfort and quality, linings protect the seams from abrasion, reduce wrinkling, prolong the garment's life, add warmth, preserve the shape of the garment, allow the garment to slip easily over other garments, reduce clinging, and protect the body from irritating fabric. Although linings are usually inconspicuous, they can be an important design feature.

Sometimes called mountings or backings, underlinings are attached to the individual garment sections before the garment is assembled. Generally used to add support and body, underlinings can change the character of the fabric. They conceal construction details from the outside of the garment, add opaqueness, reduce wrinkling, and support the garment shape. A flat lining is a combination lining-underlining. The individual garment sections are lined to finish the edges; then the garment is assembled.

LINING AND UNDERLINING FABRICS

Most fabrics can be used both for linings and underlinings; and almost all interfacing fabrics can be used for underlining.

À la Creme® (Springs Mills) is a lightweight, satin, 100 percent polyester lining available in many colors. This machine washable lining pills.

Ambiance (Logantex) is a lightweight Bemberg lining. Suitable for skirts and dresses, it is handwashable.

Batiste is a lightweight cotton or cotton/blend which shrinks and ravels. All-cotton batiste wrinkles. Compared to silk and similar synthetics, it is heavier.

Hint: *Generally, I do not like cotton linings because they are heavy; and they tend to cling to the body and to other garments.*

Bemberg is a good-quality rayon lining made by the cupramonium method and available in several weights. Compared to synthetics, it is more comfortable to wear; compared to silk, it is more durable and can be handwashed.

Butterfly (Stacy) is a lightweight, 100 percent polyester lining. Available in many colors, it is anti-static and machine washable.

Chesterfield (Logantex) is a medium-weight Bemberg lining, suitable for suits and coats.

China silk is a soft, lightweight, plain-weave silk used to line skirts and dresses. Most China silks are too lightweight and loosely woven to prevent seam slippage or to wear well.

372

Charmeuse is a lightweight silk lining used in the most expensive dresses and suits.

Chiffon is a lightweight, transparent material sometimes used for lining evening jackets or sweaters.

Ciao (Crown) is a lightweight, soft, crepe lining. Available in many colors, it is 100 percent polyester, anti-static, and suitable for lining knits, as well as woven fabrics.

Coupe de Ville (Burlington/Klopman) is a medium-weight polyester lining which wears well.

Cotton net is a lightweight underlining which adds stability without weight. Used to create foundations in couture construction, it controls and supports the body.

Crepe de chine ranges from light- to medium-weight. Available in several fibers, it is used for lining coats, jackets, and suits, as well as for matching blouses. Used in couture construction, silk crepe de chine is expensive. Skinner's polyester crepe de chine, dyed to match their Ultrasuede, is strong and durable.

Crepe-backed satin is medium-weight lining. Available in many colors, it can be rayon or acetate. Used for coats, jackets, and suits, it has nice body but ravels badly.

Earl-Glo Satin is a medium-weight acetate lining with a satin weave. Used for coats, jackets, and suits, it is smooth, with good shape retention.

Earl-Glo Twill is a medium-weight acetate lining with a twill weave. Used for coats, jackets, and suits, it wears well and adds body.

Fake-fur fabrics are heavy pile fabrics used for warmth and/or design.

Fur linings are used for warmth and design.

Jersey is a knitted lining material. Wool jersey is used to add warmth to wool jackets and coats.

King William® (Springs Mills) is an acetate twill lining. It can be handwashed and pressed with a cool iron.

Marquisette is a transparent, lightweight underlining which adds stability without weight.

Minaret® (Springs Mills) is a lightweight polyester taffeta. It has a slight rustle.

Net and tulle are transparent, lightweight underlinings which add body, as well as stability, without weight. They may irritate the skin, requiring a lining.

Milium is an acetate lining backed with milium. It adds warmth without weight.

Muslin is used to underline tailored suits and coats. Available in several weights, it can be 100 percent cotton or a cotton blend.

Organza is a lightweight, crisp, transparent fabric. Frequently used to underline luxury ready-to-wear, it adds body without weight. Silk organza splits with wear.

Polyester blouse fabrics are generally more absorbent, more comfortable, but more expensive to use as lining fabric than polyester lining fabrics.

Polyester lining fabrics vary tremendously in quality. Generally, brand-name fabrics are more absorbent and better quality than generic fabrics.

Poly SiBonne Plus (Crown) is a 100 percent polyester fabric which resembles a lightweight cotton batiste.

Quilted linings are heavy and bulky. They are used to line complete jackets and coats or partial garments, such as the body or sleeves.

Rayon linings are good choices for garments which require dry-cleaning. Compared to polyester, they are more comfortable to wear, but they are not as strong or as easy to launder.

Satin-weave linings range from medium- to heavyweight. Smooth and nonclinging, they add body; but they frequently ravel badly and slip at the seams. Satin linings are more supple than taffetas.

Sheath linings are available in natural and man-made fibers.

Silk blouse fabrics are used to line dresses and jackets. Depending on the weave and dyes, they may fade and slip at the seams.

Sunback is a satin-weave lining fabric with a napped back. Bulky and heavy, it is used in coats and jackets for warmth.

Taffeta is a firmly woven, crisp material which rustles.

Tricot knits are well-suited as lining and underlinings for knits.

Twill-weave linings are medium in weight, wear well, and add body. Rayon twills may fade and shrink.

Fabric Characteristics

- Linings are usually smooth, slippery fabrics.
- Linings should be colorfast, static free, and wrinkle-resistant.
- Linings should be durable.
- Linings and underlinings made from fibers which breathe are more comfortable to wear.
- Many lining fabrics ravel badly.

PLANNING A GARMENT

SELECTING LININGS AND UNDERLININGS

Before shopping, review the characteristics of various fibers and fabrics so you'll know what to expect from the fabric.

Choose linings and underlinings that have the same care requirements as the fashion fabric.

Linings should add strength and protection without adding bulk. Generally, the best choice for most designs is lighter in weight and slightly softer than the fashion fabric.

Choose a color which matches or complements the fashion fabric. Whenever possible, avoid whites and light colors which soil easily.

Generally, twill weaves wear well and are more durable than plain- or satin-weave fabrics. Satin-weave fabrics are easiest to slip into. For skirt linings, polyester twill-weaves are good choices.

Scrape your thumbnail across the fabric to be sure the fabric is firmly woven. Examine the cut end; if it is fraying badly, it will be difficult to sew.

Hint: *Use a fabric protector like Scotchgard on your lining fabric to reduce dry cleaning bills.*

When selecting underlinings, decide what you expect them to do—support, add body, reinforce, stabilize and prevent stretching, shape and establish a silhouette, add opaqueness or color, create a new color, add softness, or reduce wrinkling. Within one garment, use different underlinings as needed for different effects.

Like linings, the underlining should never be heavier than the fashion fabric. Do not confuse weight with crispness and thickness.

Place the underlining under the fashion fabric to check the color and texture of the two fabrics combined.

Always preshrink the lining and underlining fabrics. And adjust the pattern before cutting the lining. If you plan to fit as you sew, don't cut the lining until the garment has been fitted.

AN EDGE-TO-EDGE LINING PATTERN

Most patterns for lined garments have a traditional facing/lining. To make a pattern for an edge-

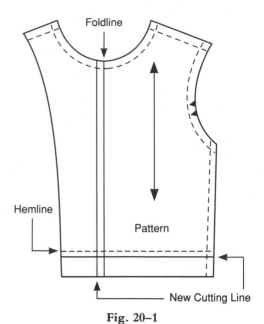

Fig. 20–1

to-edge lining, eliminate all facings and hems. Add a 5/8" seam allowance as needed at the pattern edges; duplicate the main pattern pieces.

Hint: *Use this tailoring trick so the sleeve will hang nicely if the garment is not reversible. Extend the side seams of the front, back, and sleeve 5/8" into the armscye. Connect the extended seam to the armscye notch.*

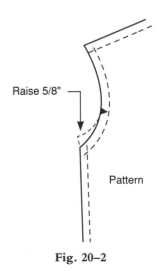

Fig. 20–2

MAKING A LINING PATTERN

To make a skirt lining, duplicate the pattern pieces for the skirt, but not for the waistband.

To make a jacket lining, use these easy directions.

1. On the jacket front pattern, pin the facing on top with the seamlines matched.

2. Trace the unnotched edge of the facing and add a 1 1/4″ seam allowance to the traced line.

3. Trace the finished hemline and add the extension at the underarm.

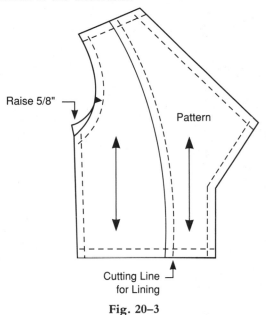

Fig. 20-3

4. Repeat to make the lining back pattern; at the center back, add a 1″-wide pleat.

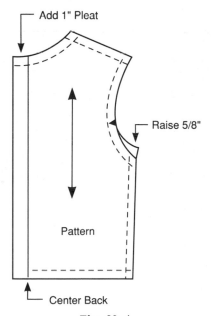

Fig. 20-4

5. For the sleeve lining pattern, add the extension to the underarm and shorten the length.

MAKING A PATTERN FOR A FLAT LINING

A flat lining is a combination lining/underlining. The individual garment sections are lined to finish the edges; then the garment is assembled.

These directions for a jacket can be adapted for skirts and slacks.

1. To make the lining pattern, trace the pattern pieces for the jacket front, back, and sleeve; transfer the matchpoints and grainlines.

2. Add an additional 5/8″ seam allowance to all vertical seamlines.

3. To flat line a section, begin right sides together. Match and pin the raw edges together. Since the lining is 1 1/4″ wider than the garment fabric, it will bubble. Stitch 1/4″ from the raw edge. Trim the seam to 1/8″ and turn the section right side out. Adjust the lining so it wraps the edge smoothly; ditch-stitch or baste to secure it. Complete the garment using 1/2″ seam allowances.

SEWING NOTES

Use Universal-H point needles in small sizes (60/8 to 80/12) when stitching.

To control slippery fabrics, spread them wrong sides together. Lay out skirt linings on the crossgrain for added strength.

LININGS

Generally linings should be slightly larger than the garment itself. Compared to the fashion fabric, the lining is much more firmly woven with little or no give; and, if it is the slightest bit smaller, the lining will cause the garment to ripple.

Since most linings are light and soft, the excess lining material can be pressed into a soft pleat.

Hint: *Edge-to-edge linings on reversible garments are the same size; and bulky linings made of fur, fake-fur fabrics, or fleece will be slightly smaller.*

375

UNDERLININGS

Pin or baste the underlining to the wrong side of the fashion fabric before assembling the garment.

Generally, like the lining, the size of the underlining is greater than the fabric section, since underlining fabrics are much more firmly woven, with less give, than most fashion fabrics. If the backing is the same size or smaller, the garment is more restricting.

Hint: *I like for the underlining to bubble just a little so the give and comfort of the fashion fabric is retained.*

When a fusible is used as an underlining, it is the same size; and when a stiffer sew-in material is used to control the shape and change the character of the fabric, the underlining must be slightly smaller, so it won't buckle.

To shape a stiff underlining, lay the garment section on the table or place it on a dress form.

Cover it with the underlining. Match the raw edges and pin them together at the center of the section. Fold along the pinned line and pin the edges; the underlining will show 1/8" to 1/4" and the section will not lie flat. Baste layers together; assemble the garment.

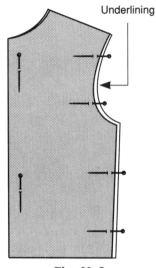

Fig. 20–5

PART FIVE

Sewing Techniques

This alphabetical mini-guide is included to avoid any misunderstandings about the techniques and terminology used elsewhere in this book. Many of the techniques are common knowledge, but a few were developed especially for this book.

To expand your knowledge of garment construction, consult my earlier book, *The Complete Book of Sewing Short Cuts*.

CHAPTER 21
Seams and Seam Finishes

Seams

ABUTTED SEAMS

Sometimes called butted seams, abutted seams are suitable for materials which don't ravel, foundation garments, and interfacings.

Abutted seams have no seam allowances and can be made with or without an underlay. And although the underlay is usually on the wrong side of the garment, it can be decorative and positioned on the right side.

ABUTTED SEAM WITHOUT UNDERLAY

Butt and zigzag the raw edges together either with a wide zigzag or with a multiple zigzag (also called a serpentine stitch).

ABUTTED SEAM WITH UNDERLAY

1. Select an appropriate underlay. Generally, twill tape is the best choice for interfacings, but decorative tapes, ribbons, leather, and synthetic suede can be used for fashion fabrics.

2. Cut away the seam allowances. Mark matchpoints with pins or a temporary marking pen.

3. For interfacings, stitch one raw edge to the

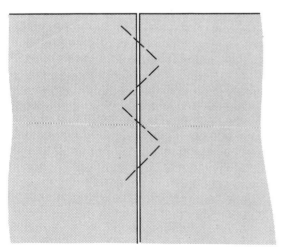

Fig. 21–1

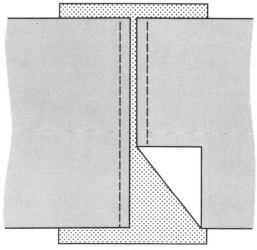

Fig. 21–2

underlay; then butt the other edge and stitch it in place.

4. For decorative seams, baste one edge to the center of the underlay; then baste the corresponding edge, matching the edges and matchpoints.

Hint: *Some machines have guide accessories to help you align the two edges perfectly.*

APPLIQUÉ SEAMS FOR LACE

Frequently used on lace fabrics, appliqué seams are a variation of the lapped seam.

1. Make duplicate pattern pieces without seam allowances.

Hint: *Use see-through pattern cloth for easier layout.*

2. Right side up, pin the pattern pieces to the lace so the motifs are positioned attractively. Align the motifs horizontally and vertically, but do not expect them to match.

3. Using the pattern as a guide, thread trace all stitching lines on the lace.

4. On the overlaps, add 3/8″ seam allowances. Examine the layout; and if the cutting line goes through any motifs, redraw it, following the edge of the design motif. Do not cut through the motifs. The cutting line will probably be quite crooked; and the seamline will actually be less noticeable if it is.

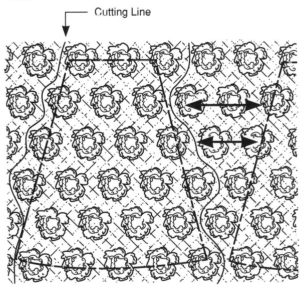

Fig. 21–3

Allow 1/4″ seam allowances on the corresponding underlaps.

5. Right sides up with the overlap on top, match and pin the traced lines (seamlines) together.

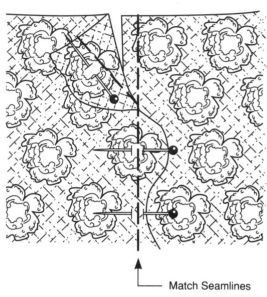

Match Seamlines

Fig. 21–4

6. Baste the new seamline, following the motif design, at the edge of the overlap.

7. Check the fit as needed and make any last-minute alterations.

8. Appliqué around the lace motifs by hand with a whipping stitch or by machine with a zigzag (W,1.5; L,1).

9. Trim away the excess seam allowances from each layer.

APPLIQUÉ SEAMS FOR WOVEN FABRICS

Suitable for woven fabrics with large motifs on solid backgrounds and for embroidered border designs, these appliqué seams do not interrupt the design motifs or require matching in the usual way.

Generally used on special-occasion garments, they are never used on ready-made garments, only expensive couture designs because they are so costly.

1. Make duplicate pattern pieces without seam allowances.

Hint: *When you don't want to trim away the seam allowances, press them out of the way.*

2. Right side up, pin the pattern pieces to the fabric, positioning the motifs attractively.

3. Using the pattern as a guide, thread trace all stitching lines on the fabric.

4. Add 3/8″ seam allowances around the design motifs and 5/8″ seam allowances in background areas.

Add 3/8" Here ⎯
Add 5/8" Here ⎯

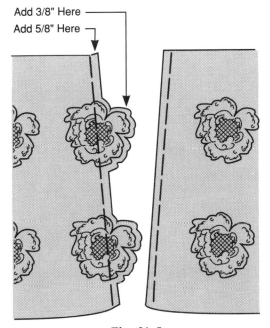

Fig. 21–5

Hint: *Examine the layout carefully before adding seam allowances. If it will enhance the design, allow the layers to alternate as overlap and underlap on the seamline.*

5. On the overlap sections, clip the seam allowances to the seamline at the beginning and end of each motif. This allows you to sew the straight areas by machine.

On the overlap, lightly press the seam allowances between the motifs to the wrong side.

6. Right sides up, match the seamlines. Using an even basting stitch placed 1/4″ from the seamline, baste the straight sections between the motifs (Fig. 21-6).

Slip baste or fell the same sections. Remove the first basting thread.

Hint: *To avoid marring delicate fabrics, use very fine needles and silk thread for basting.*

Fig. 21–6

7. Turn the sections wrong side up and machine stitch permanently. Remove the basting threads.

Hint: *Use a pair of tweezers to remove basting threads.*

8. To finish the seam, appliqué around the edges of the motifs. First turn the edge under, clipping and trimming the seam allowance as needed so the edge will be flat and smooth. Baste about 1/8″ from the edge; then, using a tiny felling or slipstitch, secure it permanently.

Basting ⎯

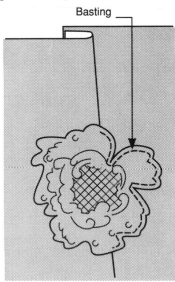

Fig. 21–7

381

9. Press the seam lightly. Wrong side up, press the straight, machine-stitched sections of the seam open. Right side up, use a press cloth to press the appliqués.

Hint: *To avoid seam imprints, use a seam roll for the straight sections. Press only with the point of the iron at the edges of the appliqués.*

10. If necessary, trim away the appliqué under-layers to reduce the bulk.

Bound Seams

Neat and narrow, bound seams are frequently used to finish armscye seams. They can also be used on the right side of the garment as a decorative seam.

BOUND SEAM ON THE WRONG SIDE OF THE GARMENT

1. Cut seam allowances 5/8″ wide.
2. For the binding, cut bias strips 1 1/4″ wide or use purchased tricot bias.
3. Right sides of the garment sections together, stitch on the seamline.
4. Trim the seam evenly to 1/4″.
5. Pin the right side of the bias strip to the wrong

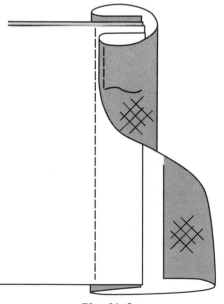

Fig. 21–8

side of the seam, matching the raw edges. Stitch again on the seamline.

6. Wrap the bias around the seam and turn under the raw edge so the fold meets the seamline. Secure it to the seamline by hand or machine.

DECORATIVE BOUND SEAM— METHOD ONE

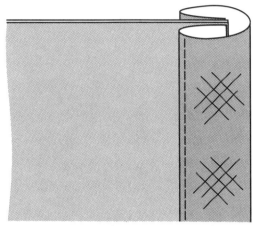

Fig. 21–9

This imaginative seam from Jeanne Marc is attractive on casual blouses, skirts, and jackets.

1. Cut seam allowances 5/8″ wide.
2. Wrong sides together, stitch on the seamline. Press and trim to 1/4″.
3. Using a wide, double-fold purchased bias binding, insert the raw edges of the seam between the folds. Match the folds to the seamline and edgestitch in place.
4. Press shoulder and side seams to the back.
5. If desired, bind the binding fold with a double-fold binding in a contrasting color.

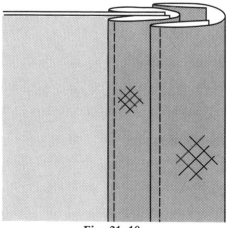

Fig. 21–10

DECORATIVE BOUND SEAM— METHOD TWO

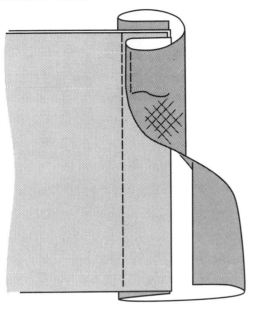

Fig. 21–11

Use this method on better garments for a smoother finish.

1. Cut a bias strip 1 1/2" wide.

2. Join the seam of the garment wrong sides together, press flat; and trim to 1/4".

3. Right sides together, match the raw edges of the seam and bias; stitch with the garment on top.

4. Wrap the bias over the seam; turn the raw edge under so the fold matches the seamline. Edgestitch the fold in place; press.

Hint: *Baste the folded edge so the bias won't ripple when you edgestitch.*

BOUND-AND-LAPPED SEAMS

Geiger uses this attractive seam on its ready-made jackets. Use it to join the front to the side panel and the sleeve to the shoulder. Generally, it is not used at the shoulder or underarm.

1. Trim the seam allowances so that they are the same width as the binding.

2. Bind the edge of the overlap with the same braid selected for the edges. Stitch permanently by hand or machine. Also bind the underlap if the garment will be reversible.

3. Right sides up, lap the bound edge over the underlap, matching the seamlines. Baste.

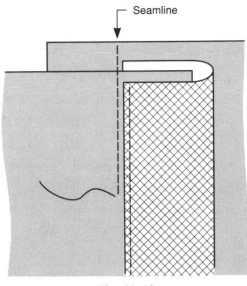

Fig. 21–12

Hint: *Generally the front laps the side panel, the bodice laps the sleeve, and yokes lap adjoining sections.*

4. Topstitch close to the edge of the braid.

BOUND-AND-STITCHED SEAMS

Used on a reversible coat designed by Jacques Griffe in the fifties, the bound-and-stitched seam is suitable for thick, bulky fabrics as well as for reversible materials and unlined garments. All edges are bound and only the bindings are stitched together for a super flat finish.

The binding can be a wool fold-over braid, a bias binding like the Griffe design, ribbon, twill tape, synthetic suede, or leather. Estimate the amount of binding required before beginning; this decorative seam requires more than you initially expect. Measure the lengths of all seamlines and multiply by two.

There are two basic methods for assembling the seams, depending on the kind of binding you plan to apply.

METHOD ONE

Use method one for bindings such as fold-over braid, ribbon, leather, suede, synthetic suedes, or twill tape which have finished edges or do not ravel.

1. Trim away the seam allowances on all edges to be bound and stitched. If the fabric is unusually thick or bulky, trim away an additional 1/8" to 1/4".

2. Experiment with the braid and fabric scraps before assembling the garment. Visualize the finished design to determine the finished width of the trim.

Theoretically, the finished width and binding width are the same; however, when the binding wraps around thicker fabrics, it shrinks in width because of the turn of the cloth. To be exact, experiment with bindings in different widths, or use this general rule. For a 1"-wide trim, select a 1"-wide binding when the fashion fabric is thin; select a 1 1/4"-wide binding for medium-thick fabrics, and a 1 1/2"-wide one for thick materials. When the binding wraps around thicker fabrics, more is lost in the turn of the cloth.

3. Fold the binding in half lengthwise; insert the edge of the fabric between the binding layers. Mark the fabric at the edges of the binding with a small clip, fabric marking pen, or straight pins. Set the binding aside; measure the distance between the raw edge of the garment section and the marked points. For example: when binding a medium-weight wool with a 1 1/4" braid, the edges of the braid measure 1/2" from the raw edges.

4. With the garment sections wrong side up, mark all edges which will be bound and stitched this distance from the edge.

Hint: *I use a temporary marking pen or machine stitching. When machine stitching, mark the distance 1/8" less (3/8") so it won't show on the finished garment.*

5. Continuing with the garment section wrong side up, align the edge of the braid with the marked pen line; or, if you've used machine stitching, position the braid so it covers the marked line 1/8". Baste the braid in place for stitching. If it's a fine garment, hand baste. When speed sewing, baste with glue or a fusible web such as Wonder Under or Transfuse II.

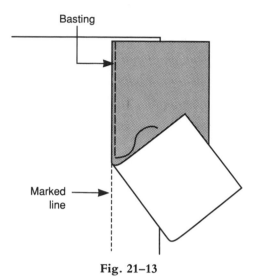

Fig. 21–13

6. Baste the braid to the remaining seam edges. When hand sewing, sew this edge of the braid permanently.

7. With the garment sections wrong sides together, match and pin the edges of the braid together. Stitch the braids together at the center. Press the seams open.

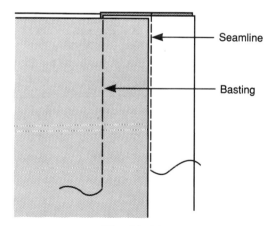

Fig. 21–14

8. With the garment right side up, edgestitch the braid to the garment by hand, straight stitching, or zigzagging. Press.

Hint: *It's easier to catch the braid on the underside when zigzagging.*

METHOD TWO

Use method two for bindings such as purchased bias, custom-made bias, and fabric strips which ravel.

1. Trim away the seam allowances on all edges to be bound and stitched. Trim away an additional 1/8″ to 1/4″ if the fabric is thick or bulky.

2. Experiment with the braid and fabric scraps before assembling the garment. Visualize the finished design to determine the finished width of the trim. For a 1″-wide trim, begin with 1 3/4″-wide bias strips when the fashion fabric is thin; 2″-wide when it's medium thick, and 2 1/4″-wide for thick materials.

3. With wrong sides up and the bias on top, match the raw edges and join with a 3/8″ seam.

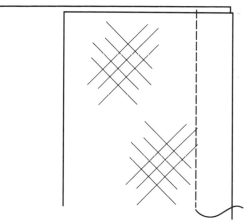

Fig. 21–15

4. Wrap the binding around the raw edge; press.
5. With the garment sections wrong sides to-

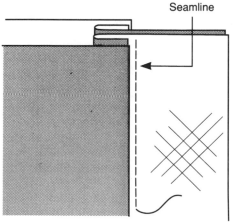

Fig. 21–16

gether, match the creased lines and pin the bias together. Stitch on the creased lines. Press the seams open.

6. With the garment right side up, turn under the edges of the bias and edgestitch the binding to the garment by hand, straight stitching or zigzagging. Press.

Slipstitch

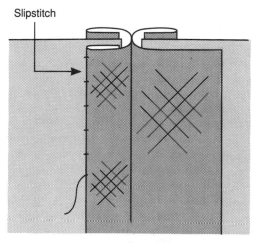

Fig. 21–17

Hint: *To prevent ripping, baste before you edge-stitch. If it's a fine garment, hand baste. When speed sewing, glue baste.*

CHANNEL SEAMS

See Slot Seams.

CORDED SEAMS

Sometimes called a piped seam or corded piping; see Piped Seams.

DECORATIVE SEAMS

Although many seams, such as piped, tucked, slot, topstitched, welt, flat-locked, and Zandra Rhodes, are designed to be decorative, many others, such as abutted, serged, bound, and French, can also be decorative. Try them all.

DOUBLE-CLOTH SEAMS

These are seams, such as plain, flat-felled, insertion, bound-and-wrapped, bound-and-stitched, and double-lapped seams, which have been adapted for double-cloth. See Reversible Fabrics.

DOUBLE-LAPPED SEAMS

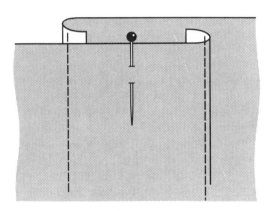

Fig. 21–18

Suitable for straight and almost-straight seams on light- to medium-weight fabrics, this is an attractive seam for reversible garments.

1. Cut seam allowances 1″ wide. Mark the seamlines at the top and bottom with a clip.

If you prefer a narrower lap, cut the seam allowances 5/8″.

2. On the overlap, press the edge under 1/4″. On the underlap, press the edge to the top side 1/4″.

Hint: *To press accurately, stitch a guideline 1/4″ from the edge.*

3. Right sides up, match the seamlines; pin, and edgestitch the overlap in place. Turn the garment over; edgestitch the underlap in place.

DOUBLE/PLY SEAMS

A double/ply seam is any seam finished with both edges together. It can be finished with a straight stitch, zigzag, multi-stitch zigzag, or serger. Suitable for a variety of fabrics, such as knits, trans-

parent fabrics, light- and medium-weight wovens, and quilted materials, it is particularly well-suited for unlined garments and seams, such as armholes, which are pressed in one direction.

DOUBLE-STITCHED SEAMS

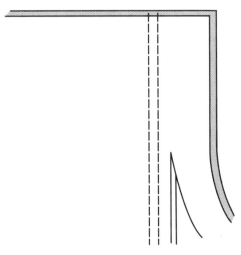

Fig. 21–19

This is a double/ply seam suitable for knits, transparent fabrics which do not fray, and seams which will be enclosed.

1. Cut seam allowances the desired width.
2. Right sides together, stitch on the seamline.

Hint: *Use a short, straight stitch (L,1–1.5) for enclosed seams.*

3. On enclosed seams, stitch again 1/16″ away. On transparent fabrics, stitch 1/8″ away.
4. Trim close to the second stitching line.

DOUBLE-WELT SEAMS

See Welt Seams.

DRAW SEAM

A type of slipstitch or ladder stitch, the draw seam is hand-stitched from the right side of the

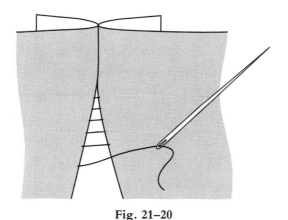

Fig. 21–20

garment. The draw seam is used most frequently to finish the gorgeline (the seamline which joins the collar and lapel facing.)

1. Trim the seam allowances of the collar and lapel facings to 1/2″.

2. Fold in the seam allowances and baste both sides 1/4″ from the folds. The folded edges will meet at the seamline.

3. Working from the right side of the garment, join the folds with a slipstitch or ladder stitch. Take short stitches, making them parallel to each other without a slant. Draw the thread taut.

DRAPERY FRENCH SEAMS

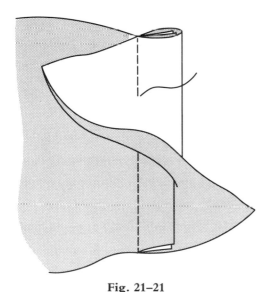

Fig. 21–21

Named for the custom-made draperies on which they were originally used, this self-finished seam is appropriate for straight and slightly curved seams on lightweight fabrics.

The drapery French seam is a substitute for the regular French seam which it resembles; but it is easier to make.

1. Cut the seam allowances 5/8″ wide.

2. Wrong sides together, stitch a 1/4″ seam.

3. Press the seam flat; then press it to one side.

4. Wrap one layer around the seam's raw edges so the right sides are together and the seamline is located 1/4″ from the folded edge.

Note: The total seam allowance is 1 1/4″—1/4″ is stitched on one layer and 3/4″ is stitched on the other, leaving 1/4″. Most of this will be lost in the turn of the cloth.

5. Wrong side up, ditch-stitch on the seamline.

ENCLOSED SEAMS

Enclosed seams are located at garment edges and around cuffs and collars. Enclosed between the garment and its facing or lining, these seams are usually left unfinished.

FALSE MERROW SEAMS

See Mock-Merrow Seams.

FALSE FRENCH SEAMS

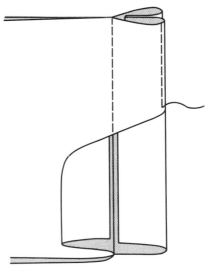

Fig. 21–22

Technically the false, fake, or simulated French seam is a seam finish, not a kind of seam. Although the finished seam requires a second look to distinguish it from the real thing, it is easier to fit and can be used on seams with more shape than real French seams.

False French seams are not suitable for medium- or heavyweight fabrics.

1. Cut the seam allowances 5/8″ wide.

2. Right sides together, stitch on the seamline.

3. Fit the garment as needed. Press the seam flat; then press it open.

4. Fold each seam allowance in half—right sides together—so the raw edges touch the seamline. Align the folded edges; baste.

Hint: *On curved seams, clip as needed so the edges will turn smoothly. If the fabric is wiry, turn in one edge; baste; repeat for the other edge.*

5. Edgestitch or whip the folded edges together.

FLAT-FELL OR FELLED SEAMS

The flat-fell seam is suitable for tailored, reversible, unlined garments, and work clothes in light- to medium-weight fabrics; and, like most self-finished seams, it is a sturdy, durable seam which will withstand heavy wear and frequent launderings.

On mass-produced ready-made garments, flat-fell seams are stitched on double-needle machines. The two rows of stitching on both sides of the garment make them easy to identify.

Flat-fell seams on luxury ready-mades and those made on home sewing machines are stitched on single-needle machines. They have one row of stitching on one side of the garment and two rows on the other. And, although one row on the outside is easier to stitch successfully and just as correct, most home sewers prefer two rows on the outside so the seam looks like a ready-made flat-fell seam.

For an outside fell with two rows of stitching on the right side, stitch the seam wrong sides together. For an inside fell with one row of stitching on the outside, stitch right sides together.

Experiment with these two methods for making flat-fell seams, to determine which method is better for you.

TRADITIONAL FLAT-FELL

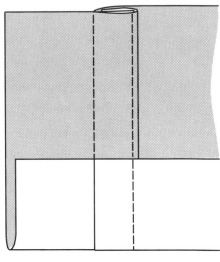

Fig. 21–23

1. Cut the seam allowances 5/8″ wide.

2. Wrong sides together, stitch a 5/8″ seam. For an inside fell, stitch right sides together.

3. Press the seam flat; then press it to one side. Press horizontal seams down, shoulder and side seams toward the back, and armscye seams toward the bodice. Press garment centers to the left on the front and to the right on the back.

4. Trim the inside seam allowance to 1/8″ and turn under the other seam allowance 3/8″.

Hint: *Wrap the wider seam allowance around the trimmed one; pin the two together so the folded edge is an even distance from the seamline and the raw edge laps the seamline. (If the distance between the seam and folded edge isn't even, the finished seam will be unattractive.) Hand or machine baste on the original seamline. When machine basting, tighten the upper tension slightly so the stitches can be removed easily.*

5. Pin or baste the seam allowance to the garment; open the garment out, then stitch again 1/4″ from the seamline.

Hint: *The seam will twist less when stitched directionally.*

6. Remove the bastings.

QUICK FLAT-FELL

Frequently overlooked as a seam for transparent fabrics, quick flat-fell seams are particularly attractive on crisp, tailored sheers. They can be used on straight and slightly curved seams.

1. Cut the seam allowances 5/8" wide.
2. Start wrong sides together for an outside fell and right sides together for an inside fell.

Note: *Hathaway shirts and Chanel silk blouses have inside fells.*

3. Stack the two layers so the lower one extends 1/2".
4. Wrap the lower layer around the upper one and stitch 3/8" from the edge.

Hint: *For a prettier seam, stitch an even distance from the folded edge, even if an occasional bit of raw edge isn't caught.*

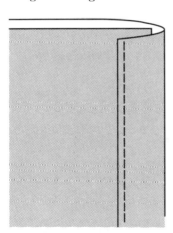

Fig. 21–24

5. Press the seam flat; then open the garment flat and press the seam to one side, enclosing the raw edge.
6. Edgestitch the seam to the garment.

Hint: *On an outside fell, use the inside of one side of the presser foot or a zipper foot as an edge-stitching guide. For an inside fell, stitch—right side up—an even distance from the seamline.*

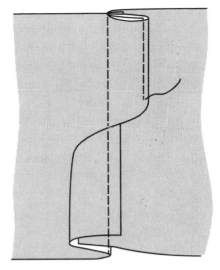

Fig. 21–25

For lightweight fabrics, cut seam allowances 1/2" wide; extend the lower layer only 3/8"; wrap and stitch it 1/4" from the fold.

For heavier fabrics, cut seam allowances 3/4" wide; extend the lower layer 5/8"; wrap and stitch 1/2" from the fold.

FAKE FLAT-FELL

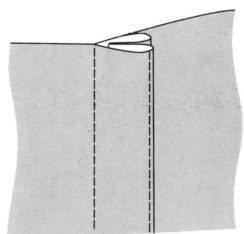

Fig. 21–26

1. Stitch a decorative French seam on the right side of the garment (see entry later).
2. Press the seam flat, then press to one side.
3. Edgestitch the seam to garment.

FLAT-LOCKED SEAMS

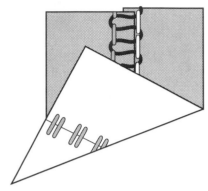

Fig. 21–27

Made on a serger, flat-locked seams are a decorative addition for fun, casual designs. Flat-locked seams are most attractive on fabrics which don't ravel.

1. For three-thread overlocks, drastically loosen the tension on the needle; tighten the tension on the lower looper. Adjust the stitch length as needed so the length is equal to the width.

2. Wrong sides together, stitch on the seamline.

3. Open the layers flat and press.

Hint: *If the seam doesn't press flat, experiment with the tensions and try again. To increase your knowledge of serger techniques, I recommend* Creative Serging Illustrated.

FAKE FLAT-LOCK SEAMS

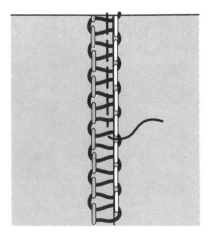

Fig. 21–28

This quick-and-easy method works best on light- and medium-weight fabrics that don't fray.

1. Serge the seam, wrong sides together; then press it to the side, upper looper threads on top.

2. Use a conventional machine to edgestitch it to the garment.

FRENCH SEAMS

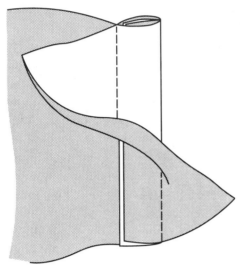

Fig. 21–29

Frequently described as a seam within a seam, the French seam is one of several self-finished seams which enclose all raw edges.

French seams are frequently used on transparent fabrics; they are appropriate for straight and slightly curved seams on sheer and lightweight fabrics. Particularly practical for fabrics which ravel and for garments which require frequent launderings, they look best when they are very narrow.

Since each seam is stitched twice, it will be slightly stiff. For a softer seam, hand sew one or both seams.

Rarely used on ready-made garments, these seams are expensive and time-consuming to sew.

1. Cut seam allowances 5/8" wide.

2. Wrong sides together, stitch a 3/8" seam by hand, machine, or overlock. When straight stitching, shorten the stitch length to 1.75–2 mm (12–15 stitches per inch).

Hint: *For a sturdier seam, use a narrow overlock stitch for the first row.*

3. Press the seam to one side, using the point of the iron.

4. Trim the seam to 1/8".

Hint: *To avoid ravelled or stray threads which show on the right side of the garment, do not trim the seam until you're ready to stitch the next seamline.*

On problem fabrics, trim only 12" at a time; stitch; repeat until the seamline is finished.

5. Reposition the layers right sides together. Press and baste as needed; stitch a skinny 1/4" seam.

Hint: *Work the seam between your thumb and forefinger to position the seamline at the fold. Clip curves as needed to flatten the seam.*

6. Press the seam flat; then press it to one side. Try to avoid pressing from the right side.

Note: French seams are difficult to alter. If the fit needs to be checked, baste the seams, right sides together. Remove the basting threads; then assemble the garment.

DECORATIVE FRENCH SEAMS

Use French seams on the outside of the garment for a novelty finish.

1. For a finished seam 1/2" wide, cut seam allowances 3/4" wide.

2. Right sides together, stitch a 1/4" seam. Press.

3. Turn the garment right side out, and stitch a 1/2" seam. Press.

FRINGED SEAMS

This decorative seam is very attractive on casual designs made of loosely woven fabrics or denim. It is not suitable for curved seams.

1. Cut the seam allowances 5/8" wide.

2. Wrong sides together, stitch on the seamline.

3. Press flat; then press the seam open.

4. Trim one seam allowance to 1/8" and press the other over it.

5. Topstitch 1/4" from the seamline.

6. Unravel the raw edge to make the fringe.

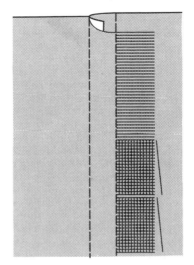

Fig. 21–30

Hint: *Using small trimmers, clip to the seamline every 3" to 4"; then pull the threads out with a needle.*

7. Clip off any threads that are caught in the seamline.

FUR SEAMS

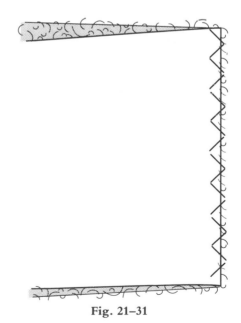

Fig. 21–31

This seam works particularly well for fur and fake fur fabrics. Use it on toys and seamlines which are not at garment edges.

1. Trim seam allowances to 1/8".

2. Brush the pile toward the garment, using a damp sponge.

3. Right sides together, position the seam so the raw edges are in the center of the presser foot. Zigzag (W,4; L,2), allowing the needle to swing off the edge.

Hint: *Overcast the edges together by hand where seamlines converge; overcast all seams if the fabric is unusually bulky. Use a glover's needle and waxed thread when sewing fur; use a regular needle for fake-fur fabrics.*

You could also serge the seams with a loosely balanced stitch. Or use an abutted seam. Begin with the sections wrong sides up. Butt the edges to be joined and zigzag (W,3; L,2) the edges together.

3. Open the seam flat, skin side up, and press the seam with the handles of your shears or a wallpaper roller. Brush the seam on the right side with a wire dog brush.

PLAIN FUR SEAMS

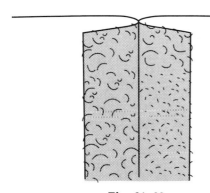

Fig. 21–32

1. If you don't have a zigzag machine, stitch a plain seam, right sides together.

2. Using small trimming or appliqué scissors to reduce the bulk, trim away the fur pile on the seam allowances.

Hint: *If the fabric has a deep pile, trim away the pile in the seam allowances before stitching. Stitch, using a zipper foot.*

3. Steam the seams open and finger press. If the seams won't stay pressed open, use a loose catchs-

titch to sew them to the garment underlining, or use a permanent glue to join the seam allowances to the backing.

Hairline Seams

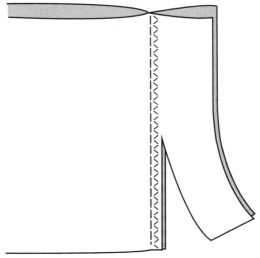

Fig. 21–33

Particularly attractive on transparent fabrics, this narrow seam can be made in any of the following three methods. Frequently used for enclosed seams at the edges of collars and cuffs, hairline seams are sturdy and wash well.

METHOD ONE

1. Cut seam allowances 5/8" wide.

2. Right sides together, stitch on the seamline, using a short, straight stitch (L,1.25–1.75).

3. Stitch again with a zigzag (W,1;L,1) close to the first stitched line.

Hint: *Stitch over cord to strengthen the seam.*

4. Press the seam flat, then to one side.

5. Trim close to the stitched line.

METHOD TWO

1. Right sides together, stitch on the seam line, using a short straight stitch.

2. Trim the seam to 1/8".

3. Set the machine to zigzag (W,1.5;L,1). Stitch

again, allowing the needle to stitch off the fabric when it swings to the right and overcasts the edge. Adjust the stitch length and width if desired.

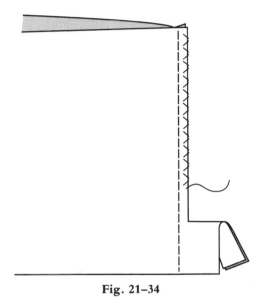

Fig. 21–34

Hint: *To reduce whiskers, stitch directionally.*

METHOD THREE

1. Set the serger for a narrow, rolled hem.
2. Right sides together, stitch on the seamline.

INSERTION SEAMS

Insertion seams of lace, eyelet, or crocheted strips can be made by either of two methods. Particularly attractive when used on sheers and soft fabrics to assemble garments inconspicuously, insertions are frequently used on lingerie and baby dresses.

METHOD ONE

These directions are for a 1/2″-wide lace. When wider laces are used, make appropriate stitch adjustments.

1. Cut away the seam allowances.
2. Right sides up, lap the lace over the raw edge 1/4″ and pin. Zigzag (W,1;L,1) the edge in place. Trim the fabric on the underside close to the stitched line. Repeat to finish the corresponding edge.

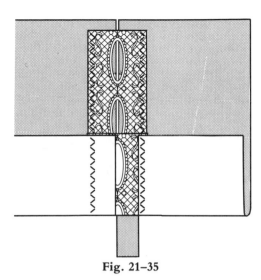

Fig. 21–35

METHOD TWO

Use this seam for a stronger seam on washable fabrics which ravel. These directions are for 1/2″-wide lace.

1. Cut away the seam allowances.
2. Right side up, fold under the raw edge of the fabric 1/4″; zigzag (W,1;L,1) over the edge. Trim close to the stitched line.
3. Butt the finished edge to the edge of the lace; zigzag again (W,2; L,2).

Hint: *Do not stretch the lace when stitching.*
To avoid being caught short, do not cut a length of the lace insertion until it is stitched to the fabric.

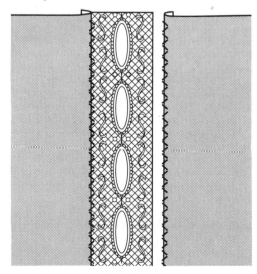

Fig. 21–36

LACED SEAMS

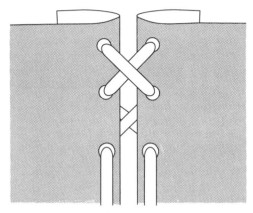

Fig. 21–37

A decorative seam which can be used as a closing, laced seams are frequently used on leather, suede, synthetic suede, and casual garments. The edges meet at the seamline and the garment sections are laced together with narrow strips of suede, leather, cord, or ribbon.

1. Cut seam allowances 5/8″ wide.
2. Cut and apply 5/8″-wide strips of interfacing to the seam allowances.

Hint: *For leather, suede, and vinyl, use a nonwoven sew-in interfacing; glue it in place. For synthetic suedes and fabrics, use a fusible.*

3. Fold and press the seam allowances under; topstitch, if desired.
4. Using a temporary marking pen, mark the locations for the eyelets.
5. Set the eyelets or grommets or machine stitch eyelets or short buttonholes.

LAPPED SEAMS

Generally, seams lap top over bottom, front over back, center over side, bodice armscyes over sleeves. Bands lap the adjoining sections: collars lap bodices, bands lap skirts, and cuffs lap sleeves. Garment centers lap right over left at the front and left over right at the back.

1. Cut seam allowances 5/8″ wide.
2. Mark the seamlines on the right side of the fabric.

Hint: *To mark the seamlines quickly and easily, use a soap sliver or chalk. Or gauge stitch 1/8″ inside the seamline. Gauge stitching has the added advantage of staying the edges so they are easier to control.*

3. On the overlap, press the seam allowance under. Clip, crimp, or baste as needed for a smooth edge.
4. Right side up, pin or baste the layers together so the seamlines match. The raw edges should be aligned on the underside. Edgestitch the seam permanently.

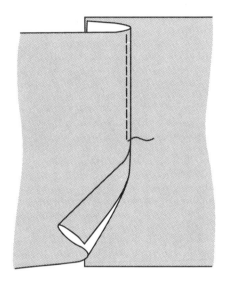

Fig. 21–38

Hint: *Use the inside edge of the presser foot or a zipper foot to edgestitch evenly.*

LAPPED SEAMS FOR INTERFACINGS

Use lapped seams to join interfacing sections and to stitch darts.

1. Mark the seamlines.
2. Lap the layers, matching the seamlines; pin. Stitch on the seamline. Trim both layers close to the seamline.

394

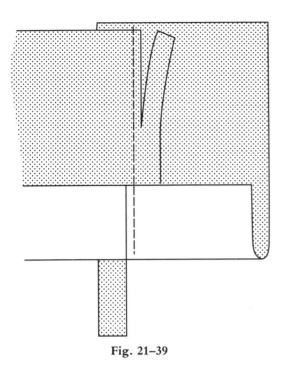

Fig. 21–39

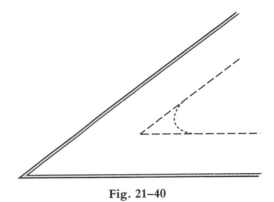

Fig. 21–40

Hint: *For a smoother finish, round sharp points on collars, cuffs, and garment edges.*

5. Clip or notch enclosed seams at edges. Apply rubber cement; and, when it becomes tacky, finger press the seam allowances against the garment. Turn the section right side out. Place the clapper just on the edge; then pound the clapper with a mallet or cloth-covered hammer.

LEATHER SEAMS

The basic leather seams, such as plain, top-stitched, and lapped, can also be adapted for non-woven materials such as synthetic suede and felt.

PLAIN LEATHER SEAMS

1. Cut seam allowances 3/8″ to 1/2″ wide.
2. Right sides together, stitch on the seamline.
3. Open the seam and press with the handles of the shears or pound with a mallet. Clip or notch as needed so seams will lie flat. To reduce bulk, bevel or skive the edges of seam allowances.

Hint: *If you don't have a mallet, use a clapper or cloth-covered hammer.*

4. Apply rubber cement to the wrong side of the seam allowances. Wait until the glue is tacky, then press the seam allowances against the garment and pound again. Test the rubber cement on a scrap first, to be certain it doesn't bleed through.

TOPSTITCHED LEATHER SEAMS

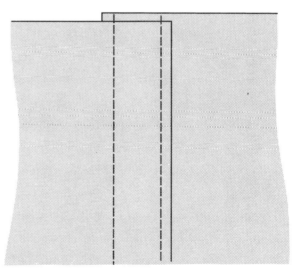

Fig. 21–41

Topstitching holds the seam allowances flat without gluing and it adds strength as well. It is particularly attractive on dressy, lightweight leathers when stitched with a regular stitch (L,2.5) 1/16″ from both sides of the seamline. Stitch sporty designs with a long stitch (L,4) 1/4″ away on one or both sides.

395

LAPPED LEATHER SEAMS

For medium- and heavyweight leathers, lapped seams are the best choice.

1. Cut no seam allowance on the overlap; cut a 3/8″ to 5/8″ seam allowance on the underlap.
2. Mark the seamline on the underlap with chalk or soap sliver.
3. Matching the seamlines, lap the seams and baste with rubber cement or a washable glue stick.
4. Topstitch 1/8″ from the garment edge. On sporty designs or outerwear, topstitch again 3/8″ from the edge.

MACHINE FELL SEAMS

See Flat-Fell Seams.

MACHINE-ROLLED SEAMS

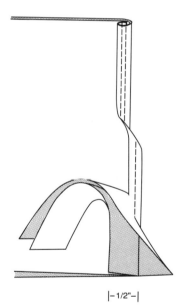

|—1/2″—|

Fig. 21–42

This narrow seam, used by designer Bill Travilla on his sheer fabric designs, is neat and easy to sew.

1. Cut seam allowances 5/8″ wide.
2. Right sides together, stitch a 1/2″ seam.
3. Fold the seam to the left on the stitched line and stitch again close to the folded edge. Trim closely.

Hint: *The secret of a super-narrow seam is to stitch as close as possible to the fold and then to trim very closely. Use the inside of the presser foot for a stitching guide; use appliqué or small trimming scissors to trim.*

4. Fold the seam again as close to the edge as possible. Edgestitch; press.

NONWOVEN SEAMS

Although most nonwoven fabrics, such as felt, Facile, and Lamous, can be seamed like regular fabrics, a few cannot because they are too thick, bulky, or wiry (for example, Ultrasuede and some vinyls). More important, the garment design may be enhanced by using these special seams for nonwoven fabrics instead.

NONWOVEN FLAT-FELL SEAMS

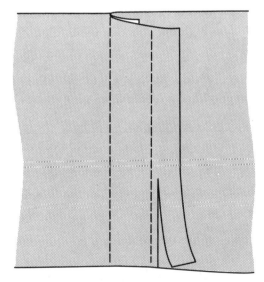

Fig. 21–43

1. Cut seam allowances 5/8″ wide.
2. Wrong sides together, stitch on the seamline.

Hint: *This is a good opportunity to check the garment fit, if you have any concerns.*

3. Press the seam flat, then to one side.
4. Trim the inner layer to 1/8″.
5. Glue or baste the other seam allowance in

place; stitch the desired distance from the seamline.

6. Trim close to the stitched line.

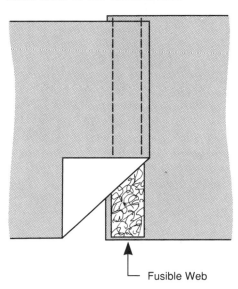

Fusible Web

Fig. 21–44

Hint: *Use appliqué or small trimming scissors for a close (1/16") trim.*

NONWOVEN LAPPED SEAMS

1. Cut no seam allowance on the overlap; cut a 3/8" to 5/8" seam allowance on the underlap.

2. On the underlap, mark the seamline on the right side of the fabric.

3. Right side up, match the raw edge of the overlap to the marked seamline; baste. Edgestitch it in place. If desired, topstitch again 1/4" away.

Hint: *Right side up, fuse 1/4"-wide strips of Wonder Under to the underlap seam allowance; fuse baste. Then topstitch.*

4. For a different look, zigzag (W,2;L,2) the overlap.

NONWOVEN SLOT SEAMS

This decorative flat seam looks great on a variety of materials, such as suede, leather, synthetic suedes, vinyl, felt, wadmal, boiled wool, and Polarfleece. They are particularly attractive for tops with yokes and gored skirts.

1. Trim away the seam allowances on the paper pattern before cutting out.

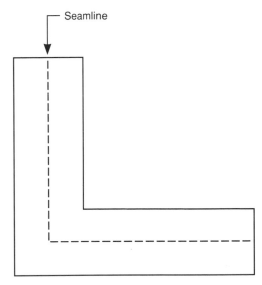

Seamline

Fig. 21–45

2. Cut 1 1/4"-wide underlay from self-fabric, another nonwoven, or a fabric which doesn't fray.

Use clips to mark the center on each end of the underlay.

Hint: *If the seamline is shaped, make a pattern for the underlay. Trace the seamline; mark the cutting lines parallel to it.*

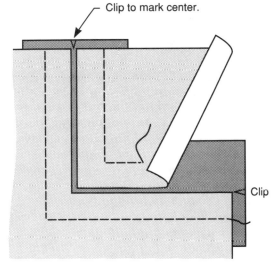

Clip to mark center.

Clip

Fig. 21–46

3. Right sides up, match the edge of the garment section to the center of the underlay. Baste; topstitch 1/4" from the edge of the underlay. If desired, topstitch again 1/4" away. Repeat for the other side of the seam. Press.

397

4. If the garment is reversible or unlined, trim the underlay close to the stitched line.

NONWOVEN LATTICE SEAMS

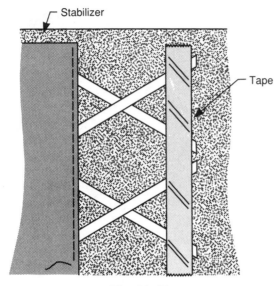

Fig. 21–47

This novelty seam is particularly attractive on tee tops, vests, and skirts; and it is one way to use small pieces of leather and suede.

1. Decide the width of the lattice.

2. On the paper pattern, trim away the seam allowances plus half the lattice width.

3. Cut enough strips, ribbon, or bias tape for the lattice design.

4. On a piece of stabilizer, draw two parallel lines spaced appropriately for the lattice width.

5. Glue or tape the lattice pieces to the stabilizer.

6. Right side up, position the garment sections on the stabilizer, with the lattice design between.

7. Edgestitch the garment to the lattice work. Tear away the stabilizer.

NONWOVEN STRAP SEAMS

Another flat, decorative seam, the strap seam can be made from nonfrayable fabrics, leather, suede, synthetic suede, or vinyl.

1. Trim away the seam allowances on the paper pattern before cutting out.

2. Use self-fabric, another nonwoven or non-frayable fabric, ribbon, or bias tape for the strap. Purchase or cut strips the desired width.

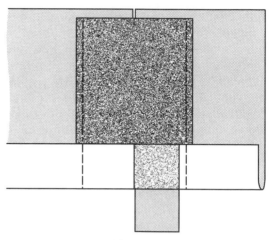

Fig. 21–48

Hint: *To cut smoothly, use a mat knife or rotary cutter and mat.*

  Use clips to mark the centers on each end of the strap and a temporary marking pen to indicate matchpoints.

  If the seam is shaped, trace the seamline; then mark the cutting lines parallel to it.

3. Wrong sides up, match the edges of the garment sections to the center of the strap; glue baste. Turn the sections right side up; edgestitch the strap in place. Press.

4. If the garment is unlined, trim the garment close to the stitched lines.

DOUBLE-STRAP OR WADMAL SEAM

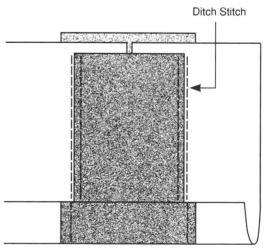

Fig. 21–49

If the garment is reversible, cut another strap 1/2″ wider than the one on the face side of the garment. Glue baste in place; then, right side up, ditch-stitch next to the strap edges.

PIPED SEAMS

This decorative seam is used to accentuate seamlines and garment edges. Unfilled or corded, the piping can be made from a variety of materials, such as fabric, bias tape, ribbon, lace, leather, suede, fringe, purchased pipings, and lip braids.

Select the piping and determine the grain for the strips. Generally, bias strips are most attractive and easiest to shape on curved and angled seams; but there are many exceptions.

Pipings made from materials which have more stretch on the crossgrain—knits, leather, and synthetic suedes—are frequently cut on the crossgrain. Pipings in some fabric patterns—stripes and diagonals—are more attractive when cut on the crossgrain or lengthwise grain.

Pipings on straight seams or very slightly curved seams can be cut on any grain since they require little or no shaping.

wise, wrong sides together. Stitch the piping width plus 1/16″ from the folded edge.

4. Right side up, place the piping on one garment section, matching the raw edges. Stitch just inside the seamline.

Hint: *To apply piping smoothly on corners and curved seams of collars, pockets, and flaps, clip the seam allowances of the piping almost to the stitching line. For more attractive corners, avoid sharp points by rounding them slightly.*

For curved seams at neckline and armscye edges, stretch the piping while easing the seam allowances to fit those of the garment.

For a square neckline, clip the seam allowances of the garment and facing to the corner before stitching. To avoid wrinkles on the finished garment, hold the piping taut when stitching the corner.

5. Right sides together, with the piping in between, match the raw edges and notches. Pin and stitch on the seamline. Press.

6. When stitching a V-neckline, begin and end at the V. Lap the piping right over left on ladies' garments and the reverse for men's designs.

PLAIN PIPING

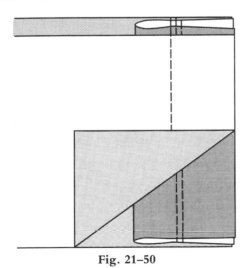

Fig. 21–50

1. Determine the width of the piping strips. Cut the strips twice the width of the piping plus two seam allowances. For a 1/4″ piping, cut the strips 1 3/4″ wide.

2. Cut the piping strips.

3. Make the piping. Fold the strips in half length-

CORDED PIPING

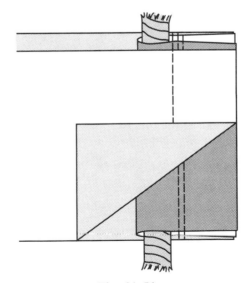

Fig. 21–51

1. To determine the width of the fabric strips, wrap and pin the bias-cut fabric around the cord. Remove the cord; add two seam allowances; then measure the total width.

399

Hint: *Sometimes it is easier to cut the piping strips wider than needed. Wrap the piping around the cord; stitch. Then trim the seam allowances to 5/8".*

2. Cord the piping. Place the cord on the wrong side of the strip. Wrap the strip around the cord, matching the raw edges; then, using a zipper or cording foot, stitch close to the cord.

Hint: *Always preshrink the cord before making the piping.*

3. Proceed as indicated for unfilled piping.
4. To reduce bulk at the ends of corded piping at garment openings, pull the end of the cord out and trim it 5/8".

RIBBON PIPING

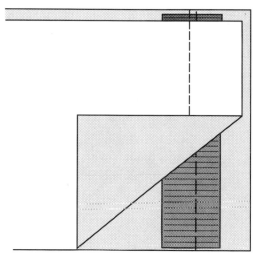

Fig. 21–52

For lace and ribbon pipings which have no wrong side, select a width that is the desired piping width plus 1/4".

1. For regular 5/8"-wide seams, pin and stitch the ribbon piping to the right side of the fabric so the edge of the piping is 3/8" from the raw edge.

Hint: *For enclosed seams, trim the seam allowances to 1/4".*

2. Complete the seams.

PLAIN SEAMS

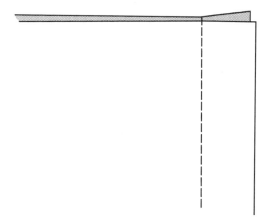

Fig. 21–53

Suitable for all types of garments and most fabrics, plain seams are the most versatile and most widely used.

1. Cut 5/8" seam allowances.
2. Right sides together, align the match points and raw edges. Pin and baste as needed; then stitch permanently on the seamline.

Hint: *For best results, stitch most seams directionally. This is usually from the hem to the waist, armscye, or neckline.*

2. Press the seam flat; then press it open; and finish the edges as needed.

REVERSED SEAMS

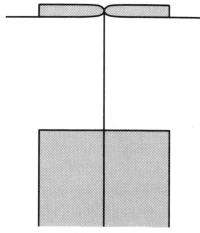

Fig. 21–54

Use reversed seams with decorative facings that lie on the right side of the garment, so the seam won't show at the garment edge.

1. On the seamline, measure and mark 1" from the cutting line of the edge to be faced.

2. Wrong sides together, stitch from the raw edge to the marked point. Backstitch.

3. Clip to the end of the stitched line; right sides together, stitch the rest of the seam. Press all seams open.

4. Stitch the facing to the garment, wrong sides up. Press, trim, and turn to the outside, covering the 3/8"-deep seam allowances.

SELF-FINISHED SEAMS

Self-finished seams, such as French, false French, flat-fell, standing-fell, bound, and machine-rolled, enclose all raw edges. See appropriate entries for instructions.

SERGED SEAMS

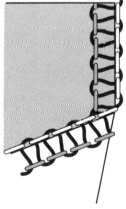

Fig. 21–55

Sometimes called safety-stitched seams, serged seams are made on serger or overlock machines. This double/ply seam is suitable for a variety of fabrics, including knits, sheers, lace, and fabrics which ravel.

DECORATIVE SERGED SEAMS

For novelty finishes, serge the seams wrong sides together with pearl cotton, yarn, woolly nylon, crochet cotton, metallic threads, or buttonhole twist in the looper. Thread the needle and lower looper

with regular thread, using the decorative thread in the upper looper.

For a more secure seam, use a conventional machine to stitch on the seamline. (For more ideas and decorative seams, see *Creative Serging Illustrated*.)

LAPPED SERGER SEAMS

This quick-and-easy lapped seam is another decorative serged seam suitable for unlined, reversible, or casual designs. Finish the edges with matching or decorative threads.

1. Allow 1/4" seam allowances.

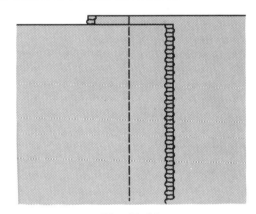

Fig. 21–56

2. Serge the edge of the overlap and underlap without reducing the seam allowances.

3. Lap the layers, matching the seamlines. Then, using a conventional sewing machine, topstitch on the seamline and, if desired, again at the edge.

SHEER SEAMS

Narrow seams, such as French, false French, flat-fell, standing-fell, machine-rolled, hairline, whipped, and double-stitched, are suitable for transparent and sheer fabrics. See appropriate entries for instructions.

SLOT SEAMS

Sometimes called channel seams, slot seams feature two tucks stitched to an underlay; they are suitable for straight, or almost straight seamlines.

On closed-slot seams, the tucks meet at the center of the underlay; on open-slot seams, the underlay is exposed 1/4″ to 1″. The underlay can be self-fabric or a different weave, texture, or color.

OPEN-SLOT SEAMS

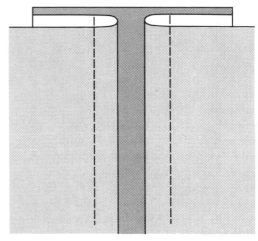

Fig. 21–58

CLOSED-SLOT SEAMS

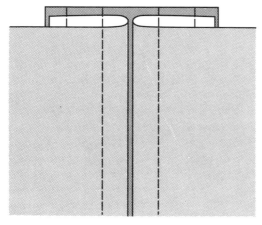

Fig. 21–57

1. Determine the width of the finished tucks.
2. Cut seam allowances the finished tuck width plus 5/8″. For 1/4″ tucks, cut seam allowances 7/8″ wide.
3. Cut the underlay twice the finished tuck width plus two seam allowances. For 1/4″ tucks, cut the underlay 1 3/4″ wide and the length of the seam.

Hint: *Use ribbons, braids, or novelty fabrics to vary the design; and if the underlay is soft or lightweight, back it with a fusible interfacing.*

4. Loosen the tension and set the machine for basting. Right sides together, baste the seamline. Press the seam open.

Hint: *To remove the basting easily, use a seam ripper to clip the threads every 2 to 3″; or use water-soluble basting thread.*

5. Wrong sides up, cover the seam with the underlay. Join each seam allowance and underlay with a 1/4″ seam.
6. Right side up, mark the tuck width on each side of the seamline; topstitch. Remove the basting thread and press.

1. Determine the width of the finished tucks and the distance between them.
2. On the garment pattern, make these changes for an open-slot seam with 1/4″ finished tucks and 1/4″ between. Draw the tuck placement line 1/8″ (half the distance between the tucks—the open slot) from the original seamline. Add 7/8″ seam allowances—the width of the finished tuck (1/4″) plus the regular seam allowance (5/8″).
3. Cut the underlay twice the finished tuck width plus the distance between and two 5/8″ seam allowances. For 1/4″ tucks with 1/4″ between, cut the underlay 2″ wide. Mark the vertical center on each end of the underlay.
4. Press the garment seam allowances under 7/8″.

Hint: *Mark the tuck foldline on the right side of the fabric with soap sliver, chalk, or temporary marking pen.*

5. Wrong sides up, match the edges of the garment sections and the underlay. Baste close to the raw edges by hand or machine; or glue baste.
6. Turn the garment over. Right sides up, mark the tuck stitching line; topstitch.

Hint: *To avoid a drag line, use hand basting through all layers to mark the stitching line.*

STANDING-FELL SEAMS

The standing-fell seam is suitable for light-weight fabrics which ravel. Sometimes called self-bound, mantua maker, wrapped, or hemmed over, this self-finished seam can be made by either of two methods.

TRADITIONAL METHOD

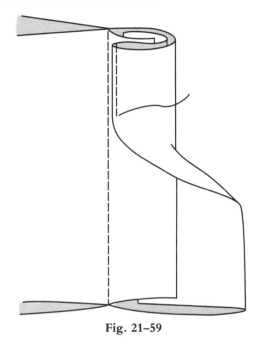

Fig. 21–59

This method for standing-fell seams is best for curved seams and close-fitting garments.

1. Cut seam allowances 5/8″ wide. Try to avoid marking with clips.
2. Right sides together, stitch on the seamline.
3. Trim one seam allowance to 1/8″.
4. Tuck the edge of the untrimmed seam allowance under the edge of the trimmed one; fold again to encase both raw edges. Hand or machine stitch the folded edge to the seamline.

QUICK-AND-EASY METHOD

Fast and easy, this method is suitable for seams which can be a hair off. I frequently use it on silk blouses which aren't closely fitted.

1. Cut seam allowances 5/8″ wide.
2. Stack the layers, right sides together, so the lower layer extends 1/4″.
3. Wrap the lower layer around the upper one;

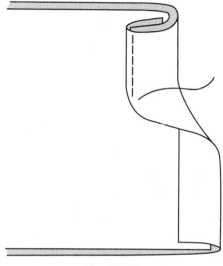

Fig. 21–60

then fold both to the left to encase the remaining raw edge. Pin and stitch through all layers close to the foldline, using the inside of the presser foot as a guide.

Hint: *When using this on underarm seams, fold the back over the front so the seams of the sleeves and bodice will align properly at the underarm.*

I use the "arrange-as-you-go" system: arrange 6″ to 8″, pin and stitch; repeat until finished.

STRAP SEAMS

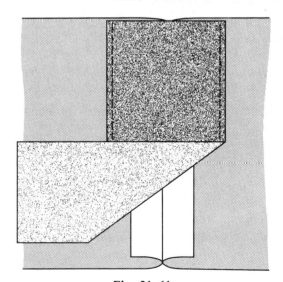

Fig. 21–61

This decorative seam is particularly attractive on reversible, unlined, and some sheer garments. The straps can be made from a variety of materials such as ribbon, decorative braid, lace, bias tape, leather, suede, felt, synthetic suede, and contrasting fabrics. And although they are usually straight, straps can be shaped.

1. Cut seam allowances 5/8" wide.

2. Straps made of ribbon, braid, bias tape, lace, and nonwovens do not need seam allowances. If the strap is a nonwoven fabric, cut it to the desired width. For a 1"-wide, nonwoven fabric strap, cut the strip 1" wide. If the strap is a woven fabric, cut it to the desired width plus two 1/4" seam allowances. For a 1"-wide, woven fabric strap, cut the strip 1 1/2" wide.

3. Wrong sides together, stitch the garment seam; trim to 1/4". Press flat, then to one side.

Hint: *For bulky fabrics, press the seam open; then trim it.*

4. Right side up, center nonwoven straps over the seam and baste; then edgestitch it to the garment.

Hint: *Use a zipper foot to edgestitch easily.*

5. When sewing woven fabrics, press the strap seam allowances under before applying the strap.

Hint: *Place a row of stitching a narrow 1/4" from each edge to use as a guideline.*

DOUBLE STRAP SEAM

Same as a wadmal seam; see Nonwoven Seams.

STRETCH SEAMS

Used most frequently on knits, stretch seams are a must for stretch fabrics. The best seaming method will depend on your equipment.

DOUBLE-STITCHED SEAMS

If you have a straight-stitch machine, the double-stitched seam can be used successfully for some stretch fabrics; however, it will not have enough elasticity for others (such as action knits), and the stitches will break when the garment is worn.

1. Cut the seam allowances 1/4" or 5/8" wide.

2. Right sides together, stretch slightly and stitch on the seamline.

Hint: *For a more elastic straight stitch, use 100 percent polyester, cotton/wrapped polyester, or woolly nylon thread and shorten the stitch length so more thread will be stitched into the seam. Loosen the tension on both the bobbin and needle threads; and, if necessary, loosen the pressure. Always begin with a new Universal-H point or ballpoint needle.*

3. Stitch again 1/8" away.

4. Trim to 1/4" when using a wide seam allowance.

ZIGZAG SEAM

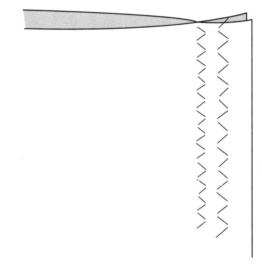

Fig. 21–62

This double/ply seam is one of several stretch seams which can be made on the basic zigzag machine.

1. Cut seam allowances as indicated on the pattern.

2. Right sides together, stitch on the seamline using a narrow zigzag (W,1; L,1.5).

Hint: *Loosen the tension and shorten the stitch length to increase the seam elasticity. Hold the fabric taut when stitching.*

3. Stitch (W,2; L,2) again close to the seamline. Trim as needed.

4. Press the seam flat, then to one side.

TWIN NEEDLE SEAM

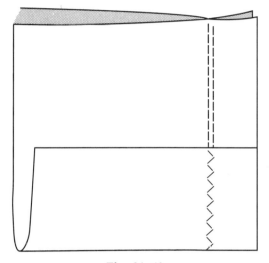

Fig. 21–63

The twin needle seam is another seam which can be used on the basic zigzag machine.

1. Cut seam allowances the desired width.

2. Right sides together, stitch, using a twin needle, so the needle on the left will be on the seamline.

Hint: *To increase the seam elasticity, use woolly nylon in the bobbin.*

STRETCH-STITCH SEAMS

If you have an automatic zigzag machine, experiment with the stretch stitches recommended in your sewing-machine manual.

1. Cut seam allowances 1/4″ wide.

2. Set the machine for a stretch stitch.

STRETCH SEAMS ON OVERLOCK MACHINES

1. Cut seam allowances the desired width. Since the overlock machine trims as it seams, seam allowances can be cut as indicated on the pattern and reduced when stitched.

2. Using the overlock manual as a guide, set the machine for seaming.

Hint: *For extra stretch, use woolly nylon thread on the loopers.*

TAPED SEAMS

Sometimes called stabilized or reinforced seams, these seams are finished with seam binding, linen or twill tape, invisible elastic, or lightweight selvage to strengthen and stabilize them. The tape can be applied several ways—either on the garment sections (Method One), or on the finished seamline (Methods Two and Three).

METHOD ONE

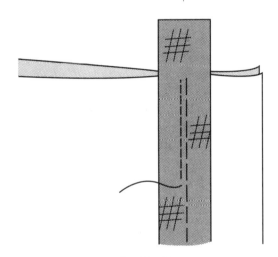

Fig. 21–64

1. Cut seam allowances 5/8″ wide.

2. Using the paper pattern as a guide, measure and mark the seamline length on the tape.

3. Wrong side up, center and pin the tape over one seamline. If the garment is longer than the tape, distribute the ease smoothly along the seamline; baste the tape in place to one layer.

4. Right sides together, with the taped section on top, stitch on the seamline.

5. Press flat; then press open.

METHOD TWO

Use this method to stabilize seams after they are stitched.

1. Press the seam flat. Center and pin the tape over the seamline. Turn the garment over and stitch again on the seamline.

2. To reduce the seam length on gaping necklines and too-long shoulder seams, ease the seamline to the tape. Pin the tape to each end of the seam and distribute the fullness as desired; baste; then stitch on the original seamline with the garment against the feed dogs. Press.

METHOD THREE

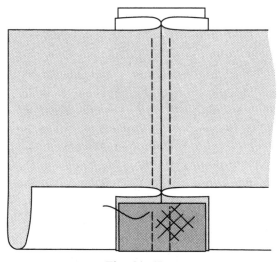

Fig. 21–65

Use this method to reinforce seams which will be stressed, such as the underarm on kimono designs.

1. Complete the seam.

2. Press the seam open. Wrong side up, center and pin the tape over the seamline.

3. Right side up, stitch through all layers—the tape, seam allowance, and garment—on both sides of the seamline.

TISSUE-STITCHED SEAMS

Tissue stitch seams with a piece of stabilizer between the fabric and feed dogs, to avoid damaging the fabric or to prevent puckered seams and underlayer creep.

Use your favorite stabilizers—typing paper, wax paper, Ziploc bags, nonwoven tear-away stabilizers, water-soluble stabilizers, or tissue paper.

Hint: *When using paper, stitch with the grain or length of the paper. Before cutting the paper*

into strips, tear it in both directions to determine which way tears easier; this is with the grain.

To remove the paper easily, tear toward the stitched line.

TOPSTITCHED SEAMS

Versatile and easy, topstitched seams are the most popular decorative seams. By changing the size, color, and kind of thread; the number and position of topstitched rows; and the stitch length, you can create an endless variety of decorative seams.

1. Cut seam allowances 5/8″ wide when topstitching 1/2″ or less from the seamline. When topstitching more than 1/2″ from the seamline, cut the seam allowances 1/8″ to 1/4″ wider than the topstitching width.

2. Right sides together, stitch a plain seam.

3. Finish the edges if necessary.

4. Press the seam flat, then press it open. Topstitch, locating the rows the desired distance—1/16″ to 1/2″—on each side of the seamline.

Or press the seam to one side; and topstitch one or more rows the desired distance from the seamline.

Hint: *Generally, press horizontal seams up, side and shoulder seams to the front, other vertical seams toward the center, and armscye seams toward the body. Press seams at garment centers to the right in front and to the left in back.*

TUCKED SEAMS

A variation of the lapped seam, this decorative seam can be made by several methods. Two of the methods are suitable for straight or slightly curved seams, while the third can be used on seams with deep curves or angles.

STRAIGHT TUCKED SEAMS—
METHOD ONE

1. Cut the seam allowances the finished tuck width, plus 3/8″. For a 1/4″-wide tucked seam, cut the seam allowances 5/8″ wide.

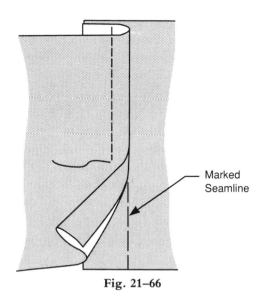

Fig. 21–66

2. Mark the seamlines on the right side of the fabric, using a soap sliver or chalk.

3. On the overlap, press the seam allowance under. Clip, crimp, or baste as needed for a smooth edge. Using a soap sliver or chalk, mark the stitching line or tuck width.

Hint: *Use a transparent plastic ruler as a guide for marking.*

4. Right sides up, pin or baste the layers together, so the seamlines match. The raw edges should be aligned on the underside. Stitch permanently on the marked line.

STRAIGHT TUCKED SEAMS— METHOD TWO

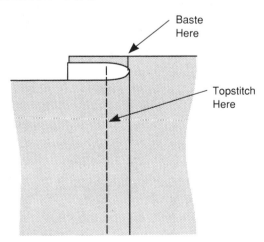

Fig. 21–67

1. Cut seam allowances the finished tuck width plus 3/8″.

2. Set the machine for a basting stitch (4 mm or 6 stitches per inch) and an unbalanced tension.

3. Right sides together, join the layers on the seamline.

4. Press the seam flat, then to one side.

5. Using a seam ripper, clip the looser basting thread every 4″ to 5″.

5. Right side up, mark the stitching line for the tuck. Stitch on the marked line.

Hint: *Don't forget to reset the tension and stitch length before topstitching.*

6. Remove the row of basting. Press.

SHAPED TUCKED SEAMS

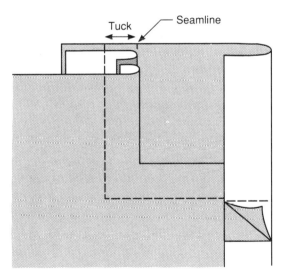

Fig. 21–68

Sometimes called a faced tuck seam, this method can be used on seams with angles or deep curves.

1. Cut the overlap seam allowance 1/4″ wide. Cut the underlap seam allowance the width of the finished tuck plus 3/8″. Cut a shaped facing for the overlap the width of the finished tuck plus 5/8″.

2. Right sides together, join the facing and overlap with a 1/4″ seam. Clip as needed; press the seam open; and turn it right side out. Facing side up, press again so the seam is at the edge. For a 1/4″-wide tuck, trim the seam 1/8″. Using a soap sliver, chalk, or temporary marking pen, mark the stitching line or tuck width.

407

3. Mark the seamline on the right side of the underlap.

4. Right sides up, pin or baste the layers together so the seamlines match. Check to be sure the raw edges are aligned on the underside. Stitch permanently on the marked line.

Hint: *For easier, straighter stitching, use a zipper foot.*

TWIN NEEDLE SEAMS

See Stretch Seams.

WADMAL SEAMS

Same as a double-strap seam, the wadmal seam is used on nonwoven and thick, bulky fabrics. See Nonwoven Seams.

WELT SEAMS

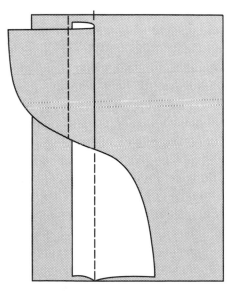

Fig. 21–69

Suitable for medium- to heavyweight fabrics, welt seams are particularly attractive on tailored designs.

At first glance, welt seams look like topstitched seams, but when examined closely, welts are thicker between the seamline and topstitched row and form a definite ridge.

1. Cut the seam allowances 5/8″ wide for 1/4″ to 3/8″ welts. For wider welts, cut seam allowances the width of the welt plus 1/4″.

2. Right sides together, stitch a plain seam.

3. Press the seam flat; then, using the guidelines for topstitched seams to determine the direction, press the seam to one side.

4. Trim the seam allowance next to the garment 1/8″ narrower than the welt. Trim to 1/8″ for a 1/4″ welt and 1/4″ for a 3/8″ welt.

5. Right side up, topstitch, or hand stitch, through the garment and the untrimmed seam allowance the desired distance from the seamline.

Hint: *Mark the stitching line with chalk, soap, or temporary marking pen.*

Experiment with a walking foot or a zipper foot to determine which produces the better results. The walking foot is better when drag lines are a problem and the zipper is preferred for bulky welts.

DOUBLE-WELT SEAMS

Sometimes called a fake flat-fell, the double-welt is topstitched twice.

1. Complete a welt seam.
2. Stitch again close to the seamline.

WHIPPED SEAM

Suitable for very fine sheers, whipped seams are time-consuming, but not difficult, to make.

1. Cut seam allowances 5/8″ wide.

2. Right sides together, stitch on the 5/8″ seamline.

3. Press flat; fold the seam allowances to one side 1/16″ from the seamline; press again.

4. Using a very fine thread, overcast the folded edge with a small stitch.

5. Carefully trim close to the stitches.

Hint: *I use Ginghers 5″ trimmers and the "palms up" technique to trim closely without cutting the stitches. Hold the scissors in your right*

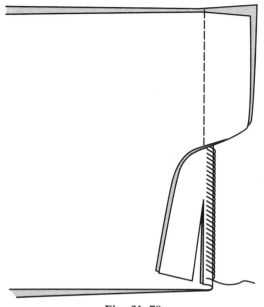

Fig. 21–70

hand in the usual way with the larger blade down. Then, with both palms up, hold the seam in your left hand with the garment bulk toward you; slip the large blade under the seam allowances and trim.

MOCK WHIPPED SEAM

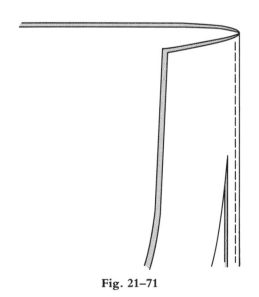

Fig. 21–71

1. Cut seam allowances 5/8″ wide.
2. Right sides together, stitch a 1/2″ seam.
3. Press flat and fold the seam allowances on the stitched line. Stitch again a narrow 1/8″ from the fold. Trim close to the stitched line.

WRONG-SIDE-OUT SEAMS

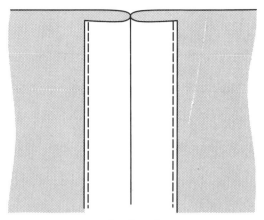

Fig. 21–72

Suitable for fabrics which have an attractive reverse side, wrong-side-out seams are used on unlined and reversible garments.

1. For nonwoven fabrics and fabrics that don't fray, cut seam allowances 5/8″ wide. Cut seam allowances on lightweight fabrics which fray 7/8″ wide.

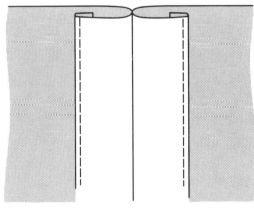

Fig. 21–73

2. Wrong sides together, stitch on the seamline. Press the seam flat, then press it open.
3. For nonwoven fabrics and fabrics that don't fray, edgestitch or zigzag (W,2; L,2) the edges to the garment. For fabrics which fray, fold under 1/4″ or serge the edges; then edgestitch the seams in place. Press.

For a novelty finish, satin stitch or serge the edges separately or together and leave them to stand upright.

409

ZANDRA RHODES SEAM

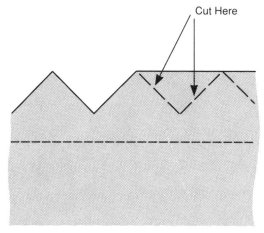

Cut Here

Fig. 21–74

This decorative wrong-side-out seam is suitable for nonwoven fabrics such as felt and synthetic suedes.

1. Cut seam allowances 1″ wide.
2. Wrong sides together, stitch on the seamline.
3. At the edge cut away triangles from both layers to make a large pinked edge.

Hint: *Use a disappearing marking pen to draw a line midway the seam allowance; then draw the triangles so they are 1″ wide at the line.*

4. Press shoulder and side seams to the back or leave them to stand upright.

ZIGZAGGED SEAMS

See Stretch Seams.

Seam Finishes

Although the primary purpose of seam finishes is to prevent or retard fraying during wear and cleaning, they can also improve the garment's appearance, strengthen seams, and make the garment more comfortable to wear.

When choosing the finish, consider the characteristics of the fabric—its weave, transparency, sheerness, bulk, roughness, and care requirements; the type, use, and quality of the garment; the shape of the seam and its location on the garment; your sewing skills; and the amount of time you have to complete the garment.

The best finishes are flat and completely invisible from the right side of the garment.

BOUND FINISH

This neat finish for unlined coats and jackets is also suitable for fabrics which ravel, irritate the skin, or shed.

1. Use seam tape, lace, net, or nylon tricot for the binding. Generally, the purchased cotton/polyester bias binding which is readily avail-

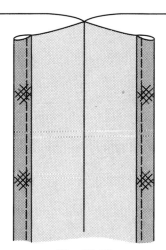

Fig. 21–75

able is too bulky and will show on the right side of the garment; however, bias custom-made from 1 1/4″-wide strips of lightweight polyester or silk blouse fabrics works well.

2. Wrong sides together, press the binding lengthwise so the bottom layer is 1/8″ wider than the upper one.

When using bias-cut strips, fold the raw edges in to meet the pressed line; and press again.

3. For a single/ply binding, stitch and press the garment seam open. Insert the edge of one seam allowance between the binding layers. Edgestitch or zigzag (W,1; L,2) the binding in place.

Hint: *Use the inside of the presser foot as a guide for straight stitching.*

4. For a double/ply binding, stitch on the seamline; stitch again through both seam allowances 1/8" away; trim the seam to 1/4". Press.
Encase the seam with the binding. Edgestitch or zigzag (W,1; L,2).

CLEAN-FINISHED EDGE

Technically, the clean-finished edge is the same as a turned-and-stitch finish; however, the term is frequently used to describe any seam finish. See Turned-and-Stitched.

FUSIBLE INTERFACING FINISH

This finish is suitable for loosely woven fabrics which ravel badly.
1. Cut narrow (1/4" to 3/8") strips of a very soft, lightweight fusible interfacing. If a fusing test shows no demarcation on the right side of the fabric, cut the strips 5/8" to 3/4" wide.
2. Align and fuse the strips to the raw edges immediately after cutting out.

Hint: *To avoid getting the fusible adhesive on your pressing pad, cover the pad with a Teflon pressing sheet.*

3. Right sides together, stitch on the seamline.

HAND OVERCASTING

Frequently used in couture construction, hand overcasting is perhaps the flattest, softest finish. Since it is time-consuming, you will want to reserve it for your finest wool, silk, and linen designs.

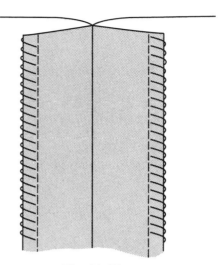

Fig. 21–76

1. For a single/ply finish, complete and press the seam open. Overcast one seam allowance, using mercerized cotton thread. Make the stitches 1/8" deep and space them 1/8" apart. Repeat for the other seam allowance.

Hint: *To make neat, uniform stitches, machine stitch a guideline 1/8" from the edge. Pull the thread taut after each stitch.*

2. For a double/ply finish, complete and press the seam open, then press it flat. Stitch again 1/8" away; trim the seam to 1/4". Overcast the edges together.

HONG KONG FINISH

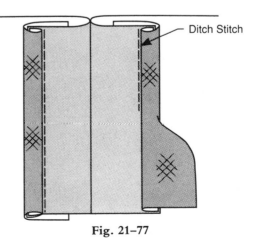

Ditch Stitch

Fig. 21–77

Although this neat finish could be used on any fabric which frays, as well as on pile fabrics and unlined jackets, it should only be used on ball gowns and luxury garments. Since this finish is only used in couture construction, never ready-to-wear, using it on the wrong type garment will immediately identify your design as homemade.

1. For the binding, use lightweight lining fabrics, silk organza, chiffon, or nylon tricot. Purchased bias bindings are too heavy and bulky.

2. Cut the bias strips 1″ wide.

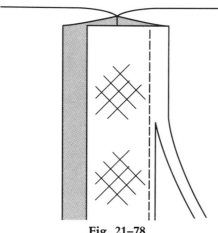

Fig. 21–78

3. Complete and press the seam open.

4. Right sides together, join the binding to one seam allowance with a 1/4″ seam. Trim to an even 1/8″.

5. Wrap the binding around the edge and press. Ditch-stitch to secure the binding.

Hint: *Stitch with the grain and baste as needed to prevent a drag line. For a softer finish, use a small running stitch to secure the binding.*

6. Repeat for the other seam allowance.

LACE BINDING

See Bound Finish.

MULTI-STITCH ZIGZAG

See Zigzag Finish.

OVERLOCKED EDGE

Frequently used on knits and sheers, this double/ply finish is sometimes called an overedge or zigzagged finish. See Zigzag Finish.

Another overlock finish is made on an overlock or serger (see Serged).

PINKED OR PINKED-AND-STITCHED

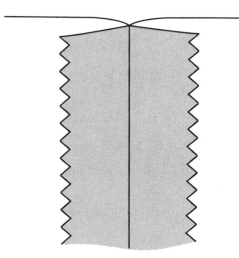

Fig. 21–79

Use pinking on firmly woven fabrics which do not fray badly.

1. Complete the seam and press it open. If the fabric ravels, stitch 1/4″ from each raw edge. Set the stitch length (2–1.25mm or 12–20 stitches per inch), depending on how badly the fabric ravels.

2. Pink the edges.

Hint: *To reduce shedding, brush the pink edges with a small, stiff brush.*

SEAM BINDING

See Bound Finish.

SEARING

This finish can be applied to any fabric which melts. It works particularly well on fabrics which ravel badly, such as nylon ripstop or nylon taffeta.

Sometimes called singeing or candling, searing is frequently used for outerwear, tote bags, and tents. Since the seared edge may irritate the skin, it should not be used on garments which are worn next to the body.

When edges are seared before sewing, the raw edges cannot be used as a seam guide. When seared after sewing, take care to avoid damaging the garment during the process of searing.

1. Set up a well-seated candle, preferably a dripless one. Open all windows in the room. Have a bucket of water ready.

2. Trim away any fraying at the garment edges, to prevent loose threads from catching fire.

3. Hold the fabric edge taut and move it quickly just above the candle to seal the edge.

Hint: *If a heavy brown bead forms, the fabric is too close to the flame or you're not moving it quickly enough.*
If the fabric should catch fire, blow it out.

SERGED

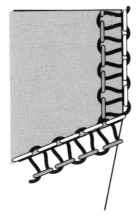

Fig. 21–80

The serged or overlocked edge is used on most ready-made garments, even some which cost more than $5000. Every sewing-machine company makes several models which allow the home sewer to duplicate this finish.

Seams can be serged single/ply or double/ply. For best results, review the serger manual and experiment with various threads and tensions.

Although serged edges are frequently wonderful, the amount of thread used makes them stiff and sometimes obvious from the right side of the fabric.

Hint: *Use fine two-ply threads designed for sergers; and for problem fabrics like silk shantung, gabardine, and tropical wools, use soft woolly nylon.*

STANDING-FELL OR SELF-BOUND SEAM

Technically, this is a seam finish, but it is usually described as a seam type. (See Standing-Fell Seams.)

TRICOT OR NET-BOUND FINISH

See Bound Finish.

TURNED-AND-STITCHED

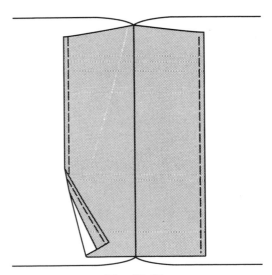

Fig. 21–81

Sometimes called an edgestitched or clean-finished seam, this finish is bulky and only suitable for lightweight fabrics. It is sturdy and can be machine washed or dry-cleaned.

413

Almost completely replaced by serging, the turned-and-stitched finish is a neat treatment for unlined jackets.

1. Cut seam allowances 3/4″ to 1″ wide.
2. Complete the seam and press it open.
3. Turn each raw edge under 1/4″ and edgestitch.

Hint *Use the inside of the presser foot as a stitching guide. On convex or outward curved edges, crimp 1/4″ from the edge so the edge will turn under smoothly.*

Unfinished Edge

Sometimes called a raw, cut, or plain edge, the unfinished edge is suitable for nonwoven fabrics, fabrics which don't fray, vinyl, leather, suede, synthetic suedes, knits, and lined garments.

Hint: *If a ridge at the edge shows on the right side of the garment, try pinking it.*

Zigzag Finish

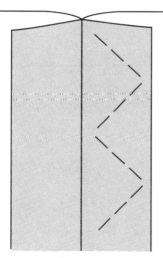

Fig. 21–82

The zigzag finish can be used on a variety of fabrics—loosely wovens, fabrics which fray, heavy materials, and knits.

1. For a single/ply finish, complete and press the seam open. Set the machine for a zigzag (W,2; L,2), or multi-stitch zigzag (W,3; 1,2), or blindstitch (W,2; L,2). Stitch the seam allowance close to the raw edge.

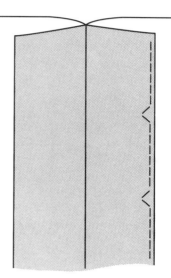

Fig. 21–83

Hint: *To reduce rolling or tunnelling, use a stabilizer or overcast foot; or set the machine for a blindstitch (W,4; L,2). Also, reduce top tension.*

2. For a double/ply finish, complete and press the seam open, then press it flat. Set the machine for a wide zigzag (W,3; L,3), multi-stitch zigzag (W,4; L,2), or blindstitch (W,2; L,2).

Hint: *When using a zigzag or multi-stitch zigzag, stitch through both plies close to the seamline. Trim the seam to 1/4″. When using a blindstitch, stitch close to the raw edge.*

3. Another way to finish double/ply seams is to trim the seam to 1/4″ before zigzagging.

CHAPTER 22
Hems and Hem Finishes

Hems

BLINDSTITCHED HEMS

Blindstitched hems can be finished by hand or machine. In either case, the stitches are placed between the hem and garment, invisible from the inside of the garment as well as from the outside. (Note: See also Machine Blindstitch.)

BLIND STITCHED BY HAND

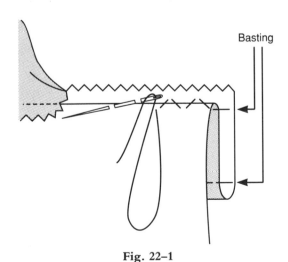

Fig. 22–1

The most frequently used hand-stitched hem, the blindstitched hem is sometimes called a tailor's

hem. Used on all better garments, the stitches should be inconspicuous from the right side of the garment.

1. Cut the hem allowance the appropriate width for the type garment, fabric, and hem shape.

2. Mark the hemline; fold the hem under; steam press the hem to remove extra fullness.

Hint: *Baste both layers 1/4" from the foldline. Use cotton basting thread or silk thread (size A). Insert brown paper strips between the hem and garment to avoid shrinking the garment.*

3. Mark the hem allowance the desired depth, and finish the edge appropriately. Baste again 1/4" from the finished edge of the hem allowance.

4. Lay the garment on a table, right side up, so the folded-under hem is toward you. Fold the garment, right sides together, at the basted line.

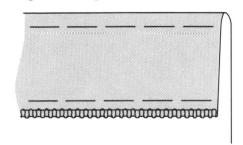

Fig. 22–2

Hint: *Fold the edge of the hem allowance back if the fabric creases easily.*

5. Working right to left, secure the thread in the hem or seam allowance. Hem the garment by picking up one thread, or part of a thread, in the garment; then pick up a small stitch in the hem 1/2" to the left. Repeat, alternating between the garment and hem to create a series of small "v's."

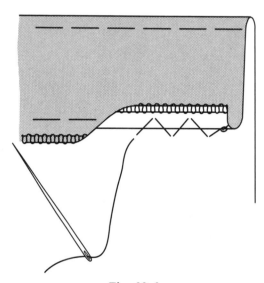

Fig. 22–3

Hint: *Use a very fine needle when hemming. Keep the stitches loose so the hem will be inconspicuous. For security, take a backstitch in the hem allowance every 4" to 5".*

Make stitches on the garment in the back of one or two yarns; hem lightly and loosely.

6. Remove basting. Press the hem. Wrong sides up, use the point of the iron to press under the edge of the hem allowance.

BLIND CATCHSTITCH HEMS

Frequently used to hem heavy fabrics, make the blind catchstitch hem using the directions above and a catchstitch.
1. To make a blind catchstitch, work from left to right. Take a small stitch on the garment right to left, then a similar stitch on the hem. This stitch is called herringbone in hand embroidery.

FIGURE-EIGHT HEM

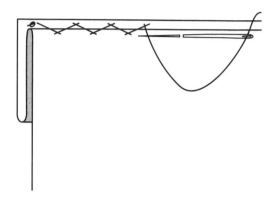

Fig. 22–4

Used to hem knits, crepes, and other difficult-to-hem fabrics invisibly, the figure-eight hem secures each stitch independently.
1. Using the directions above, work right to left.
2. Take two small stitches in the hem allowance—one on top of the other. Then take a stitch in the garment, directly opposite the stitches in the hem; take one more stitch in the hem to complete the figure eight.

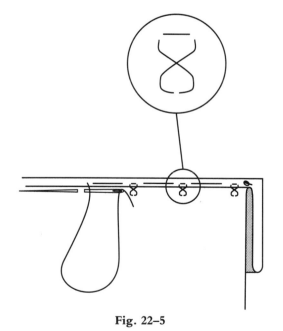

Fig. 22–5

3. Begin the next stitch 3/4" to 1" to the right. Do not pull the thread tight between stitches.

BOOK HEMS

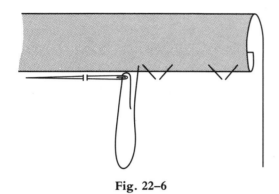

Fig. 22–6

Frequently used on coats, jackets, and children's garments, this hand-stitched hem is used when topstitching would detract from the garment's appearance and raw edges would be unsightly on the inside of the garment.

1. Cut the hem allowance 5/8″ to 2 1/4″. Use 5/8″ on lightweight fabrics, 1 1/4″ on jackets, and 2 1/4″ on coats.

2. Mark and press the hem in place. Fold the raw edge under 1/4″; baste.

3. Place the garment on a table. Hold the hem in your hand; and working right to left, secure the thread in the hem or seam allowance. Hem the garment by picking up one thread, or part of a thread, in the garment; then take a 1/2″ stitch in the fold of the hem. Repeat, alternating between the garment and hem to create a series of small "v's."

Hint: *Use a very fine needle when hemming; and keep the stitches loose, so the hem will be inconspicuous. For security, take a backstitch in the hem allowance every 4″ to 5″.*

4. Remove bastings; press.

CATCHSTITCH HEMS

Sometimes called a cross-stitched hem, catch-stitched hems have more stretch than regular blindstitched hems.

The flat catchstitch hem is frequently used for hems on tailored suits and coats.

1. Cut the hem allowance the desired width.
2. Press and baste the hem in place.

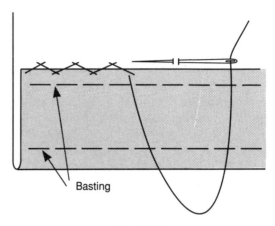

Basting

Fig. 22–7

3. Wrong side up, work from left to right; and secure the knot on the hem allowance. Make a small stitch on the garment just above the hem; then, working to the right, take a small stitch in the hem. Continue, alternating stitches between the garment and hem until finished.

4. Remove bastings; press.

DOUBLE HEMS

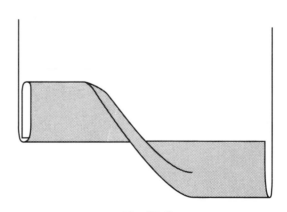

Fig. 22–8

Frequently used to shadowproof a hem on lightweight and transparent fabrics, double hems are good choices for rectangular skirts and children's garments that have a straight hemline. They can be as narrow as 1/4″ and as wide as one-third the skirt length.

Since this hem requires additional fabric, it is not used on inexpensive garments.

417

1. Cut the hem allowance twice the desired finished width.

2. Mark the hemline, using a temporary marking pen, soap sliver, or chalk.

3. Press the hem under on the marked line.

4. Remeasure the hem allowance and correct any unevenness. Trim away any whiskers on the raw edge.

5. Fold the hem allowance in half so the raw edge meets the hemline; baste and press.

6. Hem luxury garments with a slipstitch. Hem casual designs, linens, and curtains by machine, if desired.

7. Remove basting. Press.

DOUBLE-STITCHED HEMS

Use double-stitched hems on heavy or bulky fabrics, so the hem will remain invisible on the right side of the garment.

1. Cut the hem allowance the desired hem width.

2. Mark the hemline and press the hem under.

3. Finish the edge, if necessary.

4. Baste the hem, midway between the hemline and finished edge; then using a blindstitch or blind catchstitch, hem the garment at the basted line.

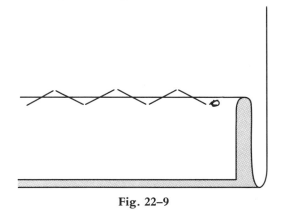

Fig. 22–9

5. Baste again 1/4″ below the finished edge and hem again. Remove bastings; press.

FACED HEMS

Use faced hems to finish shaped hemlines, reduce bulk, lengthen the garment, or increase com-

fort. The facing can be self-fabric, contrasting fabric, lining-weight material, bias strips, purchased bias facing, grosgrain ribbon, or lace.

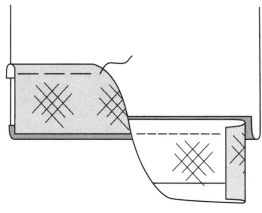

Fig. 22–10

FACED HEM—STRAIGHT EDGE

1. Cut the hem allowance 1/4″ wide.

2. Cut 2″-wide bias strips from lining-weight fabric, or use prepackaged bias tape.

3. Right sides together, pin the facing to the garment. Fold the beginning end under 1/2″; overlap the remaining end. Stitch with a 1/4″ seam allowance.

4. Wrong side up, press the hem under so the facing/garment seam is visible.

5. Fold the edge of the facing under; baste; and hem. Remove basting; press.

FACED HEM—SHAPED EDGE

1. Draw the facing pattern on the garment pattern so it is at least 2″ wide. Add a 1/4″ seam allowance at the hemline. Trace the facing pattern and grainline on a piece of pattern paper.

2. Cut out the garment and facing.

3. Complete the vertical seams.

4. Finish the unnotched edge of the facing.

5. Right sides together, pin and stitch the facing to the garment with a 1/4″ seam.

Hint: *For a smoother finish when stitching scallops, use a shorter stitch length and take one stitch across the point of the scallop.*

6. Trim the seam to a fat 1/8″; clip any points as needed. Cut triangles out of convex curves.

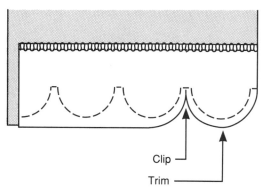

Clip

Trim

Fig. 22–11

7. Turn the hem right side out. Wrong side up, press the facing so the facing/garment seam is barely visible; baste.

8. Hem the facing to the garment. Remove basting; press.

Hint: *Most lined garments will not have to be hemmed. The lining will hold the facing in place.*

FUSED HEMS

Quick and easy, fused hems are made by melting a fusible web between the hem and the garment. Fused hems look best on nonwoven and thick fabrics, children's garments, and casual designs.

Fusing stiffens the hem; and it may bleed through to the right side on lightweight and light-colored fabrics. Experiment with different applications and several fusible webs.

Hint: *Don't overlook Wonder Under, Transfuse II, or Melt Adhesive Thread when trying different fusibles; they bond well and the finished hem is softer than webs like Stitch Witchery.*

1. When using fusible webs, cut the fusible web 1/4″ wide or slightly narrower than the hem width.

Hint: *To cut 1/4″-wide strips, roll the fusible web like a cigar; pin. Cut the strips off one end with scissors or an Olfa cutter.*

2. Cut the hem allowance the desired width.
3. Mark the hemline; and press the hem under.

4. Wrong side up, stitch fusible web strips to the top of the hem allowance. Use 1/4″-wide strips for a softer hem and strips slightly narrower than the hem width for a crisper finish.

Note: When using Wonder Under or Transfuse II, skip the stitching and just fuse the strips to the wrong side of the hem allowance. When using Melt Adhesive Thread, stitch with the fusible thread in the bobbin and the garment right side up.

5. Fold the hem under. Cover with a damp cloth; fuse the hem in place.

Hint: *To avoid a bubble at the hemline be sure the web touches the fold.*

GLUED HEMS

Frequently used on felted or leather materials, glued hems are quick and easy to make.

1. Cut hem allowances the desired width.
2. Fold and press the hem to the wrong side of the garment.
3. Glue the hem in place, using rubber cement or Sticky Stuff on leather and suede and a permanent white glue on felt.

Hint: *To avoid a bubble, be sure the glue extends to the foldline.*

HORSEHAIR HEMS

Named for the horsehair once used to make this stiff braid, today's horsehair is a transparent, synthetic braid available in several widths, from 1/2″ to 6″. Use it to add crispness and body to the hemline, to reduce wrinkling, and to make a skirt stand away from the body.

Although these directions can be used for braids of any width, they are used most frequently for narrow braids.

1. Mark the hemline carefully. On lightweight fabrics, trim the hem allowance to 1/2″; on heavier fabrics, trim to 5/8″.

Hint: *Mark, measure, and trim carefully; after trimming, the hem can be shortened but it cannot be lengthened.*

419

2. Steam press the braid to remove foldlines.

3. Right side up, match and pin the braid to the edge of the garment, overlapping the ends 1/2″. Use a short running stitch to sew the braid ends together.

Hint: *If the garment isn't lined, cover the ends of the braid with a piece of seam binding or satin ribbon so they won't snag your hose.*

Unpin a short section of the braid; wrap the binding around the ends; then hand sew the raw edges together.

4. Join the braid and skirt with a 1/4″ seam.

5. Fold the braid to the wrong side so the hem wraps around the braid; press.

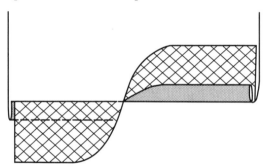

Fig. 22–12

6. Using a catchstitch, hem the braid to the garment.

Hint: *If the distance between seamlines isn't too great, as on gored skirts, hem the braid only to the seamlines, with a few hemming stitches in the middle of each skirt panel.*

When using a wide horsehair braid on shaped edges, select a braid with a gathering thread along one edge. Position the braid so it can be gathered at the upper edge.

Interfaced Hems

Interface hems on better garments to add body, prevent wrinkling, and avoid sharply creased edges.

For a crisp edge, interface with organza, organdy, muslin, hair canvas, horsehair braid, or crisp interfacing materials. For a soft, padded edge, interface with lamb's wool, Armo wool, polyester fleece, or cotton flannel.

INTERFACED HEMS ON LINED GARMENTS

1. For lined garments, cut bias strips of sew-in interfacing at least 1″ wider than the garment hem allowance.

Hint: *The interfacing width depends on the amount of shaping desired in the hemline; for ball gowns and peplum style jackets, the desired width can be several inches wider than the hem allowance.*

2. For a sharp edge, position and pin interfacing so the lower edge is along the hemline; overlap and join the interfacing ends with a short running stitch.

3. Secure both edges of the interfacing with a loose catchstitch, making it invisible on the right side of the garment.

4. Fold and press the hem in place; use a loose catchstitch to secure the top of the hem to the interfacing. Do not sew through to the garment.

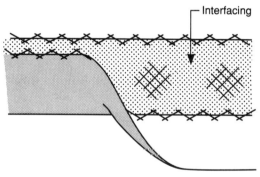

Fig. 22–13

5. For a crisp or soft edge, position and pin the interfacing so the lower edge laps the hemline 1/2″; secure the interfacing at the hemline with a loose blindstitch; and hem the garment.

Hint: *To avoid making dimples with your blindstitches at the hemline, pick up the back of the fabric yarns.*

6. Press.

420

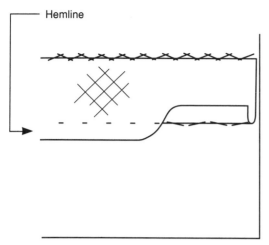

Fig. 22–14

INTERFACED HEMS ON UNLINED GARMENTS

1. For a crisp or soft edge on unlined garments, cut the bias strips the width of the garment hem; for a sharper edge, cut the strips 1/2" narrower.

2. Position and pin the interfacing strips to the wrong side of the garment so the edge meets or laps the hemline, depending on the desired finish. Catchstitch or blindstitch the interfacing to the hemline.

3. Fold and press the hem in place; use a loose blindstitch or blind catchstitch to hem the garment invisibly.

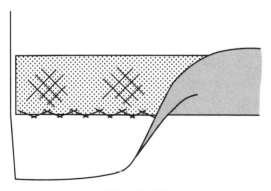

Fig. 22–15

4. When using a fusible interfacing, cut the strips to fit the hem allowance. Fuse the interfacing to the hem allowance; fold and press the hem in place. Hem the garment.

LETTUCE EDGING

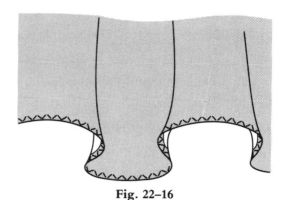

Fig. 22–16

Sometimes called lettucing or fluted edging, this hem was popularized by American designer Stephen Burrows.

To make an attractive rippled edge, use it on knits with 50 percent stretch or on bias-cut woven fabrics. When sewing knits, check—before cutting—for runs. If the fabric runs at one end, cut the garment so the fabric runs toward the hem.

1. Trim away the hem allowances.

2. Set the machine (W,3; L,1) and center the edge under the foot. Stretching the fabric as much as possible, stitch the edging; press.

3. For a smoother, firmer edging, cut seam allowances 1/4" wide. Fold the edge under on the hemline; zigzag.

MACHINE BLINDSTITCH

Frequently used on children's wear, casual designs, and everyday garments, machine blindstitched hems are strong and launder well.

1. Cut the hem allowance 1" to 3" wide.

2. Mark, press, and finish the edge of the hem.

3. If the hem is flared, baste the hem in place 1/4" below the free edge to control the fullness. If it is straight, pin the hem in place.

Hint: *To avoid catching the pin heads in the needle hole, place the pins on the right side of the garment with the heads toward the hemline.*

4. Fold the garment, right sides together, so the free edge of the hem is exposed 1/4". Repin from the wrong side of garment through all layers.

421

5. Set the machine for a blind-hemming stitch (W,2; L,2). Center the fold under the foot and stitch.

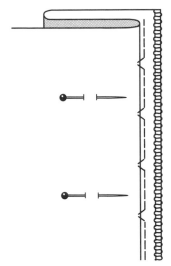

Fig. 22–17

Hint: *To make the hem invisible on the right side of the garment, use a blind-hemming foot, a very fine needle (60/8 to 80/12), and a loose upper tension. Center the fold under the foot and stitch. Fine-tune the stitch width so the needle barely catches the fold of the garment.*

6. Press.

BLINDSTITCHING ON STRAIGHT-STITCH MACHINES

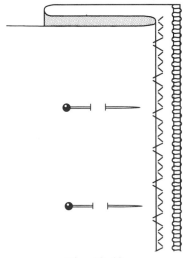

Fig. 22–18

To blindstitch on a straight-stitch machine, set the machine for L, 2–2.5 (10–12 stitches per inch). Stitch five stitches on the hem allowance; then swing the hem manually to catch one stitch on the garment. Repeat until the hem is finished; press.

STRETCH BLINDSTITCH

Many machines have a stretch blindstitch for hemming knits.
1. Cut the hem allowance 1″ to 3″ wide.
2. Mark, press, and finish the edge of the hem.
3. Pin or baste the hem in place.
4. Fold the garment, right sides together, so the free edge of the hem is exposed 1/4″.
5. Set the machine for a stretch blindstitch (W,2; L,2). Center the fold under the foot and stitch.

Hint: *Use a blind-hemming foot and a very fine needle. Fine-tune the stitch width so the needle barely catches the fold of the garment.*

6. Press.

ZIGZAG BLINDSTITCH

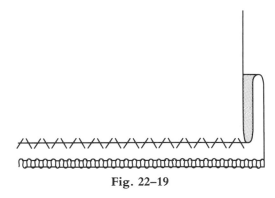

Fig. 22–19

Particularly appropriate for knits which curl, the zigzag blindstitch has more stretch than a regular machine blindstitch; and it can be used if your machine doesn't have a stretch blindstitch.

Follow the directions for the stretch blindstitch, using a plain zigzag stitch.

MACHINE-ROLLED HEM

This attractive, narrow hem is used on ready-made garments in all price ranges. It is particularly attractive for hemming flounces, collars, ruffles, scarves, circular skirts, and lightweight and sheer fabrics. Unlike the hemmer-foot hem which it imitates, it is easy to use on curves and corners.

1. Cut the hem allowance 5/8″ wide.
2. Machine stitch 1/2″ from the edge.

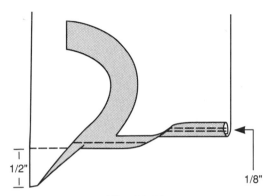

1/2″   1/8″

Fig. 22–20

3. Right side up, fold under the edge on the stitched line; edgestitch.

Hint: *The finished width of the hem is determined by how closely you edgestitch. To stitch 1/16″ from the edge, use a zipper foot, edgestitching foot, or the inside edge of the straight-stitch presser foot as a guide.*

4. Trim close to the stitched line.

Hint: *One of the secrets for a very narrow hem is to trim as closely as possible. I use appliqué scissors or 5″ trimmers.*

5. Fold the hem again; and, with the wrong side of the garment up, stitch on the last stitching line. Press.

Hint: *This is an exception to the rule to stitch from the right side of the garment. When stitching wrong side up, you are less likely to have two obvious rows of stitching—an important point when the hem is used on collars, flounces, and ruffles.*

Another solution is to use water-soluble thread in the bobbin when edgestitching the first time. Since the thread dissolves when you steam press, you can pull the other thread away easily.

6. When the edge is shaped, clip the hem allowance as needed so it will turn under smoothly.

MERROW FINISH

Sometimes called a handkerchief edging or a napkin finish, the merrow finish is named for the industrial machine that makes this edging. The merrow finish is a very narrow rolled hem made on a serger.

Using the directions in your serger manual, experiment with the tensions on your machine.

MITERED HEMS

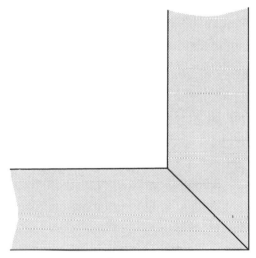

Fig. 22–21

Characterized by an angled seam at the corner, the mitered hem is used to reduce bulk at the hemline.

1. Right side up, mark the foldlines at the garment edges with chalk or temporary marking pen.
2. Finish the raw edges so they won't ravel.
3. Wrong side up, press the hem allowances to the wrong side.
4. Using chalk or temporary marking pen, mark the finished edges where they meet; draw a line from one mark point to the corner on the wrong side of the fabric.
5. Fold the fabric right sides together; and stitch on the marked line from the corner to the finished edge.

6. If the fabric is bulky, trim the seam; press.

7. Turn the corner right side out and press.

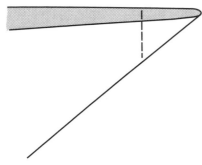

Fig. 22–22

8. For a decorative finish, make the hem wrong side out. Finish the edges with a serger (Step 2); ditch-stitch at the edge of the serging to secure the hems.

MITERED CORNERS FOR REVERSIBLE GARMENTS

Particularly attractive on light- to medium-weight unlined and reversible garments, this clean-finished hem is generally folded to the wrong side; but if the back of the fabric is attractive, fold it wrong side out.

1. Add 1/4″ to the hem allowances.

2. Right side up, mark the foldlines at the garment edges with chalk or temporary marking pen.

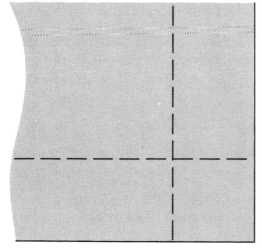

Fig. 22–23

3. Wrong side up, press the hem allowances to the wrong side.

4. Mark the raw edges with a small clip where they meet; draw a line from one clip to the corner on the wrong side of the fabric.

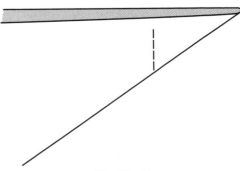

Fig. 22–24

5. Fold the fabric right sides together; stitch on the marked line. Begin at the corner and stop 1/4″ from the raw edges. Backstitch.

6. Trim the seam if needed; press.

7. Turn the corner right side out.

8. Press the raw edges of the hem under 1/4″; baste; then edgestitch the hem in place.

MITERED CORNERS ON TRANSPARENT FABRICS

1. Make a paper pattern for the mitered corner.

2. Draw the hem allowance twice the finished hem width.

3. Fold the hems in place on the paper pattern. First fold one edge; then fold the other.

4. Crease a line from the corner to the hem edge. Before you unfold the pattern, add a 1/4″ seam allowance to each side of the creased line; trim.

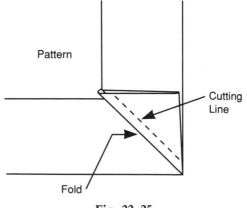

Fig. 22–25

5. Using the paper pattern as a guide, shape the garment corners.

6. To stitch the corners, stitch right sides together. Clip and press.

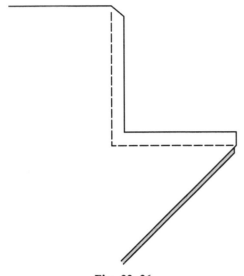

Fig. 22–26

7. Turn the corner right side out; press from the wrong side.

8. Pin or baste the hem in place; edgestitch.

MOCK-MERROW FINISH

If you don't have a serger, use these easy directions to simulate a merrow finish on a conventional zigzag machine.

1. Cut hem allowances 5/8″ wide.
2. Straight stitch on the hemline.

Hint: *For easier folding, use a twin needle and a tighter tension on the bobbin.*

3. Right side up, fold the hem under and edgestitch.
4. Trim close to the edgestitching.
5. Right side up, satin stitch (W,2–3; L, almost 0) the edge so the stitches cover the trimmed raw edge and the fold.

Hint: *Use an embroidery foot; and experiment with embroidery threads and different stitch lengths and widths until the stitch is attractive. You*

might also try using water-soluble stabilizer under the edge.

6. If you're in a hurry, eliminate the straight edgestitching; simply satin stitch, then trim. The wrong side will not be as attractive because the raw edges won't be enclosed, but it is much quicker.

Hint: *Instead of appliqué scissors, use 5″ trimmers and the "palms up" technique; you're less likely to clip the zigzag stitches.*

NARROW HEMS

Narrow hems range from very narrow hems, such as machine-rolled, hemmer-rolled, hand-rolled, and mock-merrow, to 1/4″ hems, such as shirttail and book hems. See appropriate entries for instructions.

PADDED HEM

Interface the hem with lamb's wool, polyester fleece, cotton batting, or Armo wool to soften the hemline and to add weight and body to the hem. One of the features of a well-padded hem is that it is impervious to overpressing and retains its soft edge for the life of the garment. See Interfaced Hems.

PINKED HEMS

A novelty hem for nonfrayable fabrics, felts, vinyls, silk taffetas, and satins, these hems use pinking to create a decorative edge.

Mark the hemline and pink carefully, so the pinking strokes blend together smoothly.

PLAIN HEMS

Sometimes called a flat or unfinished hem, the plain hem is made with a single fold and a flat edge finish, such as pinking, pinked-and-stitched, zigzag, multi-stitch zigzag, or serging. On materials such as vinyl, synthetic suede, leather, and suede, the edge is left unfinished.

RAW-EDGE OR CUT-EDGE HEMS

Used on nonwoven materials such as leather, suede, synthetic suedes, and vinyl, raw-edge hems have a raw edge at the hemline. Generally, these hems tend to be flimsy and are not as attractive as fused, glued, and topstitched hems or raw-edge facings.

ROLLED HEMS— HAND STITCHED

Hand-rolled hems are always beautiful, but they are time-consuming. Used for scarves, infants' wear, ruffles, flounces, and sheer fabrics, hand-rolled hems are suitable for fine quality, lightweight fabrics, such as silks, wools, cottons, laces, and handkerchief linen.

Polyesters are too wiry for these hems. Laces and embroidered fabrics are difficult to roll evenly.

There are several ways to make a hand-rolled hem. Experiment with the various methods to see which works best for you.

Hint: *If you want to learn this technique, but don't want to commit yourself to a large project, roll the edge of a scarf or ruana.*

Use a very fine needle (size 10) and extra-fine thread. Wax the threads to prevent knotting and curling; then press the threads to saturate them with the wax.

If you don't have extra-fine thread, make your own by separating the plies of a heavier silk, polyester thread, or embroidery floss.

METHOD ONE

This rolled hem is small, firm, and round.
1. Cut hem allowances 5/8″ wide.
2. Trim any seams on the garment to 1/8″ at the hemline.

3. Right side up, machine stitch 1/2″ from the edge.

Hint: *The stitched line prevents the hem from stretching on the bias or crossgrain; it also serves as a guide for an even, straight hem.*

4. Trim close to the stitched line.

Hint: *To avoid fraying, trim only 8″ to 10″ at a time.*

5. Wrong side up, roll the trimmed edge between your thumb and forefinger to enclose the stitched line.

Hint: *For a tighter roll, moisten your fingers with a little saliva before rolling. Lightweight silks and sheers make smaller rolls than lightweight wools. Laces and some jacquard-weave fabrics are difficult to roll evenly, since the background rolls more tightly than the design.*

6. Hold the rolled edge firmly over your forefinger between your thumb and middle finger.

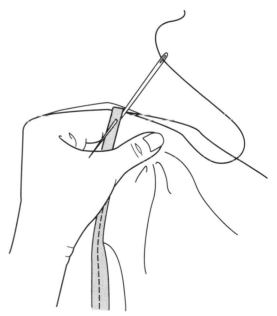

Fig. 22–27

Hint: *During the nineteenth century, needlewomen had sewing birds or hemming clamps which held the fabric firmly at one end. The left*

426

hand held the edge taut 6" to 10" away, al-
lowing the right hand to stitch quickly and
evenly.

When hemming at home, I sit at the end of
the sofa and use the arm as a pin cushion hem-
ming clamp. The edge remains taut while I
hem.

You can also buy reproduction sewing birds
or third-hand clamps.

7. Hide the knot in the roll; and hem the trimmed edge, using a slipstitch hem, fell stitch, or a small overcast stitch.

8. Trim and hem until the edge is finished.

9. Press up to the hem and steam the hem to avoid pressing the hem flat.

METHOD TWO

This rolled hem is easier to make, but it is flatter.

1. Cut the hem allowance 5/8" wide.
2. Fold under 1/2" and edgestitch.
3. Trim close to the stitched line.
4. Wrong side up, hide the knot in the hem allowance. Hem the edge with a slipstitch or whipstitch.

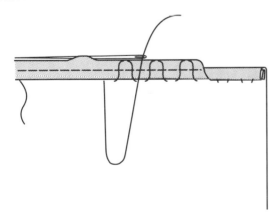

Fig. 22–28

To slipstitch the hem, take a small (1/8") stitch in the fold; then pick up one or two threads on the hemline. Work several stitches back and forth like a slipstitch; then pull the thread taut to make a roll.

To whip the edge, pick up a single thread on the garment next to the raw edge. Slip the needle point under the raw edge and bring it out at the

foldline. Repeat for several stitches; then pull the thread to tighten the stitches and create a roll.

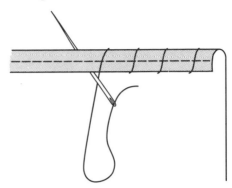

Fig. 22–29

5. Do not press the hem flat.

ROLLED HEMS—HEMMER FOOT

Frequently used on ready-made garments, these hems can be made in several widths from 3/32" to 1/4", depending on the size of the hemmer foot.

If you use narrow hems frequently, practice until you can use the hemmer foot perfectly; otherwise, make machine-rolled hems.

1. Cut the hem allowances 5/8" wide.
2. Trim garment seamlines to 1/8" at the hemline.
3. Wrong side up, machine stitch 3/8" from the edge. Trim close to the stitched line.

Hint: *To avoid fraying, trim only 8" to 10" at a time.*

4. Thread the hem into the foot's spiral. Hold the fabric firmly in front and behind the foot; and pull the hem back and forth until it is properly threaded.

Hint: *When the hem begins at an end, thread the hem into the foot about 2" from the end; then pull the hem toward the front of the machine to begin on the end. If you haven't trimmed the ends of the machine stitching, hold them in back of the foot.*

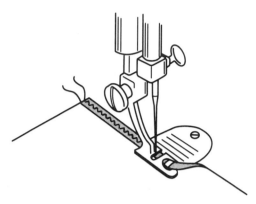

Fig. 22–30

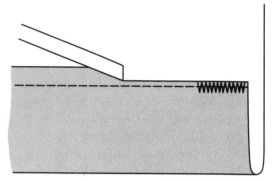

Fig. 22–31

5. Stitch the hem with a straight stitch or zigzag (W,4; L,3).

Hint: *For a scalloped finish, tighten the tension.*

SATIN-STITCHED HEMS

Some satin-stitched hems are very narrow and resemble a merrow finish (see Mock-Merrow); while others are wide and decorative.

Wide satin-stitched hems are particularly attractive on crisp, transparent fabrics and reversible designs. Hem the garment as usual or wrong side out. The raw edge of the hem and/or the hemline can be straight or shaped.

WIDE SATIN-STITCHED HEM— STRAIGHT HEMLINE

1. Cut the hem allowance the desired finished width plus 1/4″.
2. Fold the hem to the wrong side; baste.

Hint: *When pin basting, place the pins with the heads toward the hemline so they won't have to be removed during stitching.*

3. Hem side up, straight stitch (L,1.5) 1/4″ from the raw edge of the hem. Trim as closely as possible to the stitched line.

Hint: *When trimming curved edges, small 5″ trimmers are easier to use than appliqué scissors; when trimming straight edges, both work well.*

4. Using a decorative or matching thread and an embroidery foot, set the machine to satin stitch (W,2; L,.25). Right side up, stitch, enclosing both the stitched line and the raw edge; press.

Hint: *Adjust the stitch width and length as desired. For reversible designs and transparent fabrics, satin stitch with matching thread on the bobbin. Use a water-soluble stabilizer to prevent tunneling, if needed.*

WIDE SATIN-STITCHED HEMS— SHAPED HEMLINE

1. Make a faced hem (see Faced Hems).
2. Hem side up, straight stitch (L,1.5) 1/4″ from the raw edge of the hem. Trim close to the stitched line.

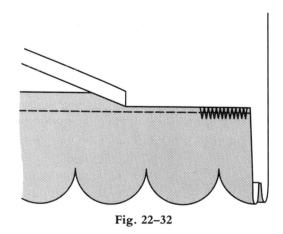

Fig. 22–32

3. Satin stitch (W,2; L,.25) the hem; press.

SCALLOPED HEMS

The scalloped hem is an attractive finish for flared skirts of soft, lightweight fabrics.

1. Cut the hem allowance 5/8″ wide.

2. If the fabric frays, finish the raw edge; then fold the hem under.

Hint: *To ensure an even hem allowance, machine stitch 1/2″ from the edge. Fold the hem under so the stitched line is 1/8″ from the fold.*

3. Right side up, zigzag (W,3; L,2) so the needle swings off the fabric.

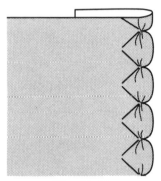

Fig. 22–33

Hint: *The fabric tends to scallop better when the hemline is on the bias.*

Experiment with different threads, tensions, stitch widths, and stitch lengths to create different looks.

4. For a fancier hem, use pearl cotton or pearl rayon. Hold the thread along the hemline so the zigzag stitch catches the decorative thread.

5. Press.

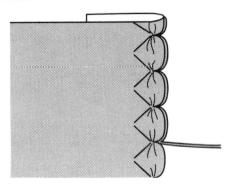

Fig. 22–34

SHEER HEMS

See Transparent Hems.

SHELL HEMS

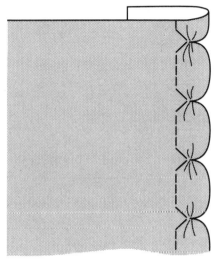

Fig. 22–35

Another decorative hem for flared skirts and soft, lightweight fabrics, the shell hem is made with a scallop stitch or blind-hem stitch.

1. Cut the hem allowance 5/8″ wide.

2. Fold the hem under. If the fabric frays, finish the raw edge first.

3. Set the machine for a shell stitch or blind-hem stitch (W,3; L,1). For a shell-stitch pattern, stitch as usual with the bulk to the left of the foot; for a blind-hem stitch, stitch with the bulk to the right. (Note: On some machines you can mirror-image the blind-hem stitch and keep the fabric bulk to the left of the needle.) Position the edge so the needle swings off the edge to make the scallop. Steam press lightly.

Hint: *Experiment with tension, stitch width, stitch length, and decorative threads held along the foldline.*

SHIRTTAIL HEMS

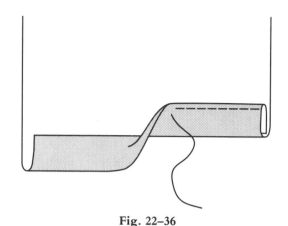

Fig. 22–36

Frequently used on blouse and shirt hems, the 1/4"-wide shirttail hem is a narrow machine-stitched hem that looks best on light- and medium-weight fabrics. When the hem is hand-finished, it's called a book hem.

1. Cut the hem allowance 5/8" wide.
2. Wrong side up, fold the edge twice to make a 1/4"-wide hem; edgestitch the hem in place.

Hint: *For best results, baste and press before edge-stitching.*

When stitching curved hems, crimp 1/4" from the edge to control the extra fullness; press the edge under; then fold again.

3. Press.

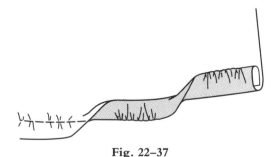

Fig. 22–37

SLIPSTITCHED HEMS

Sometimes called book hems, these hand-stitched hems are suitable for better garments made of lightweight fabrics that fray. Clean finished with a fold or turned-and-stitched finish, slipstitched hems are a good choice for many unlined designs.

Finished hem widths vary from 1/2" to several inches, depending on the skirt's flare or hemline curve. Generally, wide hems are best on straight skirts, children's dresses, and ball gowns; most hems are 1" to 2" wide.

1. Cut the hem allowance the desired finished width plus 1/4".
2. Right side up, use soap sliver, chalk, or temporary marking pen to mark the hemline. Interface the hem if desired.
3. Wrong side up, fold the hem in place and press lightly. Measure and mark the hem depth if it isn't even.
4. Clean finish the raw edge; baste the hem in place.
5. Using a slipstitch and a fine, short needle, hem the garment.

Working from right to left, hide the knot in the fold of the hem allowance. Pick up the back of one thread on the garment; pull the thread through. Then take a 1/2" stitch in the fold of the hem; pull the thread through. Repeat, alternating stitches between the garment and hem until the hem is finished.

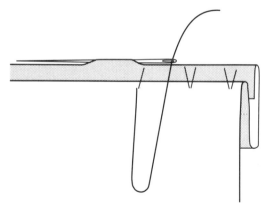

Fig. 22–38

Hint: *The finished stitches look like small "v's." For an invisible hem on the right side of the garment, hem lightly and loosely; use a fine needle and thread; pick up only the backs of the fabric yarns; and pull the thread through after each stitch.*

6. Remove basting; press.

STRETCH BLINDSTITCH

See Machine Blindstitch.

STRETCH HEMS

To avoid popped stitches, stretch fabrics require stretch hems. Most stretch hems, such as zigzag blindstitch, zigzag or multi-stitch zigzag topstitching, shell, zigzag and lettuce edgings, and twin-needle hems, are machine-stitched; while a few, such as catchstitch, blind catchstitch, and figure eight, are hand-stitched. See appropriate entries for instructions.

TOPSTITCHED HEMS

Technically, a topstitched hem is any machine-made hem which shows on the right side of the garment. It can be any width, very decorative, or inconspicuous and utilitarian.

For different looks, experiment with different threads, stitch lengths, stitch patterns, and row placements.

NARROW TOPSTITCHED HEM

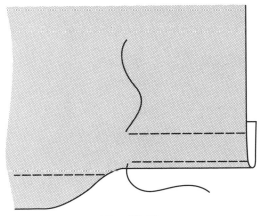

Fig. 22–39

Use this narrow hem on straight or shaped hemlines and all weight fabrics.

1. Cut hem allowances 5/8″ wide.

2. Finish the raw edge as needed; fold the hem under.

Hint: *Machine stitch 1/2″ from the raw edge. Fold the hem so the stitched line is 1/8″ from the fold.*

3. Right side up, edgestitch around the hem. Topstitch again 3/8″ to 1/2″ from the fold; press.

Hint: *To edgestitch 1/16″ from the fold, use a zipper foot, edgestitch foot, or the inside edge of the presser foot as a guide.*

NARROW TOPSTITCHED HEM— LIGHTWEIGHT FABRICS

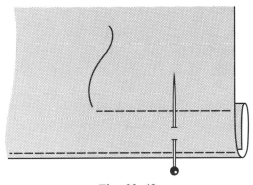

Fig. 22–40

Particularly well-suited for fabrics that fray, such as lightweight silks and polyesters, this hem has more body and hangs better than the method described above.

1. Cut hem allowances 1″ wide.
2. Fold the hem under.
3. Right side up, edgestitch around the hem.
4. Fold the raw edge of the hem in to the stitched line; pin.

Hint: *Position pins with the heads toward the fold so they can be removed easily while stitching.*

5. Right side up, topstitch again 3/8″ to 1/2″ from the fold; press.

WIDE TOPSTITCHED HEM

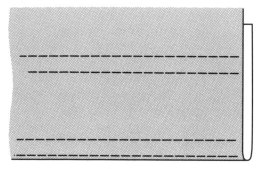

Fig. 22–41

Made famous by English designer Jean Muir, wide topstitched hems are suitable for fabrics in all weights.

1. Cut the hem allowance 2″ wide.

Hint: *To vary the stitching design, cut the hem allowance as wide or as narrow as needed. To determine the hem allowance width, decide where the hem will be stitched and measure the distance between the hemline fold and top stitching line; add 1/4″.*

2. Finish the raw edge as needed; fold the hem under; pin and baste.

Hint: *For a firmer hem, fuse the hem in place. For a softer hem, interface or pad it.*

3. Right side up, edgestitch around the hem. Topstitch again 1/4″ away; then topstitch again 1 1/4″ and 1 1/2″ from the garment edges. Press.

Hint: *To topstitch evenly, mark the machine bed with drafting tape the desired distances from the needle.*

4. Vary the stitching pattern and topstitch several evenly spaced rows.

TOPSTITCHED HEMS FOR KNITS AND TEXTURED FABRICS

When topstitching knits, use woolly nylon on the bobbin for a more elastic straight stitch.

On textured fabrics and some knits, straight stitches tend to get lost in the fabric bulk and may look crooked. Before beginning, experiment with a plain zigzag stitch in various lengths and widths and with a straight stretch stitch.

TRANSPARENT HEMS

Sometimes called sheer hems, hems that are suitable for transparent fabrics include wide double hems, wide satin-stitched hems, machine-rolled hems, hemmer-foot hems, hand-rolled hems, mock-merrow and merrow finishes, and lettuce edgings. (See appropriate entries for instructions.)

TUCKED HEMS

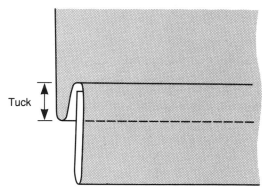

Tuck

Fig. 22–42

Tucked hems are particularly attractive on reversible and unlined garments.

1. Add 3/4″ to the hem allowance. Add more for a wider hem.
2. Fold under twice to make a doubled hem. To make the tuck and enclose the raw edge, topstitch 3/8″ from the folded edge.

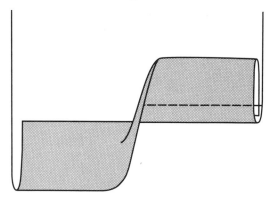

Fig. 22–43

3. Open up and press.

4. When making a tucked hem, the garment can be seamed either before or after the hem is stitched.

TWIN-NEEDLE HEMS

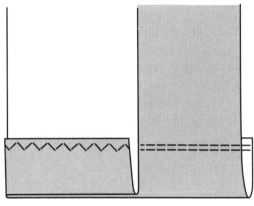

Fig. 22–44

Attractive on most fabrics, twin-needle hems are soft and elastic. Two rows of straight stitching are formed on the right side of the garment while the bobbin thread zigzags between them. These seams are well-suited for knits and stretch fabrics.

Twin needles are available in several sizes: 1.6/70, 1.6/80, 2/80, 2.5/80, 3/90, and 4/90. The first number is the number of millimeters between the needles, and the second is the size of the needles.

Use the smaller needles on lightweight fabrics, swimwear, and jerseys. Use the larger needles on heavier fabrics, sweatshirts, and elastics.

Before beginning the garment, experiment with different sized needles. If skipped stitches are a major problem, use a larger needle.

1. Cut the hem allowance the desired width, depending on the garment design, fabric weight, and personal choice.

Generally, hems on action knits are stitched 1/2″ to 1″ from the edge. Hems on other fabrics can be stitched any distance, 1/2″ to several inches from the edge.

Hint: *To determine the hem allowance, decide where the hem will be stitched. Measure this distance and add 1/2″.*

2. Fill the bobbin with polyester thread, woolly nylon, or elastic thread.

3. Set the stitch length (L,2–3). Loosen the bobbin tension to avoid a ridge between the two rows.

4. Finish the raw edge if needed; and fold the hem under. Pin or baste.

5. Right side up, stitch the desired distance from the edge.

Hint: *To prevent skipped stitches, use a needle lubricant; if that doesn't solve the problem, change to a new needle. If you still have a problem, use a larger needle.*

To increase the stretch, use a zigzag (W,2.5; L,1.25), multistitch zigzag (W,2.5; L,1), or honeycomb stretch stitch (W,2–5; L,2). Before stitching, turn the hand wheel manually to be sure the needles won't hit the foot or the needle hole.

6. If the fabric doesn't fray, trim the hem allowance close to the stitched line.

7. Press.

WEIGHTED HEMS

Some fabrics and garment designs don't have enough weight to control the hem so it will hang evenly. Use square drapery weights or a heavy chain.

CHAIN WEIGHTS

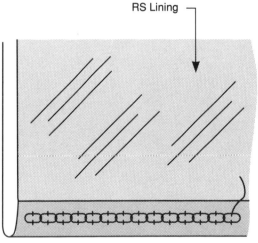

Fig. 22–45

Sometimes called a Chanel chain, since Coco Chanel used brass chains on her famous lightweight wool jackets. Sewn to the hem allowance on the inside of the garment, the chain adds enough weight to ensure that garments hang properly.

1. Hem the garment with a plain hem. Finish the garment; and give it a final press before attaching the chain.

2. Locate the chain just above the hemline, just below the lining, or somewhere in between. Most chains begin and end at the edge of the facing; however, some extend almost to the front edge.

Using waxed thread, sew both sides of the chain in place by hand.

Hint: *To avoid press marks, check with your dry cleaner. You may have to remove the chain for cleaning.*

DRAPERY WEIGHTS

Most designers use drapery weights in the hems of suits, jackets, and ball gowns to ensure straight, pucker-free seamlines.

1. If you think the weight is too large or heavy, use old scissors to cut it into smaller pieces. Then pound it flat with a hammer to eliminate ridges and sharp edges.

2. Cover the weight with organza, tulle, or lightweight lining fabric.

Hint: *Cut a fabric square three times the width and length of the weight. Place the weight in the center of the square; fold the fabric over it; and secure the raw edges by hand.*

3. Hide the weight between the hem allowance and garment; sew it to the seam allowance.

4. Hem the garment.

Hint: *Many designers use weights to control skirt vents. Complete the hem, and sew the covered weight to the hem allowance.*

Norman Norell used covered weights at the bottom of a silk crepe overblouse so it would hang nicely. Since the weights were not pounded flat, they were applied on the inside after the garment was hemmed so they could be removed for cleaning.

WIRED HEMS

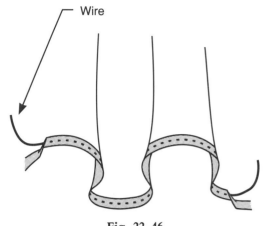

Wire

Fig. 22–46

Frequently used on permanently pleated fabrics, ruffles, flounces, bridal gowns, and costumes, wired hems make a large fluting design at the edge.

Use lightweight picture wire, fishing tackle line, and craft wires to wire such narrow hems as machine-rolled, hemmer-foot rolled, mock-merrow, merrow, and lettuce edgings.

When stitching them, hide the wire in the fold between the hem and the garment.

ZIGZAG BLINDSTITCH

See Machine Blindstitch.

ZIGZAGGED EDGES

Made famous by Sonia Rykiel, this decorative hem is used on the raw edges of knits, woven, and nonwoven fabrics.

1. Trim away all hem allowances.

2. Right side up, center the edge on the foot and zigzag (W,4; L,2).

Hint: *To minimize tunneling or rolling, use an overlock or overcast foot; or tissue-stitch, using a water-soluble stabilizer. To minimize fraying, stitch directionally.*

Norma Walters uses this finish on the col-

lars and lapels of Ultrasuede jackets. Experiment with the stitch width and length; they should look the same even if they aren't.

3. Press.

Hem Finishes

Hems can be finished with a folded edge or hem tape, as well as with all the seam finishes described in Chapter 21. Review the criteria for selecting seam finishes.

FOLDED EDGE

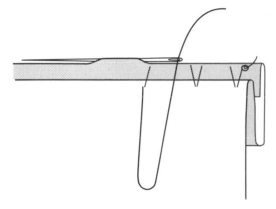

Fig. 22–47

This neat finish is suitable for lightweight fabrics, sheers, and reversible and unlined garments. Very similar to the turned-and-stitch finish, the edge is turned under, but not stitched.

When used on reversible and unlined garments, the folded edge is topstitched to the garment. When used on transparent fabrics, the hem is doubled.

SEAM TAPE

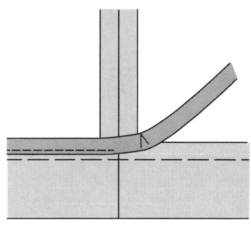

Fig. 22–48

Seam tape is suitable for washable fabrics which fray. Unlike the bound finish, which encases the edge, the hem tape is applied flat.

1. Measure and mark the hem depth.
2. Align the edge of the hem tape with the marked line. Edgestitch in place.
3. Trim away the excess fabric under the tape.

CHAPTER 23
Edge Finishes

Bands

There are many different ways to apply bands; the following are the most popular.

TOPSTITCHED BAND

1. Interface one-half the band.
2. Join the ends of the band to make a ring if there is no placket.
3. Wrong sides up, pin and stitch the uninterfaced side of the band to the garment.

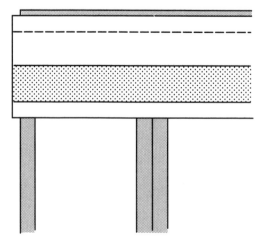

Fig. 23–1

4. If there is a placket, finish the ends right sides together.

Hint: *Trim the seam allowances at the ends of the band to reduce the bulk in the buttonhole area.*

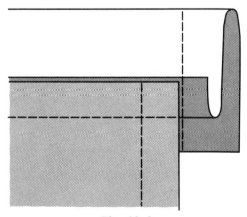

Fig. 23–2

5. Turn the band to the right side and press.
6. Fold the seam allowance under; baste and topstitch the band in place.

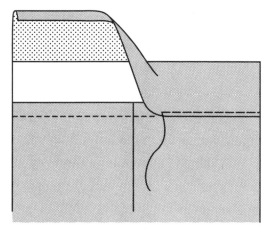

Fig. 23–3

HAND-FINISHED OR DITCH-STITCHED BAND

1. Interface one-half of the band. If it will be finished by machine, finish the long edge on the uninterfaced side.

2. Join the ends of the band to make a ring if there is no placket.

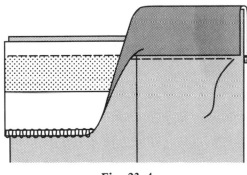

Fig. 23–4

Bindings

This facing alternative is frequently used to trim transparent fabrics, two-faced fabrics, reversible and unlined garments and high fashion designs.

There are two differences between bindings and bias facings:

1. Bindings are visible on both sides of the garment; facings are visible on only one side of the garment.

3. Right sides together, pin and stitch interfaced side of the band to the garment.

4. If there is a placket, finish the ends.

5. Turn the band right side out and press.

6. Pin the band securely; ditch-stitch or topstitch from the right side of the garment. Or fold the seam allowance under and finish by hand.

FALSE BAND

Use this easy hem to simulate a band.

1. Cut the hem allowance the width of the band plus 1 1/2″. For a 2″ band, cut the hem allowance 3 1/2″.

2. Fold under the hem, plus 1″; pin. For a 2″ band, fold under 3″.

3. Fold the garment, right sides together at the top of the hem allowance (3″); stitch a 1/2″ tuck.

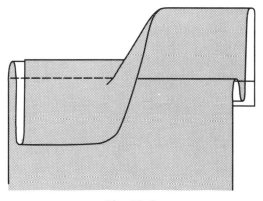

Fig. 23–5

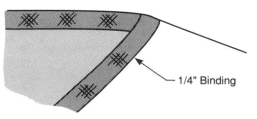

1/4″ Binding

Fig. 23–6

437

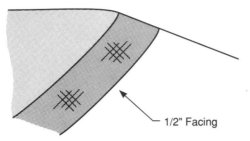

Fig. 23–7

1/2" Facing

2. The garment seam allowance is trimmed away before a binding is applied; facings require a seam allowance.

These trade secrets from Jeanne Allen, Jeanne-Marc's designer, will ensure success when applying bindings.

- Reshape the garment edges if the curves are too acute.
- Be sure the binding is wide enough. Always make a sample on a fabric scrap before cutting all the bias strips. Heavy garment and binding fabrics may require a wider bias strip.
- Bias strips must be on the true bias to eliminate rippling.

SINGLE BIAS BINDINGS

1. Trim away the seam allowances from the garment edges to be bound.
2. Cut the bias strips six times the desired finished width. Cut the strip 1 1/2" wide for a finished binding 1/4" wide.

Hint: *Strips can be cut on the crossgrain but only a few knits will shape as smoothly as those fabrics cut on the bias. Strips cut on the lengthwise grain are the most difficult to shape; however, they can be used successfully on straight edges.*

3. Staystitch the garment edge. For a 1/4" binding, stitch a skinny 1/4" from the raw edge.
4. Right sides together, match and pin the binding to the staystitched line on the garment. On straight edges, the binding and garment are the same length at the edge.

On concave or inward curves around the neckline, the bias will ripple at the curved edge.

At convex or outward curves around collars, cuffs, and pockets, the bias must be stretched or clipped at the raw edge.

Hint: *For best results, hand baste just inside the seamline.*

5. With the bias on top, machine stitch the binding in place. Remove the bastings.
6. Wrap the binding around the raw edge; press.

Hint: *For a perfect binding, hand baste in place before pressing.*

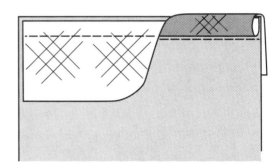

Fig. 23–8

7. To finish the binding with a raw edge on the inside of the garment, ditch-stitch from the right side of the garment. Trim the binding to a skinny 1/8".

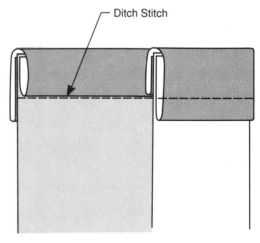

Ditch Stitch

Fig. 23–9

To clean finish the binding on the inside of the garment, fold the binding edge under so the binding is wider on the wrong side of the garment; baste. Right sides up, ditch-stitch.

To clean finish the binding by hand, trim the binding, so you'll only have 1/4″ to turn under. Fold the raw edge under so the binding fold is even with the stitched line. Hand sew the binding in place.

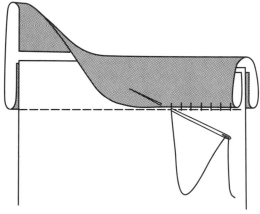

Fig. 23–10

Hint: *The hand stitches will be almost invisible if you use a fell stitch and catch the stitched line on the garment.*

BINDING CORNERS

When binding inward corners, such as those found on square necklines, reinforce the corner with short machine stitches on the seamline and clip to the corner. This allows you to coax the inward corner into a straight line for stitching. With the garment on top and right sides together, pin the binding to the garment. Hold the garment edge straight and stitch the binding in place.

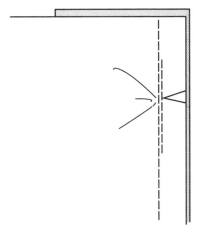

Fig. 23–11

Complete the binding application; then, on the wrong side, miter the binding at the corner by stitching a small dart.

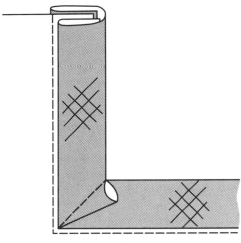

Fig. 23–12

When binding outward corners on the edges of collars, pockets, welts, and flaps, begin binding on the right edge. Stitch toward the corner; stop 1/4″—the finished binding width—from the raw edge. Backstitch and break your threads.

Refold and pin the binding strip so the raw edge matches the garment; stitch, beginning at the fold.

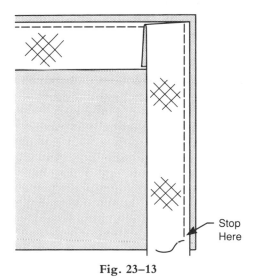

Stop Here

Fig. 23–13

Note: The binding fold which you can see is even with the other raw edge; the underfold makes a diagonal.

Wrap the binding around the edge; and use a needle to miter the corner on the underside.

439

BINDING REVERSIBLE GARMENTS

To apply single bindings to reversible garments, cut the binding five times the finished width. Stitch the right side of the binding to the wrong side of the garment. Wrap it around the garment edge; fold the binding edge under so the fold matches the stitched line; baste. Topstitch the binding in place.

Hint: *To topstitch easily, use a zipper foot positioned on top of the binding.*

DOUBLE BINDINGS

The double binding is easier to sew since both raw edges are joined to the garment; however, it is more difficult to keep the binding width even on curved edges.

DOUBLE BINDING—EQUAL WIDTH

Frequently used for reversible garments, double bindings applied using this method are the same width on the inside and outside. When finished by hand, there are no visible stitches on either side of the garment. When finished by machine, there are machine stitches on both sides of the garment.

Generally, bindings are first sewn to the right side of the garment; however, they can be applied to the wrong side.

1. Trim away the seam allowances from the garment edges to be bound.

2. Cut the bias strips seven times the finished width. Cut the strip 1 3/4″ wide for a finished binding 1/4″ wide.

3. Fold the strip in half lengthwise, wrong sides together; baste the raw edges together; and press the foldline.

4. Staystitch the garment edge. For a 1/4″ binding, stitch a skinny 1/4″ from the raw edge.

5. Right sides together, match and pin the binding to the staystitched line on the garment; stitch. The binding and garment are the same length at the raw edges if the edge is straight.

On concave or inward curves around the neckline, the bias will ripple at the raw edge. At convex or outward curves around collars, cuffs, and pock-

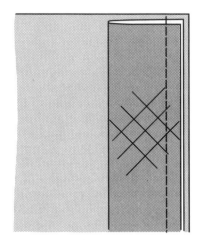

Fig. 23–14

ets, the bias must be stretched or clipped at the raw edge.

Hint: *For best results, hand baste at the staystitched line.*

5. Wrap the binding around the raw edge; press. The folded edge of the binding should match the stitched line.

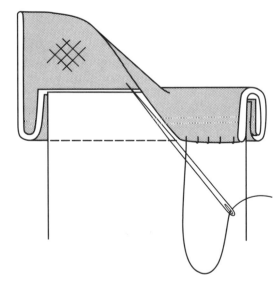

Fig. 23–15

Hint: *For a perfect binding, hand baste before pressing.*

6. Using a felling stitch, hand sew the binding to the stitched line.

Corners. When binding inward and outward corners, see Single Binding.

Machine-Finished Bindings. For a machine finish, stitch the binding to the wrong side of the garment. Wrap it around the garment edge so the fold matches the stitched line; baste. Using a zipper foot, topstitch the binding in place.

DOUBLE BINDING—UNEQUAL WIDTH

Double bindings applied using this method are wider on the inside than on the outside. Ditch-stitch to secure them. The machine stitches are inconspicuous on the right side of the garment and catch the binding on the inside.

Generally, bindings are first sewn to the right side of the garment; however, they can be sewn to the wrong side.

1. To finish the binding by machine, cut the binding nine times the desired finished width. Cut the strip 2 1/4″ wide for a finished binding 1/4″ wide.

2. Proceed as above to apply the binding.

3. Right sides up, ditch-stitch or topstitch the edge of the binding.

Hint: *Use a zipper foot set to the left of the needle to ditch-stitch. Set it to the right of the needle to topstitch.*

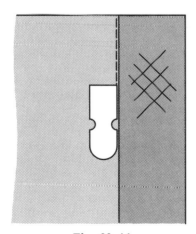

Fig. 23–16

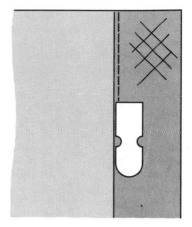

Fig. 23–17

DESIGNER BINDING

This narrow 1/8″-wide binding is only used on the finest garments made of sheer and lightweight fabrics. Even though it can be applied using the directions above, it will be easier to apply with these modifications.

1. Trim the garment seam allowances to 1/8″.
2. Cut a 1″-wide bias strip.
3. Fold the strip in half lengthwise, wrong sides together; press. Baste the raw edges together.
4. Match and pin the raw edges of the strip to the right side of the garment; baste 1/4″ from the raw edge.

Hint: *When applying to an inward curve, ease the raw edges of the bias to the garment; when applying to an outward curve, stretch the raw edges of the bias slightly.*

5. Shorten the stitch length; and stitch next to the basted line; or hand sew with a tiny running stitch with an occasional backstitch. Remove the basting.
6. Trim the seam to a skinny 1/8″.

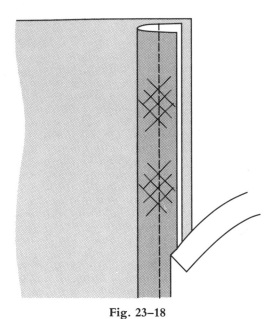

Fig. 23–18

7. Wrap the binding around the raw edge; baste; then press. The folded edge of the binding should match the stitched line.

8. Using a felling stitch, hand sew the binding to the stitched line.

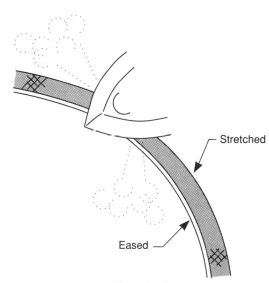

Stretched

Eased

Fig. 23–19

ONE-STEP BINDING

Purchased or custom-made double-fold bindings are quick and easy to apply using the one-step method.

1. Trim the seam allowances from the garment edges to be bound.

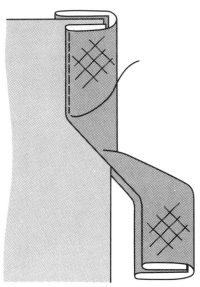

Fig. 23–20

2. Use purchased bias binding or cut the bias strips five times the desired finished width. Cut the strip 1 1/4″ wide for a finished binding 1/4″ wide.

3. Using a steam iron, shape the binding to match the curves of the garment. For custom bindings, fold the strip, wrong sides together, lengthwise so one edge is 1/8″ wider than the other; press. Open the bias and fold the raw edges so they meet at the foldline; press. One edge will be slightly wider than the other. Shape the bias to match the garment edges.

Hint: *If you have a bias tape maker, you may prefer using it; however, if your results haven't been perfect, you'll be pleased with the method above.*

4. With the wider edge on the bottom and the garment right side up, slip the garment edge into the bias binding so the edge touches the foldline; baste. Using a zipper foot, edgestitch the binding in place.

Hint: *When applying bias bindings to straight edges, it's easy to stretch the bias if you aren't careful.*

If you can't edgestitch evenly, zigzag (W,2; L,2).

NONWOVEN BINDINGS

Nonwoven materials such as leather, suede, synthetic suede, and vinyl make very attractive trims. They are especially attractive when applied to other nonwoven materials, double-faced fabrics, reversible garments and unlined designs.

When binding the edges of better garments, use the single bias binding application. When binding everyday designs, use this quick and easy method.

1. Trim the seam allowances from the garment edges to be bound.

2. Cut the binding strip twice the desired finished width plus 1/2". For a finished 1/4" binding, cut the strip 1" wide.

3. Fold the strip in half lengthwise, wrong sides together; press.

Hint: *For best results, review the pressing tips for the nonwoven material before pressing; then test press.*

4. With the garment right side up, slip the garment edge into the binding so the garment edge touches the foldline; glue baste. Stitch through all layers the desired distance from the edge. For a binding 1/4" wide, stitch slightly less than 1/4" from the edge.

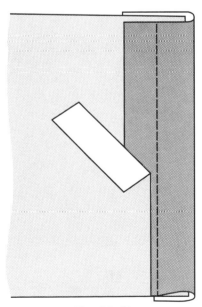

Fig. 23–21

Hint: *Change to a roller or Teflon foot before stitching.*

5. Using appliqué scissors or 5" trimmers, trim both sides of the binding close to the stitched line.

BRAID AND RIBBON BINDINGS

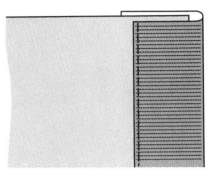

Fig. 23–22

Fold-over braid and ribbon are attractive yet easy to apply. Although most ribbons can be used on straight edges, grosgrain ribbons shape easily and smoothly around most curves.

1. Trim the seam allowances from the garment edges to be bound.

2. Select the ribbon or fold-over braid. Choose a ribbon which is twice the desired finished width.

3. Fold the ribbon in half lengthwise, wrong sides together, so one edge is 1/16" wider than the other; press.

Using a steam iron, shape the ribbon or fold-over braid to fit the garment edges.

Hint: *When shaping the binding for outward curves, use a short gathering stitch at the binding edges to draw the fullness in smoothly.*

4. With the garment right side up, slip the garment edge into the binding so the garment edge touches the foldline; baste. Using a zipper foot, edgestitch the binding in place.

FINISHING BINDING ENDS

There are several ways to finish the binding ends. Select the one most appropriate for the garment quality, your sewing abilities, and the time available.

OPEN SEAM

To finish the ends quickly and easily, leave one seam open. Stitch the binding to the garment; complete the seam; then finish the binding application.

For a neckline binding, leave the left shoulder open; for armhole bindings, leave the side seams open; for bindings on hems or jacket edges, leave the left side seam open.

Hint: *This method is particularly easy because the binding is sewn to the garment sections while they are still flat.*

OVERLAPPED ENDS

This method looks best when the binding fabric is lightweight. When the binding fabric is bulky, experiment before using it on a garment.

Complete all the garment seams before applying the binding. At one end of the binding, fold 1/2″ under before pinning it to the garment. Baste the binding in place; overlap the other end 3/8″.

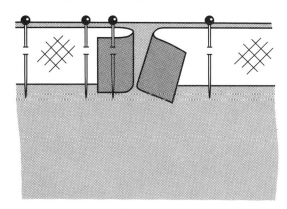

Fig. 23–23

SEAM THE BINDING ENDS

This is the best method and should be used on your finest fabrics.

Complete all the garment seams before applying the binding. At the end of the binding, fold 1/2″ under before pinning it to the garment. Make the fold on the lengthwise grain. Pin the rest of the binding to the garment and fold 1/2″ under at the other end.

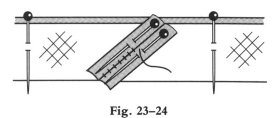

Fig. 23–24

Carefully slipstitch the binding ends together, without catching the garment.

Hint: *If you slipstitch carefully and neatly, the seam can be left without machine stitching; otherwise, you'll need to machine stitch the seam and remove the slipstitching.*

Trim the ends of the binding and press. Baste the binding to the neckline and complete the application.

Elastic

To finish edges with elastic, use a casing or an applied elastic band.

APPLIED ELASTIC

In this neat application, the elastic is hidden under the seam allowance of a waistband.

1. Leave one side seam open until the elastic is applied.

2. Choose a woven or knitted elastic.

3. Cut the elastic the desired length. Elastic, except the new invisible kind, will lose about 25 percent of its elasticity when stitched. Experiment with the elastic and fabric before sewing it to the garment.

4. Divide and mark the elastic and garment edge into quarters.

5. Pin the elastic to the wrong side of the garment, matching the marked points and the seamline. The elastic may also match the garment edge.

6. Using a ballpoint or Universal-H point needle, join the elastic to the garment with a regular or multi-stitch zigzag (W,4;L,2).

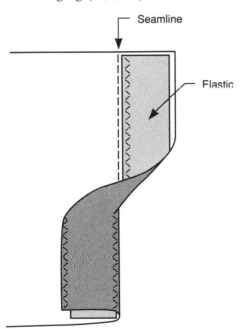

Fig. 23–25

7. Fold the seam allowance and elastic under and stitch again.

APPLIED VARIATION

In this variation, the elastic is exposed on the inside of the garment.

1. Pin the elastic to the right side of the garment, matching the marked points and seamline.

2. Join the elastic to the garment at the inside edge with a regular or multi-stitch zigzag (W,4; L,2).

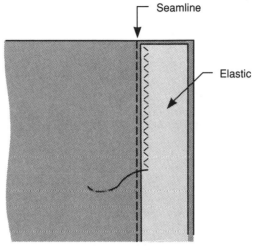

Fig. 23–26

3. Trim the seam allowance close to the zigzag.

4. Fold the elastic under and stitch again.

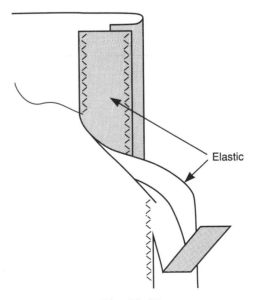

Fig. 23–27

Facings

BIAS FACINGS

Bias facings are a neat alternative to shaped facings. Particularly attractive on transparent fabrics, they are usually narrow and inconspicuous.

Use purchased bias tape, bias tricot or custom-made bias for the facings.

1. Cut bias strips 2″ wide.

Hint: *Cut using this method, bias tends to twist less than with traditional methods. To find the true bias, place a right-angle triangle on the fabric so one short side is even with the selvage; draw the bias at the long edge.*

If you don't have a triangle, fold an envelope so the bottom edge is even with one of the sides.

2. Join the bias strips as needed on the lengthwise grain.

3. Fold the bias lengthwise wrong sides together; steam press to shape it before applying it to the garment.

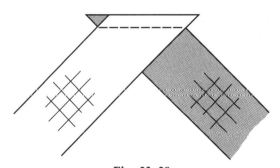

Fig. 23–28

4. Right sides together, pin and baste the bias to the garment edge; stitch on the seamline.

Seamline

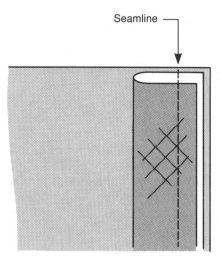

Fig. 23–29

Hint: *Bias facings are easier to stitch smoothly when the seam allowances are narrower—1/4″ or 3/8″.*

On inward curves, ease the bias slightly; on outward curves, clip the bias so it fits smoothly.

5. Say "Tea cup" to help you remember the steps: trim, clip, understitch, and press. This memory aid originated in the Bishop Method; I sometimes rearrange the order of the operations.

6. Use wider bias facings as a decorative trim on the outside of the garment or on reversible designs.

DECORATIVE FACINGS

Decorative facings are particularly attractive on quilted fabrics, unlined, and reversible garments.

1. Reverse the shoulder seams near the neckline to avoid whiskers at the garment edge.

2. Make the facing.

3. Wrong sides up, join the facing and garment.

4. Tea cup: Trim, clip, understitch, and press the garment.

Hint: *On garments made of double-faced quilted fabrics or two-faced fabrics, topstitch the finished garment instead of understitching. Eliminate understitching entirely on reversible designs.*

5. Fold the facing to the right side, turn the edge under; pin and edgestitch the facing in place.

Hint: *I prefer a faced facing which already has a finished edge.*

LACE FACING

These directions for lace facings can be used for any material with two finished edges: ribbon, leather, synthetic suede, or vinyl. The facing can be applied inconspicuously on the inside of the garment or as a decorative trim.

1. Machine stitch the garment 1/2″ from the edge.

Hint: *This not only controls stretching, but it also provides an accurate guide for placing the lace.*

2. For an inconspicuous facing, begin right side up. Place the lace so it barely covers the stitched line; pin and stitch.

Fold the lace to the wrong side of the garment; edgestitch close to the garment edge.

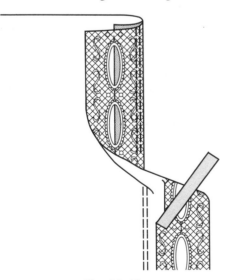

Fig. 23–30

3. For a decorative facing, begin with the garment wrong side up. Pin and stitch the lace in place. Trim the seam allowance close to the stitched line. Fold the lace to the right side and topstitch at the lower edge.

Fig. 23–31

NET FACINGS

Use net or tulle facings on transparent fabrics, lace, and net. Cut the net on the crossgrain and apply like a bias facing.

RAW-EDGE FACINGS

Use raw-edge facings on leather, suede, and synthetic suede. Some vinyls can also be finished with raw edge facings made of the same or similar materials.

1. Cut the seam allowances 1/4″ wide.

2. Wrong sides together, stitch a fat 1/4″ from the edge. Stitch again 1/4″ in.

3. Trim away the seam allowances.

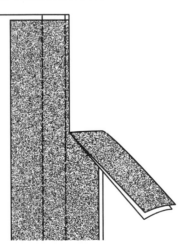

Fig. 23–32

Ribbings

1. Estimate the ribbing length. Measure and mark the estimated length before cutting.

2. Fold the ribbing in half lengthwise; pin the ends together. Try it on. It should slip on easily and fit snugly once it's in place.

Hint: *If the ribbing doesn't fit snugly, interface it with a piece of soft, flexible elastic. Cut the elastic to the desired finished length; lap the seams 1/4″ and zigzag the ends together.*

3. Cut the ribbing. Then, right sides together, join the ends with a 1/4″ seam.

Hint: *For a flat seamline, clip the seam allowance at the foldline. Fold half the seam in one direction and half in the other.*

4. Steam press lightly; fold the ribbing wrong sides together. If the ribbing is to be interfaced, slip the elastic between the layers.

5. Divide and mark the edges of the ribbing and garment into quarters.

6. Match and pin the marked points; right sides together and the ribbing on top, stitch, using the stretch seam of your choice.

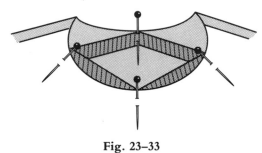

Fig. 23–33

CHAPTER 24
Closures

Button Loops

Use self-filled or corded tubing to make button loops. Although all loops should be small, round, and firm, the actual size is determined by the weight and texture of the fabric. Experiment with some lightweight silks and medium-weight wools.

Generally, button loops are set into a seamline; however, they can also be inserted into a foldline. Use an awl to make a hole for each end of the loop. From the wrong side, sew the loops to the interfacing.

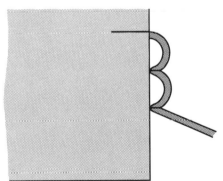

Fig. 24–1

When using button loops on light transparent fabrics, make the tubing long enough for all loops plus several inches. Hide one end in the seam or fold; then from the right side, tack the tubing to the foldline to make individual loops. Trim and hide the end.

SELF-FILLED TUBING

1. Cut a bias strip 1″ to 2″ wide, depending on the fabric weight (experiment on scraps).
2. Right sides together, fold the strip lengthwise and stitch parallel to the folded edge. The width of the tubing will vary from a fat 1/16″ for lightweight silks to a skinny 3/8″ for wool.

Hint: *Make a small funnel at the beginning so the tubing will turn easily.*

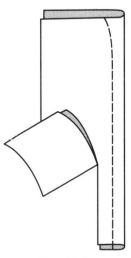

Fig. 24–2

449

When stitching, stretch as much as possible, so the stitches won't pop when the tubing is turned.

3. Trim the strip so the stitching line is in the center of the strip; at the top, trim close to the funnel.

4. Use a tapestry needle to fasten a short length of topstitching thread at the top of the funnel. Run the needle into the tubing; and turn it right side out.

Hint: *If it turns easily, it's too fat. If you have difficulty turning it, use a little saliva to dampen your fingers.*

5. Wet the tubing and squeeze dry in a towel. Pin one end to the pressing board; straighten the tubing so the seam isn't twisted. Stretch it as much as possible; pin. Leave it to dry.

Hint: *Even silks don't waterspot, because the entire tubing is wet.*

CORDED TUBING

1. Preshrink the cord; cut it twice the desired length plus 10″. Mark the midpoint on the cord.

Hint: *I use cotton postal twine.*

2. Cut the bias 1 1/2″ wide.
3. Right side up, place the cord on the bias. Match the midpoint to one end of the bias; stitch them together.

4. Wrap the bias around the cord; using a zipper foot, stitch close to the cord.

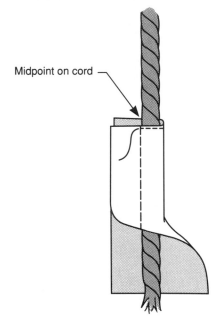

Midpoint on cord —

Fig. 24–3

Hint: *Don't stitch too closely or the finished tubing will be lumpy.*

5. Trim the seam allowances to 1/8″.
6. Hold the end of the cord securely and turn the tubing right side out.

Hint: *Smooth the tubing over the cord and straighten the seamline.*

7. Cut the tubing into buttonhole lengths.

Buttonholes

Buttonholes should be identical in length and in width, they all should be located the same distance from the edge of the garment. They are usually evenly spaced; however, the spacing may vary on designs with band collars or belts.

Generally, machine-stitched or hand-worked buttonholes are stitched on an almost-complete garment; but they can be stitched at an earlier stage.

BUTTONHOLE LENGTH

The button diameter, thickness, shape, and texture determine the buttonhole length.

To determine the buttonhole length, measure the button. Wrap a narrow piece of paper around the button and pin the ends together. Remove the button; and with the paper folded in half, measure from the fold to the pin to determine the minimum buttonhole length.

Hint: *To eliminate measuring the button every time you make machine-stitched buttonholes, make a buttonhole sampler with eight to ten button-holes in frequently used lengths. Slip the button into several buttonholes to determine the best size.*

BOUND BUTTONHOLES

Bound buttonholes should be at least 1″ long. Always make a test buttonhole, complete with fac-ing. Bound buttonholes tend to shrink; and, if they are too tight for the buttons, the ends will pull out and unravel.

There are many ways to make bound button-holes and every seamster has a favorite. Some methods are better for fabrics which ravel, while others work well for heavy or bulky materials. Among the five methods included here, you'll find one that works well on every fabric in this book.

PATCH METHOD

The patch method is appropriate for lightweight materials and for fabrics which ravel.

1. Interface the buttonhole area; mark the but-tonhole locations.

Hint: *Do not trim the interfacing out of the button-hole; it is needed for support.*

2. For each buttonhole, cut a bias patch 2″ wide and 1 1/2″ longer than the buttonhole.

Hint: *I prefer silk organza to polyester. Even if the color doesn't match exactly, it's less likely to show.*

3. Right sides together, center the patch over the buttonhole marking; pin each end. Unpin one end; stretch the patch so the welts won't ripple on the finished buttonhole. Repin and baste on the buttonhole line.

4. Stitch (L,1.5) around the buttonhole.

Hint: *Begin stitching in the center 1/8″ from the basted line. Stitch to the end. Pivot and count the stitches to the basted line; stitch the same number of stitches on the other end. Pivot*

again. Stitch to the other end; repeat. Overlap the stitches at the end 1/2″. If you have a computer sewing machine, you may be able to put this in memory.

5. Clip the rectangles along the basted button-hole line and to the corners.

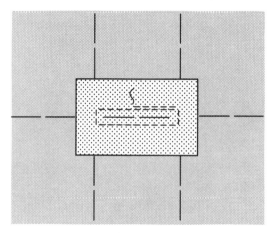

Fig. 24–4

Hint: *To clip precisely without cutting the stitches, use scissors which cut all the way to the points. Position the points exactly where the clip is to be and close the scissors.*

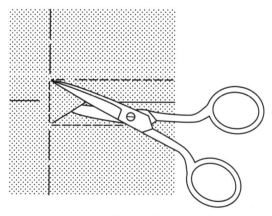

Fig. 24–5

6. Turn the patch to the wrong side.

7. Right side up, adjust the patch so it wraps around the long raw edges and doesn't show at the ends; pin.

8. Using a small diagonal stitch, baste the welts together.

451

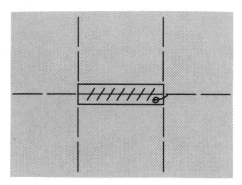

Fig. 24–6

9. Use a fine needle and tiny backstitch to ditch-stitch by hand.

10. Fold the garment back; and stitch across the triangle and welts at the end.

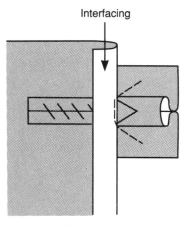

Interfacing

Fig. 24–7

Hint: *Before stitching, pull the welts sharply. To catch the corners securely, swing in slightly when you stitch.*

11. Round the corners of the patch and trim it neatly.

12. Wrong side up, press on a softly padded press board.

13. Join the front facing to the garment and baste around the buttonhole.

14. Using pins, mark the ends of the buttonhole on the facing. Carefully cut the facing between the pins.

15. Using a fine needle, turn the edges of the facing under and sew them securely.

Hint: *I use a felling stitch and sew around the buttonhole twice.*

STRIP BUTTONHOLES

This is the method I like best. The strips can be cut on the lengthwise grain, crossgrain, or the bias.

1. Interface the buttonhole area; mark the buttonhole locations.

2. For each buttonhole, make two strips 1″ longer than the buttonhole. Trim one edge of a fabric scrap on the desired grain; then fold 1″ from the trimmed edge and press. Machine stitch through both layers, 1/8″ from the edge; now trim the strip so the stitched line is in the center.

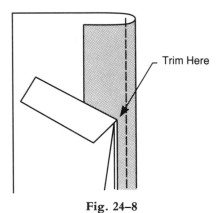

Trim Here

Fig. 24–8

3. Align the raw edges of the strip with the buttonhole marking; baste. Repeat with the other welt, butting the edges together.

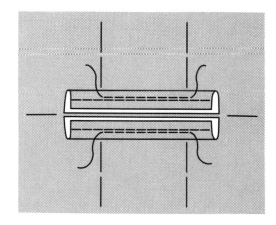

Fig. 24–9

452

Hint: *If you are matching plaids or stripes, check be- fore proceeding.*

4. Using a short stitch (L,1.5), sew on top of the previously stitched line. Fasten the stitches securely at the beginning and end with a spot tack or knot.

5. If the welts are on the bias, use a tapestry needle to run cord or wool yarn into them so they won't stretch out of shape.

6. Finish the buttonhole, using the directions for the patch method.

Note: The strip method doesn't need to be ditch-stitched (Step 9).

MODIFIED STRIP METHOD

1. Interface the buttonhole area; mark the buttonhole locations.

2. Cut two strips 1 1/2" wide and 1" longer than the buttonhole.

3. Right sides together, align one edge of the strip with the buttonhole location line; baste and stitch 1/8" from the edge. Repeat for the other strip, butting the raw edges together.

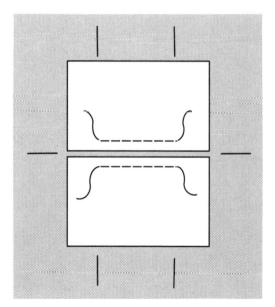

Fig. 24–10

4. Slash the opening; and, wrong side up, press the little buttonhole seams open.

5. Push the strips to the wrong side and adjust the welts so they are parallel and even in width.

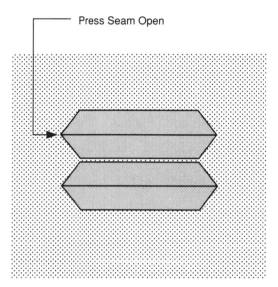

Fig. 24–11

6. Complete the buttonhole using the directions for the patch method.

WINDOWPANE METHOD

Sometimes called a window, faced, organza, or tulle buttonhole, the windowpane method is suitable for bulky, stiff fabrics and for fabrics which fray. First you make a finished opening; then you add welts.

1. Interface the buttonhole area; mark the buttonhole locations.

2. Using silk organza, tulle, or marquisette, cut a patch 1 1/2" wide and 1" longer than the buttonhole.

Hint: *Natural fiber fabrics are better, even if the color doesn't match exactly.*

3. Right sides together, center the patch over the buttonhole marking; pin.

4. Stitch (L,1.5) around the buttonhole as with the patch method.

453

5. Carefully slash the opening; push the organza through.

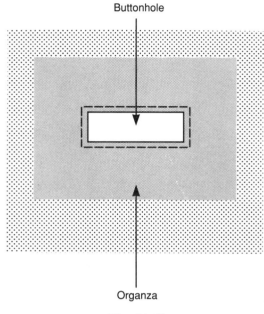

Buttonhole

Organza

Fig. 24–12

6. Wrong side up, adjust the organza so you can see the seam; press.

Hint: *Fuse a narrow strip of Wonder Under to the right side of the organza so the welts will be easy to position accurately.*

7. To make the welts, cut two rectangles on the desired grain 2″ wide and 1″ longer than the buttonhole. Right sides together, baste the centers together. Press them open.

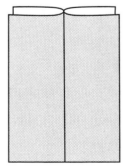

Fig. 24–13

8. Right sides up, center the welts under the windowpane; pin at each end.

Hint: *If you fused Wonder Under a couple of steps ago, steam around the buttonhole from the right side up. Use your fingers to pat and "baste" the layers together.*

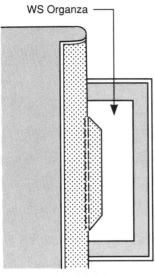

WS Organza

Fig. 24–14

9. Fold the garment back to expose the long seam at the top of the buttonhole; stitch again on the first seamline. Repeat for the bottom of the buttonhole.

10. Remove the basting from the welts.

11. Finish the buttonhole using the directions for the patch method.

LEATHER BUTTONHOLE

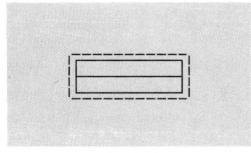

Fig. 24–15

Sometimes called a nonwoven buttonhole, the leather buttonhole is just a variation of the windowpane method.

1. Interface the buttonhole area.

2. Draw a window the exact size at each buttonhole location.

454

Hint: *On vinyls and synthetics, experiment with temporary marking pens. On leather, mark the window with drafting tape—test the tape first to be sure it doesn't lift the leather color; or use a felt-tip pen and draw on the wrong side.*

3. Using a mat knife or single-edged razor blade, cut out the window.

4. Make the buttonhole welts.

For synthetic suedes, use the windowpane method. For leather and vinyl, baste only the ends together.

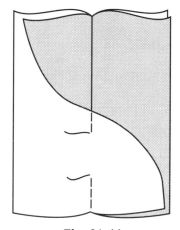

Fig. 24–16

5. Right sides up, center the welts under the buttonhole. Baste, using a washable glue stick.

6. Join the facing to the garment.

7. Right side up, edgestitch around the window to secure the welts and facing.

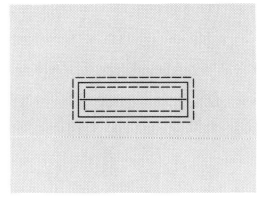

Fig. 24–17

Hint: *If you had a mental lapse and edgestitched before applying the facing, ditch-stitch around the window.*

8. Carefully slash the facing.

Hint: *I use a very sharp seam ripper and work from the right side of the garment.*

9. When sewing sherpa, machine stitch around the facing edge.

Fig. 24–18

Faced Buttonholes

Fig. 24–19

Faced buttonholes are used most frequently on fur and fake-fur fabrics.

1. Mark the buttonhole location on the wrong side of the fabric.

2. From a firmly woven interfacing or lining material, cut the facing 2″ wide and 1″ longer than the buttonhole.

3. Pin the facing to the right side of the garment. When working with pile, pin or tape the pile away from the buttonhole location first.

4. Wrong side up, shorten the stitch length (L,1.75) and stitch around the buttonhole.

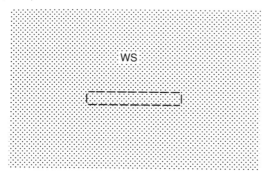

Fig. 24–20

5. Slash the buttonhole and push the facing to the wrong size.

6. Press; round the corners of the facing. On fake and real furs, catchstitch them to the fabric back.

HAND-WORKED BUTTONHOLES

Frequently used on couture designs, hand-worked buttonholes can have a bar at each end, a fan at each end, a fan at the end farther from the edge, or a keyhole at the end nearer the edge.

1. Interface the buttonhole area.

2. Mark the buttonhole location. If it is a keyhole buttonhole, draw a small triangle at the end or use a hole punch to make the keyhole.

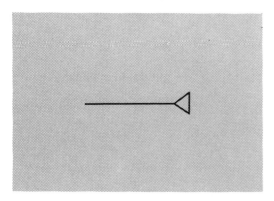

Fig. 24–21

3. Machine stitch (L,1.75) 1/16″ from each side of the marked line. For fans, extend stitches 1/16″ beyond the end.

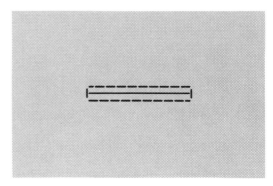

Fig. 24–22

4. Carefully cut the buttonhole on the grain.

5. Using buttonhole twists, begin the stitches at the end away from the edge. For lightweight fabrics, try regular (size 50) or machine embroidery threads.

6. If you are right-handed, work from right to left with the slit held over your forefinger so it spreads slightly. Make the stitches close together so the purls are on the top edge.

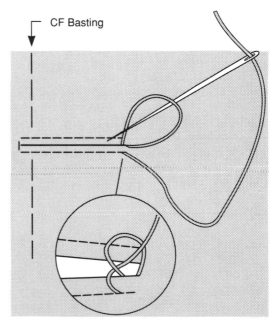

Fig. 24–23

Hint: *I can make the underside neater by making the buttonhole stitch like a stabstitch; then I pick up the loop.*

To make a traditional buttonhole stitch, wrap the thread near the eye around the needle point from right to left.

Experiment with pulling the thread out of the stitch in different directions to see how the thread controls the purl. Use your thumbnails to adjust the purls into a straight line.

Hint: *Traditional buttonholes can also be worked left to right; but you must also wrap the threads left to right. Practice using a cord until your buttonholes are perfect.*

7. For a fan, make five or seven stitches at the end. For a keyhole, make as many as needed.

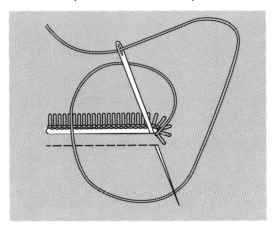

Fig. 24–24

8. Turn the work around and make stitches on the other side.

9. To make the bar tack, take three stitches across

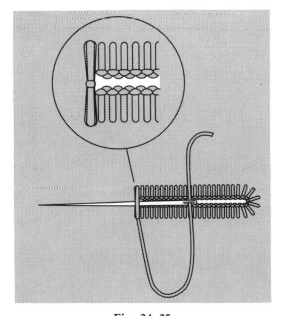

Fig. 24–25

the end of the buttonhole. Work blanket stitches over the bar.

10. Knot the thread and hide the end between the layers.

MACHINE-STITCHED BUTTONHOLES

Machine-stitched buttonholes are the most popular and easiest to make.

1. Interface the buttonhole area so the interfacing is positioned with the least amount of stretch parallel to the buttonhole.

Hint: *To avoid buttonholes that ripple when this isn't the case, interface the buttonhole with another piece of interfacing or organdy with the least amount of stretch parallel to the buttonhole.*

2. Layer and trim seam allowances in the buttonhole area so they won't impede the progress of the foot during the buttonhole process.

3. Mark the buttonhole locations on the right side of the garment. When using a buttonhole attachment, mark the end of the buttonhole near the garment edge.

When using a machine with a built-in automatic buttonholer, mark both ends of the buttonhole.

Hint: *Mark the ends with drafting tape.*

4. Use a new needle and a fine, good quality thread.

Hint: *Machine-embroidery threads, extra-fine cotton-wrapped polyester, and fine, long-staple polyester thread (100/3) make the most attractive buttonholes.*

5. Loosen the upper tension; or if there is a hole in the end of the bobbin case finger, thread the bobbin thread into it to tighten the lower tension.

Hint: *If the wrong side of the buttonhole will show when the garment is worn, do not change the tension.*

6. Change to a buttonhole foot.

Hint: *If your machine doesn't have a buttonhole foot with two parallel grooves on the bottom, experiment with feet made by other manufacturers until you find one that works well on your machine. Once you know whether your machine is a high-shank, low-shank, or slant needle, you can use feet from corresponding models. Ask your dealer.*

7. Make a sample buttonhole, using a L,.5 stitch length.

Hint: *To prevent skipped stitches, use a new needle and a needle lubricant.*

To avoid tunneling on lightweight fabrics, use a water-soluble stabilizer between the fabric and feed dogs. If the fabric will waterspot, trim the stabilizer close to the buttonhole and steam from the wrong side.

Lengthen the stitch length for bulky or heavy fabrics.

8. Position the garment under the foot with the bulk in your lap or to the left of the foot. Align the mark on the garment with the center of the foot.

Hint: *When positioning garments made of bulky fabrics, hold the presser-bar lifter up and cover the fabric with a thin plastic card.*

Begin and end the buttonhole at the end near the garment edge so the most attractive bar, which is at the other end, will be visible when the garment is buttoned.

9. With the garment right side up, stitch around the buttonhole once.

Hint: *For best results, make at least one sample buttonhole, duplicating the fabric and interfacing layers, before making buttonholes on the garment.*

Avoid a satin stitch; it is a tattletale sign of homemade. The stitches around the buttonholes should be spaced so they have a little "air" between them.

Fine tune the stitch length, when stitching in reverse, so the beads on both sides of the buttonhole are the same length.

BUTTONHOLE ATTACHMENTS

A buttonhole attachment can be used on any machine, even older straight-stitch models. The attachment utilizes templates in various lengths to control the buttonhole length; and, while the buttonholer foot or cloth clamp holds the fabric firmly, the attachment moves the fabric forward, backward, and around the ends the predetermined amount.

1. Use the manufacturer's directions to attach the foot.

2. Set the cloth clamp as far forward as possible before beginning each buttonhole.

3. Position the garment under the cloth clamp with the bulk in your lap or to the left of the foot. Align the mark on the garment with the first line on the cloth clamp.

Hint: *To position delicate and bulky fabrics easily and without damage, cover the garment with a piece of firm, transparent plastic; then slide the garment into position. Remove the plastic before stitching.*

The plastic that comes in bacon packages is a nice size. Wash it thoroughly before using, to remove all the grease.

4. Lower the presser bar.

Hint: *To avoid skipped stitches, level the cloth clamp by holding it flat against the fabric with your index finger; or balance it by placing a piece of cardboard under one side of the clamp.*

5. Stitch around the buttonhole once.

6. Raise the foot; and reposition the garment for the next buttonhole. Use the plastic protector again if needed.

7. Pull the threads to the wrong side of the garment; knot and clip them closely.

KEYHOLE BUTTONHOLES

Keyhole buttonholes are frequently used on men's and women's tailored jackets, because the keyhole, which is near the garment edge, allows a larger button shank to set better than it would on a straight buttonhole.

Generally made with a buttonhole attachment, keyhole buttonholes can also be made manually.

1. Draw the buttonhole on the right side of the garment exactly as it is to look finished.

2. Using a short stitch (L,1), stitch on the marked line. Using a mat knife, cut the buttonhole open and cut out the keyhole.

3. Beginning at the end farther from the garment edge, hold the buttonhole open; and stitch (W,3; L,1) around the buttonhole so the needle swings off the fabric each time it swings to the right. Stitch around the buttonhole again to cover the whiskers. Make a wide bar to finish the end.

CORDED BUTTONHOLES

Corded buttonholes are firmer and stretch less. Use pearl cotton, pearl rayon, embroidery floss, crochet thread, gimp, topstitching thread, or regular thread for the cording.

To make a corded buttonhole, raise the foot and loop the cord around the spur on the foot. Hold the cord taut in the channels on the underside of the foot while stitching.

When the buttonhole is finished, pull the cord into the buttonhole until the loop is hidden under the bar.

Thread the cord ends into a needle and draw them to the wrong side of the garment or in between the fabric layers. Knot and hide the ends.

Hint: *For easy threading, use a calyx-eye needle. Designed for the visually impaired, these needles have an open end and are readily available.*

CUTTING BUTTONHOLES

1. Check the placement before cutting the buttonholes.

Hint: *If you must rip a buttonhole, use a seam ripper to clip the bobbin thread on the wrong side. A lamp with a magnifying glass is particularly helpful.*

2. Using the dull side of the seam ripper, score the buttonhole between the two beads.

3. Insert a very sharp seam ripper straight down into the buttonhole at one end. Slash toward the center; repeat at the other end. Or, if you prefer, use a buttonhole cutter. Check the cutter placement carefully to avoid cutting the stitches.

Hint: *If the fabric frays when the buttonhole is cut, apply a small amount of fray retardant, diluted clear nail polish, or a thin solution of white glue to the back of the buttonhole opening. Test first to be sure it won't spread onto the fabric or leave a permanent stain.*

Use a permanent color marker to dye any interfacing that shows.

STITCHED-SLASH BUTTONHOLES

Suitable for nonwoven fabrics, leather, and suede, this buttonhole is unbelievably easy.

1. Interface the buttonhole area; mark the buttonhole locations.

2. Use a new needle and shorten the stitch length. Begin at the end nearer the edge. Stitch the end, then the top, 1/8″ from the buttonhole marking; stitch the other end, the bottom, and the first end again. Pull the threads to the wrong side; knot and hide them.

Hint: *Don't forget to count the stitches at the end (as with the patch method). Thread the ends in a calyx-eyed needle and hide them between the layers.*

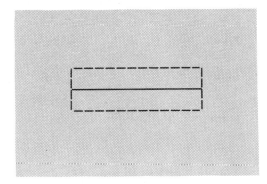

Fig. 24–26

3. Using a mat knife or single-edged razor blade, slash the buttonhole carefully.

Fly Plackets

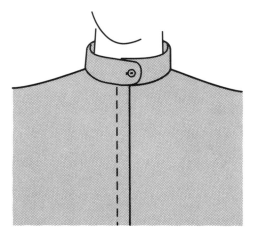

Fig. 24–27

The invisible fly placket has many applications, but it is particularly useful when you can't find buttons to match or your machine doesn't make perfect buttonholes. Generally used on blouse fronts by home sewers, many designers use it instead on the back.

1. To economize, make separate patterns for the right and left fronts.

2. On the paper pattern cut away the facing at the garment edge; then tape a piece of pattern paper to it.

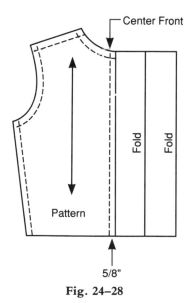

Fig. 24–28

3. Measure the distance between the center front and garment edge; it is usually 5/8″. For the right

front, multiply by eight and draw a line parallel to the garment edge and this distance (5″) away; trim on this line. For the left front, multiply by four.

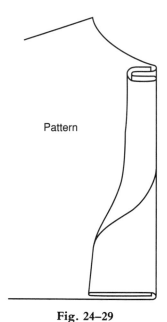

Fig. 24–29

4. Fold the cut edge in to meet the creased line; trim away the excess paper at the neckline.

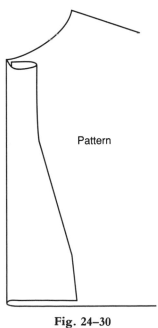

Fig. 24–30

SEWING NOTES

1. On both the right and left fronts, use small clips to mark the top and bottom of the foldlines at the garment edges.

2. On the underlap, press a foldline, using the clips as a guide. Fold the raw edge in to meet the foldline and press again; pin the layers together until the buttons are sewn on.

3. On the overlap, press a foldline, using the clips as a guide. Fold the raw edge in to meet the foldline and press again. Right side up, topstitch 1 1/4″ from the garment edge. Make the buttonholes on the underlay; then bring the folds together; pin.

Hint: *It's all right for the underlay to be slightly narrower than the fly; but it shouldn't be wider.*

4. The easiest finish at the neckline is a band or two-piece shirt collar. For a tie collar, clip the garment neckline to the stitching line at the end of the collar. Carefully trim the neckline seam to 1/4″; fold it in at the neckline and finish the edge with a slipstitch.

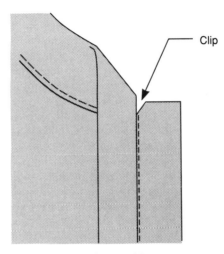

Clip

Fig. 24–32

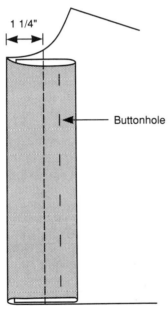

1 1/4″

Buttonhole

Fig. 24–31

Snaps

Use covered snaps on jackets, coats, special-occasion designs, or any time they might be seen.

1. For each snap section, cut a circle of light-weight lining fabric twice the diameter of the snap.

2. Using a fine needle, gather the edge of the circle with a small stitch. Place the snap face down on the wrong side of the lining; and tighten the gathering. Fasten the stitches securely then sew back and forth over the snap to flatten the edges.

3. Repeat for the other part of the snap and snap them together.

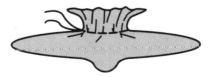

Fig. 24–33

Ties and Straps

Ties are frequently used on casual garments.

1. Cut the tie to the desired length and four times the finished width.

Hint: *Ties are usually cut on the lengthwise grain, but they can be cut on any grain.*

2. Wrong sides together, fold the tie in half lengthwise; press. Fold the raw edges in to meet the foldline and press again.

3. Edgestitch one or both sides of the ties.

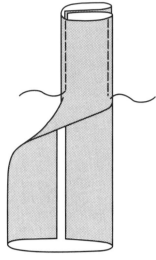

Fig. 24–34

Claire's Super-Easy Zipper

This is the easiest zipper you'll ever stitch. The directions are for a slot zipper, but they are easily adapted for a lapped application.

1. Press the seam allowances in the placket area to the wrong side.

2. Right side up, stitch around the opening a skinny 1/4″ from the fold. Looks beautiful, doesn't it?

Hint: *If this is a luxury garment, use small running stitches instead of machine stitching.*

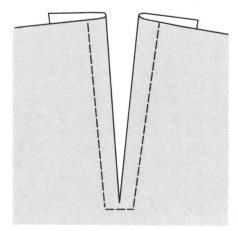

Fig. 24–35

3. Wrong side up, baste one side of the zipper to the seam allowance with the edge of the coil just inside the folded edge.

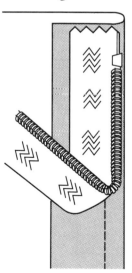

Fig. 24–36

Hint: *Use washable glue stick or water-soluble tape to baste. Close the zipper. There should be a small peak where the folds meet. If there isn't, rebaste so there is.*

4. Fold the garment back; and, using a zipper foot, stitch close to first stitched line.

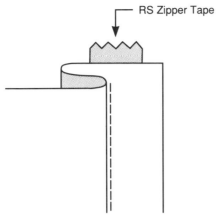

Fig. 24–37

Hint: *If you don't stitch close to the original stitching line, the placket will gap.*

5. Repeat for the other side of the zipper.

CHAPTER 25
Hand Stitches

BACKSTITCHES

The strongest hand stitches, backstitches are used to repair seams in hard-to-reach places, understitch some fabrics and couture designs, set zippers by hand, and complete garments when a machine is unavailable.

Working right to left, secure the thread. Take the stitch 1/8″ to the right of the thread, bringing the needle out 1/8″ to the left of the thread. Take the second stitch by inserting the needle at the end of the last stitch. Make the stitches longer or shorter as desired.

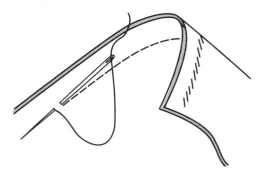

Fig. 25–1

To make half backstitches, make the stitch on the right side of the fabric half the distance to the last stitch.

To make prickstitches, use a stabstitch and make the stitch almost invisible on the right side of the fabric.

To make a pickstitch, make a very small stitch on the right side of the garment; slip the needle between the layers so the thread doesn't show on the underside.

BASTING STITCHES

Use basting stitches to hold the fabric layers together temporarily. Working right to left, secure the thread at the beginning and end with a backstitch instead of a knot.

To make even basting stitches, make short 1/4″ spaced stitches.

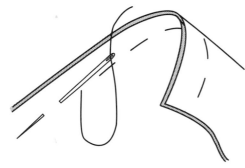

Fig. 25–2

To double baste, make a row of even basting; then make a second row, alternating the stitches and spaces with the first row.

To make uneven basting stitches, take a short stitch; insert the needle again 3/8″ to 1/2″ from the first stitch.

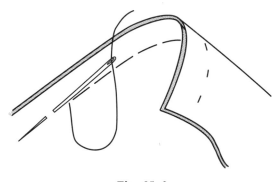

Fig. 25–3

To make diagonal basting stitches, work from top to bottom. Take small horizontal stitches, spacing them 1/4″ to 2″ apart.

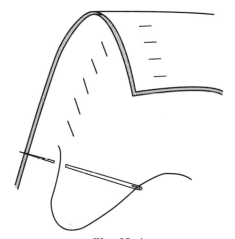

Fig. 25–4

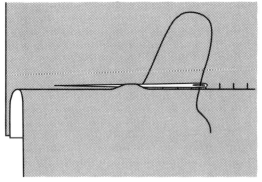

Fig. 25–5

To slip baste, work from right to left, making a ladder stitch (Fig. 25-5).

BLANKET STITCHES

These directions for using blanket stitches to finish edges can be adapted to make belt carriers and thread eyes, and to sew on hooks and eyes.

Working left to right with the garment right side up, insert the needle into the fabric 1/8″ to 1″ from the edge. Loop the thread under the needle; then pull the needle through to make a stitch at the edge.

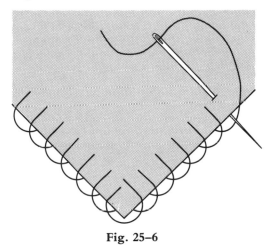

Fig. 25–6

BLINDSTITCHES

Called blindstitches because they are hidden between the hem and garment layers, they may also be called a tailor's hem.

Working from right to left, secure the thread and take a small stitch in the hem allowance; then take a tiny stitch in the garment about 3/8″ to the left. Alternate between the hem and garment to make small "v's."

Hint: *For an invisible hem, use a fine needle (size 8 or 9), pick up only the back of the garment fabric, hem very loosely, and pull the thread through after each stitch.*

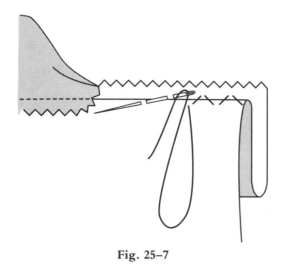

Fig. 25–7

BLIND CATCHSTITCH

The blind catchstitch is used for hemming heavyweight fabrics.

Working from left to right, secure the thread and take a small stitch in the hem allowance; then take a tiny stitch in the garment about 3/8″ to the right. Alternate between the hem and garment to make small "x's."

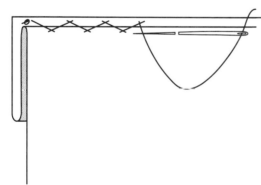

Fig. 25–8

BUTTONHOLE STITCHES

Used to secure hooks and eyes, make thread eyes and belt loops, as well as make hand-worked buttonholes, buttonhole stitches require practice.

Working from right to left with the garment right side up, insert the needle into the wrong side of the fabric 1/16″ to 1/8″ from the edge. Pull the

needle out of the fabric; pick up the thread loop at the edge. Pull the thread taut to form a purl at the fabric edge.

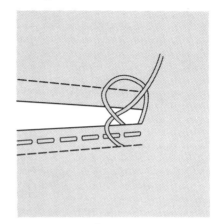

Fig. 25–9

Hint: *When making buttonhole stitches the needle points from the edge to the body of the garment.*

CATCHSTITCHES

Sometimes called cross stitches, catchstitches are used to hem garments and to secure pleats and lapels.

Working left to right, secure the thread; take a small stitch to the right and below the thread. Take the next stitch to the right and above the last stitch; alternate the stitches, spacing the equal sized stitches equidistant. In hand embroidery, these are called herringbone stitches.

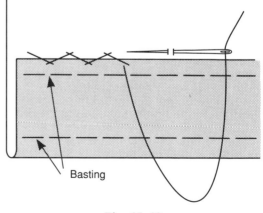

Basting

Fig. 25–10

466

FELL STITCHES

Frequently used in tailoring, fell stitches are neat vertical stitches. Use fell stitches to hem, to close seams from the right side, to appliqué, to baste difficult-to-stitch seams, and to finish bands and bindings.

When properly made, fell stitches simulate machine stitches on the right side and are inconspicuous on the wrong side.

Working from right to left, secure the thread inconspicuously. Pick up a tiny stitch in the garment opposite the thread. Slip the needle point under the fold and pick up the edge about a 1/4″ away. Pull the thread through. Depending on the security required, stitches can be spaced 1/16″ to 3/8″ apart.

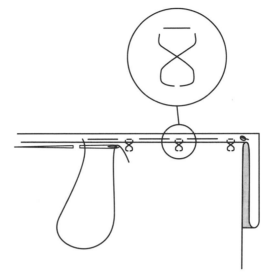

Fig. 25–12

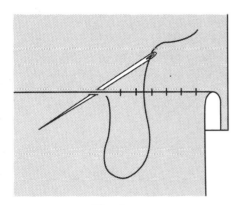

Fig. 25–11

FIGURE-EIGHT STITCHES

Used to blindhem difficult fabrics such as knits and crepes, figure-eight stitches can be spaced farther apart than other stitches.

Working from right to left, secure the thread; and take two stitches in the hem—one on top of the other. Pick up a tiny stitch in the garment directly opposite the stitch; then take another stitch on the hem to form the figure eight. Space the stitches about an inch apart.

Hint: *Keep the stitches loose.*

OVERCASTING STITCHES

The flattest, least conspicuous edge finish, overcasting stitches are used to finish the raw edges of seams and hems on fine fabrics.

Work in either direction, using mercerized cotton thread. Space the stitches about 1/8″ apart.

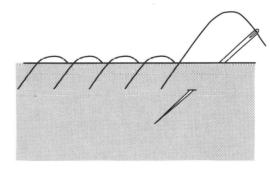

Fig. 25–13

Hint: *For neater stitches, pull the thread through after each stitch. Do not weave several stitches onto the needle before pulling the thread.*

If the fabric frays badly, "cross your hand"—make a second set of stitches in the return directions to simulate a zigzag stitch.

467

PADDING STITCHES

Used to shape tailored lapels and collars, padding stitches are small diagonal stitches.

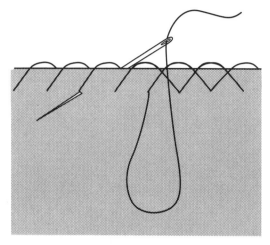

Fig. 25–14

Working from top to bottom, make a series of small horizontal stitches one below the other. Work the next row from bottom to top.

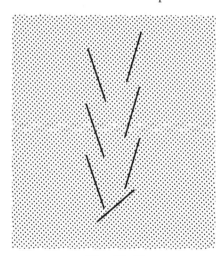

Fig. 25–15

RUNNING STITCHES

Used for gathering and tucking and for seams which don't require strength, running stitches should be very short. Proceed as for even basting, working the point of the needle up and down to take up several stitches before pulling the needle through.

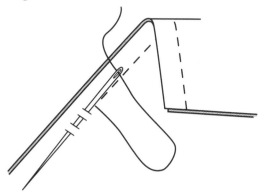

Fig. 25–16

STABSTITCHES

Used to secure shoulder pads and to set zippers, these stitches are made one stitch at a time by stabbing the fabric vertically.

Working from right to left with the garment right side up, insert the needle vertically in the fabric layers; pull the thread through. Repeat to bring the needle back to the right side.

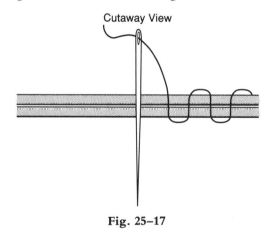

Cutaway View

Fig. 25–17

Hint: *For invisible stitches, keep the stitches loose.*

SLIPSTITCHES OR LADDER STITCHES

Slipstitches or ladder stitches are used to join two layers from the right side of the fabric. Worked properly, slipstitches look like machine stitching.

Working from right to left, secure the thread and take a small stitch. Pick up a small stitch in the garment directly opposite the thread; pull the needle out of the fabric. Make several stitches, alternating the stitches between the two layers, to form a ladder; then draw the thread tight. Space stitches 1/16″ to 3/8″ apart.

Hint: *To resemble a machine stitch, the ladder steps must be parallel to each other. Do not weave several stitches onto the needle.*

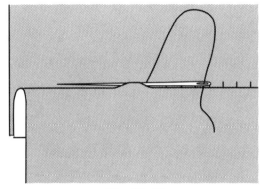

Fig. 25–18

When used to finish the gorge line on jackets, it is called a draw stitch.

TAILOR TACKS

Used to mark seamlines and matchpoints, tailor tacks are made by two methods. Use soft basting cotton or white embroidery cotton.

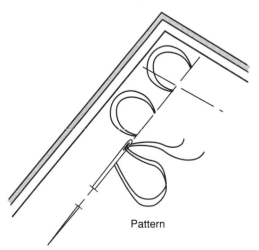

Pattern

Fig. 25–19

To mark seamlines, make loopy basting stitches. Clip the loops between each stitch; carefully separate the layers; and clip the threads between the layers.

To mark matchpoints, take a stitch at the matchpoint; take a second stitch at the matchpoint, leaving a 1/2″ loop. Clip the loop; carefully separate the layers; and clip the threads between the layers.

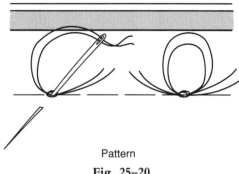

Pattern

Fig. 25–20

WHIPPING STITCHES

Whipping stitches are used to join two edges together from the right side. Working right to left, sew through two layers, proceeding as for an overcasting stitch.

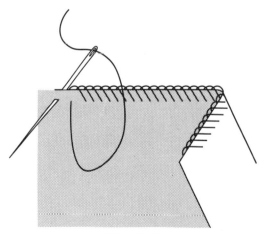

Fig. 25–21

Hint: *To avoid making a ridge, don't make the stitches too tight.*

Sometimes used for hemming, whipping stitches generally are less attractive than felling stitches.

469

PART SIX

Fabric and Fiber Dictionary

A

absorbent finish   Finish that enables fabrics to absorb moisture more readily.

acetate   (1) Synthetic fiber made from cellulose acetate; differs from rayon, which is made from regenerated cellulose. Soft and pliable, it resembles silk, but is colorfast to sunlight and perspiration when solution dyed. It is weaker when wet and frequently used with other fibers to add sheen or reduce cost. Dissolves in acetone, which is used in fingernail polish removers. According to the Federal Trade Commission, the term acetate is to be used for yarn, thread, and fabrics composed of cellulose acetate. Uses: blouses, dresses, lingerie, linings, shirts, slacks, and sportswear. (2) Acetate fabrics include brocade, crepe, double knits, faille, knitted jersey, satin, taffeta, and tricot. (3) Trade names include Acetate by Avtex, Ariloft, Avron, Celanese, Celara, Chromspun, Estron, and Loftura.

acrylic   (1) Synthetic fiber made from a combination of coal, air, water, oil, and limestone. Soft, lightweight, and warm, it is frequently used instead of wool. Washable and quick drying, it pills badly. Resistant to moths, chemicals, oils, and sunlight. Uses: dresses, infant's wear, skirts, ski garments, and sweaters. (2) Fabrics made of acrylic include fleece and pile materials, fake-fur fabrics, and knits. (3) Trade names include Acrilan, Bi-Loft, Creslan, Fi-lana, Nomelle, Or-lon, Pa-Qel, Remember, So-Lara, Wintuk, Zefran, and Zitkrome.

Agilon   Trademark of Derring Milliken, Inc., for stretch nylon. Strong, durable, and easy care. It can be made with variety of hands.

alaskine   Crisp, silk/wool blend popular in the sixties.

Alençon lace   Lace design outlined with a cord on net ground.

alligator   Reptile skin sometimes used for belts.

allover embroidery   Fabric with an allover pattern on its surface. Embroidery may be cotton, silk, linen, rayon, or nylon; background may be organdy, taffeta, broadcloth, or piqué. Uses: blouses, shirts, dresses, lingerie, and evening wear.

allover lace   Lace with pattern all over the surface; no scalloped edges. Most cannot be clipped for appliquéing. Uses: blouses, dresses, and evening wear.

alpaca   Soft, lustrous, wool fiber from the alpaca—a kind of llama raised in the Andes Mountains. Coarser than camel. Frequently blended with wool to make fabric. Uses: coats, suits, and sportswear.

angora   (1) Long, white fleece from the angora goat. Soft and smooth. Combined with other fibers and called mohair. (2) Light, fine hair from angora rabbits. Combined with other fibers to reduce the cost. Must be labeled angora rabbit.

anidex Synthetic fiber with permanent stretch and recovery. Less stretch than spandex but can withstand higher temperatures in laundering.

antelope Soft, fine-grained leather similar to deerskin.

anti-crease finish Synthetic finish to reduce wrinkling of fabrics. Used on cotton, rayon, linen, and blends.

antique satin Reversible satin-weave fabric with a lustrous face and a dull, slubbed back. Uses: evening wear and draperies.

antique taffeta Crisp, slubbed taffeta. Some are iridescent.

Antron DuPont trademark for nylon fiber.

application printing See direct printing.

appliqué Design which is sewn, embroidered, glued, or fused to the face of another fabric.

appliqué lace Lace fabric or trim with motifs which have been made separately from the background. Motifs can be clipped apart and appliquéd to another surface. Sometimes called clipped lace.

aramid (1) Synthetic fiber that is very strong and flame-resistant. Use: protective clothing. (2) Trade names include Kevlar and Nomex.

argyle Knitting design motif featuring a diamond pattern. Originally from Argyll in the West Highlands of Scotland.

armure French term for pebbled surface or embossed effect. Dress fabric made in a variety of fibers or blends.

Arnel Trademark of Celanese Corp. for cellulose triacetate. Resists wrinkles, is washable, and has good pleat retention.

art linen Plain-weave fabric used for needlework.

artificial silk Early name for rayon fabrics which imitated silk.

artillery tweed Same as whipcord.

astrakhan (1) Curly fur from the karakul sheep. (2) Woven fabric with a thick curly pile, imitating fur. Usually wool or synthetic; best quality has mohair warp to add luster and curl. Use: coatings.

athletic mesh Mesh-knit fabric with open work pattern. Sometimes called dishrag.

B

backed cloth Extra filling and/or warp woven into a fabric to define pattern, add thickness, weight, strength, or warmth. Piqué, matelassé, and satin-backed crepe are examples of a backed cloth.

bagheera Crease-resistant velvet with uncut, looped pile. Uses: evening gowns and wraps.

balanced fabric Cloth with same number of picks and ends per inch, which are identical in size and character.

balanced twill Simplest twill weave, which alternates same number of picks and ends (e.g., 2/2 or 3/3). Sometimes called even twill.

bandanna Originally a colored, cotton square with a tie-dyed design in white.

Ban-Lon Trademark of Bancroft Licensing for a process that adds bulk and stretch to synthetic yarns.

Bannockburn Tweed made by alternating single-ply and two-ply yarns. Originally made in Bannockburn, Scotland. Uses: jackets, suits, and topcoats.

barathea High-quality, fine-textured material with twill weave. Originally silk warp with worsted filling; now frequently synthetic. Uses: men's tuxedos and suits.

bark crepe Rough-textured crepe which resembles tree bark. Made in wool, rayon, and polyester. Uses: coats and evening wear.

baronet satin Satin-weave fabric with cotton warp and rayon filling. Drapes and wears well.

bars See Brides.

basket weave Variation of plain weave. Instead of interlacing single threads at right angles, it utilizes two or more threads in both the warp and filling. Used in monk's cloth and hopsacking.

bast fibers Fibers from the bark of flax, ramie, hemp, and jute.

batik Resist method of printing, originally from Java, which utilizes wax on crisp cottons. Today, batiklike designs may be used on synthetics and blends. Uses: shirts, beachwear, and casual garments.

batiste Soft, lightweight, plain-weave fabric. Originally made in linen, it may be woven in silk or wool, but it is usually cotton or a cotton/polyester blend. Durable, varies in sheerness. Uses: lingerie, baby dresses, blouses, and sometimes dresses.

Battenberg lace Lace made by joining Battenberg tape with brides.

batting Originally, carded cotton or wool sold in sheets; today, usually polyester fleece which is sold by the yard. Uses: quilting, interlining, shoulder pads, stuffings.

beaded velvet See cut velvet.

beading Lace or embroidered insertion with holes for inserting ribbon.

beaver Warm, soft, hard-wearing fur. It may be sheared or natural. Redness is undesirable. Uses: jackets, coats, and trims.

beaver cloth Expensive topcoat fabric with heavy nap on face. Similar to melton and broadcloth, but softer, with a longer nap.

Bedford cord Firm, medium-heavy fabric distinguished by cords in the warp. May be a worsted, cotton, or man-made. Uses: riding breeches, trousers, suits, and uniforms.

beetled finish Finish with a sheen produced by pounding the fabric. Beetling closes the spaces between warp and filling and produces a sheen.

Bemberg Soft, silky fabric made of cuprammonium rayon by American Bemberg Corp. Sometimes called cupro.

benares Lightweight fabric with a metallic thread pattern, made in India. May be cotton or silk.

bengaline Lustrous, cross-rib fabric; similar to grosgrain or faille, but heavier. Firm, but drapeable. Compact texture makes it a good stiffening. May be silk, wool, cotton, rayon, or blend. Uses: dresses, coats, suits, and ribbons.

billiard cloth High-quality twill- or plain-weave fabric in merino wool. Even, smooth, and durable. Uses: billiard tables and underlinings.

bird's eye A fine worsted in a dobby weave with a small indentation in the center of the pattern resembling the eye of a bird. Sometimes made of cotton or rayon. Uses: diapers and toweling.

blanket cloth Named for Thomas Blanquette (Blanket), a fourteenth-century Flemish weaver who first used it for warmth and sleeping. Heavily napped and fulled fabric made of wool, worsted, cotton, or blend. Uses: bathrobes, coats, and jackets.

blazer cloth Satin-weave fabric used for loose-fitting blazers. Traditionally striped wool flannel or melton with a slight nap on the face. Today

blazer cloth is made in other fibers, solid colors, and sometimes a plain weave.

bleach Chemical used to remove color.

bleeding dye Dyes, usually vegetable, which run or fade when wet. Undesirable, except on madras and perhaps denim.

blend Combination of two or more fibers in one yarn. Fabric made of blended yarns.

blister Puckers, crimps, or bulges on the fabric surface.

block printing Hand-printing method using carved wooden or linoleum blocks. Separate blocks are required for each color. The oldest form of printing, this is a slow and expensive process.

blotch printing A direct printing method. The reverse will be almost white.

bobbin Device that carries filling yarns in weaving.

bobbin lace Handmade lace sometimes called pillow lace. Originally made with bobbins on a pillow.

bobbinet A net fabric which simulates bobbin lace.

boiled wool A knitted wool which has been shrunk and fulled.

bolt Quantity of fabric.

bombazine A twill-weave silk and worsted fabric. Often dyed black and used for mourning cloth.

bonded fabrics Two fabrics which have been fused or glued wrong sides together to make one fabric.

bonded knit Knit fabric bonded to another fabric.

border design Printed, woven, or knitted design along one edge. Frequently used on the crossgrain for garments.

Botany Soft, but firm worsted with a twill weave. Term originally applied to merino wool from Botany Bay, Australia. Use: high-quality suitings.

bouclé Wool or worsted with loops or curls on the surface, sometimes both sides. Fabrics vary in weight as well as firmness. May be knitted or woven. Uses: dresses and suits.

braid (1) Method of making tape, trim, and elastic by plaiting. (2) Narrow plaited band made in all major fibers. Narrows when stretched. (3) Fancy narrow bands woven on a jacquard loom.

Breton lace   Net ground with heavily embroidered motifs featuring colored cords.

brides   Connecting threads in lace. Sometimes called bridges or bars.

broadcloth   (1) Originally, the name designated high quality, closely woven woolen or worsted wider than 27″ (the width of narrow cloth). Wool broadcloth, made from merino wool, is a fine twill weave (sometimes plain weave) with a velvety nap. Weight varies from light to medium. Better qualities drape well and are hard wearing. Uses: coats, suits, pants, and dresses. (2) Fine, cross-rib fabric made of silk, rayon, cotton, and blends. Light to medium weight, very durable. Uses: shirtings, dresses, pajamas, and sportswear. (3) Smooth, plain-weave fabric used for prints.

broadtail   A flat, wavy fur taken from unborn lambs. Use: jackets, coats, and evening wear.

brocade   Embossed or raised floral and scroll design woven on a jacquard loom. Fabric back is easy to distinguish by floating threads. Made from all major textile fibers and often includes metallic threads. Sometimes crisp and heavy. Uses: dresses, suits, coats, draperies and upholstery.

brocade velvet   See sculptured velvet.

brocalette   Heavy brocade fabric used for upholstery.

broderie anglaise   Means English embroidery. Fine quality, white eyelet on white cotton or cotton blend.

broken check   Woven or printed pattern with checks which are not perfect squares.

broken-twill weave   Twill-weave fabrics in which the twill changes direction. Not always a herringbone.

brushing   Finishing process to raise the nap. Used on acrylics, wool, cotton, denim, and nylon. Sometimes called scrubbing.

Brussels lace   Originally, featured handmade bobbin-lace motifs which were worked separately, then joined by a net ground which was worked around them. Today both the motifs and ground are machine-made.

buckram   Very stiff open-weave stiffening fabric. Uses: belts and hats.

buckskin   (1) The flesh or sueded side of deerskin. It is soft and lightweight. (2) Rugged, satin-weave fabric, simulating buckskin (skin from a male fallow deer). Used for riding breeches.

burlap   Coarse plain-weave fabric made of jute, hemp, or cotton, with a distinctive odor. Sometimes used for trim.

burn-out fabrics   (1) Plain-weave fabric made of two different yarns. The fabric is treated with acid to "burn out" one of the fibers, creating a pattern design. Most are lightweight blends with sheer and opaque areas; others are sculptured velvets. Uses: blouses, dresses, and evening wear. Sometimes called etched-out. (2) Lace embroidered with a schiffli machine on water-soluble material. Sometimes called guipure or chemical lace.

butcher linen   Stiff, heavy, durable linen in a plain weave; originally manufactured for butcher's aprons. Sheds dirt easily and wears well. Usually bleached white and used for aprons and laboratory coats. Term frequently used incorrectly to describe linen-look fabrics made of rayon or cotton.

C

cabretta   A popular lightweight goat skin with a fine grain and rich finish.

calender printing   See roller printing and direct printing.

calendering   Lustrous or embossed finish applied to fabric by rollers. May not be permanent.

calf   Coarse, flat fur with a sheen. Frequently dyed to imitate other animals.

calfskin suede   The underlayer of calfskin.

calico   Inexpensive, printed, plain-weave cotton. Similar to percale but coarser and poorer quality. Firmly woven, wears and launders well. Frequently printed with a small design. Originally made in Calicut (Calcutta), India, for which it is named. Easy to sew. Uses: patchwork, children's garments, and utility linens.

cambric   Lightweight, crisp, plain-weave linen or cotton. Usually bleached or plain color and finished with sizing to produce a slight shine on the face. Uses: handkerchiefs, collars, baby clothes, blouses, lingerie, and nightgowns.

camel hair   Woollike fiber, underhair of the bactrian (two-humped) camel. Lustrous and soft in natural colors from light tan to dark brown. May be mixed with merino, cashmere, or less expensive wools. Uses: suits and coats.

candlewick Heavy, plain-weave cotton fabric with coarse string tuffs. Originally made by hand.

canton crepe Silk crepe with a slight cross-rib.

canton satin Soft, heavy satin with a crepe back, heavier than crepe de chine. Very drapeable.

canvas (1) Stiff, plain-weave cloth; similar to duck and sailcloth, but lighter. Multiple ply yarns (2–14) make it very durable. Usually made of linen or cotton. Uses: awnings, director's chairs, and tote bags. (2) Term sometimes used to describe muslin.

carded cotton Cotton yarns made of short irregular fibers. Durable, but not as smooth or lustrous as combed cotton. Used for calico and muslin.

carding Process of cleaning, untangling, and straightening wool, silk, and cotton fibers.

cashmere Soft, strong, and silky wool-like hair from the kashmir (cashmere) goat. Usually mixed with wool to reduce cost and improve durability. Uses: dresses, suits, and coats.

cassimere Plain or twill-weave suiting with a clear finish.

cavalry twill Durable twill-weave fabric with distinctive 63° weave and double-twill line. Uses: jackets, trousers, and uniforms.

cellophane Thin, transparent, smooth cellulose film.

cellulose Fiber made from the cell walls of plants, used to make rayons and acetates.

chalk stripe Suiting fabric with a fine, light or white line. May be printed or woven. Uses: suits and jackets.

challis Soft, but firm, plain-weave fabric in wool, cotton, rayon, or blends. Frequently printed. Lightweight, drapes and gathers well. Uses: dresses, skirts, robes, and scarves.

chambray Plain-weave, smooth fabric with colored warp and white filling. Looks like denim but lighter weight. Originally all cotton, today it may be a synthetic or a blend. Wears and launders well. Uses: shirts, sportswear, and children's clothes.

chameleon Fabric with a changeable effect; warp of one color and double yarn filling of different colors.

chamois Soft suede originally from the chamois goat. Today it may be from other goats, sheep, or deer. Uses: skirts, jackets, blouses, and tee tops.

changeable See iridescent.

Chantilly lace Originally a bobbin lace made in Chantilly, France, with a fine net ground and elaborate floral motifs. Sometimes re-embroidered.

charmeuse Soft, satin-weave fabric with a dull back and lustrous face. May be silk, polyester, cotton, rayon, or blends. Creases, snags, and wears poorly. Uses: blouses, dresses, evening gowns, lingerie, and nightgowns.

charvet silk Soft, twill-weave fabric with a dull finish. Frequently woven in stripes and used for ties.

check Woven or printed pattern of squares. Common types include gingham, houndstooth, and Tattersall.

cheesecloth Soft, open-weave cotton used for making cheese, straining milk, jelly, etc. Frequently called gauze. Uses: shirts, blouses, and dresses.

chenille Pile fabric named, in French, for the caterpillar. Uses: bathrobes, bedspreads, casual tops and jackets.

cheviot Rough-surfaced, twill-weave wool with the same color in the warp and filling. Wears well, but loses its shape. Uses: suits and coats.

chevron A horizontal design of joined V's.

chiffon Lightweight, transparent, plain-weave fabric made with fine, highly twisted yarns. Soft, drapeable, filmy, and strong. May be plain, printed, or have a woven pattern in silk, nylon, cotton, rayon, or polyester. Uses: cocktail dresses, evening gowns, blouses, lingerie, and nightgowns.

chiffon velvet Lightweight, pile fabric in rayon or silk. Durable and drapes well, but crushes.

China grass See ramie.

China silk Inexpensive, soft, lightweight silk made in a plain weave. Not very durable. Sometimes called Jap silk. Uses: blouses, linings, and lingerie.

chinchilla Expensive, soft, bluish-white fur with dark tips. Uses: trims and evening wear.

chinchilla cloth Thick, heavily napped wool coating with a short, curly pile on the face, simulating chinchilla fur. Spongy, usually gray in color.

chino Durable, medium-weight fabric with a slight sheen on the face and a dull back. Usually a twill-weave cotton. Uses: sportswear and summer military uniforms.

chintz Closely woven, plain-weave cotton with a glazed finish. Originally imported into Britain by the East India Co. in the seventeenth century. Uses: draperies, slip covers, dresses, and jackets. Wears well. Original glazes washed out; some modern resin glazes are more permanent.

circular knit Fabric or garment knitted in a circle without a seam.

ciré (1) Originally a waxed finish used for shrouds. Sometimes used on silk and rayon to produce a smooth, lustrous finish similar to patent leather. Use: evening wear. (2) High-luster finish applied to heat-sensitive nylon and rayon. Sometimes lined or quilted for warmth. Water-repellant, not waterproof. Uses: raincoats and jackets.

cisele velvet (1) Pile fabric with cut and uncut loops. (2) Satin fabric with velvet pattern.

clear finish Finish on wool fabrics such as gabardine and serge to remove nap and fuzz, making the weave easy to see. Fabrics hold creases well, but shine with wear.

clipped lace See appliqué lace.

cloque Lightweight, woven fabric with a blistered surface. Soft and drapeable. Made in silk, rayon, and polyester. Uses: dresses, blouses, and evening wear.

cloth Material made with yarns by weaving, knitting, or braiding or by felting fibers with heat, pressure, and moisture.

Cluny lace Coarse, open lace. Uses: casual blouses, dresses, and curtains.

coated fabric Any fabric coated with a film to make it waterproof or longer wearing.

coating Fabric suitable for making coats.

colorfast Color which will not wash out, rub off, or fade in normal use.

combed cotton Fine fabrics such as organdy, lawn, percale, and batiste, made with long cotton fibers which remain after combing.

combing Process to remove short fiber lengths from cotton and man-made yarns after carding.

comfort stretch Fabrics with less than 30 percent stretch; suitable for everyday wear.

companion fabrics Manufacturer's collection of two or more fabrics designed to be used together.

continuous filament Uncut filament of silk or man-made fiber.

corded fabric Fabric with a noticeable rib. Cross-rib fabrics include bengaline, grosgrain, faille, ottoman, and poplin. Warp cords include piqué and Bedford cord.

Cordura® DuPont trademark for bulked filament nylon. Stronger and more resistant to abrasion than cotton, canvas, and vinyl. It dries quickly and is not affected by rot or mildew. Uses: luggage and outdoor wear.

corduroy Rugged pile fabric made in cotton or a cotton blend with a plain or twill weave. Called "cord of the king" and first worn by the outdoor servants of the French monarchy, the pile, formed by an extra set of filling yarns, usually forms wales or vertical ribs. Fabric weight, drape, and stiffness vary with the size of the wales, which range from very fine to thick and heavy, or 5 to 21 cords per inch. Uses: children's garments, coats, dresses, shirts, and sportswear.

cotton (1) Soft, absorbent fiber obtained from the seed pod of the cotton plant. American Peeler, American Pima, and Peruvian cottons have the longest fibers and make the finest, most lustrous fabrics. SXP has a slightly shorter fiber, but greater strength, Egyptian cotton is also frequently used for thread. Indian and Chinese cotton have short, wiry fibers. Cotton is frequently blended with other fibers. (2) Used to make bark cloth, batiste, Bedford cord, bengaline, cotton broadcloth and brocade, calico, cambric, canvas, challis, chambray, cheesecloth, chino, chintz, covert, crepe, damask, denim, dimity, dotted swiss, drill, duck, eyelet, cotton flannel, gabardine, gingham, homespun, hopsacking, lawn, madras, monk's cloth, muslin, net, organdy, oxford cloth, percale, piqué, plissé, polished cotton, poplin, sailcloth, sateen, seersucker, cotton suede fabric, ticking, voile.

cotton linters Short cotton fibers used to make rayon, acetate, and cotton wadding.

count of cloth In a woven fabric, the number of picks and ends in a square inch; in a knit, the number of wales and courses.

course One row of stitches across knitted fabric. Corresponds to crossgrain or filling in woven fabrics. Easy to see on the back of single knits.

covert Rugged, medium-weight fabric with a twill weave of highly twisted yarns. Originally made from wool or worsted, now manufactured of man-made fibers and blends. Usually two shades of a color are twisted together, creating a speckled effect. Naturally water-repellant. Uses: riding wear, rainwear, coats, and suits.

476

cowhide Smooth-grained leather in all weights.

cowhide splits Soft, sueded splits.

crash Coarse, rough-textured fabric in plain or twill weaves. May be linen, cotton, rayon, or wool. Uses: suits and sportswear.

crepe Light- to heavyweight fabric with a dull, crinkled surface. Made in silk, rayon, cotton, wool, synthetics, or blends. Crinkled surface is made by using hard-twist yarns, a crepe weave, chemicals, or embossing. Most crepes are woven; a few are knitted. Lightweight crepes include charmeuse and georgette; medium-weights, flat crepe and crepe de chine; heavier weights, four-ply, canton, marocain, satin, satin-back.

crepe-backed satin Reversible fabric with a satin-weave face and a crepe back in silk, rayon, or polyester. Sometimes called satin-backed crepe. Uses: dresses, blouses, linings, evening wear, and lingerie.

crepe charmeuse Smooth, light- to medium-weight crepe with a dull luster and slight stiffness. Drapes and clings gracefully. May be silk or polyester. Uses: dresses, evening wear, expensive linings, and blouses.

crepe de chine Fine, light- to medium-weight with crepe yarns used in the warp and filling. Term means silk from China; today the fabric may be polyester, nylon, acetate, or viscose. Uses: blouses, shirts, dresses, and lingerie.

crepon Heavy crepe with lengthwise crinkles.

crimp Waviness in the fiber. Adds bulk and warmth to the fabric and increases resiliency, absorbency, and resistance to abrasion. Natural in wool; sometimes added to man-made yarns.

crinkle crepe See plissé.

crinoline Stiff, open-weave fabric with a heavy sizing. Uses: petticoats and interfacings.

crochet knit Open-work knit made on a raschel knitting machine; has little or no strength. Usually acrylic. Uses: sweaters, tops, and dresses.

crocking Process of surface dye rubbing off onto the skin or other fabrics. Indigo dyes crock badly.

crocodile Expensive leather similar to alligator.

cross-dyeing Piece dyeing fabrics with different fibers and affinities for the dyestuff, to create different shades and heathers.

crush resistance Finish applied to pile fabrics to improve ability to spring back after crushing.

cuprammonium rayon Soft, silky rayon fiber. Frequently called Bemberg.

cupro Same as cuprammonium rayon.

cut Sample piece of fabric in a particular pattern or color to make one or more sample garments.

cut-pile Pile fabrics like corduroy and velvet made by forming extra loops on the surface, which are then cut to form the pile.

cut velvet (1) Any velvet with cut loops. (2) Brocade pattern on sheer fabric. Drapes well. Uses: evening wear, women's apparel. Sometimes called beaded velvet.

D

Dacron Trademark for polyester fiber produced by DuPont. Resists stretching, abrasion, and wrinkles. Launders well and dries quickly.

dacating Process for shrinking fabrics. Sometimes called decatizing.

damask Reversible fabric made on a jacquard loom. Features elaborate designs woven in cotton, linen, wool, worsted, silk, rayon, or man-made yarns. Usually has the same color warp and filling. Flatter than brocade, it is sometimes woven with gold or silver patterns. One of the oldest fabrics.

darned lace Design on netting.

deep pile See fake-fur fabrics.

deerskin Grain or skin edge of deer leather.

deerskin splits Sueded on both sides, these splits are soft, lightweight, and washable. Similar to chamois, but stronger.

delustering See pigmenting.

denim (1) Densely woven twill fabric with colored warp, usually indigo blue, and a white filling. First made in Nîmes, France. May have vertical stripes. Medium- to heavyweight, strong and hard wearing, stiff when new. Softens with wear, shrinks, and fades badly. Usually all cotton or a cotton blend. Uses: casual wear, jeans, suits, coats, and jackets. (2) Knitted or woven fabrics made in a variety of fibers which look like denim.

design Weave design on graph paper. The marked or black squares show the warp yarns.

diagonal weave Twill weave running from left or right on the face of the material. Most run from the upper right-hand corner to the lower left at a 45 degree angle. Steep twills may be 63, 70, or 75 degrees.

dimity   Lightweight, sheer fabric woven with multi-ply yarns to create fine, woven stripes or checks. Originally all cotton, today many are synthetics. Uses: blouses, dresses, children's and infant's wear.

direct printing   Method of printing directly onto the fabric which is usually white. Sometimes called application, commercial, roller, calender, or cylinder printing.

discharge printing   Method of printing which removes some of the dye in background, while leaving a white design. A colored design may be overprinted.

dishrag   Open-weave raschel knit used for dishrags and casual design. Sometimes called athletic mesh or fishnet. Uses: casual tops, athletic wear, and children's wear.

dobby   Fabric woven on a dobby loom with small dots, or a geometric or floral pattern. Made in cotton, rayon, silk, or man-made fibers. Uses: shirtings, diapers, and dresses.

doeskin   (1) Skin of white sheep; originally skin of deer. (2) Soft, slightly napped wool broadcloth. Uses: trousers and riding habits.

domette   British name for lamb's wool interlining fabric. Sometimes called llama wool or French wool. Uses: shoulder pads, sleeve heads, and underlinings.

Donegal tweed   Rough herringbone tweed with slubs. Originally made in Donegal County, Ireland.

dope dyeing   See solution dyeing.

dotted swiss   Sheer, crisp cotton with woven dots made by a lappet weave. Wears and launders well. Imitation dotted swiss has flocked or printed dots. Uses: blouses, dresses, nightgowns, wedding dresses, and children's garments.

double cloth   (1) Reversible fabric which can be used on either side. The two faces may differ in weave, color, yarns and/or pattern. Heavier weight fabrics with firm weave. Double-cloth fabrics, which cannot be separated without damaging the two layers, are woven with two warp sets and one filling set, one warp set and two filling sets, or two filling sets and two warp sets. (2) A reversible fabric that can be separated, woven with two filling sets and two warp sets with a fifth set of yarns which interlaces between the two. The face and reverse can have two different patterns or colors. The fabric can be sep-arated into two distinct layers by clipping the interlacing yarn. Varies in weight and crispness. Uses: coats and sportswear. (3) Two fabrics, with two separate sets of warps and fillings, which are woven together with an interlacing pile which is cut after weaving, such as velvet.

double-faced fabric   (1) Reversible fabric woven with two sets of fillings and two sets of warps. Face and reverse can have two different patterns, same colors. Cannot be separated into two distinct layers by clipping the binding yarns. Varies in weight and firmness. (2) Two fabric layers fused together to make a double-faced fabric. Uses: unlined coats and jackets, skirts, and trousers, depending on weight. (3) Single/ply fabrics which have no wrong side.

double-knit   Medium to heavy fabric, knitted on a machine with two sets of needles, so both sides look the same when there is no pattern. Fabric has little or no stretch and holds its shape well. Sometimes called double jersey. Uses: jackets, dresses, and trousers.

douppioni   (1) Uneven, irregular yarn with slubs. Originally made of silk thread from two cocoons which had nested together; synthetic fibers are also used today. Used to make douppioni, pongee, nankeen, and shantung fabrics. (2) Firm, plain-weave fabric made with douppioni yarn. Ravels badly. Uses: suits and dresses.

down   Softest, fluffiest, and shortest feathers of ducks and geese. Uses: insulation and pillows.

down-proof   Closely woven fabric which doesn't allow down to escape.

draft   Pattern for weaving.

drape   The way a fabric hangs when arranged in different positions.

drill   Durable, tightly woven, twill-weave cotton. Uses: work clothes, trouser pockets, pillow ticking, and press cloths.

drip-dry   Garments which, when hung to dry while dripping wet, dry with little wrinkling.

duchesse satin   Heavy, very lustrous silk satin with a plain back. Uses: formal wear and wedding gowns.

duck   Closely woven material similar to canvas, but heavier and more durable. Uses: trousers and sails.

dungaree   Heavy cotton with colored warp and filling, similar to denim. Originally made in India. Term frequently used to describe blue jeans or denim trousers.

duplex printing Process for printing both sides of a fabric simultaneously. Designs may be the same or different. Sometimes called register printing.

duvetyne or **duvetyn** Soft, medium-weight fabric with a velvety nap. Satin weave. Drapes and wears well; spots easily. Cotton duvetyn is sometimes called cotton suede. Uses: women's garments, hats, and military uniforms.

D.W.R A durable, water-repellent coating which will wash out in six to eight launderings.

dyed-in-the-wool Process of dyeing wool fibers before they are spun into yarn.

dyeing Process of adding color to a fiber, yarn, or fabric.

Dynel Trademark of Union Carbide for a modacrylic fiber which is strong, warm, quick-drying, and noncombustible. Used for fake furs.

E

Egyptian cotton High-quality, plain-weave cotton grown in the Nile valley, known for its long staple. Soft, but strong and hard wearing; dyes well. Uses: blouses, shirts, dresses, lingerie, and baby dresses.

elastic Cord or fabric with stretch and recovery. Made of latex, spandex, or cut rubber.

elk Soft, supple leather with a coarse grain; similar to deer but more bulky.

embossed fabric Any fabric with a relief pattern which has been pressed into it by passing it between heated rollers. Usually permanent. Used on crepe, satin, and velvet.

embroidered fabric Any fabric embellished with hand- or machine-made embroidery. The embroidery may be an allover or border design.

end (1) Warp yarn running lengthwise in cloth. (2) Fabric remnant.

end and end Weave with two colors alternating in the warp. Use: shirtings.

Entrant Tradename for a nonstretch fabric with a polyurethane coating. Used primarily for ski-wear, it is more waterproof than water-repellent. It's very flexible, tough and has a good hand and drape. It can be washed or dry-cleaned.

entredeux Narrow insertion meaning "between the two."

ermine Thick, lustrous fur from a weasel. Doesn't wear well. Winter coat is white; summer coat, golden brown. Use: evening wear.

etched-out See burn-out.

even twill See balanced twill.

extract printing See discharge printing.

eyelash Reversible fabric with clipped yarns on the fabric surface. Looks like eyelashes. Uses: blouses, dresses, children's wear.

eyelet (1) Fabric with embroidered, open-work pattern. Holes in the open-work design are punched first; then reinforced with machine-made embroidery. Usually white on white, but the embroidery or fabric may be colored. Widths vary from very narrow to 45″; many have one scalloped or finished edge. (2) The holes in knitted materials. (3) The holes in casings for ties.

F

fabric Any woven, knitted, braided, felted, or nonwoven material. Frequently called cloth or material.

fabric weight Weight of fabric according to the number of yarns per inch, size of yarns, and fiber types. Can be measured in square yards, linear yards, or number of yards per pound. Affects the hand and drape of garments.

face The side intended to be the "right" side of the fabric.

Facile Trade name of Skinner Co. for synthetic suede.

faconné (1) Fancy-weave fabric, like a jacquard. (2) Fabric, such as sculptured velvet, which is made of two fibers with different characteristics and is printed with a chemical which eats away one, leaving the other.

faille Cross-rib fabric with flat ribs, made of silk, cotton, wool, or man-made yarns. The ribs, created by thicker yarns in the filling, may be the same or different sizes. A dressy fabric, similar to grosgrain. Uses: coats, jackets, and dresses.

faille crepe Cross-rib fabric with a satin back. A smoother, duller, and heavier fabric than crepe de chine. May be silk or synthetic.

fake-fur fabric Deep pile fabrics woven or knitted to simulate real furs. Usually made of modacrylic, which is flame-resistant, or nylon fibers with a knit backing.

fancy Any fabric that isn't plain.

479

fashion fabric   Term used to describe the most visible fabric used in apparel.

fatigue factor   Loss of ability of stretch yarns to recover after stretching.

felt   Fabric sheeting produced by pounding and felting wet fibers together. Wool, fur, and mohair make the best quality felt; most are made of man-made fibers. Uses: sportswear and casual designs.

felted fabric   Woven or knitted fabric which has been shrunk to produce a felted finish. Boiled wool and wadmal are felted fabrics.

fiber   The smallest unit in all fabrics. An individual strand with a definite length before it is made into yarn—e.g., Sea Island cotton fibers are about 1-5/8" long.

fiber dyeing   Process for dyeing fibers before spinning them into yarns.

fiberfill   Fluffy batting material, usually polyester, for quilting, padding, and shoulder pads.

fibranne   French term for viscose rayon.

filament   Individual fiber of an indefinite length, before it is made into yarn. Silk, the only natural filament, can be 300 to 1,800 yards long, while a synthetic filament can run several miles.

filament fabric   Smooth fabric made of filament yarns. May be transparent or opaque, light- or medium-weight. Chiffon, taffeta, satin, ninon, and silk organza are filament fabrics.

filling   Crossgrain yarns which interlace with the warp (lengthwise yarns). May be decorative; usually weaker than the warp, with less twist. Sometimes called pick, shoot, shute, weft, or woof.

filling-face twill   Twill-weave fabric with a predominance of filling yarns on the fabric face.

filling-face satin   Satin-weave fabric with a predominance of filling yarns on the fabric face. Used for sateens and heavily napped wools.

filling pile   Fabric such as corduroy with pile created by extra set of filling yarns.

filling stretch   See horizontal stretch.

findings   Supplementary materials used in garment making: buttons, snaps, zippers, and belts. Sometimes called notions or haberdashery.

finish   Treatments to make fabrics more attractive, such as embossing, felting, crinkling, flocking, and laminating, or processes which enable fabrics to perform better by wrinkling and shrinking less, resisting flames, or repelling water.

fireproof   Fabric which will not burn.

fire-resistant   Fabric treated to resist burning and retard spreading flames. Sometimes called fire-retardant.

flameproof   See fireproof.

flannel   (1) Plain, dull-surface wools and worsteds with a light nap. Plain or twill weave. Weight, texture, and price vary considerably. Uses: *lightweights,* dresses; *heavier weights,* suits, trousers, and uniforms. (2) Lightweight, napped cotton or man-made fibers. May be napped on one or both sides. Sometimes called flannelette, outing flannel, or interlining flannel. Uses: underwear, pajamas, and children's clothes.

flat crepe   Very smooth crepe with a flat warp and twisted filling; available in silk, rayon or man-made fibers. Uses: blouses and dresses.

flat knit   Fabric knitted on a flat machine instead of a circular one.

flax   A bask fiber from the flax plant, used to produce linen.

fleece   (1) Wool from live sheep. (2) Heavy wool with deep, soft nap on fabric face. Knitted or woven. Uses: jackets, coats, and skirts.

fleece-lined   Double-knit fabric with fleece on one or both sides. Used for sweatshirts.

fleeced   A napped surface, usually on the back side of knitted fabrics.

float   Portion of the filling or warp yarns which cross two or more of the opposite yarns to form the pattern.

flock   Small bits of fibers bonded to the fabric surface in dots or patterns. Usually permanent.

Fortisan   Strong, high-tenacity rayon fiber made by Celanese.

Fortuny fabrics   Permanently pleated silks used extensively by designer Mariano Fortuny. Simulated today in synthetic fabrics and widely used by Mary McFadden.

foulard   Lightweight, printed silk or man-made fabric woven in a plain or twill weave. Uses: blouses, dresses, robes, scarves, and ties.

four-ply silk   Silk crepe with four-ply yarns in the warp and filling. Uses: dresses and suits.

fox   Long-haired fur from several different foxes. Durability and price vary. Uses: jackets, coats, and trims. Look for thick underfur and silky guard hairs. Check for rips and tears.

french back   Worsted fabric with twill-weave back, usually in cotton to add weight, warmth, and stability.

fuji silk A lightweight, cream-colored, silk woven with spun yarns.

full grain The natural grain or texture on the side of the skin from which the hair is removed.

fulling Finishing process used on wools and wool blends to felt and shrink the yarns and make the fibers swell and thicken. Utilizes moisture, friction, and pressure to produce a soft, compact fabric. Used to make boiled wool.

fur Animal pelt tanned with the hair preserved.

fur fabrics Incorrect term, according to a Federal Trade Commission Ruling. See fake-fur fabrics.

fuse To melt with heat.

fusible fabric Fabric with a fusible backing which can be bonded to another fabric. Some interfacings are fusible fabrics. Any fabric can be made a fusible fabric by bonding a fusing agent to its back.

fusing agent Web of polyamide resins which melt when heated. Wonder Under, Jiffy Fuse, Stitch Witchery, Fine Fuse Fusible Web, Sav-a-Stitch, and TransFuse II are well-known brands.

G

gabardine Firm, hard-finished twill-weave fabric. May be wool, silk, cotton, man-made fibers, or combination. May have either a right- or left-hand twill. More threads in the warp than filling. Generally very durable, cheap fabrics slip at the seams. Uses: all types of apparel, depending on fiber content and weight.

galatea Rugged twill-weave cotton fabric. Uses: uniforms and children's garments.

galloon Lace finished with scallops or finished edge on both edges.

garment suede Lightweight, easy-to-sew lambskin suede.

gauge In knitting, measure for fabric fineness and number of needles per inch. The finer the fabric, the higher the gauge.

gauze Sheer, open-weave fabric. Usually cotton, silk, acetate, or rayon in a plain weave, sometimes a leno weave.

gauze weave Leno-weave variation in which the warp yarns twist around each other, forming a figure eight.

gazar Lightweight silk fabric woven with highly twisted yarns in a tight weave. Almost opaque. Use: evening wear.

georgette A soft, sheer crepe fabric made by alternating tightly twisted S- and Z-twist yarns in both the warp and filling. Usually silk or polyester. Uses: evening wear, blouses, dresses, and scarves.

gingham Plain-weave fabric using dyed yarns to form a striped or checked pattern. Usually cotton or a cotton/polyester blend. Varies in cost from very expensive to very inexpensive.

glazing Finish for cotton fabrics like chintz to give them a shiny finish. Glue, paraffin, and sizing may not be permanent; synthetic resins are.

glen plaid A small plaid woven over a large plaid. Sometimes called a glen check.

glissade Cotton-lining fabric with a satin weave.

Glore-Valcana Trade name for a synthetic suede fabric.

goatskin Strong, durable, soft skin. Use: lacings.

Gore-Tex Trade name for a filmlike material sandwiched between breathable fabrics. It is engineered with nine billion pores in every square inch; these pores, which are too small for water to enter, allow perspiration to escape. It provides warmth and dryness without bulk or weight. Not readily available to home sewers, except by mail-order. Uses: parkas, fashion rainwear, spacesuits, and athletic wear.

grain The yarn directions on woven fabric. The lengthwise or straight grain follows the warp. The crossgrain or crosswise grain follows the filling. Off-grain describes the fabric when the filling is not at right angles to the warp. It cannot be corrected if the fabric has a permanent-press finish.

granada Fine worsted with cotton warp and mohair or alpaca filling.

grass bleaching Process of bleaching cotton and linen by spreading the fabric outdoors, on the grass, to bleach in the sun.

gray goods Fabrics which have been knitted or woven but not finished—napped, pressed, printed, dyed, tentered, embossed, bleached, waterproofed, or mercerized. Same as gray, greige, and greige goods.

grisaille French term meaning gray. Gray-looking fabric made with black and white yarns in the warp and filling.

gros de Londres Cross-rib fabric. Use: dresses.

grosgrain Rugged, cross-rib fabric. Uses: ribbons and stiffening.

ground The background of the fabric design; the basic part of the fabric.

guanaco Hair fiber from guanaco.

guipure Heavy lace, machine-made on a background fabric which is dissolved, leaving only the lace. Sometimes called chemical, burn-out, Venise, or Venice Lace.

gun-club checks Checked fabric woven with three colors of yarn.

H

habutai Soft, lightweight, ecru-colored silk woven in Japan. Heavier than China silk. Uses: dresses and jackets.

hair canvas Interfacing fabric made of wool, cotton, or rayon with goat- or horsehair woven into the filling.

hair fibers Fibers from animals other than sheep, i.e., mohair, camel, cashmere, alpaca, and angora rabbit.

hairsheep Skin from hair-, not wool-growing sheep.

hand The tactile quality of fabric. The feel of the fabric: crispness, firmness, drapeability, softness, elasticity, and resilience.

hand-blocked Technique for hand printing with wooden or metal blocks.

handkerchief linen Lightweight, plain-weave linen. Uses: blouses, dresses, lingerie, and baby dresses.

handwoven Fabric woven on a loom by hand. Frequently loosely woven with novelty filling.

hard finish Cotton, woolen, or worsted fabrics with no nap.

Harris tweed Trade name for a cloth made of virgin wool from the Highlands of Scotland, which is spun, dyed, and handwoven on Harris and the other Outer Hebrides Islands. Rough, heavy fabric. Use: tailored coats and suits.

heat-transfer printing Printing method for fine knits and lightweight fabrics. Heat and pressure are used to transfer designs from specially treated paper.

heathers Soft, muted colors made by blending different colored fibers into the yarn. Frequently used in tweeds and other sport fabrics.

Helanca Trade name for a Swiss stretch nylon fiber. Stretches 500 percent and is used for two-way stretch fabrics. Uses: leotards, swimwear, and maternity panels.

herringbone Broken twill-weave pattern which produces a chevron, striped effect. Named to denote its resemblance to the skeleton of the herring fish.

hides Skins of larger animals, such as cows.

high pile Fabric with pile longer than 1/8″.

himalaya Same as cotton shantung.

homespun Rough, plain-weave cloth which appears undyed. Originally spun and woven in the home.

Honan silk Pongee-type silk made from wild silkworms in the Honan region of China. Dyes uniformly.

honeycomb Reversible fabric with a geometric, raised weave resembling a honeycomb. Usually cotton or a cotton/polyester blend. Sometimes called waffle weave. Uses: thermal underwear, dresses for women and girls, collars, and cuffs.

hopsacking Loosely woven basket-weave wool or cotton. Uses: dresses and coats.

horizontal stretch Fabric with stretch only in the crossgrain.

horsehair Hair from the mane and tail of a horse. Used in hair canvas.

houndstooth check Broken-check wool fabric with a regular pattern.

hydrophilic fiber Fibers which absorb water, such as rayon, acetate, cotton, and wool.

hydrophobic fiber Fibers with low absorbency which repel water, such as nylon, acrylic, and polyester.

hymo Interfacing fabric made of mohair and linen.

I

illusion Any soft silk or nylon net or tulle. Very lightweight. Uses: veils and dresses.

imperial brocade Jacquard-weave fabric with gold or silver yarns.

indigo Blue dye that fades. Originally made from the indigo plant to dye denim.

insertion Lace, embroidery, or braid with two straight edges to be inserted between two fabric edges. Uses: blouses, lingerie, dresses, and children's garments.

interfacing Woven, nonwoven, or knit fabric made of cotton, wool, hair, man-made fibers or blends. Used to reinforce, to add body or support, or to stiffen the garment.

interlining Lightweight fabric layer placed between the outer fabric and lining for warmth. May be napped, wool, cotton, or polyester fiberfill.

interlock knits Closely knit fabric which looks the same on both sides. Made of cotton and man-made fibers, it wears and launders well, but runs from one end. Uses: underwear, shirts, and casual dresses.

iridescent Fabric woven with different colors in the warp and filling which changes color when the fabric is moved; same as shot and changeable.

Irish linen Fine, lightweight linen made from Irish flax and woven in Ireland. Used for handkerchiefs, collars, blouses, and dresses.

Irish tweed Tweeds from Ireland, usually a twill weave with a white warp and dark filling.

J

jacquard Reversible tapestry design produced on a jacquard loom. Colors and pattern are reversed on fabric back. Used for all major fibers.

jacquard loom Loom which utilizes plain, twill, and/or satin weaves to create intricate designs. Used to make brocade, damask, tapestry, matelassé, and jacquard fabrics.

jean (1) Sturdy fabric similar to denim. (2) Used to describe pants made from denim.

jersey Cool, lightweight, plain-knit fabric with plain ribs on the face and purl wales on the back. Made in a variety of fibers, may be 100 percent wool, cotton, silk, man-made fibers, or a blend. Good elasticity, drapes well, comfortable to wear, snags and runs. Uses: children's garments, underwear, sportswear, blouses, and dresses.

K

kasha Soft wool fabric with a slight nap made from Tibetan goat hair. Usually has a crosswise streak caused by the darker hairs. Uses: dresses and jackets.

karakul See astrakhan cloth.

Kashmir See cashmere.

kersey A face-finished cloth with a short, lustrous nap. Compared to melton, it is heavier and more lustrous.

khaki Fabric color. Hindu word meaning dusty.

kip Skins of medium-sized animals.

K-Kote finish A waterproof polyurethane coating applied in a single layer, trade name of Kenyon Industries. Called Super K-Kote when applied in a double layer, it is heavier, will withstand more water pressure, and wear longer than the regular K-Kote.

Kodel Trade name of Eastman Kodak Co. for polyester fiber that resists pilling.

L

lace Open-work, decorative fabric usually made with a netting background. May be knitted or woven and made by hand or machine. It is available in a variety of widths and can be made of cotton, nylon, polyester, silk, or rayon. Uses: bridal gowns, formal dresses, dresses, lingerie, nightgowns, and infant's garments. The most common types include: Alençon, allover, antique, Battenberg, beading, Chantilly, Cluny, guipure, Valenciennes, and Venise lace.

lambskin Soft, lightweight leather with a silky feel. It is frequently embossed or tooled.

lambskin suede A lightweight, easy-to-sew suede. Sometimes called garment suede.

lamb's wool Very soft wool taken from the first clipping, before lambs reach seven months. Used for interlinings, sleeve heads, and batting.

lamé Any woven or knitted fabric with metallic yarns in the warp, filling, or both. Lightweight and drapeable. Uses: dresses, blouses, and evening wear.

laminated fabric Fabric made by fusing two layers of fabric, film to fabric, simulated leather to fabric, simulated fabric to foam, or fabric to foam.

Lamous II Trade name of Asahi Chemical Industry Co., Ltd. for nonwoven, man-made suede.

lappet weave Utilizes extra set of warp yarns to create a pattern at fixed intervals. Resembles embroidery. Sometimes used to make dotted swiss effects.

latex Liquid rubber, natural or synthetic.

lawn Fine, crisp cotton or linen fabric with a plain weave. More closely woven and stiffer than batiste and lighter than cambric. Uses: baby dresses, blouses, collars, and cuffs.

leather Animal hide without fur.

leno Loosely woven, but firm, open-weave fabric. Uses: shirtings and novelty suitings.

leno weave Made on a leno loom. The warp yarns are paired; and while one warp is positioned like the warp on a plain weave, the other passes to its opposite side. At the same time, the second warp alternates over and under the filling. The term "leno" is used interchangeably with gauze, but they are not exactly the same.

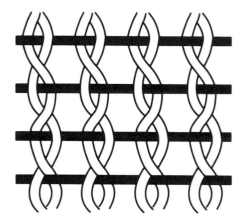

Fig. 26–1

leopard Buff-colored fur with black markings. It is illegal to sell leopard skins, even second-hand.

Liberty prints Muted-print fabrics produced by Liberty Ltd., London. Usually on lawn, silk, wool, challis, or a wool/cotton blend. Uses: shirtings and dresses.

Light Spirit Blend Trademark of DuPont for type 720W polyester. Fifty percent more breathable than cotton, it wicks well and dries quickly.

linen Fabric made from the flax plant. Strong, lustrous, and very absorbent. Plain or damask weave, it is available in various weights from fine, sheer, handkerchief linen to heavy suitings. Uses: dresses, suits, pants, lightweight coats, and handkerchiefs.

linen-look Any fabric made to look like linen. Usually firmly woven and slightly coarse in a plain weave.

lining fabric Firmly woven or knit fabric in a plain, twill, or satin weave. Usually slippery, yarns may be cotton, silk, man-made, or blends. Available in various weights, it is used to protect and hide seams, reduce wrinkling, prolong the garment's life, and improve its appearance.

linters Short cotton fibers used to make acetate and rayon.

Linton tweed Trade name of tweeds made by Linton Tweeds, Ltd., Carlisle, England. Very soft, nice hand, and variety of designs.

lizard A reptile skin.

llama Llama hair fiber. Uses: expensive coats and suits.

loden cloth Thick, soft fabric, usually dark green in color. Made from coarse, oily wool which naturally repels water. Originally woven by peasants in the Loderers, a mountainous district of Austria, during the sixteenth century. Use: coating.

London-shrunk Cold-water method of shrinking wool fabrics. Fabrics labeled London-shrunk do not need preshrinking.

loom Machine for weaving fabrics.

Lorette Brand name of Deering, Milliken & Co., for Orlon/wool (55/45) blend. Use: dresses.

Lurex Trademark of Dow Badische Co. for plastic-coated metallic yarn. Breaks easily, but does not tarnish.

Lustron Trademark for the first acetate (1916) fiber produced in United States.

Lycra Trademark of DuPont for spandex two-way stretch fiber with good strength; resists heat and perspiration.

lynx Long-haired fur from the wild cat. Expensive. Uses: coats, jackets, and trims.

Lyons velvet Stiff, short-piled velvet. Originally made with silk pile and cotton or rayon back. Today, usually synthetic and labelled Lyons-type.

M

macintosh Rubber-coated fabric named for inventor, Charles Macintosh. Originally used for raincoats, but rarely used today.

mackinac or mackinaw cloth Heavy, warm fabric with a natural water repellancy. Usually wool or acrylic plaid or check. Used for shirts and outerwear.

macramé Open-work fabric or trim formed by knotting. Technically, it is not a lace.

madras Originally imported from Madras, India. A soft, cotton fabric with a plaid, checked, or striped pattern. To be labeled madras, it must be dyed with vegetable dyes, which bleed when washed.

maline A diaphanous net.

man-made fiber Any fiber not provided by nature. The cellulosic fibers, which are made from cellulose, include rayon, acetate, and triacetate. The synthetics, which are manufactured from petroleum, natural gas, coal, alcohol, and limestone, are polyester, nylon, acrylic, modacrylic, spandex, anidex, metallic, and vinyon.

marocain A heavy, cross-rib crepe. Uses: dressmaker suits and dresses.

marquisette Lightweight, gauze fabric, made with a leno weave. Made from natural and man-made fibers. Uses: curtains and dresses.

marten Warm, soft, thick fur. Frequently available in resale stores, complete with head, eyes, and a mouth that clips. Uses: coats, jackets, and trims.

matelassé Blistered or quilted-effect fabric, made on a dobby or jacquard loom. Back has a fine, loosely woven web. Made in cotton, silk, wool, rayon, acetate, polyester, and blends. Uses: blouses, dresses, and suits.

material Same as fabric.

matte Dull surface finish.

matte jersey Dull jersey fabric knitted with crepe yarns; usually rayon.

medallions Same as motifs.

melton Nonlustrous, dense, plain-weave coating with a short nap. Very durable. Uses: coatings, suits, uniforms, pea jackets, and collar backs.

mercerized Finish to increase luster, strength, and affinity to dye. Applied to cotton and cotton/blend yarn or fabric.

merino Finest, softest wool available. From merino sheep.

messaline Very lightweight, lustrous, satin-weave silk. Use: evening wear.

mesh Open-work fabric. May be knitted or woven with natural and/or synthetic yarns. Used for a variety of garments from casual to formal wear.

metallic Any metal, plastic-coated metal, metal-coated fiber, or metal wrapped core.

metallic cloth Any fabric containing metal threads.

meter One meter is equal to 39.37 inches.

milanese knit Fine, lightweight knit fabric. Runproof.

Milium Trade name of Deering Milliken & Co., Inc., for an aluminum finish applied to the back of lining fabrics for added warmth.

mill ends Short lengths of fabric.

mink Warm, popular fur with a dark center back stripe, called the grotzen. Should have lustrous guard hairs and dense underfur. Redness is undesirable. Uses: coats, jackets, trims, linings, boas, hats, muffs, stoles, and capes.

mirror velvet Fabric with an uncut pile which is pressed flat.

mixture Same as blend.

modacrylic Modified acrylic, synthetic fiber. Soft, resilient, and quick drying. Very flame-retardant. Resistant to acids and alkalies. Trade names include Dynel, Elura, Verel, SEF, and Taslan. Uses: fake furs.

modified fibers Fibers modified to eliminate undesirable qualities or to add desirable characteristics.

mohair (1) Long, lustrous fibers from the Angora goat, stronger than wool. (2) Spongy, plain-weave fabric made in a mixture of mohair and wool. Uses: jackets, coats, shawls.

moiré A rippled, watermark pattern applied to fabrics like silk and acetate by calendering or printing. Usually permanent on acetate; may not be permanent on other fibers.

moiré taffeta Taffeta with moiré pattern. May be rayon, acetate, or silk. Moiré pattern may or may not be permanent.

momie weave Tight, irregular weave producing a rough, pebblelike surface. Sometimes called crepe or granite weave.

monk's cloth Coarse, basket-weave fabric in cotton or linen. Ravels badly.

monofilament Single thread of man-made fiber.

moreen Plain-woven worsted with a moiré finish.

Morocco Fine, long-wearing goatskin. It has a rich red hue.

moss crepe Rayon or polyester crepe with a mosslike surface.

motif Pattern or design.

mountain cloth   A nylon/cotton poplin with a durable water-repellant finish. Uses: skiwear, windbreakers, parkas, and rainwear.

mousseline or **mousseline de soie**   Sheer, lightweight, quality fabric with a crisp hand. French term meaning muslin. Originally made in silk, now made in a variety of fibers.

mouton   Fur from sheared sheep. Short to medium length, dense pile. Uses: jackets and trims.

muga silk   Fine, wild silk from India.

multifilament   Man-made yarn with several filaments twisted together.

muskrat   The "poor woman's mink." Dyed to look like many other furs.

muslin   Inexpensive, plain-weave fabric in cotton and cotton blends. Uses: sample garments and press cloths.

N

nacré velvet   Iridescent velvet with one color in the background and another color in the nap.

nainsook   Soft, fine, lightweight cotton in a plain weave. Slightly coarser than batiste, wears and launders well. Uses: blouses, lingerie, and infant's garments.

naked wool   Very light, sheer woolen.

nankeen   Same as shantung.

nappa leather   Sheep or goatskin tanned with oil.

nap   (1) Fuzzy fibers on the surface of a fabric, produced by brushing. (2) Pile and hair on fabrics which have a definite "up" and "down." (3) One-way design, with a definite top and bottom, printed on a fabric.

napa   Soft, thin leather used for fine garments. It may be skin or suede.

napped fabric   (1) Warm fuzzy fabric. Uses: coatings, casual clothes, suits, and linings. (2) Any fabric which must be cut with the pattern pieces in the same direction, including hair fibers, knits, piles, and printed fabrics with a one-way design.

napping   Finish used to raise fibers on one or both sides of a fabric by brushing with fine wires.

narrow goods   Fabric woven on looms no wider than 27".

Naugahyde   Vinyl resin-coated fabric made by U.S. Rubber Co.

needlepoint fabric   Novelty wool fabric.

needlepunch   Method of making fabrics by using needles to punch and entangle a web of fibers.

net   An open-weave, knotted fabric. Made in cotton, rayon, silk, polyester, and nylon. May be very sheer to very heavy. Uses: background of lace, evening gowns, bridal veils, and laundry bags.

ninon   Sheer, lightweight, plain-weave voile in rayon, acetate, nylon, or polyester. Uses: dresses and curtains.

noils   Short fibers left after combing and carding. Added to longer fibers to make yarn. Silk noils also add luster.

nonwoven fabric   Fabric, such as Ultrasuede and nonwoven interfacings, made from a web of fibers without knitting, weaving, or felting.

novelty yarns   Decorative yarns, such as slubbed, thick and thin, bouclé, and metallic, used to create structural designs.

nub   Same as a slub.

nun's veiling   Lightweight, sheer; silk and worsted. Uses: veils, blouses, and dresses.

nutria   Fur from a small animal similar to the beaver. Uses: linings and reversible garments.

nylon   (1) First synthetic fiber. Very strong, supple, lustrous, wrinkle-resistant, and easy to wash. Resists abrasion, oils, and many chemicals. Accepts dye readily. Low moisture absorbency. Used for blouses, dresses, lingerie and foundation garments, raincoats, skiwear, suits, and windbreakers. (2) Trade names include A.C.E., Anso, Antron, Blue "C," Cadon, Cantrece, Caprolan, Captiva, Celanese, Cerex, Cordura, Courtaulds Nylon, Cumuloft, Eloquent Luster, Eloquent Touch, Enkacrepe, Enkalon, Enkalure, Enkasheer, Lurelon, Multisheer, Natural Touch, Natural Luster, No Shock, Qiana, Shareen, Shimmereen, Softalon, T.E.N., Ultron, Zefran, Zeftron.

nylon Antron taffeta   A plain-weave fabric made with Antron nylon fibers. Available in varying thread counts and deniers, it is lightweight, water- and wind-repellent, quick drying, and easy-care. Compared to regular nylon taffetas, it has more sparkle. It can be machine washed and dried on low heat, or dry-cleaned.

nylon pack cloth   A lightweight water-repellent fabric with finer yarns in the warp than the filling. Uses: backpacks and suit bags.

nylon taffeta   A tightly woven, smooth, plain-weave fabric. Uses: jackets, windbreakers, rainwear, running suits, vests, and stuff sacks.

O

ocelot Similar to leopard. Also illegal to sell.

oilcloth Early waterproof fabric treated with linseed-oil varnish.

olefin Synthetic fiber made from polyethylene or polypropylene. Uses: Home furnishings, fashions.

opaque Fabric that you can't see through.

opossum Interesting fur from the opossum. Use: sport garments.

organdy Transparent, lightweight, plain-weave cotton cloth with a stiff finish which may or may not be permanent. Used for interfacing, dresses, evening gowns, infant's and little girl's designs.

organza Similar to organdy, but made in silk, rayon, or polyester. Usually not as crisp as organdy. Uses: blouses, dressy dresses, evening wear, little girl's dresses, facings, and interfacings.

Orlon Trade name of DuPont for acrylic fiber.

osnaberg Coarse cotton cloth.

ostrich Leather made from ostrich skin, which has a characteristic rosette or spiral marking made when the ostrich plumes are plucked. It is rarely available to home sewers.

otter Short, thick, lustrous brown fur. Very durable. Uses: jackets, coats, and trims.

ottoman Cross-rib fabric. Ribs can be small, medium, or large. Fabric weight varies with rib size. Uses: dresses, jackets, and coats.

ottoman cord Cross-rib fabric with ribs in several sizes.

outing Soft, cotton fabric with nap on the face and back. Usually lightweight. May be plain or twill weave. Sometimes called outing flannel. Uses: sleepwear, underlinings, and infant's wear.

overplaid Sometimes called double plaid.

overprint Print applied on top of a piece-dyed fabric or fabric which has already been printed.

oxford cloth Soft, basket-weave fabric made in cotton, man-made fibers, or a blend. Usually has a colored warp and white filling, but it may have the same color in both. Uses: shirtings, skirts, and sport dresses.

oxidation Exposure to air, which changes some dyes and weakens some fibers.

P

pailletes Large sequins with a single hole in the center. Usually plastic or metal. Uses: to embellish evening fabrics.

paisley Printed, elaborate scroll design. Originally used on fine wool shawls woven in Paisley, Scotland, to imitate the cone design woven on shawls from Kashmir. Uses: skirts, dresses, and shawls.

Palm Beach Expensive, lightweight, summer suiting. Originally cotton warp and mohair filling; today many fiber variations. Trademark of Palm Beach Company, Inc.

palmering Soft finish applied to rayon satins, taffetas, and lining twills.

panama Lightweight, plain-weave suiting with cotton warp and worsted filling. Cool and wrinkle-resistant. Usually a solid color. Uses: dresses and trousers.

panné velvet Soft, short-pile, high-luster velvet with the pile flattened in one direction. May be knitted or woven. Usually polyester or rayon. Comfortable to wear. Uses: evening wear and leisurewear.

paper fabric Nonwoven fabric, resembling paper. Uses: pattern making.

paper taffeta Lightweight, very crisp, plain-weave taffeta.

patchwork Design resembling early American patchwork quilts, in which small sections were joined to make a large piece. May be seamed, woven, or printed. Usually cotton or cotton/blend. Uses: casual garments.

patent leather Made by applying a solution to leather, which then becomes hard and shiny.

pattern (1) Design or motif which is woven, knitted, or printed on the fabric. (2) Printed paper guide for cutting out garments.

peasant lace Coarse Cluny lace. Uses: casual garments.

peau d'ange (1) Medium satin-weave fabric with a dull finish. Usually silk and heavier than peau de soie. Uses: evening wear and cocktail suits. (2) A type of Chantilly lace.

peau de soie French term meaning skin of silk. Medium-weight, satin-weave fabric with a dull finish. May be made of silk, polyester, or other man-made fibers. Uses: bridal gowns and formal dresses.

pebble Grainy, rough-surfaced fabric formed by two different methods: (1) highly twisted yarns that shrink when wet or (2) a special weave.

peccary leather Sheepskin made to look like pigskin.

pekin Stripes in the fabric length. Usually equal in width.

Pellon Trade name of Pellon Corp. for nonwoven interfacings.

pelt Another term for hide or skin.

percale Closely woven, plain-weave fabric with a smooth finish. Wears and launders well. May be cotton or cotton/blend. Uses: shirtings, sleepwear, and sheets.

permanent finishes Finishes applied to the fabric that will last a lifetime—i.e., glaze, stiffness, pleating, and permanent press.

permanent press Finish to retard wrinkling on fabrics which are machine washed and dried. Sometimes called durable press.

Persian lamb Soft, curly fur from young karakul lambs. Same as astrakhan.

petersham Narrow, ribbed belting, similar to grosgrain. Uses: stiffen belts and waistbands.

photographic print Method of printing using a photographic image.

pick glass Magnifying glass for counting the number of yarns in the warp and filling.

picks Filling yarns which run crosswise in woven fabrics.

picots Decorative loops along the fabric edge. Frequently found on lace and ribbon.

piece dyeing Dyeing finished fabric. Cross-dyeing is a form of piece dyeing.

piece goods Fabrics sold by the yard. Same as yardage, yard goods, and fashion fabrics.

pigment printing Method of printing with titanium to reduce luster.

pigmented taffeta Dull-surfaced taffeta made with delustered yarns, which are called pigmented.

pigskin Leather from the skin of pigs. Easily identified by its clusters of three small holes. May be smooth or napped.

pile fabric Knit or woven fabric with cut or uncut loops on one or both sides. Common pile fabrics include terry, corduroy, velvet, velveteen, and candlewick. Technically, not a napped fabric, but must be cut with a nap layout.

pile weave Weave utilizing an additional set of warp or filling yarns to create a pile. Corduroys and velveteens are made with an extra set of filling yarns; velvets and velours are made with an extra set of warp yarns. Both are cut. Terry has uncut loops on one or both sides.

pills Small fiber balls which appear with wear on the fabric surface. A frequent problem on woollens, polyesters, and acrylics, which can be reduced in the processing and finishing of the fabric.

pillow ticking Tightly woven cotton fabric used for making pillows. Sometimes used for jackets, leisurewear, and casual garments.

Pima cotton Fine, extra-long-staple cotton grown in America.

pin check Very small, checked pattern. May be woven or printed.

pin stripe Fabric with a very small stripe; may be woven or printed. Popular worsted pattern. Use: suits.

pinwale Very small wale or rib; usually found on corduroy.

piqué Light- to heavyweight cotton with a woven, raised design. Usually a lengthwise rib, but it may be another geometric pattern. Uses: shirtings, collars, cuffs, tennis wear, women's and children's wear.

plaid Woven or printed pattern of stripes crossing at right angles. Term originally described the cape worn by the Scottish Highlanders. Today it describes the fabric pattern.

plain knit Simple, flat-surfaced knit with vertical rows of plain ribs on the face, and horizontal rows of purl wales on the back. Looks like the hand-knit stockinette stitch.

plain weave Simplest, most frequently used weave, in which each filling yarn passes alternately over and under one warp yarn. Some plain-weave fabrics are crepes, shantung, organdy, taffeta, and flannel. Sometimes called tabby weave.

Fig. 26–2

plissé Lightweight cotton or cotton-blend fabric with blistered stripes or pattern. Usually created by printing the fabric with caustic soda. Uses: loungewear, nightgowns, summer dresses and blouses.

plonge Leather from Japanese cows fed on a beer diet. Moderately priced, with few imperfections, it drapes and feels like expensive luxury leathers.

plush Compact, deep-pile fabric made in silk, cotton, wool, and combinations. Uses: coats, casual designs, and robes.

ply Number of individual threads twisted together to make yarn.

point d'esprit Net with rectangular dots positioned at regular intervals.

pointed twill Same as herringbone.

polished cotton Plain-weave cotton with a permanently glazed finish; usually has less sheen than chintz.

polka dots Woven, knit, or printed circular design repeated at regular intervals. Dots range in size from pin dots to very large.

polyester (1) Versatile synthetic fiber. Very strong and resistant to wrinkles, shrinkage, moths, mildew, and abrasion. Retains heat-set pleats and creases. Pills and attracts lint. Many polyesters don't breathe, making them clammy in winter and hot in summer. Uses: blouses, shirts, children's wear, dresses, suits, sportswear, lingerie, and slacks. (2) Trade names include A.C.E., Avlin, Caprolan, Crepesoft, Dacron, Encron, Fortrel, Golden Glow, Golden Touch, Hollofil, Kodaire, Kodel, Kodofill, Kodolite, Kodosoff, Lethasuede, Matte Touch, Natural Touch, Ply-

loc, Polyextra, Shanton, Silky Touch, Strialine, Terylene, Trevira, Ultraglow, and Ultra Touch.

polynosic rayon Process for making rayon, making it stronger when wet or dry, as well as less likely to shrink or stretch when wet. Trademark of American Enka Corp.

polyurethane Synthetic fiber used in foam which is sometimes laminated to other fabrics. A component of Ultrasuede, spandex, and Genay.

pongee Lightweight, plain-weave fabric with a slight slub. May be silk or man-made. Uses: blouses and dresses.

poodle cloth Soft, bulky fabric with yarn loops on face, resembling poodle fur. Originally wool and mohair; today, may be man-made fibers. Uses: jackets, coats, and dresses.

poplin Fine cross-rib fabric. Lightweight, plain-weave fabric with the same size warp and filling yarns. Poor-quality fabrics slip at the seams. Originally silk warp and wool filling; today may be cotton, cotton/blend, silk, or man-made fibers. Uses: shirtings, sportswear, and dresses.

power stretch Fabrics with 30 percent to 50 percent stretch in one or both directions. Uses: skiwear, swimwear, leotards, tights, and foundation garments. Sometimes called action stretch or power net.

preshrunk Finishing process to reduce shrinkage in fabrics and garments.

printing Process for adding a solid or decorative pattern to fabric. Some printing methods are application, block, blotch, burn-out, direct, discharge, duplex, heat transfer, overprinting, photographic, resist, screen, shadow, stipple, and warp.

progressive shrinkage Shrinkage that continues to occur with repeated washing or cleaning.

puckered nylon Lightweight fabric produced by several different methods. One fabric, similar to seersucker, is woven with preshrunk and unshrunk yarns while another, similar to plissé, is printed with phenol.

purl knit Horizontal ridges on both sides of the fabric.

PVC Abbreviation for polyvinyl chloride, a waterproofing agent. Usually a plain fabric sprayed with PVC. Uses: aprons, raincoats, tote bags, and pillowcases.

python skin Snakeskin with a beautiful scale pattern.

Q

Qiana   Trade name of DuPont nylon.

qiviut or qiviet   Rare wool fiber from the domesticated musk ox.

quilted fabric   Fabric machine-quilted to a layer of padding. Usually has a backing added before quilting. The backing may be a thin nylon jersey, gauze, or an attractive contrasting fabric. Uses: robes, casual designs, children's wear, coats, vests, and belts.

quilting   Multiple rows of decorative stitching through more than one layer of fabric. May be hand- or machine-made.

R

rabbit   Popular, inexpensive fur for children's wear. Sheds and is not very durable.

rabbit hair   Soft, lustrous fiber from rabbits; blended with wool and other fibers.

raccoon   Long-haired, warm fur used primarily for trims, linings, jackets and coats.

rajah   May be silk or synthetic. See shantung.

ramie   Lustrous, bast fiber similar to flax, but more brittle. Mixed with other fibers. Same as China grass.

raschel knit   Warp knit made on the versatile raschel knit machine. Variety of designs, lace, netting, and open-work. Stretch varies from minimal to maximal.

ratiné   Bulky coating with a rough, fuzzy surface. Sometimes called éponge, frisé, or sponge cloth.

ravel   Tendency of fabric to fray at cut edges. Same as unravel.

raw silk   (1) Silk fiber as it comes from the cocoon before processing. (2) Frequently, but incorrectly, used to describe wild silk, a dull silk with a rough texture.

rayon   (1) First man-made fiber, made from regenerated cellulose. Soft and comfortable to wear, weaker when wet. Leaves a soft, gray ash when burned. In the United Kingdom, the term rayon has been replaced by viscose. (2) Trade names include Avril, Avsorb, Beau-Grip, Bemberg, Coloray, Courtaulds Rayon, Cortaulds HT Rayon, Courcel, Durvil, Enkaire, Enkrome, Fibro, Fortisan, Jetspun, Polynosic, and Zantrel.

recovery   Ability to return to original shape after stretching.

recycled wool   Used after 1980 to replace the terms reprocessed and reused wool.

reeled silk   "Raw" silk with only a slight twist, made by winding filament directly from several cocoons.

re-embroidered lace   Lace with design embroidered on the surface. Embroidery may be with cording, ribbon, sequins, or beads.

register printing   Same as duplex printing.

remnants   Ends of fabric originally sold by the yard.

rep or repp   Medium- to heavyweight, cross-rib fabric. Similar to faille.

repeat   A complete pattern which is repeated at regular intervals on the fabric. May be printed, woven, or knit. Size varies from a fraction of an inch to several feet.

reprocessed wool   Term used before 1980 for fabric made from wool scraps, samples, and mill ends which have not been worn.

reptile skins   Small skins from snakes and reptiles.

residual shrinkage   Amount of shrinkage remaining after shrinking process.

resiliency   Natural property of wool and silk to spring back when crushed.

resin finish   Finish on cottons to produce different textures—glazing, embossing, and pleating—or to improve resistance to soil, water, and wrinkling.

resist printing   Method of printing in which a substance that resists color is applied before the fabric is dyed. This prevents the dye from penetrating the fabric. After dyeing, the resist is removed. Resist printing, tie dyeing and batik are forms of resist dyeing.

reused wool   Term used before 1980 for fabric made from a mixture of old rags, clothing, and new wool. Now called recycled wool. Used in inexpensive ready-made garments.

reverse knit   Back side of a plain knit used as the right side.

reversible fabric   Fabric which can be used with either side as the face. Easy-to-identify reversibles include double-faced, jacquard, damask, knit ribbing, antique satin, and crepe-backed satin. Uses: coats, capes, and wrap skirts.

reversible twill   Twill running from upper right to lower left.

rib (1) Raised cord formed in the weaving. Can be horizontal, vertical, or diagonal. (2) Ridged, vertical design or wale on knit fabric.

rib cloth Fabric with a rib in either the warp or filling, including corduroy, poplin, ottoman, rep, Bedford cord, and grosgrain.

rib knit Same as ribbing.

rib weave Variation of plain weave with larger yarns in the warp or filling.

ribbing Reversible fabric with alternating rows of ribs and wales. Very elastic. Uses: cuffs, waistbands, and neckline finishes.

ribbon Narrow fabric used as a trim.

ribbon-embroidered lace Lace with narrow ribbon applied to the face in an elaborate pattern.

richelieu An open-work embroidery.

ripstop Fabric designed to prevent rips and tears from spreading. Uses: windbreakers, lightweight outerwear, tote bags.

ripple cloth Coarse woollen fabric finished to form ripples.

Robia Trade name of Tootal for cotton voile fabrics.

roller printing Method of printing with cylindrical rollers. Same as direct printing.

romaine Lightweight, plain-weave silk or rayon fabric with a dull luster and crepe texture.

Roman stripe Narrow, vertically striped fabric. May be reversible.

rough Lightweight linen. Use: underline suits.

rubber Fiber made of natural or synthetic rubber, including Lastex, Lactron, Revere, Darleen.

running yard One yard of cloth in any width.

rustle Crunching noise made by taffeta. Sometimes called scroop.

S

S-twist Left-hand twist of yarns so they look like the middle of the letter "S."

sable Luxurious, dark brown fur. Uses: coats, jackets and trims.

sailcloth Very strong, firmly woven canvas made of cotton, linen, or nylon.

Salisbury White English wool flannel.

salt and pepper Term used to describe tweed fabric with black and white yarns.

Sanforize Trade name of Cluett, Peabody and Company for preshrinking treatment to reduce residual shrinkage to less than 1 percent.

sari Rectangular piece of fabric 45″ wide and six yards long worn by Hindu women. May be woven of cotton, silk, or man-made fibers with a woven or embroidered border on one end and along one long edge. Worn by Indian women, it is wrapped around the waist, then thrown over the shoulder.

Sarille Rayon fiber, trade name of Courtaulds.

sateen Firmly woven, satin-weave cotton. May have filling floats which are made by passing over several warp yarns, then under one warp. Uses: dresses, underlinings, and linings.

satin Firmly woven, satin-weave fabric with a very smooth face. Made of silk, rayon, acetate, nylon, and polyester. May be light or heavy, sometimes slippery. Uses: evening wear, bridal gowns, dresses, and linings.

satin back Reversible fabric with satin-weave back and dull-finished face.

satin-backed crepe Same as crepe-backed satin.

satin crepe Soft, lustrous, satin-weave fabric. Uses: dresses, formal wear, negligees, lingerie.

satin weave One of three basic weaves. Weave with long warp floats, which produce a very smooth, lustrous surface. Usually made by passing filling yarns under several warp yarns, then over one warp. When used to make sateen, the filling yarns usually pass over several warps, then under one.

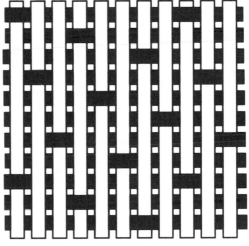

Fig. 26–3

Savina DPR A polyester/nylon blend which is woven 66″ wide, then shrunk to 48″. Almost waterproof and wind-repellent, it has no coating and breathes. It is softer, more lustrous, and more drapeable than densely woven polyester/nylon blends. It is used for running wear, bicycle wear, fashion rainwear, and outerwear.

Saxony Heavy, fine-quality woollen with a plain weave. Originally made in Saxony, Germany, and similar to flannel.

schiffli embroidery Machine-made embroidery which duplicates a wide variety of hand-embroidered stitches.

Scotchgard Colorless finish used for soil and water repellency.

screen printing Printing method utilizing screen(s) of silk or nylon gauze. All areas of the screen, except the design to be printed, are coated with a nonporous substance. With the screen set on the fabric, the dye is forced through the uncoated areas to print the fabric below. Each color requires a different screen.

scroop Same as rustle.

scrubbed Same as brushed.

sculptured velvet Patterned velvet with high and low pile.

Sea Island cotton Lustrous, high-quality cotton.

seal Warm, sheared fur, always dyed. Very unpopular because of unfavorable publicity about the hunting of the Newfoundland harp seal, which was never used by the American fur industry. Uses: jackets and coats.

seam slippage Fabric pulling away at the seams.

seersucker Durable, firmly woven fabric with puckered stripes alternating with flat ones. Created by alternating groups of tight warp yarns with groups of loose ones. May be woven in cotton, man-made fibers, or blends. Available in plain colors, stripes, and plaids. Launders well, usually with no ironing. Not the same as plissé. Uses: casual clothes, children's garments, and loungewear.

selvage Long, woven edge on each side of the fabric which does not ravel. Frequently different from the body of the cloth. Sometimes called self-edge or selvedge.

serge Smooth, twill-weave fabric, made of wool, worsted, or blends. Durable. Tailors and drapes well. Holds creases, but shines with wear. Originally made of silk. Uses: suits and trousers.

sericin Natural gum in silk.

shadow printing See warp printing.

shadow stripes Subtle stripes created by weaving the stripes with the same-color yarn with a different twist, weave, or with blended yarns slightly lighter or darker.

shantung Plain-weave fabric with irregular yarns and slubs in the filling. May be dull or lustrous. Originally only silk, now made in all major fibers and blends. Sometimes called nankeen, rajah, or tussah. Uses: blouses, dresses, suits, and slacks.

sharkskin (1) Fine quality worsted in fancy weaves that frequently resembles skin of a shark. Wool sharkskin wears well. Use: suits. (2) Medium- to heavyweight fabric with a sheen. Usually acetate or triacetate and white in color. Uses: tennis dresses and skirts with permanent pleats.

shearing (1) Method of removing the wool from the animal. (2) Trimming the fabric pile as needed to the desired height.

shearling Sheep or goat skin with wool left on. Reversible material used for coats and jackets. Very bulky. Same as sheepskin and sherpa.

sheepskin Suede from sheep which grow hair, not wool. Sometimes called cabretta. See shearling.

sheepskin suede Suede similar to lambskin.

sheer (1) Lightweight fabric. (2) Transparent fabric woven in natural, man-made fibers, and blends. Weaves can be very tight or quite open.

sherpa Same as shearling.

sheeting Very wide, plain-weave fabric in plain colors and prints. Used for sheets, tablecloths, and linings.

shepherd's check Twill-weave, black and white fabric with a 1/4″ (6 mm) check. Made in wool, cotton, and man-made fibers. Sometimes called shepherd's plaid. Uses: coats, suits, capes, shawls, shirts, sportsclothes and children's garments.

Shetland wool Originally very soft, expensive woollens made only from yarn pulled from the undercoat of sheep raised on the Shetland Islands, Scotland. Now it includes soft woollens which look as if they were made from Shetland wool.

shirred fabrics Fabrics with elastic fullness along one edge. Usually cotton or cotton blends. Uses: casual skirts and sundresses.

shirting Lightweight, closely woven fabrics suitable for shirts and blouses. Sometimes called top-weight. Typical shirtings include oxford cloth, dimity, voile, batiste, end and end, handkerchief linen, Pima and Sea Island cottons, and silk broadcloth.

shirting suede A soft, chrome-tanned suede similar to deerskin.

shoddy (1) Fabric made from reprocessed wool or old rags. (2) Poor quality or poorly made fabric.

shoot Same as filling.

shot Same as changeable and iridescent.

shrinkage control Treatment to minimize shrinkage in the finished fabric.

shute Same as filling.

shuttle Part of weaving loom that carries the filling yarns.

silesia Lightweight, loosely woven cotton twill used for linings and pocket sacks.

silicone Material used to improve stain and wrinkle resistance.

silk (1) A protein fiber made by silkworms. The only natural filament fiber. (2) Luxury fabric made in a variety of weights, weaves, and qualities.

silk floss Short fibers of waste silk.

silk noil Cross-rib silk with bits of cocoon left in the slub.

silk suede A lightweight suede that feels like silk.

silk twill Soft, twill-weave silk. Usually printed. Uses: blouses, skirts, scarves, shawls, linings, and men's ties.

single knit Same as plain knit.

sizing Starch, gelatin, or resin finish added to a fabric for body and smoothness. May be temporary or permanent.

skein A length of yarn.

skins Skins of small animals.

Skinner's Satin Trade name by William Skinner & Son for satin.

skip-dent (1) Variation of plain-weave fabric with long filling floats at regular intervals. (2) Occasional fabric defect.

skiver Splits of calf-, pig- or sheepskin.

slipper satin Tightly woven, medium- to heavyweight, satin-weave fabric. Rather stiff. May have metallic threads or jacquard motifs. Sometimes called panné satin. Use: evening wear.

slub Small, thick section of yarn which gives the fabric a rough texture. Slubs in silk are natural imperfections, while slubs in man-made fibers are manufactured. Sometimes called nub.

snakeskin Skin from snake; usually whipsnake or python. Uses: trims, belts, and accessories.

soft Quality of fabric hand. Drapeable and sometimes clingy. Opposite of crisp. Chiffon, batiste, charmeuse, and tricot are soft fabrics.

soil release Finish applied to man-made fibers to release dirt and oil-based stains.

solution dyeing Process for dyeing man-made fibers before the solution is made into filaments. Very colorfast. Same as dope and spun dyeing.

space dyeing Process for dyeing different sections of yarn different colors.

spandex Man-made elastic fiber made from polyurethane. Good stretch (500 percent) and recovery. Uses: skiwear, swimwear, skating costumes, foundation and exercise garments.

spinnerette Showerhead-type of device used to make man-made filaments.

spinning Process of twisting fibers together into a continuous thread.

splits Thin layers of leather made from one thick skin. Usually sueded on both sides. Sometimes called garment splits.

sponging Process for shrinking wool fabrics. Unnecessary if the fabric is labeled "needle-ready," "sponge shrunk," or London shrunk.

spun dyeing See solution dyeing.

spun fabric Fabric made of spun yarns. Usually opaque and not as smooth as filament fabrics. May be light- to heavyweight. Uses: suitings, gabardine, and serge.

spun rayon Fabrics made from yarns spun from rayon staple or cut rayon waste.

spun yarn Yarn made from man-made filaments which have been cut into short lengths to imitate natural fibers.

square cloth Any fabric having the same number of warp and filling yarns per inch.

square fabric Fabric one yard long and one yard wide.

squirrel Soft, silky fur. Uses: coats, jackets, linings, and children's wear.

stain- or **spot-resistant** Finish to retard staining.

stable knit Knit with little or no stretch, including raschel and double knits.

staple (1) Short lengths of cotton or wool fibers. (2) Man-made filaments which have been cut into short lengths.

steerhide Heavy, crinkle-grain leather.

stencil printing Method of printing using metal or paper stencils to block areas which are not to be printed. A different stencil is required for each color.

stretch fabrics (1) Fabrics woven with stretch fibers in either the warp or filling. (2) Fabrics woven or knit so they will stretch.

stretch fibers (1) Elastic, strongly crimped fibers (stretch nylon and stretch polyester), rubber, spandex, and anidex. (2) Trade names include Agrilon, Fluflon, Superloft, Taslan, Helanca, and Lycra.

stretch nylon Tightly coiled yarn, heat-set into long-lasting springs.

stretch polyester Tightly coiled yarn, heat-set into long-lasting springs.

structural design Design woven, not printed, into a fabric, including plaids, stripes, brocade, tapestry, and jacquard.

studs Decorative metal objects used to embellish fabric surface.

stuff Same as fabric.

suede Leather skin which has been treated so the flesh side is used as the face.

suede fabric (1) Soft, woven fabrics with a nap, simulating the look of real suede. (2) Nonwoven fabrics with a nap such as Ultrasuede, Lamous, Facile and Caress. Same as synthetic suede.

suiting Medium- to heavyweight fabric used for suits. Includes many weaves, textures, and all fibers and blends. Flannel, tweed, piqué, faille, linen, and worsted are typical suitings.

Superwash 100 percent wool which will not shrink when machine washed.

Supima Trade name of fine, extra-long-staple cotton; grown in U.S.

surah Soft, printed, twill-weave fabric. Made from silk, acetate, and polyester. Does not wear well. Uses: blouses, dresses, scarves, linings, and ties.

swatch Small sample of fabric to show pattern and color. Used by designers to identify specific fabric for a design, as well as by retailers to describe a fabric for customers.

sweatshirt fabric Medium-weight, knit fabric with a smooth face and fleeced back. May be cotton, acrylic, polyester, or blend. Uses: casual wear, jackets, sweat pants, robes, sleepwear, or sweatshirts.

Swiss batiste High-luster, plain-weave cotton batiste.

swivel weave Utilizes extra filling to create eyelash effects. May come out with wear.

synthetic fiber Man-made fiber such as polyester and nylon created in the laboratory.

synthetic suede Nonwoven fabric developed to simulate suede. Ultrasuede, Lamous, Facile, Caressa, and Glore-Valcana are synthetic suedes.

T

tabby Same as plain weave.

Tactel A trade name for texturized nylon with an acetate coating and matte finish. It is very wind- and water-repellent and breathes well. Lighter weight than Taslan. Uses: skiwear, rainwear, windbreakers, and fashion outerwear.

taffeta Smooth, crisp, plain-weave fabric made of silk, acetate, rayon, nylon, polyester, or blends. Does not wear well, has a characteristic rustle, and holds its shape when draped. Uses: dresses, evening wear and petticoats.

tapestry Decorative fabric with woven design which may be floral or tell a story. Uses: coats, jackets, and handbags.

tarnish-resistant material Material which absorbs sulphur to retard silver tarnish.

tartan Twill-weave, checked designs belonging to individual Scottish clans. Frequently used for kilts, although the word "tartan" evolved from the Spanish "tiritana," which means colored cloth. Available in a variety of weights. Usually wool, but may be silk.

Taslan A textured nylon with a rough texture and matte finish. It looks like cotton, but is stronger, quick drying, wind- and water-repellent. Uses: skiwear, mountain wear, parkas, outerwear, jackets and pants.

tattersall check Two-colored overcheck pattern. Named for Robert Tattersall, who used it for a horse blanket.

Teklan Modacrylic fiber made by Courtaulds.

tentering Process for stretching and straightening fabric.

terry cloth Plain or printed warp-pile fabric with uncut loops on one or both sides. Most absorbent when made of cotton or rayon. Sometimes called Turkish towelling. Uses: robes, beachwear, and casual garments.

Terylene   Trade name of Imperial Chemical Industries Ltd. (England) for a fiber similar to Dacron.

textiles   All fibers and fabrics, as well as items made from them.

texture   Look and feel of fabric—smooth, rough, soft, crisp.

Thai silk   Heavyweight, textured silk made in Thailand. Frequently iridescent. Uses: suitings, coats, and evening gowns.

thermal   Honeycomb-weave fabrics which trap the air for added warmth. Uses: pajamas and underwear.

thermoplastic   Heat-sensitive fibers like synthetics, which can be changed when heat is applied.

thick and thin   Fabric with yarns of uneven sizes.

thread   (1) Continuous length of twisted fibers used for sewing. (2) Term sometimes used instead of yarns in weaving.

thrums   The fringe of warp threads left over after the woven cloth has been cut off.

ticking   Same as pillow ticking.

tie dyeing   A form of resist dyeing utilizing knots and strings to create patterns.

tie silk   Silk used to make ties.

tissue   Lightweight fabric in any fiber with some body.

tissue taffeta   Very lightweight, transparent taffeta. Uses: dresses, blouses, and evening wear.

toile   (1) French word meaning cloth. (2) Sample garment. (3) Printed design.

toweling   Any fabric meant to be used for drying.

tracing cloth   Transparent, nonwoven fabric, printed with a dotted grid. Use: pattern making.

traditional fabrics   Fabrics which have been manufactured and used with little or no change for many years.

transparent velvet   Lightweight velvet which is translucent when held up to the light. Drapes well, but tends to crush. Uses: evening wear and suits.

Trevira   Trade name of Hoechst Fibers, Inc., for polyester.

triacetate   (1) Modification of acetate fiber, which is stronger when wet, with greater resistance to heat, shrinkage, wrinkling, and fading. (2) Trade names include Arnel and Courpleta.

triblends   Blends of nylon, polyester, and cotton. Fast drying, lightweight and durable, they have a low luster and can be washed or dry-cleaned. Uses: jackets, pants, shirts, or jumpsuits.

tricot   Warp knit with ribs on the face and wales on the back.

triple sheer   Tightly woven, sheer fabric that gives impression of being opaque.

tropical suiting   Lightweight, crisp suiting that pleats and creases well. Cool to wear.

tubular knits   Fabrics knit in a tube on a circular knitting machine.

tuft   Group of yarns pulled to the surface.

tulle   Very fine net. May be cotton, silk or nylon. Uses: bridal veils and evening gowns.

Turkish toweling   Thick, very absorbent terry cloth. Uses: robes, press cloths, and drying.

tussah   Fabric made with filament from uncultivated silkworms; or synthetics made to look like silk. Sometimes called wild silk, shantung, or rajah.

tweed   Rough-textured fabric with slubs or knots on the surface. Usually yarn dyed, with fibers of different colors added before spinning. Originally woollens woven by the country people near the Tweed River, which separates England and Scotland; may be any fiber or combination today.

twill fabric   Fabric with a diagonal weave.

twill weave   One of the three basic weaves; has a diagonal rib. Each filling yarn always passes over or under two or more warp yarns. Can be right- or left-handed.

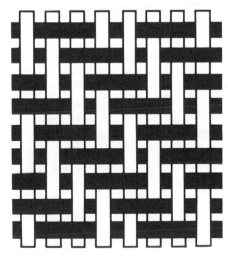

Fig. 26–4

twist   Term to describe the direction the yarn is rotated as it is manufactured. Yarns with an "S" twist are turned to the left, while yarns with a "Z" twist are turned to the right.

two-faced fabric   See double-faced fabric.

two-way stretch   Fabric with stretch in both the warp and filling.

U

Ultrasuede   Trade name of Springs Mills, Inc., for synthetic suede.

unbalanced stripe   Stripe which, when folded in half, is not the same on both sides of the center. Sometimes called uneven stripe.

unbalanced plaid   Plaid pattern which, when folded in half, is not the same on both sides of the center. Sometimes called uneven plaid.

uncut velvet   Velvet fabric with uncut loops. Sometimes called terry velvet.

uniform cloth   Serviceable fabric. Use: uniforms.

union dye   Process of dyeing fabric made of two fibers to produce two different shades.

unravel   Same as ravel.

V

val lace   Originally a bobbin lace made with linen thread. Same thread used for design and ground. Sometimes called Valenciennes.

Valenciennes   See val lace.

vat dyeing   A kind of wash-fast dye.

veiling   Net made from silk, rayon, or nylon. Use: veils.

Velcro   Trademark for hook and loop fasteners.

velour   French word meaning velvet. Knit or woven fabric with a thick, short, warp pile. Usually made of a man-made fiber or blend. Not as absorbent as terry cloth. Uses: coats, robes, leisurewear and towels.

velvet   Luxurious fabric with a short (less than 1/8″) pile on a knit or woven background. Made with an extra set of warp yarns. May be silk, rayon, nylon, or cotton. Ranges from lightweight transparent velvet to heavy upholstery velvet. Uses: dresses and evening wear.

velveteen   Cut pile, made with an extra set of filling yarns, on a woven background. Made of cotton and man-made fibers. Uses: dresses, pants, skirts, suits, and evening wear.

velveteen plush   Cotton velveteen with longer pile.

Venetian lace   A kind of guipure lace.

Venise lace   A kind of guipure lace.

vertical stretch   Fabric with lengthwise stretch.

Verel   Trade name of Eastman Kodak for modacrylic fiber.

vicuna   Luxurious hair fiber.

vinal-vinyon   Fiber similar to acrylic. Soft and flame-retardant. Use: children's sleepwear.

vinyl   (1) Abbreviation for polyvinyl chloride (PVC). (2) Any fabric with a vinyl base. (3) Fabric covered with vinyl-based coating.

virgin   Used to describe wool made from new fibers. Sometimes called 100 percent wool or all wool.

viscose   Term used in United Kingdom to describe all rayons made by the viscose process.

viscose rayon   Cellulose fiber made from wood pulp or cotton linters by the viscose process. Soft and absorbent, but very weak when wet. Same as viscose.

Viyella   Trade name for soft, twill-weave fabric made of 55 percent lamb's wool and 45 percent cotton. First produced by William Hollins in Britain in 1893. Uses: dresses, blouses, and children's clothes.

voile   Lightweight, sheer, plain-weave fabric. May be cotton, polyester, or blend, plain or printed. Uses: shirtings, dresses, and children's clothes.

W

wadding   Lightweight batting made of cotton. Uses: quilting and shoulder pads.

waffle weave   Same as honeycomb.

wale   Vertical row of loops on knit fabrics or pile ribs on corduroy. Corduroy wales vary in size from 5 to 21 per inch.

warp   Set of yarns put onto the loom to run the length of the cloth and parallel to the selvage. Same as the ends and woof.

warp knit   Flat, dense knit. Less elastic than jersey. Tricot and raschel are examples.

warp print Fabric with warp threads printed before weaving. Sometimes called shadow printing.

warp stretch Fabric with lengthwise stretch.

wash and wear Fabrics which can be worn with little or no ironing when washed. Same as durable press and permanent press.

waste silk Waste or short filaments spun into thick and thin yarn.

waterproof Fabric impervious to water. Warm and clammy to wear. Plastic, rubber, vinyl, and coatings of lacquer, synthetic resin, or rubber are waterproof.

water-repellent Finish, usually wax or silicone resin, which resists water and retards soiling.

water-resistant Same as water-repellent.

weave Method of making fabric by interlacing yarns at right angles. The three primary weaves are plain, twill, and satin.

weft Same as filling and picks.

welt Finished edge on bands and ribbings.

wet look Shiny fabrics such as vinyl and ciré that look wet.

wet strength Fabric strength when wet; important in swim- and exercise wear.

whipcord Twill-weave fabric using bulky yarns in the warp to create a sharply defined upright diagonal on the face. Originally rugged wool or worsted fabric, now available in all fibers and a variety of weights. Uses: topcoats, suitings, trousers, riding and sports clothes, children's garments.

whipsnake An attractive, affordable snakeskin.

white-on-white White design woven or embroidered on white fabric. Uses: shirtings, dresses, and children's wear.

wide wale Corduroy with large wales (5 per inch).

wigan Interfacing or backing, a plain-weave cotton fabric used in tailoring.

wild silk Rough, uneven silk from uncultured silkworms. Textured fabrics with a dull finish.

woof Same as warp or end.

wool Hair fiber with natural felting ability like the fleece from sheep. Comfortable to wear; very easy to sew and press. Other wools include hair fibers from angora, cashmere goats, and llamas. Technically hair fibers and fur from other animals are not wool because they do not felt naturally.

Woolblend mark Fabric composed of more than 60 percent wool, which has been quality tested.

woollen Fabric made from loosely twisted woollen yarns which have short, fluffy fibers. Nap frequently obscures weave. Doesn't shine or hold crease. Tweeds, flannel, and fleece are woollens.

Woolmark Trademark which assures the consumer that the product is 100 percent new and meets the quality standards of the International Wool Secretariat.

worsted Fabric made from high-twist, worsted yarns which have long, smooth fibers. Crisp with a clear-finished surface. Holds a crease and shines easily. Gabardine, crepe, and serge are worsteds.

woven stretch Fabric woven with stretch yarns.

Y

yard Thirty-six inches.

yard goods Same as piece goods.

yarn Continuous strand spun from fibers or filaments, used to weave or knit into fabrics.

yarn dyed Process for dyeing fibers which have already been spun into yarn but not made into fabric. Considered more colorfast than piece dyeing.

Z

Z-twist Right-hand twist of threads or yarns so they look like the middle of the letter "Z." Sometimes called right twist.

Zantrel Trade name of American Enka for high-wet-modulus rayon fiber.

Zefran Blend of acrylic, nylon, and polyester fibers, trademark of Dow Badische.

Zepel Trade name for stain-resistant finish.

zephyr Very lightweight gingham.

zibeline Heavily napped coating fabric. Usually camel or mohair blended with wool or man-made fiber. Use: coats.

Zirpro Treatment for wool to improve flame-resistance.

Appendix

Recommended Equipment and Supplies

alcohol (rubbing) Removes fusible web residue.

auxiliary light Mine has a flexible arm and magnifying glass.

awl Pointed tool which makes holes without cutting; knitting needles can be substituted.

basting tape Use only the water-soluble type.

beeswax Strengthens thread for hand sewing. Press thread to melt the wax into the fibers.

bias tape maker Optional tool for making bias binding.

brown paper Strips of grocery bag paper *without printing*, used in pressing.

brush Keeps your machine clean.

canned air Keeps your machine clean. Can also use a cool hair dryer.

cardboard cutting board Resilient surface with a marked grid.

chalk and chalk wheel Marking aids.

clapper Essential pressing aid; frequently the base of a point turner.

drafting tape Marking aid; do not confuse with masking tape.

dual tracing wheel Tracing wheel which marks one line while tracing another.

fray retardant Lacquerlike liquids and sprays like Fray Check and Fray-No-More that retard fraying.

fusible web Web which melts to bond two fabrics permanently.

glue stick Washable, used for basting.

hot-iron cleaner A real sanity saver; can also be used on presses.

iron Use a good quality iron; I prefer the gravity flow types even though they are very expensive.

marking pencil Chalk pencil used for temporary markings.

meter stick or yardstick Essential for marking hems and for pattern making.

needle lubricant Generally used to prevent skipped stitches; can be used when hand sewing densely woven fabrics.

needle threader Helpful for large threads. Wire needle threaders can be bent at right angles and used on sewing machine needles.

needles Crewel or embroidery needles for hemming and finishing garments; cotton darners, sharps, or milliner's needles for basting; tapestry needles for turning button loops; glover's or leather needles for sewing leather; calyx-eyed needles for hiding threads.

499

No More Pins   A temporary glue to hold pattern pieces in place.

pattern cloth   Nonwoven material with a grid.

physician's examining table paper   Good source of pattern paper.

pin holder   I like the magnetic ones for cutting and a wrist pin cushion for fitting. At the machine, I have one on a piece of elastic around the machine arm.

pins   Keep a variety of good-quality pins on hand: glass headed or flower pins for loosely woven fabrics, fine pleating pins for fine fabrics, and small safety pins for lightweight or slippery fabrics.

point presser   Essential pressing tool for difficult-to-reach seams.

point turner   Helpful tool for turning corners.

press cloths   A variety of cloths—muslin, diapers, wool, and drill—for pressing.

pressing mitt   Useful mitt for pressing; a clean oven mitt can be substituted.

release sheet   Nonstick sheet which allows you to bond fusible web to one fabric.

rotary cutter and mat   Available in a variety of sizes; they work particularly well on some fabrics.

ruler   I like the see-through plastic type with a 1/8″ grid printed on it.

seam ripper   Be sure it is extra sharp.

scissors   The essentials are three pairs of scissors or shears: a large pair of good-quality, well-sharpened shears for cutting out fabrics; a pair of paper scissors which can be sharpened for cutting metallics and sequins; and a small pair of 5″ trimmers. Optional, but very nice: appli-qué scissors, lightweight shears, and pinking shears. I've used Gingher products for several years and find that the design and weight of their products is as good as the quality.

seam roll   Essential pressing tool.

see-through ruler   Plastic ruler with a 1/8″ grid. I prefer those made by C-Thru Ruler Co.; many other brands are not always accurate.

sleeve board   Small pressing board which allows you to press sleeves and other difficult-to-reach sections.

soap sliver   Marking aid.

soleplate for iron   Nonstick plate for the iron, to reduce slicking and scorching fabrics.

steamer   A lightweight "iron" with a plastic soleplate—e.g., the Steamstress by Osrow.

tailor's ham   Essential for pressing. (Directions for making one are in my earlier book, *Sew A Beautiful Gift*.)

tape measure   A must for measuring and marking. Make sure yours is accurate.

temporary marking pens   Water-soluble and air-erasable pens for marking fabrics temporarily.

thimble   A must for hand sewing.

tracing wheel and tracing carbon   Marking aid for most fabrics.

triangle   An isosceles triangle with a 90° angle and two equal sides; used to determine true bias.

wax chalk   Marking aid for wool.

wax paper   Convenient source of pattern paper.

weights   Aids for holding pattern pieces in place. Small cans, ashtrays, and silver dinner knives work well.

white vinegar   Sets and removes creases.

Sewing Machine Needles

all-purpose needle   See universal needle.

ballpoint needle—705-SUK (Schmetz)   Designed for bulky knits, elastics, and spandex, the tip is more rounded than the H point. Available in sizes 70/10 to 110/18.

jeans needles—705-HJ (Schmetz)   Engineered for stitching densely woven fabrics and denim, it has a blue shank, a very sharp point, and a stiffer shaft, to resist deflection. Available in sizes 90/14 to 110/18.

leather needle—705-HLL or NTW (Schmetz)   This needle has a wedge-shaped point which cuts through leather and vinyl, instead of tearing it. Available in sizes 80/12 to 120/20.

Red Band Needle (Singer)   This sharp-point needle is recommended for sewing woven fabrics, and works particularly well on outerwear fabrics. Available in sizes 75/11 to 100/16.

self-threading or slotted needle   Designed with slotted-eye needle to make threading easier for the visually impaired. Available in sizes 80/12 to 100/16.

serger needles Needles designed for sergers. See your manual for type. (Some sergers use sewing-machine needles.)

Skip-Free Needle (J & P Coats) Engineered for skip-free stitching, this needle has a slightly rounded point and a shaved shank. It has a deeply cut shank and breaks easily. Available in sizes 75/11 and 90/14.

stretch needle—705-HS (Schmetz) Engineered with a hump above a very small eye, this needle is electroplated blue. It has a shaved shank and works well on older machines. Available in sizes 75/11 or 90/14.

topstitching needle—130N This needle has a larger eye than universal needles of the same size to accommodate heavy threads. Available in sizes 80/12 to 110/18.

triple needle Needle for decorative stitching.

twin needle Two needles on one shank. Originally designed for decorative stitching, twin needles can be used for stretch seams and hems. Available in sizes 1.6/70 to 4/100.

universal needle—705H (Schmetz) This all-purpose needle has a slightly rounded point for sewing knit and woven fabrics. It works well on most machines and is sometimes called a universal ballpoint. Available in sizes 60/8 to 120/20.

wing needle This needle is used for decorative stitching. Available in one size—100.

Yellow Band Needle (Singer) This all-purpose needle has a slightly rounded ballpoint needle with an elongated scarf and shaved shank. It works well on older machines. Available in sizes 75/11 to 110/18.

NEEDLE CHART

Use this handy needle and thread chart as a guide when machine stitching different fabrics.

Fabric Type: Very Lightweight Woven Fabrics

Batiste, chiffon, fine lace, marquisette, net, voile, organza, georgette, transparent fabrics.

Needle Type: Universal-H or Red Band.
Needle Sizes: 60/8 to 70/10.

Stitching Thread: Synthetics—polyester 100/3 or fine cotton-wrapped polyester; silks—mercerized cotton, size 60.

Fabric Type: Lightweight Wovens

Challis, chambray, charmeuse, crepe, dimity, dotted swiss, handkerchief linen, cloque, silk blouse fabrics, satin, eyelet, lace, velvet, pleated fabrics, taffeta, lightweight wools, lightweight polyesters.

Needle Type: Universal-H or Red Band.
Needle Sizes: 60/8 to 80/12.
Stitching Thread: Synthetics or blends—polyester 100/3 or fine cotton-wrapped polyester; silks—mercerized cotton, size 60.

Fabric Type: Lightweight Knits

Double knit, interlocks, jersey, mesh, panné velvet, metallics, rib knits.

Needle Type: Universal-H, ballpoint (SUK), stretch (HS), or Yellow Band.
Needle Sizes: 60/8 to 80/12.
Stitching Thread: Polyester or cotton-wrapped polyester.

Fabric Type: Light- to Medium-Weight Wovens

Metallics, sequinned fabrics, elasticized fabrics, chambray, gingham, percale, loosely woven fabrics, seersucker.

Needle Type: Universal-H or Red Band.
Needle Sizes: 60/8 to 90/14.
Stitching Thread: Synthetics or blends—polyester or cotton-wrapped polyester; silks—mercerized cotton.

Fabric Type: Light- to Medium-Weight Knits

Raschel, sweater, sweatshirt, two-way stretch, power net, velour.

Needle Type: Universal-H, ballpoint (SUK), stretch (HS), or Yellow Band.
Needle Sizes: 70/10 to 90/14.
Stitching Thread: Polyester or cotton-wrapped polyester; for extra stretch—woolly nylon thread.

Fabric Type: Medium-Weight Wovens

Broadcloth, brocade, linen, matelassé, piqué, shantung, silk suitings, chintz, faille, ottoman, velveteen, tufted fabrics, felt, felted fabrics, single/ply reversible fabrics, polyester blends, acrylics, woollens, worsteds, washable wools, fleece, gabardine, outerwear fabrics.

Needle Type: Universal-H or Red Band; densely woven fabrics—jeans (HJ).
Needle Sizes: 70/10 to 90/14.
Stitching Thread: Synthetics or blends—polyester or cotton-wrapped polyester; silks—mercerized cotton; outerwear fabrics—polyester thread.

Fabric Type: Medium- to Heavyweight Wovens

Denim, drapery fabrics, guipure lace, twill-weave fabrics, ticking, corduroy, terry, velour, fake fur, double-faced fabrics, quilted fabrics, outerwear.

Needle Type: Universal-H or Red Band; densely woven fabrics—jeans (HJ)
Needle Sizes: 70/10 to 100/16.
Stitching Thread: Synthetics or blends—polyester or cotton-wrapped polyester; silks—mercerized cotton; outerwear fabrics—polyester.

Fabric Type: Medium- to Heavyweight Knits

Fake fur, double-knits.

Needle Type: Universal-H or Yellow Band.
Needle Sizes: 70/10 to 100/16.
Stitching Thread: Polyester, cotton-wrapped polyester, topstitching thread.

Fabric Type: Heavy Woven Fabrics

Canvas, coatings, duck, awning fabrics.

Needle Type: Universal-H, jeans (HJ), or Red Band.
Needle Sizes: 80/12 to 100/16.
Stitching Thread: Synthetics or blends—polyester or cotton-wrapped polyester; silks—mercerized cotton.

Fabric Type: Synthetic Suedes

Needle Type: Universal-H, jeans (HJ), Yellow Band, or Red Band.
Needle Sizes: 65/9 to 90/14.
Stitching Thread: Polyester, cotton-wrapped polyester.

Fabric Type: Vinyl

Needle Type: Universal-H, jeans (HJ), leather (HLL), stretch (HS), Red Band.
Needle Sizes: 70/10 to 90/14.
Stitching Thread: Polyester, cotton-wrapped polyester; clear vinyl: monofilament nylon.

Fabric Type: Leather, Sherpa, Fur

Needle Type: Universal-H, jeans (HJ), leather (HLL).
Needle Sizes: 70/10 to 100/16.
Stitching Thread: Polyester.

Threads

all-purpose See long-staple polyester.

bargain-priced (spun polyester) Poor-quality thread spun from short fibers. Lint and knots are a problem. Cheap thread has little or no stretch and frequently causes puckered seams. Uses: None.

basting (cotton) A soft finished cotton thread; available in several colors on a cardboard spool. Dark and bright colors crock. Uses: Basting, tailor tacks. Do not use dark colors on light fabrics or for permanent stitching.

cotton-wrapped polyester (size 50) (Dual Duty or Duet—J & P Coats) A polyester core wrapped with fine cotton. Compared to 100 percent polyester, it has less static, is easier to sew, and withstands higher temperatures, but it rots and mildews. Compared to cotton, it has more stretch and is stronger and more durable. Uses: Most fabrics. Do not use on lightweight fabrics, leather, suede, fur, or rainwear.

decorative Rayon, silk, and metallic threads for decorative stitching.

elastic Elastic thread for elasticized shirring. Loses its elasticity more quickly than elastic.

extra-fine, cotton-wrapped polyester (Extra Fine, Dual Duty—J & P Coats) Fine, polyester core with cotton wrap. Uses: Most lightweight fabrics. Do not use on silk.

glazed cotton Heavy-duty thread with a glaze. Uses: Machine gathering, seaming canvas or coarse abrasive fabrics.

long-staple polyester (size 50) Sometimes called all-purpose; popular brand names include Drima (Coats and Clark), Gutermann, Metrosene Plus,

Molnlycke, Seralon (Amann Thread), Suisse (American Thread). Good-quality polyester thread is made with long fibers. Compared to cotton, it is stronger, more durable, more resistant to abrasion and chemicals, but it's more difficult to sew; puckered seams and skipped stitches are frequent problems. Uses: Most fabrics, leather, suede, and fur. Do not use on silk, lightweight fabrics, and transparent plastic.

long-stable polyester (Metrosene Plus) A strong, but fine (100/3), good-quality thread. Uses: Lightweight fabrics. Do not use on silk.

machine embroidery (sizes 30/2 and 60/2) Very lustrous 100 percent Egyptian cotton thread; available in two sizes: regular 30/2 and fine 60/2. Uses: Machine embroidery, machine-stitched buttonholes, decorative stitching. Generally, these two-ply threads are not durable enough for garment construction.

melt adhesive Thread with a fusible coating that melts when pressed. Uses: Any application requiring a narrow strip of fusible web.

mercerized cotton (50/3) All-cotton thread, mercerized to give it a luster and to prevent shrinkage. Little or no lint. Compared to polyester, it is easier to sew, but is not as strong or durable. Uses: Natural fiber fabrics. Do not use on knits, stretch fabrics, synthetics, or blends.

mercerized cotton (60/3) Fine all-cotton thread; limited colors. Uses: Lightweight silks.

nylon monofilament Single filament of nylon; very wiry, stiff, and transparent. It has no twist and the ends are scratchy. Uses: Fluted hems and transparent plastics.

Nymo B (Corticelli) Very strong, transparent, 100 percent nylon thread. Uses: Heavy-duty seaming, gathering, leather, suede, fur, transparent vinyl.

Nymo BST (Corticelli) Prewaxed 100 percent nylon thread. Uses: Hand sewing heavy fabrics, leather, fur, buttons, beads.

quilting (40/3) Fine Egyptian fiber, 100 percent cotton. Uses: Quilting and hand sewing, hand-worked buttonholes on lightweight cottons and linens.

serger Two-ply polyester threads for finishing without bulk.

silk (size A) Very lustrous, fine thread. Uses: Hand sewing, finishing, and hems on silk garments, topstitching, buttonholes, bastings which will not be removed before pressing. Rarely used for seaming.

silk buttonhole twist (size D) Heavy, lustrous silk thread. Uses: Topstitching, buttonholes on very heavy fabrics. Do not use for buttonholes on lightweight fabrics.

topstitching Thick, heavy polyester thread. Sometimes called buttonhole twist. Uses: Topstitching, heavy-duty sewing, sewing heavy furs and leathers. Do not use for buttonholes.

Wonder A clear lightweight, soft nylon thread. Uses: Soft rolled hems, joining lace strips, soft seam finishes, serging.

woolly nylon or polyester A woolly stretch thread made of texturized nylon or polyester. After stitching, some are fluffier and have better coverage than others. Compared to regular thread, it has more stretch, resists abrasion, and makes flatter seams. Uses: Finishing edges, stretch seams, decorative stitching.

The Sewing Clinic

Sooner or later, everyone has stitching problems; but, even though these glitches are frustrating, they are easy to solve with a little knowledge and patience. This section includes common, everyday problems, some of their causes, and the solutions which work for me and my students.

Problem:
Machine doesn't stitch properly.

CAUSES

Dirty machine.

Improper threading.

Needle damaged, dull, wrong size, or wrong type.

SOLUTIONS

Keep your machine clean and well oiled. Clean it at the end of each sewing day; if needed, clean it periodically during the day. Today's synthetic fabrics shed large amounts of lint and fibers. Since the needle hole is larger, lint collects much more rapidly inside zigzag machines than in older straight-stitch machines. These fibers can cause permanent damage to the machine, as well as temporary frustration for you. Fortunately, newer machines are usually easy to clean.

Most machines don't need to be oiled every time they are cleaned; but all should be cleaned before they are oiled. If your machine requires oil, oil it after eight cumulative hours of stitching.

Rethread the machine.

A damaged or dull needle can affect stitch quality. When in doubt, change the needle. Check the size and type before stitching. (Keep a magnifying glass handy to read the size on the needle shank.) Keep an assortment of needles on hand in a variety of sizes and types. I use the smallest recommended size first; why make a big hole when a little one works?

Problem:
Machine skips stitches.

Causes	Solutions
Dirty machine.	Clean and oil the machine, including the bobbin case.
Improperly threaded machine.	Rethread the machine.
Needle damaged, wrong type or size.	Use a different size or type of needle, i.e., ballpoint, lingerie, topstitching, or leather.
Fabric not held firmly, so it clings to the needle, raising the top thread loop and causing it to be missed by the bobbin shuttle hook.	Change to a straight-stitch, roller, or jeans foot and a small-hole needle plate to hold the fabric more firmly. If that isn't possible, cover the large hole on the zigzag throat plate with drafting tape; or decenter the needle. When zigzagging, use an all-purpose zigzag foot, except when embroidering, appliquéing, or satin stitching, when you should use an embroidery foot. Wash fabrics to remove undesirable finishes; hold the fabric taut when stitching. Tissue-stitch seams with the stabilizer of your choice. Use a needle lubricant on the needle tension disks, thread, and bobbin: test first for spotting.
Needle doesn't make a large enough hole.	Use a larger needle.
Needle makes too large a hole.	Use a smaller needle.
Needle incorrectly set.	Remove and reset needle.
Thread too thick for needle.	Use smaller thread or a larger needle.
Thread tension too tight.	Loosen the upper tension.

Problem:
Seams are puckered.

Causes	Solutions
Thread "shrank."	Fill bobbins with polyester thread on slow speed. When filled too quickly, the thread stretches. Once stitched into the seamline, it relaxes and appears to shrink.

CAUSES	SOLUTIONS
Fabric is lightweight, wash and wear, or tightly woven.	Use a stabilizer under the fabric. Hold fabric taut when stitching.
Needle damaged, wrong size or type.	Change to a new needle, a different size or type needle.
Fabric not held firmly.	Change to a straight-stitch, roller, or jeans foot and a small-hole needle plate to hold the fabric more firmly. If that isn't possible, cover the large hole on the zigzag throat plate with drafting tape; or decenter the needle. When zigzagging, use an all-purpose zigzag foot, except when embroidering, appliquéing, or satin stitching, when you should use an embroidery foot.
Seamline on the lengthwise grain.	Redraw seamline so it is not on the lengthwise grain.
Tension too tight.	Correct the tension. Lighten the pressure.
Stitches too long.	Shorten the stitch length.
Operator (you) in a hurry.	Change to low speed or stitch slowly.
Thread too large for the needle or fabric.	Use a finer thread or a larger needle.
Different threads on the bobbin and needle.	Use the same size and kind of thread on the needle and bobbin.

Problem:

Underlayer creeps.

When stitching, the feed dogs move the underlayer toward the back of the machine, while the presser foot pushes the top layer forward.	Use an even-feed or roller foot.
Pressure too heavy.	Lighten the pressure.
Fabric layers lock together.	Pull the underlayer forward with the right hand, while pushing the upper layer back with the left hand. Use the scissor points or screwdriver to push the upper layer toward the needle or to hold it firmly against the underlayer.
Presser foot sticks to the fabric.	Spray the bottom of the presser foot with a Teflon spray. When topstitching leather or vinyl, rub the fabric surface with talcum powder or a needle lubricant before stitching.

CAUSES	SOLUTIONS
Garment sections different lengths.	When stitching a short section to a longer section, stitch with the longer piece on the bottom. Double-baste seam lines.
Garment sections cut on different grains.	When stitching a bias to a straight section, stitch with the bias on the bottom.

Problem:
Machine jams.

Dirty machine.	Clean and oil the machine, including the bobbin case.
Incorrectly threaded machine.	Rethread the machine.
Damaged needle.	Use a new needle.
Lint or thread around the bobbin case.	Check for lint between the tension disks.
Threads not held when beginning.	Hold threads when beginning.
Bobbin inserted incorrectly.	Remove the bobbin and replace correctly.
Needle inserted incorrectly.	Remove the needle and reset correctly.
Presser bar not down.	Lower the presser bar.
Static electricity pulls fabric into needle hole.	Spray the fabric with Static Guard: rub your hands with hand lotion.
Hole in needle plate too large.	Use a small-hole needle plate or cover the large zigzag hole with tape.
Wrong type foot.	Change to correct presser foot.
Foot can't move over satin stitches.	Use an embroidery foot when satin stitching.
Fabric not held firmly.	Change to a straight-stitch, roller, or jeans foot and a small-hole needle plate to hold the fabric more firmly.

Problem:
Tension is unbalanced.

Dirty machine.	Clean and oil the machine.
Machine improperly threaded.	Rethread the machine.
Damaged needle, or wrong type of needle.	Use a new needle, or a different size and type needle.

CAUSES	SOLUTIONS
Thread has slipped out of take-up lever or tension disks.	Check the tension disks for lint; rethread.
Thread catching on the thread spool slash.	Turn the thread spool over so the slash is on the bottom. Use a horizontal spindle or a thread cap.
Needle set incorrectly.	Remove and reset the needle.
Bent or rusted bobbin.	Use a new bobbin.
Operator forgot to reset tension after making buttonholes, gathers, etc.	Adjust tension as needed.
Operator forgot to replace embroidery bobbin case with regular bobbin case.	Replace regular bobbin case.
Wrong bobbin for the machine.	Use bobbins recommended by the manufacturer.
Bobbin improperly or unevenly wound.	Fill an empty bobbin with the machine set on slow. (Remove all polyester thread from bobbins if you've been filling them on high speed.)
Layers of several different threads on bobbin.	Remove all threads before filling the bobbin.
Bobbin pigtail—thread end—sticking out.	Cut off the bobbin pigtail.
Bobbin case screw worked out.	Replace screw.
Damaged spring on bobbin case.	Replace a damaged bobbin case. To avoid damaging the spring, cut the thread close to the spring before removing the bobbin from the case.
Different threads on the needle and bobbin.	Use the same thread on the top and bobbin.
Thread poor quality, too coarse, too fine, dry, old, or brittle.	Throw away poor-quality thread. Soak mercerized cotton thread in water. (Since it is stronger when wet, you can even sew before it dries.)
Thread catching on rough surfaces on the thread guides, throat plate, or thread spindle.	Check your machine, thread guides, throat, and thread spindle for rough surfaces. Use an emery cloth to smooth them or ask your dealer to replace them.

Problem:
Upper thread breaks.

Dirty machine.	Clean the machine.

CAUSES	SOLUTIONS
Machine improperly threaded.	Rethread the machine.
Needle poor quality, damaged, too small, or wrong type.	Use good quality needles; a new needle, a larger needle, and/or the right type needle.
Needle set improperly.	Reset the needle.
Tension too tight.	Adjust the tension.
Thread wrong size for fabric or needle.	Change the thread.
Thread poor-quality.	Discard poor-quality threads.
Take-up lever in wrong position at beginning.	Be sure the take-up lever is down when beginning to stitch.
Stitching over pins.	Don't stitch over pins. When it can't be avoided, turn the hand wheel manually and walk the machine over pins.
Thread caught on thread spool slash.	Turn the thread spool over. Use a horizontal spindle or thread cap.
Thread catching on rough surfaces on the thread guides, throat plate, or thread spindle.	Check your machine, thread guides, throat, and thread spindle for rough surfaces. Use an emery cloth to smooth them or ask your dealer to replace them.
Operator pulling fabric.	Don't pull the fabric during stitching or when the needle is in the fabric. Practice holding the fabric firmly without pulling it.

Problem:
Machine won't run.

Machine not plugged in.	Plug machine in.
Machine not turned on.	Turn machine on.
Outlet switch not turned on.	Check outlet switch.
Circuit breaker tripped.	Check circuit breaker.
Machine clogged with wrong type oil or fray retardant.	Have machine cleaned professionally; use only recommended sewing machine oil.
Machine rusted.	Do not store machine in an unheated, unair-conditioned, or damp garage, basement, or attic. Get professional service for rusty machine.

Problem:
Needles break.

CAUSES	SOLUTIONS
Bent needle.	Use a new needle.
Poor-quality needle.	Use good-quality needles.
Needle too fine for fabric.	Use a larger needle; needles are available up to size 120/19.
Needle improperly set or loose.	Insert needle correctly and tighten set screw.
Wrong needle for machine.	Use type of needles recommended by sewing machine company.
Loose presser foot.	Tighten the presser-foot screw.
Wrong foot or needle plate for zigzag stitching.	Check foot and needle plate before zigzag stitching.
Changing needle position with needle in the needle hole.	Do not change the stitch width or needle position while the needle is in the needle hole.
Stitching over pins or zipper.	Try to avoid stitching over pins, zippers, snaps, hooks and eyes; when that isn't possible, turn the hand wheel manually to avoid breaking or damaging the needle.
Bobbin or bobbin case incorrectly set.	Set the bobbin and bobbin case correctly.
Operator pulls fabric without raising presser foot lever.	Do not pull the fabric without raising the presser foot.
Operator pulls fabric toward the front.	Do not pull the fabric forward.
Operator pulls fabric with needle in the fabric.	Do not pull the fabric when the needle is in it.
Upper tension too tight.	Loosen the upper tension.
Material too thick.	Avoid thick, heavy fabrics; or purchase a machine which will handle them.

Problem:
Machine noisy.

CAUSES	SOLUTIONS
Dirty machine.	Clean and oil the machine.
Dull needle.	Use a new needle.
Damaged machine.	Take the machine to an authorized dealer/repair center.

510

Tips for Topstitching

- Begin with a clean, well-oiled machine and a new needle.
- Before topstitching the garment, experiment on fabric scraps with different types and sizes of needles, different threads, several machine feet and adjustments, and stitching techniques.
- Use a presser foot which holds the fabric firmly. Straight-stitch and jeans presser feet are best; but the all-purpose zigzag foot and roller foot are better than an embroidery foot.
- To avoid drag lines, use an even-feed foot or roller foot.
- Other aids for holding the fabric firmly are a small-hole needle plate, tape over the needle hole, decentering the needle, or tissue-stitching.
- When stitching over uneven thicknesses next to seamlines, at garment edges, and around pockets, use a zipper foot or level the foot with a shim or piece of cardboard under one side of the foot.
- To level the foot when crossing seamlines, use a shim or cardboard under the heel as you approach the seam; place it under the toes as you descend.
- For straight, uniform topstitching, use a most convenient gauge: line up the garment edge or seamline with the outer or inner edge of the foot; then stitch. Change the distance between the needle and foot by changing the needle position or by using different feet.
- Other marking aids include soap sliver, chalk wheel, temporary marking pens, drafting tape, double basting, or cardboard template.
- To gauge wide distances at garment edges, place a piece of drafting tape, magnet, rubber band or T-gauge on the machine base. Position it the desired distance from the needle.
- When topstitching with two strands of regular thread or topstitching thread, use a larger needle.
- Shorter stitches are less likely to look crooked than long ones.
- When stitching tweeds and heavy fabrics, try a short, narrow zigzag if straight stitches look crooked.
- Check the amount of thread on the bobbin and spool before topstitching, so you don't run out.
- When using polyester thread, fill the bobbin slowly.
- Topstitch right side up.
- Stitch directionally unless the fabric has a nap.
- Always stitch with the nap.
- Always stitch both sides of a seam or two corresponding seams in the same direction.
- Hold the garment firmly in front and back of the foot when stitching.
- Stitch slowly at an even speed; or, if your machine has a speed regulator, shift into low.
- Stop and relax. Stop periodically, with the needle in the fabric; raise the foot and allow the fabric to relax. Lower the foot; then continue.
- To give individual stitches more definition, loosen the upper tension, use a different color thread on the bobbin, use a heavier thread, or use a straight stretch stitch.
- If the needle can't handle a heavier thread, wind the thread on the bobbin; topstitch, wrong side up.
- When topstitching difficult fabrics, lubricate the fabric with a soap sliver, pound thick seams with a cloth-covered hammer to soften the fibers, or use a needle lubricant.
- Using needle lubricant, make several vertical rows on the spool thread before beginning; periodically, add a drop between the tension disks and at the top of the needle. Always test for spotting first.
- If you have only 5″ or 6″ more to topstitch and you run out of thread, tie the thread end to the thread on another spool and continue stitching. You should be able to finish before the knot reaches the eye of the needle.
- If you run out of thread in the middle of a line of topstitching, resume stitching by inserting the machine needle precisely into the last hole stitched. Later, pull the thread ends to the back, knot, and hide the thread ends.
- To solve machine stitching problems, consult the Sewing Clinic.

Glossary

air-erasable marking pen See fadeaway marking pen.

align To match raw edges, fabric pattern, or matchpoints.

all-purpose zigzag foot Zigzag foot with a small indentation on the bottom.

appliqué (1) Design applied to the surface of another fabric. (2) To apply designs to the surface of another fabric.

appliqué scissors Scissors designed to trim close to a stitched line. Made by Gingher, Inc.; sometimes called pelican or rug shears.

apply To join one section to another.

armscye Armhole.

arrow Symbol on pattern pieces indicating the lengthwise grain, the direction for stitching, or the direction for folding pleats and tucks.

assemble To sew the garment.

backing See underlining.

backstitch Technique for stitching backwards to secure the threads at the beginning and end of a seam.

band Strip at garment edge to finish or trim the garment.

bar tack Hand or machine stitch to reinforce areas of stress—i.e., end of zipper, pocket openings, end of buttonhole.

baste To hold fabric layers together temporarily.

bias Any cut which is not on the lengthwise or crossgrain. *True bias* is a line at a 45° angle to the lengthwise grain.

bias binding Binding made of bias fabric, used to finish the edge.

bobbin-stitching Technique of stitching with the bobbin thread pulled up through the needle, needle thread guides, and upper tension.

bottom weight Heavier weight fabrics suitable for skirts, slacks, and jackets.

bound pocket Inset pocket with two equal welts. Looks like a large bound buttonhole.

butt To match the edges or folds so they touch.

canned air Pressurized can of air used to clean sewing machines and camera lenses.

casing Hem or tuck through which elastic or ties are threaded.

chain stitch To stitch from one fabric or garment section to another without cutting the threads. Sometimes called continuous stitching.

clapper Wooden tool used in pressing.

clean finish A method for finishing the raw edges of hems and seams. Generally, it describes all hem/seam finishes; specifically, it describes a folded edge or a turned-and-stitched finish.

clearance above the eye Flattened area above the eye of the needle. Same as the needle scarf.

coil Narrow, synthetic coil that secures a zipper. Same as the zipper teeth.

complete pattern See duplicate pattern.

cording Narrow, corded piping inserted into a seam.

couching Sewing a decorative cord, thread, or yarn to the surface of the fabric by zigzagging over the cord with the machine or overcasting by hand.

course   Horizontal rows on the back of single-knit fabrics.

crimping   Technique for easing fabric into the seamline. Sometimes called ease-plus, stay-stitching plus, or crowding.

crock   Dye color rubs off.

crooked straight stitch   Very narrow zigzag (W,.5; L,2).

crossgrain   The filling threads which run from selvage to selvage; sometimes used to describe the course on knits.

crowding   See crimping.

dart   Stitched fabric fold, tapering at one or both ends. Used to shape the flat fabric to the contours of the figure.

decenter   To change the machine needle position to stitch at the extreme right or left.

demarcation line   Ridge or shadow that shows on right side of fabric at the edge of interfacings, fusibles, and linings.

design ease   Amount of ease allowed by the pattern designer to make the garment not only loose enough to wear, but fashionable.

directional stitching   See stitch directionally.

ditch-stitch   Technique of stitching inconspicuously from the right side in the well of a seam or next to a seamline.

double/lay   Two layers of fabric, spread for cutting.

double/ply   Seams which have both seam allowances stitched or finished together.

dropped shoulder   Design with shoulder extended over the top of the arm.

duplicate pattern   Pattern with pieces for both the right and left sides of the garment so the design can be cut in a single/lay.

ease basting   A temporary stitch used to ease excess fullness into a seamline. Using a regular stitch length, a tight bobbin tension, and a heavier thread on the bobbin, stitch—right side up—just inside the seamline and again midway between the raw edge and seamline. Pull both threads up together so they won't break.

ease-plus   See crimping.

edgestitch   Topstitching 1/16″ from the edge or seamline.

embroidery foot   Sewing-machine foot with a wide slot or V on the bottom, which allows the foot to move freely over satin stitching.

embroidery hoop   Special hoop for machine embroidery.

enclosed seam   Seam enclosed between two layers of fabric—i.e., the seam at the garment edge.

even-feed foot   Machine foot which feeds the top layer of fabric at the same rate as the bottom.

expanded pattern   See duplicate pattern.

extended facing   Facing cut in one piece with garment section. To make an extended facing pattern, pin the facing pattern to the garment pattern, matching the stitching lines.

eyelet   (1) Small round opening in fabric. (2) Small metal ring.

face   (1) Right side of the fabric. (2) To finish garment edge with a facing.

faced facing   See interfaced facing.

facing   Piece of complementary, lining-weight, or self-fabric applied to finish the edge. Generally, it folds to the underside; but it can fold to the right side.

fadeaway marking pen   Type of temporary marking pen which usually disappears within forty-eight hours. Sometimes called an air-erasable or 48-hour pen.

fashion fabric   Face or outer fabric used for the garment. Sometimes called garment or shell fabric.

fasteners   Devices used at garment openings to close the garment.

feed dogs   Pointed metal or rubber bars located under the presser foot that move the fabric backward or forward.

fell   To finish with a felling stitch.

filling   Threads that run back and forth between the selvages.

findings   Linings, underlinings, interfacings, zippers, buttons, thread, snaps, toggles, grommets, eyelets, etc.

finish   (1) Any method for neatening the edges of seams, hems, and facings. (2) To apply the appropriate finish to raw edges. (3) To complete the work.

flagging   The clinging of the fabric to the needle as the needle moves up and down.

flat finish   Finishes, such as overcast, zigzag, multistitch zigzag, serged, raw edge, and seam tape, which are flat.

flat lining   A method of underlining.

flounce   Circular-shaped ruffle.

fly placket Any placket which conceals the fasteners—zipper, hooks and eyes, or buttons and buttonholes.

fray retardant Lacquerlike liquid which retards fraying. Discolors some fabrics.

fusible web A weblike material which melts when you apply heat and moisture. Stitch Witchery and Wonder Under are popular brands.

garment fabric See fashion fabric.

garment shell Outermost layers of the main garment sections, excluding hems and facings.

gather To pull excess fullness into a seamline.

gathering rows Stitched lines used for gathering. Using a regular stitch length, a tight bobbin tension, and a heavier thread on the bobbin, stitch—right side up—just inside the seamline; stitch again midway between the raw edge and seamline. Pull both threads up together so they won't break.

gauge stitch A line of machine stitching to help you gauge a distance accurately.

glover's needle Needle with a wedge point used for sewing leather and fur.

gore Garment section; usually larger at the bottom than the top.

gorge line Diagonal seamline which joins the the collar and lapel.

grading Reducing bulk of enclosed seams by trimming the individual seam allowances different widths, clipping inward curves and corners, notching convex curves, and trimming away excess fabric at outward corners.

grainline Generally refers to the lengthwise grain.

grommets Large metal eyelets.

groove of the seam See well of the seam.

hemline The lower edge of the garment.

inside Part of the garment toward the body.

interfaced facing Interfacing applied to the facing. Frequently seamed, right sides together, at the unnotched edge. Usually called a faced facing.

interfacing Fabric placed between the garment and facing to add body, strength, or shape.

interlining Fabric layer applied to the wrong side of the garment or lining for warmth.

jeans foot Machine foot for Bernina machines which holds the fabric very firmly when straight stitching.

join (1) To stitch together. (2) A seamline.

knock-off Adaptation of a more expensive garment.

(L,2) Stitch length in millimeters.

lapel Turned-back facing at garment edge between the first button and neckline.

lay Layer of fabric for layout.

layout The placement of pattern pieces on the fabric for cutting.

lengthwise grain The warp threads which run parallel to the selvage.

lining Fabric used on the inside of the garment to conceal the construction. Usually lightweight, a lining enhances the appearance, improves comfort and shape retention, and extends the garment's use.

loft Batting thickness.

miter (1) To join two edges at an angle, frequently a 45 degree angle. (2) A diagonal seam at a corner.

mm Millimeters.

mounting See underlining.

needle lubricant Silicone-like liquid which eliminates skipped stitches on fabrics, as well as eliminating sticking on leathers and vinyl. Sewers' Aid, Needle Glide, and Needle-Lube are popular brand names.

No More Pins Spray or liquid which temporarily bastes pattern to pattern.

nonwoven fabric Fabric which is neither woven nor knit.

notches Matchpoints on cutting lines of the paper pattern.

notions Sewing supplies and equipment needed to complete the garment.

open lay See single lay.

outside (1) Right side of the fabric. (2) Part of the garment seen when the garment is worn.

overcast or **overedge foot** Special machine foot which holds the fabric flat during zigzagging.

parallel Two lines evenly spaced.

pattern cloth Nonwoven fabric, plain or grid, used to make patterns.

pattern repeat The vertical distance required for one complete design on the fabric pattern.

perpendicular Two lines meeting at a right or 90° angle.

pick-up line Foldline at the center of a dart or tuck.

piecing Joining two pieces together to make one piece wider or longer.

piping Decorative strip sewn into a seamline.

pivot To turn the fabric with the needle inserted into it.

placket Any finished opening in a garment.

pocket sacks Portion of the pocket on the inside of the garment. Sometimes called pocket bags.

ply Used to describe number of fabric layers or thread strands.

preshrink To treat fabric before cutting by laundering or steam pressing to prevent shrinking later.

quarter To divide and mark section into quarters.

raw edge Unfinished or cut edge of the garment.

reinforce To strengthen a section with short machine stitches, fabric scrap, or tape.

release sheet A Teflon-like film which allows you to bond fusible web to a single layer of fabric. Trade names include TransFuse and Appliqué Pressing Sheet. Wonder Under and TransFuse II are already bonded to a release sheet.

rip To remove unwanted stitches. Using a small seam ripper, clip the needle thread every fifth stitch, then pull the bobbin thread out.

roller foot Special machine foot which grips top fabric and reduces underlayer creep.

rotary cutter and mat A cutting tool with a round cutting blade, to be used with a mat.

ruffle Decorative fabric band, gathered or pleated at the edge or in the center before it's sewn to the garment.

RTW Ready-to-wear.

satin stitch Zigzag stitch of any width with a very short length (L,.5 or less).

seam allowance The width of fabric between the stitching line and the cutting line.

seamline Stitching line.

secure To fasten threads permanently.

see-through ruler Plastic ruler with a 1/8″ grid. Manufactured by C-Thru Ruler Co.

self Same as the fashion fabric.

selvage Finished edges on each side of a woven fabric; runs parallel to the lengthwise grain. Sometimes called selvedge or self-edge.

shim Leveling device to use when machine stitching layers of uneven thicknesses. Available at sewing-machine dealers.

shrink To make smaller.

sleeve heads Narrow strips placed at the top of the sleeve cap to support the cap and make a smooth line. Usually bias-cut organza, interfacing materials, cotton batting, lamb's wool, or polyester fleece.

spi Stitches per inch.

stabilized seam Seam stabilized with lightweight selvage or seam tape. Same as taped seams (see seams).

stay Strip of lightweight selvage, seam tape, twill tape, tricot bias, or bias tape to hold the seam or edge as desired.

stitch-in-the-ditch See ditch-stitch.

stitching line Seamline.

single/lay Single layer of fabric spread for cutting.

spot tack Knot made by machine at the end of the stitching line by setting stitch length on 0 or by lowering the feed dogs.

stabilizer Tissue paper, nonwoven materials, or water-soluble materials which reduce stitching problems. Nonwoven stabilizers include Tear-Away, Stitch 'n Tear, Trace Erase; Aqua-Solv and Solvy are water-soluble stabilizers.

staystitch To straight stitch a single layer of fabric just inside the seamline.

steamer Pressing device with a plastic soleplate which only steams. The Steamstress brand is a good-quality steamer.

stitch directionally Stitch with the grain; generally, stitching from wide to narrow.

straight-stitch foot Foot used for straight stitching. Generally toes are uneven in length and width.

strike through Fusible seeps through to right side of fabric.

swatch Small fabric piece.

tack Permanent stitches to hold fabric layers permanently.

teeth Metal or nylon parts that hold the zipper together.

temporary marking pen Water-soluble and fadeaway marking pens designed to mark fabrics temporarily.

test To try on a fabric scrap.

thread trace Hand basting used to mark stitching lines, detail location lines, grain lines, and garment centers on both the right side and wrong side of the fabric.

tissue-stitch To stitch with tissue or stabilizer between the fabric and feed dogs.

topstitch To stitch on the right side of the garment.

topweight Lighter weight fabrics suitable for blouses and dresses.

trim To cut away excess fabric.

515

turn of the cloth Amount of fabric which is "lost" because of the fabric thickness when an edge is folded or turned right side out. Must be allowed for in calculating hem and seam allowances.

true bias A line midway between the warp and filling threads; a 45 degree angle from both.

underlap Part of garment which extends under another part.

underlining Fabric layer applied to the wrong side of the garment fabric before the seams are sewn. Sometimes called a backing or mounting.

understitch Technique of stitching, by hand or machine, through the facing and seam allowances.

(W,2) Stitch width in millimeters.

(W,2; L,2) Stitch width and stitch length in millimeters.

wales The lengthwise ribs on knit fabrics.

warp Threads parallel to the selvage.

water-soluble marking pen See temporary marking pen.

well of the seam The seamline on the right side of the fabric.

welt Visible part of a bound buttonhole, bound pocket, or welt pocket.

welt pocket Inset pocket with one band on the outside of the pocket. A double-welt pocket is the same as a bound pocket.

wick Ability of fiber to carry moisture away from the body without absorbing it.

wrong side Inside of the garment or back side of the fabric.

zigzag (1) The movement of the needle sideways. (2) To stitch, using a stitch with width as well as length.

zipper foot Special machine foot with one toe, which allows you to stitch close to or on top of a raised edge.

Bibliography

Books

Alderman, Sharon D., and Kathryn Wertenberger. *Handwoven, Tailormade*. Loveland, CO: Interweave Press, Inc., 1982.

Alexander, Patsy R. *Textile Products*. Boston: Houghton Mifflin Co., 1977.

American Fabrics and Fashion Magazine, ed. *The New Encyclopedia of Textiles*. Englewood Cliffs, NJ: Prentice-Hall, Inc., 1980.

American Wool Council. *See Yourself in Your Own Wool Fashions*. Denver, CO: American Wool Council, 1964.

Ashbrook, Frank G. *Furs—Glamourous and Practical*. New York: D. Van Nostrand Co., Inc., 1954.

"Attractive Hems." *Bernina Sewing Club*, Spring/Summer 1985, pp. 36–37.

Bailey, Rick, ed. *Sewing: The Complete Guide*. Tucson, AZ: HP Books, 1983.

Bane, Allyn. *Creative Clothing Construction*. New York: McGraw-Hill Book Company, 1973.

Bane, Allyn. *Creative Sewing*. New York: McGraw-Hill Book Company, Inc., 1956.

Bane, Allyn. *Tailoring*. New York: McGraw-Hill Book Co., 1968.

Barker, Linda. *That Touch of Class: Machine Embroidery on Leather*. Evanston, WY (Rt 1, Box 48).

Beaulieu, Robert J. *Fashion: Textiles and Laboratory Workbook*. Encino, CA: Glencoe Publishing Co., 1986.

Belck, Nancy, Marjory L. Joseph, and Marlene Wamhoff. *Textiles: Decision Making for the Consumer*. East Lansing, MI: Michigan State University Press, 1984.

Bendure, Zelma, and Gladys Pfeiffer. *America's Fabrics*. New York: Macmillan Co., 1947.

Betzina, Sandra, *Power Sewing*. San Francisco, CA: 1985.

Bishop, Edna Bryte, and Marjorie Stotler Arch. *Super Sewing*. Philadelphia, PA: J. B. Lippincott Co., 1962.

Brown, Gail, *Sensational Silk*. Portland, OR: Palmer/Pletsch Associates, 1982.

Brown, Gail, and Karen Dillon. *Sew A Beautiful Wedding*. Portland, OR: Palmer/Pletsch Associates, 1980.

Cabrera, Roberto, and Patricia Flaherty Meyers. *Classic Tailoring Techniques: A Construction Guide for Men's Wear*. New York: Fairchild Publications, 1983.

Carmichael, W. L., George E. Linton and Isaac Price. *Callaway Textile Dictionary*. La Grange, GA: Calloway Mills, 1947.

Coats & Clark, Inc. *Action-Packed Sewing*. Stamford, CT: Coats & Clark, Inc., 1982.

517

Coats & Clark, Inc. *Denim*. Stamford, CT: Coats & Clark, Inc., nd.

Coats & Clark, Inc. *Lingerie: Sewing on Tricot*. Stamford, CT: Coats & Clark Inc., nd.

Coats & Clark, Inc. *Quilted Fabrics*. Stamford, CT: Coats & Clark, Inc., 1982.

Coats & Clark, Inc. *Successful Sewing with Wash and Wear Fabrics*. New York: Coats & Clark, Inc., 1960.

Coats & Clark, Inc. *Stretch Terry and Velour*. Stamford, CT: Coats & Clark, Inc., nd.

Cotton from Field to Fabric. Memphis, TN: The National Cotton Council of America, 1981.

Cook, J. Gordon, ed. *Handbook of Textile Fibres: 1. Natural Fibres* and *2. Man-Made Fibres*. Durham, England: Merrow Publishing Co., Ltd., 1984.

Craig, Hazel Thompson. *Clothing: A Comprehensive Study*. Philadelphia, PA: J. B. Lippincott Co., 1968.

Crompton-Richmond Company, Inc. *A Pile Fabric Primer*. Edited by William Gaddis. New York: M. J. Gladstone, 1970.

Crown, Fenya. *The Fabric Guide for People Who Sew*. New York: Grosset and Dunlap, 1973.

DeLong, Marilyn Revell. *The Way We Look*. Ames, IA: Iowa State University Press, 1987.

Devereaux, Laverne. *Sew Lovely Lingerie: Girdles and Bras*. Minneapolis: Sew Lovely Publications, Inc., 1971.

Devereaux, Laverne. *Sew Lovely Lingerie: Slips and Panties*. Minneapolis: Sew Lovely Publications, Inc., 1971.

DuPont Fiber Facts. Wilmington, DE: E. I. du Pont de Nemours & Co.

Earnshaw, Pat. *A Dictionary of Lace*. Aylesbury, England: Shire Publications Ltd., 1982.

Eddy, Josephine F., and Elizabeth C. B. Wiley. *Pattern and Dress Design*. Boston, MA: Houghton Mifflin Co., 1932.

Ein, Claudia. *How to Make Your Own Wedding Gown*. Garden City, NY: Doubleday & Co., Inc., 1978.

Eisinger, Larry, ed. *The Complete Book of Sewing*. New York: Greystone Press, 1972.

Emery, Irene. *The Primary Structures of Fabrics*. Washington, DC: The Textile Museum, 1980.

Erwin, Mabel D., Lila A. Kinchen and Kathleen A. Peters. *Clothing for Moderns*. New York: Macmillan Publishing Co., Inc., 1979.

Facts About Man-made Fibers. New York: Celanese Fibers Marketing Company.

Fales, Anne. *Dressmaking*. New York: Charles Scribner's Sons, 1917.

Fanning, Robbie and Tony. *The Complete Book of Machine Quilting*. Radnor, PA: Chilton Book Co., 1980.

Fanning, Robbie and Tony. *The Complete Book of Machine Embroidery*. Radnor, PA: Chilton Book Co., 1986.

Fisher, Joan. *The Creative Art of Sewing*. London, England: Hamlyn, 1973.

Focus on Man-Made Fibers. Washington, DC: Man-Made Fiber Producers Association, Inc., 1985.

Geijer, Agnes. *A History of Textile Art*. London, England: Sotheby Parke Bernet Publications, 1982.

Giles, Rosalie. *Dressmaking with Special Fabrics*. London, England: Bell & Hyman, 1982.

Gioello, Debbie Ann, and Beverly Berke. *Fashion Production Terms*. New York: Fairchild Publications, 1979.

Gioello, Debbie Ann. *Profiling Fabrics: Properties, Performance & Construction Techniques*. New York: Fairchild Publications, 1981.

Gioello, Debbie Ann. *Understanding Fabrics: From Fiber to Finished Cloth*. New York: Fairchild Publications, 1982.

Goldsworthy, Maureen. *Dressmaking with Leather*. London, England: B. T. Batsford, 1976.

Gross, Catherine E. *The Fabric Thesaurus*. Louisville, KY: Baef Fabrics, 1988.

Guide to Man-Made Fibers. New York: Man-Made Fiber Producers Association, Inc., 1971.

Hardingham, Martin. *The Fabric Catalog*. New York: Pocket Books, 1978.

Hollen, Norma, Jane Saddler, Anna L. Langford, Sara J. Kadolph. *Textiles*, 6th ed. New York: Macmillan Publishing Co., 1988.

Home Cleaning Guide for Articles Containing Du Pont Textile Fibers. Wilmington, DE: E. I. du Pont de Nemours & Co., (Inc.), n.d.

Hooey, Hazel Boyd. *Silks 'n Satins*. Canada: Tex-Mar Seminars and Publications, 1986.

Hudson, Peyton B. *Guide to Apparel Manufacturing*. Greensboro, NC: MEDIApparel, Inc. 1988.

Hutton, Jessie. *Singer Fashion Tailoring*. New York: Golden Press, 1973.

Hutton, Jessie and Gladys Cunningham. *Singer Sewing Book*. New York: Golden Press, 1972.

Johnson, Mary. *The Easier Way to Sew for Your Family*. New York: E. P. Dutton & Co., Inc., 1972.

Jorgensen, Kirsten. *Making Leather Clothes*. New York: Van Nostrand Reinhold Co., 1972.

Joseph, Marjory L. *Essentials of Textiles*. New York: Holt, Rinehart and Winston, 1980.

Keenan, Nance B. *The Boiled Wool Jacket and Vest*. McMurray, PA: A. Raphael Knitte, 1985.

Kefgen, Mary, and Phyllis Touchie-Specht. *Individuality in Clothing Selection and Personal Appearance*. New York: Macmillan Publishing Co., Inc., 1981.

Komives, Margaret. *Sewing Tricks*. Milwaukee: Line Tone Litho Inc., 1974.

Krinke, Dolores. *The Feminine Art: Lingerie Sewing*. The Croixside Press, 1972.

Ladbury Ann. *The Dressmaker's Dictionary*. New York: Arco Publishing, Inc., 1982.

Ladbury, Ann. *Fabrics*. London, England: Sidgwick & Jackson, 1985.

Ladbury, Ann. *Make the Most of Your Sewing Machine*. London, England: B. T. Batsford, Ltd., 1987.

Ladbury, Ann. *Quick Casual Clothes*. Garden City, NY: Doubleday & Co., 1985.

Lawrence, Judy, and Clotilde Yurick. *Sew Smart in the Classroom*. Minneapolis, MN: Burgess Publishing Co., 1977. (Clotilde, Inc., 237 S.W. 28th St., Ft. Lauderdale, FL 33315.)

Ledbetter, N. Marie, and Linda Thiel Lansing. *Tailoring: Traditional and Contemporary Techniques*. Reston, VA: Reston Publishing Co., Inc., 1981.

Lee, Artefebas. *901 Super Quick Sewing Tips*. Fresno, CA: Artefebas, 1985.

Levey, Santina M. *Lace: A History*. London, England: The Victoria and Albert Museum, 1983.

Lewis, Virginia Stolpe. *Comparative Clothing Construction Techniques*. Minneapolis, MN: Burgess Publishing Co., 1976.

Lippman, Gidon, Dorothy Erskine. *Dressmaking Made Simple*. London, England: Heinemann, 1974.

Lyle, Dorothy Siegert. *Focus on Fabrics*. Silver Spring, MD: National Institute of Dry Cleaning, 1964.

Lyle, Dorothy Siegert. *Modern Textiles*. New York: John Wiley & Sons, 1982.

Man-Made Fibers—A New Guide. Washington, DC: Man-Made Fiber Producers Association, Inc., 1984.

Man-Made Fibers Fact Book. Washington, DC: Man-Made Fiber Producers Association, Inc., 1978.

Mansfield, Evelyn A. *Clothing Construction*. Boston, MA: Houghton Mifflin Company, 1953.

Martensson, Kerstin. *Kerstin Martensson's Kwik-Sew Method for Sewing Lingerie*. Minneapolis: Kwik Sew, 1978.

Mason, Gertrude. *Tailoring For Women*. London, England: Adam & Charles Black, 1946.

Mayer, Anita Luvera. *Handwoven Clothing—Felted to Wear*. Couperville, WA: Shuttle Craft Books, 1988.

O'Hara, Georgina. *The Encyclopaedia of Fashion*. London, England: Thames and Hudson, 1986.

Palmer, Pati, Gail Brown, and Sue Green. *Creative Serging Illustrated*. Radnor, PA: Chilton Book Co., 1987.

Palmer, Pati, and Susan Pletsch. *Sewing Skinner Ultrasuede Fabric*. Eugene, OR: Palmer/Pletsch, 1974.

Perry, Patricia, ed. *Everything about Sewing Knits*. New York: Butterick Fashion Marketing Co., 1971.

Perry, Patricia, ed. *Everything about Sewing Leather and Leather-Like Fabrics*. New York: Butterick Fashion Marketing Co., 1971.

Person, Ann. *Get Physical*. Eugene, OR: Stretch & Sew, 1984.

Person, Ann. *Lingerie*. Eugene, OR: Stretch & Sew, 1982.

Person, Ann. *Sew Active*. Eugene, OR: Stretch & Sew, 1984.

Person, Ann. *Sew Splashy*. Eugene, OR: Stretch & Sew, 1984.

Person, Ann. *Sew Tops*. Eugene, OR: Stretch & Sew, 1984.

Person, Ann. *Sew T-Riffic!* Eugene, OR: Stretch & Sew, 1985.

Person, Ann. *Sewing Sweaters*. Eugene, OR: Stretch & Sew, 1983.

Phillips, Joan Kunze, and Jean Kunze Sullivan. *Needle Knows about Ultrasuede*. Phoenix, AZ: Needle Knows, 1982.

Potter, M. D. *Fiber to Fabric*. New York: Gregg Publishing Co., 1945.

Rivers, Lucille. *Better Homes and Gardens Sewing Book*. Des Moines, IA: 1977.

Schwebke, Phyllis, and Margery Dorfmeister. *Sewing with the New Knits*. New York: Macmillan Co., 1975.

Schwebke, Phyllis, and Margaret B. Krohn. *How to Sew Leather, Suede, Fur*. New York: Collier Books, 1970.

Sewing with Durable Press Fabrics. New York: Simplicity Pattern Co., Inc., 1967.

Sewing Tips for Modern Fabrics. New York: Eastman Chemical Products, Inc., 1972.

Shaeffer, Claire B. *Claire Shaeffer's Sewing S.O.S.* Menlo. Park, CA: Open Chain Publishing, 1988.

Shaeffer, Claire B. *The Complete Book of Sewing Short Cuts.* New York: Sterling Publishing Co., Inc., 1981. (Autographed copies available: Box 157, Palm Springs, CA 92263.)

Shaeffer, Claire B. *Sew A Beautiful Gift.* New York: Sterling Publishing Co., Inc., 1986.

Shaeffer, Claire B. *Sew Successful: 1001 Super Sewing Hints.* New York: Avon Books, 1984.

Shaner, Jane. *Sewing with Leather and Suede.* McMurray, PA: The Silver Thimble, 1984.

Shaner, Jane. *Ultrasuede and What to do with it.* McMurray, PA: The Silver Thimble, 1978.

Simmons, Melissa A. *Buying and Caring for Your Fabulous Fur.* New York: Fawcett Columbine, 1986.

Simplicity's All About Plaids. New York: Simplicity Pattern Co., Inc., 1979.

Singer Reference Library. *Sewing Activewear.* Minnetonka, MN: Cy DeCosse Inc., 1986.

Singer Reference Library. *Sewing Specialty Fabrics.* Minnetonka, MN: Cy DeCosse Inc., 1986.

Singer Reference Library. *Timesaving Sewing.* Minnetonka, MN: Cy DeCosse Inc., 1987.

Tandy Leather Co. *Sewing with Leather.* Fort Worth: Tandy Leather Co., 1986.

Textile Handbook. Washington, DC: American Home Economics Association, 1974.

Thomas, Debbie. "Mixing Prints and Textures," "The Selvage." Minneapolis: The American Sewing Guild, June/July 1983, p. 9.

Tortora, Phyllis G. *Understanding Textiles.* New York: Macmillan Publishing Co., Inc., 1982.

Vogue Sewing. New York: Butterick Fashion Marketing Company, 1982.

Vogue's Book of Smart Dressmaking. Conde Nast Publications, Inc., 1936.

Weiland, Barbara, and Leslie Wood. *Clothes Sense.* Portland, OR: Palmer/Pletsch Associates, 1984.

Wilson, Kay. *A History of Textiles.* Boulder, CO: Westview Press, 1979.

Wingate, Isabel and Jane F. Mohler. *Textile Fabrics and Their Selection,* 8th ed. Englewood Cliffs, NJ: Prentice-Hall, Inc., 1984.

Wool Bureau, Inc. *The Story of Wool.* Denver, CO: American Wool Council and The Wool Bureau, Inc., 1968.

Woman's Institute Library of Dressmaking. *Sewing Materials.* Scranton, PA: Woman's Institute, 1926.

Zieman, Nancy with Robbie Fanning. *The Busy Woman's Sewing Book.* Menlo Park, CA: Open Chain Publishing, 1988.

Magazines

Through the years, I've read and clipped numerous articles from the following newsletters and magazines.

Butterick Sewing World, Butterick Co., 161 Ave. of the Americas, New York, NY.

Handwoven, Interweave Press, 306 N. Washington Ave., Loveland, CO 80537.

McCall's Patterns, The McCall Pattern Co., 230 Park Ave., New York, NY.

Sew It Seams, 333 11th Place, Kirkland, WA 98083.

Sew News, PJS Publications, P.O. Box 1790, Peoria, IL 61656.

Sewing Update (newsletter), 2269 Chestnut, Ste. 269, San Francisco, CA 94123.

Silver Thimble (newsletter), 311 Valley Brook Rd., McMurray, PA 15317.

Simplicity Today, 200 Madison Ave., New York, NY.

Threads Magazine, Taunton Press, P.O. Box 355, Newton, CT 06470.

Vogue Patterns, see *Butterick Sewing World.*

Index

Page numbers in *italic* indicate information in illustrations. For terminology and definitions, *see also* Fabric and Fiber Dictionary, p. 471, and the Glossary, p. 512.

abutted seams, 379–380
accordion pleating, 227
acetate, 63–65
  care of garments, 64
Acrilan, 74
acrylics, 74–76
  in wool blend, 58
action knits, 184–187
activewear, 167
A jours, 242
à la Creme, 372
albatross, 45
Alençon lace, 240, 244, 245
all-bias nonwoven interfacings, 354
allover lace, 240, 243, 244
alpaca, 50
  fiber from, 60
aluminized Mylar needlepunch, 369
Amara, 96
Ambiance, 372
American Peeler cotton, 18
American Pima cotton, 18
angora rabbits, 61
antelope, 80
antique satin, 212, 217
antique taffeta, 221
Antron, 65
appliqué seams, 380–382
appliquéd darts, in lace, 245–246
appliqués
  fusing, 248
  lace, 242, 247–248
  by machine, on sweatshirt knits, 168
Armo Wool, 369
  as underlining, 284
arnel, 64
artificial silk, 62
astrakhan, 50, 112
asute, 234–235
athletic mesh, 168, 197, 198
Avisco XL, 63
Avril, 63

Avril Prima Fibers, 63
Avron, 63
awning stripes, 338

background, of lace, 242
backings, 372
backstitches, 464
bagheera velvet, 267
baize, 50
balanced alternating stripes, 338
balanced plaids, 326
  layout for, 330–333
balanced stripes, testing for, 339
bale, of silk, 27
Balmain, Pierre, *27*
bands, as edge finishes, 436–437
Bannockburn tweeds, 47
Barker, Linda, *That Touch of Class;*
    Machine Embroidery on Leather, 91
baronet satin, 212
basket-weave fabric, 7
  vs. plain-weave, 125
basting, 14
  and avoiding imprint, 223
  on leather, 86
  on plaids, 335–336
  removing, 381
  on silk, 30
  stitches for, 464–465
  on Ultrasuede, 100
bathrobes, 167, 273
batiste, 18, 45, 197, 372
Battenberg lace, 242
batting, 369–371
  for custom quilting, 323
bead edge, of lace, 242
beaded fabric, 235–238
beading, 242
beads, gluing, 249
beaver, 112
Bedford cord, 338
bedspreads, 262

Beene, Geoffrey, 17, 51, 52, 312
Bellana, 57
Belleseime, 96
belts, for fake furs, 283
bemberg, 30, 63, 372
bengaline, 217
Biagiotti, Laura, 38, 51, 53, 323
bias collars, from plaids, 332
bias-cut designs, from plaids, 332–333,
  334
bias facings, 446
  vs. bindings, 437–438
bias seams, double-fold, 315
bias tape, and knits, 153
bias trims, from diagonal reversible
  fabric, 346
bindings
  from braid, 443
  designer, 441–442
  double, 440–441
  as edge finishes, 437–444
  finishing edges of, 443–444
  in knits, 153
  from nonwoven fabric, 443
  ribbon for, 443
  one-step, 442
  on Ultrasuede, 105
  for velvet, 270
Bion II, 142
blanket stitch, 465
blankets, as batting, 370
Blass, Bill, *125, 228, 258, 355*
bleeding, reducing, from ribbing, 179
blends, 7, 139
  of cotton, 18
  of silk, 29
blindstitch
  hand, 465
  hemming with, 161, 192, 415–416
  machine, 421–422
blocking, sweater knits, 176
Blue C, 77, 188

521

bobbin
  for knits, 152
  lightweight polyester and, 72
  winding, 141
bobbinet, 250
bobbin-stitching darts, 203
Bohan, Marc, *154*
boiled wool, 148, 287, 288
  process for making, 290
  purchase of, 289
bolivia, 50
bonded batting, 369
book hem, 417, 430
books, of silk, 27
border designs, 341–343
bouclé, 7, 133
bound-and-lapped seams, 383
  for quilted fabric, 315
bound-and-stitched seams, 383–385
bound buttonholes, 54, 101–102,
    451–455
  on double cloth, 307
  patch method for, 451–452
  strip, 452–453
  on striped fabric, 341
  windowpane, 453–454
bound seams, 382–385, 410–411
  for quilted fabric, 314–315
braid bindings, 443
braided straps, 173
Breton lace, 241
bridal gowns, 214
  storing, 250
bridal veils, 252
brides, in lace, 242
bridesmaids' dresses, 204
broadcloth, 7, 18, 125, 217
  interfacings for, 362
  silk, 30
broadtail, 112
brocade, 19, 64, 223–224, 231
brocaded velvet, 267
brocatelle, 223, 224
brushed denim, 255
bubble skirts, 252
buckskin, 80
bunting, 148, 287, 288, 369
burn test, for fiber identification, 6
burned-out lace, 241
Burrows, Stephen, 421
butted seams, 379–380
Butterfly, 372
button links, 308
button loops, 54, 102, 283, 449–450
  for transparent fabrics, 205
buttonholes, 54, 450–459. *See also*
    bound buttonholes
  corded, 459
  cutting, 459
  faced, 282–283, 307, 455–456
  on fake furs, 282–283
  hand-worked, 308, 456–457
  on handwovens, 138
  inseam, 308
  in jersey, 156
  keyhole, 458–459
  leather, 454–455
  length of, 450–451
  in linen garments, 24
  machine-stitched, 208, 457–459
  on plaids, 336
  in raschel knits, 166

  in ribbing, 180
  in satin, 216
  stitch-slash, 95, 459
  on striped fabrics, 341
  thread for, 457
  on velvet, 270
buttonhole stitch, by hand, 466
buttons, 4
  on fake furs, 283
  full ball, 216

cabretta, 81
calf, 112
calfskin suede, 81
calico, 125
camel's hair, 50, 60, 255
camping gear, 142
candling, 413
canton crepe, 217
canton satin, 212
canvas, 130
capes, 278, 289, 298
Cardin, Pierre, *65, 71, 77, 130, 167,*
    175, 182, 273
care of garment, 7
  of acetate, 64
  of cotton, 21
  of fake furs, 284
  insulated, 371
  of lace, 250
  of linen, 24–25
  of nylon, 67
  of polyester, 70
  prepleated, 231
  sequinned, 238
  of silk, 31
  of suede, 92
  of triacetate, 65
  of velvet, 271
Caress, 96, 105
carpet beetles, 21
Carven, *133*
Cashin, Bonnie, *91*, 91
cashmere, 50, 59–60
casings, for elastic in tricot, 172
cassimere, 48
catchstitches, 466
  blind, 416, 466
  for hems, 417
cavalry twill, 50
chalk, 11
challis, 18, 45, 125, 197
chambray, 125
chamois, 81
Chanel chain, 434
Chanel suits, 138
changeable taffeta, 221
channel seams, 401
Chantilly, 240, 244, 245
  vs. Alençon lace, 240
charmeuse, 7, 30, 32, 212, 373
  evaluating, 33
charmeuse batiste, interfacings for,
    360–361
checks, 337
  woven vs. printed, 5
chemical lace, 241
chenille, 257, 275
Chesterfield, 372
cheviot, 48
chevron, diagonals and, 344, 346
chiffon, 197, 208

interfacings for, 360
  as lining, 373
chiffon velvet, 267
children's garments, 167, 226, 262,
    263, 266, 289
  fabric for, 4
China grass, 26
China silk, 30, 31, 32, 372
chinchilla, 50, 112
chinella, 287, 288, 371
chino, 128
Ciao, 373
cire, 212
clean-finished edge, 304
clean-finished seams, 301–302, 413
Cleerspan, 77, 188
clips, 11
cloque, 223, 224
closed-slot seams, 402
closures, 449–463. *See also* buttonholes
  in action knits, 186
  button loops as, 449–450
  for coatings, 54
  for denim, 132
  for double knits, 162
  for fake furs, 282–283
  on felt, 287
  fly plackets for, 460–461
  for fur, 118
  on handwovens, 138
  for lace, 247
  on leather, 88
  for prepleated fabric, 230
  on reversible garments, 296,
    307–309
  for satin, 216
  for silk, 36
  snaps as, 461
  ties and straps as, 462
  in transparent fabrics, 205, 210–211
  on Ultrasuede, 101–103
  for velvet, 270
  for velveteen, 266
  on vinyls, 110
  zippers as, 462–463
Cluny lace, 240, 244
coatings, 50–57
  closures for, 54
  collars on, 55
  facings for, 52
  interfacings for, 54
  planning, 50–51
  pockets on, 55–57
  sewing, 52–57
  topstitching on, 54
coats, 278, 289, 319
collars
  bias, from plaids, 332
  from fake furs, 281
  of fur, 118
  on coatings, 55
  organdy, 207–208
  on reversible garments, 310–311
  on Ultrasuede, 103–104
colors
  and figure flattery, 4
  setting, 38, 179
comfort, 7
Comiso, 63
Complete Book of Sewing Short Cuts, 2
concertina pleating, 231
continuous bound placket, 211

Cool Wool, 45
corded buttonholes, 459
corded piping, 399–400
corded tubing, 450
cordonnet, 242
Cordura, 65, 142
corduroy, 18, 257, 261–264, 338
    vs. velveteen, 262, 265
corners
    applying piping to, 399
    binding, 439
    in linen, 24
    mitered, 424
cortex, of wool fiber, 39
cottons, 7, 17–21
    batting of, 369
    care of, 21
    crepe of, 125
    interfacings for, 362
    net of, 373
    organdy of, 205
    planning garment with, 18–19
    satin of, 212
    sewing, 19–20
    silk blend with, 29
    straightening, 19
    vs. linen, 23
couching, 119
Coupe de Ville, 373
Courreges, 159, 256, 340
courses, in knits, 149
covert, 48, 128
cowhide, 81
creases
    in double knits, 160
    in knits, 151
    setting, 192
creeping, reducing, 183
crepe, 45, 64
    evaluating, 33
    wool, pressing, 44
crepe-backed satin, 212, 373
crepe chiffon, 197, 208
crepe de chine, 30, 32, 373
    interfacings for, 360
crepe tricots, 170
Crepela, 57
Creslan, 74
crochet-type knits, 197
crocking, testing denim for, 131
cross-stitched hem, 417
crotch lining, 172
crushed velvet, 267
cuffs, on Ultrasuede, 101
cupramonium rayon, 63
Curel, 77, 188
curling
    reducing, 183
    reducing, in jersey, 156
curtains, acrylic for, 75
custom-knit fabric, 176
custom-pleated skirts, 230–231
custom quilting, 322–323
cut-edge hems, 426
cut velvet, 212, 267, 341
cutouts, of lace, 249
cutting, 11
cycling costumes, 184

D.W.R., 142
Dacron, 67
damask, 7, 292

dance costumes, 184
darts
    appliquéd, in lace, 245–246
    changing bias to underarm, 345
    in linen, 24
    on reversible garments, 306
    on silk, 30
    in transparent fabrics, 203
    in wool, 42
de la Renta, Oscar, 224, 337, 344
decorative seams, 385
    bound, 382–383
    French, 391
decorative surface fabric, 223–227
deerskin, 81
Delphos, 227
denim, 129–133
    brushed, 255
    closures for, 132
    hems in, 132
    interfacings for, 362–365
    reducing fading in, 133
    sewing multiple thicknesses of, 131
design
    changes in, 9–10
    ideas for, 8
designer binding, 441–442
diagonal patterns, 343–346
Diana, 57
dimity, 197–198, 217, 338
Dior, Christian, 46, 51, 59, 113, 121,
    154
dishrag knits, 168, 197, 198
ditch stitched band, 137
dobby weaves, 19
doeskin, 81, 255
Domette, 370
Donegal tweeds, 47
dotted Swiss, 19, 197, 198–199, 205
double bindings, 440–441
double-cloth fabrics, 292, 297–311
    flat-fell seam for, 302
    lapped seam for, 303–304
    layout for, 299, 301
    piped edges for, 305
    self-bound edges for, 306
double-faced fabrics
    quilted, 311–318
    satin, 212
double-fold bias seams, 315
double-fold finish, for reversible
    garments, 304–305
double hems, 417–418
double knits, 64, 147, 148, 157–162,
    292
    edge finishes for, 161
    hems in, 161
    interfacings for, 161, 362–366
    layout, cutting and marking, 160
    linings and underlinings for,
    161–162
    recovery of, 158
    seams in, 160
double-lapped seams, 386
double/ply seams, 386
double sheer, 199
double-stitched seams, 386
    stretch, 404
    for hems, 418
double-strap seams, 398–399
double-welt seams, 408
doupion silk, 26

douppioni, 217
down, 369, 371
draperies, 20
    acrylic for, 75
drapery French seams, 387
drapery weights, 434
drape
    of silk, 28
    of wool, 40
draw seams, 386–387
draw stitch, 469
dress shields, for silk garments, 31
drill, 128
Duchesse satin, 212
duck, 130
duffcl, 287
durability
    in children's clothes, 4
    of cotton, testing, 18–19
    of wool, 40

Earl-Glo Satin, 373
ease, in sleeve, reducing, 73
Easy-Knit, 170
edge finishes, 436–448
    bands as, 436–437
    bindings as, 437–444
    for double knits, 161
    edgestitched, 413
    elastic, 186, 444–445
    facings as, 447–448
    on fake furs, 281
    fluted, 230
    on fur, 117
    interfaced, 358
    on jersey, 156
    on knits, 153
    on lace, 246
    for prepleated fabric, 230
    on quilted fabric, 316–317
    for raschel knits, 166
    for reversible garments, 296,
    304–306
    ribbing for, 178, 448
    for sequinned fabric, 237
    shaped, faced hem for, 418–419
    for stretch terry and velour, 183
    in transparent fabrics, 203
    on vinyls, 110
    zigzagged, 434
edges, unfinished, 414
edge-to-edge linings, 204
edgings
    handkerchief, 423
    lace, 242, 243
    lettuce, 186, 421
Egyptian cotton, 18
Egyptian mummy cloths, 23
elastane, 188
elastic
    on action knit edges, 186
    in casing for knit skirts, 178
    as edge finish, 444–445
    in tricot, 172
elastic stitches, for knits, 152
elasticity, in straight stitch, 404
elasticized fabrics, 192–193
elastine, 184
elastique, 48
elk, 81
embossed fabric, 224, 226
embroidered designs, 7

on border, 341
on net, 252
on sweatshirt knits, 168
enclosed seams, 387
Encron, 67
English net, 250
Entrant, 142
epicuticle, of wool fiber, 39
epidermis, of wool fiber, 39
ermine, 112
Eskimo, 370
even plaids, 325, 326
    layout for, 330–333
even stripes, 339
evening gowns, 155, 214, 340
eyelash voile, 197, 199
eyelet, 18, 197, 199, 341

fabric
    evaluating, 4
    preparing, 10
fabric bands, on lace, 246
fabric notebook, 3
fabric softener sheets, 70
fabric weight
    and needle size, 20
    and stitch setting, 20
face side
    of cotton, 19
    of silk, 29
    of wool, 40
faced buttonholes, 282–283, 307,
    455–456
faced hems, 282, 418–419
faced tuck seam, 407
Facile, 96, 105
facings, 446–447
    for coatings, 52
    for corduroy, 263
    decorative, on quilted fabrics, 316
    faced, 358
    in fake furs, 279
    net and tulle as, 252
    for polyester, 70
    securing, for double knits, 161
    on terry or velour, 274–275
    for transparent fabrics, 207
    for velvet, 269–270
faconné velvet, 267
fading, reducing, 21
faille, 64, 217
faille taffeta, 221
fake flat-fell seams, 389
fake furs, 76, 276–284
    layout, cutting and marking, 279
    as lining, 373
    purchasing, 277
    seams for, 280–281
false band, 437
false French seams, 387–388
fan pleating, 231
feathers, 120–121
Featherwool, 57
fell stitches, 467
felt, 285–287
felted fabric, 287–291
    process for making, 290–291
Feraud, Louis, 48, 288
Ferragamo, 305
fiber content, 5
    burn test for, 6
fiber length, of cotton, 18
fibroin, 26

figure type
    flattering, fabrics for, 4–5
    large, 209
    and prints, 348
    and stripes, 340
figure-eight stitches, 467
    hemming with, 416
filament fiber, 26
filet, 241
filling-face twills, 127
filling knits, 147
fishnets, 198
flannel, 48, 64
flaps, on coatings, 55
flat hem, 425
flat lining, 372
    pattern for, 375
flat-fell lapped zippers, 132
flat-fell seams, 388–389
    for double-cloth fabric, 302
    for nonwoven fabric, 396–397
    for quilted fabric, 313–314
flat-locked seams, 390
flax, vs. cotton, 18
fleece, 50, 166, 257
    polyester, 370
    sweatshirt, 255
flocked dotted Swiss, 19
flowers, of lace, 249
fluted edges, 230, 421
fly plackets, 460–461
folded edge, for hems, 435
footing, of lace, 242
Fortrel, 67
Fortuny, Mariano, 227
Fortuny, Mario, 230
foulard, 32
four-way stretch knits, 148–149
fox, 112
fray retardant, 151, 226
    on metallics, 233
fraying, testing for, 5
French seams, 390–391
    drapery, 387
    false, 387–388
frieze, 287
fringed hem, 137–138
fringed seams, 391
Fuji silk, 32
full ball buttons, 216
fur, 112–119
    cleaning, 115
    fake, 276–284
    purchasing, 114–115
    seams on, 117, 391–392
fur-bearing animals, 60–61
Fur Products Labeling Act of 1951, 61
fused hems, 419
fusible interfacings, 36, 353
    for corduroy, 263
    evaluating, 356
    for seam finish, 411
    on transparent fabrics, 203
    as underlining, 376
fusible resins, removing from iron,
    254
fusible webs, 354, 369

gabardine, 7, 48, 128
gabardine coating, 50
Galanos, 13, 205
galloons, 242
    insertions of, 248

garment planning, 3–8
garment care, 8
    for velveteen, 266
garment split, 83
garment suede, 81
gathers, in pile fabric, 260
gauze, 45, 197, 199
gazar, 199, 205
Geiger, 287
georgette, 197, 199, 208
    interfacings for, 360
gingham, 18, 337
girdle fabric, action knit lining, 186
Glore-Valcana, 96
Glospan, 77, 188
glue, temporary, for pattern, 34
glue stick, 356
    for basting, 335
glued hems, 419
goats, hair fibers from, 59–60
    goatskin, 81
Gore-Tex, 142
gorgeline, 387
grain, changing, ribbed fabric and, 219
grease spots, removing, 31, 37
Great Lakes Mink Association, 113
gros de Loudres, 217–218
grosgrain, 217
grotzen, 113
ground, of lace, 242
guanaco, fleece from, 60
guard hairs, 116
Guatemalan cotton, 21
guipure, 241
guipure lace, 243, 245
    underlinings for, 246

H_2O wool, 57
hair canvas, 354, 367
hair fibers, 59–61
    hairline seams, 392–393
hairsheep, 81
half backstitches, 464
Halston, 96
hand, of silk, 28
hand knitting, 147
hand overcasting, for seam finish, 411
hand stitches, 464–469
    backstitching, 464
    basting, 464–465
    blanket, 465
    blind, 415, 465
    blind catchstitch, 466
    buttonhole, 54, 308, 456–457, 466
    catchstitches, 466
    fell, 467
    figure-eight, 467
    ladder, 468–469
    overcasting, 467
    padding, 468
    rolled hems, 426–427
    running, 468
    stab, 468
    whipping, 469
hand-stitched zippers, 309
hand-tailored collars, 310–311
handkerchief edging, 423
handkerchief linen, 25–26, 197, 199
    interfacings for, 360–361, 362
hands, smoothing roughness in, 215
handwovens, 133
    plaids, 328–329
    seams on, 136–137

staystitching on, 136
stripes on, 135
Harris tweeds, 47, 48
Hayes, David, 33
Helanca, 66
hem bands, for sequinned fabric, 237–238
hemline, reducing rolling at, 183
hemming clamps, 426
hems, 13–14, 415–435
  avoiding limp, 247
  blindstitched, 192, 415–416
  book, 417
  on border designs, 343
  catchstitch, 417
  in denim, 132
  double, 417–418
  in double knits, 161
  double-stitched, 418
  faced, 282, 418–419
  on fake furs, 281–282
  figure-eight, 416
  finishes for, 435
  fringed, 137–138
  fused, 419
  glued, 419
  horsehair, 419–420
  interfaced, 420–421
  in jersey, 156
  for knits, 152–153
  on lace, 246
  on leather, 87–88
  on lightweight polyester, 72
  in linen garment, 24
  machine-rolled, 422–423
  mitered, 423–425
  in net, 252
  padded, 425
  pinked, 425
  plain, 425–426
  for prepleated fabric, 229–230
  for raschel knits, 166
  raw-edge, 426
  in ribbing, 180
  rolled, 426–428
  on satin, 215
  satin-stitched, 428
  scalloped, 429
  for sequinned fabric, 237
  shell, 429
  shirttail, 430
  on silk, 30, 36
  slipstitched, 430
  stretch, 431
  topstitched, 431–432
  in transparent fabrics, 203, 210, 432
  tucked, 432–433
  twin-needle, 433
  on velvet, 269
  weighted, 433–434
  wired, 434
Herrera, Carolina, *233, 250, 253*
herringbone, 47, 127, 416
hides, 81, 84
Hollofil, 370
homespuns, 48, 50
Hong Kong seam finish, 411–412
hook and loop tape, and action knits, 184
hooks, hiding small, 247
hopsacking, 133
horsehair, 61
horsehair hems, 419–420

House of Balmain, 267
huarizo, fleece from, 60
HWM (hig-wet-modulus) rayons, 63

ice skating costumes, linings in, 186
illusion, 250
imperial brocade, 224
inseam buttonholes, 308
inseam pockets, 166, 204
insertion seams, 393
  for double-cloth fabric, 302–303
insertions, 242
  joining, 243
  lace-border, 247
insulating fabric, 369–371
interfacings, 4, 353–368
  additional fabric for, 73
  applying, 358
  checklist for, 360–368
  for coatings, 54
  cutting, 357
  for double knits, 161
  for edges, 358
  as facings, 183
  for fake furs, 283
  fusing process for, 359
  on hems, 420–421
  for jersey, 157
  for knits, 153
  for lace, 246
  lapped seams for, 394
  for leather, 89
  library of, 357
  for linen garment, 24
  net and tulle as, 252
  for polyester, 70
  preshrinking, 357
  reasons for, 353
  removing, 359
  selecting, 354–357
  self-fabric, 358–359
  for silk, 30, 36
  specialty, 368
  stretch in, 356
  for stretch-woven fabric, 192
  for sweater knits, 178
  in transparent fabrics, 203–204
    for velvet, 269–270
interlock knits, 147, 149, 162–163
  milanese knits vs., 175
Interspan, 77, 188
inventory system, 3
iridescent taffeta, 221
  nap layout for, 222
iron, cleaning, 254

jabutai, 32
jackets, 163
  lining for, 375
jacquard, 19, 30, 32, 292
Jameson, Rosemary, 186
jersey, 64, 147, 149, 153–157
  edge finishes on, 156
  face side of, 19
  hems in, 156
  interfacings and linings for, 157
  layout, cutting and marking, 155–156
  as lining, 373
  recovery of, 154
  reducing curling in, 156
  seams in, 156

vs. interlocks, 162
vs. tricot, 153–154

K-Kote, 142
Kamali, Norma, 167
Keenan, Nancy, *The "Boiled Wool" Jacket,* 290
kersey, 50
keyhole buttonholes, 458–459
Keyon's Wash Cycle, 146
khaki, 128
King William, 373
kip, 81
Kleibacker, Charles, 36, 209, 213
Kleibacker Group, 272
knit garments, planning, 150–151
Knit Shape, 170
knits, 5, 147–189
  action, 184–187
  crease line in, 151
  determining stretch of, 151
  double, 292
  edge finishes on, 153
  face side of, 19
  filling, 147
  grainline of, 152
  hems for, 152–153
  interfacings for, 362–365
  layout of, 151
  milanese, 175
  off-grain, 151
  preparing, 151
  preventing runs in, 151
  seams in, 152
  selecting, 150–151
  stitching tips for, 152
  topstitched hems for, 432
  vs. wovens, 149–150
  warp, 147
  weft, 147
knitted straps, 173
knitting, hand, 147
Kodel, 67
Krizia, 47

labeling, of wool, 38
lace, 7, 64, 197, 199, 231, 238–250, 341
  appliqué of, 247–248
  appliqué seams for, 380
  appliquéd darts in, 245–246
  border appliqués of, 247
  border insertions of, 247
  closures for, 247
  cutouts of, 249
  as facing, 447
  flowers of, 249
  hems in, 246
  layout, cutting and marking of, 244–245
  pressing and care of, 250
  right side of, 244
  ruffles of, 249
  seams on, 245
  tea dyeing of, 249–250
  three-dimensional effects with, 249
  whitening old, 249
lace insertions, 248
lace seam binding, for double knit hems, 161
laced seams, 308–309, 394
  on reversible garments, 296–297
ladder stitches, 468–469

Lamaire, 107
lamb's wool, 255, 370
　as underlining, 284
lambskin, 81
lamé, 231
Lamous, 86
Lamous-Lite, 96, 105
Lana Silk, 57
lapels
　from fake furs, 281
　plaids and, 331–332
　on Ultrasuede, 103–104
lapped seams, 303–304, 394
　on leather, 87
　for nonwoven fabric, 396–397
large figure types, 209
lattice seams, for nonwoven fabric, 398
lawn, 197, 199
layout, 11
　for fake furs, 279
　for pile fabrics, 259–260
　for Ultrasuede, 98
　for wool, 42
leather, 80–95
　basting on, 86
　buttonholes of, 454–455
　care of, 91–92
　closures on, 88
　hems on, 87–88
　interfacings for, 89
　and knits, 153
　lapped seams for, 396
　layout for, 85
　linings for, 89–90
　pockets on, 89
　purchasing, 84
　seams for, 86–87, 395–396
　trims of, 91
Leavers machine, 238, 243
Lee, William, 147
leno, 197, 199
leopard, 112
leotards, 184
lettuce edging, 186, 421
lightweight fabrics
　polyester, 70–74
　silks, 32–37
　synthetic suedes, 105–106
　wool, 45–46
linen, 21–26
　handkerchief, 25–26
　interfacings for, 355, 362
　pressing, 24
　sewing, 23–24
　vs. cotton, 23
lingerie, 155, 171, 214
　straps for, 173, 215
linings, 4, 372–376
　for action knits, 186–187
　for corduroy, 263
　crotch, 172
　for double knits, 161–162
　edge-to-edge pattern for, 374–375
　for fake furs, 284
　of fur, 118
　for jersey, 157
　for knits, 153
　for lace, 246
　for leather, 89–90
　for lightweight polyester, 73–74
　for linen garment, 24
　for quilted garments, 322

for satin, 216
　selecting, 374
　for silk, 30–31, 36–37
　for stretch-woven fabric, 192
　for sweater knits, 178
　for transparent fabrics, 204
　for velvet, 269–270
links, button, 308
linters, 18
Litrelle, 63
llama, fleece from, 60
loden, 50, 287
London shrunk wool, 41
loosely woven fabric, 133–139
loungewear, 171, 319
Lurex, 231
Lycra, 77, 188, 190
lynx, 112
lyons velvet, 267

machine appliqué, on sweatshirt knits, 168
machine-rolled hem, 422–423
machine-rolled seams, 396
machine-stitching
　blindstitch, 421–422
　buttonholes, 54, 457–459
magic lined patch pockets, 56–57
maline, 199, 250
man-made fiber fabrics, 62–79
　rayon, 62–63
　silk blend with, 29
Manhattan, 57
mantua maker, 403
marabou, 120–121
Marii, 227
marking, 11–13
　prick and pounce, 324
　white fabric, 253
marking pens, temporary, 12
marocain, 218
marquisette, 197, 199, 373
　as interfacings, 355
　interfacings for, 360
marten, 112
matelasse, 223, 224, 231
McFadden, Mary, 66, 227
medallions, 242
medulla, of wool fiber, 39
Melt Adhesive Thread, 419
melton, 50, 255, 287
mercerized cottons, 18, 19
merino wool, 287
merrow finish, 423
　mock, 425
mesh, 168–170
messaline, 212
metallic lace, 241
metallics, 231–235
Metlon, 231
milanese, 147
milanese knits, 149, 175
milanese lace, 242
mildew, 21
milium, 373
　for lining, 370
milliner's rose, 173–174
Minaret, 373
mink, 112
mirror-image stripes, 338–339
mirror stripes, 341
mirror velvet, 267
misti, fleece from, 60

mitered hems, 423–425
mock-merrow finish, 425
mock whipped seam, 409
modacrylics, 76
mohair, 59, 255
　pressing, 44
moiré faille, 218, 221
moiré taffeta, 218, 221
　nap layout for, 222
moisture, and sequins, 235
moisture absorbency, 140
　testing, 69
monk's cloth, 133
morocco, 81
Mortensen, Erik, 27, 174, 267
moth balls, and wool, 45
moths, 21
motifs, 242, 349, 380
Mountain Cloth, 142
mountings, 372
mousseline, 199
mouton, 112
Moynel, 63
multi-ply yarns, 7
mushroom pleating, 227
muskrat, 112
muslin, 125
　as lining, 373
　silk, 199
Mutation Mink Breeders Association, 113
Mylar needlepunch, aluminized, 369

nacre velvet, 267
naked leather, 81
naked wool, 45
nap, 255–257
　determining direction of, 257
　and stretch terry color, 183
　wool with brushed, pressing, 44
napa, 81
napkin finish, 423
natural fiber fabrics, 3, 17–61. See also
　cotton; linen; silk; wool
　ramie, 26
　serviceability of, 5
neckline
　of ribbing, 180–181
　stabilizing, 310
needle hole in machine, preventing fabric in, 202
needle holes
　in plain-weave fabrics, 127
　on suede, 86
　on Ultrasuede, 100
needle size
　fabric weight and, 20
　and stitch setting, 20
needlepunch, 370
　aluminized Mylar, 369
needle-ready wool, 41
needles, 11
　for jersey, 154
　for knits, 150, 152
　for nylon, 66–67
　for outerwear fabric, 145
　for polyester, 69–70
　for silk, 30
　for wash-and-wear fabrics, 141
　for wool, 42
negligees, 214
net, 197, 199, 250–252
　as lining, 373

power, 188–189
as underlining, 205
new wool, 38
ninon, 199
No More Pins, 34, 233
nonwoven buttonholes, 454
nonwoven fabric
bindings of, 443
interfacings of, 353
seams for, 396–399
Norell Coat, 57
Norell collar, 310
notebooks, 2, 3
Novarese, Michael, 249
Novel, Norman, 434
Numa, 77
nun's veiling, 199
Nuna, 188
Nupron, 63
nutria, 113
nylon, 7, 65–67
in wool blend, 58
vs. polyester, 69
Nylon Antron Taffeta, 142
Nylon Pack Cloth, 142
nylon/spandex blends, 185
Nylon Taffeta, 143

ocelot, 113
odors
removing from polyester, 70
on wash-and-wear fabrics, 141
off-grain fabric, knits as, 151
old quilts, 312, 313
olefin, 78–79
open-slot seams, 402
open-weave fabric, 7, 197
open-work raschel knits, 199
opossum, 113
organdy, 7, 197, 199
care of, 201
cotton, 205
as interfacings, 355
organdy collar, 207–208
organza, 31, 197, 199
as lining, 373
silk, 205
Orlon, 74
ostrich, 81
otter, 113
ottoman, 50, 218, 338
outerwear fabric, 142–146
overcasting stitches, 467
overlock machines, stretch seams on, 405
overlocked edge, 413
Oxford Cloth, 18
oxford stripes, 338

padded hem, 425
padding stitches, 468
panné, 64
panné satin, 212
panné velvet, 267, 271–272
paper taffeta, 221
Parallele, Emanuel Ungaro, 292, 347
parkas, 142
patch method, for bound buttonholes, 451–452
patch pockets, 56, 104
on mesh, 169
patent leather, 82

patterns
choosing, 4
duplicating pieces of, 9
preparing and adjusting, 8–9
selection of, 8–14
up-to-date, 8
peau d'ange, 212, 241
peau de soie, 212
peccary leather, 82
Pellon's Stitch-n-Tear, 168
pelt, 82
percale, 125
permanent-pleated garments, 70
permanent press, 139
Persian lamb, 113
perspiration stains, avoiding, 215
Peruvian cotton, 18
pickstitches, 54, 464
picots, 242
pigmented taffeta, 221
pigskin, 82, 92
pile fabrics, 257–261
tufted, 275–276
pillow ticking, 128, 338
pinked finish
hems, 425
seams, 412
pins, 11–13
pinstripes, 48, 338
pinwale piqué, 218
piping
on double-cloth edges, 305
in seams, 399–400
on Ultrasuede, 105
placket, continuous bound, 211
plaids, 292, 325–336
basting techniques for, 335–336
bias collars from, 332
estimating extra fabric for, 328
even vs. uneven, 325–326
handwoven, 328–329
layout for, 329–334
seams for, 335
selecting, 327–328
woven vs. printed, 5, 328
plain knit stitches, 147
plain-weave fabrics, 125–127
planning garments, 3–8
with cotton, 18–19
with knits, 150–151
with linen, 23
with silk, 28–29, 33–34
play clothes, 193. See also children's garments
pleats
kinds of, 227
setting, in linen, 24
sunburst, 231
plissé, 7, 223, 224, 226
plonge, 82
plush, 259
pockets
on coatings, 55–57
in fake furs, 278, 283
inseam, 166, 204
on leather, 89
patch, 104, 169
on plaids, 334
on quilted fabrics, 317
on reversible garments, 306–307
on striped fabric, 341
on terry or velour, 274–275
in velvet, 270

of velveteen, 266
Yamamoto inseam, 296
point d'esprit, 199, 250
point de Venise lace, 241
Polarfleece, 287, 288, 371
polarguard, 370
Polarlite, 287, 288, 371
Polarplus, 287, 371
polo cloth, 50
Poly SiBonne Plus, 373
polyester, 7, 67–74
batting of, 370
in bunting, 148
fleece of, 370
lightweight, 70–74
as lining, 373
needles for, 69–70
organdy of, 205
sewing, 69–70
vs. nylon, 66, 69
in wool blend, 58
Polynosic, 63
polypropylene, 78–79
in bunting, 148
ponchos, 278, 289, 298
pongee, 27, 32, 218
poplin, 18, 218
interfacings for, 362–365
power net, 149, 188–189
as action knit lining, 186
prepleated fabric, 227–231
closures for, 230
flattening, 230
hems for, 229–230
press cloths, 37, 43
napped, 184
for wool, 50
presser foot, on vinyls, 109
pressing, 14
of fake furs, 284
of knits, 153
of linen, 24
of pile fabric, 260
of silk, 31
of sweater knits, 178
of velours, 184
price, 7–8
prick and pounce marking, 324
prickstitches, 464
Prima, 63
prints, 346–349
prom dresses, 214
Pucci, Emilio, 157, 185, 342
puckered seams, 70
pullovers, 289
purl knit stitches, 148
python skin, 82

quality of fabric, 5
quallofil, 370
Quiana, 65
quilted fabrics, 7
custom, 322–323
double-faced, 311–318
single-faced, 319–322
for linings, 370, 373
quilts, 171
quiviut, 61

rabbit, 113
raccoon, 113
raincoats, 142
ramie, 26

raschel knits, 147, 149, 163–166, 184, 198
  buttonholes in, 166
  edge finishes for, 166
  seams and hems for, 166
ratine, 50
raveling, testing for, 40, 213
raw silk, 27
  interfacings for, 362–365
raw edges
  on facings, 447
  on hems, 426
rayon, 18, 62–63
  acetate vs., 64
  for lining, 373
  in wool blend, 58
  vs. cotton, 18
rayon challis, 197
recovery, of double knits, 158
re-embroidered lace, 241
reinforced seams, 405
reinforcement buttons, 54
release sheets, 354
repeat, of plaid, 326
repp, 218
reprocessed wool, 38
reptile skins, 82
reseau, 242
resiliency, testing for, 5
reused wool, 38
reversed seams, 400–401
reversible fabric, 292–318
  diagonal, 346
reversible garments
  binding, 440
  closures on, 296, 307–309
  collars on, 310–311
  darts on, 306
  edge finishes for, 296, 304–306
  mitered corners for, 424
  pockets on, 306–307
  seams for, 295
  sleeves on, 297, 311
Rhodes, Zandra, 286
rib knit stitches, 148
rib knits, 149
ribbed fabrics, 217–220
ribbed piqué, 338
ribbings, 147, 178–181, 448
  hems in, 180
  neckline of, 180–181
  waistbands in, 180
ribbon
  for bindings, 443
  for piping, 400
ribs, in knits, 149
ripstop nylon, 143
RIT, Fast Fade, 131
robes, 289, 319
rolled hems, 426–428
rough hands, smoothing, 215
rubber cement, 87
ruffles
  of lace, 249
  pleated trims for, 230
  to prevent drooping skirts, 215
running stitches, 468
runs, preventing in knits, 151, 177
Rykiel, Sonia, 434

sable, 113
safety-stitched seams, 401
Saint Laurent, Yves, 219, 331, 340

Saint Laurent Rive Gauche, 50, 261
salt and pepper wool, 47
sateen, 212
satin, 7, 64, 212–216
  storage of, 213–214, 216
satin-stitched hems, 428
satin-stripe sheers, 213
satin tricot, 170
satin-weave fabric, 7
  for lining, 373
Savin DP, 143
Savina, 142
Sayres, Don, 22
scale layer, of wool fiber, 39
scalloped hems, 429
Schiffli lace, 241
Scotchgard, 142, 146
  for linings, 374
sculptured velvet, 267
seal, 113
seam imprints, avoiding, 14
seam roll, 14
seam sealer, 145
seam slippage, testing for, 5, 28, 33, 200
seam tape, for hems, 435
seams, 13, 379–410
  abutted, 379–380
  in action knits, 186
  adding, 9–10
  on border designs, 343
  bound, 314–315, 382–385
  bound-and-lapped, 315, 383
  bound-and-stitched, 383–385
  clean-finished, 301–302
  decorative, 385
  double-fold bias, 315
  in double knits, 160
  double-lapped, 386
  double/ply, 386
  double-stitched, 386
  drapery French, 387
  draw, 386–387
  eliminating, 10
  enclosed, 387
  for fake furs, 280–281
  false French, 387–388
  on felted fabric, 290
  finishes for, 410–414
  flat-fell, 302, 388–389
  flat-locked, 390
  French, 390–391
  fringed, 391
  on furs, 117, 391–392
  hairline, 392–393
  for handwovens, 136–137
  insertion, 302–303, 393
  in jersey, 156
  in knits, 152
  in lace, 245
  laced, 394
  lapped, 303–304, 394
  for leather, 86–87, 395–396
  on lightweight polyester, 72
  in linen garment, 24
  machine-rolled, 396
  for metallics, 233
  in net, 252
  for nonwoven fabric, 396–399
  piped, 399–400
  for plaids, 335
  plain, 400
  in power net, 188–189

  preventing stretched, 210
  puckered, 70, 213
  for quilted fabrics, 313
  for raschel knits, 166
  reversed, 400–401
  for reversible garments, 295, 301–304
  in satin, 215
  sequin-appliqué, 236–237
  serged, 401
  on silk, 30, 34
  slipstitched, 301–302
  slot, 401–402
  standing-fell, 403
  strap, 314, 403–404
  in stretch terry and velour, 183
  stretch, 191, 404–405
  in sweater knits, 177
  taped, 405–406
  tissue-stitched, 406
  topstitched, 406
  in transparent fabrics, 203, 207
  in tricot, 171–172
  tucked, 406–408
  twin needle, 405
  on velvet, 269
  wadmal, 398–399
  welt, 408
  whipped, 408–409
  wrong-side-out, 136, 409
  Zandra Rhodes, 410
  zigzag, 404
searing, 413
seersucker, 7, 223, 224, 226, 338
  interfacings for, 362–365
self-bound edge, for double-cloth fabric, 306
self-bound seams, 403
self-fabric
  for bindings on action knits, 186
  for interfacings, 358–359
selvage, as seam allowance, 210
sequinned fabric, 235–238
  border designs on, 341
serge, 48, 128, 255
serged finish, 13, 34, 177, 401, 413
sericin, 26
sericulture, 26–27
serpentine stitch, 379
serviceability of fabric, 5, 7
set, of laces, 242
sew-in interfacings, 353
sewing, successful, 10
sewing birds, 426
shantungs, 7, 27, 218
  interfacings for, 362–365
shaped edges, faced hem for, 418–419
shaped tucked seams, 407
sharkskin, 48, 64
shearling, 82, 92–95, 113
sheath linings, 373
sheepskin, 82
sheer fabric. See transparent fabrics
shell hems, 429
sherpa, 80, 92–95
Shetland tweeds, 47
shine on wool, 43
Shinn, Gail, 36
shiny fabrics, 4
shirtings, 197
  interfacings for, 362
  suede as, 82
shirttail hems, 430

shoulder pads, 205
shrinkage
    of knits, 150
    of sweatshirt knits, 168
    testing wool for, 41
    of wool gabardine, 227
Silicon finishes, 143
Si-Ling-Chi (Chinese Empress), 26
silk, 7, 26–39
    blends of, 29
    characteristics of, 27–28
    handwashing, 38
    interfacings for, 355, 362
    layout for, 30
    lightweight, 32–37
    needles for, 30
    pressing, 31
    satin-faced, 213
    selecting, 33
    sewing, 29–31
    steaming to preshrink, 29
    testing for, 29
    washability test for, 31
    washing, 31–32, 37–38
    wild, 218
silk batting, 370
silk broadcloths, 30, 32
silk garment
    care of, 31, 37–38
    planning, 28–29, 33–34
silk muslin, 199
silk organza, 205
    as interfacings, 355
    interfacings for, 360
silk sheers, care of, 201
silk suede, 82
silkies, 70
silverfish, 21
Silvia, 57
Simpson, Adele, *325*
singeing, 413
single knits, 149, 153–157
sizing, testing for, 23, 200
skating costumes, 184
skeins, of silk, 27
Skinner satin, 213
skins, 82, 84
skipped stitches
    on knits, 152
    on silk, 34
    on Ultrasuede, 99
skirt vents, weights for, 434
skirts
    avoiding drooping, 215
    bubble, 252
    custom-pleated, 230–231
    lining for, 374
    from plaids, 331
skiver, 82
skiwear, 184, 289
sleepwear, 214
sleeve vents, on Ultrasuede, 101
sleeves
    from fake furs, 281
    in linen garment, 24
    of nylon, 66
    from plaids, 330–331
    on reversible garments, 297, 311
    reducing ease in, 73
slipper satin, 213
slipstitches, 468–469
    on edges, 304
    for hems, 430

for seams, 301–302
slot seams, 401–402
    for nonwoven fabric, 397
snaps, 461
soap, for insulated garments, 371
soap sliver, 12
Sofrina, 107
Soft Skin, 107
Spandelle, 77, 188
spandex, 76–78, 184, 188
Spanzelle, 188
special-occasion fabrics. *See* decorative
        surface fabric; prepleated fabric;
        ribbed fabrics; satin; taffeta
splits, 82, 84
sportswear, 190, 262
spots
    on silk, 31
    on wool, 45
squirrel, 113
stabilizers, 34, 354, 369, 405, 406
stable knits, 149
stabstitches, 468
standing-fell seams, 403
static electricity, eliminating, 171
Stavropolous, 205
staystitching
    on handwovens, 136
    on knits, 152
steaming, to preshrink silk, 29
steerhide, 83
Sticky Stuff, 87
stiff fabrics, 5
stitch setting
    fabric weight and, 20
    needle sizes and, 20
stitched-slash buttonholes, 95,
        459
    on Ultrasuede, 102
straight stitch, elasticity in, 404
straightening fabric, 10, 19
strap seams, 403–404
    for nonwoven fabric, 398
    for quilted fabric, 314
straps, 462
    for lingerie, 173
stretch blindstitch, 422
stretch fabric, 190–193
    corduroy, 261
    knits, 148–149
    needlepunch, 370
    terry, 149, 181–184
    velour, 149, 181–184
    wool, pressing, 44
stretch hems, 431
stretch interfacings, 354
stretch seams, 191, 404–405
strip bound buttonholes, 452–453
stripes, 292, 338–343
    tucking, 340
    types of, 338–339
    woven vs. printed, 5
Style Patterns, 98
suede, 21, 64, 80, 96, 255
    cleaning, 92
    interfacings for, 355
    with nap, 85
    needle holes on, 86
    purchasing, 83
    synthetic, 96–106
suede chamois, 81
Suedemark, 105
Suedemark II, 96

suitings
    interfacings for, 362–365
    worsted, 48–50
sun dress, 340
sunback, 370, 373
sunburst pleating, 231
sweater knits, 147, 149, 175–178
    custom-knit, 176
    pressing of, 178
    preventing runs in, 177
    seams in, 177
sweaters, 163, 167
sweatshirt fleece, 255
sweatshirt knits, 147, 149, 166–168
sweatshirts, 163, 289
swimwear, 184
    linings in, 186
Switzerland, cotton from, 18
synthetic fabrics, 62
    interfacings for, 362
synthetic suede, 96–106
    and knits, 153
    lightweight, 105–106

Tactel, 142, 143
taffeta, 64, 218, 220–223
    as lining, 373
    storage of, 221
    testing weave of, 221
tailor tacks, 12, 469
tailor's ham, 14
tailor's hem, 415, 465
tana lawn, 199
tanning, 80
tape, 12
tape lace, 242
taped seams, 405–406
tapestry, 223, 224, 225
tarlatan, 199
tartans, 336
Taslan, 142, 143
tea dyeing, of lace, 249–250
Teflon release sheet, 354
temporary marking pens, 12
terry, 18, 64, 259, 273–275
    stretch, 149, 181–184
Terylene, 67
textured fabric, 4
    topstitching, 153, 432
    wool, 46–48
    Thai cotton, 21
*That Touch of Class; Machine
    Embroidery on Leather* (Barker), 91
Thermax, 370
Thermolite, 371
Thinsulate, 370, 371
thread
    for knits, 150, 152
    for leather, 86
    water-soluble basting, 336
thread bubbles, avoiding, 210
thread count, 7
thread tracing, 12
ticking, 128, 338
tie closures, 462
    for reversible garments, 297,
        308–309
tights, 184
timesavers, 7
tissue-stitched seams, 406
tissue taffeta, 221
toile, 242
topstitching, 10, 13, 406

on coatings, 54
on hems, 431–432
on leather, 395
on quilted fabric, 316–317
on satin, 215
on stretch terry and velour, 184
on terry, 274
textured knits, 153
towels, 273
toys, from fake furs, 280
tracing carbon, 13
tracing wheel, 13
transfer sheets, 369
Transfuse II, 52, 354, 419
transparent fabrics, 197–211
characteristics of, 200
crisp, 205–208
hems for, 432
interfacings for, 355, 360–361
mitered corners for, 424–425
satin-stripe, 213
soft, 208–211
velvet as, 267
Trevira, 67
triacetate, 63–65
triblends, 143
tricot, 64, 147, 149, 170–174
determining right side of, 171
elastic in, 172
milanese knits vs., 175
sheer, 197
vs. interlocks, 162
vs. jersey, 153–154
tricot bow, 173
tricot knit interfacings, 354
tricot knits, 184
as lining, 373
tricotine, 48
trims
custom-pleated, 230
of fur, 119
of leather, 91
tropical worsteds, 45, 48
trousers, 190
T-shirts, 155, 163
tubing, corded, 450
tucked hems, 432–433
tucked seams, 406–408
tucks, in linen, 24
tufted piles, 275–276
Tuftex, 142
tulle, 199, 250
fusing lace motif to, 248
as interfacings, 355
as lining, 373
as underlining, 205
turned-and-stitched finish, 413–414
tussah, 218
tussah silkworms, 27
twill-weave fabric, 7, 127–133, 343
for linings, 373
vs. plain-weave, 125
twin-needle seam, 405
twin-needle hems, 433
twisted straps, 173
two-faced fabric, 292–297
planning for, 294
two-way stretch knits, 149

Ultraleather, 107
Ultrasuede, 96–105
basting on, 100
closures on, 101–103

layout for, 98
patch pockets on, 104
unbalanced even stripes, 339
unbalanced plaids, 325–326
layout for, 333
unbalanced stripes, 341
unbalanced uneven stripes, 339
undergarments, 155, 205
underlay, abutted seam with, 379–380
underlinings, 372–376
for double knits, 161–162
for fake furs, 283–284
for fur, 118
fusible as, 376
on handwovens, 138
interfacings for, 359
for knits, 153
for lace, 246
for lightweight polyester, 73–74
for linen garment, 24
net and tulle as, 252
for satin, 216
selecting, 374
for silk, 30–31, 33, 36–37
for sweater knits, 178
for transparent fabrics, 204–205
underwear, 155
Unel, 77, 188
uneven plaids, 326–327
uneven stripes, 339
unfinished edge, 414
unfinished hem, 425
Ungaro, Emanuel, 345
uniforms, 190
upholstery fabric, 218, 219, 224, 225

Val lace, 242
Valenciennes, 242
Valentino, Mario, *81, 93*
veils, 252
velour, 64, 259, 273–275
knits, 5
stretch, 149, 181–184
velvet, 5, 64, 259, 267–271
cut, 212, 267, 334
vs. velveteen, 265, 268–269
velveteen, 259, 264–266
vs. corduroy, 262, 265
vs. velvet, 268–269
Venet, Philippe, *239, 299, 300*
Venise lace, 241
ventilation, in outerwear fabric, 146
vents
skirt, 434
sleeve, 101
in vinyls, 110
vests, 142, 289, 298, 319
vicuna, fleece from, 60
Vincel, 63
vinyls, 107–111
virgin wool, 38
viscose process, 62
viyella, 197, 199
voided velvet, 267
voile, 45, 197, 199
as interfacings, 355
interfacings for, 360–361
Vycron, 67
Vyrene, 77, 188

wadmal, 287
wadmal seams, 398–399, 408

waistbands
in action knits, 186
interfacings for, 368
in ribbing, 180
wales, 261
Walters, Norma, 434
warp, 11
warp-face twills, 127
warp knits, 147
warp stitches, 148
wash-and-wear fabrics, 139–142
washability test, for silk, 31, 37
washable wools, 57–59
washing, cloth bag for, 216
water-repellent fabric, 142
water-soluble basting thread, 336
water-soluble doublestick tape, 335
water-soluble stabilizer, for
embroidering net, 252
waterproof fabrics, 142
wax, 13
wax chalk, 11
weft-insertion interfacings, 354
weft knits, 147
weighted hems, 433–434
weighted silk, 27
welt seams, 408
welts, on coatings, 55
whipcord, 48
whipped seam, 408–409
whipping stitches, 469
whipsnake, 83
white fabric, 253–254
wicking quality, 69, 140
wide lace, 242
wild silk, 27, 218
windowpane bound buttonholes,
453–454
wired hems, 434
Wonder Under, 52, 100, 354, 419
wool, 38–59
boiled, 148, 287, 288
characteristics of, 39–40
coatings, 50–57
darts in, 42
drape of, 40
durability of, 40
face side of, 40
interfacings for, 355, 362, 366
layout for, 42
lightweight, 45–46
needles for, 42
preparation of, 41
pressing, 43–44
sewing, 41–43
shine on, 43
shrinking, 41
silk blend with, 29
stretching and shrinking, 44
testing shrinkage of, 41
washable, 57–59
wool batting, 370
wool blankets, 370
wool fibers, anatomy of, 39
wool flannel, 255
wool gabardine, shrinkage of, during
pleating, 227
wool poplin, 48
Wool Products Labeling Act, 38
wool stretch fabric, pressing, 44
woolly nylon, 192
threading needle with, 180
Worksheet, 3

530

worsteds, 7, 39
worsted suitings, 48–50
woven dotted Swiss, 19
woven fabrics, 125–146
  appliqué seams for, 380–382
  felted, 287
  for interfacings, 353
  of plaids, 328
  quality of, 5
  vs. knits, 149–150
wrinkling, reducing, in linen, 24
wrong-side-out seams, 136, 409

Xena, 63

Yamamoto inseam pocket, 296
yarn
  for stabilizing neckline, 310
  twist of, 5

Zandra Rhodes seam, 410
Zankara, 63
Zantrel, 63
Zefran, 74
Zepel, 142

zigzag stitch, 414, 434
  blindstitch, 422
  for stretch seams, 404
zigzag twill, 127
zippers, 462–463
  on fake furs, 283
  flat-fell lapped, 132
  in jersey, 156
  on leather, 88
  on reversible garments, 309
  in satin, 216
  on Ultrasuede, 102-103

FABRIC WORKSHEET

(Photocopy this page)

Fabric: _____

Manufacturer: _____

Width: _____ Length: _____

Care: Washable   Dry-clean only

Information on Bolt End: _____

Date Preshrunk: _____

Date purchased: _____

Where purchased: _____

Cost per yard: _____

Other: _____

_____

Place swatch here

FABRIC DESCRIPTION

For easy reference, circle all applicable sections and the appropriate page numbers.

FIBER CONTENT

Cotton—p. 17	Hair Fiber—p. 59	Rayon—p. 62	Acrylic—p. 74
Linen—p. 21	Leather—p. 80	Acetate—p. 63	Modacrylic—p. 75
Ramie—p. 26	Suede—p. 80	Triacetate—p. 63	Olefin—p. 78
Silk—p. 26	Fur—p. 112	Nylon—p. 65	Spandex—p. 76
Wool—p. 38	Feathers—p. 120	Polyester—p. 67	

FABRIC STRUCTURE

Woven—p. 125   Knit—p. 147   Stretch wovens—p. 190

FABRIC CHARACTERISTICS

Transparent—p. 197	Quilted—p. 319	Diagonals—p. 343
Special occasion—p. 212	Plaids—p. 325	Synthetic suede—p. 96
Napped—p. 255	Stripe—p. 338	Vinyl—p. 107
Felt—p. 285	Prints—p. 346	
Reversible—p. 292	Border—p. 341	

GARMENT HISTORY

Completed: _____

Pattern name & number: _____

Interfacing: _____

Lining: _____

Underlining: _____

Trims: _____

Notes: _____

_____

Place photo here

(From *Claire Shaeffer's Fabric Sewing Guide*, Chilton Book Co., 1989.)